NORTH KOREA AND THE WORLD

NORTH KOREA AND THE WORLD

HUMAN RIGHTS, ARMS CONTROL,
AND STRATEGIES FOR NEGOTIATION

Walter C. Clemens Jr.

UNIVERSITY PRESS OF KENTUCKY

Published by the University Press of Kentucky,
scholarly publisher for the Commonwealth, serving Bellarmine University, Berea College, Centre College of Kentucky, Eastern Kentucky University, The Filson Historical Society, Georgetown College, Kentucky Historical Society, Kentucky State University, Morehead State University, Murray State University, Northern Kentucky University, Transylvania University, University of Kentucky, University of Louisville, and Western Kentucky University.

Editorial and Sales Offices: The University Press of Kentucky
663 South Limestone Street, Lexington, Kentucky 40508-4008
www.kentuckypress.com

Maps and figures by Richard A. Gilbreath, University of Kentucky Cartography Lab. Photographs by Jeremy Hunter (www.jeremyhunter.com) and Steve Gong (www. stevegongphoto.com).

Library of Congress Cataloging-in-Publication Data

Names: Clemens, Walter C., author.
Title: North Korea and the world : human rights, arms control, and strategies
    for negotiation / Walter C. Clemens Jr.
Description: Lexington, KY : University Press of Kentucky, 2016. | Includes
    bibliographical references and index.
Identifiers: LCCN 2016018538| ISBN 9780813167466 (hardcover : alk. paper) |
    ISBN 9780813167626 (pdf) | ISBN 9780813167633 (epub)
Subjects: LCSH: Korea (North)—Foreign relations-21st century. | Human
    rights—Korea (North) | Human rights—Korea (North)—International
    cooperation. | Nuclear weapons—Korea (North) | Nuclear
    nonproliferation—Korea (North)—International cooperation. | Korea
    (North)—Foreign relations—United States. | United States—Foreign
    relations—Korea (North)
Classification: LCC DS935.7778 .C54 2016 | DDC 327.5193—dc23
LC record available at https://lccn.loc.gov/2016018538

For my family, East and West,
and in memory of Robert A. Scalapino
and Stephen W. Bosworth

Contents

IV. Policy Options amid Uncertainty

Abbreviations, Acronyms, and Special Terms

ASEAN	Association of Southeast Asian Nations
DMZ	demilitarized zone
DPRK	Democratic People's Republic of Korea (North Korea)
GRIT	graduated reciprocity in tension-reduction
Han'gŭl	Korean alphabet
HDI	Human Development Index
HEU	highly enriched uranium
IAEA	International Atomic Energy Agency
ICBM	intercontinental ballistic missile
JSA	Joint Security Area
Juche	self-reliance and independence
KEDO	Korean Peninsula Energy Development Organization
LEU	low-enriched uranium
LWR	light-water reactor
NDC	National Defense Commission (DPRK)
NGO	nongovernmental organization
NLL	Northern Limit Line
NMD	National Missile Defense
NPT	Nuclear Nonproliferation Treaty
NSC	National Security Council (U.S.)
Paektu	volcanic mountain, alleged birthplace of Korean people and Kim Jong Il
PRC	People's Republic of China
PSI	Proliferation Security Initiative
pyŏngjin line	concurrent development of WMD and economy (guns and butter)
RF	Russian Federation
ROK	Republic of Korea (South Korea)
SDI	Strategic Defense Initiative
sŏn'gun	military-first orientation
UNDP	United Nations Development Programme
WMD	weapons of mass destruction
Yusin	ROK "rejuvenation" constitution, 1972–1979

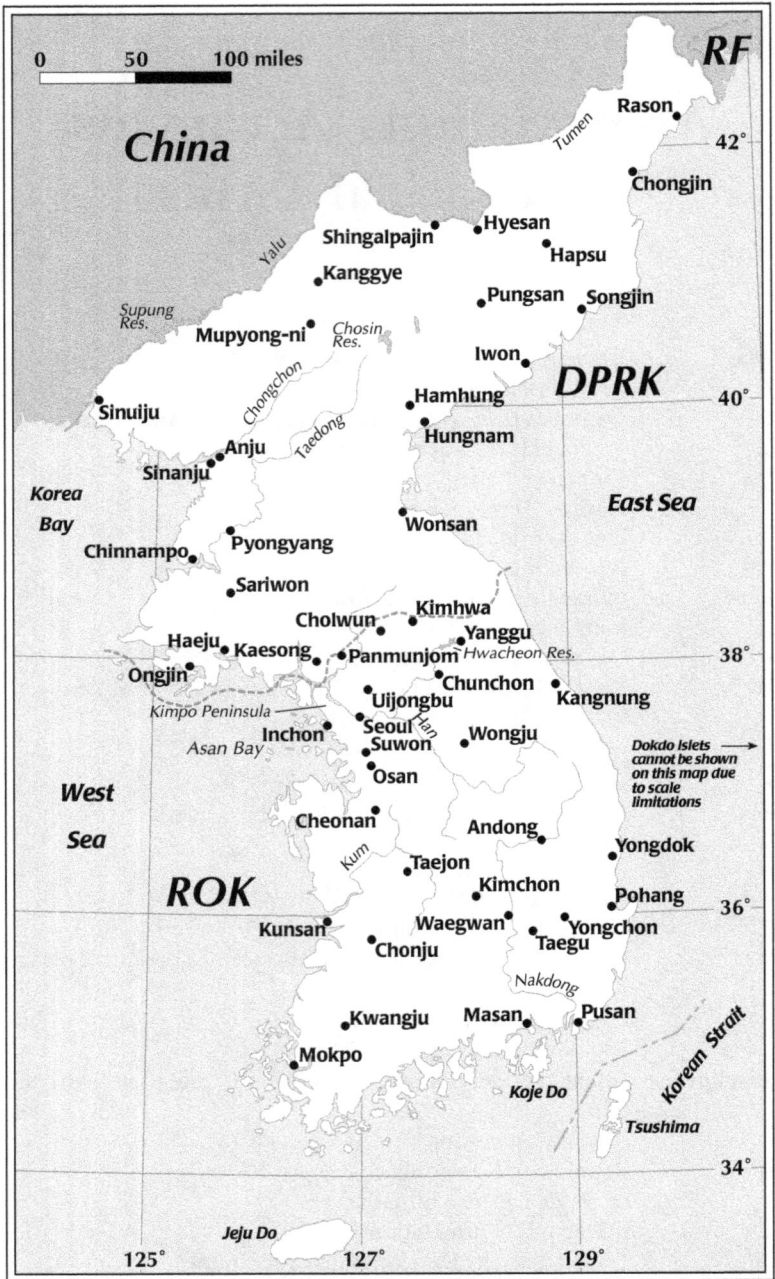
Map 0.1. The Korean peninsula

Prologue

From Vienna and Moscow
to Panmunjom

December 12, 1952. Soviet troops patrolled their zone not far from central Vienna, where existentialist philosopher Jean-Paul Sartre gave the opening address to the World Congress of the Peoples for Peace. Sartre later called the congress one of the three experiences in his life that gave him hope.[1] For me, a nineteen-year-old foreign student, an aspiring artist with a press pass from the *Cincinnati Times-Star,* the congress provided my first opportunity to meet people from Asia and Africa. Drawing on my high school French, I translated for Vietnamese who were anxious to tell English-speakers about their national liberation struggle. I dined several times with Japanese student delegates to the congress. They were slim and ate very little, they said, because their stomachs were accustomed to meager fare. The Japanese students had mixed feelings about the United States and Korea. Budgets were tight in Japan and, as war raged in Korea (1950–1953), they sold their blood every month for wounded U.S. soldiers.

The peace congress convened just as Pyongyang and Beijing resumed accusations that the United States was using biological weapons to spread disease and death in North Korea and China. I joined other congress participants in watching a North Korean film purporting to expose U.S. germ warfare—insects and voles (rodents larger than mice) stuffed into canisters dropped from airplanes by American soldiers whose huge noses outdid most stereotypes. The propaganda was primitive but seemed to convince many viewers.

Beijing and Pyongyang had begun in May 1951 to blame the United States for an epidemic that was spreading across northern China and North Korea. The accusations halted in July 1951 when armistice talks showed promise, but they resumed after truce talks collapsed in February 1952. Beijing then conflated its stories about poisons spread by Americans with the need to punish and purify Chinese guilty of embracing bourgeois values. An American army doctor who entered North Korea surreptitiously, however, discovered that the epidemic was the "Black Death," a virulent form of smallpox, against which Chinese and North Korean authorities soon mounted a huge vaccination program.

Chinese and DPRK authorities refused to permit the International Red Cross to inspect their accusations against the United States. Instead, Mao Zedong invited Joseph Needham, a well-known biochemist from Cambridge University, and N. N. Zhukov-Verezhnikov, a vice president of the Soviet Academy of Medicine, along with left-leaning scientists from Italy, France, Brazil, and Sweden to review the evidence. Both Needham and Zhukov-Verezhnikov had earlier joined Chinese scientists in analyzing the evidence of Japanese experiments with biological weapons on Chinese subjects during World War II.[2] The scientists arrived in China in June 1952 and presented their report in September 1952—a few months before the peace congress opened in Vienna. Needham and colleagues conducted no scientific investigations, but instead listened to testimonials and looked at evidence collected by Chinese scientists—voles, spiders, and other insects. Their report confirmed the Chinese version of what happened.[3] It preceded the peace congress and added credibility to the film we saw there.

In 1951–1952 the Chinese alleged that the Americans were using the same techniques deployed by Japanese experimenters a few years earlier. Needham later admitted that he had been deceived. As we shall see in chapter 5, however, in spring 1953 the Soviet government told Beijing and Pyongyang that Moscow knew the allegations were false.[4] Even the Kremlin seemed embarrassed by this Big Lie.

The grand finale of the congress helped me appreciate groupthink. When more than a thousand delegates chanted and clapped anti-U.S. slogans, I could barely resist joining the crowd's applause even though I disbelieved and disagreed with them. I described all this in essays mailed to my hometown newspaper, the *Cincinnati Times-Star*. I suggested that the United States take part in such congresses to make its position known, but my thoughts were not published.

Meanwhile, some of my high school and college buddies were fighting in Korea, while I held a student deferment. More than sixty years later, I still see veterans bearing scars from their time in Korea. One (who became an FBI agent) displayed an auto license plate: "The Chosin Few"—named for a reservoir where U.S. troops defied a much larger Chinese force in late 1950 before retreating. The American soldiers' encounters with Communist forces in the early 1950s were less uplifting than the speeches in Vienna that inspired the ivory tower existentialist from Paris.

The peace congress and other experiences in Vienna gave a new direction to my life. My year in Vienna included many encounters with Soviet occupation troops, who several times came close to shooting me and once arrested me due to misunderstandings on their part or mine. These interactions deepened my awareness of the roles played by misperception and poor communication in world affairs. Not only the still broken Stephansdom and Wiener Staatsoper but, even more, the many Austrians skiing on one leg whom I saw that winter in the Alps underscored for me the horrors inflicted in World War II. I resolved to learn Russian and do what I could to prevent another war—especially one waged with nuclear arms. Meanwhile, the drunken jailer in the final scene of *Die Fledermaus* stumbled on his lantern and muttered, "Poor little Austria. They [the Soviets] have taken all your oil!"

Of course the Korean War changed or ended life for millions. It helped the author of *Angela's Ashes,* Frank McCourt, get an education. McCourt left his job sweeping the lobby of the Biltmore Hotel to join the U.S. Army. He later used the G.I. Bill to get into college without a high school diploma. He jokingly thanked Mao Zedong for dispatching Chinese volunteers and expanding the war.[5] When I started graduate school at Columbia in 1955, many of my colleagues were Korean War veterans studying thanks to the G.I. Bill. Many seemed older and more serious than their years.

Should Americans and others in the West try to build bridges to the Communist world or labor to destroy it? This question arose sharply for me in Vienna and continues to resonate in many pages of this book. A framework for answering the question took shape in summer 1954 when I studied at Harvard under Zbigniew Brzezinski, Paul Sigmund, and Bruce Larkin in a seminar organized by the U.S. National Student Association and financed by a front for the CIA. The USNSA aimed to prepare twenty or so American students to mobilize resistance to the International Union of Students and World Federation of Democratic Youth— Communist fronts based in Eastern Europe financed by the same Soviet sources as the World Congress of the Peoples for Peace in Vienna. The American students' task was to win the hearts and minds of young leaders in the Third World lest they be seduced by Communist promises and propaganda. We learned about the machinations of Communist regimes and fronts, but—influenced by Swiss theologian Karl Barth—I wrote a paper on the pros and cons of bridge-building. Barth's question undergirds nearly every chapter: If all persons are tainted by Original Sin, is anyone entitled to throw the first stone against those accused of sin? Apart from theology, if all persons and governments have their faults, then do any have grounds to be self-righteous? Still, if we think that some regimes are much worse than others, what kinds of policies should we then pursue?

Questions like these were Ivory Tower with few practical consequences. For the German pastor Dietrich Bonhoeffer, however, they were matters of life and death. Influenced by Karl Barth and by contacts at the Union Theological Seminary in New York, Bonhoeffer in 1933 protested Hitler's anti-Jewish laws and later became a declared pacifist. Still, the Nazi regime permitted him to serve in military intelligence—until he provided a moral justification for a plot to kill the Führer. When the conspiracy failed, Bonhoeffer was arrested and executed along with other plotters.[6]

For the rest of the 1950s and 1960s I studied Russian and Soviet politics. One of the first American graduate students to do research in the USSR under an exchange set up in 1958, I studied the origins of Soviet disarmament policy under Lenin.[7] Prevented from using the basic documents in Moscow, I found them the next year at Stanford's Hoover Institution and completed my dissertation at Columbia in 1961.[8] Two years later, at a time when Senator Hubert H. Humphrey and President John F. Kennedy could convince Congress that policy should be grounded in knowledge, the U.S. Arms Control and Disarmament Agency awarded MIT a contract to study Soviet arms policy. The Center for International Studies at MIT invited me to be the principal researcher. In 1966 our findings were published in a book called *Khrushchev and the Arms Race: Soviet Interests in Arms Control and Disarmament, 1954–1964*.[9] At MIT I worked under Lincoln P. Bloomfield, William E. Griffith, and Jerome B. Wiesner, who became my mentors for life. Moving across the Charles River to Boston University in 1966, I continued to study and write about Soviet and Sino-Soviet relations and how the West could and should deal with the unfolding challenges and opportunities in the Communist world.[10]

Puzzling how to break the spirals of tension in U.S. dealings with Communist states, I thought back to 1962, when I heard psychology professor Charles E. Osgood lecture on his book *An Alternative to War or Surrender*.[11] The alternative was what Osgood called "GRIT"—graduated reciprocity in tension-reduction. Osgood's ideas struck me as both commonsensical and profound. They were echoed by other scholars as President John F. Kennedy sought to push U.S.-Soviet relations away from Armageddon.[12]

In an era when Congress still funded Enlightenment values, the U.S. Information Agency (1953–1999) sent me in 1970 to Korea and other Asian and Pacific rim countries to lecture on Soviet foreign policy.[13] In Korea I traveled to Panmunjom and learned how one U.S. Army lieutenant had tried—and failed—to break the tit-for-tat treadmill of mutual hostility with North Korea: "Whatever they do, we do—and more, if possible." I began to think about what had worked—and failed—in negotiations between the Western democracies and the Soviet Union. Were there lessons there that might help reshape the democracies' dealings with North Korea? My first essay was called "GRIT at Panmunjom"[14]—updated nearly half a century later as chapter 11 below.

I continued to ponder the potential of true GRIT to redirect world affairs. It seemed to me that two master diplomatists, Henry Kissinger and Zhou Enlai, had used a version of GRIT to normalize U.S.-Chinese relations. A student from China at Boston University wrote about the role of GRIT in improving ties between Beijing and Taipei.[15] Becoming more engaged in analysis of North Korea after the collapse of Soviet communism, I wrote in 2004 about what Washington and Pyongyang could learn from Professor Osgood as well as from Lenin and Bill Clinton.[16]

Is Peace and Goodwill a Chimera?

Starting in the 1990s, moments emerged—synergies between key individuals, forces, and good timing—when relations between North Korea and the democracies appeared to shift in positive directions. But these moments were often followed by one or two steps backward—relapses when ostensible agreements disappeared, when biting words became more biting, and when contacts diminished. Leaders in the democracies wondered if they could ever reach meaningful understandings with North Korea. Still, if the democracies could achieve useful accords with regimes led by the likes of Nikita Khrushchev and Mao Zedong, could they not do so also with the Kim dynasty in Pyongyang? Could they not mitigate the dangers the Kim dynasty posed to world peace and to its subjects? There were no certainties—no solid grounds to say yes or no. Still, the record demonstrated the dangers of hubris—on all sides—and the ways that enlightened self-interest could lead all parties away from chaos and toward a brighter future.

I

Roots of
Twenty-First-Century Problems

1

Why Care about North Korea?

No man is an island,
Entire of itself,
Every man is a piece of the continent,
A part of the main. . . .
Because I am involved in mankind,
And therefore never send to know for whom the bell tolls;
It tolls for thee
                              —John Donne, "Meditation XVII"

Why worry about people living on a narrow peninsula in Northeast Asia squeezed by much larger neighbors? Not long after the Korean War halted, U.S. secretary of state Dean Acheson gave this answer: "Never has fate been secreted in so unlikely a receptacle." Reviewing recent history, Acheson wondered: How could so much in world affairs depend on what happened in Korea?[1] On the eve of the war, a cultural anthropologist supported by Acheson wrote, "It may be said of Korea that there is no country of comparable significance concerning which so many people are ignorant."[2] Nearly seven decades later, in a world more closely linked and interdependent than ever, a smile or a grimace in Korea reverberates around the globe.

Why should the world care about North Korea? Because the regime in Pyongyang is a menace to its own people and to peace. This book seeks to analyze those threats—how and why they emerged and what the United States and others, beginning with North Korea's neighbors, could do to mitigate the dangers.

ARE WE OUR BROTHERS' AND SISTERS' KEEPERS?

People do terrible things to one another everywhere. What can one do about it? Cain, the realist, spoke back to the Lord sarcastically with the question "Am I my brother's keeper?" (Genesis 4.9). Others, such as idealist John Donne, asserted that we are all "involved in mankind"—so that suffering anywhere diminishes everyone.

How should outsiders deal with a regime believed to abuse its own people and menace world order? Can—should—must those concerned with human rights and security try to bridge their differences with individuals and groups whom they regard as evil? Is an accommodation feasible, or even desirable, between parties who differ profoundly on notions of right and wrong? Are some regimes so evil that it is wrong and unwise to engage with them—even on matters of shared concern? If actors believe it worthwhile to bargain with a perceived devil, should they deploy or demand special safeguards? Lest we view the problem from just one side, we must recall that similar questions confront North Koreans. How should they deal with outsiders who, the North's leaders say, have brutalized and betrayed them for decades?

The United Nations Security Council in 2006 adopted resolution 1674 affirming the "Responsibility to Protect." This norm holds that every state has a duty to protect its own people from genocide, ethnic cleansing, crimes against humanity, and war crimes. The international community has a duty to assist every state to fulfill this responsibility. If a state manifestly fails to protect its citizens from mass atrocities, and if peaceful measures have failed, then the international community must intervene with economic pressures and, if necessary, military force.[3] The U.S. State Department *Quadrennial Diplomacy and Development Review* in 2010 explained why U.S. interests support the Responsibility to Protect: "Situations that threaten genocide or other mass atrocities warrant very high priority for prevention. Such extreme violence undermines our security by fueling state and regional instability, prolonging the effects of violence on societies, and entrenching murderous regimes that perpetuate other threats. The moral values we cherish are breached, and the legal and normative structures we champion and depend upon for continued order are undermined."[4]

How does the Responsibility to Protect relate to North Korea? The Commission of Inquiry established by the UN Human Rights Council recommended in February 2014 that the UN Security Council take action to punish and prevent crimes against humanity in the Democratic People's Republic of Korea.[5] The commission reported that "the DPRK is a state where the commission of human rights violations and crimes against humanity is ingrained into the institutional framework" controlled and led by Supreme Leader Kim Jong Un. The commission's findings and subsequent UN actions are detailed in later chapters. Suffice it here to say that they underscore why the entire international community should be concerned with North Korea.

A United Nations inquiry in 2014 defined one aspect of the DPRK's challenge to humanity: "Systematic, widespread and gross human rights violations have been, and are being committed by the DPRK, its institutions and officials." Some violations "constitute crimes against humanity. These are not mere excesses of the state. They are essential components of a political system that has moved far from the ideals on which it claims to be founded. The gravity, scale and nature of these violations reveal a state that does not have any parallel in the contemporary world. Political scientists of the 20th century characterized this type of political organization as a totalitarian state: A state that does not content itself with ensuring the authoritarian rule of a small group of people, but seeks to dominate every aspect of its citizens' lives and terrorizes them from within."[6]

The DPRK is a totalitarian system, ruled by "a single party, led by a single person," based on an ideology called *Juche*—independent self-reliance—or, on occasion, "Kimilsungism-Kimjongilism." As the UN study put it: "The keystone to the political system is the vast political and security apparatus that strategically uses surveillance, coercion, fear and punishment to preclude the expression of any dissent. Public executions and enforced disappearance to political prison camps serve as the ultimate means to terrorize the population into submission. The state's violence has been externalized through state-sponsored abductions and enforced disappearances of people from other nations. These international enforced disappearances are unique in their intensity, scale and nature."[7]

North Korea's Challenges to Regional and Global Security

While Koreans at times ruled Manchuria, they seldom encroached on their neighbors. On the other hand, outsiders—Chinese, Japanese, Mongols, Manchus, Russians—took turns trying to dominate Korea. As CIA analysts put it: "Victimized by its strategic location throughout history," Korea has been and continues to be "the scene of competition for dominant influence by its powerful neighbors."[8]

Korea served as the focus of many wars. In the late sixteenth century, for example, Japan ravaged Korea for six years before being driven back by Chinese troops and Korean ironclad "turtle" boats. Three centuries later, however, in 1894–1895, Japan defeated China in a struggle to control Korea and access to Manchuria. A decade later, in 1904–1905, Japan defeated Russia in a fight for hegemony over Manchuria and Korea.

The expansionist policies of China, Japan, and Russia were joined in the nineteenth century by those of Europeans, led by France, followed by the United States. Despite long distances and dangers, Americans engaged in trade and in mortal combat with Koreans. America's first encounters with Korea were violent: U.S. gunboats shot their way into the Han River in 1871. Soon, however, Korean leaders looked to the United States to help in modernizing and protecting their country.

Many U.S. policies were shaped by what policymakers conceived as the realities of power—bolstered by pressures from firms hoping for business in Asia. For most of America's aspiring realists and merchants, however, relatively small Korea was less important than its neighbors. Washington readily sacrificed Korea to America's larger concerns with Japan and, later, with the USSR. Officials in Washington paid little heed to American diplomats, missionaries, educators, and physicians in Korea who were concerned with the country's well-being and who wished to preserve its independence.

Americans used their good offices to mediate Japan's peace treaty with China in 1895 and with Russia in 1905. As we shall see in chapter 3, however, Washington acquiesced in Japan's absorption of Korea in return for Tokyo's acceptance of U.S. control of the Philippines. London did the same to protect its position in Singapore. No U.S. president spoke the word "Korea" in public from 1911 to 1942! The White House did not condemn Japan's colonization of Korea until after Pearl Harbor.

When the Japanese departed in 1945, one Korea became two—divided north and south—in part because Washington had done nothing to foster a free and independent Korea or prepare for an enlightened occupation, as in Japan. The outbreak of the Korean War in June 1950 soon changed all that. Washington came to see Korea as a battleground between the Free World and the Communist. The Korean War pitted UN forces, led by the United States, against North Korea, China, and—behind the lines—the USSR. Three to four million soldiers and civilians died in the fighting, in a war that barely altered the North–South boundary.[9]

Why worry about North Korea now? Another war in Northeast Asia waged with twenty-first-century weapons could well be far more destructive.

For some observers, the Korean War showed that containment of Communist expansion, boosted by collective security, could succeed. Critics countered that the Korean War initiated a string of unwinnable wars in Asia and the Middle East chosen by U.S. presidents with almost no participation by Congress or the broader U.S. public.

The Korean War Armistice was signed on July 27, 1953, by DPRK, Chinese, and UN/U.S. representatives. A month or so later the United Nations established a Northern Limit Line (NLL) to demarcate the DPRK-ROK border in the West Sea.[10] Starting in 1973, the DPRK challenged the legality of this demarcation. The DPRK also had unresolved border disputes with China—in the West Sea, in the north near Mount Paektu, and regarding certain islands in the Yalu and Tumen rivers. Both the DPRK and the ROK rejected Japan's claims to Liancourt Rocks (Dokdo in Korean, Takeshima in Japanese) in the East Sea (Sea of Japan), where fish abound and natural gas deposits were likely.

Korea could still spark a war dragging in the great powers. Despite an armistice in 1953, more than half a century passed with no formal peace agreement. Instead, North Korean troops continued to face off against UN troops along Korea's demilitarized zone (DMZ). Bloody incidents occurred regularly at sea along the NLL.

The DMZ. Bill Clinton called it the "scariest place on earth." (Photo by Jeremy Hunter)

Despite some occasional respites, tension often strangled moments of détente as North Korea moved to join the nuclear weapons club. Washington worried not only that Pyongyang might acquire the means to destroy portions of South Korea, Japan, and North America, but also that North Korea's actions would encourage Iran and other states—including Japan—to go nuclear.[11]

North Korea's confrontation with the United States constituted "the first twenty-first-century conflict between a failed state relying on the threat of nuclear weapons and their proliferation to ensure regime survival, and a world power intent on preventing such flexing, blackmailing, and transfer of weapons of mass destruction (WMD) to potential terrorists."[12]

For more than six decades North Korea acted as one of the most aggressive actors on the world stage and the most repressive at home—doing little even to address mass hunger and other basic human needs. The DPRK became the first state after World War II to invade and seek to annex another state. North Korea probably achieved the modern world's record for state sponsorship of kidnapping and assassination. The Pyongyang regime dealt harshly not only with its own subjects and with the ROK but even with its patrons in Moscow and Beijing. No other government treated so shabbily the relief agencies whose programs saved millions of its citizens from acute hunger and disease.

As for North–South friendship, would any other government kill an authorized guest—and then demand an apology? In July 2008 a DPRK soldier shot and killed a South Korean tourist as she walked along a beach in an area that Pyongyang later claimed was marked as off limits to foreigners. The killing took place on the very day that ROK president Lee Myung Bak spoke in favor of more North–South engagement without preconditions. Not swayed by the president's message, Pyongyang's authoritative newspaper *Rodung Sinmun* (July 27, 2008) asserted that the "Lee Myung Bak group of traitors [meaning the ROK government] is touting 'pragmatism' and the policy of confrontation with the DPRK based on it," which the DPRK oracle called a "fundamental factor bedeviling north-south relations." Pyongyang expressed no regret for the incident, but instead demanded that Seoul apologize for the transgression.

The DPRK menaced the world not only with its weapons but also by its economic and political fragility. Washington and Tokyo worried about North Korea's military strength; Beijing and Seoul feared its weakness as well as its threats to security. All these concerns were justified: the DPRK could become a failed state equipped with nuclear weapons. North Korea sold missiles and proffered its nuclear technology. The regime's bellicose words and deeds raised doubts whether any outsiders could reach an accommodation with Pyongyang on issues of high politics (security issues such as weapons and boundaries) or even "low" politics (trade, the environment, culture, fishing rights). For a failing state, nearly everything is high politics, including human rights.

Was there good reason for the United States and its partners to pursue nuclear arms negotiations with Pyongyang? No, said neorealists such as the late Kenneth N. Waltz. They argued that nuclear spread is both inevitable and desirable, because nobody attacks a nuclear power. Any dangers from proliferating nukes can be managed. No matter how crazy North Korea's leaders might sometimes appear, they did not want to perish in a nuclear exchange.[13]

Proponents of arms control did not argue that nuclear arms are safe in the hands of the United States and other existing nuclear weapons states. Arms controllers worried that the emergence of *any* additional actor equipped with nuclear weapons raised the probability that nuclear arms will be used—whether by accident, by a miscalculation, or by a madman. Individuals of any ethnic, cultural, or political hue can make grievous mistakes. Westerners and Russians had no grounds for self-congratulation. Both the Russian and the American nuclear arsenals and command systems suffered many nearly cataclysmic accidents over the decades. No "Nucflash" happened in the United States, but there were dozens of very close calls, known as "Broken Arrows."[14] Some officials try to learn from past mistakes, but human fallibility knows no limits. In 2007 what the Pentagon called a "Bent Spear" event took place when the U.S. Air Force lost track of six nuclear-armed cruise missiles between two of its bases in North Dakota.[15] In 2013 Air Force officers entrusted with the launch keys to long-range nuclear missiles twice left open a blast door intended to keep out terrorists or other intruders from entering their underground command post. The top American ICBM commander, a two-star general, was fired in 2013 for going on a drinking binge and for personal misbehavior during a visit to Russia. In 2014 the Air Force accused other missileers of using narcotics and cheating on proficiency exams. If such mishaps occurred regularly in a technologically advanced America, what were the risks in India, which had twice the number of industrial accidents as the United States, or in Pakistan, where the rate was four times higher? Officials in Vladimir Putin's Russia and Putin admirers in 2014–2015 actually talked of using nuclear weapons as a way to "de-escalate" if a conventional war broke out with NATO.[16]

On a more positive note, the record showed that nuclear spread could be stopped and even reversed. John F. Kennedy in 1963 worried that by the 1970s there could be fifteen to twenty-five states with nuclear arms.[17] By 2015, however, there were eight—nine if we include North Korea; and 185 states had signed or acceded to the Nuclear Nonproliferation Treaty.[18] They included South Africa, Ukraine, Belarus, and Kazakhstan, which gave up their nuclear arms. Libya surrendered its nuclear plant as part of a grand bargain. Iraq was disarmed by force. Iran in 2013–2015 agreed to freeze and perhaps reverse its production of enriched uranium in return for reduced sanctions. Three of North Korea's neighbors, the ROK, Japan, and Taiwan, abjured nuclear arms, at least for the time being, despite having an ability to produce them. Stopping nuclear spread would depend on trends in China as well as North Korea, and the credibility of the U.S. deterrent.

Arms controllers hoped that North Korea would limit, if not eliminate, its nuclear weapons and capacity. Pyongyang countered that it would not repeat the mistakes made by Iraq and Libya. Had Saddam Hussein and Muammar Gaddafi possessed a nuclear deterrent, DPRK commentators asserted, then their regimes would not have fallen to outside forces. In this same vein, some Ukrainians in 2014–2015 wished they still had nuclear arms to keep Vladimir Putin's Russia at bay.

Can meaningful arms controls be negotiated? The record is analyzed in chapter 9 and subsequent chapters. Here we note only that if top leaders do not *want* an accord, then their negotiators do not *fail* if they reach no agreement. The negotiators' assigned task may have been to buy time by dragging out the talks or merely to save face and embarrass the other side.[19]

If the rulers of the DPRK insist on maintaining their claim to be a nuclear-weapons state, could it be wise to seek renewed negotiations on arms control? Why validate North Korea's nuclear status through government-to-government initiatives? Would this not add dignity to Kim Jong Un's regime and its nuclear claim? Even efforts at greater economic engagement could add credibility to Pyongyang's *pyŏngjin* line, asserting the feasibility and desirability of developing the DPRK economy while enhancing its nuclear and missile weapons.

Given these dilemmas, the International Crisis Group in June 2015 recommended a long game of principled engagement. Yes, containment and deterrence would still be needed, but the risks of miscalculation and war would not go away. "To reduce these risks, the international community needs to develop other channels of communication and cooperation that are not contingent on progress toward denuclearization." Actors on many levels—governments, international organizations, the private sector, and civil society—needed to find ways to produce cooperative outcomes and avert catastrophes while avoiding doing harm.[20]

Despite potential abuses of negotiations, arms controls can reduce the danger of war, save money, and limit damage if war erupts. They can open the way to a positive relationship as well as a negative peace. Reviewing the record of arms talks with North Korea should help us to understand what succeeds and what fails in such efforts. It may suggest ways to turn from a dead end to an open road.

LOCATION, LOCATION, LOCATION

Size isn't everything. But in world affairs, as in real estate, value is often shaped by location. Korea is the hub of security concerns in Northeast Asia and beyond—a crossroads for commerce but also a caldron for war. A map of Korea shows a potential dagger pointed at Japan, China, and Russia, but also a narrow peninsula readily accessed by three of the most powerful actors on the world stage.[21]

Both the ROK and the DPRK are medium-sized countries with long coastlines. North Korea borders China, Russia, and South Korea, whereas the South is surrounded by water, except on its land border with the North. The more than 25 million people in the North live in a mountainous space with deep valleys and some coastal plains covering 121,000 square kilometers (a little smaller than Mississippi). The South's population is nearly twice as large—49 million, living in a hilly land with wide coastal plains covering 97,000 square kilometers (slightly larger than Indiana). By the size of its population, the North ranks 49th in the world; by the extent of its territory, 99th. The South's population is 25th largest in the world; its area, 109th.

Proximity counts: As a Chinese general noted, "China and Korea are separated by only a river. They depend on each other like lips and teeth. What concerns one concerns also the other. The security of China is closely connected with the survival of Korea."[22] China dominated Korea for centuries but lost its hold in the late nineteenth century to a rising Japan. Having annexed Korea in 1910, Japanese forces parted only in 1945. Still, Japanese interest in Korea remained. An early Japanese version of the Microsoft encyclopedia *Encarta* had 216 articles on Korea—compared to just 46 in the U.S. edition. A single comic book on North Korea's "Dear Leader" Kim Jong Il (portrayed as a depraved despot) published in Japan in 2003 sold half a million copies in a few months—probably more than all the books ever published on Korea in English.[23]

The presence of U.S. troops in Korea long after the Korean War reassured some South Koreans but angered others.[24] Some South Koreans wanted closer ties with China to counter U.S. influences. North Korea's leaders usually demanded withdrawal of U.S. troops from the Korean peninsula but on occasion allowed that American forces might stay. A near constant in DPRK policy, however, was a quest for normalized ties with the United States. It is possible that Pyongyang might have renounced its quest for nuclear weapons if it had acquired diplomatic recognition and nonaggression assurances from Washington. One DPRK objective was to offset China's heavy presence. "It would be good for the United States," a visitor to Pyongyang was told, to have North Korea "as a buffer state in this dangerous area. Who knows, perhaps there are ways in which the United States could benefit from our ports and our intelligence if we become friends."[25] One high-ranking DPRK minister told an American diplomat, "We could be your base to contain China." Another said, "We could be your 'Israel in East Asia.'" As of 2015, however, officials in the United States were unsure about the DPRK and its strategy. Policy analysts in Pyongyang probably had similar questions.

LESSONS FOR THE WORLD?

Another reason to think about Korea is to understand better why some states fail while others prosper. Both Koreas proclaimed their independent statehood in 1948; both joined the United Nations on the same day in 1991; North and South Koreans share the same genes, cultural traditions, and language. Still, the two Koreas became and remained two different states with distinct ways of life. The economic strength of North Korea plateaued in the 1970s and began to decline relative to South Korea. Its greatest political achievement was to institutionalize and sacralize a ruling dynasty across three generations. By the twenty-first century the Republic of Korea offered a model of economic dynamism, self-government, educational excellence, and "wired" infrastructure. Its pop culture animated Japan, China, parts of the United States and Europe, and even—underground—North Korea.

What complexity science calls *societal fitness*—the ability to cope with complex challenges and take advantage of opportunities—declined in the North even as it increased in the South.[26] One indicator of societal fitness is a country's ranking on the Human Development Index (HDI) prepared by the UN Development Programme. The HDI seeks to gauge the conditions that enhance human choice—what Aristotle might term the capacity to actualize each person's potential. To measure those conditions, the UNDP Human Development Index collects and aggregates data on health, education, and incomes. Western or Westernized countries dominate the top ranks on the index. In 2014 Norway placed first; Australia and New Zealand ranked second, and the United States, fifth. The only Asian

A woman who works at a restaurant in Pyongyang watches over her son, who explores a pack of biscuits given to him by a Chinese tourist. (Photo by Stephen Gong)

country in the top ten was Singapore, at ninth. The ROK and Hong Kong tied at 15th; Japan, 17th; Israel, 19th; Russia, 57th; China, 91st; India, 135th; and Pakistan, 146th. Following Afghanistan, ten African countries were at the bottom—ranked from 170th to 179th, with Guinea last.[27]

Due to lack of data, the UNDP did not rank the DPRK but merely listed it with other countries such as Somalia and Sudan. The DPRK regime cultivated high rates of literacy and school attendance, but left North Korea unfit by many indicators. The regime did little to advance the realm of choice for most North Koreans. According to the UNDP, infant mortality was high in the North. Some 23 babies died for every 1,000 live births—nearly eight times the rates in South Korea and Japan (3 of 1,000) and nearly four times the U.S. rate (6 per 1,000). On the other hand, the DPRK rate was low relative to India (44 per 1,000) and Pakistan (69 per 1,000). The UN also reported severe malnutrition and stunting in 28 percent of North Korean children aged five and under—compared with 9 percent in China, virtually none in South Korea and Japan, and 44 percent in India and 69 percent in Pakistan. The UN reported that the DPRK had a food deficit of 238 calories—high, though only half of Burundi's. Challenging any expectation of an authoritarian calm, the DPRK homicide rate was 15.2 per 100,000 persons—much higher than in South Korea (2.6) or the United States (4.7).[28]

```
        Exploitation                          Mutual Gain
       /            \                              |
      ↙              ↘                             ↓

 Law of the jungle    Top-down rule          Self-organization

    Anarchy            Dictatorship             Democracy

    Sterility            Sterility               Creativity

  Random chaos        Rigid hierarchy           Complexity

       ↘              ↙                             ↓
         Low Fitness                            High Fitness
```

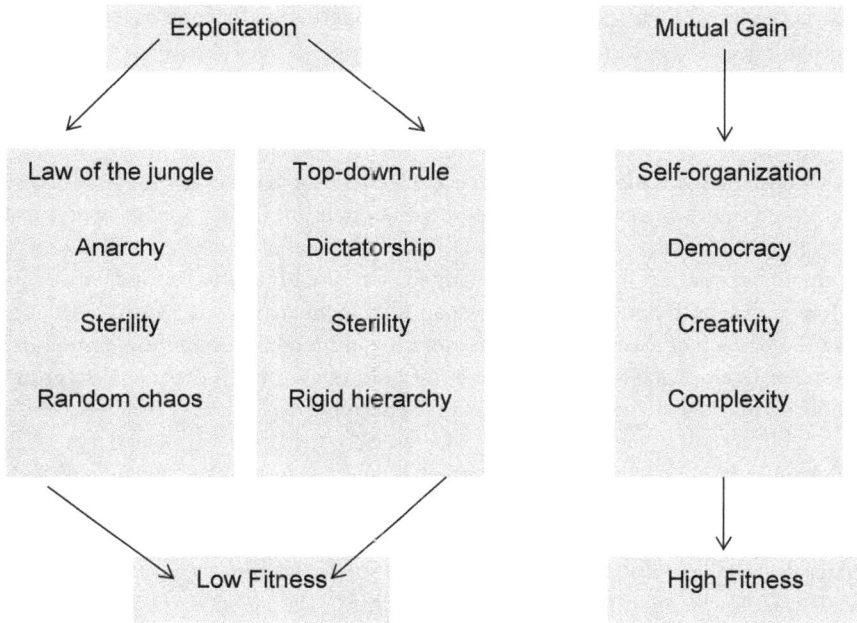

Figure 1.1. Exploitation, mutual gain, and fitness: likely linkages

Evaluative rankings by other agencies—Freedom House, Transparency International, and the Bertelsmann Foundation—are summarized below in chapter 10. With few exceptions, they dovetail with the HDI.

What accounts for the very different trajectories of North Korea and its neighbors? This book argues that Northeast Asia's experience provides another case of a pattern that has beset humanity for millennia: *The Kim dynasty's policies illustrate how extractive policies by the ruling elite for its private interests can harm the development of entire societies.*[29] *Rooted both in self-seeking and mutual distrust, the North's policies reflect a myopic, zero-sum orientation that usually serves to degrade the well-being of extractive polities.*[30]

As Figure 1.1 suggests, exploitative policies spawn low fitness, while policies oriented toward mutual gain nurture high fitness. The evidence for this proposition may be found in my previous books but will also emerge in many chapters that follow—especially in chapter 10, on why North Korea is not the South.[31]

IMPLICATIONS OF INTERDEPENDENCE AND COMPLEXITY

Neither the democracies nor the authoritarians involved in Northeast Asia can ignore the challenges and opportunities in a world of growing interdependence. A wise policy must take account of this growing interdependence in every domain. Mutual dependence signifies mutual vulnerability—a relationship so close that moves by any party can harm or help the other. The realities of global interdependence reinforce the reasons for developing a strategy aimed at creating values for all parties.

Interdependence is rarely symmetrical. North Korea occupies one-sixth more space than South Korea but possesses less than half the ROK population and just a fraction of its material wealth. The DPRK is far smaller and weaker than any of its other negotiating partners—the United States, China, Russia, and Japan. Its only ace relative to South Korea and Japan is its inchoate nuclear arsenal. Still, the DPRK and each of these parties share not only vulnerabilities but also a potential for mutual gain. Such asymmetries are not unique. Actors on the global stage are seldom equal. Even the U.S. and Soviet "superpowers" had very different assets and liabilities. One was more than twice as rich; the other, twice as large. Still, Washington and Moscow recognized their shared needs and the utility of collaborating in many realms.[32]

An understanding of interdependence combined with insights about complex systems could contribute to a new paradigm for social studies more useful than realism or idealism with all their "neo" variants.[33] The fledgling science of complex systems suggests that every society's well-being—its overall fitness—depends on its ability to cooperate as well as compete. To sustain life-support networks, humans need to collaborate—not free ride, like a parasite, or otherwise exploit one another. Harnessing complex interdependence can make a participant stronger than the sum of its parts. Interlocking ties can resemble a coral reef where diverse life forms find mutual protection in a sustainable ecosystem. Self-organization and self-healing are processes found in nature that can also be emulated by humans.[34] These principles are used in chapter 10 to illuminate differences between South Korea and the North.

The actors in Northeast Asia could benefit from adapting to interdependence in the ways pioneered within the European Union and between the United States and Canada. Between the United States and the DPRK meaningful cooperation may exist only as a mental image in the early twenty-first century—still, such a vision could push policy in more positive directions.

Each actor in Northeast Asia could utilize interdependence to seek unilateral advantage or mutual gain. In our world of escalating interdependencies, an effective foreign policy needs to follow three axioms. First, policymakers must develop a "smart" mix of hard and soft power plus conversion power—the ability to apply them effectively.[35]

Second, each actor's deepest interests are more likely to be advanced by policies meant to create mutual gain with others than by value-claiming policies aimed at unilateral gain. Exploiting others may achieve short-term gains, but this approach tends to boomerang over time so that the costs outweigh the benefits. In addition, the time during which exploitation can pay has become ever shorter, thanks to modern communications and interdependence. The history of evolution shows that the capacity to cooperate is vital for species fitness.

Of course a mutual gain strategy requires reciprocity. If any actor merely pockets the other's concessions and then asks for more, then value-creating will be a losing strategy. Both North Korea and its interlocutors complain that their gestures of goodwill have been abused by the other side. How to induce reciprocity in relations between longtime antagonists quite different in assets and outlook is explored in the chapters that follow.

Third, the more that all actors communicate with each other and with their own publics, the greater the prospect of finding solutions useful to all sides. The most successful U.S. foreign endeavor of all time, the Marshall Plan, was organized and conducted in full view. Both its inputs and its outputs were mutual. The more complete the public discussion of policy—based on *accurate* information—the lower the danger of counterproductive adventures such as the Indochina and Iraq wars. For a dictatorship, open discussion of the facts and policy alternatives may not be feasible, but even an authoritarian regime can profit from sharing its objectives, assets, and needs with foreign interlocutors. Without shared knowledge of each side's desiderata, their optimal accommodation is unlikely.

The prospects for better mutual understanding are improved by the fact that, in today's world, countries communicate not only through their government officials but also through their unofficial representatives—rock stars, athletes, evangelists, au pairs, bloggers, and ordinary tourists. We have not only Track 1—official diplomacy between governments—but also Track 2, or "private citizen," diplomacy. With North Korea there is also Track 1½: diplomacy conducted by private citizens and off-duty or retired officials. Thus, representatives of the Nautilus Institute have discussed energy issues with North Korean specialists while U.S. officials have observed and taken notes.[36] Negotiations by business and commercial interests constitute a kind of Track 3, with some ability to leapfrog political hang-ups.

The many forms of diplomacy now available contribute to a major hope for peace—relationships of complex interdependence. While interdependence can exist in just one area of vulnerability (e.g., nuclear deterrence), *complex* interdependence is marked by three features: first, the parties interact on many levels—not just at the summit (as among heads of state); second, their agendas touch many shared concerns with no clear hierarchy; and third, given these linkages, discord over any particular agenda item or items could never give rise to war. Where complex interdependence is strong, as in today's Europe, violence as a way to resolve disputes becomes unthinkable.[37] The ROK "Sunshine Policy," initiated in the late 1990s, aimed to create such relationships with the DPRK but encountered many obstacles. Critics faulted it for not insisting on reciprocal actions by the North.

Ostensibly angered by South Korean rhetoric and by ROK-U.S. military exercises, Pyongyang shut down the last vestige of the Sunshine Policy, the Kaesong Industrial Park, in April 2013, only to call for its reopening a few months later. Responding to new DPRK bomb and missile tests, the ROK terminated all its operations at Kaesong in early 2016.

Détente would make the integration of Northeast Asia far easier. Higher levels of prosperity and human development across the region could be reached if political conditions encouraged investment, education, and commerce. No country needs such conditions more than North Korea, where a "military-first" policy shortchanged every other aspect of life.

If the Korean peninsula became a zone of peace, then it could radiate economic benefits in all azimuths. The industrial South could gain from access to the North's mineral riches and educated workforce, while the North could benefit from the South's know-how in agriculture, business, and technology. North Korea's disciplined labor force could become another ingredient in lowering production costs for multinational firms—while raising living standards in the North. All Koreans, as well as Japanese, Chinese, and Russians, could gain if the oil and gas riches of Siberia could flow freely down the peninsula instead of being first loaded and unloaded on heavy ships. Improved rail links between Siberia and North Korea could fillip trade and bring both Koreas and China closer to all Eurasia and Europe.

Protection of rare and threatened species—whooping cranes and fishes—would be facilitated by regional stability.[38] The relatively pristine nature sanctuary created by the demilitarized zone between North and South Korea could be enhanced and enlarged.

These and other alternative futures are discussed here. Worst-case as well as win-win scenarios are analyzed. For example, a nuclear-armed North Korea could trigger an Asian arms race and war. On the other hand, if the lessons of history contributed to enlightened policies, then the prospects for mutual gain could improve.

Whatever we learn about conflict resolution in Northeast Asia could have broader implications. Hostile antagonists around the globe need to learn how to manage their differences, foster shared interests, and convert swords into plowshares.

2

How Korea Became Korea

To comprehend political or nuclear Korea we must also know something of social Korea, cultural Korea, and ethnic Korea.[1] Historically speaking, Korea is younger than China but older than Japan. The history of Korea reveals many forces and features shared by both South and North Korea. To understand and deal with North Korea, we must be familiar with the trends of Korea's development before 1945.[2] These trends included a drive for self-mastery and resistance to foreign influences—roots of North Korea's Juche ideology—succinctly expressed by a DPRK poet:

> Even when we were tightening our belt,
> We did not drink Coca-Cola.
> Even when we were drinking muddied water,
> At least we drank our own water.[3]

The DPRK regime extolled Juche not only to rail against foreign influences but also to justify self-sacrifice for the state and submission to god-king rulers, who were alleged to represent the will of the North Korean people. Each dynast—Great Leader Kim Il Sung; his son, Dear Leader Kim Jong Il; and his grandson, Kim Jong Un—claimed, in effect, "*L'etat, c'est moi*": "I am the state and its people live through me." Nearly every topic discussed in this book—from the Korean War to nuclear weapons to human rights—was and continues to be shaped by the Juche quest for self-assertion and self-reliance.

GOD-KINGS AND JUCHE

Korea's long history anticipated many of the conflicts and opportunities confronting policymakers and diplomats in the twenty-first century. Although Koreans constituted one of the world's most homogeneous peoples, with a distinct culture and a unique language, they often vied for supremacy among themselves. Koreans also faced powerful and menacing neighbors. The techniques by which

Kim Il Sung. The "Great Leader," said to be "The Light of Human Genius" and "North Star of the People." (Photo by Jeremy Hunter)

Paying respects to the Great Leader. (Photo by Jeremy Hunter)

Koreans manipulated both foes and putative allies emerged from centuries of life-and-death struggles. The smaller fish, to survive among sharks, often played off one adversary against the other. But the smaller fish often fought each other to the death.

Korea's past consecrated the idea of authoritarian rule. Korean myths, summarized in this chapter, help explain why North Korea is the only Communist country that experienced a dynastic succession and why these putative demigods can adorn themselves in superhuman superlatives even as they exploit and abuse their subjects.

Thus, Kim Il Sung and his successors taught North Koreans to believe that the people and their supreme leader are one. The rationale for this view borrowed from Japanese ideology as well as from Korean mythology. As Charles F. Armstrong observed, "Meiji Japan was the first East Asian state to promote the idea of 'national essence,' or *kokutai,* the nation as a collective self (personified in Japan by the emperor), subsuming the individual within." Kim Il Sung's regime kept the form of "Japanese corporatism, with its god-like leader, invisible mass, and sacred national purpose, linked together in an organic whole."[4]

Kim switched places with Hirohito and became the reigning monarch in North Korea after 1945. Kim developed the state ideology of Juche to justify his own needs. The term is loosely translated as "self-reliance," but its etymology connotes "rule the body" or "master the essence." Juche breaks from materialist determinism to emphasize subjective factors—willpower, the state, and sovereignty. The term reflects Korea's long history of proud nationalism and determination to fend off foreign influence. The policy emerged from the *Ch'ollima undong* (Galloping Horse Movement) initiated by Kim Il Sung in 1957—a call to push forward rapidly but without mimicking China or the USSR. Kim first extolled Juche in a speech to some 400 top leaders of the Korean Workers' party in December 1955. Entitled "On Eliminating Dogmatism and Formalism and Establishing Juche in Ideological Work," the speech called on Koreans to do their own thing—not to ape the USSR, which in 1955 appeared to seek better relations with the capitalist world. It also served as a vehicle to pillory Kim's potential rivals—North Korean Communists he accused of being too close to Moscow or to Beijing. The speech was not publicized until later but became heavily propagated after the mid-1960s.[5]

Juche implies that North Korea should rule itself—without dictation by outsiders. This outlook strengthened as Korean nationalists, left and right, sought to throw off Japanese colonial dominion, but it also colored Korean attitudes toward Chinese, Russians, and Americans.[6] Juche became a quasi-theological concept linked to the quasi-divine personage of the top leader. It links sovereignty with individual dignity, or "face." To lose face means shame in a deep, Confucian sense. Given this outlook, North Korea defends its sovereignty against any slight.[7] Failure to take account of this attitude led Americans during the Korean War to regard

Kim Il Sung as a Soviet puppet. A similar failure kept the Chinese from grasping why Kim resisted military advice from PRC marshals. Reluctant to admit the extent of Soviet and Chinese assistance, Pyongyang barely acknowledged it. As comrades in the cause of Communism, Kim and his offspring expected help from other Communists, but showed little gratitude for it.

While the foregoing interpretations suggest that Juche has served to mobilize North Korean citizens to respect, honor, and obey the country's rulers, a professor of Korean studies in Seoul argues that Juche propaganda is meant mainly for foreign consumption. The North's real ideology, according to B. R. Myers, is nationalism rooted in a radical form of racism.[8] Devotion to one's race and to national sovereignty, however, could overlap and feed on each other. At odds with the foreign consumption thesis, the official DPRK calendar starts with the year of Kim Il Sung's birth in 1912. What most of the world calls 2012, for North Koreans, is Juche 100 or Juche 101. As shown in note 17 to this chapter, the official Korean Central News Agency dated its dispatches using both calendars.

AN IMAGINED COMMUNITY: FOLKLORE AS FAKE LORE

The entire edifice of North Korean culture can be understood as an effort to form and shape an imagined community.[9] Selecting what to include, emphasize, or downgrade makes folklore more like fake lore.[10]

Korean mythology holds that the Korean people emerged from the Paektu volcanic mountain, the highest point in Korea at 2,744 meters. Nearly half of Mount Paektu stands in China, however, and Chinese also revere the mountain and appreciate its beauty. Tourists from each side converge at the crater lake atop the volcano, the source of both the Yalu and Tumen rivers. Some nationalists in China and in Korea claim the entire mountain as their own. Some Koreans recall that their ancestors once ruled much of Manchuria to the northwest of their sacred volcano.

Kim Il Sung is said to have fought the Japanese occupation from a cabin at Mount Paektu. His son, Kim Jong Il, was reportedly born "in a secret camp in Mount Paektu and grew up to be the son of Mount Paektu, hearing gun reports as a lullaby, and wearing clothes made of the power-reeking military uniform of his mother, the anti-Japanese war hero Kim Jong Suk, using patched quilt."[11]

When Kim Jong Il died in December 2011, the Korean Central News Agency reported that a snowstorm hit the mountain; the ice at the lake near his birthplace cracked; and a message appeared carved in the rock—"Mount Paektu, holy mountain of revolution, Kim Jong Il"—where it remained until sunset. The Korean Central News Agency (KCNA) reported that a crane also mourned the demise of Kim Jong Il. It flew down in the dead of a cold night to adopt a posture of grief near the statue of the late leader's father in the city of Hamhung.

Juche ideology says that ordinary North Koreans acquire the status of sovereign being by connecting with the sovereign leader. To die for him is the highest and most noble goal in life. As Sonia Ryang put it: "The Great Leader's endless love is not the reason why North Koreans love him, but his love is the reason for them to love themselves."[12] Somewhat like the way many Christians see God, each North Korean is free to follow the charismatic leader, who personifies each person's higher, superior self. The ties between a man and woman can become true love only if they triangulate in loving the leader.[13]

A viable state requires a viable society, but this was destroyed in the 1990s famine and its aftermath. North Korea became a "theater state" in which shows of state strength took the place of a viable political economy. Theater perpetuated the charisma of the revolutionary regime and helped to carry on hereditary rule. Displays of power also justified dedication to sŏn'gun—"military first"—over real economic development.[14]

North Korea's ideology became a gumbo containing several contradictory ingredients. The leadership paid obeisance to Marxism but ranked subjective power above material determinism. It praised the collective will but conflated it with the will of the supreme leader. The most noble act for the individual was said

Tower of the Juche Idea. A tourist attraction, thanks to its 360-degree view from the top, with memorials submitted by DPRK supporters from Malta to Nigeria. (Photo by Jeremy Hunter)

Monument to the Korean Workers' Party, 50 meters high with three gigantic hands in a circle, holding not only a hammer (worker) and sickle (peasant) but also a brush (intellectual) to symbolize the three pillars of the state. The three objects are connected by a circular band with the slogan "Long live the Workers Party of Korea, which organizes and guides all victories for the Korean people!" (Photo by Jeremy Hunter)

Ryugyong Hotel. Called the "105" building for the number of its floors. Construction of the hotel began in 1987 to attract Western business people and tourists, and to compete with a hotel in Singapore built by South Koreans. Not completed for years, "105" was sometimes airbrushed out of printed material. There were plans to open the hotel in 2016. (Photo by Jeremy Hunter)

to be the sacrifice of his or her life for the leader. Thus, the official press praised a man who, as his home and family were swept away in a flood, risked the safety of his children to save portraits of two god-kings.[15] As some North Koreans discovered, however, the demigods and their entourage were stuffing themselves while the masses endured a Long March.

Juche stressed the power of subjectivity, but under Kim Jong Il it became a barrel-of-a-gun philosophy, dedicating all resources to building up military strength. Barrel-of-a-gunnism was sacralized by the tale of three pistols. Kim Hyung Jik, the father of Kim Il Sung, was said to have given him two pistols in the 1920s to fight the Japanese. A generation later, Kim Il Sung was said to have given a single pistol to his ten-year-old son, Kim Jong Il, in 1952 (during the Korean War). "The Great Leader passed over to his son the heritage of our revolution through this revolver, following what [his father] had done in earlier times. Contained in the gun was the Great Leader's dearest wish for a continuous Korean revolution across the generations and according to the glorious tradition of the Mankyung-dae [legendary birthplace of Kim Il Sung] revolutionary family."[16]

After less than one year on the throne, Kim Jong Un demanded that his dynasty be worshipped: revolutionary schools should educate students to "trust

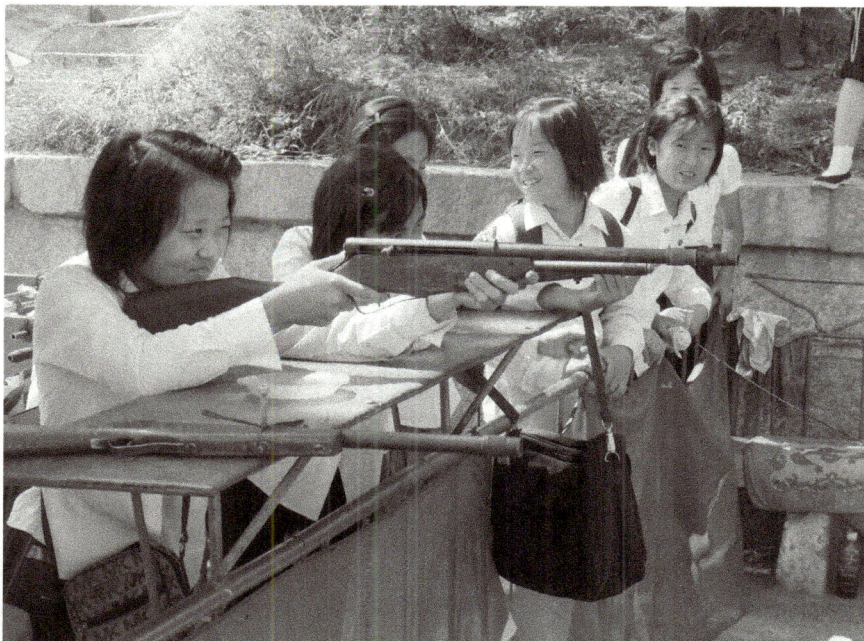

Shooting range. "In our country, everyone knows how to fire a gun."—Kim Il Sung (Photo by Jeremy Hunter)

Streets of central Pyongyang—a country "left deserted by some invisible plague," according to a Chinese official when he saw the empty streets of the DPRK capital in 1991. By 2016, traffic was much heavier. (Photo by Jeremy Hunter)

and follow only the Party and the leader that have brought them up." Young people should give "steady continuity to the blood line of Maygyondae, the bloodline of Mt. Paektu," as befits the sons and daughters "who grew up under the care of the three commanders of Mt. Paektu." They must become persons "strong in faith and the sense of obligation, who will hold fast to the red flag of the revolution, the flag of the glorious Party, even though they have to abandon their lives."[17]

CHINESE LEGEND AND DPRK MYTHOLOGY

North Korea's rulers adopted and adapted ancient legends to legitimate dynastic rule in the DPRK. Korea's past and present are illuminated but also distorted by legend. The earliest political entity on the Korean peninsula documented by historical records was the Kingdom of Koguryŏ (first century BCE–seventh century CE). Regarded as the first great representative of Korean civilization, Koguryŏ extended from the middle of the peninsula into Manchuria. This entity materialized from the consolidation of protostates and statelets in the first century BCE. But legend traces the origins of Korea to 2333 BCE, when king Dan'gun founded the kingdom of Old Chosŏn. He was said to be the son of the Spirit King and a "she-bear" who mated at Mount Paektu. Thus, Dan'gun was Korea's first theocrat.[18] Dan'gun reigned for 1,500 years and taught a previously wild and untutored people all the arts of living. His capital, a walled city built near today's Pyongyang, was shaped like a boat. Since a boat will sink if a hole is bored into its bottom, it was "forbidden in those early times to dig wells inside this boat city. That is why the people there had to carry all their water a long way"[19]—a harbinger perhaps of future hardships under Japanese and then under Communist rule.

Legend holds that Dan'gun was succeeded by the sage Kija, a refugee from China. A high official in the Zhou dynasty, Kija was unhappy with the wicked emperor there and wanted to rule where people could live safely and in peace.[20] Kija crossed the Duck Green (Yalu) River beneath the Ever-White Mountains, bringing with him 5,000 "good Chinese"—doctors, scholars, mechanics, carpenters, fortune tellers, and magicians; also the precious worms that spin silk; plus rice and barley. Chinese influences became strong early in Korean life.[21] Kija made the walled city of Pyongyang his capital in 1122 BCE. He gave his subjects the Five Laws, laying out their duties. Those were golden days, when travelers were safe from robbers and gates could be left open.

Dan'gun gave Korea its basic culture, including kimchee (fermented cabbage and spices); Kija introduced high culture and built an autonomous civilization that borrowed from, but was distinct from, China.[22] His dynasty, the Ki-Jun, lasted until 4 CE.

Many historians doubt whether Kija ever existed. The story of Kija and his 5,000 "good Chinese" may well have originated as Chinese propaganda, but today it has been adapted to fit North Korean mythology. The tale confirms the idea that a father figure created a great dynasty. DPRK guides assert that Kija's tomb can still be seen near Pyongyang, close to the place where the founding father of today's DPRK, Kim Il Sung, reposes in a mausoleum—one that is much grander than those housing the mummies of Lenin and Mao Zedong.

Korean kings wanted sons as successors and sometimes acquired them in strange ways. A legend told in North Korea, but not in the South, relates that Chu-mong, the legendary founder of Koguryŏ, was conceived when the wind of a passing cloud placed an egg inside the dress of a royal wife. This boy's jealous brothers tried to kill him, but he fled south. He used magic to cross the dark-green waters of the River Aprok (Yalu) and then charm its waters to swallow up his pursuers. He ruled from 37 to 19 BCE.

EMERGENCE IN THE SHADOW OF CHINA

Koreans chafe at their dependency—in North Korea vis-à-vis China and Russia, and in South Korea, toward the United States. China in the early twenty-first century became the major trading partner of South as well as North Korea. China remained the most steadfast supporter of the DPRK on the international stage, though Chinese officials increasingly criticized the North's behavior. As we shall see in later chapters, Pyongyang needed help from China in many fields but often complained that Beijing was niggardly.[23] South Korea's deepening economic ties with China helped to offset the ROK's dependency on the United States for military security. Many South Koreans were pleased—others unhappy—regarding their alliance with the United States.[24]

Interacting with their powerful neighbor to the west, Koreans acquired a hate-love relationship with China. Koreans imported much of their religion, science, and technology from China. They depended at times on China for protection from what Chinese called "barbarians" and from the Japanese. Koreans thought of themselves as members of a universal system—what Harvard's John Fairbanks called "the Sinic Zone." As such, Koreans also regarded themselves as caretakers of Chinese culture.[25] Internally they endeavored to unite the power of clan chiefs and establish the foundation of a ruling system. But ancient Korean states strove to free themselves from Chinese cultural forces and to remain intact in their struggles against other peoples outside the Great Wall.[26]

The first ruler of Korea recorded in contemporaneous records is Wi-man, a Chinese or Chinese-born Korean, who seized power in the Old Chosŏn kingdom in 194 BCE. Chinese forces subsequently conquered the eastern half of the peninsula and made Lolang, near modern Pyongyang, the chief base for Chinese rule. Chinese sources recall how China used not only military force but also assassination and divide-and-conquer tactics to subdue Chosŏn and divide the territory into four commanderies.[27]

The complicated history of Korea is simplified and summarized in figure 2.1.

By the first century CE a native Korean kingdom, Koguryŏ, arose on both sides of the Yalu River. By the fourth century CE, Koguryŏ conquered Lolang and occupied much of what is now Korea and northeastern China. In 612 CE Koguryŏ forces wiped out an invading Chinese army in the Great Battle of Salsu River. But two rival kingdoms emerged in the south—Paekche in the west side of the peninsula and Silla in the east. Allied with Tang China, Silla conquered both Paekche and Koguryŏ by 668, and then expelled the Chinese and unified much of the peninsula. Having ruled most of Korea for centuries, Silla fragmented and then surrendered to the Koryŏ dynasty in 935.

A Chinese account in the ninth century CE told how the Chinese emperor sought hegemony over barbarians in the "Nine Zones of Submission," which spread eastward as well as westward. "When Koguryŏ became refractory and rebellious, Wei sent an army detachment to visit chastisement upon them. The army went to the end of the earth in exhaustive pursuit" until it "gazed eastwards upon the great sea." The peoples there had strange faces from their proximity to the sun. They also had strange customs but retained the shape of ritual vessels as in

CHINA	KOREA
PRC (1949–>)	DPRK (1948–>) ROK (1948–>)
Republic of China (1912–>)	Soviet military gov't U.S. military gov't (1945–1948) Japanese rule (1910–1945)
Qing (1664–1912)	Chosŏn (1392–1910) European and U.S. ships enter Korea (1860s–1870s) Christianity introduced (1776) Japanese invasions (1592–1597) Han'gŭl invented (1444)
Ming (1368–1664)	
Yuan (1271–1368)	Koryŏ (918–1392) Mongol Domination (1250s–1360s)
S. Sung (1127–1279)	
N. Sung (959–1126) Liao (907–1125)	
Tang (618–906)	United Silla Kingdom (668–935) Balhae (698–926)
Sui (581–618)	Three Kingdoms in Conflict: Koguryŏ, Paekche, Silla (400s–600s)

Figure 2.1. Chronology of Chinese and Korean history. *Sources:* Cornelius Osgood, *The Koreans and Their Culture* (New York: Ronald Press, 1951), 168; Patricia B. Ebrey, Anne Walthall, and James B. Palais, *East Asia: A Cultural, Social, and Political History* (Boston: Houghton Mifflin, 2006), v–vi; Kyung Moon Hwang, *A History of Korea: An Episodic Narrative* (New York: Palgrave, 2010), xiv.

China—confirming the saying "When the Middle Kingdom has lost the rites, seek them among the Four Barbarians."[28]

Koreans became a racially and linguistically homogeneous people during United Silla (668–935). They lived in a well-defined territory administered by a centralized bureaucracy. Their shared traditional and cultural values made them well aware of their special position toward China and Japan. Under Silla's rule, Korea prospered and the arts flourished.

In 918, however, the Silla dynasty was overthrown by Wang Kon, founder of the Koryŏ dynasty (an abbreviated form of *Koguryŏ* and source of the name *Korea*). Koryŏ Korea (918–1392) was Buddhist. Having entered Korea from China in the fourth century, Buddhism became dominant in Korea's spiritual life. During the Koryŏ period, literature flourished; and, even while Buddhism remained the state religion, China's Confucian bureaucracy became the model for Korean government. Under the influence of China, a patrilineal philosophy subtly superimposed itself upon the originally cognatic Korean system. This brought a slow reduction in the range of choices the traditional social system had granted to an individual and his or her group. Flexibility was narrowed by patrilineally calculated rules. This development, promoted from the top, prepared the ground for Neo-Confucianism.

As in China and Russia, Mongols dominated Korea for much of the thirteenth and fourteenth centuries. The Mongols virtually annexed Korea and used it as a base to invade Japan. The Mongol invasions of Japan in 1274 and 1281 were ultimately defeated by storms, but they left a mark on Japanese thinking. The fact that typhoons—regarded as divine winds (*kami-kaze*)—came to Japan's aid confirmed the traditional Japanese belief that theirs is a sacred land. But the Mongols' onslaught also instilled in the Japanese the fear that Korea might again become a springboard for attack against them.[29]

Conflict between the Koryŏ king and aristocracy escalated after the collapse of Mongol domination in the 1350s, as each faction sought more power and influence. This struggle deepened factional strife among aristocrats. As officials were purged and banished, military leaders gained ascendancy.

Having dominated the peninsula for nearly five centuries, Koryŏ was succeeded by the Chosŏn, or Yi, dynasty in 1392. An alliance between Yi Song-gye, a military hero, and Neo-Confucian scholar-officials led to the founding of the Chosŏn dynasty, which endured until Japan annexed Korea in 1910. Military weakness pressed for change. Yi Song-gye saw that Chosŏn could not defeat the Ming regime in China and so opted to bow to it. He backed land reforms that stripped land from large Buddhist establishments and other large estates so that the state owned all land and could distribute it to others for cultivation. Brutal in establishing his dynasty, Yi managed to reduce domestic strife and improve relations with China and Japan. He moved the capital to Seoul in 1394.

The change agents who founded the Chosŏn dynasty in 1392 were not rebellious peasants. Some harbored economic grievances, but nearly all were aristocrats with sufficient wealth to sustain themselves during the long preparations for the civil service examinations. Success in the exams plus an illustrious family background gave them access to the central bureaucracy, which, however, was overstaffed and subject to factional strife. The highest offices continued to be occupied by descendants of well-established, aristocratic kin groups. The deepest driving force for them was the Neo-Confucian canon—a literature that envisioned a new sociopolitical order grounded on moral principles. The key text was the *Ta-hsüeh*, which sustained the Neo-Confucians' claim to complete mastery over the totality of public and private life. Referring to the sage-kings of Chinese antiquity, it justified the way the Korean Confucians went about their tasks. The Confucian Academy encouraged disputation—not the rote, dull routine of traditional scholarship. It contained elements of a moral and political plan of action.[30]

Neo-Confucianists claimed to apply classic Confucian teachings to the present situation and problems. They took Neo-Confucianism as the universal basis on which the state must rest. Renewal of society through Neo-Confucian principles, concrete and pragmatic, differed sharply with Buddhism and with earlier Confucian values. While Buddhism and Confucianism had coexisted in Koryŏ, Neo-Confucianists believed that Buddhism had to be eradicated to remake society. In later times, Communists, also seeking to remake society, sought to wipe out all religion except Kimilsongism.

The alliance of a military hero with Neo-Confucian scholars helped restore kingly influence and create a new political order. The leading scholar-official was Chŏng To-jŏn, a polymath whose oeuvre eclipsed that of his contemporaries. Neo-Confucian scholars talked of learning as the tool for bringing people under control by activating their moral nature. The new learning meant action, not just recitation or contemplation. It stimulated the process of self-realization to find the Way in oneself. So that everyone could know his proper station, Neo-Confucian texts spelled out the proper relations between ruler and subject, father and son, old and young, and friends. Kwôn Kûn wrote the *Iphak toseol* (Illustrated Treatises for the Beginner) in 1390, a booklet with diagrams and commentaries to guide the reader through the maze of Neo-Confucian philosophy. But this was a treatise for the intelligentsia, not a primer for beginning readers in the vein of *Orbis Pictus*, produced in 1658 by John Comenius (Jan Komenský in Czech).

Like Kim Il Sung in the late 1940s and 1950s, the founders of the Chosŏn dynasty wanted to establish a new system with a new ideology. The new order blended the ideology of progressive reform with the pragmatic aims of the military. It amounted to a Korean rendition of the Confucian concept of renovation, or *yusin*—the name later attached to South Korea's new constitution in 1972, rammed through by another general turned politician, Park Chung Hee.

The Chosŏn dynasty maintained a special relationship with China characterized by *sadae*—"respect for the senior state" (also translated as serving the superior). Korea accepted a junior status and observed all the ritual practices of a tributary state (including at least two long and arduous pilgrimages to Beijing each year). Dependency, however, was mutual, for China could not allow Korea to fall into hostile hands.[31]

King Sejong in 1419 subdued Japanese marauders based on the islands of Tsushima. He then permitted the Japanese to trade at three Korean ports. Nearly two centuries of peace were shattered when Japan invaded Korea in 1592. Japan's ruler, Toyotomi Hideyoshi, called on Korea to submit to Japan and to collaborate in the conquest of China. Koreans rebuffed the demand, saying that "to invade another nation is an act of which men of culture and intellectual attainments should feel ashamed." But Japanese troops overran Korea. When they fought their way to the Yalu River, the Chinese arranged a truce and used the interval to mobilize. When the truce expired, Chinese troops swarmed across the Yalu with numerically superior forces. The Japanese then agreed to discuss peace terms. In 1593 Hideyoshi proposed a division of Korea. The north would be a self-governing Chinese satellite; the south would belong to Japan. (European relations with Korea began that same year, when a Spanish Jesuit arrived to minister to Christians among the Japanese troops.) China rejected the offer, and four more years of fighting laid waste to Korea. Chinese troops with Korean ironclad "turtle ships" finally compelled the Japanese to withdraw in 1597 after Hideyoshi's death.[32]

In contrast to the *sadae* relationship with China, for most of the seventeenth century Korea maintained only "neighborly" relations (*kyorin*) with Tokugawa Japan. The daimyo of Tsushima enjoyed a monopoly on trade with Korea, but his ships had to carry a seal certified by Korean authorities. Only Japanese merchants were allowed to land at the single port open to foreign trade, Pusan; no Japanese government officials were allowed to join them.

Meanwhile, the Manchus invaded Korea in 1627 and 1636 and compelled the Korean king to kowtow to the Manchu conqueror and sue for peace. The Manchus proceeded to defeat Ming China and establish the Qing dynasty there. Korea then became a tributary state of Manchu China.

From the first half of the seventeenth century to the second half of the nineteenth, Korea became a virtual "hermit kingdom." In the eighteenth century Chosŏn experienced some material prosperity and a cultural rebirth, but did not recover from the previous Japanese and Manchu invasions. Unlike Japan, Korea failed to develop an effective government. During this period Korea limited its foreign contacts and, longer than China or Japan, resisted commerce and other influences from the West. No foreigners except certain envoys and merchants were allowed to visit. Nor were Koreans permitted to go abroad or to associate with illegal entrants. Manchu China, meanwhile, failed to live up to its responsibilities as "older brother" to Korea. Devastated by the Opium Wars of the mid-nineteenth century, China forfeited suzerainty, and Korea became virtually independent in the third quarter of the nineteenth century.

Confucianism and Risk-Taking in Korea

Confucianism became the state religion of Korea in the late fourteenth century. In the spirit of Max Weber,[33] the late political scientist and Asian scholar Lucian W. Pye pondered the impact of Confucianism on Korean culture. Pye's analysis is controversial, but, if on target, it helps us understand not only how Korea became Korea but also why Koreans—in both the North and the South—behave as they do. Reading Pye's analysis of centuries past, we must remember that Confucianism in Korea was not a static phenomenon. It changed over time and shared ideological space with folk religion, Buddhism, and various forms of Christianity. Each faith shaped and was shaped by the state and its activities.[34] Since Pye's analysis is disputed, readers should probably take it as heuristic rather than as a proven theory.

Pye argued that Confucianism in Korea contributed to a risk-taking style of behavior unlike its analogues in China or Japan.[35] He wrote, "The Korean model of government was a peculiar combination of the Chinese ideal of dignity, secure in its monopoly of authority, and the Japanese reality of competitive authority."[36] Uncertainty about who constituted the legitimate elite created a dynamic insecurity and produced people who were self-starters—risk-takers like the Protestant entrepreneurs described by Max Weber. According to Pye, Confucianism made Koreans aware of standards of excellence foreign to their culture to which they could aspire. In so doing, however, Confucianism created aspirations for acceptance and anxiety about unworthiness that led Koreans to audacious exploits as they conducted enterprises to test and prove their worth. Those in power tended to have a vivid sense of their own virtue and the wickedness of their opponents, so that it was proper to strike the foe and make him suffer. Confucian confidence that spirit can overcome physical limitations may also have contributed to Korean War excesses. The brutality of that war and post-1953 insecurities "legitimized" the use of harsh methods by Korean officials against perceived foes.[37]

Pye saw a Confucian background in Koreans' strong attachment to discipline and formal manners, to deference, and to a stiff and aloof style of authority. On the other hand, he noted, Korean culture also tolerates brashness and cockiness toward authority, boldness of action by top leaders, and self-assertiveness by practically everyone. The gentle Confucian scholar-superior could at any moment become a brusque and cruel authority. "Koreans came to see power, even in its Confucian-ethical guise, as entailing a series of struggles unrelated to either serious policy choices or ideological disagreements."[38] Such behaviors, of course, have also occurred in many times and places outside of Korea.

Pye pointed to ways that Korea differed from other Confucian cultures. The mandarin, or *yangban,* class was supposed to be a harmoniously united brotherhood of scholarly officials. In time, however, the *yangban* became an arrogant aristocracy, torn by rivalries and conflicts. The term *yangban* meant "two orders" and was supposed to distinguish the civil from the military bureaucracy. Yet it came to comprise both scholars and, ranked lower, army officers. Thanks both to the adoption of competitive exams and to increasing corruption, the number of aristocrats increased. The *yangban* quickly became too numerous for the land available for estates, which the new aristocrats expected to possess, as well as the bureaucratic posts available for assignment. Seeking to contain the explosion in numbers, *yangban* factions conspired with the Korean king to exterminate rival *yangbans.* Several "massacres of scholars" ensued in the sixteenth century.[39]

A Korean academic, Yurim Yi, however, believes that Pye's views reflect Japanese colonial propaganda meant to disparage Korea. The massacres, she says, had to do with struggles over property and did not arise from Confucianism. She notes that times change and meanings evolve. Part of the *yangban* heritage may be seen in the determination of today's young Koreans to acquire a higher education. The term *yangban* has come to signify a gentle person. It is also used by a wife who speaks kindly of her husband. A novel about life under Kim Jong Il, however, uses the term *yangban* to refer to North Korea's bureaucratic elite, few of whom appear gentle.[40]

Pye noted another feature he said was particularly Korean. In the Korean family there was no mistaking the superior role of the patriarch, who expected to make decisions without the restraints customary in Japan. Korean rulers, like family patriarchs, were expected to be embattled but masterful at all times—lone figures, aloof and able to cope single-handedly with problems while demanding total obedience. Modifying the patriarchal culture, Korean mothers played a more autonomous decision-making role than did mothers in China or Japan. Korean children learned how to play the two family authorities against each other, but they also regarded home as a sanctuary to which they could retreat after going out and assuming high risks.

The Confucian sense of family underscored the differences between the internal "we" and the foreign "they." The norms that govern relations among the ingroup need not apply to outsiders. As the two Koreas became estranged under anti-Communist and Communist rule, each side saw the other increasingly as foreign.

Having observed life in South Korea (focusing on rice-producing villages) in the late 1940s, Yale anthropologist Cornelius Osgood concluded that Koreans accentuated the Confucian primacy of the family patriarch and the subordinate status assigned to women. Korean culture, Osgood argued, left people hungry for emotional satisfaction and with a "smoldering violence in their nature, struggling against an environment in which for each brief victory there was a period of severe constraint." At puberty the young Korean was cut off from the few sources of manifest affection that had been available. The typical Korean "hates his dominating father" and is deprived of intimacy with the female sex. Lacking both physical satisfactions and ego gratification he turns to "violence and sadistic tendencies." The quest for ego gratification showed itself in "the frequency with which Koreans demonstrate or verbalize their desire to undertake actions of heroic proportions. They will risk the most cruel punishments for the sake of a religious belief or a political cause," as did early Christians and campaigners for independence against Japanese rule. The young Korean's approach to "the field of finance or art is typically the same": he will be satisfied only by "becoming a Rockefeller or Rachmaninoff. However he may achieve it, the Korean goal is to be a hero."[41]

Confucian tradition became a tool for those in South Korea, Japan, and China who opposed regional cooperation and integration in a globalized world. For centuries, according to Gilbert Rozman, Confucianization fostered universal values in China, Japan, and Korea—in some ways *abetting* premodern development. But it also served to entrench particularism and to *block* modernizing influences from the West—prompting reformers and revolutionaries to call for de-Confucianization. Still, some elements of Confucianism survived and contributed to modernization and the rise of Asian "tigers" in the 1980s and 1990s.[42] While Mao Zedong tried to throttle and extirpate Confucian influences, his successors in the twenty-first century paid their respects to Confucian order and endeavored to deploy their version of Neo-Confucianism as an instrument of soft power abroad.[43]

The blend of pre-Communist Korean traditions with borrowings from Stalinism added to the roadblocks to modernization of North Korea. Indeed, the Kim Il Sung dynasty perverted the Confucian emphasis on discipline and reciprocal obligation to help the regime command and control. The Communist dynasts saw obligation as a one-way street by which to extract goods and services from most North Koreans to benefit a few. To be sure, the tradition of patriarchal hierarchy impeded the forces of modernization. In the early twenty-first century, however, the Kim dynasty's family business networks prevailed over incipient pluralism.[44]

Confucianism, along with Christian and other traditions, has shaped all of Korea, but most vestiges of hierarchy were undermined by the forces of modernity in South Korea—as was the case also in Hong Kong and other parts of the sinic universe.

THE VORTEX OF POWER

North Korea's political and economic system borrowed heavily from the USSR, but Kim Il Sung's adaptations of Stalinist models embellished a centralized system of power developed over many centuries. The Korean political system was never that of a city-state. Usually it was a centralized oligarchy within an agricultural framework. The amalgam of racial and cultural homogeneity and centralized bureaucratic rule fostered a politics of the vortex. Like moths to a flame, aspiring elites struggled to reach the center, even though many who did so suffered—as some were expropriated, some exiled, and some killed. Centralization and uniformity worked against pluralism, democracy, and modernization. Focused on their political struggles, elites neglected economic development—a pattern characteristic of North Korea.[45]

The atomized updraft toward central political power impeded cohesion of society below the vortex crest. At the top, Korea's king derived his legitimacy from Beijing's emperor—his court and bureaucracy cast in the Sino-Confucian image. At the top of the updraft was a council of respected elders, or *yangban*, that wielded power in Koryŏ times, under Mongol domination, and in Chosŏn. The Korean king was weak relative to China, and the council strong—especially in the fourteenth and fifteenth centuries, when it took the form of the Censorate, composed of *yangban*. This body was charged with criticizing public policy, scrutinizing the conduct of officialdom, rectifying mores, redressing public wrongs, and preventing forgery and misuse of credentials. It offered daily Confucian critiques to the monarch and channeled complaints against government officials, but had no administrative responsibilities. The Censorate absorbed star Confucian zealots fresh from the National Academy. Full of idealistic, often doctrinaire, Confucian zeal, the Censorate was part legal chamber, part theological council—an ideal rostrum for a captious and persuasive vocation.[46]

The number of councils increased. By the nineteenth century they often contradicted each other and paralyzed decision-making. There was little leadership within the councils. They criticized but did not take responsibility for acting. Surveys of fertile lands along the Yalu were debated for centuries. Re-surveys were called for, but rarely accomplished. In a similar spirit, the ROK National Assembly in the 1950s often criticized the executive office of President Syngman Rhee.[47]

The ROK National Assembly lost power first to political parties and then, after Park Chung Hee took power, to the Korean Central Intelligence Agency (KCIA). Unlike earlier versions of the *yangban*-led council, the KCIA allied with the president and became his adviser and administrator. As before, it recruited bright young people seeking access to power. From this chrysalis arose the government's political organization, the Democratic Republican Party. Agents of the KCIA, as in Taiwan's Kuomintang and in Communist regimes, formed a strong secretariat to manipulate those selected as representatives of the ruling party. Many South Koreans concluded that no political groups merited their loyalty. The DPRK, by contrast, achieved cohesion through the disciplines of Stalinism. Kim Il Sung became king and eventually destroyed whatever resemblance remained between his entourage and the Chosŏn Censorate.

Language, Power, and Politics

By the twenty-first century the RCK had become a leader in science and a major innovator in technology. In 2011 South Korea ranked just behind Japan in the number of patents granted per million citizens; somewhat ahead of the United States; and far ahead of China, Europe, Russia, and North Korea.[48] South Korea's eminence in learning stemmed in part from a strong if uneven tradition of academic excellence and wide literacy.[49] By 2015 South Korea pupils (grades 4 to 8) ranked first in the world (just ahead of Japan) on the Pearson Index of Cognitive Skills and Educational Attainment—up from number two in 2012 (just behind Finland).[50] Pearson attributed Koreans' achievements to their Confucian heritage, parental pressure, and an average of nine hours tutoring a week. While Finland had short school days, little homework, and a focus on "helping children understand and apply knowledge, not merely repeat it," the South Korean system emphasized exams, rote learning, discipline, long hours of study, and private cram schools.[51]

Korea's traditional dedication to learning remained also in the Communist North. Part of a foreign peace delegation to Pyongyang in 1994, Mark Berry recalled that Kim Il Sung turned to what seemed a favorite theme of his: what made the DPRK different from the Soviet Union, China, and other Communist states. According to Berry, Kim said, "After 1945, I tried to find intellectuals to rebuild the country, but could only locate a handful. The partisans who fought with me against the Japanese knew how to fight, but not how to build institutions.' The Japanese in their thirty-five-year colonial rule left no college functioning in the North. 'So I had to start my own, which became Kim Il Sung University, and then other schools. Today [1994], there are 1.76 million intellectuals out of a population of 20 million, almost one out of ten citizens.'" Kim showed the delegates a card of the Korean Workers' Party. As Berry recalled, Kim "pointed to the large gold-stamped party emblem, consisting of the usual hammer and sickle, but also a calligraphy brush in the middle. Kim said that 'in 1946, I created this emblem for our party. The brush symbolizes our highest commitment to intellectual pursuits in every discipline. Our emblem is unique among communist parties in the world. This is an example of Juche, doing things our own way. We did everything in our own way.'"[52]

In 2012 the Pyongyang regime required twelve years of education for all citizens. Starting in 2010, it permitted outsiders to establish and teach at the Pyongyang University of Science and Technology, a potential MIT for 500 sons of the elite, founded by Dr. James Chin-Kyung Kim, a Korean-American entrepreneur, and funded by Evangelical Christians in the United States and South Korea. But even this crème de la crème lacked access to the Internet.

The Kim dynasty wanted to foster education and science, and managed—with few resources—to produce nuclear explosions and long-range rockets. But top-down controls over every facet of thought and inquiry could only blunt its educational efforts.

Both North and South Korea inherited strong traditions of learning. Buddhist texts were printed in Korea as early as 751 CE using wooden blocks. By the early thirteenth century Koreans printed books using metal type—some 200 years before Gutenberg's Bible.[53] In the fourteenth century the Chosŏn dynasty set up a well-planned system of schools to offer Confucian education to qualified students—not only in Seoul but in every county. For advanced study there was a National Academy and special schools for military affairs, law, mathematics, medicine, and foreign languages. These schools were well endowed by the state. From the mid-sixteenth century on, private academies were organized in the countryside and funded by private donations and a grant of books, land, and servants from the government.[54]

Until the fifteenth century, the Korean language for more than 1,000 years had been written using Chinese ideograms—Korean sounds represented by Chinese characters with similar pronunciations.[55] Since the Chinese writing system is not phonetic, this system was very difficult to learn, and few Koreans were literate. The situation resembled that in Europe, where sacred scriptures and many government documents were in Latin, a language incomprehensible to most people, and where, struggling to change things, Wycliffe, Hus, and Luther labored to translate the Bible into the vernacular. In a similar vein, the Chosŏn dynasty's "Great King" Sejong in the 1440s commissioned scholars to invent a phonetic and phonemic script that common people could quickly learn and use. He wrote, "The sounds of our language differ from Chinese and are not easily communicated by using Chinese ideographs. Therefore, many are ignorant . . . unable to communicate [by writing]."[56]

The scholars in 1443–1444 devised a system called *HunMinChongUm—Correct Sounds for the Instruction of the People.* Originally it was made up of 28 letters, but the modern system, known as *Han'gŭl,* contains just 24 letters. Han'gŭl means "unique, great, and correct." As in much of Europe, however, some Korean scholars and some later kings preferred to keep the masses in the dark. A leading scholar wrote in 1444 that Korea had always "respected the senior state and consistently followed the Chinese system of government." Some people say that "barbarians are transformed only by adopting Chinese ways; we have never heard of the Chinese ways being transformed by the barbarians. Historically, China has always regarded our country as the state that has maintained the virtuous customs bequeathed by the sage-king Kija and has viewed our literature, rituals, and music as similar to its own." Barbarians in Japan, Mongolia, and Tibet have their own writing systems, but that is not Korea's way.[57]

Until the early twentieth century, Han'gŭl was denigrated as vulgar by many of the literate elite, who preferred the traditional *hanja* writing system. They gave the new alphabet such names as *Achimgeul* ("writing you can learn within a morning"), *Eonmun* ("vernacular"), and *Amgeul* ("women's script"). Thanks in part to pressures by Protestant missions that arrived in Korea in the nineteenth century, however, Han'gŭl became the standard script used in the church schools and other private schools for wealthy Koreans just before the Japanese takeover. Korea's Japanese rulers saw Han'gŭl as nationalistic and tried to suppress it. The Japanese expanded public schools, but with instruction in Japanese.

After the Korean War, the ROK adopted Han'gŭl as its official script. Koreans celebrate Han'gŭl day every October 9—they are probably the only people who commemorate the invention of their writing system. Up to the 1980s, however, children in South Korean schools continued to learn Chinese characters (*Han-Cha*) because they were still used in some newspapers and in academic manuscripts. The use of Chinese characters was discouraged by ROK leaders in the 1970s and 1980s but given more scope under Kim Dae Jung in the late 1990s. The continued use of Chinese characters in South Korea was criticized by linguistic nationalists but defended by cultural conservatives, who feared that the loss of character literacy would isolate younger Koreans from their cultural heritage.[58]

The "Standard Language" (*p'yojuno*) of South Korea derived from the language spoken in and around Seoul. Korea's partition since 1945 led to linguistic divergences north and south of the DMZ. The North's language became more Orwellian and developed a system of honorific deferences to refer to the Kim Il Sung dynasty. The DPRK leadership attempted to eliminate as many foreign loanwords as possible. It treated Chinese characters as symbols of "flunkeyism" and systematically eliminated them from all publications. Starting in 1949, *Kullo-ja* (The Worker), the monthly Korean Workers' Party journal, used only Han'gŭl.[59] The DPRK government introduced new words of exclusively Korean origin and encouraged parents to give their children Korean rather than Chinese-type names. Nonetheless, approximately 300 Chinese characters are still taught in North Korean schools. North Koreans refer to their language as "Cultured Language" (*munhwa*), which uses the regional dialect of Pyongyang as its standard. North Korean sources vilified the Standard Language of the South as "coquettish" and "decadent," corrupted by English and Japanese loanwords and full of nasal twangs.[60] North Korea's rejection of Chinese characters and disdain for other foreign influences arose from an "oppositional nationalism" that fed both the ideology of self-reliance (Juche) and a historical revisionism (suggesting, for example, that much of Manchuria rightly belongs to Korea).[61]

CHRISTIANITY, EGALITARIANISM, EDUCATION, DEMOCRACY

In Korea, as in China and Japan, European and American missionaries spread Western medicine and education along with Christianity. Their message and labors buttressed Korean drives toward social equality and self-rule. Missionaries got minimal help from official Washington, but they helped open the doors to American business interests and good relations with the U.S. government. Many Americans in Korea protested U.S. acquiescence in Japanese rule over Korea, but many stayed on even after 1910. Their support for Han'gŭl and other things Korean boosted Koreans' sense of nationhood and their resistance to foreign rule.

In Korea, as in China and Japan, many political authorities and elites in the nineteenth century viewed Christianity as a danger to their privileged positions—either as a potential internal rebellion or as a link to a foreign threat. But Christianity also appealed to impoverished lower classes and to alienated elites, who saw it as a path to modernization of the state and society.[62]

The seeds of Christianity were sown in 1603 when a Korean diplomat, having converted to Catholicism, returned from Beijing and spread ideas contained in theological books written by a Jesuit missionary in China. Korea's Confucian rulers wanted no challenge to their ideology. Accordingly, the mainstream academic establishment and court officials in Korea denounced these unconventional beliefs. However, scholars belonging to the Silhak ("practical learning") school were attracted to the egalitarian values of Christianity. They advocated a social structure based on merit rather than birth and opposed Neo-Confucian formalism. They provided a substantial body of educated opinion sympathetic to the Catholic faith. Catholicism was outlawed in 1758, but Silhak scholars remained a deviant minority. Many Catholics were killed in the Sinyu Persecution of 1801. This event marked the end of the church of scholar-aristocrats and the beginning of an underground, persecuted church of the people. Self-evangelization became the norm as Christianity grew from the bottom up. Persecution of Catholics continued every twelve or so years and peaked in the Great Massacre of 1866–1868, which killed more than 8,000 adherents—about half of the country's Catholics, including nine French missionaries. Korea has one-fourth of the Catholic martyrs in the world. Pope Francis beatified 124 of them when he visited Korea in 2014.

The accession of King Kojong in 1871 began the gradual opening of Korea to the outside world. It brought toleration for Catholics and also introduced Protestantism. Decades of persecution left a ghetto mentality among Catholics and little concern for social issues around them. Accurate counts of believers are problematic, but some estimates say that by 1882 there were 12,500 Catholics, an increase of 5,500 persons since the end of the Great Persecution. Two decades later, in 1910, the number of adherents had grown to 73,000—cared for by fifteen Korean priests and fifty-six foreign clergy. (These and most other estimates of religious affiliation in Korea are estimates—sometimes distorted by an up or down bias.)

In the 1880s John Ross, from the United Presbyterian Church of Scotland mission in Manchuria, translated the New Testament into Korean using Han'gŭl. His converts established the first Protestant communities in northwestern Korea.

Like Catholicism, Protestantism grew by self-evangelization. Because the propagation of Christianity was prohibited by the anti-Christian edict of 1866, most overt missionary work until the mid-1890s was accomplished through educational and medical institutions. Indeed, many of Korea's medical institutions and printing establishments trace their origins to this period. Meanwhile, baptisms took place and some church organizations developed surreptitiously in the 1880s.

The Protestant missionary enterprise in Korea, as in China and other mission fields, consisted of a triad of efforts: evangelism, education, and medicine. The first American Presbyterian missionary in Korea, Horace Newton Allen, born and educated in Ohio, arrived in Korea in 1884 from China. A trained physician, Allen introduced Western medicine to Korea and founded a medical center that evolved into Yonsei University. Founded as a Christian college, Yonsei aimed to send liberally educated Christian graduates to claim leading positions not only in the church but also in business and other walks of secular life.

Dr. Allen became close to the royal family and in 1877 accompanied the first Korean legation to Washington. In the 1890s he became secretary to the American legation in Seoul and then U.S. minister and consul general. Allen arranged for U.S. firms to build Korea's first electric and water works, trolley and railway systems. In 1905, however, Allen's appeals for U.S. intervention to stop the Japanese takeover of Korea led to his recall.[53]

Protestant clergy in Korea adopted a strategy devised by John L. Nevius, a Presbyterian missionary in Shandong. The Nevius principles called for creating a self-propagating, self-governing, and self-supporting church. The first goal was to concentrate on the conversion of people from the lower classes rather than the higher classes. The second was to focus on women and girls because of their influence in society. The third was to translate the Bible to the Han'gŭl vernacular. Accordingly, missionaries generated a Korean–English dictionary, Han'gŭl translations of devotional works such as *The Pilgrim's Progress,* and a standard Han'gŭl translation of the Bible to replace the Ross translation. A Great Revival swept from Pyongyang into Manchuria in 1907. In the decade leading up to Japan's annexation of Korea in 1910 the Protestant community grew to more than 10,000 persons—a larger fraction of the population than in Japan. Parts of the Bible were published in Korean in 1882; the New Testament in 1887; the entire Bible in 1911.

요한복음서

1 태초에 말씀이 계셨다. 그 말씀은 하나님 과 함께 계셨다. 그 말씀은 하나님이셨다. ○ 그는 태초에 하나님과 함께 계셨다. 모든 것이 그로 말미암아 생겨났으니, 그가 없이 생겨난 것은 하나도 없다. ○ 그의 안에서 생겨난 것은 생명이었으니, 그 생명은 모든 사람의 빛이었다. ○ 그 빛이 어둠 속에서 비치니, 어둠이 그 빛을 이기지 못하였다. 하나님께서 보내신 사람이 있었다. 그 이름은 요한이었다. ○ 그 사람은 빛을 증언하러 왔다. 그 증언으로 모든 사람을 믿게 하려는 것이었다. ○ 그 사람 자신은 빛이 아니었다. 그는 그 빛을 증언하러 온 것뿐이다.

"In the beginning was the Word. . . ." The opening page of the Gospel according to Saint John in Han'gŭl.

Nationalism, progress, and Christian faith became linked in the minds of many young and progressive Koreans. They valued Christianity's support for education and medicine and rejected a Confucian heritage that left the state corrupt and ill-prepared to meet the challenges of the times. Many hoped to restore national sovereignty and dignity by raising the educational level of the nation. Christians started 293 schools, which admitted girls, and universities that came to include three of Korea's top five academic institutions.[64]

Democracy was fostered by the example of Christian missionaries. Presbyterians governed themselves through elected representatives. Their boards of deacons and elders give many church members leadership positions and prestige in their communities. Pastors were subject to "presbyteries," and all were subject to a national Presbyterian assembly of elected delegates. By the late 1930s the major Protestant denominations were self-governing.

As Japan started building elementary schools in Korea, many Korean Christians opted to stay with their church-related academies. Christians also played major roles in resistance of Japanese rule. Many took part in the 1919 Independence Movement. Fifteen of the thirty-three signers of the Declaration of Independence were national Christian figures. Christians clashed with the colonial government in the 1930s when they resisted worshipping the spirits at Shinto shrines. The pressure continued through the years of the Second World War. Many Christian leaders and intellectuals were forced to choose between prison and support for Japanese dominion.

The trauma of Japanese conquest eroded faith in Confucian or Buddhist traditions: Koreans could relate to Israel's sufferings in the Old Testament. Yet by 1945 only 2 percent of Koreans were Christian—many in the North. The advent of Communist rule drove many Christians from the North to the South. By 2014 some 15 million South Koreans were Christian—nearly 30 percent of the population. Roughly 18 percent of the population was Protestant and 11 percent Catholic.

According to the Korea National Statistical Office in 2003, 53.9 percent of the South Korean population over the age of fifteen reported a religious affiliation. Of those, 47 percent were Buddhists, 36.8 percent were Protestants of various denominations, and 13.7 percent were Roman Catholics. The concentration of Christians in the general population also varied by region, with more Christians in Seoul and the southwestern Chôlla provinces, and more Buddhists in other regions.[65]

By 2014 some 5.4 million of South Korea's 50 million people were Roman Catholics and 9 million were Protestants, which included the Yoido Full Gospel Church (with one million members, the largest Pentecostal congregation on earth); the Unification Church, founded by the late Sun-myung Moon; and the sect established by the late Yoo Byung-eun, the shifty and versatile tycoon behind the ferry *Sewol*, which sank in April 2014.[66]

Women buttressed Korean Christianity since its beginnings in secret Catholic congregations. When the Protestants arrived, they included women missionaries who sought to attract women to Christianity. Mary F. Scranton founded the

Ewha School for Girls in 1886. By the late twentieth and early twenty-first centuries Ewha Woman's University had become the largest school for women in Asia. South Korean women had to contend with many sexist barriers, but a woman was elected ROK president in 2012. Taking office in 2013, Park Geun Hye was named the world's eleventh most powerful woman and the most powerful woman in East Asia by *Forbes* magazine.[67]

As Max Weber might have anticipated, Christianity waxed along with South Korea's economy. As Weber interpreted the Protestant ethic, worldly success signified God's blessing. As Edward Gibbon argued, rapid social change often produces spiritual ferment. Entrepreneurs such as Moon and Yoo were saviors for some and charlatans to others. Prophet and profit blurred: both men did time for fraud. Even Yoido's founder, David Cho, was convicted in February 2014 of embezzling $12 million.

But Korea also bred its own liberation theology lauding the poor and oppressed. The Christian concept of individual worth found expression in a lengthy struggle for human rights and democracy in Korea. Based on the "image of God" concept expressed in Genesis 1: 26–27, a Korean version of liberation theology took hold in the 1970s. Known as Minjung theology, it depicted commoners as the rightful masters of their own destiny. *Minjung* signifies "oppressed masses." As used in the Yi dynasty that ended in 1910, the term referred to all those not part of the *yangban* class. Under Japanese rule *Minjung* applied to most Koreans except collaborators with the Japanese. In the 1970s it referred to commoners and also to intelligentsia fired from their jobs by the military dictatorship. Though initiated in the 1920s and revived in the 1970s, the Minjung orientation recalled the egalitarian demands of the late eighteenth- and early nineteenth-century Silhak society and the Tonghak rebellion in the late 1800s. Two ROK presidents, Kim Young Sam, a Presbyterian, and Kim Dae Jung, a Catholic, subscribed to Minjung theology. Both men spent decades opposing military governments in South Korea and were frequently imprisoned as a result. In the 1970s Minjung theology gave rise to movements regarded as foes by Park Chung Hee: the Catholic Farmers Movement and the Protestant Urban Industrial Mission, which campaigned for better wages and working conditions. Minjung helped energize the 1980 Kwangju uprising in the province that was home to Kim Dae Jung.[68]

In 2012 only 52 percent of South Koreans claimed to be religious—down from 56 percent in 2005. But only the United States sent out more missionaries. Korean Christians were seized in Afghanistan, beheaded in Iraq, and stopped by their embassy from hymn-singing in Yemen. Many worked undercover in China. Some helped North Koreans to flee: as many as 1,000 had their Chinese visas canceled. Others had a grander ambition, to spread Christianity in the North, where Protestantism had been strong in Japanese days. Indeed, the Kim dynasty permitted Christians to establish the private Pyongyang University of Science and Technology, which, starting in 2010, educated North Korea's future elite, but with no preaching. Given Korean Christians' energy and tenacity, *The Economist* (August 12, 2014) predicted that one day Pyongyang's skyline would be as studded with neon crosses as Seoul's.

Religion can close or open horizons. Christian influences in the North help explain why Kim Il Sung met the Reverend Billy Graham in 1992 and 1994. The DPRK leader is said to have been close to his grandmother, a devout Presbyterian. The wife of the Reverend Graham, Ruth Bell Graham, attended a missionary school in Pyongyang for three years in the 1930s. She departed Korea for North Carolina in 1937 but returned to Pyongyang for a visit in 2007, fondly recalling school friends there and skating on the frozen river. Ruth's father had served as a surgeon at a Presbyterian Hospital 300 miles north of Shanghai for twenty-five years before moving to Pyongyang.[69] Reverend Graham's son, Franklin, head of the Billy Graham Evangelical Association and Samaritan's Purse, visited the DPRK several times, including 2008 and 2009, and donated medical and dental equipment to hospitals there.

Neither Kim Jong Il nor Kim Jong Un seemed to harbor any soft spots for Christianity. In 2015 four churches stood in Pyongyang—two Protestant, one Catholic, and one Russian Orthodox. These churches accommodated expatriates, but they were more for show than for devotion. Actual believers—perhaps as many as half a million—were reported to sometimes attend services in underground churches. But churchgoing could be construed as treason. In April 2013 Korean-American missionary Kenneth Bae was sentenced to fifteen years' hard labor. In May 2014 a DPRK court sentenced a South Korean Baptist missionary, Kim Jun Wook, to hard labor for life after he admitted to anti–North Korean religious acts and "malignantly hurting the dignity" of the country's supreme leadership. There were also reports that thirty-three North Koreans were executed for working with Kim Jun Wook to overthrow the regime by setting up 500 underground churches.

CULTURE AND POLITICS

Confucian culture instilled discipline and respect for authority. Across most of Asia, traditional people saw power as residing in the *person* of high officials—not in their offices or in institutions. Respect for the paterfamilias prepared people to esteem the country's supreme leader. Encouraged by Christianity and modernizing influences, shoots of self-organization emerged in Korea and did much to boost economic and social development and enhance societal fitness. As detailed in chapter 10, the near absence of self-organization in the North since the late 1940s stunted development and curtailed fitness.

The fusion of politics and religion in North Korea did much to encourage fantasies about cause and effect. Political leaders were expected to have superhuman powers. If they did not deliver, then some scapegoat had to be found. Pyongyang blamed North Korea's problems on the machinations of Washington and its "puppets" in Seoul.

The World Values Survey placed South Korea relatively high on the scale moving from traditional toward secular-rational values—a bit lower than China and much lower than Japan. Survival values were somewhat stronger in South Korea than those of self-expression. The world leaders in secular and self-expression values were Japan, Sweden, and Norway. The United States placed fairly high on self-expression but was closer to traditional than to secular-rational values.[70] The DPRK was not ranked, but North Korea defied any simple dichotomy. It was traditional in demanding deference to authority and in mobilizing national pride and a nationalism. On the other hand, traditional religion and family values were supplanted by official dedication to the Kim regime and its ideology. Survival values—for individuals and the state—certainly outweighed self-expression. Still, those with license to create, like retired painters who had spent decades glorifying the regime, showed a desire and ability to express themselves using classical idioms.

Less than Japan but more "modern" on average than China or India, and equipped with ultrasound technology to determine the sex of embryos, South Korea by 1990 had developed the greatest gender imbalance in the world—116.5 male babies to 100 females. As democratic and feminist values strengthened in the 1990s, however, the ratio of female to male babies moved toward the global normal. Gone was the patriarchal belief that a son was essential to inherit property, worship ancestors, care for parents, and continue the family lineage. In 2014 South Korea's gender ratio returned to the global average of 105 males born for every 100 females. Even though the ROK had elected a female president, however, the World Economic Forum ranked South Korea 125th of 142 countries for income equality between men and women.[71]

Starting in the 1980s, Korean women on average gave birth to fewer than two babies. By 2014 the average fell to 1.21—far below replacement level. The speed of aging of the South Korean population had no known precedent. In 2014 the structure of the population resembled not a pyramid but a diamond—with more persons in the age thirty to fifty bracket than in any other grouping. The elderly dependency rate was 18 percent. The future costs and other problems of dealing with an aging population would be huge.[72]

Demographic trends in North Korea were obscured by shortages of reliable statistics. Long after the Korean War, women appeared to outnumber men. In 2014, among North Koreans over sixty-five, women were far more numerous than men. Higher than in South Korea, total fertility in North Korea declined from about 3.0 children per woman in 1980 to about 2.5 babies per woman in the years 2005–2010—thus permitting a small growth (0.53 percent in 2015) in population.

The structure of the population in 2014 resembled more a pyramid than a diamond, but with bulges for those aged twenty to twenty-four and those aged forty to fifty. The elderly dependency rate was 13.8. percent. The total population in the DPRK appeared likely to stabilize at 34 million persons in 2045 and then gradually decline. South Korea's population, by contrast, was expected to stabilize at 52.6 million in 2023.[73]

The implications of all this for peace and prosperity were mixed. The highly confident and dynamic South balked at directions from the United States.[74] The highly centralized but stagnating North needed outside help, but the regime feared outside influences that might upset the existing system. Both ROK and Chinese leaders wanted stability on the Korean peninsula, but they also saw enormous business opportunities if North Korea opened up and became more pragmatic. Russia and Japan also perceived vast commercial prospects but tended to keep their distance as from a hot stove. Such was the broad context facing U.S. and other world leaders as they deliberated policy toward a deeply divided Korea.

3

How Korea Became Japan

The second half of the nineteenth century saw a rising Japan struggle against China and Russia to dominate Korea. Starting in the 1860s, Washington's usual stance on Korea amounted to less-than-benign neglect. Official U.S. policy generally followed the rule set out in 1888 by Secretary of State Thomas Bayard: U.S. interest in Korea is "merely the protection of American citizens and their commerce."[1] In 1905 the United States and Great Britain acquiesced in Japan's takeover of Korea in exchange for Tokyo's acceptance of U.S. rule in the Philippines and British rule in Singapore. Not till World War II did the democracies denounce Japan's cruel occupation of Korea.

AMERICA AS ELDER BROTHER

As outsiders hovered over Korea, a U.S. adviser to the Korean emperor described the struggles for influence by China, Japan, and other countries in Korea. He noted that Korea was "the weakest of Far Eastern countries, not only weak internally but also by having no undisputed official protector or friend among the Western powers."[2] To be sure, many American diplomats, missionaries, educators, and businesspeople based in Korea wanted to help Koreans resist domination by outsiders. The *Korean Review* (published in Seoul) informed readers in 1902 not only about the price of sorghum but also about the success of the Bible Society in distributing the Old and New Testament in Korean.[3] Letters home from missionaries in Korea helped spur U.S. newspapers to editorialize against Japanese encroachments. Americans could also read descriptions of Korean life by Europeans. An Englishwoman made several grueling trips across Korea and described in 1897 how her own feelings turned from abhorrence to affection and admiration.[4] An English artist engaged to paint portraits of aristocrats described everything he saw, from kite flying and leopard hunts to exorcisms and crucifixions.[5]

While some Americans in Korea—missionaries, diplomats, educators, businesspeople—wanted to help Korea resist domination by outsiders, Secretary of

State Bayard declared that agitation for Korean independence was "neither desirable nor beneficial."[6] Notwithstanding many U.S. rebuffs, Korea's reformist King Gojong told Washington's minister in Seoul in 1890 that "we feel that America is to us as our Elder Brother."[7]

U.S. policies toward Asia and elsewhere were often conflicted by contradictory impulses of idealism and realism.[8] Idealistic fervor fed on official proclamations such as the Open Door in 1898, the Fourteen Points in 1917, the Nine-Power Treaty in 1922, the pact to outlaw war in 1928, the Stimson Doctrine in 1932, and the Atlantic Charter in August 1941—all implying that law and morality trumped greed and power in U.S. foreign policy. When push came to shove, however, official Washington usually bowed to realpolitik and commercial pressures. Top U.S. policymakers tended to relegate Korea to the status of a rook, a knight, or even a pawn, while treating the region's major powers as queens, if not kings. Thus, President Theodore Roosevelt did not object to Japan's absorbing Korea—provided Tokyo allowed the United States untrammeled control of the Philippines. Forty years later, another Roosevelt—Franklin D.—seemed ready to give Joseph Stalin whatever he wished in Asia to secure Soviet entry into the war against Japan. When World War II ended and Communist forces crossed into Korea, the United States did nothing to stop the Sovietization of North Korea.[9] Once the great divide hardened in Korea, the Free World's hegemon took roughly the same stance toward South Korean politics as it did in Central America: "The top leader is an S.O.B., but he is our S.O.B." Free elections did not become the norm in South Korea until the 1990s—nearly half a century after partition; they never took place in the North.

Why did the United States issue idealistic pronouncements while cutting realpolitik deals on spheres of interest? First of all, self-righteous hubris, which permitted actions undertaken despite ignorance of local realities, fueled a disdain for Koreans bordering on racism. Next was the difficulty of projecting finite military muscle halfway around the world. There was also greed, driven by a belief that business opportunities in China and Japan far outweighed any economic gains available in Korea. Partisan politics in the United States also undercut any hope for a consistent and enlightened U.S. approach to Korea. Top officials devoted their energies to other causes. Whatever they did in Korea could be held against them, while hardly anyone would condemn a ban on war or a call for "freedom."

WHERE DO WE COME FROM? WHAT ARE WE? WHERE ARE WE GOING?

As China's sway over Korea weakened in the nineteenth century, Korea's regent,[10] father of the boy king Gojong, sought to resist penetration by foreign powers. As noted in chapter 2, Korean authorities killed many Catholic converts—more than

8,000 in 1866, along with nine French missionaries. Responding to the massacre, the French chargé d'affaires in Beijing declared that China had forfeited suzerainty over Korea and that France intended to conquer Korea. This assertion was followed by the arrival of a French naval expedition at the approaches to the Han River, passageway to Seoul. But shots from a Korean fort and the mauling of French marines by a regiment of Korean tiger hunters compelled the French to retreat.

The United States also sought to open up Korea for commerce—much as Commodore Matthew Perry had done in Japan in 1854. Earlier, in 1834, a U.S. agent advised the secretary of state to open Japan to U.S. commerce so that Korea could also be accessed. In 1845 the House of Representatives discussed (but did not pass) a resolution to open both Japan and Korea to trade.[11] Meanwhile, in the years 1855 to 1866 many American ships were wrecked on the Korean coast. Usually their crews were well treated and eventually sent to the U.S. consul in China. But an American-led expedition to Korea in 1866 (just a year after America's Civil War ended) met a worse fate than the French. The entire crew of a privately owned gunboat, named the first practitioner of "total war," *General Sherman,* was killed as it tried to sail up the Taedong River to Pyongyang and persuade Korean authorities to permit both foreign trade and Christian proselytizing.[12] Their bodies were hacked to pieces and some parts used for medicine. The anchor chains of their vessel were hung at the Great East Gate of Pyongyang as a warning to other foreigners (a model for the display of the USS *Pueblo,* which was captured by the DPRK in 1968 and subsequently made part of the Fatherland Liberation War Museum in Pyongyang). Secretary of State William H. Seward learned of the *Sherman* incident in January 1867 from the French, who discovered the destroyed vessel while investigating the massacre of French missionaries in 1866. Seward proposed to the French minister in Washington that the two powers unite in a joint expedition to Korea, but this scheme never materialized.

The same fort at the straits leading into the Han River that drove off the French in 1866 also fired on six U.S. gunboats in 1871. The Americans shot back and silenced the fort. A U.S. officer noted that the Koreans fought until they were overwhelmed and died at their posts heroically. "The men of no nation could have done more for home and country."[13] Three Americans died, along with 250 or more Koreans—the largest body count of Asians killed by Americans until the Filipino insurrection at the end of the nineteenth century.[14]

Ulysses S. Grant reported the incident to Congress in December 1871—the first occasion when a U.S. president spoke publicly of Korea:[15]

> Prompted by a desire to put an end to the barbarous treatment of our shipwrecked sailors on the Korean coast, I instructed our minister at Peking to endeavor to conclude a convention with Korea for securing the safety and humane treatment of such mariners. . . . Admiral Rodgers

was instructed to accompany him with a sufficient force to protect him in case of need. . . . A small surveying party sent out, on reaching the coast was treacherously attacked at a disadvantage. Ample opportunity was given for explanation and apology for the insult. Neither came. A force was then landed. After an arduous march over a rugged and difficult country, the forts from which the outrages had been committed were reduced by a gallant assault and were destroyed. Having thus punished the criminals, and having vindicated the honor of the flag, the expedition returned, finding it impracticable under the circumstances to conclude the desired convention. I leave the subject for such action as Congress may see fit to take.

Grant's report in 1871 captured the leitmotif of American policy for nearly eight decades to come. He disparaged Korea, but paid deference to Japan and China. In Grant's words:

With Japan we continue to maintain intimate relations. The cabinet of the Mikado has since the close of the last session of Congress selected citizens of the United States to serve in offices of importance in several departments of Government. I have reason to think that this selection is due to an appreciation of the disinterestedness of the policy which the United States have pursued toward Japan. It is our desire to continue to maintain this disinterested and just policy with China as well as Japan. . . . There is no disposition on the part of this Government to swerve from its established course.

In the nineteenth century, as in the twenty-first century's "six-party talks," Washington sometimes looked to Korea's neighbors to mediate U.S. relations with Korea. In April 1878 Senator A. A. Sargent of California introduced a joint resolution to appoint a commission to negotiate a treaty with Korea "*with the aid of the friendly offices of Japan*" (emphasis added). This resolution failed. In 1882, however, the treaty by which the United States entered diplomatic relations with Korea was drawn up in Tientsin by U.S. commodore Robert W. Shufeldt and the Chinese governor-general, Li Hung-chang.[16] China, however, did not wish to surrender suzerainty over Korea. Li wanted to include in the treaty the phrase "Chosŏn being a dependent state of the Chinese Empire," which Shufeldt did not accept. These differences were finessed by a compromise: a letter from the king of Korea to the U.S. president stating that the treaty had been made by consent of the Chinese government.[17]

As we have seen, a French official declared in 1866 that China no longer enjoyed suzerainty over Korea. By signing the treaty of peace and commerce with

Korea in 1882 (known as the Shufeldt Convention), the United States became the first Western power to recognize Korea's independent statehood.

China, however, continue to assert its suzerainty over Korea. In 1887 the Chinese government demanded that Washington recall from Seoul the U.S. chargé d'affaires *ad interim,* who had opposed Chinese interference in Korea, and the United States promptly acquiesced Later that year, however, when the Chinese government sought to prevent the departure of the appointed Korean minister to the United States, Washington did not give in. The minister was received in January 1888 "on a footing of diplomatic equality with the representatives of other States." One year later, Secretary of State James G. Blaine informed the U.S. minister resident in Seoul that the king of Korea remained "under some form of feudal subjection to the Chinese crown" on internal matters, but not with respect to foreign affairs. Washington wanted to bolster U.S. commercial rights in Korea without becoming entangled in regional power plays.[18]

By 1882, when the Shufeldt Convention was signed, things had changed in Korea. King Gojong and Queen Min wanted to reform and modernize Korea, and sought help—in a sequence that began with Japan, the United States, China, Russia, and then back to America again. The Korean royals began to follow the advice given by a Chinese counselor on how to resist Russian expansion: "Be intimate with China, unite with Japan, and ally with the United States," which the adviser depicted as a powerful Christian country with no territorial ambitions abroad.[19] In 1883 Queen Min established English-language schools in Seoul with U.S. instructors. That same year the queen sent a special mission to the United States. The delegation carried the newly created Korean national flag, visited many American historical sites, heard lectures on U.S. history, and attended a gala event for the mission given by the mayor of San Francisco. Later the mission dined with President Chester Arthur and discussed U.S. investment in Korea and the growing threat posed by Japan. The head of the delegation, a relative of the queen, reported to her: "I was born in the dark. I went out into the light, and your Majesty, it is my displeasure to inform you that I have returned to the dark. I envision a Seoul of towering buildings filled with Western establishments that will place [Korea] back above the Japanese barbarians. Great things lay ahead for the Kingdom, great things. We must take action, your Majesty, without hesitation, to further modernize this still ancient kingdom."[20]

In 1885 President Grover Cleveland affirmed U.S. amity toward Korea, "whose entrance into the family of treaty powers the United States were the first to recognize. I regard with favor the application made by the Korean Government to be allowed to employ American officers as military instructors, to which the assent of Congress becomes necessary, and I am happy to say this request has the concurrent sanction of China and Japan."[21]

In 1888 Cleveland noted that a "diplomatic mission from Korea has been received, and the formal intercourse between the two countries contemplated by the treaty of 1882 is now established." Cleveland later reported an agreement "between the representatives of certain foreign powers and the Korean Government in 1884 in respect to a foreign settlement at Chemulpo [Inchon]."[22]

Korea's treaty with the United States served as a model for its treaties with Britain and Germany in 1883, Italy and Russia in 1884, France in 1886, and Austria-Hungary in 1889. But Cleveland exaggerated U.S. primacy, for Korea had already signed with Japan the Treaty of Ganghwa in 1876.[23] Whereas Korea's rulers had been strongly pressured to accept the unequal treaty with Japan, they sought the pact with the United States.

The relationship with America meant far more to the Korean than to the U.S. government. The 1882 treaty contained a "good offices" clause that both sides came to interpret quite differently. It provided that, "if another power deals injustly or oppressively with either Government, the other will exert [its] good offices, on being informed of the case, to bring about an amicable arrangement, thus showing their friendly feelings." Viewing the clause as a firm commitment, King Gojong several times invoked it to request America's backing against intimidation by Korea's neighbors. But the U.S. government denied that the clause created any obligation to assist Korea or even to mediate when outside powers intruded.[24]

While Washington kept its distance politically, American businesspeople quickly leapt into the arena. King Gojong saw the United States as a progressive and moral country that could guide Korea's modernization and protect its independent place on the world stage. In 1882 the king dispatched a delegation to inspect American industry. One of its first stops was Boston's Hotel Vendome, recently lit up by the (Thomas) Edison Lamp Company. Soon, Korea permitted Edison to establish a subsidiary in Korea. By 1887 the Edison team had electrified the royal palace in Seoul—a model for illuminating Tokyo's Mikado Palace and Beijing's Forbidden City two years later.[25]

JAPAN'S AMBITIONS

Japan and the United States had mostly good relations until the 1930s. Determined to modernize Japan and resist Western domination, Japanese reformers also looked to the West for ideas, guidance, and techniques. They employed more than 3,000 "hired foreigners"—most of them residing in treaty ports. But in 1876 the reformers invited William S. Clark, president of the Massachusetts Agricultural College (later the University of Massachusetts, Amherst), to establish the Sapporo Agricultural College (later Hokkaido University, one of seven national universities in Japan). Clark worked directly under Kuroda Kiyotaka, governor of Hokkaido. Both men had been officers in war, and got along well. Clark contributed many ideas to the prefecture's colonization. A painting of Clark's departure from Hokkaido, rendered in 1971, hangs in the Prefectural Capitol building in Sapporo and includes a version of his parting words (still well known and honored in Japan): "Boys, be ambitious! Be ambitious not for money or for selfish aggrandizement, not for that evanescent thing which men call fame. Be ambitious for that attainment of all that a man ought to be." Clark returned to Massachusetts after eight months in Japan. The exchanges between his colleges in Amherst and Sapporo became the first technological assistance relationship between a U.S. and a foreign university and continued strong into the twenty-first century. A statue of Clark greets visitors to Hokkaido—a reminder of American soft power. Before becoming prime minister in 1888–1889, Kuroda served as a diplomat. Dispatched as an envoy to Korea in 1875, he negotiated Japan's treaty with Korea in 1876.

The Japanese could view Korea as a menacing dagger or as a bridge to the riches of Manchuria and Siberia. Much like the British Isles, the Japanese archipelago sits at a comfortable distance from the mainland—not too close, not too far. Also like Britain, Japan lacks raw materials to feed its industry. Dominion over Korea would help Japan to extract that country's resources and access those of Manchuria, while denying the peninsula to Russia and other competitors. Japan's desire to occupy Korea and China was central to its march to the Yalu in the late sixteenth century. As noted in the previous chapter, Chinese and Korean forces compelled Japanese troops to withdraw in 1597.

Just as the United States had opened Japan to outside influencers with visits by Matthew Perry's flotillas in 1853–1854, some Japanese resolved to open Korea to Japan.[26] Both shocked and inspired by Perry and America, young radicals in Japan abolished the shogunate and established the Meiji emperor in 1868. The radicals' slogan was "Enrich the state, strengthen the military."

In 1876 Japan concluded its Ganghwa Treaty with the Kingdom of Chosŏn. The treaty effectively terminated Korea's status as a Chinese tributary, referring to the kingdom as an "independent state"—a phrase that evoked no protest from China. The treaty required Korea to open three ports to trade and permit foreign residence.

In 1889 U.S. president Benjamin Harrison noted Japan's "advancement . . . evidenced by the recent promulgation of a new constitution, containing valuable guaranties of liberty and providing for a responsible ministry to conduct the Government." Implicitly recognizing Japan's growing influence in Korea, Harrison's next paragraph dealt with Korea. He "recommended that our judicial rights and processes in Korea be established on a firm basis by providing the machinery necessary to carry out treaty stipulations in that regard."[27] In 1892 he sent to Congress for its review and possible "revision a copy of the regulations for the consular courts of the United States in Korea, as decreed by the minister of this Government at Seoul."[28]

Korea soon became a key target as Japan fought first China and then Russia for hegemony there.[29] Russia became a major player in Northeast Asia when a much weakened China ceded eastern Manchuria to St. Petersburg by treaties in 1858 and 1860. This huge "maritime province" gave Russia direct access to Korea by a seventeen-mile strip along the Tumen River, giving Russia a short border with Korea—much used (or abused) in 1950–1953. Starting in 1860, Russia built the port city of Vladivostok, "power of the East." Starting in 1863, Koreans migrated to Siberia looking for work. Substantial numbers remained there into Soviet and post-Soviet times.

The port of Vladivostok permitted Russian ships to sail out through Korea's East Sea to the East China Sea and the Pacific Ocean. Russia started to build its Trans-Siberian Railway (*magistral'*) in 1891. But China's continued possession of northern Manchuria blocked a direct route to Vladivostok. Russia, however, built and controlled the Chinese Eastern Railway, which went south from Chita (Siberia) to Harbin (Manchuria) and continued to Port Arthur (now Lushun), on the Kwantung (now Liaodong) Peninsula. China in 1896 ceded to Russia a strip of land to build a rail link from Harbin to Vladivostok. Two years later China leased Port Arthur to Russia, finally giving Russia a year-round, warm-water port. These and other rail connections across Manchuria, completed in 1903, looked ominous to Japan and helped provoke its attack on Port Arthur in 1904. After 1905 the southern portion of the Chinese Eastern Railway became part of the Southern Manchurian Railway, owned and operated by Japan. A single-track railroad connecting Vladivostok with St. Petersburg across Russian territory was completed only in 1916–1917.

When other actors—Russia and Great Britain as well as China and Japan—competed to dominate Korea in the late nineteenth and early twentieth centuries, Washington stood aside. Washington rejected proposals from London for joint action to prevent war between China and Japan. When Japan attacked Chinese troops in Korea in 1894, President Grover Cleveland told Congress that both sides had requested that "agents of the United States should within proper limits afford protection to the subjects of the other during the suspension of diplomatic relations due to a state of war"—a "delicate office" he accepted. The war did not directly threaten the United States, Cleveland said, but raised concern for U.S. commerce in both countries and the safety of U.S. citizens in China. As for Korea, Cleveland wanted "at the beginning of the controversy to tender our good offices to induce an amicable arrangement of the initial difficulty growing out of the Japanese demands for administrative reforms in Korea, but the unhappy precipitation of actual hostilities defeated this kindly purpose."[30]

Confronted with a broad-based rebellion (known as the Tonghak upheaval), the Korean government in 1894 requested Chinese military assistance to restore order. The Qing dynasty informed Japan that it would intervene to bring order in its traditional "vassal state." The Japanese replied that they did not regard Korea as a Chinese vassal and dispatched their own army. Since the 1870s the Japanese military had looked for a pretext to fight China. A Japanese expeditionary force thrashed Chinese troops in Korea and moved on into Manchuria.

In November 1894 the United States tendered its good offices to both China and Japan to bring the war to a close. Mediated by Americans in Beijing, the Treaty of Shimonoseki (Chinese, *Maguan*) in 1895 required China to recognize Korean independence.[31] Soon, Korea became subject to "direction" and "assistance" from Japan. The same treaty ceded Taiwan and the Pescadores to Japan—as well as the Liaodong Peninsula, although Russia, France, and Germany soon pressured Japan to re-cede it to China in return for a larger indemnity. Seeing Queen Min as a bulwark against Japanese penetration of Korea, dozens of Japanese agents stormed through the palace in October 1895, killed her and other women, and burned her corpse, whereupon the king and the crown prince took refuge in the Russian embassy.

In 1903 Theodore Roosevelt endorsed the recent U.S. commercial treaty with China for helping to open "the great Oriental Empire" for U.S. traders, miners, and missionaries. "And," he added, "what was an indispensable condition for the advance and development of our commerce in Manchuria, China, by treaty with us, has opened to foreign commerce the cities of Mukden, the capital of the province of Manchuria, and An-tung [Dandong], an important port on the Yalu River, on the road to Korea."[32]

Russia's finance minister, Sergei Witte, convinced Tsar Nicholas II to summon the Hague Peace Conference in 1899 in a bid to limit the arms race. Russia was falling behind other European powers militarily. It could not readily compete with Austria-Hungary, which was perfecting rapid-fire artillery. Witte urged that Russia invest more in economic development and less on arms. Against Witte, the tsar's minister of war contended that more and better arms—not words—were needed to achieve Russia's aims in the Far East and at the Turkish Straits. Russia's ally, France, also opposed arms limitation. Paris informed the tsar that France would attend the Hague conference only if France could be assured that no arms limits would emerge.[33]

Seeking to organize knowledge about Korea, the Russian Ministry of Finance in 1890 published a virtual encyclopedia about Korea—everything from shamanism to language to trade statistics.[34] But the real target for both Russia and Japan was Manchuria.[35] In 1897 Russia coerced a lease of Liaodong from China and gained railroad right-of-way to join the peninsula with the city of Harbin. In 1900–1903 Russian troops poured into Manchuria. The Russians virtually annexed the peninsula and proceeded to fortify Port Arthur. If Russia could block Japan's advance into Korea, then Russia's hold on Manchuria would be more secure. Accordingly, Russian troops began covertly to cross over into Korea. At the same time, St. Petersburg proposed "neutralization of the Korean territory" north of the thirty-ninth parallel, a proposal that could keep Japan in the south. A few days later, in reply, Tokyo demanded that St. Petersburg explicitly recognize that Korea and its littoral were outside Russia's sphere of interest.[36]

Alarmed by Russian penetration into Manchuria, Tokyo sought to clarify with St. Petersburg their respective roles there.[37]Asserting that the Russian negotiators were both hypocritical and inflexible, Japan broke off diplomatic relations on February 6, 2004. On February 8 Japan launched a surprise attack on the Russian fleet at Port Arthur.

Having destroyed much of the Russian fleet, Japan declared war against Russia on February 10, 1904. Japan asserted that Russia was plotting to annex Manchuria and, if that happened, Korea's independence could not be maintained. Because peace in the Far East was at stake, the Japanese statement alleged, Tokyo had tried for six months to reach a negotiated settlement with St. Petersburg. Russia's diplomats, however, had stalled even as its military prepared for war. Tokyo asserted: "The safety of Korea is in danger: the vital interests of our Empire are menaced. The guarantees for the future, which we have failed to secure by peaceful negotiations, we can now only seek by an appeal to arms."[38]

Two weeks after the Russo-Japanese War began, Japan signed a protocol with the emperor (or king) of Korea guaranteeing the independence of Korea and pledging to defend the country against "aggression of a third power or internal disturbances." To this end, Japan could occupy as needed "such places [in Korea] as may be necessary from strategic points of view."[39]

The United States acquiesced in Japanese hegemony over Korea to check Russian expansion, bolster ties with Japan, and secure Tokyo's acquiescence in American occupation of the Philippines. Some Americans believed that Koreans (like Filipinos) were not capable of governing themselves and would be better off under foreign rule.

U.S. officials understood that the protocol established a Japanese protectorate over Korea, but few worried that Korea was becoming a Japanese colony. The U.S. legate in Tokyo assured Washington in February 1904 that Japan intended to maintain the "Empire of Korea intact, although its administration would continue to be under the close Japanese supervision which has already begun."[40] For his part, the U.S. secretary of state seemed more concerned that Korean soldiers, after an accident in a snowstorm, had damaged an American-built streetcar of the Seoul Electric Company than with Japan's tightening grip on Korea. Anxious to give no offense, the Korean minister of foreign affairs apologized for the incident to the U.S. legate in Seoul.[41] Washington's minister in Seoul, Horace Newton Allen, protested American failure to oppose the Japanese takeover and was fired for challenging official U.S. policy.

Theodore Roosevelt, despite his education and wide travels, embraced racist theories that helped inspire U.S. expansion during and after the Spanish-American

War.[42] "I should like to see Japan have Korea," the then–Vice President Roosevelt wrote in 1900. After Japan attacked Russia, TR cut off relations with Korea, turned the U.S. legation in Seoul over to the Japanese military, and deleted the word "Korea" from the State Department's record of foreign relations, replacing it with the word "Japan."

Historian Tyler Dennett later summed up TR's views on Korea: "Japanese control was to be preferred to Korean misgovernment, Chinese interference, or Russian bureaucracy."[43] TR seemed to harbor no reservations about a Japanese regime that assassinated the queen of Korea. Roosevelt admired Japanese vigor while disdaining the leaders of Korea, Russia, and Germany. He wanted Japan to contain Russian expansion but not interfere with U.S. commerce in China or with U.S. operations in the Philippines.

Japan defeated Russia on land and at sea, but—exhausted and strapped for credit—in June 1905 welcomed Roosevelt's offer to mediate (secretly requested by Tokyo). The same Sergei Witte who in 1899 had urged the tsar to limit arms found himself at Portsmouth, New Hampshire, negotiating an end to the Russo-Japanese War.

The Treaty of Portsmouth, signed by Japan and Russia in September 1905, placed Korea, the Kwantung peninsula (today's Liaodong), and the Southern Manchurian Railroad under Japanese control. Russia ceded southern Sakhalin and the Kurile Islands to Japan. Both Russia and Japan pledged to evacuate their troops from Manchuria.

In November 1905 Japan imposed the Eulsa (or Ŭlsa) Treaty on Korea. It made Japan responsible for Korea's foreign affairs and its ports. In short, Korea became a Japanese protectorate. King Gojong and several ministers refused to sign the treaty, putting its legitimacy in doubt.

Meanwhile, as preliminary arrangements were being made for the Portsmouth conference, U.S. secretary of war William H. Taft, stopping off on his "imperial cruise," reached a secret understanding in July 1905 with Japanese prime minister Taro Katsura. Their memorandum, which President Roosevelt upheld by a telegram, recorded a U.S. pledge to recognize Japanese suzerainty over Korea while Japan disavowed any aggressive designs on the Philippines. A nearly full text of the Taft-Katsura memorandum (omitting Taft's name, to avoid embarrassing him) was not published until 1924—in the magazine Current History.[44] Expatriate Korean nationalist Dr. Syngman Rhee, who knew Woodrow Wilson at Princeton University, denounced this "sale" of Korea's right to self-determination.[45]

The imperialist zeitgeist fostered a deep malaise. In August 1905 Great Britain and Japan reached an accord similar to the Taft-Katsura deal as they renewed their alliance: London recognized Japanese dominance in Korea, while Tokyo pledged not to threaten Singapore. Adopting a kind of Monroe Doctrine, Tokyo wanted to dominate East Asia as the United States did the Caribbean and Latin America.

For helping to end the Russo-Japanese War, the U.S. president received the Nobel Peace Prize in 1906. Koreans felt victimized by Roosevelt as well as by Japan. Some Russians and many Japanese felt they had been shortchanged. Anti-peace groups in Japan denounced the Portsmouth peace as a betrayal. Forty years later, Stalin complained that the United States had helped Japan tear away Russian territory.[46] The longest-serving Soviet foreign minister ever, Andrei A. Gromyko, recalled that his own father—having returned from serving in the Russo-Japanese war—termed Roosevelt a "clever president." Andrei's father added that America became richer than other countries by taking their wealth. A neighbor added, however, that Roosevelt was not only "sly" but also "wise."[47] Seeking to learn from history, a future Soviet ambassador to Washington wrote his doctoral dissertation in 1947 on U.S. policy in the Russo-Japanese War.[48]

As Japan moved to incorporate Korea, Washington ignored or rebuffed numerous appeals by King Gojong for U.S. intervention. Roosevelt in his December 1905 message to Congress did not mention Korea at all, though he spoke in favorable or neutral terms of Japan and China—five or six times each.[49] Amid all this bonhomie, the U.S. and Japanese "legations" were raised to the status of "embassies" in January 1906.

The U.S.-Japanese deal resembled the August 1939 Ribbentrop-Molotov pact, which partitioned Eastern Europe and secured a temporary peace between Germany and the Soviet Union—a deal warmly greeted by both Adolf Hitler and Stalin.

Having defeated Russia in the Far East, Japan tightened its grip on Korea. In January and February 1906 Japan's imperial government "abandoned" its legation in Seoul and set up a "residency-general" there to handle Korea's foreign affairs. Alleging in June 1906 that Korea had no "judicial system in the sense understood in civilized countries," Japan claimed a duty to reform Korean courts. Tokyo also abolished extraterritorial rights for foreigners in Korea and put them under Japanese jurisdiction. The Japanese press reported how Japan's resident-general in Seoul bullied the Korean emperor, replaced his palace guards with hundreds of Japanese police, and demanded expulsion from the court of "intriguers" whose machinations imperiled the friendship between Japan and Korea. Japanese ordinances placed Kwantung and the South Manchurian Railway under a Japanese general subject to Japan's minister of war.[50] U.S. officials seemed—or tried—to accept at face value Tokyo's assurances that it would safeguard the independence of the "emperor of Korea" and his country's sovereignty.

Washington acquiesced in Japanese annexation of Korea and penetration into Manchuria in part because U.S. officials felt they lacked any tangible means to contain Japanese expansion. They ignored not only America's moral clout—what we now call "soft power"—but also its economic and financial muscle. Japan, after all, was nearly bankrupted by its war with Russia. Indeed, famine seized Japan's northeastern provinces in early 1906—so severely that U.S. offers of financial assistance were accepted, regardless of "face," and gratefully acknowledged by the emperor himself.[51]

The sham ended in 1910 when Tokyo made Korea part of the Japanese empire. Japanese occupation sought to destroy Korean nationhood—a policy tantamount to cultural genocide, as defined in the subsequent 1948 convention—that is, actions intended "to destroy, in whole or in part, a national, ethnical, racial or religious group, as such." Koreans could not use their own language in schools or publications—not even in conversations with neighbors. They were required to use "Japanized" names, render obeisance at Shinto shrines, and hail the Japanese emperor as their overlord. The brutality of the Japanese occupation, which lasted until 1945, left bitter memories that continued to resonate in the early twenty-first century—in North as well as South Korea.[52] Chang Ki-jin, a resident since 1942 of a leper colony established by Japan on Sorok Island in 1916, recalled in 2007 that the Japanese commander of the leper colony "carried a big bat and would hit us whenever we rested" from carrying bricks. "He was really vicious." When Chang's legs froze one winter, they were amputated.[53]

President William Howard Taft's message for 1910 noted that Japan had annexed Korea, "the final step in a process of control of the ancient empire by her powerful neighbor that has been in progress for several years past." Taft reported Japanese "assurances of the full protection of the rights of American citizens in Korea under the changed conditions."[54] Taft later spoke of the "satisfactory adjustment . . . of the questions growing out of the annexation of Korea by Japan."[55]

"Hear no evil, see no evil"—this became Washington's principle. Thus, Taft in 1910 also welcomed the gradual establishment of "representative government" in China and the conclusion of a Japanese-Russian agreement regarding Manchuria. The U.S. president noted also that his secretary of war had toured the Philippines and then visited Japan and China, accompanied by many U.S. business representatives.

In 1911 Taft reported that the 1894 U.S.-Japanese trade treaty had been renegotiated and all outstanding issues resolved. He recalled that Washington had provided warm receptions to both Chinese and Japanese officials, including Admiral Count Togo (who, having studied naval science for seven years in England, sank an English ship carrying Chinese troops during the Sino-Japanese war and then led the decisive attack on Russia's navy at the Tsushima Strait in 1904). Taft said nothing about how U.S. efforts to gain markets and financial influence in China and Manchuria were challenging European and Japanese vested interests and adding to tensions in the region.

Then, amazingly, *for the next thirty-one years—from 1911 until 1942—the word "Korea" disappeared from public statements by U.S. presidents.* Korea seemed to vanish not only from maps but also from official American consciousness.

Engaged elsewhere—including in Mexico, Europe, and Russia—the United States paid little attention to Korea under Japanese rule. When Walter Lippmann led an extensive inquiry in 1918–1919 for Woodrow Wilson on how to reorder the world, his experts on the Far East and the Pacific rim considered Japan and China in some detail but failed even to mention Korea. (The documents on their deliberations were not published until 1942—by which time another war had enveloped and changed everything that Lippmann's group had been concerned with more than thirty years earlier.)[56]

The Japanese stood ready and willing to exploit the opportunities that emerged as its giant neighbor fragmented. China fell into near anarchy after the dowager empress died in 1911 and a republic was formed in 1912. The republic's second president, more dictator than democrat, Yuan Shih-kai (who had also been China's last resident in Korea, 1885–1894), died in 1916. Soon China had a war-lord government in Beijing and a republican government in Nanjing, headed by Sun Yat-sen, later regarded by both Nationalists and Communists as the "father of modern China."[57]

Sun Yat-sen sought to merge Western and Chinese ideals, but got no backing from Washington. When Sun and his compatriots failed to obtain aid and diplomatic recognition from Western governments, they turned to Soviet Russia for assistance. Sun died in 1925, one year after two other giants in their countries' development, Woodrow Wilson and Vladimir Lenin.

Sun Yat-sen's story anticipated that of Syngman Rhee, the father of the Republic of Korea and a Princeton PhD, who got more frustration than help from Washington until 1950. The U.S. government refused appeals for aid by Rhee and other leaders of Korea's nationalist movement. The Department of State instructed the U.S. ambassador to Japan in April 1919 that the U.S. consulate at Seoul "should be extremely careful not to encourage any belief that the United States will assist the Korean nationalists in carrying out their plans."[58] When Korean nationalists sought to organize resistance to Japanese rule, Tokyo blamed these actions on Wilson's doctrine of national self-determination.

The United States accepted Japanese restrictions on foreign trade with Korea and the abolition of extraterritoriality and foreign settlements in treaty ports in Korea. Concerned that Washington was giving away too much, the Senate in 1916 adopted a resolution requesting the correspondence between representatives of the U.S. and Korean governments relative to the Japanese occupation of Korea. Secretary of State Robert Lansing then made a "judicious selection" of the correspondence for delivery to the Senate.[59]

Japanese imperial policies resembled those of the Russian and European imperialists, but they were exceptionally brutal in Korea. Looking back after World War II, the former U.S. secretary of state Cordell Hull wrote that Japan's record in Korea and elsewhere was that of a "highway robber."[60] As a result, Korean animosity toward Japan persisted long after Japanese troops withdrew in 1945. Whereas most of the former colonies of Portugal, Spain, France, and Great Britain came to welcome close ties with their erstwhile metropoles, both North and South Korea remained bitter toward Japan.

FROM WORLD WAR I TO WORLD WAR II

As Europeans waged their own civil war, Japan seized the Shantung peninsula from Germany. Tokyo expected no challenge to its position in Korea but wanted the Paris Peace Conference in 1919 to give a green light to further Japanese expansion. The U.S. ambassador in Tokyo reported in late 1918 that eminent financier Baron Shibusawa demanded recognition of Japan's "absolute superiority in China." The baron cautioned that America, "the Champion of Democracy," might try to check Japan's military expansion. The journal *Chuwo* warned America "that if she becomes conceited and attributes the defeat of the enemy to her own strength . . . she will be doomed as Germany is now doomed." Presciently, if prematurely, the journal predicted that if America "recklessly attempts to display her strength . . . the result will be the unhappiness of mankind." Another periodical called for Vladivostok to be converted into a free port and the Chinese Eastern Railway to be placed under Japanese control. One leading politician wanted special recognition of Japanese interests in Manchuria and Mongolia.[61]

Having emerged from World War I as the world's creditor, the United States employed its material might with caution. Secretary of State Charles Evans Hughes convened the Washington Naval Conference in 1921 and persuaded the conferees to limit tonnage of capital ships and to recognize the "open door" in China. A leading U.S. historian noted that the Washington treaties signed in 1922 set America's "diplomatic frontier way out into Manchuria. But we did not put our military frontier out there; in fact, we disarmed west of Hawaii. That meant we had an imbalance between what we were promising and what we were capable of achieving. When the Japanese moved back into China in the 1930s we were unable to do anything about it."[62]

Like "Korea," the word "Manchuria" disappeared from presidential statements from 1911 to 1942—save one mention by President Herbert Hoover in 1931 after Japan annexed Manchuria. Even though Hoover rejected calls for sanctions against Japan, Secretary of State Henry Stimson in January 1932 enunciated what became known as the Stimson Doctrine: the United States would not recognize any Japanese-Chinese agreements that "may impair the rights of the United States or its citizens in China, including those which relate to the sovereignty, the independence, or the territorial and administrative integrity of the Republic of China, or to the international policy relative to China, commonly known as the open door policy."[63] The legal basis for this position was the Nine-Power Treaty signed in Washington by Japan and others in 1922. But a broader principle was enunciated in the final sentence of the doctrine: The United States would not recognize any political or territorial changes accomplished by force.[64] The legal justification for this position was the 1928 Paris Pact outlawing war, signed by most of the world's governments.

Washington never applied the Stimson Doctrine to Korea, even though its principles had been implicit, and sometimes explicit, in U.S. policy since the mid-nineteenth century.[65] The Stimson Doctrine did not dislodge Japan from territories it seized in the 1930s. Japan was driven from Korea only in the final days of World War II. Even then, Korea remained under foreign rule. Against the will of most Koreans—for the first time in many centuries—the country was split into two warring kingdoms.

When World War II ended, U.S. and Soviet authorities learned that Unit 731 of the Japanese armed forces, based in Harbin, had practiced vivisection without anesthesia on thousands of Chinese, Russian, and Korean prisoners, including women and infants. The declared purpose was to determine the effects of plague and other disease agents by which they were deliberately infected. Having studied the effects, Japan proceeded to drop biological weapons on China—killing perhaps 200,000 Chinese.

The vivisections, along with the issue of comfort women, added to other negative feelings among Chinese and Koreans toward Japan. As egregious actions by heartless aggressors, they ranked with the assassination of Queen Min. While Soviet authorities tried and executed some of the Unit 731 personnel, the United States did not. Instead, it gave them stipends in exchange for information about their experiments.[66]

Despite America's growing strength relative to all other countries in the twentieth century, the United States acquiesced in a cruel Japanese occupation and colonization of Korea—egregious violations of President Wilson's Fourteen Points and other ostensible U.S. principles.

4

How One Korea Became Two

One month after Pearl Harbor, a U.S. president finally spoke truth to power. In February 1942 Franklin D. Roosevelt accurately depicted Japan's occupation of Korea as part of a "scheme of conquest" launched by Tokyo in 1894—a reality that a series of U.S. presidents had heretofore passed over in silence. Roosevelt spoke of Japan's harsh despotism in Manchuria and Korea. Still, the United States did little to help Korea become an independent and united member of the world community. Their country divided at the 38th parallel in August 1945, authoritarian leaders in the North and in the South sought to unify the peninsula under their own rule. When the North invaded the South in June 1950, United Nations forces led by the United States fought North Korean and Chinese armies to a draw. An armistice signed in July 1953 sealed Korea's division into the twenty-first century.

INDEPENDENCE IN "DUE COURSE"

Even as the United States and its allies waged war across the Pacific, Washington rejected pleas of Korean leaders that their homeland be restored to independent statehood with membership in the United Nations.[1] Roosevelt's only vision for Korea was to place it under an international—that is, foreign—trusteeship. The Cairo Conference held by Roosevelt, Winston Churchill, and Chiang Kai-shek in November 1943 endorsed the trusteeship idea but assured the world that the three allies coveted no gain for themselves.[2] Mindful of the enslavement of Korea, they were "determined that *in due course* Korea shall become free and independent" (emphasis added).[3]

These high hopes got nowhere. Within a decade, World War II had ended but a global Cold War had erupted; Chiang Kai-shek had been driven offshore to Taiwan; and a divided Korea had experienced three years of intense warfare.

Official U.S. insouciance to Korea, as we have seen, began in the nineteenth century. But many factors shaped FDR's policies toward Korea and the entire postwar world. The president wanted to use whatever aid the USSR could muster to defeat Germany and Japan as quickly as possible. Wishing to avoid any discord with "Uncle Joe" Stalin, the U.S. president tended to put off detailed postwar planning—even for Berlin. At Tehran in 1943 and Yalta in 1945 he gave Stalin a virtual free pass to retake the three Baltic republics, even though Washington had refused to recognize their absorption into the USSR in 1940. Roosevelt was equally cavalier toward Soviet claims on Finland, Poland, and the Far East. FDR's generosity with other people's futures was greatly appreciated by Stalin.[4] When Roosevelt approved Russia's retaking Sakhalin and the Kurile Islands, Stalin practically danced with joy—even though (or because?) this implied the USSR would have to join the war against Japan.[5]

Harry S. Truman, who succeeded Roosevelt in April 1945, also wanted to draw the USSR into the final battles with Japan. When this happened, as experts knew, the Red Army plus two divisions of Soviet-trained Korean troops would cross into the Korean peninsula before U.S. forces could get there in large numbers. Anti-Communist Korean exiles and Nationalist Chinese based in Chungking warned American officials that Korean forces backed by Moscow would try to sovietize North Korea and conquer the South.[6] U.S. planners were suspicious of Moscow's intentions but gave little thought to how America might cope with Soviet and Soviet-backed Korean forces once they entered Korea.

Syngman Rhee and some other Korean exiles urged Washington to recognize the Korean Provisional Government, based in Chungking as well as in the United States, as Korea's legitimate government. However, the U.S. ambassador to the Nationalist Chinese government in Chungking advised Washington not to do so. Recognition of the "Korean Provisional Government composed of professional revolutionaries constantly quarrelling among themselves," he wrote, would not stop Communist forces from sovietizing Korea.[7] A Nationalist Chinese expert put it more bluntly: The Korean exiles in China and the United States, said Chu Hein-ming, had no roots or support in Korea itself, where the Japanese occupiers and their local puppets had destroyed political life. On the other hand, those Koreans trained in the USSR and who survived the purges there in 1937–1938 had been fully incorporated into the Soviet administration. Their expertise and the prestige of their backers would help them to dominate Korea when the USSR finally joined the war against Japan. When the Soviets begin to fight Japan, Chu added, they might aid the Chinese Communists even though they despised them.[8]

Rhee pressed for Korea to become a founding member of the United Nations. But Washington said no. His Provisional Korean Government did not even get observer status at the April 1945 San Francisco conference that finalized the UN Charter. The U.S. stance was equally tough on Italy. Neither in Korea nor in Italy, American officials said, was there an established government that could claim to lead the country.[9]

As President Truman prepared for the Potsdam (Berlin) Conference with

Stalin and Churchill in July 1945, an aide summarized for the new president the place of Korea in FDR's deliberations: "There was no reference to Korea in Map Room messages or documents until the Yalta Conference. On 8 February 1945, during a discussion on the Far East when Churchill was not present, President Roosevelt explained his intentions with regard to Korea." Roosevelt envisioned "for Korea a trusteeship composed of a Soviet, an American and a Chinese representative"—an arrangement that "might last from *20 to 30 years*" (emphasis added). Stalin replied: The shorter the trusteeship period, the better.[10] When Roosevelt opined that Great Britain should be excluded from the trusteeship, Stalin countered that, if excluded, London's "resentment would be strong [so] the British should be invited."[11] Stalin's often liberal internationalist stands on Korea in 1943 and again in the first seven months of 1945 do not fit the image of a greedy imperialist.[12] Were they merely a façade or a sincerely held outlook that changed as new conditions emerged?

By the time that presidential adviser Harry Hopkins met Stalin at the Kremlin on May 28, 1945, Washington had adopted Stalin's view that Britain should take part in a four-power trusteeship for Korea. Its duration, however, had not been fixed. Hopkins said the trusteeship "might be twenty-five years; it might be less, but it would certainly be five or ten." Stalin replied that a trusteeship would be desirable but said nothing about its duration. As to China, Stalin assured Hopkins that the USSR had no territorial designs on Manchuria or elsewhere and would back the Nationalist leader Chiang Kai-shek. Stalin saw him as "best of the lot" and more likely than Communist leaders to unify China.[13] Two weeks later, Truman informed Chiang Kai-shek that there would be a four-power trusteeship for Korea.[14]

As World War II entered its final months, jockeying for postwar advantage intensified. Harbingers of future conflicts multiplied. Contrary to what Stalin told Hopkins in late May, in early July 1945 the Soviet leader told Nationalist Chinese foreign minister T. V. Soong that the USSR should own and manage both the Chinese Eastern and the South Manchurian railroads, though they could be supervised by a joint Soviet-Chinese board. Soong countered that ownership should be Chinese, though the railroads could be operated by a joint Soviet-Chinese company. Stalin wanted Dairen (Dalny) to be managed by Russians, though half of the port could be Chinese. Soong responded that Dairen should be a "free port" under Chinese administration, with technical assistance from Russia. Stalin proposed that the USSR and China share the use of Port Arthur. Stalin wanted arrangements for the railroads and ports to last for forty-five years.

Discussing Korea with Soong, Stalin reiterated his agreement to a four-power trusteeship. V. M. Molotov interjected that this would be an unusual arrangement for which there was no parallel. Hence, he said, there should be a detailed understanding. Adding a major proviso Stalin said there should be no foreign troops or police in Korea. As Soong later warned the Americans, even with a four-power trusteeship, the USSR could then dominate Korea by means of Korean troops and police trained in the USSR.[15]

Meanwhile, specialists in the U.S. State Department prepared briefing books for the new U.S. president, who would soon meet Stalin and Churchill in Berlin. Still expecting that Japan would fight for a long time, the State Department urged that liberation of Korea take place by joint Allied land and sea operations, conducted under a single Allied command. Given Korean hostility to outsiders, the State Department thought it inadvisable for any one country to invade Korea to drive out the Japanese. State worried that, having occupied Manchuria and North China, an advancing Soviet Union might try by unilateral action to establish a "friendly government" in Korea. State therefore advised Truman to seek confirmation of Moscow's adherence to the Cairo Declaration. This would mean international trusteeship for Korea under the United Nations or by the four Allied powers. If the USSR were to become the main voice in Korea's administration, then State wanted the trusteeship to be under the United Nations. Any kind of territorial disposition should be based on prior consultation and agreement.[16]

Truman, Stalin, and two British prime ministers (Churchill followed by Clement Atlee) meet in Berlin from July 17 to August 2, 1945. Henry Stimson, then secretary of war, advised Truman one day before the conference opened that the one or two Soviet-trained divisions of Korean troops would "probably gain control, and influence, the setting up of a Soviet dominated local government [in Korea], rather than an independent one. This is the Polish question transplanted to the Far East." Stimson suggested that Truman press for a trusteeship, and that "at least a token force of American soldiers or marines" be stationed in Korea during the trusteeship.[17] The Potsdam Declaration, issued a few days before the conference ended, promised implementation of the 1943 Cairo principles, which included Korean independence "in due course." The Potsdam Declaration was issued on July 26, but the Kremlin did not accede to it until August 9—the same day the Soviet Union declared war on Japan.[18]

ORIGINS OF THE 38TH PARALLEL

Having suffered two nuclear bombings and facing a Soviet onslaught, Japan accepted the Potsdam Declaration terms and surrendered on August 15, 1945. "The suddenness of the Japanese surrender forced emergency consideration by the Department of State and the armed services of the necessary orders to General MacArthur . . . about the Japanese surrender." So began a memorandum written in 1950 by Dean Rusk, a participant in the surrender deliberations of the State-War-Navy Coordinating Committee (SWNCC), which took place from August 10 to 15. The State Department wanted U.S. forces to receive the Japanese surrender "as far North as practicable." Rusk (then age thirty-six) and a military colleague were tasked to "come up with a proposal which would harmonize the political desire to have U.S. forces receive the surrender as far North as possible and the obvious limitations on the ability of the U.S. forces to reach the area." As Rusk recalled later, they "recommended the 38th parallel even though it was further north than could be realistically reached by U.S. forces in the event of Soviet disagreement, but we did so because we felt it important to include the capital of Korea in the area of responsibility of American troops.' The SWNCC accepted this recommendation, and it was agreed to "internationally." One historic capital, Pyongyang, lay north of the dividing line while Seoul, the capital prior to Japanese annexation in 1910, lay a short distance to the south. Rusk was "somewhat surprised that the Soviet [sic] accepted the 38th parallel," since he thought "they might insist upon a line further south in view of our respective military positions."[19] Before the Russo-Japanese war, as we saw in the previous chapter, Russia proposed to Japan the neutralization of Korea north of the 39th parallel Speaking on Soviet radio on September 2, the date of Japan's formal surrender, Stalin expressed glee that Japan had been routed and the "stain" of Russia's defeat in 1905 wiped out. Stalin may have accepted the American presence below the 38th parallel as a bulwark against a renewed Japanese threat to Russia.[20]

Surrender arrangements to north and south of the 38th parallel were enshrined in General Order No. 1 issued by "The Imperial General Headquarters of Japan under Order from the Supreme Commander for the Allied Powers [Douglas MacArthur]," dated September 2, 1945. The order directed Japanese forces in Manchuria, Korea north of 38 degrees, Karafuto, and the Kurile Islands to surrender to Soviet forces in the Far East. Commanders of Japanese forces in Japan, Korea south of 38 degrees north latitude, Ryukyus, and the Philippines were to surrender to the commander in chief of U.S. forces in the Pacific. Nothing was said of Taiwan.[21]

The Department of State regarded the surrender arrangements as a temporary expedient and pressed for the administration of civil affairs to be combined "so that the whole of Korea would constitute a centralized administrative area"— perhaps under a council made up of the commanding officers of the occupying powers.[22]

In 1945 and as late as 1947 there were signs that Stalin wished to preserve the spirit of wartime cooperation with Washington. To be sure, the USSR in 1945 broke its Yalta commitments on Poland and shifted from four-power collaboration in Germany to sovietization of the Eastern zone.[23] On the other hand, Stalin also agreed to a proposal from President Truman for a joint withdrawal from Czechoslovakia, even though the Americans were preparing to pull out unilaterally. The Cold War intensified in 1946, but in 1947 Stalin could still advise U.S. secretary of state George C. Marshall not to take a "tragic" view of U.S.-Soviet relations but to understand that differences would arise and could be negotiated. We do not know if Stalin planned all along to use unilateral action to achieve his goals or whether new developments triggered a shift away from wartime unity. Possible triggers for a change included contention over Poland, U.S. refusal to commit to a specific sum of German reparations, American reminders of the U.S. nuclear weapon monopoly, discord over Turkey and Iran, and Washington's refusal to include the USSR in the occupation of Japan.[24]

Years away from possessing a nuclear deterrent, Stalin sought to avoid provoking a U.S attack on the USSR. Still, following Japan's surrender, the Kremlin's policy hardened in Korea. Soviet representatives spurned appeals for competitive politics and free elections to establish an all-Korean government. Tellingly, three of the most important Soviets in administering North Korea were Red Army veterans of the Russo-Finnish War of 1939–1940. One of them, Col. Gen. Terentii F. Shtykov, became known as Moscow's "Mr. Korea." With direct access to Stalin, he served as the first Soviet ambassador to North Korea and was instrumental in formulating and directing Soviet policy there.[25]

The Kremlin gave far more attention to China and Japan than to Korea. The first Soviet troops to enter Korea raped and pillaged. Australian observers reported that Russian excesses in the North managed to unite Koreans and Japanese for the first time in forty years. By late September 1945, however, Soviet commanders imposed discipline and posed as protectors of private and public property. No evidence has surfaced of a master plan to sovietize the North or take over the entire country. Still, many reports reached U.S. authorities in Seoul in 1945 about Soviet suppression of non-Communist political groups in the North. For example, when Soviet troops entered the city of Syn-wi-ju (at the mouth of the Yalu River) on August 30, their commander replaced a local "Self-Rule Council," which had been organized immediately after Japan's surrender, with a "People's Political Committee," in which two minuscule Communist groups were given the dominant position.[26] They were then allowed to form a Communist Party while the Soviets disbanded an opposition "Democratic Party." In time, however, as in East Germany, the Red Army stripped North Korea of industrial equipment. The Soviets organized sham joint stock companies that took Korean minerals to the USSR. Moscow set the terms of trade to its advantage.

Washington also gave more attention to Japan and China than to Korea. U.S. policy south of the 38th parallel showed no sign of a master plan. Official Washington made little or no effort to analyze Korea during World War II or before it proposed dividing Korea at the 38th parallel. There was no Korean analogue to the wartime studies of Japan and Germany or Cold War analyses of the USSR sponsored by the U.S. government.[27] The closest parallel was probably *The Koreans and Their Culture* by a Yale anthropologist who specialized in Native Americans and China. He conducted an on-site study of a South Korean village for a few months in 1947 and did extensive historical research. But his book was not published until 1951 and contained no policy recommendations for outsiders.[28]

In August 1945 the War Department assigned Lt. Gen. John R. Hodge to head the occupation of the U.S. zone. It instructed him to prepare Koreans for eventual self-determination but did not give him enough troops to govern an occupation zone where many people clamored for independence. Hodge distrusted Soviets in the north and Korean leftists in the south and felt he needed conservative Koreans, including some who had earlier collaborated with the Japanese, to stabilize that part of Korea occupied by U.S. forces. With the acquiescence of the U.S. viceroy in Tokyo, General Douglas MacArthur, Hodge undercut the trusteeship idea pushed on him by the State Department.[29] Whereas the Communists tightly controlled the North, U.S. authorities in Seoul permitted Communist groups and newspapers to vilify the United States and Syngman Rhee's "provisional government" in Chungking. When Hodge allowed Rhee and two associates to return to Seoul, they returned only "in their individual capacities." They could join the Advisory Board to the U.S. occupation, but only on the same terms as existing members.[30]

As in divided Germany, U.S. and Soviet talks to unify divided Korea broke down. Washington authorized the U.S. commander in Korea to negotiate with his Soviet counterpart "regarding the rationalization of communications, commerce, finance, and other outstanding issues in Korea"—for example, resumption of rail and other traffic between the two zones, establishment of uniform fiscal policies, and policies to deal with displaced persons, including the Japanese. In October and November 1945, however, the Soviet commander refused to negotiate working agreements with the U.S. commander until given authority by Moscow.[31] The Soviet consul general in Seoul accepted American food and services, but rebuffed any effort to solve practical problems. Instead, the Soviets labored behind the scenes to discredit the United States in Korean eyes.[32]

Secretary of State James Byrnes discussed Korea and other issues with V. M. Molotov and British foreign minister Ernest Bevin at the foreign ministers meeting held in Moscow in December 1945. Molotov several times put off U.S. proposals on Korea for further study, but finally submitted a proposal on December 20 to create a "provisional, democratic Korean government" to develop the economy and "national culture of the Korean people." Molotov proposed a joint commission drawn from the U.S. and Soviet commands to assist the provisional government. Moscow also called for a four-power trusteeship for Korea, to last up to five years (much shorter than FDR had contemplated).

Molotov's proposal looked constructive. Byrnes naïvely approved it with only minor revisions, even though it contained two potential deal-killers: First, the joint U.S.-Soviet military commission was obliged to "consult with Korean democratic parties and social organizations." The Soviet idea of a democratic party or social organization, of course, was that it be Communist oriented—thus barring non-Communist organizations in the North and the South. Second, the commission's decisions had to be approved by the four trustee governments—a formula for infinite delay.[33]

The man who later became North Korea's "great leader" was not Moscow's first choice for the job. The Kremlin's first choice spurned Communist policies. A second potential candidate was from Seoul and not well known in the North. A third was deemed too close to Chinese Communists. That left Kim Il Sung, who arrived in the North Korean port city of Wŏnsan from the USSR a month after the Japanese surrender. While still in his twenties, Kim Il Sung in the 1930s had led small units of ethnic Koreans fighting the Japanese in Manchuria.[34] He later became a captain in the Red Army after it incorporated Korean guerrillas to gain intelligence about Japanese forces. The Soviets in October presented Kim Il Sung, then thirty-three years old, at a rally in Pyongyang as a national hero and "outstanding guerrilla leader." Some in the audience called him a "fake" with nothing to say. Still, he remained Moscow's man. In December Kim became head of the Provisional People's Committee in Pyongyang. In parts of the Soviet occupation zone, however, rioters—farmers, students, and others—called for an end to Communist and Soviet military rule. They were suppressed, but more than a million refugees from Manchuria and the Soviet zone of Korea fled to the U.S. zone, many claiming to have originated there.[35] In response, Kim Il Sung called for a merger of all "democratic forces" in the North and brought local Communist cells under central control. The process began in which over the next decade Kim Il Sung put down dissent and purged all rivals.[36]

In the 1940s Kim Il Sung respected Stalin and adopted a Soviet model for governing. This included "democratic centralism" (in practice: the center gives orders and everyone else executes them) and an assumption that politics is a question of "*kto kovo*—who will do in whom?" As we shall see, however, Kim Il Sung became disaffected when he perceived that Stalin put the security and economic interests of the Soviet state over Communist internationalism and the needs of Korean Communists. Perceived grievances came to outweigh Kim Il Sung's respect for Stalin and the USSR. A pawn of the mighty, however, he could do little without Soviet permission and assistance.

Kim Il Sung also came to resent Communist Chinese policies toward his regime. North Korea provided much help to Chinese Communists as they fought the Nationalists in Manchuria in the late 1940s. North Korea provided a refuge for wounded Chinese and a conduit for Chinese goods and troops. The Chinese Communist Party had a Northeast Bureau in Pyongyang that coordinated all this. China in turn sent huge quantities of grain to North Korea and helped Kim Il Sung build an army from ethnic Koreans who had served in China. But Kim Il Sung thought Mao Zedong owed him a great deal.

DID U.S. POLICY INVITE AGGRESSION?

Tensions in divided Korea reflected and contributed to the global confrontation between the West and the Communist powers. In March 1946, however, the SWNCC recommended that the United States provide only limited military aid to South Korea's National Civil Police Force—"equipment adequate for the internal police requirements of that country"—until U.S. and Soviet occupying forces had been withdrawn or a responsible Korean government had been created.[37] As the Cold War became more intense, the Joint Strategic Survey Committee in April 1947 advised the Pentagon that it should extend military assistance according to a country's importance to U.S. national security. Eleven of the first twelve countries listed were in Europe. Korea ranked fifteenth—just below Japan and Nationalist China and just above the last, the Philippines (sixteenth).[38]

A year later, in March 1948 (following the Communist coup d'état in Czechoslovakia), Korea's importance rose a little in the eyes of official Washington. The director of European affairs at the State Department disagreed with the joint chief of staff that priority should be accorded to Italy, Greece, and Turkey for military assistance. He argued for the "equally vital importance of the Greek-Turkish, Italian, Iranian, and probably also Korean and Chinese situations"—with each individual program considered in relation to America's limited capabilities.[39] By September 1948 Greece and Korea were the only country concerns on the task list for the U.S. delegation to the UN General Assembly—and both were assigned to the future secretary of state, John Foster Dulles.[40]

Meanwhile, negotiations to unify the two Koreas got nowhere. In 1948 the Americans sponsored creation of a Republic of Korea south of the 38th parallel. The Soviets, in turn, formalized their client state as the Democratic People's Republic of Korea. Here was the Cold War pattern in divided Europe recapitulated in Korea. As in East Germany, the Soviets sponsored and equipped their client with a fighting force far superior to what existed across the dividing line.[41] The USSR and the United States withdrew most of their forces from Korea in 1948–1949. The Kremlin, however, provided the DPRK with tanks and other arms far superior to anything possessed by the South. The Americans helped put the South on the road to economic takeoff but left the ROK with an army far smaller and weaker than the North's. By early 1950 only 500 or so U.S. troops remained in Korea.[42]

American efforts to form a republican government in South Korea were inept. Syngman Rhee became president of the ROK in May 1948 and kept the post until 1960.[43]

Rhee was the first of many strong individuals, military and nonmilitary, to lead South Korea.[44] By 1949 Rhee had purged from political life many Koreans who had resisted Japanese rule, many of them leftists, and brought into his administration many who had collaborated with the Japanese. Washington's clients in Europe and Japan were becoming more democratic; not so in Korea.

SINO-SOVIET RELATIONS AND KOREA

North Korea could call on the world's two largest counties for support. The USSR had the largest territory; China, the largest population. Each bordered the other as well as North Korea. The DPRK was one of the first countries to recognize Communist rule in China—on October 6, 1949. But relations between Russia and China had been strained for centuries and did not improve when Communists rose to power in each country. Starting in the 1920s, Stalin's policy to China favored Chiang Kai-shek's Nationalists over Mao Zedong's Communists. After Communist forces drove the Nationalists off the mainland to Taiwan in October 1949, however, the governments of the world's two largest countries appeared to seek a fresh start. Andrei A. Gromyko led a Soviet delegation to the PRC to discuss formation of joint Soviet-Chinese oil and metal enterprises in Xinjiang (Sinkiang) province. When Gromyko returned to Moscow and reported how conflicted the talks in China had become, Stalin heatedly told the Politburo that the Chinese did not want to collaborate with the Soviet Union. This episode left a mark, according to Gromyko.[45]

Stalin saw reasons to worry that Mao Zedong hoped to distance China from the USSR and establish relations not only with Great Britain but also with the United States. The style and content of Soviet demands that the United Nations seat Communist China gave rise to suspicions that Stalin's diplomacy hoped to lock Beijing into greater dependence on Moscow. Taiwan was also an issue. Having failed to take Taiwan in October 1949, Mao realized that his forces could not accomplish this task without Soviet assistance. Even though the USSR had just tested a nuclear bomb, the USSR now confronted a North Atlantic alliance formed earlier in 1949. Given all this, Stalin did not want to risk war over Taiwan with Chiang Kai-shek's patrons in Washington.

PRC leaders wanted a new set of relationships with Moscow, different and less onerous than those provided in the Treaty of Friendship and Alliance the Kremlin had signed with Nationalist China in August 1945. Having traveled to the USSR by train, a PRC delegation headed by Mao Zedong stayed in Moscow from mid-December 1949 until mid-February 1950. Besides many contentious issues between the two states, personal animosities aggravated the negotiations. Suspecting that Stalin preferred relying on the PRC commander in northeast China, Gao Gang, to himself, Mao decoupled from the train a baggage car carrying gifts for Stalin's seventieth birthday from Gao and Lin Biao and ordered their gifts returned to them.[46] Disputes over many issues were so deep and prolonged that Mao considered departing Moscow in early 1950 without a treaty. Still, the two sides managed to sign an alliance on February 14, 1950, which lasted—at least on paper—for thirty years (1979).[47] Stalin and Mao barely talked to one another at the banquet to celebrate the alliance—an oddity noticed by many in the room, according to Gromyko.[48]

Tensions between Stalin and Mao affected their willingness and ability to assist and channel Kim Il Sung's North Korea. Even when weak and unsteady, both the DPRK and the ROK usually managed to go their own ways. Both Seoul and Panmunjom proved adept at manipulating the larger states that financed, armed, and backed them diplomatically.

All this formed the context for the increasingly important roles played by North and South Korea on the global stage.

5

How a Civil War Became Global

He calls it Reason, but uses it only to act more beastly than any animal.
(Er nennt's Vernunft und braucht's allein, nur tierischer als jedes Tier zu sein.)
—Mephistopheles to the Lord in Goethe's *Faust* (lines 285–286)

The partition of Korea left the peninsula with two governments, each determined to unify all Koreans under its rule. Korea was not a priority for the Kremlin or the White House: each focused more on its nuclear arms competition and on Europe. Still, Stalin gave a green light and equipped the DPRK to invade South Korea in June 1950. Despite earlier signs that Korea lay beyond the U.S. defense perimeter, the Truman administration dispatched U.S. forces and acquired UN approval to drive back the North Korean invaders. Feeling threatened, China joined the fray. The USSR sent pilots as well as arms to sustain DPRK and Chinese forces. After three years of combat, the parties signed an armistice in July 1953. The putative lessons and consequences of the Korean War ricocheted around the globe.

NORTH KOREA PLAYS ITS SOVIET AND CHINESE CARDS

Each leader—Kim Il Sung in the North and Syngman Rhee in the South—struggled to unify Korea under his own rule. Starting in 1949, if not earlier, Kim Il Sung importuned Stalin on several occasions for permission to march North Korean forces across the 38th parallel and unify all Korea. The DPRK leader assured Stalin that Communists in the South would mobilize popular support for unification with the Communist North. However, neither Stalin nor Mao Zedong wanted a war on the Korean peninsula that might bring U.S. forces to their doorstep. Stalin initially rejected Kim Il Sung's appeals, but changed his stance after the USSR successfully conducted a nuclear explosion and after Communists took control of

China. In January 1950 Stalin instructed Soviet ambassador Terentii F. Shtykov to inform Kim Il Sung that the USSR stood ready to assist his campaign to liberate the South, provided that it be organized to avoid U.S. intervention. Stalin authorized the dispatch of 400 senior Soviet officers to plan the war. He also dictated such details as whether the DPRK could issue a bond, form an additional three infantry divisions, convene the Supreme People's Assembly, or send textile workers to the Soviet Union for training. Still, Stalin did not want a major war on the Soviet doorstep that could also lead to war with the United States or a renewed threat from Japanese militarism.

Kim Il Sung assured Stalin that the United States would not join the war. After all, the Americans had not intervened to save Chiang Kai-shek in the Chinese civil war, and now they would be deterred by the alliance concluded between Moscow and Beijing in February 1950.

In April the ever-cautious Stalin warned that if the DPRK needed direct assistance, it would have to come from China—not from the USSR. Kim Il Sung traveled to China in May and informed Mao of his plan to attack the South. Mao Zedong said he would prefer to take Taiwan before engaging in other adventures. But when Mao received a telegram from Stalin confirming that he supported the invasion, Mao gave his approval as well. He also offered Chinese assistance—which, for the time being, was rejected. Mao declined to enter an alliance with Pyongyang until Korea was unified. Mao's coolness grated on Kim's sensitivities.[1]

Unlike the Allies and Central Powers in 1914, Stalin and Mao did not feel linked to each other or to Kim Il Sung as in a chain gang, where every actor's fate was inseparable.[2] Instead, each sought to pass the buck. Each Communist power practiced the parasitic logic of collective action—exploiting others to reduce burdens on itself. Beijing helped North Korea only when China felt endangered. Though resentful of each other, each Communist regime usually, but not always, held its tongue. Costs, as we shall see, were not shared equally.

The War Begins

North Korean forces crossed the 38th parallel on June 25, 1950, and pushed south. Soviet advisers helped plan and supervise the DPRK attack, but Pyongyang's leader lacked the courtesy even to inform Beijing that war had begun. The Chinese learned of it from foreign news sources.

Did the United States Invite the Attack?

America looked strong in Europe: The Marshall Plan and NATO were taking hold. In most of Asia, however, Washington appeared irresolute. Less-than-benign neglect proved costly.

Korea lay beyond the U.S. defense perimeter as defined by General Douglas MacArthur on March 2, 1949, and by Secretary of State Dean Acheson on January 12, 1950. America's defense line used to run along its West Coast, said MacArthur. "Now the Pacific has become an Anglo-Saxon lake and our line of defense runs through the chain of islands fringing the coast of Asia"—from the Philippines through the Ryukyus to Japan and the Aleutian chain to Alaska. Acheson's line was identical to MacArthur's, but started with Alaska and ended with the Philippines. Neither mentioned Korea—or Taiwan, both of which President Harry S. Truman in June 1950 decided to defend. In regard to "other areas of the Pacific," Acheson declared, "it must be clear that no person can guarantee these areas against military attack. . . . Should such an attack occur . . . the initial reliance must be on the people attacked to resist it and then upon the commitments of the entire civilized world under the Charter of the United Nations." Acheson urged people not to become obsessed with military considerations in the Pacific and Far East. Military means could not solve economic dislocations or susceptibility to Communist penetration.[3]

Acheson distinguished U.S. responsibility and opportunities in the northern part of the Pacific from the southern. "In the North, we *have* direct responsibility in Japan and we *have* direct opportunity to act. The same thing to a lesser degree is true in Korea," he declared. While Acheson used the present tense to describe an ongoing obligation to Japan, he used the past tense to describe U.S. responsibility in Korea and present tense to portray opportunity. In Korea, he said, "we *had* direct responsibility and there we *did* act, and there we *have* a greater opportunity to be effective than we have in the more southerly part." There, "the direct responsibility lies with the peoples concerned." American aid could be effective only when it supported the missing component in a situation that might otherwise be solved. He welcomed the dawn of a new day in Asia when "Asian peoples are on *their* own" (all emphases added).

Critics said that, with this statement, Acheson had flashed a green light for the North to invade the South, which happened six months after he spoke. They charged that Acheson had conveyed to Communists in Pyongyang and elsewhere that, if they marched across the 38th parallel, Washington would do nothing. Defenders of Acheson said the speech reflected a faith that containment could be achieved short of military means and did not signify abandonment of the peninsula.

Acheson's adviser George F. Kennan had argued that containment of the USSR should be accomplished primarily with political and economic tools. In June 1949 Kennan called on Congress to provide economic assistance to South Korea, but he also warned against any military involvement there. Acutely aware of the limitations of U.S. resources, Kennan urged that priority be given to areas of the greatest geopolitical significance. These included Japan, Manchuria, and Siberia—but not

Korea. Speaking as Nationalist Chinese forces were retreating to Taiwan, Kennan argued that the United States should hold the line in Korea to bolster Japan and other nations across the great crescent of Asia against communism.

Acheson contended later that the critique of his perimeter speech was unjusti-fied—part of a larger "attack of the primitives" on the Truman administration. The attack was "specious, for Australia and New Zealand were not included either, and the first of all our mutual defense arrangements was made with Korea." If the Rus-sians were watching for signs of American intentions, said Acheson, they would have paid little heed to his speech and far more to two years' agitation for with-drawal of U.S. combat troops from Korea, the recent defeat in Congress of a minor aid bill for Korea, and the increasing U.S. focus on concluding a peace treaty with Japan.[4] In truth, Acheson for several years had argued the importance of support-ing and funding South Korea, against the prevailing views in Congress and the Pentagon.

Still, Acheson's speech added to other signs that Washington had written off Korea as a vital American interest. As in 1904–1905 and again in 1919, there were few strong voices in Washington to support Korea against external threat. Ache-son's perimeter was identical to MacArthur's. But the world had changed radically in the ten intervening months. In Asia it was moving leftward. By October 1949 the Communists had won mainland China and driven the Nationalists offshore. The USSR had tested an atomic bomb. Rhee's government in South Korea was doing little to improve life for its people but wanted to attack the North.[5] Stalin reportedly cited all these factors when he explained in April 1950 why he was giv-ing a go-ahead for the North to invade the South.[6]

United States/United Nations Intervention

Neither Stalin nor Mao nor Kim Jong Il had expected the United States to join the fray. What started as a civil or local war quickly became a global conflict that could explode into a nuclear war.[7] Making an analogy to Munich in 1938 and following his own instincts, President Truman agreed with Acheson that the United States had to fight what Washington saw as Soviet-inspired, Communist aggression. Accused by Republicans of having "lost China," the White House was determined to avoid any hint that it was soft on communism. Truman would not "pass the buck," as did France and Britain in the 1930s. The Truman administration acted unilaterally but also mobilized international support. The UN Security Council, by a vote of 9 to 0, with one abstention (Yugoslavia) and one absent (the USSR), declared that an "armed attack" had taken place in Korea and called for an imme-diate end to hostilities and the withdrawal of North Korean forces from the South. Two days later the Security Council adopted a U.S. resolution calling on all mem-bers to furnish such assistance as necessary to repel the armed attack.

The United States led a United Nations force, consisting of South Korean troops and token forces from more than thirty UN member-states, to fight North Korea and—in effect—its Soviet and Chinese backers. The Soviet Union could not use its veto to stop the Security Council from authorizing collective security actions against North Korea, because the Soviet delegate was absent. Starting in January 1950, the Soviet delegate had absented himself to protest the UN's failure to give the PRC the seat assigned to China (which was occupied by the delegate from Taipei). When asked by Czechoslovak Communist leader Klement Gottwald to explain the Soviet absence at the Security Council, Stalin replied on August 27, 1950, that the Kremlin had wanted America to become "entangled in a military intervention in Korea" where it would "squander its military prestige and moral authority." When the United States became "distracted from Europe to the Far East," Stalin said, the "global balance of power" shifted to "us." Stalin expected (before China intervened in the Korean War) that America, like any other country, would be unable to "cope with China." He averred that the global shift in power would delay a third world war and give the Communists time to consolidate their strength in Europe while the "struggle between America and China would revolutionize the entire Far East."[8]

In early August Mao told his Politburo that China must help the DPRK if U.S. troops threatened China.[9] Indeed, some 14,000 ethnic Koreans in two divisions of the China's People's Liberation Army (PLA) crossed into Korea on August 25, 1950, nearly two months before the large-scale intervention of Chinese "volunteers." The Chinese Koreans kept their weapons and structure but were incorporated into the 33rd Regiment of the North Korean People's Army (NKPA) Twenty-Sixth Division. The NKPA was more Russianized than the PLA. It had an officer ranking system that the Chinese did not have until 1955. North Korea had inherited weapons from the Soviet forces that had departed in 1948. As a result, NKPA tanks, heavy artillery, and automatic weapons were superior to the equipment available to the Chinese Koreans in China's PLA.

In late August the Chinese Koreans participated in the NKPA's fourth major offensive, which pushed ROK and UN troops into a small corner of land around the port city of Pusan on Korea's southeast coast. For six weeks NKPA forces sought, but failed, to break through the "Pusan perimeter," a 140-mile defensive line around the port. Bolstered by more troops and equipment landed at Pusan, UN forces came to outnumber NKPA troops. Overstretched and outnumbered, NKPA troops began to retreat northward by mid-September. Driven from Seoul on September 28 by advancing UN troops, some NKPA troops dispersed as guerrilla units. They suffered from the severe winter of 1950–1951 no less than UN forces.[10]

The author of America's containment policy found himself divided on Korea. George F. Kennan saw both the limitations on U.S. capabilities, which argued for restraint, and America's need to affirm its reliability as a bastion against Communist expansion. So he supported U.S. military action to turn back the North Korean advance. Two months *after* the Korean War began, however, Kennan advised Acheson that the United States lacked the means to "keep Korea permanently out of the Soviet orbit" and that "the Koreans cannot really maintain their own independence in the face of both Russian and Japanese pressures." Kennan deemed it preferable "that Japan should dominate Korea. . . . But Japan, at the moment, is too weak to compete [with Russia]." Therefore, he concluded, the United States should acquiesce in gradual Soviet domination of Korea so that the United States could be freed "from involvement in that unhappy area."[11] This was the realpolitik conclusion by an authority who disparaged "legalism-moralism" in past U.S. policy to Asia.

Writing in August 1950 just before he left the State Department for Princeton's Institute for Advanced Study, Kennan recommended that the United States "terminate our involvements on the mainland of Asia as rapidly as possible, on the best terms we can get." He proposed an accommodation with the USSR that included neutralization and demilitarization of Japan; establishment of UN "control" over Korea for a year or two after withdrawal of North Korean troops from the South and pullout of U.S. troops from Korea; and demilitarization of Formosa (Taiwan) under UN control, as well as a plebiscite to determine Formosa's future.

This proposal, Kennan wrote, did "not imply any written agreement with the Russians. In fact, to negotiate anything of that sort would probably be disastrous. It implies only a general meeting of the minds." If the Russians became too tactless and reverted to harsh measures, as when North Korea attacked the South, then America's "sanction" would be to reintroduce U.S. troops into Japan. Given the American public's mood and complaints (especially by Republicans) about "losing China," Kennan conceded it would be difficult to persuade Americans to adopt his recommendations. Still, he felt obliged before resigning from government service to present his views to the secretary of state. Acheson rejected Kennan's views, and they did not get a public hearing. Some critics judged Kennan naïve, but his views were no more singular than those of U.S. experts who said that China was too weak to enter the Korean War or others who called for nuclear bombs to halt Communist advances.[12]

General Douglas A. MacArthur, named commander of the UN forces, sent U.S. forces in Japan to bolster those still in Korea. While the U.S. Eighth Army established a defensive perimeter around Pusan, U.S. Marines (the X Corps) assembled in Japan and prepared for an amphibious assault at Inchon on Korea's west coast.

The tide of battle changed after September 15, 1950, when the United States landed waves of troops at Inchon and threatened to sever the supply lines of the DPRK troops retreating from Pusan. Kim Il Sung had not prepared to defend

Inchon, in spite of warnings from many quarters that an American invasion there was imminent. The Inchon landing was a brilliant strategic move, but U.S. troops then took ten days to reach and liberate Seoul. During that time, many DPRK troops managed to retreat northward.

The American success at Inchon and the northward advance of UN forces compelled both Mao Zedong and Stalin to reassess their options.[13] Beijing's contingency planning for China's possible entry into the Korean War began well before the UN advance northward. The Chinese leadership had already decided in early July to relocate troops near to the Korean border to prepare for a possible intervention. Apprised of this decision, Stalin told Mao in July that "we will do our best to provide air cover" for Chinese troops if Americans crossed the 38th parallel. "Doing our best," of course, was not a firm commitment to act.

Stalin and his Politburo agreed in early October 1950 that the USSR should avoid war with the United States, even if this meant abandoning North Korea. As Nikita S. Khrushchev later recalled, Stalin said he was resigned to the annihilation of the DPRK. If the American forces stood on the border with the USSR, "so what?" said Stalin. "Let the United States of America be our neighbors in the Far East. They will come there, but we shall not fight them now. We are not ready to fight."[14]

Like Kennan in August, Stalin was prepared in October to write off Korea. On Stalin's instructions, the Soviet delegation proposed to the UN General Assembly on October 2, 1950 a ceasefire in Korea, the withdrawal of all foreign troops from the peninsula, and a general election under UN supervision that would produce a united Korea. Flush with recent military successes, the United States persuaded the General Assembly to reject the Soviet proposal.

Had the UN General Assembly passed the Soviet proposal of October 2, 1950, Syngman Rhee might well have become president of a united Korea. If the United States and the Soviet Union had agreed in 1950 to stop the fighting, then more than a million lives and much of Korea's buildings and infrastructure would have been spared destruction. Of course we cannot know whether the country would have been unified under a Communist or an anti-Communist regime. Either way, a unified Korea would probably have concentrated on internal development and posed no threat to its neighbors. If Communist, it might have resembled Tito's Yugoslavia; if anti-Communist, an expanded South Korea. With no fighting in Korea, Washington might well have come to terms with Communist China two decades earlier and avoided the Indochina debacle (plus deficit spending) it spawned.

But reality took a different fork. Having invited trouble by appearing weak before June 25, 1950, the United States embraced the opposite course.[15] President Truman and the Joint Chiefs of Staff authorized MacArthur to send UN troops across the 38th parallel. Interpreting his mandate quite freely, MacArthur appeared

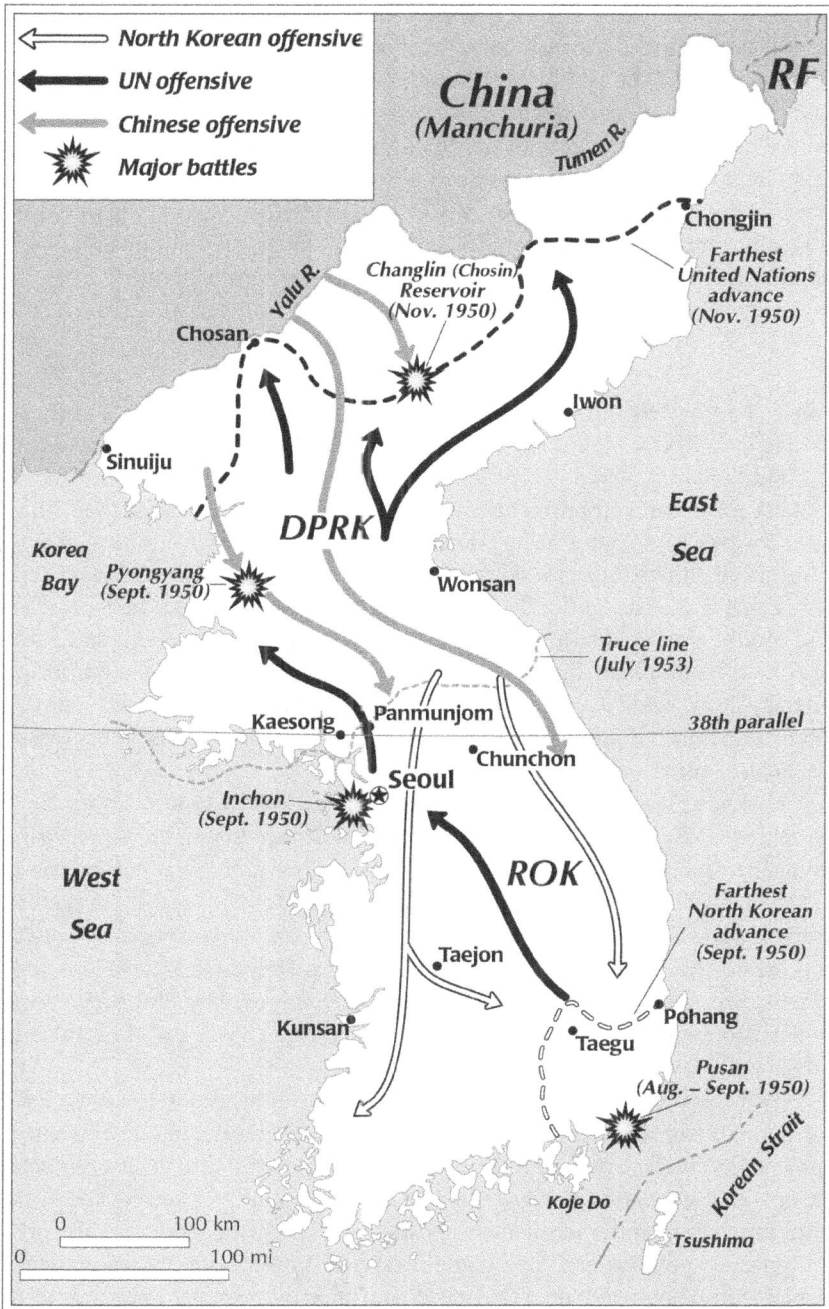

Map 5.1. The Korean War in 1950 and truce line, 1953

determined not only to destroy the North Korean regime but also to invade China. Map 5.1 shows the armies' marches up and down the peninsula

On October 7 the UN General Assembly passed a resolution calling for the unification of Korea. It called for conditions of stability under a unified government followed by a prompt withdrawal of foreign troops. UN forces "should not remain in any part of Korea longer than necessary once the goal of achieving stability and a unified democratic Korea" was achieved. The resolution played down the significance of the 38th parallel and permitted the UN commander to be guided by tactical considerations when he reached the parallel.

CHINA CROSSES THE YALU

In early October Mao informed Kim Il Sung that a force of Chinese "volunteers" would fight in Korea. He did not tell Kim, however, that China's entry into the war was conditional on Soviet air cover. Mao then sent Zhou Enlai and Lin Biao to ask Stalin for a firm commitment of air support. Having talked with the Chinese envoys for two days, Stalin turned down their request. Mao then informed Stalin on October 12 that China would not bail out Kim Il Sung. That same day Stalin learned that a U.S. naval flotilla was approaching North Korea's west coast and could mount another amphibious assault. All this led Stalin to command Kim Il Sung to retreat into Manchuria. Hours later, Mao changed his mind and informed Kim that China would assist the DPRK with or without Soviet air cover. Stalin was content and Kim Il Sung remained in Korea, albeit quartered in dugouts close to the Chinese border to escape U.S. saturation bombing.

Unbeknownst to the UN command, some 260,000 Chinese troops began crossing the Yalu River on October 19. Some U.S. analysts had anticipated this contingency, but their warnings were ignored.[16] When UN forces moved toward the Yalu in November, they encountered the Chinese, who quickly forced the Americans and South Koreans into a desperate retreat. Many UN forces were cut off in the northeast and had to be evacuated by sea. Desperate, MacArthur urged Truman to recognize that a "state of war" had been imposed by China. He recommended dropping thirty to fifty atomic bombs on Manchuria and cities in mainland China.[17]

When asked if the United States would use the atomic bomb in Korea, President Truman told reporters on November 30, 1950, that he would take "whatever steps are necessary" to deal with the situation and indicated that the use of nuclear weapons had "always been [under] active consideration."[18] When he added that the military commander in the field would be "in charge of" their use, the president ignited a political and diplomatic firestorm. In response, the White House clarified within hours that only the president could authorize use of nuclear weapons.[19] Despite hints to the contrary in public, Truman in private refused to use nuclear weapons in the war. For example, he turned down a proposal to destroy a large dam in North Korea with an atomic bomb.[20]

Elite Soviet pilots began training would-be pilots from North Korea on Soviet soil. Later, Soviet pilots disguised as Chinese flew patrols to project bridges linking China and North Korea. They shot down many U.S. bombers, but American Saber jets were superior to Russian MiG 15s in aerial combat.[21] Stalin insisted that his minions avoid any direct pretext for America to expand the war into Soviet territory. The United States played along with this fiction. It bombed Soviet bases in Manchuria and waged aerial combat over Chinese territory but denied doing so. Khrushchev later blamed Stalin for giving insufficient help to Kim Il Sung. The impetuous personality that conceived the Cuban missile gambit in 1962 also blamed Stalin for failing to invade Hokkaido in 1945.[22]

The fact that the terms of Chinese entry into the war were set in Moscow—that the PRC would provide troops, the USSR would contribute some matériel and advisers, and China would pay the Soviet Union for military supplies—engendered considerable bitterness on the part of the Chinese leadership. A Chinese delegation sent to buy arms and military technology in mid-1951 encountered what one delegate termed "great reserve" in Moscow. The Chinese thought the Soviets "overcautious"—afraid of provoking war with the United States. Also, Stalin worried that "China could become a second Yugoslavia"—another defector from the Soviet camp. Accordingly, the Soviets took four months to negotiate arms deliveries that would not be completed for three years. Not till the last minute did the Soviets agree to provide some military technology to help China become more self-reliant. Soviet representatives were impatient, rude, and demeaning, even though the Chinese intended to buy the weapons and pay a fair price for them. The marshal heading the Chinese delegation sometimes choked with anger. Never expecting the talks to drag on for four months, the Chinese had no clothes for cold weather. The marshal himself developed pleurisy and had to be hospitalized before his train reached Beijing.[23]

A year later, in September 1952, Zhou Enlai met with Stalin and other Soviet leaders to discuss armistice negotiations. Former foreign minister V. M. Molotov asked Zhou about Chinese debts. Molotov wanted to be sure that he had understood Zhou correctly: that China would pay in full—not just half—for Soviet weapons delivered for sixty Chinese divisions according to the rates established for countries other than China; also, that this obligation was *not* covered by the military credit granted by the Soviet government to China on February 1, 1951. Zhou replied that Molotov understood him absolutely correctly. Stalin then interjected that both sides should sign a special agreement to this effect.[24]

Stalin then brought up the issue of gifts from China to the Soviet government. Zhou replied that having visited the "museum of gifts" and seen gifts sent to Stalin for his seventieth birthday by other countries, the Chinese "feel they must make up for what they were not able to do before." Stalin then pledged to present the Chinese delegation with automobiles made in the USSR.[25] Whatever resentments he may have felt toward Stalin, Zhou was quite obsequious. He insisted on treating everything Stalin said as an "instruction" even though Stalin repeatedly said he was only making "suggestions."

Expecting the United States to stay out of the war, the DPRK had prepared no air defenses. But UN commander MacArthur on November 5, 1950, made all cities and villages in North Korea targets of the American bombers. When U.S. bombers began to pummel the North, Kim Il Sung and his comrades were shocked and groped frantically for practical responses. In November 1950 the Pyongyang leadership called on people to build and live in "dugouts or mud huts." But even these were bombed. As the fighting continued, most North Koreans lost their dwellings and had to endure living in cramped quarters with no light or water. Many, if not most, were mobilized to restore industries and transportation facilities at nighttime.

Despite suffering heavy losses, Chinese troops continued to push UN troops southward and away from the Yalu River. Given that U.S. troops were retreating and U.S. diplomats were seeking some kind of cease-fire, Stalin changed course. In December 1950 he told Soviet diplomats to string out peace talks and urged Beijing to continue fighting. Once the war stabilized into a kind of standoff, Stalin preferred to keep it going indefinitely to tie down and wear down U.S. power.

Back in Washington, Acheson was glad to have Kennan return from Princeton for a week in December 1950 to advise him on Soviet affairs and buck up spirits—for example, by predicting that the Chinese push south would outstrip its logistical capabilities.[26]

In early 1951 UN forces gradually drove back the Chinese and North Koreans. By April, UN forces were again approaching the 38th parallel. President Truman (in agreement with Britain's prime minister, Clement Attlee) proposed a cease-fire to the Communists. This displeased MacArthur, who desired to continue his advance. MacArthur proceeded to broadcast an ultimatum to the enemy commander, a move that subverted Truman's plans. Furious that MacArthur had preempted a presidential prerogative, Truman sacked him and replaced him with General Matthew Ridgeway, who was already commander of the Eighth Army.

In May 1951 Chinese forces drove some American forces south of the 38th parallel but then suffered huge losses when they were surprised by a U.S. attack to the west and north of Seoul. The failed offensives by Chinese and North Korean troops in April and May forced the Communist allies to consider opening negotiations with the UN command. Nonetheless Stalin on June 5 informed Mao that "the war in Korea should not be speeded up, since a drawn out war, in the first place, gives the possibility to the Chinese troops to study contemporary warfare on the field of battle and in the second place shakes up the Truman regime in America and harms the military prestige of Anglo-American troops."[27]

Stalin conducted an orchestrated set of moves by which Chinese and DPRK representatives negotiated in ways that bought time during which their forces could prepare for renewed offensives in November 1951.[28] Talks began at Panmunjom in July 1951 on an armistice, the demarcation line, a demilitarized zone, supervision of the truce, and arrangements for prisoners. But bitter fighting continued for two more years. The delay resulted from discord over repatriating prisoners of war, and possibly because Stalin—assured that the conflict would not escalate—was in no hurry to end it at this juncture.

While the major actors continued to "fight and talk," North Korean partisans waged unconventional war on DPRK and Chinese forces from redoubts on several islands in the West Sea. Though not officially part of UN, U.S., or ROK forces, they received logistical support from the U.S. Eighth Army. In 1952, one unit trained by a U.S. first lieutenant managed to destroy a DPRK 76-mm AT gun and a heavy machine gun pillbox in an operation backed by a UK warship and U.S. Marine aircraft. To counter nearly 20,000 partisans offshore in 1953, North Korea deployed some 200,000 troops. Many partisans opposed a negotiated settlement, cutting short their efforts to liberate the North. U.S. officers organized two groups of partisans that infiltrated the North after the July 27, 1953, armistice, but they were disbanded in 1954, as described in Ben S. Malcom, *White Tigers: My Secret War in Korea* (Washington: Brassey's, 1995).

Talk and Bomb

By February 1952 Kim Il Sung wanted to sign an armistice and turn over any unresolved questions to a committee. There was no point arguing about the return of prisoners of war (many of whom, he said, had fought for Chiang Kai-shek's Nationalists) when U.S. bombers were killing more Koreans than those imprisoned by the Americans. Stalin and the Chinese, however, argued for continuing the war, because it distracted and weakened the United States. The North Koreans, Stalin said, had lost nothing except their casualties(!).

Not just bombing but cold winters, epidemics (typhus, cholera, meningitis), and hunger killed many North Koreans. Many people lived in dugouts, where lack of fresh air and heat aggravated health problems. Some ate frozen roots of cabbage unearthed from the snow. Livestock, not abundant before the war, declined, in many cases forcing humans to pull plows. High government taxes and arbitrary decrees (such as "Grow cotton!") added to human suffering. Many North Koreans did not know how to tilt politically lest they be persecuted by South Koreans or by returning DPRK and Chinese forces. Frequent bombing compelled DPRK agencies to function in dugout buildings. The official newspaper operated from an abandoned coal mine.[29]

While negotiators sparred, the United States intensified its bombing campaigns. Starting in June 1952, the American "air pressure strategy" treated all buildings and inhabitants of villages and cities as targets. Any building could conceal supplies and provide shelter for troops and workers. North Korean repair crews worked on broken railroad tracks at night. Between Sinanju and Pyongyang, for example, the North had track-walkers spot rail cuts and then recruit citizen labor to fill the bomb craters as soon as possible after a strike. With nightfall, experienced military repair crews, with materials and equipment, repaired ties and rails.[30] American and other UN airplanes nearly crippled four hydroelectric plants, drastically reducing electricity in the North. The bombers also flattened Pyongyang and ravaged mining and other industrial facilities in the North, but failed to stop all shipments of industrial goods from China and the USSR.

North Korean and Chinese portrayals of American biological warfare during the Korean War showed the Americans using the same kinds of canisters with flies and rodents actually used by the Japanese against Chinese targets in the 1940s.[31] The North Korean and Chinese allegations were seconded by Soviet and some Western scientists, but they turned out to be another big lie. In spring 1953 the Soviet government told Beijing and Pyongyang that Moscow knew the allegations were false.[32] Even Lavrentii Beria (presented to FDR by Stalin as "our Himmler") seemed upset that Moscow's reputation for honesty would be sullied![33]

Stalin expressed his deepest feelings about the United Nations in September 1952 when discussing the Korean armistice and other issues with Zhou Enlai. Stalin stated that the UN "is an American organization and we should destroy it, while keeping up the appearance that we are not against the UN; we should conduct this with an appearance of respect to the UN, without saying that it should be destroyed, weakened, but in reality weaken it." Stalin recalled his earlier suggestion that China take the initiative in creating a continental or regional UN. Besides the current UN, Stalin favored creation of separate organizations for Asia, Europe, and other regions. "Let America create an American organization, Europe—a European one, Asia—an Asian one, but parallel to the UN, not in lieu of the UN." Zhou said China had no interest in the UN and agreed that China should initiate creation of a continental organization. He added that Beijing was holding a peace congress in October and sought Indian and Japanese participation.[34]

ARMISTICE

Each party continued its version of fight and talk, but battle fatigue was pervasive. A concatenation of events in the first months of 1953 pushed for a deal.

President-elect Dwight D. Eisenhower went to Korea before he was inaugurated in January 1953, but the trip provided him with no clear solution for ending the war. The president and his advisers considered mounting a renewed offensive northward, perhaps using tactical nuclear weapons, but worried about expected costs and possible dangers. American officials attempted to send indirect hints to the Chinese government that Eisenhower might expand the war into China or even use nuclear weapons, but Mao and his associates seemed defiant.[35] Despite all this, Washington never came close to tactical use of the atomic bomb in Korea. Not a single American nuclear weapon was deployed within usable distance of the fighting.[36]

The evidence is contradictory, but it suggests that by late 1952 Stalin was ready to halt the war—a shift that pleased Kim Il Sung but not (at that time) Mao Zedong. Moscow's position became clear when, soon after Stalin's death on March 5, 1953, his successors pressed for peace.[37]

Chinese negotiators signaled a change in policy in April when they accepted the UN proposal for an exchange of sick and wounded prisoners and then recommended turning nonrepatriates over to a neutral state. As armistice talks dragged on, the United States in May 1953 bombed dams and irrigation systems in North Korea, and President Eisenhower threatened to expand the war using nuclear weapons. Showing both strength and defiance, however, Chinese forces in late May and early June attacked positions defended by ROK troops along the front line, accompanied with measured attacks on U.S. forces but none on UK units, perhaps because British policies were deemed less objectionable than American.[38]

Having expended more blood, both sides made concessions on the issue of repatriating prisoners of war, and the armistice was signed on July 27, 1953, by the commanders of the UN forces, the Korean People's Army, and the Chinese People's Volunteers—but not by the ROK. The signatories agreed to establish a demilitarized zone four kilometers wide between North and South. Starting southwest of Panmunjom, the partition line slanted to the northeast of the 38th parallel—adjustments that each side claimed improved its strategic position.[39]

As ROK president Syngman Rhee had feared, his government was excluded not only from the negotiations but even from the signing ceremony, though the ROK was part of the UN command. Nonetheless Rhee used the war and the negotiations to enhance his own and South Korea's influence in world affairs. Many Koreans admired his manipulation of Americans, such as his unauthorized release of 28,000 prisoners of war in June 1953 to frustrate negotiations for an armistice in the Korean War, and his successful bargaining for massive American economic and military support as his price for acquiescence in the truce.

Costs

Three to four million soldiers and civilians died in the fighting in Korea, in a war that barely altered the North–South boundary.[40] More than 35,000 U.S. servicemen and servicewomen lost their lives.[41] More than 1,000 UK troops and about 2,000 from other UN member-states also died in the fighting. The Republic of

Korea lost at least 600,000 soldiers and up to a million civilians. North Korea, which started the war and had the smallest population of the major combatants, lost at least 1.3 million—half of them civilians.

Chinese casualties totaled 1,010,700—at least 152,000 soldiers and civilian personnel killed; 383,000 wounded; 450,000 hospitalized; 21,700 taken prisoner; and 4,000 missing in action. China also lost 400 airplanes and 13,000 vehicles. China spent up to 10 billion yuan (some $3.3 billion at then-current exchange rates)—half of it owed to the USSR for weapons, a debt not repaid fully until 1965. War outlays consumed from 34 to 43 percent of government expenditures.[42]

A reluctance to become involved in another such conflict helped account for China's devotion to the 1955 Bandung Spirit and its later low-profile involvement in the Vietnam War. Beijing's efforts to modernize the PLA were stalled when Mao Zedong fired Peng Dehuai in 1959 for opposing Mao's radical domestic policies, and by other partisan wars within the leadership.[43]

Apart from deaths caused by land combat and aerial combing, many civilians were simply massacred in both South and North Korea. Civilian deaths were uncounted, though a Soviet report claimed that 280,000 North Koreans had been killed by U.S. bombing—about 250 a day. "Most of the towns were just rubble or snowy open spaces where buildings had been. . . . The little towns, once full of people, were unoccupied shells," according to General William Dean, the commander of the 24th division, who was captured and imprisoned in the DPRK for much of the war.[44] A Hungarian diplomat reported to Budapest in 1954 that the American bombing of the North had been unexpected, and that nothing was left standing—no buildings or machines or anything else.[45] Scholars estimated that the war reduced the South's GDP per capita by 10 percent and the North's by 45 percent; they further estimate that the North's population decreased (from emigration as well as violence) by more than 10 percent, from 9,622,000 in 1949 to about 8,490,000.[46] Since more men than women died in combat, gender ratios became skewed. By 2002 there were two women for every man among those aged 65 and over.[47]

Famine struck North Korea again in the mid-1950s. Lack of rain added to the problems caused by Kim Il Sung's policy of building up heavy industry by taxing the countryside—an approach very much like Stalin's in 1928 through the early 1930s. Thanks to widespread sacrifices and to aid from other Communist countries, in the years that followed Pyongyang began to look like a modern city, and the North's economy rebounded faster than the South's until about 1970. Still, a Hungarian diplomat reported in 1977—twenty-four years after the war ended—that life for most North Koreas remained a desperate struggle to make ends meet. Most had no strength or opportunity to meet freely and have informal conversations. Their only desire was to sleep. They did not want "to rise up," but many were demoralized and hungry.[48]

Relations among the three Communist regimes did not improve as a result of their struggle against the U.S. and UN forces. Essentially, Pyongyang complained that Moscow and Beijing had not done enough, while Soviet and Chinese officials saw the Kim Il Sung regime as ungrateful and unwise in many of its actions. Though many North Koreans and Chinese died in the fighting and very few Soviets, Moscow insisted that Beijing pay for aid rendered during the Korean War. Close economic and military ties between Pyongyang and Beijing developed only after the Chinese entered the Korean War. Each of the three Communist dictatorships found fault with the others. Pyongyang criticized China for not joining the war earlier. Chinese and Soviet officials, in turn, blamed Kim Il Sung for many reckless decisions. Beijing urged Kim Il Sung to accept a unified command under China's Marshal Peng Dehuai. Kim resisted; but, pressed by Stalin, he finally gave in. Still, this did not end Chinese–North Korean wrangling. Peng at one point told Kim, "You are gambling with the fate of people"—Chinese as well as Koreans. Even though Kim Il Sung resented Stalin's haughty attitude and the fact that Stalin treated him like a puppet, Kim was always quite fawning when addressing the Soviet leader. He was not deferential toward the Chinese.

LONG-TERM CONSEQUENCES

At the end of the war, Korea remained divided close to the same boundary where the conflict began in 1950, except that Kaesong now lay in the DPRK. Though a Communist dictatorship continued in Pyongyang, many American strategists saw the Korean War as a victory for the U.S. strategy of containment. North Korea and its Communist allies had been contained and South Korea given an opportunity to develop in relative peace. Some U.S. policymakers in the 1960s took a similar approach to Vietnam. American defense of the South, they reasoned, would check Communism and permit South Vietnam to follow South Korea's example. They had, at least, learned one lesson from the Korean War: they avoided any actions that might provoke China to join the Indochina war.

A very different interpretation is that the Korean War set a precedent for U.S. presidents to take the country into undeclared and unwinnable wars. Vietnam and the twenty-first century's "war on terror" followed the same pattern. For domestic as much as for foreign political reasons, the U.S. president in each case misled Congress and the public, mobilizing and consuming vast resources. For each war the White House spun a rationale, but what appeared political was often personal as well. Like Lyndon Johnson and George W. Bush after him, President Truman wrestled with personal insecurities and private demons—including a decades-long hostility toward MacArthur. When the American public perceived that the Korean, Vietnam, and other wars were unwinnable, these wars became unsustainable.[49]

U.S. tank in diorama of Korean War at the Victorious Fatherland Liberation War Museum, Pyongyang. (Photo by Jeremy Hunter)

For North Koreans, the struggle became a war of identity—their nation against America, a war that the DPRK claimed to have waged mainly on its own. To make the point, the North obliterated Chinese grave markers. Though North Koreans and Chinese suffered huge losses, their high birth rates meant that the extensive human losses did not stop population growth. Mao Zedong could claim that the Korean War put China on the diplomatic map; Stalin, that it trapped America in endless labors; Kim Il Sung, that his regime had fought America to a stalemate and survived. More than seven decades later, his family still ruled. If memories of the war persisted, North Koreans had reason to hate and fear the United States.

Some months after the Korean armistice, Pyongyang and Beijing on November 3, 1953, signed an agreement on economic and cultural cooperation. As Sino-Soviet tensions mounted, the DPRK signed a mutual assistance treaty with China on July 11, 1961. It was renewed for twenty years in 1980 and again in 2001. Article 2 of the treaty committed each side to immediately render military and other assistance by all means to its ally against any outside attack. Caveat emptor: That eleven years passed between the entry of Chinese forces into the Korea War (1950) and a formal alliance (1961) spoke volumes about tensions between leaders in Beijing and Pyongyang.

The Korean War intensified the global Cold War and served to bolster what President Eisenhower in 1961 termed America's "military-industrial complex." Believing that the USSR pulled the strings in North Korea, Washington sharply expanded U.S. military spending; reintroduced conscription; and did what it could to make America's NATO allies a real fighting force. Washington opted to unleash West Germany's industrial potential. In 1955 the Federal Republic of Germany joined NATO, and Japan, despite its so-called "pacifist constitution," became a forward base for U.S. forces in Asia. Japan's industry also gained from and contributed to the Korean War effort.[50]

After Stalin's death in 1953, Moscow and Beijing explored another fresh start. But a troubled honeymoon soon led to altercations and then to a divorce. By the early 1960s the erstwhile allies were denouncing each other in public. Beijing tested its first nuclear weapon in October 1964—the same month that Khrushchev's opponents ousted him for "hare-brained schemes." Soviet planners considered attacking China and its nuclear facilities in 1970–1971 but did not. Their major military engagements were confined to skirmishes along the long Sino-Soviet border in 1969.

Relations between Beijing and Moscow remained frigid until M. S. Gorbachev initiated a détente in the late 1980s. In the post-Soviet 1990s, however, China and Russia remained at odds. When Vladimir Putin took the helm in Moscow in 1999–2000, Sino-Russian relations improved. In 2015 Russian and Chinese ships conducted their first joint exercises in the Mediterranean. Putin also tried to improve Russia's ties with North Korea. He met with Kim Jong Il and worked out some joint economic projects. In April 2015, however, Kim Jong Un canceled his plan to attend the Kremlin's victory over Germany celebrations in May. The reason given, according to a Russian official, was "internal Korean affairs."

6

How North Korea Got the Bomb

North Korea tested its first nuclear device in 2006. Within a few years it claimed to be a nuclear weapons state. How did it acquire the necessary materials and know-how? The story began more than a half century earlier. Soviet and East European documents reveal a long-standing drive by DPRK leadership to obtain nuclear weapons, coupled with a growing reluctance on the part of North Korea's professed allies to assist this effort. Pyongyang's ostensible comrades probably feared that the DPRK could use nuclear weapons in ways that generated unwelcome dangers.

The collapse of the Soviet Union and the emergence of closer ties to South Korea in Beijing as well as in Moscow deepened Pyongyang's determination to acquire its own nuclear capability. It accomplished this goal with limited foreign aid. In the 1990s Pakistan provided know-how and some equipment for uranium enrichment, but North Korea's first nuclear devices were fueled by plutonium. The near absence of external support reinforced the Kim dynasty's dedication to self-reliance and its "military first" priority.

NORTH KOREA'S INTEREST IN ALL THINGS NUCLEAR

Any actor's decision to acquire nuclear weapons is irrational in the sense that the consequences of possessing and using them are incalculable.[1] Even if rational, such a decision may be questioned on moral grounds.[2] Still, a mix of fear and pride can drive what Etel Solingen terms "oppositional nationalists," such as the DPRK leadership, to seek nuclear weapons.[3] As early as the mid-1950s Kim Il Sung initiated a quest for nuclear weapons—in part to counter nuclear threats from the United States.[4] DPRK leaders devoted the country's resources to making sure that they never again experienced this type of coercion.[5] Washington never used nuclear weapons in Korea, but a sort of nuclear inferiority complex came to pervade DPRK strategic thinking.

North Korean anxieties deepened when the United States began to deploy nuclear artillery shells and Honest John missiles into South Korea in 1958—

probably a violation of the 1953 Armistice Agreement, which banned the introduction of new types of weapons into Korea.[6] The number of U.S. nuclear weapons
deployed in Korea rose to about 1,000 in the mid-1960s and fell to around 100 in
the 1980s before being withdrawn in 1991.

In the 1950s the DPRK leadership began to organize a strong national cadre
of nuclear technicians and scientists. In 1955 North Korea established an Atomic
Energy Research Institute and sent members of the DPRK Academy of Sciences to
attend a nuclear energy conference in Moscow. In 1956 the DPRK signed an agreement on nuclear research with the USSR. Soon, North Korean scientists, along
with many from China and other Communist countries, began arriving in Moscow to study at the Nuclear Research Institute in Dubna.[7]

The Kremlin's ostensible hospitality may well have been a response to President Dwight D. Eisenhower's call in December 1953 to share "atoms for peace,"
which led to establishment of the International Atomic Energy Agency (IAEA) in
July 1957. The work at Dubna appeared to focus on peaceful uses of nuclear power.
In time, however, both the Soviets and the Americans learned to regret their promotion of nuclear research. They found that atoms for peace could become atoms
for war.

Despite Dubna, the Soviets tried to keep *military* nuclear know-how to themselves. Having mastered the atom, neither Moscow nor, later on, Beijing wanted to
share nuclear secrets with others—not even with nominal allies. Whatever nuclear
or other assistance the USSR provided the DPRK, it was transmitted grudgingly
and with many strings attached—as was the case also with Soviet aid to China.
Soviet assistance to China's nuclear power program began about the same time as
to North Korea—in 1954–1955.

But China claimed that the Soviets had practiced deceit. Beijing asserted
on September 6, 1963, that the USSR on October 15, 1957, had signed a "New
Defense Technology Pact" with China. According to Beijing, the pact committed the USSR to assisting China's nuclear weapon program—even to delivering a
"sample atomic bomb."[8] A few weeks later, Mao Zedong endorsed Soviet leadership of the Communist movement at the Moscow Conference of Communist and
Workers' Parties. Having pocketed Mao's support, the Khrushchev regime stalled
on its commitment and finally suspended the deal on June 20, 1959—citing prospects for arms limitations with the United States. It appeared that Khrushchev
played a double game—never intending to give real support to China's nuclear
weapon program.[9] This interpretation was later confirmed by the memoir of the
marshal who supervised China's development of nuclear weapons and missiles.[10]

Khrushchev's refusal to honor the New Technology Pact drove a stake into the
heart of the Sino-Soviet partnership. The Kremlin withdrew all Soviet assistance to
China in 1960. Public signs of a serious rift emerged in 1960, but Beijing revealed
the story of the New Defense Technology affair only in 1963—one element in Bei-

jing's denunciations of the Khrushchev regime for signing a limited nuclear test ban with Washington and London, which China portrayed as a nonproliferation pact.

Despite halting aid to China's nuclear program in 1959, earlier Soviet assistance put the Chinese on the road that led to their first nuclear explosion in 1964. The Kremlin did not want to repeat its Chinese blunder with North Korea. Still, Moscow wanted to keep Pyongyang on its side in the emerging conflict between the USSR and China. So the Kremlin in September 1959 agreed to train North Korean personnel in nuclear-related disciplines and to help establish a nuclear research center, code-named The Furniture Factory, on the bank of the Kuryong River, eight kilometers from the town of Yongbyon. The Soviets built a 2 MW IRT nuclear research reactor at Yongbyon, which began operation in 1969.[11]

From 1953 to 1959 China trained some 1,500 North Korean apprentices in industrial and mining sectors. They were expected to contribute to North Korea's postwar reconstruction. Chinese authorities gave high priority to these programs as a way to help the DPRK economy and to resist the United States. But Chinese authorities complained that the DPRK often departed from the agreed rules for these programs. Occasionally the trainees arrived in China with health problems or educational shortfalls expressly forbidden in the agreements. Sometimes the Koreans asked to change the content and location of training programs even after the trainees had arrived. For their part, some Chinese refused to train the Koreans because Koreans in the Japanese army had committed war crimes in eastern China. Other Chinese refused to provide the level of care for the North Koreans mandated by the official agreements. In the mid-1950s, however, China's "internationalist education" improved relations between the Korean trainees and their Chinese tutors.[12]

Exploiting the Sino-Soviet rift, the DPRK persuaded China in 1959 to sign an agreement on nuclear cooperation. China then began to train North Korean scientific workers and engineering personnel. The DPRK did not join the anti-Chinese chorus in the early 1960s, and the training of North Koreans in China continued. After 1965, however, relations between China and North Korea deteriorated while those between North Korea and the Soviet Union improved. By 1967 the DPRK stopped sending trainees, and China suspended all training programs for North Koreans. The PRC First Machine Building Ministry warned that "being devoid of a correct political viewpoint is the same as not having a soul." Its statement explained how to "handle contradictions among the people." In short, the training of North Koreans proved to be a barometer of the Sino–North Korean alliance.[13]

As the Sino-Soviet rift foreclosed more help from Moscow, the DPRK sought help from Communist regimes in Eastern Europe. In August 1963 the East German ambassador to Pyongyang told the Soviet ambassador that the North Koreans were "asking whether they could obtain any kind of information about nuclear weapons and the atomic industry from German universities and research institutes" (Document 1).[14] The East German diplomat surmised that the DPRK request was on behalf of China, but it could well have reflected Pyongyang's quest for nuclear know-how.

In September 1963 the Soviet ambassador in Pyongyang, Vasily Moskovsky, talked with three Soviet specialists who were analyzing uranium ore in the DPRK. They reported that "the Korean side insistently tries to obtain information about the deposits and quality of the uranium ore mined in the Soviet Union. But our comrades have been instructed on this account, and know how to evade answering such questions." The report went on: "Our specialists reported that the Korean uranium ore is not rich and is very scarce. The mining and processing of such ore will be extremely expensive for the Koreans. But from conversations with the Korean specialists they learned that the Koreans, despite all odds, want to develop the mining of uranium ore on a broad scale." The Soviet specialists thought it probable that "uranium ore mined in the DPRK will be supplied to China" because just a small quantity of uranium ore would suffice for a North Korean nuclear reactor. The Soviets were trying to persuade the North Koreans that it "would be much easier for the economy of the DPRK to satisfy all internal needs by means of purchasing a small amount of the necessary processed 'product.'" But the Koreans replied that they needed to extract uranium ore in large quantities. Moskovsky concluded: "*I think that by sending specialists to the DPRK from the Soviet Union we are helping China, and at the time of the current struggle against the Chinese splitters, one should not do this*" (emphasis added) (Document 2).

The North Koreans were often rude to the very parties on whom they depended for assistance. The Hungarian ambassador to Pyongyang, József Kovács, reported to Budapest on January 11, 1964, that Soviet ambassador Moskovsky told him that in 1963 that North Korean "officials had demanded fingerprints from the Soviet technical experts who worked on the construction of a radio station, an experimental nuclear reactor, and a weaving mill (!) that were being built with Soviet assistance and co-operation, and made [the Soviet experts] fill out a form of 72 questions, in which they had to describe their circle of relatives and friends in detail, with addresses! A Korean 'colleague' told one of the technical experts, 'if we cannot get you for some reason, we will get your relatives; this is why [the questionnaire] is needed!'" (Document 3).

1965: A SMALL REACTOR AT YONGBYON

Despite the end of Soviet nuclear assistance in June 1959 and the withdrawal from China of thousands of Soviet specialists in 1960, China detonated its first nuclear device in October 1964. Pyongyang then sent a delegation to Beijing to request Chinese assistance in nuclear matters, but Mao Zedong sent the Koreans away empty-handed. One year later, however, the USSR sold the DPRK a small 2- to 4-megawatt research reactor, built in the vicinity of Yongbyon. It began operation in 1967.

1966–1967: INGRATES WHO DEMAND EVER MORE

North Korea pocketed foreign aid and then demanded more. It used its existing debts as a bargaining tool to demand yet more assistance. But the Soviets continued to say *nyet.*

The Hungarian ambassador to DPRK, István Kádas, reported to the Hungarian Foreign Ministry on March 13, 1967, that the Soviets had recently "rejected a Korean request for the delivery of a *nuclear power plant*" (emphasis in the original). The request began with an "incognito visit that Comrade Kim Il Sung made to Moscow" in late 1966. The "delegation was received by the [top Soviet party leader] L. Brezhnev and [Prime Minister] A. Kosygin, while the head of the Soviet delegation was First Deputy Premier Mazurov." The Hungarian ambassador gave no specific reason for the Soviet rejection except to note that an "experimental nuclear reactor . . . established with Soviet assistance . . . opened approximately one and a half years ago, and since then the Soviet comrades have hardly any data about its operation" (Document 4).

1967: AN END-RUN DEFLECTED IN BERLIN

Late in 1967 the DPRK tried to persuade the East Germans to do what the Soviets refused. The delegation from Pyongyang was led by the vice-chairman of the DPRK Atomic Energy Commission. It sought to sign an agreement with the German Democratic Republic in the field of nuclear research; obtain equipment needed for the construction of a nuclear power plant; purchase equipment needed for producing radioactive isotopes; conduct an exchange of nuclear scientists; send nuclear science trainees to the GDR; purchase certain secret equipment used in nuclear research; and acquire copies of articles on nuclear research in Western scientific journals. The East German reply was a long and diplomatic "*nein*"— unless the Soviets approved (Document 5).

1968

The year 1968 saw turbulence across the globe. Mao Zedong's Cultural Revolution was reaching fever pitch. Chinese placards screamed "Fry Brezhnev and skin Kosygin!" In January, while Communists in Vietnam launched their Tet offensive, North Korean forces attacked the ROK president's Blue House in Seoul. When the attackers perished, Pyongyang said they had been South Korean partisans. Needing to mask or deflect its aggressive actions, the DPRK protested U.S. aggression

USS *Pueblo* with a naval officer who says he participated in the capture of the U.S. intelligence gathering ship in January 1968. (Photo by Jeremy Hunter)

and seized an unarmed U.S. spy ship, the *Pueblo*. Faced with a strong response from the Johnson administration that seemed to challenge Moscow's Far Eastern fleet and Soviet interests in Northeast Asia, the Kremlin appeared to support the DPRK. President Lyndon Johnson backed down. Behind the scenes, however, the Soviets ordered Kim Il Sung to return the U.S. crew. But he did not. Instead, the DPRK regime began to evacuate its capital and mobilize the entire population. Next, Kim Il Sung called on the Soviet Union to honor its alliance. This Leonid Brezhnev refused to do and, instead, summoned Kim to Moscow. Kim did not go, but he eventually canceled the evacuation and returned the U.S. crew.[15]

The Nuclear Nonproliferation Treaty (NPT), drafted mainly by Soviet and U.S. diplomats and submitted to all UN members for signature in 1968, added to tensions between the DPRK and the USSR. It appeared that the Soviets stood ready to provide nuclear power assistance only to clients who were both faithful and sufficiently advanced to deal with nuclear technology—Bulgaria, Czechoslovakia, the GDR, and Hungary. Often-defiant Romania and North Korea were excluded; so was Vietnam—obedient, but not ready for high tech. When a Romanian delegation visited Pyongyang in February 1968, both sides agreed that "the big countries that have nuclear capacity should ensure that the small countries would also be able to utilize atomic energy for peaceful purposes. The small countries should not suffer a loss as a consequence of the [nonproliferation] treaty" (Document 5). After raising many objections to the NPT in 1968, Bucharest signed the treaty, while Pyongyang refused to do so until 1985 and put off a safeguards agreement with the IAEA until 1992.

In summer 1968 the DPRK asked Moscow for a large increase in economic and military aid. Constrained by the Sino-Soviet rift, Moscow complied with some requests. The USSR could not intervene in North Korea's domestic affairs, as it did in 1956, when it sheltered anti-Kim Communists in the Soviet embassy. In 1968 Moscow "continued to provide North Korea's essential security while asking little in return." As Kathryn Weathersby writes, this nexus "made it possible for Kim Il Sung to transform the *Juche* idea into a full-blown nationalist ideology."[16]

1969: TILTING TOWARD BEIJING ON NUCLEAR PROLIFERATION

The newly appointed Hungarian ambassador to Pyongyang stopped in Moscow on November 10, 1969, and talked with two Soviet experts on North Korea. They told him that "patient and persistent persuasion was needed to get the Korean position closer to our common position on the big issues of international politics." On nonproliferation, the Soviets said that Pyongyang understood the dangers if Japan acquired nuclear arms. But otherwise the North Koreans did not oppose nuclear proliferation—thus giving "veiled support" to the Chinese position (Document 6).

1973–1974

Pyongyang's interest in acquiring nuclear power mounted when the price of oil jumped in the 1970s. When the USSR raised the price of oil to its clients, the DPRK complained of Soviet "exploitation," even though Moscow charged Pyongyang much less than world market prices. While Washington helped the ROK develop nuclear power, however, the Kremlin did little to assist North Korea on this path.

North Korea also took note of India's "peaceful" nuclear explosion in 1974. India's example showed how even poor nations could develop nuclear weapons with materials gathered from far and wide—in India's case, a Canadian reactor using heavy water from the United States. India, like Israel, would be treated as a de facto nuclear-weapon state. North Korea tried to follow suit.

Throughout the 1970s North Korea continued to develop its nuclear capabilities, pursuing a dual track: While seeking to obtain light-water reactors (LWRs) from the Soviet Union, North Korea conducted its own studies on graphite-moderated gas-cooled reactors, using publicly available information. North Korea also carried out plutonium separation experiments at its Isotope Production Laboratory and successfully separated plutonium. The North Koreans also worked on the design of a reprocessing plant modeled after a plant in Europe. When negotiations to acquire four LWRs from the Soviet Union failed, North Korea had already embarked on its indigenous nuclear program.[17]

1975: KIM IL SUNG AS MILITARY ADVENTURER

In the mid-1970s both the USSR and China sought détente with the United States and did not want North Korea to rock the boat. Kim Il Sung, however, hoped to emulate Vietnam's Communists and unite his divided country by force. Many details emerged from a report on July 30, 1975, by János Taraba, a top Hungarian diplomat in the DPRK, who informed Budapest that "China is wary of a second Korean War, whereas Kim Il Sung makes it clear that military force is an option" (Document 7). The DPRK acquired military technology and equipment when a delegation led by Kim Il Sung traveled in spring 1975 to China, Romania, Algeria, Mauritania, Bulgaria, and Yugoslavia. Kim also wanted to visit the Soviet Union and Czechoslovakia, but the dates he proposed did not suit the leaders in Moscow or in Prague. His intention to visit Moscow, Taraba wrote, showed that the DPRK was trying to balance "the Chinese party and our parties" (Document 7).

The Vietnamese ambassador in Pyongyang told Taraba that, according to Chinese sources, the DPRK wanted "to create the kind of military situation in South Korea that came into being in South Vietnam" before the Communist North took over the entire country. "Taking advantage of the riots against the dictatorial regime of Park Chung Hee and invited by certain South Korean [political] forces, the DPRK would have given military assistance if it had not been dissuaded." China held back and opposed "any kind of armed struggle that might shake the position of the USA in Asia. A new Korean War would not be merely a war between North and South [Korea]." The "Chinese side strongly emphasized the importance of the peaceful unification of Korea. . . . For his part, Kim Il Sung said nothing, or hardly anything, about his own proposals to find a peaceful solution. On the contrary, he declared that if a revolution flared up in South Korea, the DPRK could not remain indifferent; it would give active assistance to the South Korean people. And if the enemy started a war, it would be met with a crushing repulse. In such a war the DPRK could lose only the cease-fire line, but it might achieve the unification of the country, he said" (Document 7).

Taraba believed that, of the six visits made by the DPRK delegation, "the ones made to China and Yugoslavia were also important in regard to the military equipment and military technology made available to the DPRK. China provides the People's Army of the DPRK with many kinds of military equipment and arms." Taraba's language was opaque, but he implied that North Korea had asked China for tactical nuclear weapons to offset the American nuclear forces in South Korea. Taraba noted that a deputy minister of the People's Armed Forces in Pyongyang who received Hungarian officers "vacationing" (*sic*) in North Korea alluded on June 11 to the DPRK's hope of obtaining tactical nuclear arms from China. Taraba added that Yugoslavia helped the DPRK, "primarily in the field of naval forces" (Document 7).

An outsider can only be amazed at the assumption that China, *if* it possessed tactical nuclear weapons in the mid-1970s, might share them with the DPRK—especially given its worries about Kim Il Sung's bellicosity. As for Yugoslavia, its capacity to help any country's naval forces was surely minimal at that time, even though Belgrade was still engaged in its own clandestine effort to develop nuclear weapons.[18]

Another meeting of socialist countries took place in Minsk on August 26, 1975. The North Koreans at that time asked the Hungarian delegation to mobilize the socialist countries to prevent the IAEA Technical Assistance Program from establishing a reprocessing plant for the Far Eastern region in South Korea. If anywhere, Pyongyang suggested it be built in the Philippines.

1976: Ultimatums from the Demander

Pyongyang's demands on its Communist comrades reached a new level of intensity in 1976 at the same time that it stepped up belligerent actions. On April 7 two North Korean tanks entered the DMZ, where they remained for four hours. On August 18 DPRK troops killed two U.S. officers in a "tree-cutting" incident within the DMZ. Two days earlier, while the Nonaligned Nations were meeting in Colombo, Sri Lanka, the DPRK had asked the UN General Assembly to put the Korean question on its agenda.

Unfazed by the cool reception it had received in Beijing and Moscow in 1975, a DPRK delegation visited Moscow in January–February 1976 and again demanded that the USSR build a nuclear power plant for North Korea. The Hungarian embassy in Pyongyang learned from a Soviet comrade that "for various reasons—primarily military considerations and the amount of investment—the Soviet side declared that this [request for a nuclear plant] was now inopportune and proposed to come back to it only in the course of the next [five-year] plan. The Korean side was very reluctant to accept this Soviet decision and [Moscow's] rejection of a few other investment demands" (Document 10).

The Hungarian embassy also learned that, as the two sides discussed credit, "the head of the Korean delegation—Deputy Premier Kang Chin-t'ae—behaved in an extremely aggressive way, definitely crude and insulting in certain statements vis-a-vis his Soviet counterpart, Deputy Premier Arkhipov. He declared several times that if the Soviet Union was unwilling to make 'appropriate' allowances for the 'front-line situation' of the DPRK, and did not comply entirely with the Korean requests, the DPRK would be compelled to suspend its economic relations with the Soviet Union" (Document 10).

When Kang Chin-t'ae visited the Kremlin, Soviet prime minister Aleksei

Kosygin rebuked him, saying that the Soviet Union did not accept ultimatums. "It was only after his visit to Comrade Kosygin that Kang Chin-t'ae changed his conduct, and thus it became possible to sign the agreements" (Document 10).

When a DPRK delegation visited the Hungarian Foreign Ministry in early 1976, it exaggerated North Korea's military prowess—telling bald-faced lies even to its nominal partners in the Communist realm. The North Koreans told the Hungarians that "Korea cannot be unified in a peaceful way. . . . If a war occurs in Korea, it will be waged with nuclear weapons, rather than conventional ones. The DPRK is prepared for such a contingency: the country has been turned into a system of fortifications, important factories have been moved underground (for instance, recently they relocated the steel works in Kangson), and airfields, harbors, and other military facilities have been established in the subterranean cave networks. The Pyongyang subway is connected with several branch tunnels, which are currently closed but in case of emergency they are able to place the population of Pyongyang there" (Document 8).

Implying some worry about the possibility of a U.S. nuclear attack, the North Koreans were not above bluffing. The North Koreans assured their Hungarian comrade: "*By now the DPRK also has nuclear warheads and carrier missiles, which are targeted at the big cities of South Korea and Japan, such as Seoul, Tokyo, and Nagasaki, as well as local military bases such as Okinawa*" (emphasis added). When the Hungarian diplomat asked "whether the Korean People's Army had received the nuclear warheads from China, they replied that [the North Koreans] had developed them unaided through experimentation, and they had manufactured them by themselves" (Document 8).

A few days after this meeting in Budapest, the Hungarian ambassador in Pyongyang reported details of a study by the Far Eastern Institute in Seoul. South Korean researchers reported that "the DPRK spent 60, 165, 135, and 140 million dollars on the purchase of arms in 1970, 1971, 1972, and 1973 respectively. During this time the manpower of the army underwent the following changes: it was 438,000 in 1970, 450,000 in 1971, 460,000 in 1972, and 470,000 in 1973. That is, military preparations continued in the period of [North–South] dialogue as well. The army of the DPRK has 1,100 T-55 tanks and a substantial number of surface-to-surface missiles. The DPRK ordered a substantial amount of diving suits and facilities in Japan. . . . The number of MiG fighter planes is 200, but they also have Su-7 [fighter-]bombers" (Document 9).

The Hungarian ambassador also asserted that the "the DPRK wants to construct nuclear reactors, and is having talks about this issue in order to become capable of producing atomic weapons in the future" (Document 9). The source for this claim was not clear. But it jibed with the report of a Russian intelligence officer that, in the late 1970s, Kim Il Sung instructed the Ministry of Public Security to initiate a nuclear weapons program at expanded Yongbyon facilities.[19]

Not inclined to take *nyet* for an answer, DPRK deputy premier Kang Chin-t'ae again demanded a nuclear power plant when DPRK and Soviet officials met at the thirteenth session of the Intergovernmental Consultative Committee, held in Moscow from June 8 to 11, 1976. Hungarian officials reported home that the USSR refused to deliver a nuclear power plant to the DPRK in the current five-year (1976–1980) plan because it had long-term commitments to construct such plants elsewhere. Also, the USSR refused "for the time being" to extend its agreement with the DPRK on lumbering in Siberia by three years, because ecological surveys were taking place there (Document 11).

The Hungarians said that North Korea "attempted to evade the questions related to foreign trade, for that was a thorny issue." The Soviets, however, complained that "in 1976 Korean shipments had substantially decreased in comparison with the same period of earlier years; the [DPRK's] failure to deliver the raw materials that were planned to be imported from Korea caused stoppages in the operation of important Soviet industrial plants, seriously jeopardizing the continuity of production." The North Koreans did not deny that a slowdown had occurred, but promised to make up for underfulfillments in the second half of the year. The Soviets believed that scanty rainfall in 1975 and 1976 had severely reduced electricity production in North Korea, where hydroelectric power plants provided half of existing power capacity (Document 12).

When they wished, DPRK officials could be polite. Their behavior and its motivations were described by the chairman of Hungary's National Commission of Atomic Energy in a report dated August 31, 1976. A few days earlier two North Korean officials had given him some small gifts and thanked him for "the very valuable advice" they had received from the Hungarian delegation at a meeting of socialist countries two years before. As a result of this advice, "the DPRK obtained IAEA membership without any difficulty" (Document 13).

The ability of DPRK representatives to switch from harsh demands and ultimatums to smiles and ostensible gratitude conformed more with the expectations of cynical realists than those of cultural anthropologists observing high-context diplomacy, which required personal trust and mutual respect (as discussed below in chapter 11).

1977: MUTUAL CONCERNS ABOUT EXPLOITATION TO GET HARD CURRENCY

By early 1977 the North Koreans made it clear to the USSR that the DPRK did not intend to fulfill its obligations set down in the long-term trade agreement signed in 1976. A Hungarian report from Moscow on January 20, 1977, said that the Soviets expected to hear soon from a DPRK delegation that the "DPRK intends to relieve its serious economic situation by not fulfilling its obligations . . . with regard to the export of goods that are saleable on non-socialist markets as well." At the same time, North Korea "constantly insists on the uninterrupted and punctual fulfillment of Soviet export obligations" (Document 15).

The Soviets claimed that they had fulfilled their obligations under the 1976 accord but that the DPRK fell far short—delivering only 90 million rubles' worth of provisions instead of the agreed 216 million rubles' worth of cement, fire-resistant bricks, and other goods. This shortfall caused "considerable difficulties" in the Soviet Far East, because such goods could not be obtained elsewhere without substantial delays. The Hungarian embassy believed the North Koreans would "probably attempt to convert the deficit . . . into a Soviet credit"—which, a skeptic might infer, would evolve into a gift (Document 15).

Meanwhile, the North Koreans opposed application of price policies used in COMECON (Council for Mutual Economic Assistance)—where the DPRK had only observer status—to Soviet transactions with the DPRK. "The Soviet side did not manage to achieve the COMECON price level in its relations with Korea" in 1976 and did not expect to do so in 1977 (Document 15).

The Hungarian embassy also reported Moscow's belief that the DPRK intended to divert some Soviet oil deliveries into hard currency earnings. "The Korean side constantly announces new demands (in addition to the agreements), and impatiently presses for their fulfillment. They repeatedly and very emphatically urge, at every level, that Soviet shipments of crude oil be increased to two million metric tons per annum," which the Soviets expected would be sold as processed petroleum derivatives in capitalist markets (Document 15).

Pyongyang continued to press for a nuclear power plant, citing "reasons of prestige." But the current Soviet Five-Year Plan made no provision for this kind of assistance. North Korea ignored Soviet statements that the USSR could not "deliver loss-making articles over the quantity specified in the plan." Adding insult to injury for the USSR, the Soviets believed that DPRK domestic propaganda blamed North Korea's economic difficulties on Soviet exploitation of the DPRK by raising prices and refusal to deliver goods needed for economic development, preferring to sell them to the capitalists (Document 15).

1977: Diverging Assessments in Eastern Europe

On January 25, 1977, the DPRK issued a four-point proposal for a North–South nonaggression pact in tandem with a U.S. troop withdrawal from Korea. Pyongyang immediately launched an international campaign to win backing for its declaration and, the Czechoslovak Foreign Ministry worried, would soon ask socialist countries for their official support. The Hungarian authorities treated the DPRK declaration as nothing more than another call for the peaceful and democratic unification of Korea. This is how the declaration was portrayed in the Hungarian press. When the DPRK ambassador visited the Hungarian foreign ministry, he was satisfied with its assurances and did not ask for a public endorsement of the declaration. But the Czechoslovak embassy in Pyongyang perceived an extremely threatening tone in the declaration—for example, in its description of the situation on the Korean peninsula as one that might lead to the outbreak of a global nuclear war. The embassy also saw a hint that the DPRK was equipping itself with nuclear weapons. Prague could not support Pyongyang's démarche, apparently fearing it could be a harbinger of DPRK adventurism. Hungarian officials often took note of worrisome developments in North Korea, but disagreed with their Czechoslovak comrades in this case (Document 16).

When Soviet and DPRK delegations met in September 1977 in Pyongyang to discuss economic and scientific matters, they agreed not to mention North Korea's difficulty in repaying its debts to Moscow or the Soviet refusal to supply a nuclear power plant to North Korea. They deferred important decisions to higher levels of authority, but the Soviets were satisfied with the atmospherics. This, at least, is what the Hungarian ambassador to the DPRK, Ferenc Szabó, conveyed to the Hungarian Foreign Ministry in November (Document 17).

In 1979 the DPRK again tried to bypass the Kremlin. Prague's ambassador to Pyongyang informed Szabó that on February 12 a North Korean official asked Czechoslovakia to deliver uranium-mining equipment to the DPRK and to construct a 440-megawatt nuclear power plant in the DPRK. Szabó also heard from the Soviet ambassador that the DPRK had two uranium quarries—one where the uranium content of the ore was 0.26 percent and another with 0.086 percent (Document 18).

Meanwhile, the Soviet government revealed little to the public about its dealings with the DPRK. Nevertheless, Andrei Lankov recalls, "rumors about North Korea circulated widely among educated Soviet people. They were aware of Kim Il Sung's deification, his omnipresent police apparatus, and strained relations with Moscow. To a large extent, the North Koreans damaged their own standing by flooding the USSR with exceptionally bad propaganda." The bottom line was that "nobody in Soviet intellectual circles of the 1960s or 1970s felt positive toward either Mao Zedong or Kim Il Sung." Soviet Party leader Brezhnev and most Soviet diplomats disapproved of Pyongyang's brutal and inefficient Stalinism and saw North Korea as an unreliable, costly, and scheming ally.[20] Officials and the intelligentsia in Czechoslovakia and other East European states probably shared these attitudes.

THE 1980S

Displeased with the help received by outsiders, the DPRK in 1979 began what the IAEA termed the "indigenous phase" of its nuclear development. This phase commenced with construction of a 5 MW(e) natural-uranium, graphite-moderated reactor in Yongbyong, followed by an ore-processing plant and a fuel-rod-fabrication plant. By the time the 5 MW(e) reactor became operational in 1986, the DPRK began construction of the first of two larger gas-graphite reactors, and, around 1987, construction of a radiochemical laboratory with a sizable reprocessing capacity.[21] The DPRK also worked on developing mechanisms to trigger a nuclear device.

In March 1981 the Soviet ambassador to Pyongyang told his Hungarian colleague about recent discussions between DPRK and Soviet officials in Moscow. The North Koreans repeated their request for a nuclear power plant, which the Soviets deflected, saying that if the DPRK sought an East European–type arrangement, then they would have to contribute to the cost—to which the North Koreans could "give no genuine" reply. The North Koreans also asked for "special technology"—probably for nuclear weapons—which the Soviets said would be considered by "competent authorities." Moscow agreed to extend more credits but insisted the interest rate jump from 2 to 4 percent after 1985. Serious differences emerged over Pyongyang's friendly treatment of Cambodia's Prince Sihanouk—mere "hospitality," said the North Koreans, who professed not to know that a book by Sihanouk with anti-Soviet remarks had been published in various languages and sold in Pyongyang (Document 19).

In 1981 North Korea continued to ask East European governments to accept dozens of North Korean postgraduates to study nuclear energy. Authorities in Budapest, Berlin, and Prague rejected these requests, even when Pyongyang offered to pay the students' expenses, because the information sought was "confidential." Indeed, "the Korean side was forced to recall" five graduate students from Czechoslovakia in 1980 because the topics they tried to study were "strictly confidential." The East Germans offered only to send two language instructors to North Korea and to consider some DPRK students in social sciences, to which Pyongyang gave no recorded answer (Document 20).

In 1983 the DPRK asked the Hungarian Academy of Scientists to train technicians to operate North Korea's first nuclear power plant, which was soon to be constructed (Document 21). The Hungarian foreign ministry, in a letter of April 6, told the academy to say no. Hungary's power plant "is being built on the basis of Soviet documents and with direct Soviet support; its machinery is also largely Soviet made. For some time it will be operated with the support of Soviet experts, as the training of Hungarian experts has just gotten underway." Hence, the North Koreans were advised to make their "request directly to the competent Soviet authorities" (Document 22).

Anxious and resentful in the 1980s that its nuclear program lagged not only South Korea's but also those in Eastern Europe, the DPRK began work on a 20- to 30-megawatt research reactor in the Yongbyon area not far from the much smaller reactor earlier supplied by the USSR. A U.S. satellite spotted a large hole, probably intended for the second reactor. The U.S. Central Intelligence Agency could not say in 1982 whether the second reactor at Yongbyon was being built by North Koreans alone or with Soviet help. As of May 1983 the CIA had "no basis for believing that the North Koreans have either the facilities or materials necessary to develop and test nuclear weapons."[22]

While China proved reluctant to deliver advanced technology to North Korea, one expert reported that Beijing gave or sold an atomic bomb design to Pakistan in 1982, which Pakistani scientists redesigned to make it fit on one of their own missiles. China sold some of its by then obsolete liquid-fueled CSS-2 missiles to Saudi Arabia in 1988.[23]

In 1984 relations between Pyongyang and Moscow improved. The USSR provided North Korea weaponry it had refused in 1981 to supply—SAM-5 missiles as well as MiG-29, and Su-25 jet fighters. The USSR also agreed in 1984 to build a nuclear power plant in North Korea. Details of this project were discussed by a team from GOSPLAN visiting Pyongyang in February 1985—a month before Mikhail S. Gorbachev took the helm in Moscow. DPRK authorities again explained that they wanted the plant to offset the reactor already operating in South Korea and to secure economic prestige. North Korea agreed to share the plant's cost and to accept IAEA inspection. The Soviets offered a $2 billion loan at 4 to 6 percent interest, while Pyongyang wanted to pay only 2 percent. The North Koreans wanted the plant to be built in five years, while the Soviets said it would take ten to twelve years. Soviet specialists would need two years just to decide on the best of six sites. The Soviets would operate the plant for five years; train DPRK technicians; supply enriched uranium; and help survey for uranium in North Korea (Document 23).

Why did the Soviets change course? Moscow's policy shift could have reflected the Soviet Union's diplomatic isolation in the early 1980s and increased pressures from the Reagan administration. The three top Soviet leaders in the years before Gorbachev were old, fragile, and susceptible to hard-line influences. But the Kremlin may also have concluded that the DPRK was going great guns in nuclear affairs and that Moscow should monitor the situation. By the end of 1984 the Yongbyon reactor and adjoining buildings were nearing completion—over a year before Soviet assistance even began. In 1986 the Yongbyon reactor commenced operations. While some facts implied a high-level decision in Pyongyang to use this reactor to make a bomb, the DPRK did not produce plutonium for long periods and failed to put the facility underground, as it did many other potential targets for U.S. attacks.

After a brief thaw in DPRK-Soviet relations in 1984–1985, tensions again mounted. Gorbachev in 1986 called for "new thinking" in Asia—to include a collective security system for the region and elimination of nuclear weapons. When the USSR agreed to attend the Olympics to be held in South Korea in 1988, this marked a Rubicon for Pyongyang. Its agents placed a bomb in a South Korean airliner that killed 115 persons in 1987—a warning to anyone wishing to attend the games.[24]

Three years after the Soviet-DPRK project was signed, the two sides had still not settled on the construction site. The North Koreans in April–May 1988 wanted production to begin at the reactor's first block by 1993. But the Soviets said safety had to be the sole standard and blamed North Korea for the delays (Document 24).

Were the Soviets going slower now that Gorbachev was courting not only the West but also South Korea? Or were the North Koreans refusing to implement some of their obligations as understood by Moscow? Possible answers are speculative because documentation from the Soviet and Hungarian archives stops in 1988.

The DPRK reprocessing facility at Yongbyon was detected by the CIA in 1989 and observed firsthand by IAEA director Hans Blix in 1992. This facility would permit the North to process the nuclear waste from its reactor and extract the small amounts of plutonium produced in the nuclear reactor—plutonium that could then be used to manufacture nuclear weapons. In the late 1980s U.S. satellites detected, at Yongbyon, tests conducted with conventional explosions of the kind needed to design a nuclear warhead. The head of the Soviet KGB, Vladimir Kyruchkov, reported in 1990 that North Korea had completed "development of [its] first atomic explosive device." When the buildings at Yongbyon were roofed over, however, American intelligence could only guess at what was going on inside.[25]

When DPRK and ROK representatives signed the Joint Declaration on the Denuclearization of the Korean Peninsula in December 1991 and ratified it in early 1992, North Korea's facilities for producing fissile fuels for nuclear weapons had already been operational for years. By that time the North also had two additional (50 MWe and 200 MWe) graphite-moderated gas-cooled reactors under construction. As of 1992 U.S. intelligence officials believed that North Korea had conducted as many as seventy explosive tests at Yongbyon.[26]

At Soviet insistence, Pyongyang acceded to the Nuclear Nonproliferation Treaty in 1985. Earlier, in 1977, the DPRK had signed a "Type 66" safeguards agreement with the International Atomic Energy Agency (IAEA), governing two nuclear research facilities—the "IRT" research reactor dating from 1967 and a critical assembly. In 1992 the DPRK signed a more comprehensive safeguards agreement with the IAEA, which Pyongyang promptly violated. The IAEA reported as follows:

After the DPRK had submitted its initial report to the IAEA under its Safeguards Agreement in May 1992, inspections began. Shortly thereafter inconsistencies emerged between the DPRK's initial declaration and the Agency's findings, centering on a mismatch between declared pluto-nium product and nuclear waste solutions and the results of the Agency's analysis. The latter suggested that there existed in the DPRK undeclared plutonium. In order to find answers to the inconsistencies detected and to determine the completeness and correctness of the initial declaration provided, the IAEA requested access to additional information and to two sites which seemed to be related to the storage of nuclear waste. The DPRK, however, refused access to the sites.[27]

Thus, it appeared that Pyongyang, with malice aforethought, violated both its NPT and IAEA commitments as well as its Declaration on Denuclearization recently signed with the ROK.[28]

Hoping that perestroika might save the Soviet system but in great need for cash and credits, the Gorbachev regime agreed with Seoul to establish diplomatic relations in September 1990. Informed of this, the DPRK threatened retaliation. Pyongyang warned it would feel free to act on its own without consulting Moscow and to build its own nuclear weapons. It might extend diplomatic recognition to breakaway Soviet republics. Seoul insisted on, and got, a substantial quid pro quo: an end to Soviet military aid to the DPRK. Consequently, in 1991, Moscow's military support to the DPRK, which had guaranteed the country's security since its inception, abruptly evaporated.[29] The DPRK press howled: "Diplomatic Relations Sold and Bought with Dollars."

An Enriched Uranium Track

North Korea appears to have also violated the denuclearization agreement with the South by actively pursuing uranium enrichment in the 1990s, tapping into the pro-liferation schemes of Pakistan's master bomb maker, Abdul Q. Khan. According to former Pakistan president Pervez Musharraf, Khan delivered "nearly two dozen P-1 and P-2 centrifuges to North Korea" along with "a flow meter, some special oils for centrifuges, and coaching on centrifuge technology including visits to top-secret centrifuge plants."[30] DPRK engineers received training at Khan's laboratories under a government-to-government deal on missile technology established in 1994—the same year that the DPRK signed the Agreed Framework with the United States (details below in chapter 12). North Korea probably received blueprints for centri-fuges and other related equipment from the Khan network. (The terms and nature of the required bribes are detailed in the appendix to this chapter.)

In the late 1980s, North Korea acquired from a German company vacuum pumps that could be used for enrichment experiments. North Korea's procure-ment activities in the late 1990s to the early 2000s demonstrated a goal to achieve an industrial or semi-industrial scale enrichment capacity based on a more efficient Pakistani P-2 centrifuge design. Thus, in 1997 the DPRK tried to acquire large amounts of maraging steel suitable for manufacturing centrifuges. In 2002–2003, North Korea successfully procured from Russia and the United Kingdom another essential ingredient for making centrifuges—large quantities of high-strength aluminum. A simple tally of the amounts and types of equipment and material sought by North Korea suggested plans to develop a 5,000-centrifuge-strong enrichment capacity. This undertaking would probably require workshops and facilities besides those visible to outsiders at Yongbyon.[31]

Having reviewed the exchanges between Pakistan and the DPRK, one specialist summed up their import. During the time that the DPRK plutonium program was frozen by the 1994 Agreed Framework with the United States, "we get almost a firsthand glimpse of Jon Byong Ho, Kim Jong Il's champion arms salesman and nukes acquisition specialist, going behind America's and South Korea's backs to acquire a different fissile material production technology, one they had forsworn in the Joint Denuclearization Declaration of 1992." We also see "A.Q. Khan organizing the payment of bribes to Gen. Jehangir Karamat and Lt. Gen. Zulfiqar Khan . . . so he could swap gas centrifuge technology for missile production technology. . . . Within no more than a year or so of this letter, Khan was already trying to sell missiles to a third country. And within a couple of years, he was organizing the shipment of North Korean uranium hexafluoride to his customers in Libya."[32]

Given that even Pyongyang's professed allies in Russia and China were subjected to continual evasion and subterfuge, the record augured poorly for any arms control regime with non-Communist governments requiring trust. The North Koreans, no less than their erstwhile Soviet backers, excelled at *maskirovka*—camouflage and other deceptions. The more that Pyongyang sought to hide, the more intrusive would be the inspection needed to verify any agreement.

Appendix: North Korean Bribes for Pakistani Technology

Pyongyang and Islamabad established diplomatic relations in the 1970s and soon began to trade conventional arms. Both assisted Iran as it fought Iraq in the 1980s. They signed a defense treaty after Prime Minister Zulfikar Ali Bhutto visited Pyongyang in 1993. Soon there were reports that Pakistan's centrifuge technology was being traded to the DPRK in exchange for missile technologies.[33]

In the late 1990s, according to Abdul Qadeer Khan, the founder of Pakistan's nuclear bomb program, the DPRK bribed top military officials in Islamabad to access nuclear technology. Khan displayed a letter from a DPRK official in 2011 showing that he (Khan) personally transferred more than $3 million in payments by North Korea to senior officers in the Pakistani military to win their approval for providing technical know-how and equipment to the North Koreans.

Khan detailed the alleged payments in written statements that Simon Henderson, a senior fellow at the Washington Institute for Near East Policy, shared with the *Washington Post*. Henderson said he acquired the letter and other statements from Khan in the years after Khan's 2004 arrest by Pakistani authorities.

The retired Pakistani officers named as recipients of the bribes, Bu Jehangir Karamat and Lt. Gen. Zulfiqar Khan, called the letter a fabrication intended to deflect responsibility for the transactions from Khan. Western experts disagreed on the letter's authenticity. But Olli Heinonen, a twenty-seven-year veteran of the IAEA who led its investigation of Khan, said the letter (without a letterhead) was similar to other North Korean notes he had seen or received. Heinonen also reported hearing similar accounts from senior Pakistanis of clandestine payments by North Korea to Pakistani military officials and government advisers.[34]

The letter, with no letterhead, carries the apparent signature of North Korean Workers' Party secretary Jon Byong Ho. In the letter, Jon first thanked Khan for his assistance to North Korea's then-representative to Islamabad, General Kang Tae Yun, in the aftermath of a bizarre shooting incident in which an assailant supposedly gunning for Kang accidentally killed Kang's wife. Jon presumed that the CIA, South Korean intelligence, and Pakistan's Inter-Services Intelligence (ISI) were involved in the assassination. He noted that Pakistan's intelligence agency quickly released the assassin. (Some Western accounts suggested that Kang's wife worked for U.S. intelligence.) Since General Kang's life was in danger, Jon wrote, Kang was being replaced by a Mr. Yon, who had served in Iran, Egypt, Syria, and Libya (all beneficiaries of DPRK missilery).

But the heart of Jon's letter concerned two key transactions: the provision of a kickback to speed overdue Pakistani missile-related payments; and additional payments for the nuclear-related materials. The letter released by Khan is dated July 15, 1998, and is marked "Secret." It states: "The 3 millions [*sic*] dollars have already been paid" to one Pakistani military official, and "half a million dollars" and some jewelry had been given to a second official. The text also says: "Please give the agreed documents, components, etc. to Mr. Yon to be flown back when our plane returns after delivery of missile components." Jon goes on to congratulate Khan on Pakistan's successful nuclear test that year and wishes him "good health, long life and success in your important work."

According to Khan, Jon Byong Ho met Pakistani president Farooq Leghari in the 1990s, toured Pakistan's nuclear laboratory, and arranged for dozens of North Korean technicians to work there. Born in 1926, Jon had long been a powerful member of North Korea's National Defense Commission in charge of military procurement. He supervised North Korea's first nuclear explosion in 2006.[35] In August 2011 the U.S. Treasury Department imposed financial sanctions on his department for its ballistic missile work. He retired from political work in 2012.

According to Khan's written account, the swap of North Korean cash for sensitive Pakistani technology arose during a squabble in 1996 over delays in Pakistan's payment to North Korea for some medium-range missiles. U.S. officials said they had heard of this dispute. The logic is baffling. Apparently Pyongyang bribed some Pakistanis so they would make good on overdue payments for DPRK missiles and to make sure that Pakistan sent nuclear equipment to North Korea.

Khan, in his written statements—including an eleven-page narrative he prepared for Pakistani investigators while under house arrest in 2004, later obtained by the *Washington Post*—said the idea for the kickback came from a Pakistani military officer.

Khan reported that DPRK General Kang delivered a half-million dollars in cash in a suitcase to a top Pakistani general, who declined it. Khan said Karamat, a more senior officer at the time, then said: "I [that is, Khan] should arrange with Gen. Kang to pay this money to him [Karamat] for some secret [Pakistani] army funds. He would then sanction the payment of their outstanding charges."

Khan wrote: "I talked to Gen. Kang, and he gave me the $0.5 million in cash, which I personally delivered" to Karamat. But this payment only whetted appetites. Karamat, who had just become chief of the army staff, "said to me that he needed more money for the same secret funds and that I should talk to Gen. Kang."

According to Khan, Kang then started bargaining, saying that his superiors "were willing to provide another $2.5 million, provided we helped them with the enrichment technology." Once the details of that assistance were worked out, Khan continued, "I personally gave the remaining $2.5 million to Gen. Karamat in cash at the Army House to make up the whole amount." Khan said he transferred all the funds on two occasions in a small canvas bag and three cartons, in one case at the chief of army staff's official residence. On the top of one carton was some fruit, and below it was $500,000 in cash, Khan wrote in a narrative for Henderson. Inside the bag was $500,000, and each of the other two cartons held $1 million, according to Khan.

The documents do not reveal the ultimate destination of the $3 million. Pakistani officials said in interviews that they found no trace of the money in Karamat's accounts. But the military was known to have used secret accounts for various purposes, including clandestine operations in the disputed Kashmir region.

Karamat asserted that such a delivery would have been impossible and that he "was not in the loop to delay, withhold or sanction payments" to North Korea. He called Jon's letter "quite mind-boggling."

The letter also stated that Zulfiqar Khan, Karamat's colleague, received "half a million dollars and 3 diamond and ruby sets" to pave the way for nuclear-weapons-related transfers.

Zulfiqar Khan was among those who had witnessed Pakistan's nuclear weapons test six weeks before the letter was written. Z. Khan denied having any connection to North Korean contracts. A senior Pakistani official said A. Q. Khan was seeking revenge against Karamat and Zulfiqar Khan because they were "amongst the first" to accuse A. Q. and his colleagues of illegal proliferation.

The entire affair implied that individual Pakistanis and even units of the military and scientific establishment might share nuclear know-how, and even a bomb, with anyone for the right price. This imbroglio, together with Pakistan's alleged support for Al Qaeda outside the country and even with Osama bin Laden, led many observers to wonder why Washington continued to fund such a putative partner.

II

Policy Dilemmas

7

Human Insecurity and
the Duty to Protect

The depths of human insecurity in North Korea are captured in Adam Johnson's novel *The Orphan Master's Son* (2012). Johnson describes how concentration camps and perpetual anxiety over one's personal and family security blend with the unpredictability of political life in North Korea. Thus, a former confidante of Kim Jong Il speaks to her new mate (a regime-selected replacement for one who vanished): "Let me tell you about the Dear Leader. . . . When he wants you to lose more, he gives you more to lose." When her new spouse demurs and asks what reason Kim Jong Il would have to send a goon to beat him up, she counters: "There is the proof that you don't understand any of this. The answer is that the Dear Leader doesn't need reasons."[1] Johnson's depiction of a living hell may seem incredible to outsiders, but his surrealist fiction parallels the realities portrayed in multitudes of firsthand reports of life and death as dictated by the Kim dynasty.[2]

ROBOTS OR SENTIENT HUMAN BEINGS?

Are the inhabitants of North Korea sentient humans suffering from oppression but kept in line by intimidation? Or—as in Aldous Huxley's dystopic novel *Brave New World*—have they become state-manufactured automatons, indoctrinated in utero or in test tubes to follow orders in a strictly hierarchical society? The robot thesis is suggested by *Inside North Korea,* a National Geographic documentary from 2006. The film follows a Nepalese eye doctor who goes to Pyongyang and in ten days removes cataracts from the eyes of more than one thousand North Koreans who had been blind for years in one or both eyes. Later, with his patients gathered in a large hall, the doctor removes the bandages from each person's eyes and tests his or her vision. They can see! One by one they file to the front of the room and bow before images of Kim Jong Il. They do not thank the Nepalese doctor but the "Great General." A thirty-five-year-old woman promises the general, "I will work hard in the salt mines to bring you happiness." Their sight restored, the patients raise their hands in joy to shout in unison, "Thank you, Great General!"

A bevy of DPRK slogans embodies the same spirit: "Flowers of His Great Love Are Blooming!" "He Gave Us Water and Sent Us Machines!" "He Hugged Us Still Damp from the Sea!" "The Iron-Willed Brilliant Commander . . . Who Unfolded Paradise!"[3] In March 2014 the DPRK Writers' Union provided poetic slogans to encourage North Koreans to vote; for example, "The Billows of Emotion and Happiness, We Break into Cheers from the Bottom of Our Heart and We Go to the Polling Station."

How much of this is new? An English visitor to Korea in the 1890s reported that in Seoul there was "a sharp and well-regulated body of police, always ready to pounce on outlaws of any kind." These guardians of the peace did not wear any particular uniform but were dressed just like the merchant classes. They mixed with people of all sorts and worked as detectives and police combined. Having become the bosom friend of someone who deviated from the rules, the agent arrested the culprit. Punishments were severe and often conducted in public—flogging, torture, crucifixion, and beheading. Imprisonment was not a favorite punishment in Korea because it incurred expenses. Accused culprits from the upper class might be banished from the city or even the country and their property confiscated.[4] One consolation, the Englishman believed, was that Koreans and other Asiatics seemed to feel pain and fear death less than Europeans.[5]

Some North Koreans do regard their supreme leaders (father, son, and grandson) as demigods. But most citizens are long-suffering, sensitive individuals kept in line by harsh economic conditions, stern discipline, and intimidation. Of course few dare talk of their feelings unless they have escaped the watchful eyes and ears of the regime. But the stories defectors have told to UN and other investigators converge. The DPRK has long committed crimes against its own people—crimes against humanity. And so has the regime's major patron—China.[6] The evidence for these claims follows in this chapter.

While most analysts focus on North Korea's ruling circles, some study the linkages between state-centric security and human security—issues such as gender, energy, and food.[7] The DPRK epitomizes the linkage "insecure state, insecure individual." Focused on Juche and sovereignty, North Korea endures a vicious cycle between national insecurity and human insecurity. Thus, the DPRK has failed to develop adequate supplies of energy and food—thereby weakening both national and human security. All the evidence shows a persistent deficit in human security. For example, the disintegration of the North Korean economy led many women to leave the state sector and take up free-market activity. This form of liberation, however, placed women in limbo, if not hell, because their responsibilities and burdens increased—all in a context of great and unremitting political uncertainty.

A North Korean defector recalled how hunger forced one woman to sell her daughter for 100 won—about one dollar.[8]

She was desolate.
"I Am Selling My Daughter for 100 Won."
With that placard on her neck
with her daughter by her side
the woman standing in the market place—
she was mute.
People looked at the daughter being sold
and the mother who was selling.
The people cast their curses at them
but keeping her eyes downcast
she was tearless.
Even when the daughter
wrapped herself
in her mother's skirt
shouting, screaming
that her mother was dying
the woman kept her lips
tight and trembled—
she did not know how to be grateful.
"I'm not buying the daughter
I want to buy the motherhood."
That soldier came by
with a 100 won note in his hand.
The woman who ran off with the money,
she was a mother.
With the money
she got for her daughter
she bought a loaf of bread
and put a chunk of bread
in her daughter's mouth
as they said goodbye.
"Forgive me," she cried.
She was desolate.

ECONOMIC REPRESSION

Tracking developments in North Korea in the early twenty-first century, the annual surveys of political freedom and civil rights by Freedom House consistently ranked the DPRK the least free country in the world, while the Index of Economic Freedom declared its economy one of the most repressed. Economic policies dictated by the whims of top leaders inflicted needless hardship. In response to widespread hunger and other problems in the DPRK economy, the Kim Jong Il regime began in the mid-1990s to permit some free-market activity. Basing their findings on surveys of North Korean refugees, Stephan Haggard and Marcus Noland concluded that the partial marketization of the DPRK economy was a by-product of state failure rather than the result of deliberate reform.[9]

By 2003 the regime feared that economic liberalization had gone too far and started to curtail marketization. In 2007 Kim Jong Il complained that the markets had become "a birthplace of all sorts of non-socialist practices." In 2008 the leadership took still stronger measures. On November 30, 2008, the state decreed that a new, more valuable won would replace the old won, but that families could trade only 100,000 won—about $30 at the black-market rate—for the new one. The move effectively wiped out private stores of money. The currency devaluation diverted the proceeds of North Korea's vast entrepreneurial underground to its cash-starved government businesses. But markets had turned into the sole source of income for many North Koreans. In theory everyone except minors, the elderly, and mothers with young children worked for the state. But state enterprises had been withering for decades, and many North Koreans sought work elsewhere. Farmers tended their own gardens as weeds overtook collective farms. Urban workers ducked state assignments to peddle everything from metal scavenged from mothballed factories to televisions smuggled from China.

Interviews with North Koreans living in China conducted by the *New York Times* in 2010 underscored the popular anger over the currency devaluation and growing political uncertainty as Kim Jong Il sought to install his third son as his successor. Some North Koreans with political connections avoided the worst outcomes. One woman from Hamhung, the second largest city in the DPRK, said the local bank director allowed her relatives to exchange three million won—thirty times the official limit. Not surprisingly, refugees engaged in market activity harbored more negative attitudes toward the regime than the general populace and were more willing to risk communicating their dissent to others.[10]

North Koreans had become inured to struggle and heartbreak. For some DPRK citizens, however, the currency reform was the worst disaster since the famine that killed more than one million in the mid-1990s. A construction worker told how his state employer had not paid him for so long that he had forgotten that he was supposed to have a salary. Indeed, he bribed his boss to be listed as a dummy worker so he could leave his work site to scrape out a living selling small bags of detergent on the black market. When DPRK officials devalued the official currency, his life savings of about $1,560 shrank to $30. News of the coming devaluation drove the worker's family to salvage whatever they could of the family's nest egg. The worker emptied the living-room cabinet drawer with their savings and split it with his wife and daughter, telling them, "Buy whatever you can, as fast as you can." The three bicycled furiously to Chongjin's market. "It was like a battlefield," he said. Thousands of people frantically tried to outbid one another to convert soon-to-be worthless money into something tangible. Some prices rose 10,000 percent, he said, before traders shut down, realizing that their profits soon would be worthless, too. The three said they returned home with 66 pounds of rice, a pig's head, and 220 pounds of bean curd. The construction worker's daughter had managed to purchase a small cutting board and a used pair of khaki pants. Together, he said, they spent the equivalent of $860 for items that would have cost less than $20 the day before. His daughter tried to comfort him. "Father, I will keep this pair of pants until I die!" she pledged. He told her the cutting board would be her wedding gift. "At that moment I really wanted to kill myself," he said. Looking at bright lights of the Chinese city Yangi through the safe house window, he said, "Here, it is not a big deal to make money. There [in North Korea], it is suffering and sacrificing." He could not forgive himself for rejecting—before the devaluation—his daughter's request for a navy track suit. She had said it put her thick winter sweater and plain trousers to shame. He had put her off because the cheapest ones *then* were nearly $15. When she kept asking for it, he had cursed and shouted, "People in this house need to eat first!" Voice trembling, he said, "I cannot describe how terrible I feel that I didn't buy that for her."

A picture of great privation was painted by North Koreans from many places in society—illegal traders, a prison escapee, people looking for work, the wife of an official in the ruling Workers' Party. Still, dissatisfaction seemed not to mutate into active opposition to the regime. Indeed, some interviewees hewed to the official line that North Korea was a victim of die-hard enemies—its impoverishment a Western plot and its survival threatened by the United States, South Korea, and Japan. The party official's wife asserted that Seoul's accusation that the DPRK sank the ROK corvette *Cheonan* in 2010 was part of the plot. "That's why we have weapons to protect ourselves," she said while visiting relatives in northern China and earning spare cash as a waitress. Her hair softly curled and a knockoff designer purse by her side, the woman boasted about her six-room house in the DPRK with two color televisions and a garden. In the next breath, she praised devaluation as well-deserved punishment of those who had cheated the state, even though she acknowledged that devaluation had led to chaos. She also noted that a top finance official was executed for mismanaging the operation. "A lot of bad people had gotten rich doing illegal trading with China, while the good people at the state companies didn't have enough money," she said.

Other refugees were more skeptical of government propaganda; but a former schoolteacher stated, "We always wait for the invasion. My son says he wishes the war would come because life is too hard, and we will probably die anyway from starvation." About half of those interviewed said they planned to return to North Korea; the other half hoped to defect to South Korea.[11]

"If you don't trade, you die," said the former teacher, who went from being an obedient state employee to a lawbreaking trader. She taught primary school for thirty years in Chongjin, North Korea's third largest city (with some 500,000 residents). But her all-day employment shrank in 2004 to morning duty as schools closed at noon. At least fifteen of fifty students dropped out or left after an hour, too hungry to study. Teachers were hungry, too. Her monthly salary scarcely bought two pounds of rice, she said. A university graduate, she pulled her own child out of the third grade in 1998, instead sending her to a neighbor to learn to sew. The longtime teacher quit teaching in 2004 to sell corn noodles near Chongjin's main market, where traders sold Chinese goods such as toothpaste and sewing needles along with DVDs of banned South Korean soap operas. Because selling noodles was barely profitable, the former teacher tried a riskier trade in state-controlled commodities—pine nuts and red berries used in a popular tea. That scheme collapsed when the guard at a checkpoint confiscated all the sacks of goods she and her partners had collected from a village—leaving her with a $300 debt. After her creditors took all her money, the former teacher walked across the frozen Tumen River at night and into China to seek help from her relatives there. Famished and terrified, she said she banged randomly on doors until a stranger helped her contact them. Feeling safe with relatives in China, the former teacher marveled that they could enjoy delicacies such as cucumbers in winter. However, temporarily deserting her son and daughter, both in their mid-twenties, left her so guilt-ridden that she sometimes could not swallow the food set in front of her. "I don't know whether my children have managed to get some money, or whether they have starved to death," she said, her eyes brimming with tears.

Like the schoolteacher, the construction worker figured that private enterprise was his family's only salvation. On paper, he worked for a Chongjin state construction company, but it had few supplies and no cash to pay its employees. Like more than a third of the workers, the worker paid roughly $5 a month to sign in as an employee on the company's daily log—and then seek to earn money elsewhere. Later, the firm became more active when the state decided to resurface Chongjin's only paved road and to build a hospital and a university to honor the 2012 centennial of Kim Il Sung's birth. To obtain surfacing materials, however, each family had to deliver more than a dozen bags of pebbles every month to its local party committee. The construction worker enlisted his elderly parents to scour creek beds for rocks that the family then smashed by hand into grape-size stones. In October the off-duty worker sold squid caught from a boat he piloted in treacherous coastal waters. In other months he bicycled about twenty miles every day looking for goods to sell—typically detergent bought from a factory that his wife resold at a 12 percent markup on a purple tarpaulin outside the main market.

The stories told by North Koreans in China in the last years of Kim Jong Il dovetailed with accounts by economists and political analysts. Citing aerial photos of plumeless smokestacks, economists reported that roughly three of every four North Korean factories were idle. The economy staggered.

All the refugees surveyed by Haggard and Noland left the North after 1990. The number of defectors who made it through China to South Korea rose steadily in the early twenty-first century, reaching nearly 3,000 per year in 2009. Haggard and Noland estimated in 2011 that fewer than 100,000 North Koreans remained in China or another country. Many were forcibly repatriated to the DPRK, where they were severely punished, as detailed later in this chapter. In 2012–2014 Kim Jong Un tightened border controls, and the number of North Koreans fleeing the country dwindled.

North Koreans who never crossed into China had few ways to make sense of their tribulations. There was no Internet; television and radio receivers were soldered to government channels. Slowly, however, information seeped in. Traders back from China reported that people there were richer and freer—South Koreans even more so. Some traders had cell phones linked to the Chinese cellular network that could be surreptitiously borrowed for exorbitant fees. But punishment for watching foreign films and television shows was stiff. One trader said a thirty-five-year-old neighbor spent six months in a labor camp after he was caught watching *Twin Dragons,* a farcical Hong Kong action film. To the dismay of the former teacher, her twenty-six-year-old son took similar risks. Her sister was married to a Pyongyang government official, but was not a fan of Kim Jong Il. The sister confided, "People follow Jong Il because of fear, not because of love." The construction worker, interviewed alone, said that people in the market now say openly, "The government is a thief." While the DPRK remained an Orwellian nightmare, the impact of cell phones and greater access to computers and other information sources will probably erode the impact of centralized controls.[12]

Harvests in North Korea increased in 2012, but hunger continued to stalk the land. A United Nations report in 2012 said that food supplies in the DPRK had improved: the food gap stood at 207,000 tons, the lowest figure in many years. But people's intake of protein decreased, and uneven distribution meant malnutrition or famine for some North Koreans. Food markets were full, but many products were too expensive for most people to buy. Apart from construction of more pig farms, however, no major agricultural initiatives were reported.

Interviews with North Koreans in China indicated that in 2012 the state no longer distributed food rations and even some soldiers went hungry. An interviewee said he knew "one family, a couple with two kids, who committed suicide. Life was too hard, and they had nothing to sell in their house. They made rice porridge, and added rat poison. White rice is very precious, so the kids ate a lot. They died after thirty minutes. Then the parents ate. The whole family died."[13]

HUNGER, HEALTH, AND POLITICS

Infant and maternal mortality rates in the DPRK jumped at least 30 percent from 1993 to 2008, and life expectancy fell by three years during the same period, to sixty-nine or seventy, according to North Korean census figures and UN statistics. The UN World Food Program (WFP) in 2013 estimated that 28 percent of children under five in the North suffered from chronic malnutrition and 4 percent were acutely malnourished. More than one in four persons needed food aid, but only one in seventeen would receive it, partly because donors were loath to aid a country developing nuclear weapons.

The WFP reported that in Ryanggang province, where the situation was most acute, nearly half the children were stunted from malnutrition. Even in the showcase capital, one in five children was stunted. In April 2012 the DPRK military lowered its minimum height requirement to 4 feet 7 inches—just slightly taller than the average South Korean fourth-grade student. The CIA *World Factbook* reported that roughly 4 percent of North Koreas were obese, but that more than one-fifth of children were underweight, a telling measure of social-economic inequality.

Some observers thought that the partial opening to markets, even with signs of price inflation, was positive news. For many North Koreans, however, coping with daily hunger and other material challenges remained a source of great anxiety. Even those able to sell food in stalls described difficulties with beggars, thieves, and corrupt officials.

In summer 2013 a Korean-American student tourist struck up a conversation with a DPRK officer stationed at the DMZ. He covered his mouth with a folder and looked the other way to mask his interaction with a foreigner. Fifty-some years old, he asked the Korean-American in her mid-twenties if he looked like her father. "Am I as tall as him? Same face?" She held back tears and joked "about how handsome the military officer was." In reality, she found the officer much shorter, thinner, and wizened than her father. She felt, "I was standing in front of the flesh and blood that was the result of a divided country, sixty years later, in human form." Her father could have easily been born in North Korea, but instead was born thirty-five miles south of the DMZ. Her father's fate, she reflected, "could not have been more different than [that of] the man I was standing in front of." The officer and student winked at each other as her bus moved on.[14]

COULD OUTSIDERS HELP?

Having spent time in North Korea over seven years, a Swiss businessman concluded that outside interventions by the United Nations and other busybodies were unnecessary and counterproductive. Felix Abt, a self-proclaimed capitalist, concluded that UN and U.S. sanctions obstructed the growth of legitimate businesses and encouraged black-market operations. The people he saw in Pyongyang seemed to lead comfortable lives, spending Sundays in the park pretty much like South Koreans.[15] Yet two concerned scholars denounced the United States for focusing on issues of WMD and thus supporting an inhuman status quo "rather than risk chaos on the peninsula."[15]

Both views were far from the mark. Most residents of Pyongyang belonged to one of the regime's upper castes. Realizing that they presently enjoyed a privileged existence, most avoided any actions that could rattle the system. Most North Koreans, however, had no access to subways, water parks, luxury stores, or even to adequate food. And while the United States focused on Pyongyang's nuclear weapons, Washington did not ignore the suffering of North Korea's people. As we shall see in later chapters, president George W. Bush refused for years to negotiate with Pyongyang because he loathed the brutal ways of its dictator. Seeing that Bush's approach got nowhere, president Barack Obama sought to link food aid to arms control. Only when that approach also failed did Obama settle into "strategic patience."[17]

With North Korea, as with many other less developed countries, there was a real policy dilemma: refuse aid because it will not reach those in need, or extend aid that deepens dependency and strengthens the regime?

The hard reality was that state insecurity probably contributed to human insecurity. Outsiders could try to lessen the regime's sense of insecurity while providing emergency relief, if needed, and buttressing development of energy and food production—prerequisites for human security. But the DPRK regime seems unmoved by United Nations condemnations of its military and human rights policies. Indeed, criticism by outsiders could strengthen Pyongyang's determination to go its own way. When starvation loomed, the regime sometimes deigned to accept food assistance. When harvests improved, the regime sometimes expelled UN agencies, NGOs, and other would-be do-gooders.

Despite its usual insouciance, the DPRK leadership began in the 1990s to seek and receive medical assistance from the Eugene Bell Foundation to cope with tuberculosis—particularly the kind resistant to most drugs. Financed largely by South Koreans and ethnic Koreans abroad as well as by the ROK government, the foundation provided material support to medical staff and facilities, mainly in rural areas but also in Pyongyang and Nampo. The foundation sent representatives (often including Americans and other Westerners) twice a year to North Korea to assess whether the medicines it provided were properly used. Sometimes, however, the DPRK did not grant Bell representatives entry permits when requested and then obstructed their efforts to reach rural clinics. On March 22, 2013, the foundation sent North Korea 678 million won ($604,267) worth of tuberculosis medicine. The consignment left Pyeongtaek Harbor and arrived at Nampo Harbor on April 4, 2013, by way of Dalian, China. By 2014 the foundation sponsored some forty hospitals, which were responsible for one-third of North Korea's population.[18]

Newly elected ROK president Park Geun Hye said in 2013 that her trust-building process for the Korean peninsula did not link humanitarian aid with the North Korean nuclear weapons issue. However, she also pledged to respond sternly to any provocations. Her Ministry of Unification reported in November 2013 that total aid sent from South to North Korea that year, including donations to international organizations, amounted to 17.8 billion won (nearly $17 million)—a 26 percent increase over the 14.1 billion won offered in 2012 when Park's predecessor, President Lee Myung Bak, was still in office. The increase took place against a background of rising tensions, including a third nuclear test by the North and DPRK threats to attack Seoul and Washington.

In 2013 fifteen local charity groups, including the Eugene Bell Foundation and Korea Sharing Net, provided 4.3 billion won—a quarter of all aid to the North, with the rest coming from the ROK government. South Korea's government donated 13.5 billion won to the World Health Organization and the United Nations Children's Fund in 2013. An ROK official said the government was considering matching funds to private charity organizations wanting to help the North.[19]

In July 2013 the UN World Food Program approved a two-year program of $200 million of food aid for North Korea, targeting the country's most vulnerable people, who remained dependent on external assistance. The program aimed to help 2.4 million people—children, pregnant women, and nursing mothers—with about 207,000 metric tons of food assistance, largely food manufactured in the North using ingredients imported by the WFP.

Reluctant to deliver more aid to the North without discerning positive change in the North, the ROK in 2014 waited to see if Pyongyang would follow through on the family reunions that were to take place in February at the Mt. Kumgang resort built by Hyundai in North Korea. The North had hinted that the reunions might not happen unless the ROK and the United States canceled or delayed their annual training exercises, planned to begin at the end of February. Despite these threats, more than 100 elderly persons arrived at the resort as scheduled. And one day after the reunions began, the ROK government approved a new shipment of medicine and powdered milk for the North, and promised more to come. For South Korea, the reunions were a humanitarian gesture and an attempt to lower tensions; for the North, they helped win food aid. Seeking a propaganda boost, Pyongyang's official Korean Central News Agency (KCNA) reported that the relatives had been separated for a long period "owing to the national divisions imposed on them by foreign forces. . . . Those from the north told with deep emotion . . . about their dignified and proud lives under the care of the DPRK." The KCNA also reported that persons from the South were deeply moved by what those from the North told them and by seeing the "orders and medals they had received for devoted services made for the prosperity of the country." Fewer than 300 separated relatives met for a few days at the reunion. The South chose participants by lottery; the North, probably by political criteria. Because the official exchanges were so constricted, many thousands of Koreans from both sides would never see their kinfolk again. When the South tried to plan more visits in the future, the North demurred: "Not now."

Would outside aid help to nourish and perhaps liberate the North, or would it reinforce the status quo? How would Kim Jong Un choose between guns, butter, and investment? Should outsiders subsidize a regime so it could continue to prioritize military spending? Noland estimated that the country's nutrition deficit could be closed by reallocating just 1 percent of the country's military budget—about 0.2 percent of national income.[20]

Would Kim Jong Un continue to repress markets, or would he permit some liberalization? Prospects were unclear. The official 2012 New Year message renewed the regime's promise to create a prosperous country that year to honor the 100th anniversary of Kim Il Sung's birth. The message called for accelerated development in light industry, agriculture, and science, but Kim Jong Un also introduced a new motif: his regime claimed it would pursue and achieve both military prowess and prosperity—in effect, guns and butter.

If the North Korean economy were stronger, then food aid by outsiders would be less needed. But skeptics have complained that most UN and NGO aid programs in North Korea, as in other developing countries, are counterproductive. These programs provided valuable nutrients in the 1990s, when the North suffered severe famine. But they have not resulted in the North's becoming more open to market solutions. To justify their own existence and maintain their perks, aid agencies reinforced—sometimes deliberately—a mentality of dependency. Their approach differed from capitalist enterprises that sought to develop resources for a market economy. With no pressure to make a profit, humanitarian organizations were less efficient than profit-seekers.[21] Aid programs also needed to take account of the context in which they operated. A South Korean agronomist cautioned that the ROK "should not compel developing countries to adopt Korean-style rural development nor think of enlightening, or even remodeling the minds of, the people in developing countries. It should halt material and facility-centered exhibitory ODA [official development assistance] projects and shift to sustainable projects where it can contribute to mid- to long-term rural development and poverty eradication. Rather than a unilateral approach that categorizes people in developing countries as ignorant, lazy, and in need of enlightenment, cooperation should be pursued through mutual respect and mutual learning."[22] His message was relevant to North Korea as well as to other countries in Asia and Africa.

All these issues arose again when the DPRK announced in June 2015 that drought again had dried up its rice paddies—the most severe drought in 100 years.

Pyongyang had made such claims before, but photos showed cracks in dry soil that needed water to grow anything.

SYSTEMATIC AND GROSS VIOLATIONS OF HUMAN RIGHTS

Not only did the DPRK leadership permit millions of its subjects to go hungry for decades, but it also deliberately used food as a weapon to compel their obedience. The North's food policies were part of a larger system of human rights abuses. These were among the conclusions reached by a Commission of Inquiry established by the UN Human Rights Commission in 2013 to investigate reports of gross human rights violations in the DPRK. The commission reported its findings on February 7, 2014:

> The state's monopolization of access to food has been used as an important means to enforce political loyalty. The distribution of food has prioritized those who are useful to the survival of the current political system at the expense of those deemed to be expendable. Citizens' complete dependency on the state led to one of the worst cases of famine in recent history. The authorities have only recently come to tolerate the fact that markets can no longer be fully suppressed. However, instead of fully embracing reforms to realize the right to food, the DPRK maintains a system of inefficient economic production and discriminatory resource allocation that inevitably produces more unnecessary starvation among its citizens.

Why are there persistent food shortages? The commission answered:

> The root causes of the food shortage and mass starvation that has killed, at a minimum, hundreds of thousands of people in the DPRK, particularly in the late 1990s, lie in a series of policies dating back to the establishment of the DPRK. These policies imposed a planned economy that overly focused on heavy industry, an input-intensive collectivized agriculture system and tight control over individual livelihood choices without respecting relevant principles of participation and good governance. It is also grounded in misguided spending priorities, which maintained an oversized and unsustainable security apparatus and discriminatory patterns of food distribution that served political imperatives. These policies appear to have been adopted and maintained by the DPRK authorities in reliance on the Soviet Union, China and other socialist nations continually making up for the resulting shortfall in the DPRK's own production of food and related agricultural inputs. The violations

of the right to food and other human rights intrinsic to these policies created the environment in which crimes against humanity would then unfold.[23]

The UN Human Rights Council mandated its Commission of Inquiry to assure accountability for crimes against humanity. Not allowed into the DPRK, the commission heard public testimony in Seoul, Tokyo, and other cities from eighty witnesses. It also conducted 240 nonpublic interviews with individuals who feared reprisals against families in the North. The commission heard from

> ordinary people who faced torture and imprisonment for doing noth-
> ing more than watching foreign soap operas or holding a religious belief.
> Former officials . . . previously involved in the [DPRK] propaganda appa-
> ratus related how they had to systematically manipulate free access to
> information. Women and men who exercised their human right to leave
> the DPRK and were forcibly repatriated spoke about their experiences of
> torture, sexual violence, inhumane treatment, and arbitrary detention.
> Family members of persons abducted from the Republic of Korea and
> Japan described the agony they endured ever since the enforced disap-
> pearance of their loved ones at the hands of [DPRK] agents . . . a course
> of state conduct that was partly admitted by the former ruler of the coun-
> try. The Commission listened to political prison camp survivors who suf-
> fered through childhoods of starvation and unspeakable atrocities, as a
> product of the "guilt by association" practice, punishing other genera-
> tions for a family member's perceived political views or affiliation. In
> addition to the violations in the political prison camps, the commission
> heard reports of deliberate starvation and other serious abuses occurring
> in other types of detention facilities and the suffering of an entire popula-
> tion recurrently facing malnutrition.[24]

The commission accused North Korea's government of crimes against human-ity, including murder, enslavement, torture, rape, forced abortions, and persecu-tion on political, racial, and religious grounds. "The gravity, scale, and nature of these violations reveal a state that does not have any parallel in the contempo-rary world." The commission estimated that up to 120,000 political prisoners were detained in four camps and that starvation was used to control and punish, both in the camps and in the general population. There was complete denial of freedom of thought, religion, and movement. Women were forcibly trafficked from North Korea to China for forced marriages and prostitution.

Outstripping the imagination of Zamyatin, Orwell, or Huxley, the commis-sion heard the following testimony:

- A young woman, forcibly repatriated and imprisoned for leaving the DPRK, witnessed a female prisoner forced to drown her own baby in a bucket.
- A man was forced to help load corpses of prisoners who had died from starvation, put them in a pot, and burn them, scattering their ashes and remains on the nearby vegetation fields.
- Parents of a young abduction victim from Japan appealed to the Supreme Leader: "You have a family . . . and you know how important is family love. Tell us where our daughter is. Is she alive? Is she happy? Is she dead?"
- A young woman told the commission how she "missed an entire semester of university education because her class was required to practice for six months, ten hours a day, for a short segment of a parade. . . . Some participants fainted from exhaustion. . . . Anyone who made repeated mistakes was made to remain on the training ground until midnight as a punishment." Her teachers invoked the example of a boy of seven or eight years of age who had practiced through the intense pain of an appendicitis attack, and then died because he did not receive timely medical care. The dead child was treated as a hero because he had dedicated his entire life for an event that would be witnessed by Kim Jong Il.
- Another witness told how children had to gather weekly at "confession and criticism" sessions and "take turns standing up and describing their activities for the previous week, showing how they were living in accordance with the teachings of the Kim philosophy. . . . Children must berate themselves if they have failed . . . such as being absent from class or not having made a contribution as expected. They must then make a commitment to become better. They are also expected to describe the failings of at least one of their peers in the same group. Until they identify someone for criticism, they are not allowed to stand down."
- In each and every household in the DPRK, there must be at least three framed pictures on display: one of Kim Il Sung, one of Kim Jong Il; and one showing the two together, as if consulting. (A portrait of Kim Jong Un had not yet entered mass production.) One witness described how his father had unintentionally soiled an image of Kim Jong Il, which was printed in an old newspaper he had used to mop up a spilled drink, and was consequently sent to a political prison camp (*kwanliso*). The rest of the family was spared this fate, but was labeled as a family with "hostile" *songbun*—lowest of the low in the DPRK political caste system (*songbun*) and sure to trigger harsh official discrimination.[25]

These stories were not isolated cases, but were representative of large-scale patterns of systematic and gross human rights violations.[26] The testimony tallied with confidential interviews with victims of repression in the DPRK who feared to speak publicly. They were also consistent with a large body of written documents and expert testimony gathered by the UN Commission.

The commission reached the following conclusions:

- The state was carrying out a systematic and widespread attack against religious believers, persons who tried to flee, and anyone considered a threat to the political system of the DPRK.
- The state attacked the general population by knowingly aggravating starvation and sacrificing the lives of large numbers of innocent, ordinary citizens in order to preserve the political system and its leadership.
- The state abducted and forcibly disappeared a large number of persons from other countries in a systematic and widespread manner in order to gain labor and skills to enhance the DPRK and strengthen it in the struggle for supremacy on the Korean peninsula.
- DPRK authorities committed and continued to commit crimes against humanity in its political prison camps, including extermination, murder, enslavement, torture, imprisonment, rape, and other acts of grave sexual violence and persecution on political, religious, and gender grounds.
- Inmates of the DPRK's political prison camps were victims of the crime of enforced disappearance. They were stripped of their citizenship rights and detained incommunicado in remote political prison camps.
- The DPRK authorities consistently denied access to, or information about, the camps to UN human rights bodies. The authorities falsely claimed that the camps and their inmates do not exist.
- The intentional killings of individual inmates in the DPRK's political prison camps, through summary executions, beatings, infanticide, deliberate starvation, and other illegal means, all amounted to the crime of murder.
- Inmates in political prison camps were virtually enslaved.
- A central political objective of the DPRK's political prison camps was the elimination of three generations of factionalists and class enemies.
- Inhumane acts in the DPRK's political prisons formed part of an overarching state policy. Across the various political prison camps in the DPRK and over six decades, hundreds of thousands of inmates suffered a similar pattern of starvation, forced labor, and other inhumane acts. As of the date of the commission report, between 80,000 and 120,000 prisoners were being detained in political prison camps; this represented approximately 1 in every 200 citizens of the DPRK. (The rate in the United States was similar or higher—about 7 per 1,000, while other industrial democracies averaged 1 per 1,000.)[27]
- Conditions imposed on inmates in the DPRK's ordinary prison camps (*kyohwaso*) differed only in degree, not in principle, from those in political prison camps.

- The violence and heavy punishment inflicted on those who practiced their religion outside the state-controlled churches were at the core of the state-sponsored discrimination that Christians experience.
- The camp system was controlled from the highest level of the state. In some cases, the commission was able to trace orders to cause the disappearance of individuals to the camps to the Supreme Leader.

PRINCIPAL FINDINGS OF THE COMMISSION

The UN Human Rights Commission's inquiry concluded with several findings:

- The commission found that crimes against humanity had been committed in the DPRK, pursuant to policies established at the highest level of the state. These crimes against humanity were ongoing because the policies, institutions, and patterns of impunity that lie at their root remain in place.
- Persons detained in political prison camps (*kwanliso*) and other prison camps, those who tried to flee the country, adherents to the Christian religion, and others considered to introduce subversive influences were being subjected to crimes against humanity. These took place as part of a systematic and widespread attack of the state against anyone who was considered to pose a threat to the political system and leadership of the DPRK. This attack was embedded in the larger patterns of politically motivated human rights violations experienced by the general population,
- In addition, crimes against humanity had been committed against starving populations. These crimes resulted from policies that violate the universal human right to food. They were taken to sustain the present political system, in full awareness that they would exacerbate starvation and contribute to related deaths. Many of the policies remained in place, including the deliberate failure to provide reliable data on the humanitarian situation in the DPRK, denial of free and unimpeded international humanitarian access to populations in need, and discriminatory spending and food distribution.
- Finally, the commission found that crimes of enforced disappearance were still being committed against persons from the Republic of Korea, Japan, and other countries who were systematically abducted or denied repatriation to gain labor and other skills for the DPRK.

In addition, the commission found that "the decision-making process in the DPRK is highly centralized, in particular regarding those areas where gross human rights violations and crimes against humanity are being committed. It is dominated by the Supreme Leader and a small group of people, who lead the central organs of the Workers' Party of Korea and the National Defence Commission. Many of these individuals hold high military rank and occupy key positions in the military and security apparatus. Some of them are relatives of the Supreme Leader."

CHINA AND THE RESPONSIBILITY TO PROTECT

Beijing in 2005 signed the World Summit Document and in 2006 UN Security Council Resolution 1674, proclaiming the responsibility of all states and the international community to prevent and stop genocides, war crimes, ethnic cleansing, and crimes against humanity.[28] Like Russia, however, China has appeared unwilling to implement this commitment. The UN Commission of Inquiry detailed many abuses to which China contributed.

When North Koreans sought to escape the DPRK, they usually did so via China. Chinese authorities permitted some to stay or travel further, but they repatriated many North Koreans, with horrific consequences.

In its report of February 2014, the UN Commission of Inquiry on Human Rights in the DPRK stated:

> On 16 December 2013, the Commission wrote a letter to the People's Republic of China, in which it summarized its concerns relating to China's policy and practice of forced repatriation of DPRK citizens. The Commission expressed particular concern about Chinese officials providing specific information on such persons to DPRK authorities. The Commission urged the Government of China to caution relevant officials that such conduct could amount to the aiding and abetting of crimes against humanity where repatriations and information exchanges are specifically directed towards or have the purpose of facilitating the commission of crimes against humanity in the DPRK.

The commission noted that the DPRK "systematically uses violence and punishment to deter its citizens from exercising their human right to leave the country. Persons who are forcibly repatriated from China are commonly subjected to torture, arbitrary detention, summary execution, forced abortions and other sexual violence." The commission called on the DPRK to "abolish the de facto prohibition on foreign travel imposed on ordinary citizens. Decriminalize illegal border crossings and introduce border controls that conform to international standards. Renounce orders to shoot and kill at the border. Cease to regard citizens repatriated from China as political criminals or to subject them to imprisonment, execution, torture, arbitrary detention, [and] deliberate starvation."

China was said to share responsibility for hunger in North Korea, because it helped to perpetuate a system both inefficient and inhume. According to the commission report:

> The root causes of the food shortage and mass starvation . . . lie in a series of policies dating back to the establishment of the DPRK. . . . These policies appear to have been adopted and maintained by the DPRK authorities in reliance on the Soviet Union, China and other socialist nations continually making up for the resulting shortfall in the DPRK's own production of food and related agricultural inputs. The violations of the right to food and other human rights intrinsic to these policies created the environment in which crimes against humanity would then unfold.

What to do about all this? The Commission of Inquiry recommended that

(a) Respect the principle of non-refoulement. Accordingly, abstain from forcibly repatriating any persons to the DPRK, unless the treatment there, as verified by international human rights monitors, markedly improves. Extend asylum and other means of durable protection to persons fleeing the DPRK who need international protection. Ensure that such persons are fully integrated and duly protected from discrimination. Stop providing information on activities and contacts of persons from the DPRK living in China to the State Security Department and other security agencies in the DPRK. Allow persons from the DPRK free access to diplomatic and consular representations of any state that may be willing to extend nationality or other forms of protection to them.

(b) Provide the United Nations High Commissioner for Refugees, and relevant humanitarian organizations, full and unimpeded access to all persons from the DPRK seeking such contact.

(c) Request technical assistance from the United Nations to help meet the obligations imposed under international refugee law and ensure the effective protection of persons from trafficking.

(d) Adopt a victim-centric and human rights–based approach to trafficking in persons, including by providing victims with the right to stay in the country and access to legal protection and basic services, such as medical treatment, education, and employment opportunities equivalent to those afforded to their own citizens.

(e) Regularize the status of women and men from the DPRK who marry or have a child with a Chinese citizen. Ensure that all such children can realize their rights to birth registration and Chinese nationality where applicable and access to education and healthcare without discrimination.

(f) Take immediate measures to prevent agents of the DPRK from carrying out further abductions from Chinese territory. Prosecute and adequately punish apprehended perpetrators of abduction and demand the extradition of those giving such orders so that they may be tried in accordance with law. China should raise with the Supreme Leader of the DPRK and other high-level authorities the issues of abductions, the infanticide of children entitled to Chinese nationality, forced abortions imposed on repatriated women, and other human rights violations that target persons repatriated from China.

The commission also recommended that states with "historically friendly ties with the DPRK, major donors and potential donors, as well as those states already engaged with the DPRK in the framework of the Six-Party Talks, should form a human rights contact group to raise concerns about the situation of human rights in the DPRK and to provide support for initiatives to improve the situation."

Given the basic human needs of most North Koreans, UN member-states "should not use the provision of food and other essential humanitarian assistance to impose economic or political pressure on the DPRK. Humanitarian assistance should be provided in accordance with humanitarian and human rights principles, including the principle of non-discrimination. Aid should only be curbed to the extent that unimpeded international humanitarian access and related monitoring is not adequately guaranteed."

WHAT NEXT?

On March 28, 2014, the UN Human Rights Council approved a resolution (A/HRC/25/L.17) endorsing the commission's report on North Korea and called on the UN General Assembly to refer the issue to the UN Security Council for consideration of sanctions and referral for criminal indictment with respect to crimes against humanity. The vote was 30 in favor, 6 against, and 11 abstentions, with few surprises. Those voting in favor were largely a coalition of developed- and developing-country democracies; those opposed were China, Cuba, Pakistan, Russia, Venezuela, and Vietnam. Given that the commission also condemned China for complicity in North Korea's abuses of human rights, any actions by the Security Council would confront a Chinese, and perhaps a Russian, veto.

The official North Korean news agency, KCNA, shot back on March 31, 2014, calling the United States the "worst human rights abuser in the world." Citing official U.S. statistics, Gallup polls, and U.S. newspapers, the KCNA stated that 47 million Americans were impoverished; some 43 percent viewed the issues of starvation and housing as serious social problems; some 48 million were unable to receive proper health care. It said that Americans experienced more than 1.2 million high-profile crimes each year. Nearly half of Americans did not go to the polls for the 2012 presidential elections. U.S.-style "liberty" led to widespread corruption and excessive alcohol use. More than 85 percent of persons arrested in New York City, KCNA reported, were of African or Hispanic descent. More than 100,000 children were trafficked each year. America trampled religions abroad, stirred up sanctions campaigns, and labored to topple foreign governments. Many of these charges were exaggerated, but rooted in fact. Still, they did not add up to crimes against humanity orchestrated by a nearly monolithic regime. Many, if not all, U.S. officials were trying to correct America's human rights failings. In South Korea, meanwhile, a spate of suicides in the ROK armed forces, along with reports of systemic abuse of conscripts, led President Park Geun Hye in August 2014 to demand stronger measures to control violence within the military.

In December 2014 the UN General Assembly voted 116 to 20, with 52 abstentions, to urge the Security Council to refer the human rights accusations against the DPRK regime to the International Criminal Court (ICC). The DPRK representative argued that the UN report on human rights in his country was "fabricated" and demanded that the United Nations instead focus on "CIA torture crimes committed by the United States."

On December 22, 2014, the Security Council for the first time discussed human rights in the DPRK as an agenda item separate from the nonproliferation issue. It did so by a procedural vote (not subject to veto), over an objection by China that the council was not mandated to consider human rights issues. Russia joined China in voting against, while Chad and Nigeria abstained. Argentina voted in favor, along with the ten Security Council members who requested the meeting. A majority of council members said the Security Council should consider the Commission of Inquiry's recommendation to refer the situation in the DPRK to the ICC. Some also called for targeted sanctions against those found most responsible for crimes against humanity.[29]

In January 2015 the UN special rapporteur, Marzuki Darusman (from Indonesia), told a Japanese audience that the UN Security Council had now placed the abduction issue on its permanent agenda along with the broader problem of human rights in the DPRK. In February he added that the closing of camps for political prisoners required the dismantling of the North's "cult leadership" and replacement of the Kim family regime.[30] North Korea was so worried that Kim would be personally named in the ICC referral that it offered Darusman an opportunity to visit the DPRK if the leader's name was omitted from the resolution. Pyongyang had previously declined to extend such an invitation. Darusman, who had never been to North Korea, rejected the offer.[31]

The DPRK National Defense Commission on February 14, 2015, denounced the "impudent" and "gangster" Obama administration for trying to "pull down" the DPRK social system by fabricating a nonexistent human rights issue, by war drills, by escalating sanctions, by cyber warfare, and by organizing with South Korea special military units to disable and dismantle the North's nuclear weapons and missiles. Given all this, the DPRK no longer saw any reason to negotiate with the United States and pledged to answer a conventional attack with conventional arms and a nuclear onslaught with nuclear retaliation.[32]

Was this pressure or renewed dialogue? A group of Asian and European political leaders and human rights activists on February 18, 2015, called for an international strategy that combined accountability, pressure, and engagement. Given the practical realities of the Russian and Chinese veto power, the group called for building on a DPRK offer made during the recent Security Council debate.[33] "The UN should establish a dialogue group, to initiate a framework for engagement with Kim Jong Un's regime precisely on human rights concerns, taking up his offer of a visit to North Korea by the UN Special Rapporteur on Human Rights in North Korea, the European Union, or others. Such engagement must not supersede accountability measures, but instead complement them. It should include issues of war and peace, seeking an end to the armistice. . . . It should include open discussion of abductions, separations and disappearances as well as the horrific conditions in the prison camps."[34]

Should—can—must the international community negotiate with evil? The debate continued.

8

Facing Up to Evil

What is tolerance? It is the consequence of humanity. We are all formed
of frailty and error; let us pardon reciprocally each other's folly—that is
the first law of nature.

—Voltaire

We are negotiating with evil all the time, if only in the form of the
unwise part of our own minds.

—Jack Rendler, on a Buddhist perspective on evil

Is evil commonplace—even banal?

—Hannah Arendt, *Eichmann in Jerusalem*

"Evil" is all around us, even at work. . . . One out of every 25 human
beings has no conscience, no sense of right or wrong, no empathy, no
ability to understand emotion—no soul. Worse, while they can mimic
emotion, they see other humans as mere pawns or saps, to be used for
their benefit or amusement, or both.

—Davia Temin, "The Sociopath in the Office Next Door"

The real issue is not whether to talk to the bad guys but how—under
what conditions, with which mix of pressures and conciliation, and
with what degree of expectations that the bad guys will keep their
word.

—Lesley H. Gelb, former State Department planner,
Washington Post, April 27, 2008

Can we—should we—must we try to negotiate our differences with individuals
and groups we regard as evil?[1] Is an accommodation feasible, or even desirable,
between parties who differ profoundly on notions of right and wrong? Are some

regimes so evil that it is wrong and unwise to engage with them—even on matters of shared concern? If actors believe it worthwhile to bargain with a perceived devil, should they deploy or demand special safeguards?

Around the globe contending groups characterize each other as "bad guys." Some assert that their foes have blood on their hands and are led by monsters. If evil permeates the other side, is it not foolish to behave as if negotiation could reach positive results? Accused of crimes against humanity, the DPRK regime can be seen as evil. Pyongyang, in turn, portrays its accusers as evil. How should North Koreans see and deal with a superpower that, their leaders say, has brutalized and betrayed them for more than half a century?

Even when facing a "devil," an expert on negotiation advises that one should have a bias toward seeking a deal and consider closely whether a negotiated agreement could advance one's interests. The crucial question for Washington then becomes: Are there issues on which DPRK cooperation would be helpful—perhaps even essential—to American objectives?[2] Despite mutual animosity, could a deal be reached for mutual gain?

IS EVIL REAL?

In April 2007 presidential aspirant Barack Obama was asked—out of the blue—"Have you ever read Reinhold Niebuhr?" Obama replied, "I love him. He's one of my favorite philosophers." Asked what he took away from Niebuhr, Obama answered in a rush of words: "The compelling idea that there's serious evil in the world, and hardship and pain. And we should be humble and modest in our belief we can eliminate those things. But we shouldn't use that as an excuse for cynicism and inaction. I take away . . . the sense we have to make these efforts knowing they are hard, and not swinging from naïve idealism to bitter realism."[3] In these few words Obama laid out a worldview that recognized evil but that also demanded humility. Niebuhr's views underwent several seismic shifts during his long life (1892–1971), but Obama extracted the essence of his mature thought.[4]

Some politicians warn, however, that bargaining with a putative "devil" can raise false hopes and give legitimacy to a regime that deserves to be resisted—not cajoled. In this vein, Vladimir Lenin for many years denounced any effort to negotiate arms limitations with bourgeois regimes, because, he said, capitalist systems could never disarm. Bourgeois appeals for arms negotiations, Lenin added, were pure hypocrisy meant to foster pacifist illusions. He concluded that Communists should not negotiate disarmament (*razoruzhenie*) but actively disarm (*obezoruzhit'*) the bourgeoisie.[5] In a similar spirit, speaking after the 9/11 attacks on the United States, Vice President Dick Cheney stated, "I have been charged by the president with making sure none of the tyrannies of the world are negotiated with. We don't negotiate with evil; we defeat it."[6] Both Lenin and Cheney pointed to the deepest reason not to negotiate with the enemy: to do so could mask and strengthen evil.

Against this line of thought, those who favor "jaw, jaw" over "war, war" contend that if disputes are ever to be resolved without war, then every player must be brought into the solution. If this is so, how and under what circumstances can the so-called bad guys be productively engaged? When should pragmatic expediency outweigh moralism and legalism? These are momentous questions that defy simple answers based on general principles. Wise answers depend not only on the facts of the case but also on priorities and frames of reference.

Before dealing with specific issues in world affairs, we must wrestle with several deep questions. First: Is evil an essential reality, or is it a construct of our imagination? A law professor and chair of the Harvard Negotiation Project defined the terms: "*an act is evil when it involves the intentional infliction of grievous harm on another human being in circumstances where there is no adequate justification.*" An "enemy" is not an ordinary competitor but "someone who has deeply wronged us (or can harm us) and poses a threat to our well-being."[7]

Is evil in human affairs relative or absolute? Are all humans and their institutions equally blemished? Is everything relative, or are some humans and systems intrinsically evil? Is "evil" nothing more than criminal or immoral behavior, an abuse of power—perhaps explicable by an unhappy childhood?[8] Could it be that "criminal behavior is only a left-handed form of human endeavor," as the crooked lawyer Alonzo Emmerich assured his wife in the 1950 film *Asphalt Jungle*?[9] Evil characters, such as Milton's blazing Satan and Shakespeare's scheming Iago, can upstage good-goodies.[10] But twenty-first-century writers tend to avoid such characters, perhaps because "the whole category of Evil seems too theological or because modern psychology assumes that every bad act can be traced to childhood neglect or abuse and thus be explained away."[11]

Against the theory of childhood neglect, two leaders of the New York Senate, along with their grown sons, faced federal criminal charges in 2014–2015.[12] Could childhood neglect explain why thousands of Americans chose to hide their taxable dollars in Swiss banks and why agents of Credit Suisse and UBS helped them to do so? Did the Chinese officers accused of cyber theft from U.S. industries in May 2014 suffer from unhappy childhoods?[13] Did Vladimir Putin's fables about his government's noninterference in Crimea derive from some childhood trauma? Some of these malefactors justified their actions by some noble cause; some simply followed orders; still others said, "I will do whatever is good for me."

Are some actions so evil that their perpetrators must stand beyond the bounds of human compassion? Or should we accept the all-purpose justification, "*Tout savoir, c'est tout pardonne*—To know everything is to pardon everything"?[14] If we knew and understood everything, would we then forgive whatever some actor has done? Is a society such as Stalin's USSR or Hitler's Germany the innocent victim of circumstances exploited by a peculiar set of maniacal leaders? Or do some cultures and societies tolerate and even *spawn* evil? The more we know about the circumstances in which Stalin and Hitler grew up and emerged, the better we understand them.[15] Still, environment does not explain everything. Pascal was probably correct: "The heart has its reasons that reason cannot fathom" (*Le coeur a ses raisons que la raison ne connait pas*).

Each man—Hitler and Stalin—behaved as if possessed by a demon. The Lenin-Stalin regime put to death at least 50 million Soviet citizens by execution, starvation, exile, or consignment to the gulag, where they labored in freezing conditions with little food or medical care. Some 40 million died in a war made more costly by Stalin's purge of the Red Army's officer corps in the 1930s and by his unwillingness to offend Hitler in 1939–1941—a toll the Kremlin tried to mask.[16] Not only did Hitler attack most of Europe and the USSR, but at the same time, he exterminated some 6 million Jews along with many homosexuals and Roma—at least one-third of the Jews murdered not in concentration camps but in forests, wells, quarries, and in the streets of their own villages or in their own homes, often with enthusiastic help from the locals, as in parts of Lithuania.[17] One scholar has catalogued the twentieth century's leading democidists (killers of their own people): Stalin, Mao Zedong, Hitler, Chiang Kai-shek, Lenin, Tojo Hideki, Pol Pot, and Yahya Kahn.[18] No laggard, Mao Zedong sat by while his Great Leap Forward killed 30 to 40 million Chinese. The DPRK leadership invested in jet fighters and other military devices when that money could have purchased food for the 5 to nearly 10 percent of the North Korean population who starved to death in the 1990s.

Apart from killing their own people, many polities have practiced genocide—exterminating "others" for their ethnicity or culture. North Korea's ideology holds that its people are the purest of races,[19] but since few non-Koreans live under Pyongyang's rule, DPRK rulers have had almost no opportunity to commit genocide. The political caste system established by Kim Il Sung, however, favors a few North Koreans and discriminates against those deemed politically unreliable. Since the lower castes get less food, they live undernourished and sometimes die from hunger. Most politically favored persons dwell in Pyongyang, while those outside the capital suffer.

When we recall the horrendous actions of leaders such as Stalin and Hitler, could we possibly forgive them? If they were still in power, would that forgiveness affect our approach to negotiation? If they still functioned in the twenty-first century, should they not be indicted and brought before the International Criminal Court (along with Vladimir Putin, for his wars in the Trans Caucasus and aggressions in Ukraine)?[20]

Let us recall how theology has shaped politics. Some leaders may find their opposite number so repulsive that they find it difficult to sit and talk with them.[21]

In January 2002 President George W. Bush asserted that North Korea, along with Iraq and Iran, constituted an "axis of evil." Bush let it be known that he loathed the DPRK leader who permitted huge numbers of his subjects to starve. A recovered alcoholic and a reborn Christian, Bush gathered support for many of his policies from those Christians who expected Armageddon—a final battle between the forces of righteousness and of evil.

But can—should—we regard some people and institutions as benign and others as evil? Can any individuals or institutions claim a mantle of innocence? Have not most societies had wicked leaders and policies?

Some religions and philosophies perceive a never-ending struggle between forces of Good and Evil—Light and Darkness.[22] Given this struggle, some faiths believe that humans can exert their free will so as to do good and fight evil. But other faiths are fatalistic. Some Christians accept that Providence has divided humanity into the Elect, who are predestined for heaven, and the Goats, who will never be saved. Against such dualisms, one version of Christianity asserts that all humanity has been stained by Original Sin. One sect holds that humans can and must *earn* salvation; another, that redemption comes only by God's grace.[23]

Can there be salvation outside the one true faith? Should believers practice tolerance toward unbelievers or strive to destroy them? These questions arise not only for Christians and Muslims but also for adherents of Buddhism, Hinduism, and other faiths, most of which are divided and subdivided.

Religious and ideological zealots often accuse their former comrades of succumbing to evil. Protestant divines denounced the "the whore of Babylon wearing the papal tiara." Incensed at the Swiss theologian's differences with Luther's own theology, Martin Luther wrote Huldrych Zwingli that Satan must have taken control of his mind.[24] Soviet and Chinese Communists in the 1960s accused each other of betraying Marxism and Leninism. Sunni and Shia militants and their offshoots stop at nothing to destroy each other.

History—ancient and recent—gives many illustrations of evil. Edward Gibbon concluded that history is "the register of the crimes, follies, and misfortunes of mankind." More to the point, as Mephistopheles reminded the Lord in *Faust,* humans call it "reason, but use it only to be more beastly than any beast."[25] Folklore recorded by the Brothers Grimm also confirms the pervasiveness of evil—for example, the cruelty of Hansel and Gretel's stepmother; it also describes how evil beings may deceive—wolves wearing sheep's clothing. *Destiny and Desire* by Carlos Fuentes tells of two dueling siblings in contemporary Mexico whose lives track the tragedy of Cain and Abel.[26]

Some versions of Christianity espouse tolerance; others urge a hard line— even holy war—against infidels. In February 2011 a group of Baptists from Kansas sought to disrupt the funeral of a nine-year-old shooting victim in Tucson because her family was Catholic. Those who honored the child and those who demonstrated probably saw each other as evil. Other faiths also offer conflicting guidelines. Some Muslims claim that Islam means and requires peace. Some mullahs, however, preach jihad against nonbelievers and even against other branches of Islam. Some interpret the Koran to mean that "anything goes" in dealing with infidels. Some authorize self-martyrdom against civilians. Young lawyers in Pakistan have demanded laws requiring the death penalty for blasphemy. If we accept, as poet Robert Burns put it in 1785, that "Man's inhumanity to man / Makes countless thousands mourn!" what can or should we try to do about it?

Goethe's Herr is patient. He tells Mephistopheles that so long as humans strive, they will go astray—*Es irrt der Mensch, solang er strebt.*[27] In the end, Faust is lifted into heaven even though he once sold his soul to Satan. Why? Because of his good works. Toward the end of his life, Faust built dikes that would help people live better. Even the Lord cheated, Satan inferred. God's angels got to the corpse first.

THREE WAYS TO VIEW HUMANITY

Should we assume that some people are basically good and others basically evil? Or that all humans are flawed? Or that humanity ranges up and down a bell curve, from the few people who are saintly to others who appear profoundly evil?[28]

This third view is probably correct—for entire societies as well as for individuals. Societies can be ranked from excellent to poor in their observance of human rights and in their capacity to foster human development. Freedom House ranks countries from one to seven on their support for political freedom and civil liberties—a scale where North Korea ranks as worst in the world. Other agencies—Human Rights Watch, Amnesty International, and the U.S. State Department—conduct annual surveys of human rights performance. Transparency International ranks countries by the absence or presence of corrupt practices. The UN Human Development Index (HDI) identifies what amounts to evil as well as incompetence. It reveals that some governments have vast resources and a high GDP but do little to increase average life expectancy and provide wide access to education. Russia ranked fifty-seventh of all countries on the HDI in 2013 despite its profits from oil and gas exports. Because North Korea was opaque, it did not figure in most UN and other rankings, but probably ranked among the worst performers worldwide.

There are even more explicit measures of evil—tabulations of journalists and human rights activists attacked, jailed, or murdered. Females are treated worse than males in most countries. In North Korea and elsewhere, female entertainers have been treated as sex slaves.[29]

But mores change. For millennia, many societies encouraged xenophobia and did not punish cruelty to nonmembers. As late as the seventeenth century, Hugo

Grotius, an architect of international law, taught that it was proper to treat prisoners of war and their offspring as slaves—with no limits on the effects of this law. Only in the nineteenth century did some governments and international institutions outlaw slavery and, between individuals, dueling. Only in the twentieth century did governments agree to ban aggression, to respect civilians in war, to deal humanely with prisoners, and to observe political and social rights of their citizens. We now have an International Criminal Court that tries and sometimes finds guilty individuals charged with crimes against humanity. Optimists, such as Jacques Maritain, argued that humanity's awareness of what is right has deepened over time. Steven Pinker recorded a long trend toward less violence and more mutual respect in human relations.[30] Ian Morris concluded that war has spawned peace.[31] Still, pessimists point out that wars are still waged for resources, that they are often egged on by religious differences, and that governments in China and Russia—each a permanent member of the UN Security Council—still arrest and even kill critics of their policies. In 2014–2015 both Beijing and Moscow seized and occupied what was not theirs according to international law.

IF EVIL EXISTS, SO WHAT?

Here our focus is on Northeast Asia: Should policymakers in Washington explore an accommodation with the ruling dynasty in Pyongyang that has abused its own people for decades and acted the rogue's rogue in world affairs? Would such a regime ever reciprocate a conciliatory move to improve relations? Is it not going to devour any sign of goodwill and demand more?

History overflows with cases of aspiring despots who killed not only one another but also their longtime friends and advisers; some exploited not only foreign lands but their own people to extract wealth for their personal comfort and power; some broke treaties with adversaries and scuttled alliances with ostensible partners. The infighting and purges conducted by the Kim dynasty in Pyongyang resemble not only Stalin's machinations but those of the brutal despots who founded the Tudor dynasty in England (Henry VIII and others) and the Romanov dynasty in Russia. The Kim family's brutality is no worse than that of those African leaders who used child soldiers and the threat of amputation to extract blood diamonds for their personal wealth. If nothing else positive, the Kims, at least, fostered mass literacy.

Does anyone have the right to throw the first stone?[32] American leaders have often portrayed their country as good—the "city on the hill" and the "indispensable nation"—and its opponents as evil. Taking the opposite tack, the Iranian theocrat Ruhollah Khomeini on November 5, 1979, described the United States as "the Great Satan, a wounded snake," responsible for imperialism and corruption throughout the world.

Americans and other Westerners needed to understand why many observers regarded their policies toward less developed countries as wicked. Whatever the rationales for these policies—from "salvation of souls" to "white man's burden" to anti-Communism to "war on terror"—European and U.S. actions often perverted and aborted the ideals of Western civilization.[33] Evil can spring from social systems—religious as well as political and economic—as well as from the personal drives of individuals. The logics of free enterprise spawned growing economic and social inequality not only in the United States but also in China and Russia. Haves are often indifferent to the misery of have-nots, even when they are victims of the haves.

Champions of liberty and equality, Americans allowed and profited from slavery; conducted physical and cultural genocide against Indians; enslaved Africans; and repressed Filipinos and others who sought national self-determination.[34] In return for a free hand in the Philippines, Washington raised no objection to Japan's takeover of Korea.

Speaking in Orlando, Florida, on March 8, 1983, President Ronald Reagan advised the National Association of Evangelicals that, when discussing nuclear freeze proposals, they should not blithely declare themselves above it all and label both sides in the Cold War "equally at fault." Those who preach the "supremacy of the state" and predict its "eventual domination" of the globe, he said, "are the focus of *evil* in the modern world." Do not "ignore the facts of history and the aggressive impulses of an *evil empire*." Do not simply call the arms race a giant misunderstanding and thereby remove yourself from the struggle between right and wrong and *good and evil*" (emphases added).

The logic of "states' rights" led Washington to shy away from or qualify its commitments to many human rights treaties. Having considered whether President George W. Bush had violated the Constitution or any laws, his attorneys asserted that if the president does something, then it must be legal.[35] Such leaders reckon that their lofty goals justify nearly any means. Politicians often put narrow interests above principle. Inside the Washington beltway, members of both parties cave to pressures from the National Rifle Association to block restrictions on assault weapons that have sometimes produced mass mayhem. In the United States and elsewhere some church leaders seem to care more about the image of their institutions than protecting their flock from sexual abuse.[36] In October 2011 a grand jury indicted Robert W. Finn, Catholic bishop of Kansas City–St. Joseph, for criminal failure to report child abuse by a priest he supervised. Two years later, the *National Catholic Reporter* (October 30, 2013) noted that Pope Francis had still not removed Finn from his bishopric. Finn resigned in April 2015, but he remained a bishop and presided over several ordinations.

It may be that some people are indifferent to evil or even do evil because they are evil. But others coddle evil or do evil for reasons of expediency or out of misunderstanding.[37] Expediency—pursuit of the national interest or some economic interest—often led the United States to align with dictators at the expense of ostensible U.S. values.[38] Washington for decades cooperated with many authoritarian regimes, such as the family-run enterprise of Tunisian president Zine el-Abidine Ben Ali, who exploited and repressed his subjects until overthrown in the Arab Spring. The Tunisian regime, unlike that in Pyongyang, pursued many policies that seemed congruent with U.S. values and interests.[39] Washington could rationalize, as it sometimes also did in Central America, that Ben Ali "is an S.O.B., but he is our S.O.B."

While waging a strictly defensive war can be justified, initiating an elective war is far more difficult to rationalize—for example, U.S. actions in Cambodia in 1970 and the "shock and awe" attack on Iraq in 2003. And while many U.S. presidents have endorsed international arbitration, international law, and international organization, the George W. Bush administration "unsigned" the Clinton-era commitment to the International Criminal Court.

North Koreans have cause to regard each of their neighbors as well as the United States as evil. All Koreans remember the arrogance of imperial China and Russia and the brutality of Japan's occupation.[40] North Korean elites resent the bullying by Moscow and Beijing they experienced during and after the Korean War. North Koreans are taught that the United States started the Korean War (false) and then bombed the country without mercy (true), and that Washington manipulates Seoul like a puppet (mostly false). The mix of fact and myth leaves many North Koreans believing that their cause is just and their opponents evil.

Why recite all the grievances that peoples can and do hold against one another? To caution against the self-righteous assumption that our side is good and the other evil—that our hard line is totally justified and that tough actions by the other side are not. The moral problem resembles the security dilemma: steps one side takes for "defense" can appear bellicose and threatening to the other side. One root of these attitudes, this book argues, is hubris.

SHOULD WE BARGAIN WITH THE DEVIL?

To the question "Should we bargain with a putative devil?" Professor Robert Mnookin answers, "Not always, but more often than you feel like it."[41] Why the presumption in favor of negotiation? Wise policymakers will avoid two kinds of traps—*negative* traps that keep us from negotiating when we should, and *positive* traps that push us to negotiate when we should not. The first kind of trap is often moralistic; the second, relativistic. A negative trap can result from a desire for vengeance and a tendency to demonize the other side. We may misjudge if we attribute "evil" to the other side on the basis of a few incidents without considering their context. But a positive trap may develop if we rationalize everything by context, as in "People will be people" and "The job of business is to make profit"—or if we trust excessively in the power of redemption or the inevitability of win-win outcomes. If the other side is out to hurt you, then your diffidence is not paranoia.

Our attitudes to policy issues are shaped by intuition (which is quickly responsive to nonverbal signals) and by rational analysis (which is slower, more disciplined, and systematic). We need some of both for effective decision-making. A wise policymaker will be pragmatic and not focus on revenge. If the negotiator seeks justice for the other side's past misdeeds, this attitude can obstruct resolving the conflict and advancing the negotiator's own interests.

According to Mnookin, a wise policymaker will neither fight nor flee, except as a last resort. He or she will follow four other guidelines. (1) Compare the likely costs and the benefits of negotiation. (2) Get advice from a variety of experts with different perspectives. (3) Presume that it is worthwhile to negotiate but let this presumption be rebuttable. (4) When making recommendations to others, let pragmatism outweigh moralism.

Bargain with the devil? Mnookin argues that Winston Churchill was right in May 1940 not to negotiate with Hitler, even though Germany had already conquered much of Europe and was about to attack a weakened Great Britain. Why was he right not to negotiate? Experience showed that Hitler was not a reliable partner. If negotiations broke down, then it would be harder to rally the British public to fight. By contrast, Nelson Mandela was wise in 1985 to initiate negotiations with South Africa's apartheid regime, even though he felt it necessary to do so in secret because many colleagues would have opposed talking with such an evil opponent. The ruling National Party was under increasing pressure to change its racist policies, and Mandela believed the time was ripe for negotiation.

If evil exists, does it matter for negotiators? Whether we think the other side is good, bad, or a blend, do we not negotiate simply to advance our own interests? If so, why not go for any deal that seems to meet our needs? If a car dealer offers us a new model with just the right features and price, do we care whether the dealership or its salesperson has a spotty record? *Probably we should care.* Most contracts require us to trust as well as verify. An unscrupulous auto dealer may sell a car knowing it has subpar equipment. No matter how closely we inspect the vehicle, we may overlook defects that could be life-threatening. Also, the dealer could be here today and gone tomorrow—unavailable to back up any warranty. If the car dealer is simply a poor businessperson or decides to retire, or the city puts a highway through the dealership, then the warranty may also prove worthless.

Most arms agreements, of course, are far more complicated than automobile purchases. If a new technology or political opportunity emerges, then an opportunistic regime indifferent to its reputation may jettison or evade its arms control obligations. Experience showed that the DPRK often exploited every ambiguity in its agreements with the United States. An opportunistic government determined to obtain nuclear weapons may *fake* an interest in arms control while using nego-tiations as a tool to gain time in the laboratory or test site. The opportunist may use negotiations to soften the other side's vigilance; to win political support at home and abroad; to divide its adversaries; and, if an accord is reached, to protect its own assets—future as well as current—while weakening its foes. All these con-siderations underlay Soviet diplomacy in the 1920s.[42] Like the Soviet regime and many other actors on the world stage, the DPRK has also contrived to divide its adversaries and push them against each other.

The less basis for trust, the greater the need for verification. The DPRK often resisted measures to increase transparency and found reasons to retreat from its arms control commitments. It uttered half-truths or outright falsehoods. Given this record, the guideline for U.S. negotiators should not be Ronald Reagan's "Trust but verify" but *"Verify because there is little trust."* If 100 percent reliable verifica-tion is not attainable and trust is lacking, these limitations will constrain the scope of any deal the prudent negotiator can consider.

In most arms accords between Moscow and Washington, each side usually retained ample weaponry and production facilities to deter or counter aggression if the other side cheated. But rough symmetry of this kind is lacking between Pyong-yang and Washington. If these two parties enter an agreement, each must assess the possibility the other may default. The stronger party, of course, can devise and maintain countermeasures far more easily than the weaker. The George W. Bush and Obama administrations insisted that Pyongyang limit or eliminate its nuclear deterrent, while the United States and its partners offered—when their demands were met—only to provide political and economic rewards or make marginal reductions in their military deployments. Thus, the DPRK faced far more sub-stantial risks.

Washington's dealings with Pyongyang differed from White House–Kremlin relations in other ways. First, the DPRK regime for decades appeared less stable than did the Soviet during the Cold War. Second, Pyongyang's treatment of its own people was far more abusive than the Kremlin's in the decades *after* Stalin's death. Washington and its partners therefore were compelled to ask whether any accom-modation with the DPRK would endure and whether, if it lasted, it would not pro-long the suffering of most North Koreans.

WHAT DOES IT TAKE TO MAKE PEACE WITH TOUGH GUYS?

While some faiths are Manichean, others accept that all persons are flawed—an outlook that should constrain self-righteousness and foster efforts to see how oth-ers look at things. For his part, the devout Baptist Jimmy Carter was unwilling to throw the first stone. Even when campaigning for the presidency, Carter acknowl-edged to *Playboy* what he saw as a flaw in his own makeup: "lust" in his heart.

As president, Carter mediated the Camp David accords, which stopped warfare between Israel and Egypt. Having left the White House, private citizen Carter facilitated peaceful resolution of conflicts around the globe. A mediator, he said, should leave opinions about the disputants outside the meeting room. A mediator should focus the parties on whether and how an agreement could advance their interests. "People in conflict have to be willing to talk about ending it, or at least changing it, and there has to be someone willing to talk to them, however odious they are—and that's where I come in."[43]

Critics objected to the ex-president's meddling in government affairs and his willingness to get up close and personal with dictators. If results count, however, the record shows that Carter's interventions helped Nicaragua to make a peaceful transition to democracy and to persuade Haiti's junta to leave office peacefully. But Carter's greatest achievement, described below in chapter 12, was to turn the United States and North Korea away from war in 1994 and to outline terms for their Agreed Framework, which froze DPRK plutonium production in return for economic aid and the prospect of normal relations.[44]

Both Carter and Kim Il Sung believed in high-level contacts. If Kim Il Sung could not meet the existing president, then he seemed anxious to meet with an ex-president, one who—as president—had reduced the U.S. troop presence in South Korea. Many observers were surprised that a part-time Baptist preacher could find any rapport with a Communist dictator. But Carter's faith acknowledged that no humans or regimes are perfect.

Kim Il Sung's understanding with Carter suggested that lowering barriers—rather than raising walls—could facilitate negotiations with North Korea. The impact of Carter's positive demeanor is difficult to measure for many reasons, including the background: his negotiating breakthrough in Pyongyang (as in Port-au-Prince) emerged in tandem with strong threats of U.S. military intervention.

Carter's mediations responded to significant danger to peace and security. He was not alone in perceiving these threats, but his outlook both permitted and drove him to action. His outlook encouraged him to ignore the reputations of his interlocutors. It led him to take on missions that others spurned.

Still, effective peacemaking does not require religious ardor. Other idealisms or skillful professionalism may suffice—especially if backed by muscular hard power. Like Carter, the veteran diplomat Richard Holbrooke accepted difficult missions. He did not like Slobodan Milošević and some other leaders in the former Yugoslavia, but did whatever he thought could end fighting in the Balkans. While Carter tended to be Mr. Nice, Holbrooke used a full quiver of diplomatic tools—carrots and sticks, sobriety and fiery šljivovica (brandy), duplicity and straight-talking—to get his way. Having brokered and virtually imposed peace terms for the former Yugoslav republics in the 1990s, Holbrooke later tried to do the same in Afghanistan-Pakistan. Whatever the driving forces behind Holbrooke's diplomacy, he made no public reference to his own religion. He did, however, take note of the ways that organized religions helped foster turmoil in the Balkans and in Southwest Asia. A secular humanism, if not a religious faith, helped to inspire Holbrooke. Away from the Balkans, he mobilized businessmen to finance HIV-AIDS relief and programs to control malaria.

While Carter's religious views helped him to deal with very tough characters, a self-righteous Woodrow Wilson stubbornly opposed those—even his friends—who held to different principles. These included associates at Princeton University, political figures in New Jersey, other world leaders at the Paris Peace Conference, and Republican senators in Washington. Wilson's intransigence hurt his own health and subverted many causes he espoused.[45] The black-and-white world views of other U.S. leaders—for example, John Foster Dulles and George W. Bush—also undermined U.S. interests and influence on the world stage. Was it a coincidence that the fathers of Wilson, Dulles, and Condoleezza Rice (national security adviser to George W. Bush) were all Presbyterian ministers? And that Bush himself was a born-again Christian—thanks in part, he said, to the Reverend Billy Graham? The fact that Graham's meetings with Kim Il Sung helped pave the way for Jimmy Carter's underscores the often Janus-faced role of religious faith: it can bolster self-righteous Manicheanism or acceptance of human foibles.

No one seemed to inspire the outrage of U.S. secretary of state John Kerry, at least in 2015, not even his worst negotiating partners. "I think they want to be valued for who they are and understood for where they come from and what their life is about," he told *New Yorker* editor David Remnick. "I think if people have a sense that you know what they're about, they can build some trust with you. . . . I think if you can show them that you understand what their challenge is, how they have to sell it at home or how they have to, what it means, the sacrifice they might have to make to do X, Y, or Z." This attitude helped Kerry negotiate the July 2015 nuclear deal with Iran (summarized below in chapter 17) and sustained his positive approach to efforts to resolve conflicts in Syria and between Israel and its neighbors.[46]

In and out of the White House, Barack Obama tried to bridge ethnic, cultural, and political divides.[47] His motives probably arose in part from his Christian faith, but he did not make a big display of his religious views. The influence of Reinhold Niebuhr could be seen in Obama's remarks at the January 12, 2011, memorial service in Tucson for those murdered a few days before. The president stated that "at a time when our discourse has become so sharply polarized—at a time when we are far too eager to lay the blame for all that ails the world at the feet of those who think differently than we do—it's important for us to pause for a moment and make sure that we are talking with each other in a way that heals, not a way that wounds." Referring obliquely to the doctrine of Original Sin, Obama noted that "scripture tells us that there is evil in the world, and that terrible things happen for reasons that defy human understanding. In the words of Job, 'when I looked for light, then came darkness.' Bad things happen, and we must guard against simple explanations in the aftermath."

Obama provided good advice for a creative approach to reconciliation. "Rather than pointing fingers or assigning blame, let us use this occasion to expand our moral imaginations, to listen to each other more carefully, to sharpen our instincts for empathy, and remind ourselves of all the ways our hopes and dreams are bound together." Like the Oglala Sioux medicine man Black Elk, Obama urged that we begin any effort at peacemaking by putting our own lives in order and dealing in a loving way with those close to us.[48] "We may not be able to stop all evil in the world, but . . . how we treat one another is entirely up to us. I believe that for all our imperfections, we are full of decency and goodness, and that the forces that divide us are not as strong as those that unite us."[49]

Reviewing Obama's speech, columnist David Brooks cautioned that "even a great speech won't usher in a period of civility." He suggested that civility requires humility—an awareness of our limitations and shortcomings.[50] Brooks worried that "over the past forty years or so we have gone from a culture that reminds people of their own limitations to a culture that encourages people to think highly of themselves." People "have lost a sense of their own sinfulness. Children are raised amid a chorus of applause. Politics has become less about institutional restraint and more about giving voters whatever they want at that second." As a result, "the roots of modesty have been carved away." For civility to prevail there must be "a return to modesty."

Brooks cited Niebuhr: "Nothing that is worth doing can be achieved in our lifetime; therefore, we must be saved by hope. . . . Nothing we do, however virtuous, can be accomplished alone; therefore, we are saved by love. No virtuous act is quite as virtuous from the standpoint of our friend or foe as it is from our standpoint. Therefore, we must be saved by the final form of love, which is forgiveness."

But this inference by Brooks goes too far. It also contradicts the mature views of Niebuhr—that evil must be confronted.[51] Yes, we should love and forgive where possible. But can we love—and even forgive—an Adolf Hitler, a Joseph Stalin, a Kim Jong Il? Yes, we should try to understand the circumstances that shaped their lives, views, and actions. Each probably had an unhappy childhood. But people of goodwill must oppose evil. Indeed, Niebuhr said "there was a difference between being a 'fool for Christ' and a plain damn fool."[52] As a young man Niebuhr admired socialism until he saw it deformed by Hitler and Stalin. Yes, he conceded that imperialist ideologies had triggered wars. But he rejected pacifism and live-and-let-live complacency, which he believed arose from a vapid liberal culture still marked by tacit Christian values. Like Hans Morgenthau, dean of U.S. political realists, Niebuhr believed that we should muster whatever assets are available to resist those who would destroy what we hold dear.[53]

Bottom Lines

"We are good and they are bad" is dangerous as an approach to foreign affairs. But it also wrong and dangerous to assume that all actors are equally malevolent. It does not follow that if someone smiles and looks us in the eye, that he or she will be a dependable partner. Moral relativism can initiate a slippery slope—whether for individuals, governments, or businesses. Whether or not the top leaders in Pyongyang have been intrinsically evil, many of their actions at home and abroad violated widely approved standards of behavior. All this presented a dilemma for those who would build bridges. An unscrupulous actor may exploit any concessions to counter or even assault the peacemaker.

To balance realism and hope is a difficult art. Neither cynics nor martyrs can win in real-world situations that resemble the game theory exercise of Prisoner's Dilemma. Cynics are blind to what may be positive in relationships; martyrs, to what is negative and even dangerous.

As Niebuhr might have put it, we must recognize the motes in our own eyes but also confront the great evils on the world stage. If we side with St. Augustine against the Manicheans, we will avoid self-righteousness and cultivate empathy. We may find grains of humanity inside the hardest hearts. Even Stalin was touched by Roosevelt's illness at Yalta. Leaving FDR's room, Stalin questioned Andrei Gromyko, "Tell me, how is this man worse than others that nature [*priroda*] punishes him so?"[54] At times, Stalin could appear large-hearted. Toward the end of a meeting of the Big Four Foreign Ministers in April 1947, Stalin advised Secretary of State George C. Marshall "to have patience and not become pessimistic." Disagreements among the ministers, said Stalin, were "only the first skirmishes and brushes of reconnaissance forces. . . . Differences had occurred in the past on other questions. . . . As a rule, after people had exhausted themselves in dispute, they then recognized the necessity of compromise." According to Marshall, Stalin "thought that compromises were possible on all the main questions, including demilitarization, political structure of Germany, reparations, and economic unity."[55]

A black-and-white view of the world ignores what complexity science tells us about world global affairs. International relations is not just a complicated process; it is also an interactive, nonlinear one. Many moves by leaders in Pyongyang are shaped in part by their perceptions of the United States and other actors.[56] If either side sees the other as duplicitous, it will probably take precautionary measures.

How we deal with evil regimes and their actions will shape not only our own narrow interests but those of all humanity—indeed, of all life. But there is a standard to guide us through this maze. *Peace is the sine qua non for everything else.* It follows that if a cruel dictatorship is willing to negotiate security arrangements likely to limit arms competition and make war less likely, then democratic governments should engage and do what is necessary to obtain verifiable arrangements.

We can hope that both believers and secular nonbelievers can move toward a common sense of morality. To hold through thick and thin, however, our moral beliefs need an anchor. For some, the higher order is God-given; for others, it is the wonder of life in an expanding universe.[57] Human development and advancement can grow in a widening circle of compassion. Respect for individual dignity and the biosphere require each other. Our world may be the one truly sacred place.[58] Without this transcendent sense of morality, whether viewed through religious or secular eyes, "politics remains a messy form of tribal or national religion."[59]

If this view is correct, then the United States and all the actors in Northeast Asia needed to downplay, if not resolve, their differences and get on with a quest for mutual gain.

9

Must We Choose between Peace and Human Rights?

Which is more important: peace or human rights? Must we choose, or can each of these values strengthen the other? Decades of negotiations between the USSR and Western democracies showed that greater security and deeper respect for human rights could produce a positive synergy. Arms control and détente could reduce the danger of nuclear war and, at the same time, help open a closed society and liberate its people. The outcome was not the best of imaginable worlds, but proved to be better for everyone than a life "nasty, brutish, and short"—a world "wherein men live without other security, than what is their own strength." Without order, as Thomas Hobbes warned in 1651, there would be the war of all against all and "no account of Time; no Arts; no Letters; no Society; and which is worst of all, continuall fear, and danger of violent death." Could Western experiences with the USSR be relevant to North Korea?

Better Dead than Red?

Germans in the 1930s debated *"Lieber tot als rot?"*—"Better dead than Red?" People across the Western world argued the same question in the 1950s. One of humanity's sharpest minds, Bertrand Russell, sided with those who would choose "Red" over "dead." After the Cuban confrontation eased, however, a new era began in 1963. Angst diminished, and few people still feared they had to choose between Communist tyranny and nuclear Armageddon. The new era was symbolized by the scene of Nikita Khrushchev hugging W. Averell Harriman, scion of the Union Pacific Railroad and former ambassador to Moscow, as Harriman returned to the USSR to negotiate a nuclear test ban.

Despite the "Spirit of Moscow" in 1963, both superpowers continued to improve and increase their engines of destruction. Fears faded, but the danger of a nuclear holocaust did not disappear. The USSR remained a totalitarian dictatorship, and each superpower kept adding to its nuclear arsenal. Given the mind-sets of Nikita Khrushchev and his successors, could Western governments hope to find in the Kremlin a responsible and responsive partner in negotiations to control the arms race? Two Soviet citizens, each a Nobel Prize winner, expressed opposing conclusions. Aleksandr I. Solzhenitsyn answered *"nyet,"* because a regime that oppressed its own people could not be trusted—especially with foreigners. But Andrei D. Sakharov answered *"da,"* because the stakes for humanity were so high.[1] Solzhenitsyn nominated Sakharov for the Nobel Peace Prize in 1973 but made clear his own values. "Coexistence without wars" was not enough, Solzhenitsyn maintained. Real coexistence required also a life "without violence, or anyone's telling us how to live, what to say, what to think, what to know, and what not to know."[2]

Solzhenitsyn put human rights first; Sakharov, the survival of humanity. Both men knew the realities of the Soviet system. Still, the particular aspects of each man's experiences influenced his perspective. Recipient of many awards by Stalin and then by Khrushchev, Sakharov helped develop the Soviet hydrogen bomb and worried about lethality. Having calculated how many people would die from the pollution caused by another thermonuclear test, Sakharov in 1961 pressed Khrushchev not to proceed with another H-bomb test. While Sakharov (1921–1989) had enjoyed a somewhat pampered life under Stalin and Khrushchev, Solzhenitsyn (1918–2008) had spent years in what he called the gulag archipelago.[3] The gulag survivor knew firsthand how arbitrary and cruel could be the Kremlin's approach to anyone who questioned its legitimacy or judgment. He had reason to doubt that any real accommodation was possible with a regime so evil as the Soviet.

If human rights are fundamental, then Solzhenitsyn was probably correct.[4] If peace is essential, Sakharov made the stronger case. As history played out, however, it was not necessary to choose. American negotiations with the Soviet Union probably benefited both peace and human rights. The same negotiations that advanced peace also bolstered human rights in the USSR and its allies. Besides his campaign for arms control, Sakharov became the leading defender of human rights in the Soviet Union. For him, the two causes were inseparable. Peace and human rights can reinforce each other. The first Sakharov Prize for Freedom of Thought awarded by the European Parliament went to Nelson Mandela in 1988; in 2013 it went to teenager Malala Yousafzai for her defense of the right of all children to be granted an education; in 2014, to gynecologist Denis Mukwege for his support for victims of gang rape. In 1993 Mandela and F. W. de Klerk received the Nobel Peace Prize for peaceful termination of apartheid; in 2013 it went to Yousafzai.

EVIL CLOSE UP

Can—should—must we strive for peace and arms control with an evil regime? This question haunted me throughout my time at Moscow State University in

1958–1959 as I researched the origins of Soviet disarmament policy. Understanding this topic better, I hoped, could shed light on how to prevent a nuclear war. Of course I had already read a great deal about Soviet realities, but the sheer brutality of Communist rule nearly overwhelmed me when I saw it close up. The first Saturday I spent in Moscow was on a gauzy evening in late summer. Crowds walked and sometimes danced across Manezh Square near the Kremlin. Marked as an American by my clothes, Russians were soon asking me questions about the United States—especially its treatment of blacks and the poor. In the small crowd around me stood a boy, nine or ten years old, dressed in a sailor suit. He listened to questions and answers for half an hour when suddenly two burly men pulled him into an alley. I heard an automobile engine revving up. A large car careened out of an alley with the boy sitting between his two assailants in the back seat. My mouth dropped open in astonishment. "Doesn't your FBI act the same way?" asked one of my interlocutors. "Not with children," I murmured. Another bystander pointed out that the hour had passed 10:00 p.m., when children should be off the streets. But another countered that the curfew was seldom enforced. I concluded that the authorities wanted to give this child a traumatic experience so he would never again get close to an American. For more than a year the Kremlin had been trumpeting "Peace and Friendship—*mir i druzhba,*" but many of the Soviets I met in 1958–1959 fell into serious trouble for taking the slogan seriously. At least three students were expelled from Moscow State University for associating with me.

Was this the society—the system—with which I hoped for peace and understanding? My academic adviser acted like a sophist, defending Soviet policy. When the History Department typed up my thesis outline, authorities changed the title from my noncommittal "Soviet Policy on Disarmament" into a propagandistic "Soviet Struggle [*Bor'ba*] for Disarmament." Later I learned that my professor, Boris Efimovich Shtein, had for years been a deputy to Soviet foreign commissar Maksim Litvinov. Both men, of Jewish descent, had been repressed after World War II. Shtein had just recently been rehabilitated and now found himself dealing with an American whose curiosity could get both the professor and the student into trouble. Shtein blanched when I told him that I wanted to explore how Lenin's concept of morality shaped Soviet policy.

It later dawned on me that the same professor Shtein who seemed like a spokesman for evil was himself a victim of an evil system. How far back could we trace such links? Were the men who bullied the child in the sailor suit also victims of the system? No doubt they had been indoctrinated for years—probably decades. Perhaps they had few better options than to work for the KGB (Committee on State Security). The entire system was headed by Nikita Khrushchev, who (in 1958) had just recently vanquished his last competitor to become first among equals in the leadership. Of course Khrushchev's behavior and that of his associates were also shaped by their upbringing, the Soviet system, and the Cold War.

How Individuals and Forces Fostered—
and Neutered—Accord

Khrushchev made some effort to foster a thaw in the mid-1950s. Soviet diplomats on May 10, 1955, accepted in principle British and French disarmament proposals, which Washington had already endorsed. At about the same time, Moscow also agreed to Austria's independence. Détente was in the air. In July 1955 leaders of Great Britain, France, the Soviet Union, and United States would meet at the "summit" in Geneva.

President Dwight D. Eisenhower wanted to explore whether Stalin's successors really wanted to dampen Cold War tensions and improve Soviet-U.S. relations. But he too was constricted by circumstances. He had to cope with hawks in both parties and an American public brought up to fear, or even hate, the USSR. Ike sought advice from a panel of experts in psychological warfare that convened at the Quantico Marine base. They suggested that the president at Geneva propose "Open Skies"—aerial reconnaissance of the USSR and United States. As could be expected, this proposal embarrassed and frustrated a Kremlin regime opposed to openness and jealous of its secret strengths and weaknesses. The Kremlin's rejection of this proposal helped underscore the closed and secretive nature of Soviet rule. But the proposal also suggested to Moscow that the Eisenhower administration did not really want arms control, because it walked away from previous Western initiatives after a positive Soviet response. Great Britain and France also made proposals that had nothing to do with their previous positions, which had been given provisional acceptance by Moscow on May 10. Unable to agree on anything at the summit, the four top leaders authorized their foreign ministers to continue deliberations in October.[5]

Washington had more second thoughts. Eisenhower's disarmament negotiator, Harold E. Stassen, in September 1955 placed a "reservation" on all previous U.S. positions. In October two arch hawks—Soviet foreign minister V. M. Molotov, a leftover Stalinist, and U.S. secretary of state John Foster Dulles—smothered any fresh breezes still lingering from the summer's "Spirit of Geneva." As Eisenhower recovered from a heart attack in autumn 1955, he realized that Dulles had "inadvertently" omitted the fundamental quid pro quo that Ike wanted to offer for a Soviet concession at the foreign ministers' meeting in Geneva.

The coup de grâce for the Spirit of Geneva emerged in 1956 as Soviet tanks crushed Hungarian freedom fighters and Khrushchev threatened nuclear war if London and Paris did not stop their invasion of Egypt—which they had already done, responding to pressures from Eisenhower and the UN General Assembly.

So who or what killed the momentum toward détente? A mélange of Machiavellian scheming, partisan politics, political culture, business as usual by poorly coordinated governmental bureaucracies, pressures from the military-industrial complex, and—not least—individuals' particular behavior. Driven by a strong propensity for risk-taking, Khrushchev in 1958–1961 endangered world peace with his Berlin ultimatums and in 1962 by his Cuban missile gambit. But this same gambler was also capable of farsighted deals with the United States on security and other issues. My presence and that of nineteen other U.S. graduate students in Moscow and Leningrad was possible only because Khrushchev's regime agreed in January 1958 to a multifaceted cultural exchange with the United States—a program that over the course of four decades bolstered freer access to information, free thought, and free expression.[6] The net effect was to subvert the Soviet system. One of the Soviets who studied at Columbia in 1958–1959, Aleksandr N. Yakovlev, was exiled for years to Canada for his heterodox views but later contributed to Mikhail S. Gorbachev's "new thinking," glasnost, and perestroika.[7]

From Evil Empire to Partner in Peace

Other blends of competing forces and idiosyncratic behaviors generated and then eviscerated subsequent movements toward U.S.-Soviet détente—the "Spirits" of Camp David in 1959, Moscow 1963, Glassboro 1967, Moscow 1972, San Clemente 1973, and Vienna 1979. In each case top leaders seemed to believe that détente and arms control could benefit their countries, but then permitted other individuals and forces to seize control and push U.S.-Soviet relations back toward confrontation. Not until Ronald Reagan and Mikhail Gorbachev met each other in the late 1980s did enlightened self-interest gain control in the White House and Kremlin.

Reagan in 1983 described the USSR as an "evil empire." By 1985–1987, however, Reagan adopted a more nuanced view. He thought the Kremlin might bargain based on the realities of power. He came to see that the two superpowers were engaged in an *interactive* process that reflected not only ideology and power but also perceptions and misperceptions of each other. Reagan's evolving worldview—along with Gorbachev's—set the stage for several major arms controls agreements and the near ending of the Cold War. In terms of international relations theory, Reagan shifted from neorealism to constructivism—from a focus on what power exists to how we see and think about it.[8]

A similar evolution commenced in the 1990s between Washington and Pyongyang, as we shall see in chapter 12. When the Clinton administration saw that DPRK leaders might be ready to bargain, the White House deliberated what it could offer Pyongyang in exchange for freezing its plutonium production. When Jimmy Carter and, later, William J. Perry and Madeleine Albright interacted with top DPRK leaders, they too saw how each side's words and actions shaped the other's behavior. Despite some apparent accords between Washington and Pyongyang, however, there was never a prolonged détente/entente like that between Washington and Moscow in the late twentieth century.

IS ARMS CONTROL A CHIMERA?

Starting in the late 1950s, the Kremlin and White House concluded dozens of arms control and other security accords. But did these agreements reduce the danger of war, curtail the costs of defense, or limit the likely damage if war erupted? A related question: Did they obstruct or enhance movement toward greater human rights?

Both arms control skeptics and supporters found grist for their arguments. Skeptics said that Moscow and Washington were limiting only their obsolete or redundant weapons. Thus, the 1972 SALT accords set ceilings on the number of strategic delivery vehicles each side could deploy, but put no restraint on the number of warheads, which then multiplied exponentially. The 1972 package included severe limits on antiballistic missile (ABM) defenses. But the Soviets tried to build radars, a kind banned by the treaty; and the Reagan administration sought to violate the treaty by erecting a strategic missile defense ("Star Wars") astrodome over the United States. Intent on fulfilling Reagan's dream, the George W. Bush administration unilaterally withdrew from the ABM treaty in 2001–2002, thereby destroying the keystone for limits on offensive missiles.

Arms control supporters replied that the 1987 Intermediate-Range Nuclear Forces (INF) Treaty required Moscow and Washington to destroy several classes of their newest and most formidable weapons. By the treaty's deadline of June 1, 1991, a total of 2,692 of such weapons had been destroyed, 846 by the United States and 1,846 by the Soviet Union. Under the treaty both nations were allowed to inspect each other's military installations. But the treaty permitted each side to keep and recycle the missile warheads and guidance systems.[9] Each nation was permitted to render inoperative and retain 15 missiles, 15 launch canisters, and 15 launchers for static display.

Critics noted that the INF Treaty left untouched the long-range missiles and bombers of each side. In 2007 the Putin regime said the INF treaty no longer suited its needs and warned that it might withdraw if the United States persisted with plans to deploy ABM systems in Poland and the Czech Republic—ostensibly aimed at Iran but which might be upgraded to weaken the Russian missile deterrent.[10] (The Obama administration later switched its plan for midcourse interception of Iranian missiles to defenses based at sea or in Romania.) But the Kremlin also complained that the INF treaty prevented it from developing a new type of cruise missile that could target future U.S. antimissile sites and from possessing weapons like those China was developing and fielding. Still, on October 25, 2007, the United States and Russia reaffirmed their support for the treaty and called on all UN members to join them in renouncing the missiles banned by the treaty. In 2012–2014, however, Moscow and Washington accused each other of trying to sidestep the INF treaty. Thus, Russia was developing a ground-based cruise missile

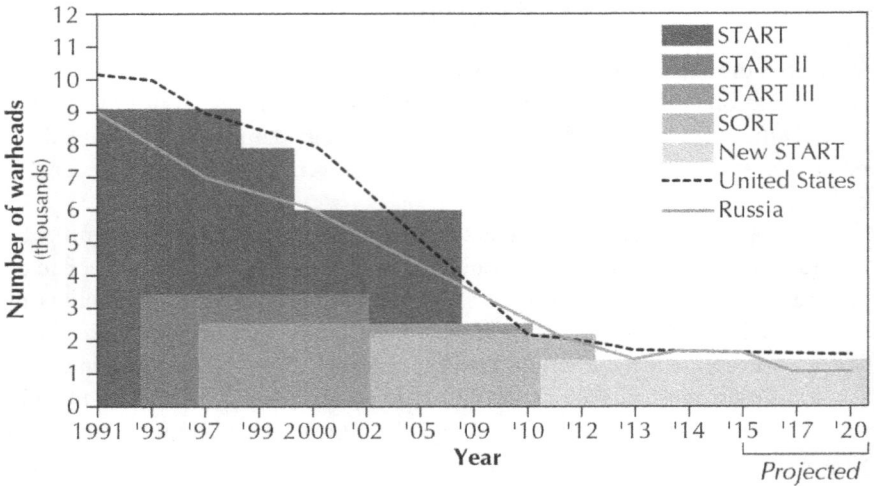

Figure 9.1. The reduction of U.S. and Russian strategic nuclear forces. START = Strategic Arms Reduction Treaty; SORT = Strategic Offensive Reductions Treaty. *Source*: Alexei Arbatov, "An Unnoticed Crisis: The End of History for Nuclear Arms Control?" June 15, 2015, at http://carnegie.ru/2015/06/16/unnoticed-crisis-end-of-history-for-nuclear-arms-control/ians?mkt_tok=3RkMMJWWfF9wsRojvKXPZKXonjHpfsX57u 8kXqOg38431UFwdcjKPmjr1YYFT8R0aPyQAgobGp5I5FEIQ7XYTLB2t60MWA%3 D%3D (accessed 6/23/2015).

with an intermediate range and a sort of ICBM whose range would fall within INF limits. For its part, the Pentagon was considering a submarine-launched intermediate-range missile armed with conventional explosives—part of a Prompt Global Strike mission to hit any target anywhere within one hour.

A leading Russian analyst in 2015 charted the progress made in arms control (see figure 9.1). Regardless of the ups and downs of U.S.-Russian relations, the arsenals of each side had declined for decades.

The skeptics are correct: neither individuals nor governments act like angels. Many make and observe contracts that serve their interests but then cheat or renege as their interests change. Still, wise planners do not allow the perfect to act as enemy of the good. World security and world health are on a stronger footing thanks to arms control. Antarctica has not been militarized; nuclear testing in the atmosphere has stopped; few states have acquired nuclear weapons since the nuclear nonproliferation treaty entered force in 1970, and several have abandoned their nuclear weapon programs. The DPRK, however, joined the NPT and later withdrew—the only state to do so. On occasion Pyongyang has invited and then expelled international inspectors.

Arms control negotiations became a channel for communication and confidence building between Moscow and the West regardless of the rise and fall of détente. Arms deliberations became one of the many shared concerns linking Moscow and Washington—a web that included human rights. Security interests meshed with human rights at the Conference on Security and Cooperation in Europe (CSCE) in 1974–1975. The CSCE brought together the United States, Canada, the USSR, and all European countries except Albania. Its Final Act, signed in Helsinki by thirty-five states in 1975, registered agreement on three "baskets" of interrelated issues—(1) political-military security; (2) cooperation in economics, science, and technology; and (3) human rights—including freedom of emigration, freedom of thought and conscience, and self-determination of peoples. A fourth basket formalized plans for follow-up meetings and implementation. Soviet leader Leonid Brezhnev hoped the Final Act would solidify the Soviet empire. Instead, the ensuing "Helsinki Process" authorized nongovernmental movements to monitor human rights observance, which helped to weaken Communist regimes. The process led to establishment of the Organization for Security and Cooperation in Europe (OSCE), which took an active role in mediating and monitoring conflicts across borders, as between Armenia and Azerbaijan. However, the OSCE had no army, and its observers were turned away by Russian troops when they sought to investigate Russia's efforts to absorb Crimea in 2014. Thus, an institution that had served both security and human rights for many decades proved less than perfect when put to an extreme test, as "Weimar Russia" behaved increasingly like Nazi Russia.[11]

Was the glass half empty or half full? Arms negotiations with Russia did not produce what Dr. Pangloss termed the best of all possible worlds, but they did foster conditions better than might otherwise have existed. As in Thomas Hobbes's state of nature, fear of death led actors to curtail their reliance on self-help. The fact that leaders in Moscow and Washington believed that each side feared a nuclear exchange reduced chances of a panicked response to an unfamiliar object speeding across a radar screen.[12] The Kremlin continued to harass and lock up dissidents, but Moscow's realm experienced a trend toward greater freedom. The trend owed much to improving communications technology but was also spurred by human interaction at all levels.[13]

Despite positive movement toward greater freedom in Russia in the late twentieth century, the trend was strangled by Vladimir Putin starting in 1999. Journalists and others who challenged Putin and his policies were killed or jailed. Kremlin controls over TV and Internet communication steadily tightened. Government propaganda switched from portraying the United States as a constructive partner to an imperialistic ogre. In 2014–2015 cooperation between Washington and Moscow on arms control and other issues skidded to a halt.[14] Some analysts, myself included, concluded that Putin should be indicted and tried before the International Criminal Court for genocide, war crimes, and crimes against humanity.[15]

Russian and Russian-backed forces annexed Crimea and tried to tear away eastern Ukraine. They shot down a Malaysian airliner and carried out extrajudicial executions of opponents. A single Russian leader, backed by other hard-liners, reversed the synergistic movement toward peace, economic and political freedom, and human rights. Should Washington try to negotiate with such a leader, contain his expansion, or seek to destroy his regime?[16]

Russia's efforts to tear away Crimea and other portions of Ukraine illustrated the Janus-face of arms control. Supporters of arms control praised Russia and the United States for persuading Ukraine, Belarus, and Kazakhstan to disgorge their nuclear weapons in the early 1990s. Thus, in January 1994 presidents Clinton, Boris Yeltsin, and Leonid Kravchuk of Ukraine agreed that all nuclear weapons on Ukrainian soil would be returned to Russia. In an imaginative swap, the highly enriched uranium from the warheads would be blended down to low enriched uranium, fabricated into fuel rods, and returned to Kyiv for use in its nuclear power plant to produce electricity. In 2012 Ukraine's president, Viktor Yanukovych (deposed in February 2014), announced that Ukraine had finally eliminated its fifteen nuclear weapons' worth of nuclear weapons material. Reviewing these developments, former Pentagon official Graham Allison recorded what he saw as "Good News from Ukraine: It Doesn't Have Nukes."[17] Whatever happened there, Ukrainian actions could not trigger a nuclear war. Some Ukrainians, however, took a different view. They said that if Kyiv had retained its nuclear weapons, then Putin would never have dared to attack Ukraine. Russia in 2014 violated the December 1994 pledge by Washington and Moscow to respect the political independence and territorial integrity of Ukraine. Left to its own devices by the United States and the rest of NATO, Ukraine had limited means to repulse or evict the invaders.

Pyongyang could only infer that Ukraine—like Libya—had been foolish to surrender its nuclear capability in exchange for empty promises. From a human rights or international law perspective, Ukraine's increased vulnerability to Russian pressure was a negative. Still, if U.S. policy aimed at reducing the chances of a nuclear Armageddon, denuclearization of Ukraine, Belarus, and Kazakhstan was movement in the right direction. And while southeastern Ukraine remained a virtual war zone in 2014-2015, most Ukrainians enjoyed more democratic freedoms than in previous times. Had a nuclear exchange taken place, many if not most would have perished.

Should Washington Fear to Negotiate?

Like Soviet leaders in the Cold War, authorities in Pyongyang often expressed their willingness to engage with the United States. If security and human rights had advanced on parallel tracks in U.S.-Russian relations, could they not progress in a similar way in Northeast Asia?

Given these patterns, what advice would Solzhenitsyn and Sakharov proffer? Solzhenitsyn would probably argue against security talks with a regime accused of crimes against its own people. Instead, he would favor efforts to overthrow the DPRK dictatorship. Sakharov, though quite critical in his 1968 memorandum on Mao Zedong's radical policies, would probably favor arms talks with Pyongyang.[18] Not only would U.S.-DPRK negotiations offer some hope of containing the arms race, but they could also contribute to a climate in which North Koreans would enjoy more openness and freedom, as happened in the Soviet Union.

A stark ethical dilemma emerged: Should outsiders do everything possible to avoid a potential holocaust? Or do whatever they can to exterminate a clear and present evil? *The U.S. experience with the Soviet Union suggested that ways could be found to buttress peace and human rights at the same time.*

North Korea was less threatening to outsiders but intrinsically more evil than what President Reagan called Moscow's "evil empire." Even with some nuclear warheads, the DPRK was far less menacing than the Soviet Union when John F. Kennedy took office. Facing a Kremlin that still crushed dissent and boasted of producing missiles "like sausages," Kennedy in January 1961 addressed "those nations who would make themselves our adversary." He called on both sides to "begin anew the quest for peace, before the dark powers of destruction unleashed by science engulf all humanity in planned or accidental self-destruction." He denied that "civility" meant weakness and cautioned that "sincerity is always subject to proof." Kennedy's bottom line: "Let us never negotiate out of fear, but let us never fear to negotiate." He urged that "both sides explore what problems unite us instead of belaboring those problems which divide us." He called on both sides to "formulate serious and precise proposals for the inspection and control of arms, and bring the absolute power to destroy other nations under the absolute control of all nations."

Not fearing to negotiate, Kennedy and other presidents after him defused many conflicts with Moscow. Similarly, Richard M. Nixon and Jimmy Carter normalized relations with Beijing. If the United States could negotiate not just a modus vivendi but a many-sided cooperative relationship with two giant, one-party adversaries, could it not do the same with the DPRK? No U.S. president would choose to bargain from weakness, but surely the United States was never weak relative to North Korea.[19] When Pyongyang's leaders call for negotiations, they might be bluffing. To test their intentions and possibilities, a long, persistent stretch of give-and-take dialogue would be needed. Given the problems besetting the DPRK across three generations, some willingness to compromise might emerge. Why not explore and promote this possibility?

10

Why Is North Korea
Not the South?

A glance at the day's news could push any thoughtful person to believe in chaos theory. To grasp global politics is like trying to measure how a butterfly's flight in Kansas will affect winds in Mongolia. But complexity scientists do try to make sense from apparent chaos. Nurtured by physicists, economists, biologists, and anthropologists at the Santa Fe Institute and several other research centers, complexity science looks for and claims to find patterns in the ebb and flow of life in all spheres. Enlarging Darwin's view of evolution, biologist Stuart Kauffman and other complexity scientists analyze the factors that shape the fitness of organisms and entire species.[1] But Kauffman also urges intellectual humility. The Newtonian paradigm that has reigned in science for three centuries, Kauffman says, does not apply to biological evolution and human relations. No prestatable laws entail the becoming of the biosphere. Still less do they exist and operate in economic, legal, social, or cultural systems. The adjacent possibles in an expanding universe open the way to emerging developments that are hard to understand, much less predict. Enablement—not entailing causal laws—explains the evolution of world affairs.[2] Let us adapt these perspectives to compare the fitness of North and South Korea.[3]

What Is Fitness? How Can It Be Measured?

Fitness is the capacity to cope with complex challenges and opportunities so as to enhance one's own survival and other interests. Fitness is not the same as resilience—the ability to buffer change. Resilience connotes a defensive stance, while fitness suggests an ability not only to withstand pressure but also the capacity to create values and alter the environment. The concept of fitness offers a framework for understanding how to enhance adaptive and creative capacities in a complex world of rapid transformations.

160

For nonhumans, fitness can be measured by reproductive health and survival. For humans, the criteria are far more nuanced. Material markers, such as the growth of population, the expansion of territory, and the growth of GDP, do not adequately measure societal fitness. The United Nations Human Development Index (HDI) is probably the best single measure of societal fitness. It evaluates the conditions that enhance human *choice*. The HDI measures health (life expectancy) and education (years of schooling) as well as command over resources (income per capita). To get a fuller picture of fitness we can draw on other measures, such as the Social Progress Index, which adds "opportunity" to other indicators; the Bertelsmann Transformation Index, which evaluates free choice in political as well as economic life; the civil and political freedom measures of Freedom House; the Economic Freedom Index of the Heritage Foundation; and the Corruption Perceptions Index of Transparency International, which measures another dimension of human development—honesty; and gauges of happiness.

By 2014 the ROK ranked fifteenth of 187 countries on the HDI (having risen rapidly from twenty-sixth in 2007).[4] Given the lack of reliable data, the HDI did not rank North Korea. Its meager GDP and poor health statistics would push the DPRK toward the bottom, though its extensive school enrollment would raise the North's aggregate score. The UN Development Programme offered no data on the DPRK except to note that life expectancy at birth in the North was seventy—nearly eleven years lower than in the South.

In 2014 South Korea's life expectancy at birth was 80.5; its mean years of schooling, 11.8, and expected years of schooling, 17.0; gross national income per capita, $30,345. South Korea's rank on gender equality was seventeenth from the top (Slovenia was number one). South Korea's rank was much higher than that of Japan (twenty-fifth) and the United States (forty-seventh!). The major difference was in maternal mortality: In the ROK there were 16 deaths of mothers per 100,000 live births compared with 21 in the United States.

South Korea's HDI numbers rose rapidly in the late twentieth century. The country's absolute score in 1980 was 0.634—far below the Organization of Economic Cooperation and Development (OECD) average then of 0.749. But the ROK narrowed the gap with the OECD in 1990 and 2000 and finally scored higher than the OECD average in 2005 (0.866 versus 0.860). By 2011 the gap was still larger (ROK, 0.897, versus OECD, 0.873). If income were omitted (thus giving more weight to health and education), the country's HDI score in 2013 increased from 0.909 to 0.949. Like the other advanced industrial countries, the ROK advanced more slowly in the early twenty-first century.

The downside: South Korea's rapid rise economically left many of its citizens behind. Income inequality in the ROK was greater even than in the United States. South Korea placed twenty-eighth from the most equal score on the inequality-adjusted HDI in 2011 while the United States placed twenty-third. Seniors in the ROK were the most destitute of any rich country. Half lived in poverty; many were deserted by their offspring despite traditions of filial piety. Despite occasional government promises, pensions and welfare benefits remained meager. Some elderly chose to work as parking attendants; others, as prostitutes. The suicide rate among South Korea's elderly rose five times from 1990 to 2011. It was four times higher than the rich-country average; more than double the rate in Japan; and probably 25 percent higher than in China.[5] The chimera of rapid development pressed many South Koreans to risk personal happiness by taking on the burdens of mounting debt.[6]

The World Economic Forum ranked South Korea the nineteenth most competitive of 144 countries in 2012–2013—behind Switzerland, ranked first; Singapore, second; the United States, seventh (down from first a few years before); Hong Kong, ninth; Japan, tenth; and Taiwan, thirteenth. But the ROK ranked well ahead of three of its neighbors: China (twenty-ninth); Russia (sixty-seventh); and Mongolia (ninety-third). North Korea was not listed.[7]

Freedom House ranked the DPRK as one of the least free societies in the world. The South's relative fitness resulted in part from freedom in many spheres. Freedom House gave the ROK a 1 for political rights and a 2 for civil liberties.

The Social Progress Index (SPI) for 2014 gave South Korea a lower rank than the HDI, finding it twenty-eighth in the world. This index used many indicators to evaluate a society's ability to meet the basic human needs of its citizens, establish the building blocks that allow citizens and communities to enhance and sustain the quality of their lives, and create the conditions for all individuals to reach their full potential. The SPI placed New Zealand and Switzerland 1st and 2nd; Japan, 14th; the United States, 16th; Russia, 18th; China, 19th; and, at the bottom, Chad, 132nd. The ROK ranked high on many indicators, but relatively low in access to higher education, tolerance, individual opportunity, personal rights, and number of employees in environmentally sustainable occupations. North Korea was not ranked, but would probably rank lower than China and closer to Chad.[8]

The Bertelsmann Foundation Transformation Index (BTI) evaluates political as well as economic development in developing and transitional countries. In 2012 it put North Korea at 125th of 128 countries, with Somalia at the bottom. South Korea ranked eleventh on his list, behind the Czech Republic (first), and Taiwan (second), but ahead of Singapore (twenty-ninth), Russia (sixtieth), and China (eighty-fourth). South Korea did better on economic indicators (seventh) than on political (twelfth). The measures employed are summed up in figure 10.1.[9] It shows that the web of fitness in the South reached wide, while the North appeared strong only in "stateness," an asset that could prove shallow and feeble.

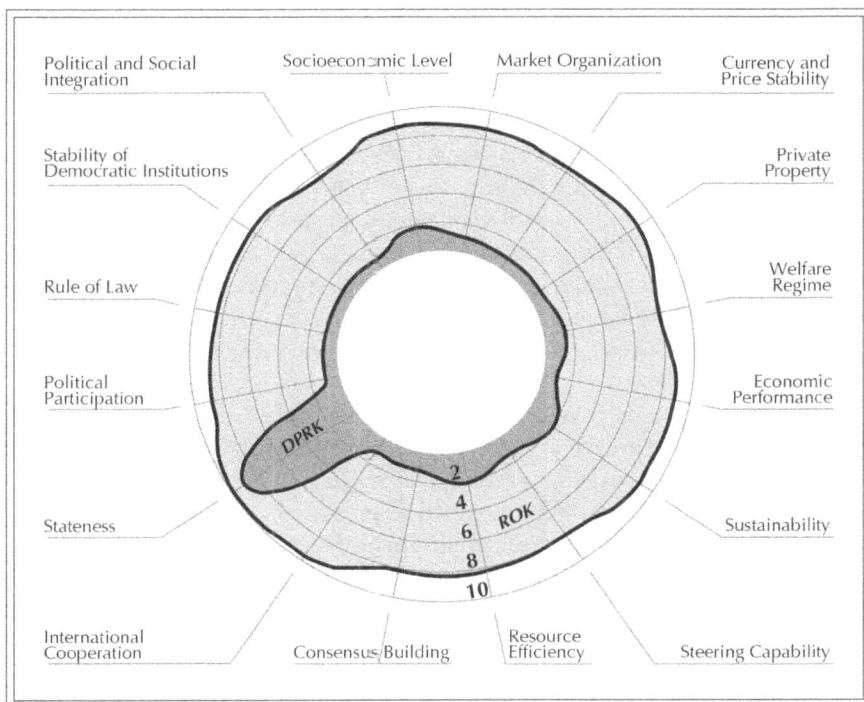

Figure 10.1. North Korea compared to South Korea, as measured in the Bertelsmann Transformation Index: http://www.bti-project.org/country-reports/aso/ (accessed 2/27/2013). The North's scores close to 1 on the inner circle are the lowest possible; the South's scores close to 10 on the outer circle are the highest possible.

How to Achieve Fitness: The Role of Self-Organization

Complexity science notes three ways to promote and maintain fitness. First, *natural selection*. Small-scale genetic mutations and recombinations help some individuals and, in time, larger groupings to adapt, survive, and multiply in their ever-changing environment. Some players coalesce for shared purposes—for example, the tendency of states worried about the rise of China's and North Korea's nuclear tests to gravitate toward Washington.

Second, *historical contingency*. Evolution, for complexity science, is too narrow a concept to explain fitness. We need rather to think in terms of *coevolution*—the ways that organisms, species, and societies interact with one another *and* with their ever-changing environment. Adaptation depends on basic resources and ingenuity (smart power), but also on contingency. Thus, the Soviets backed Kim Il Sung to lead North Korea after their first choice, Cho Man Sik, a sixty-two-year-old Presbyterian lawyer famous for defying Japan, refused to be a Soviet puppet and turned down the job.[10] (For more on the role of contingency in Korea, see chapter 18.)

Third, *self-organization*—the capacity by members of a group to cooperate for shared goals without top-down commands. Complexity science holds that fitness will not be found in a rigid order or in its polar opposite, anarchy. Fitness incubates somewhere between these extremes, but grows best close to the edge of chaos—just short of the precipice. The key is self-organization in all spheres. Fitness requires more than the formalities of democracy, such as free elections. It needs the spirit and practice of cooperation for mutual gain in many domains—political, economic, social, cultural, and scientific. These, in turn, depend on trust and mutual respect.

Fitness taps the creative and cooperative energies of a society—a family, a business, a country, a system of states, or a network of nonstate actors. A fit society will encourage cooperation to create shared values and not pillage resources for private gain. Value creation will strengthen societal fitness in a virtuous circle. This process can be obstructed or even derailed by bad guys who try to exploit system vulnerabilities for unilateral advantage. The upshot is that smart political leaders must mobilize their soft-power assets to encourage cooperation, but be ready with hard-power tools to prevent exploitation and crush aggression.

Self-organization can take place without natural selection or climactic historical events. A coral reef, for example, is a complex adaptive system that provides mutual gain for its inhabitants—corals, polyps, fishes, mollusks, worms, crustaceans, sponges, and other life forms that cohabitate in positive symbiosis. Even closer integration is practiced by ants and termites as they build their nests, feed, and procreate. Humans can think and plan what kind of order to pursue, but they often coordinate their actions with no discussion or commands from above.

Self-organization often gives rise to power laws in social systems because of "preferential attachment"—the principle that, in a network, a node with more connections is likely to attract more connections in the future. This explains why the rich get richer. But it also helps account for the spread of Psy's "Gangnam Style" music and dance from South Korea to diverse settings and applications across the globe.[11]

The ways that self-organization can conduce to freedom, creativity, and fitness in every realm are outlined in table 10.1.

Self-organization does not exist in a pure form anywhere in the world, except perhaps among tribal groups in remote jungles or mountains.[12] The need for specialization and the emergence of inequality inexorably push for some forms of hierarchy. Even the "land of the free" United States could not have developed as it did without government-supported land grants, transportation systems, schools and colleges, and research programs. Neither Boeing nor its rival Airbus could

Political condition	Anarchy	Top-down rule	Self-organized polity
Stability/instability	Unstable chaos	Rigid but fragile stability	Dynamic equilibrium near the edge of chaos
Outlook	Zero-sum	Zero-sum	Variable-sum, but seeks mutual gain
Value orientation	Self-help value-claiming	Self-help value-claiming	Create values to expand the pie
Legal climate	Law of the jungle	Diktat	Impartial justice
Social consequences	War of all vs all fostering demands for top-down rule	Repression with risk of insurgency	Consensual democracy
Creativity	No art, technology, or science	Limited art, technology, and science	Innovation in art, technology, and science
Wealth and income	General poverty with a few pockets of wealth	Some wealth, but with great inequality	High incomes with relative equality
Human Development Index	Very low rank (e.g., Somalia)	Low to medium rank (e.g., Russia)	High rank (e.g., Norway)
Fitness	Unfit: no collective capacity to cope with challenges and opportunities	Unfit: little capacity to cope with challenges and opportunities	Fit: strong capacity to cope with challenges and opportunities
Role in world affairs	Negative and destabilizing	An obstacle to development and danger to peace	Positive

Table 10.1. Alternative Scenarios Posited by Complexity Science

take off and stay aloft without massive government subventions. Still, some modern societies practice self-organization in many domains while others experience totalitarian dictatorship.

Authoritarian Ways versus Fitness in South and North Korea

Complexity science explains that North Korea ranks low on societal fitness indicators because its top-down system has stifled creativity, enterprise, cooperation, and even hard work. At first glance the high fitness achieved in the South appears to have arisen without much self-organization. The society's political and economic development took place under strong authoritarian rule from 1945 until the early 1980s.

Many South Koreans respected President Syngman Rhee because of his age, status, and nationalist credentials; but complaints about a rigged election forced him to resign in 1960. His successor, Yun Bo-Seon, was soon deposed by Park Chung Hee, a military officer who seized power in 1961. Park Chung Hee had served in the Japanese army in 1944–1945. He became a general in the ROK army during the Korean War and then trained in the United States for six months. He was elected president three times, only to be assassinated by his own intelligence chief in 1979.

Following Park's murder, Prime Minister Choi Kyu Hah became acting president. He promised democratic elections and a new constitution to replace the authoritarian *Yushin* constitution. Choi was elected president in late 1979, but soon lost control of the government to Major General Chun Doo Hwan, who staged a coup d'état in early 1980 and declared martial law. Following the massacre of hundreds in the Gwangju Democratic Movement in May 1980, Choi resigned. Chun was then elected president in September 1980 and served until 1988. In late 1987 Chun's colleague, General Roh Tae Woo, won the country's first free presidential election. In 1993, Roh's successor, Kim Young Sam, led an anticorruption campaign that saw Roh and Chun Doo Hwan tried and found guilty for their roles in the 1979 coup and the 1980 Gwangju massacre. Both were pardoned by President Kim Young Sam and released from prison in December 1997.

Liberals again won the presidency with the election of longtime dissident Kim Dae Jung in 1998, followed by that of self-educated human rights lawyer Rho Moo Hyn in 2003. Roh complained in 2004, "We are still unable to rid ourselves of the historic aberration that the families of those who fought for the independence of the nation were destined to face impoverishment for three generations, while the families of those who sided with Imperial Japan have enjoyed success for three generations."[13] Conservative leader Lee Myung Bak won the presidency in 2008, however, and Roh—indicted for financial crimes—jumped off a cliff in 2009. Park Chung Hee's daughter, Park Geun Hye, won the presidency in 2012.

The South's GDP began its rapid advance under Park Chung Hee's dictatorship.[14] Looking beneath the surface, however, we find that self-organization in South Korea began with land reforms that were launched by U.S. military authorities in 1948 and continued by President Rhee even during the Korean War.[15] These reforms, like those in Japan and Taiwan, helped South Korea begin its transition from a limited-access to an open-access society in the political as well as the economic sphere. The reforms reduced disparities in wealth and generated private funds for educating a new generation of civil servants and entrepreneurs. They enabled a democratic student revolution in 1960 that demanded an end to corruption and to the Rhee presidency.

Threats from the North and competition with the DPRK helped to limit extreme forms of rent seeking and corruption in South Korea. Land reform opened access to economic opportunities and facilitated a state monopoly of violence critical to later economic and political development. It also contributed to expanding education and establishing meritocratic and autonomous bureaucracy.[16]

The "developmental state" of Park Chung Hee was organized from the top down to promote industrial development. Even under Park's dictatorship, however, self-organization emerged at a grassroots level. The Planned Parenthood Federation of Korea began in the 1960s to organize "Mothers' Clubs" to promote family planning and community development. Following trends in civil society, the ROK government in the 1970s launched the "New Village Movement" to mobilize human and material resources. The movement was the result of a desire by farmers to overcome poverty and the government's effort to respond to that desire. One observer noted, "The government provided villages with free cement and evaluated their infrastructure improvement projects. The rural population gained experience and confidence through building and improving basic infrastructure in this initial period, and increased agricultural productivity."[17] The relatively open-access economy not only brought about rapid and sustained economic growth but also created increasing pressures for a more open politics that led, over time, to the democratic transition of the late 1980s.

Resistance to authoritarian rule peaked in the May 18, 1980, democratic uprising in Kwangju, hometown of future ROK president Kim Dae Jung. Responding to the declaration of martial law by General Chun Doo Hwan, demonstrators declared Kwangu independent of the military regime. When thousands joined the protests and local police lost control, Chun Doo Hwan ordered a paratrooper brigade to restore governmental control. The ensuing bloodbath killed hundreds of demonstrators and led to an upsurge in anti-Americanism as protestors blamed the United States for siding with a regime that imposed order.[18] The Chun Doo Hwan administration blamed Kim Dae Jung as well as Communists for fomenting the disorder. Kim Dae Jung was condemned to death but was later allowed to go into exile in the United States, where he served on the Harvard faculty for several years.

The paroxysm of violence bolstered movement toward self-organization. Laws passed in the mid-1990s required that the government not lay the first brick on a new construction project without consulting everyone affected. Responding to popular protests, the Ministry of Construction and President Kim Young Sam canceled a proposed dam at Youngwol. By the late 1990s and early twenty-first century labor unions became more powerful and women's rights achieved greater respect. The 1997 financial crisis was a critical point at which Korea could have reverted back to a limited-access order. But the ROK weathered the 1997 storm and went on to become an open-access society where democratic rule became the norm.

Still, family-owned business conglomerates—*chaebols* (a term that combines the words for "wealth" and for "clan") remained the key actors in South Korea's economic life, exerting great influence over politics. The Samsung Group in 2007 had revenues comparable to Malaysia's GDP; Hyundai, to New Zealand's.[19] For South Korea, as for all the Asian "dragons" and "tigers," the term "self-organization" must be understood as the collaboration of private sector elites with government officials and agencies to advance their own personal and institutional interests, with trickle-down benefits for the rest of the country—leaving pockets of poverty.

The model for such collaboration was set by the lower- and middle-ranking samurais who installed the Meiji emperor as the figurehead for Japanese unity in 1866. Theirs was more than a palace coup, for the agents of change in Japan pushed through educational reforms that quickly achieved universal literacy and military reforms, including universal conscription. A dynamic system of economic collaboration emerged, the *zaibatsu*, a set of companies with interlocking business relationships and shareholdings. The member firms owned shares in each other's companies, centered on a core bank, thus insulating each entity from stock market fluctuations and takeover attempts, thereby enabling long-term planning in innovative projects. The U.S. occupation authorities decided in 1945–1946 to abolish these networks, but soon opted to revive them in in a less vertically integrated form, known as *keiretsu*, to make Japan a strong partner against Communism. American-sponsored land reforms also helped integrate Japanese farmers in the body politic.

Arrangements similar to the keiretsu emerged in Singapore, Taiwan, South Korea, and—with deep differences—in Communist China after 1979. While South Korea's chaebols were modeled after Japanese groups, the Park Chung Hee regime gave the ROK's conglomerates more direct funding and controlled them more tightly than happened in Japan.[20] Conglomerates in Japan and South Korea in time became publicly owned companies, but the founding families of Samsung and Hyundai kept more control over these businesses than did their Japanese counterparts.

Still, the differences between the ROK (and Japanese) systems and North Korean practice remained profound. The DPRK system was, and remains, similar to that of the Stalinist USSR. All productive enterprises are owned and controlled by the state and run by government employees. The government came to tolerate some private trading and black market activities, but the political elite kept a tight fist on the economy and other aspects of life.

A lingering feature of authoritarian rule in the South was the continuing influence of the intelligence apparatus in civil institutions, including political parties, the legislature, ministries, and media firms. Critics said that maneuvers by ROK intelligence agencies helped Park Geun Hye prevail in the 2012 elections. Also, politicization of the agencies reduced their ability to provide objective assessments of external threats to ROK security. What they said and did, for example, in the realm of cyber warfare amounted to creating their own foreign policy.[21]

The Costs of Corruption

Partnerships between economic and political elites generate risks as well as advantages. They can inhibit as well as stimulate innovation. If "one hand washes the other," then one hand can also dirty the other. Some leaders of the largest South Korean chaebol, Hyundai, welcomed ROK president Kim Dae Jung's effort to meet DPRK leader Kim Jung Il in 2000. Pragmatic interests as well as ideals motivated Hyundai officials, for they hoped that better ties with Pyongyang might help Hyundai to employ North Korean workers at low wages. Kim Dae Jung received the Nobel Peace Prize in 2000 for his "Sunshine Policy," but a major scandal soon erupted. Investigations revealed that the Hyundai Asan Corporation had given half a million dollars to the North just before the summit, an act that many South Koreans saw as a bribe. Apparently in response to the scandal, the head of Hyundai Asan, the fifth son of Hyundai founder Chung Ju Yung, committed suicide in 2003. At the request of the ROK National Assembly, an independent counsel was established to investigate the alleged payoff. Kim Dae Jung's chief of staff, Park Jie Won, who served as culture minister in 2000, was found to have taken $12.6 million from Hyundai in April 2000. But after the first seventy-day stage of the investigation, ROK president Roh Moo Hyun rejected a request by the independent counsel to prolong the probe to uncover still other facts. In 2009 Roh Moo Hyun, by then retired, also committed suicide after he as well as his associates and family members were themselves accused of seeking and taking bribes.

Interlocking business and political associations can abet corruption, sloppy construction, and supervision.[22] While South Korea climbed ever higher on many measures of human development, its rating for honesty improved but remained low. The Corruption Perceptions Index of Transparency International in 2015 ranked South Korea 43rd from the top in its list of honest countries in the world— up by ten places since 2013. To be sure, North Korea ranked much lower—tied with Somalia at the bottom, 174th.[23] However, the ROK did better on some measures of transparency. On financial secrecy, for example, it ranked twenty-eighth in 2013, much higher than on corruption and bribery.

More revelations of corruption surfaced as the presidency of Lee Myung Bak came to an end in 2012. His elder brother, Lee Sang Deuk, was arrested in July 2012, accused of accepting more than half a million dollars in bribes to help two banks avoid a government audit. Lee Sang Deuk had earlier served six terms as a parliamentarian and had been vice speaker of the National Assembly. He had enjoyed an unofficial role as kingmaker and a great problem solver. Prosecutors said the bankers had paid Lee to stop government regulators from shutting their savings banks down for lax oversight and capital shortages. The bankers were themselves charged with embezzlement and bribery, and their banks' operations suspended. Responding to the scandal, Kim Geo-sung, chairperson of Transparency International Korea, stated that the ROK needed to develop more effective "ethics and anti-corruption awareness education programs" and build a culture in which citizens naturally feel a sense of social responsibility.

The revelations in 2012 undercut any influence the sitting president might have enjoyed in nominating his successor. The woman whom Lee Myung Bak defeated when contending for the party's nomination in 2007, Park Geun Hye, won its backing in 2012 and went on to win the presidency in the December election. Her biggest problem, said a *Korea Times* commentator, did not arise from the economy or foreign affairs. Her worst enemy was widespread skepticism that she would serve the people—not the elites. Park's predecessor, Lee Myung Bak, achieved a great deal, but he ignored advice from his own experts and scoffed at signs that his associates were corrupt. Before him, the late President Roh Moo Hyun called his administration a "participatory government" but failed to broaden a support base for his initiatives. The *Korea Times* analyst declared, "We don't need a leader we can call a father or mother. That time is gone. We need a peer as leader. We don't need our new president to be an updated version of Park Chung Hee, who had led our 'Miracle on the Han River.'" Instead, Koreans wanted a partnership with their president in which "we are equal stakeholders in national prosperity."[24] Fair or not, such views showed that some thoughtful persons believed that self-organization was still weak in South Korea.

PUNCTUATED EQUILIBRIUM AND CRITICALITY

History usually moves more like a ponderous freighter than a nimble kayak. The life cycle of political and other systems is often characterized by punctuated equilibrium—a pattern of rapid growth, followed by a long plateau, terminated by an often rapid decline or upsurge—sometimes brought about by critical threshold effects. Change may come suddenly like a thief in the night.

Complexity science adapts the theory of criticality to explain such changes. Fitness may increase rapidly but later fall like a sand pile. It gains stature as one grain of sand is added to another. Building on a low base, any inputs (more education, more capital, more labor, better health care) can raise the quality and quantity of societal fitness. At some point, however, a *critical* threshold is reached at which adding just one more burden—like a grain of sand—causes the pile to collapse.

More grains of sand or a "last straw" can make entire systems lurch in a nonlinear fashion into a new-phase space. This concept may help explain the rise and fall of states and empires as well as movements and fashions. The USSR disappeared quickly, not with a bang but a whimper. In the early twenty-first century the United States shifted in just a few years from being a widely respected or feared hyperpower to a country that was widely despised and sometimes ignored. Both the USSR and the United States suffered from many small and large burdens, including the consequences of military and political overreach.

Do the Theories of Punctuated Equilibrium and Criticality Apply to Korea?

Both North and South Korea were devastated by the war that raged in 1950–1953. Starting slowly from a low base, the South's fitness began a rapid ascent in the 1970s and 1980s. Starting in the 1990s, economic growth spurred higher HDI rankings for the ROK. The country's overall fitness continued to rise but began to plateau. It grew at a slower pace and with some setbacks. Complexity science allows that the South's trajectory could persist for some time, but predicts that at some point it will either rise sharply or fall.

Complexity science eschews detailed predictions. It does a good job when explaining past and present trends; it offers some guidance to policymakers, for example, on how to cultivate fitness; but it cannot forecast when South Korea or some other entity will reach the critical threshold that triggers a shift up or down. Looking at the United States, for example, complexity science can track and help explain the rapid descent in American fitness that began in 2000. While mindful of the many enabling factors ("adjacent possibles") that can close or open avenues to further change, the science cannot predict whether human agency and *fortuna* will push the United States down or up.

How does complexity science appraise North Korea's prospects? Clearing away the ruins caused by U.S. bombings, Kim Il Sung's regime in the mid-1950s found remnants of an industrial infrastructure established earlier by Japan in northern Korea, close to the country's mineral riches. Building on this base, which was much stronger than that in the South, the DPRK economy grew faster than the ROK's in the late 1950s and 1960s. But then the North's development plateaued—stagnated—from the 1970s into the first decades of the twenty-first century. Despite the regime's devotion to Juche, the North remained highly dependent on China and Russia for inputs of industrial know-how and machinery, oil, and food. Self-reliance in the North achieved little except where the regime prioritized its drives for nuclear weapon and missile development. Meanwhile, both Beijing and Moscow tried to keep Pyongyang on a short leash. Limited fuel supplies meant that North Korean pilots could train very few hours—a mere twenty per year—in flight relative to those in neighboring countries.[25] Limited fuel supplies made it harder for a would-be defector to reach South Korea or Russia—and more perilous, because ejection seats were disabled in peacetime. Still, the North appeared to maintain a fleet of Ukrainian-made Colt aircraft to ferry two regiments of sniper brigades to attack rear areas in the South.

Will the North's decade-long fitness plateau continue indefinitely? Complexity science says no, but it cannot predict when a sharp change will occur or in what direction. The replacement of a frail and dour demigod by his much younger and more animated son in 2011–2012 encouraged hopes that the new leader would give greater emphasis to raising living standards in the North and cultivate a more cheerful, if not more liberal, atmosphere. Whatever his stage appearances, however, the deeds of Kim Jong Un pointed to a tightening of political controls at home, more hostile rhetoric toward the ROK and the United States, and more displays of WMD prowess.

Kim Jong Un may continue the fitness plateau realized under his father and grandfather. His stand-pat policies did not promise an upward shift in DPRK fitness. At best they helped the regime hold onto power and compelled its subjects to keep their shoulders to the wheel and avoid outward displays of discontent. In the second decade of the twenty-first century the North could repeat portions of the Soviet experience in the 1970s and 1980s: growing WMD assets accompanied by persistent economic and social stagnation; mere lip service to ideology; frequent reliance on food imports; and haphazard efforts to buy, copy, and steal foreign technology. A would-be savior of the Soviet system, Mikhail Gorbachev, appeared in 1985, but his reforms proved too little and too late. The Russian state remained strong after 1991 but the putative superpower disappeared and lost more than half its former citizens and all its foreign subjects. In any event, Kim Jong Un is not another Gorbachev.

As in the former Soviet Union, any serious reforms in the DPRK will court the threat of rising expectations. This peril rises as information about the outside world penetrates Kim Jon Un's polity. Development requires being wired—not only at home but worldwide. Opening to the world, however, risks both regime and state security. Authorities try to tighten censorship but find it difficult to do so effectively. Tight controls can kill the golden goose of global networking, while porous dikes let in waves of information that challenge the regime's raison d'être. China's opening to the world did not dethrone the Communist Party. But China's opening was gradual and closely monitored. Sooner or later, however, more information and freedom may jeopardize top-down rule. Having waited so long to liberalize, North Korea might find it hard to open up without destabilizing the regime.

Andrei Lankov writes that state socialism "is as dead in North Korea as it is in China." The DPRK economy has gradually improved since the 1990s. The number of political prisoners may have halved. The DPRK elites have transformed into a bunch of entrepreneurs and corrupt officials living off kickbacks from genuine entrepreneurs. "Keeping this new elite of entrepreneurs and corrupt officials content has become a major preoccupation for the regime—and a hard one to balance."[26]

FITNESS LANDSCAPES

The fitness peaks of nations can be visualized as a coevolving landscape. Their peaks can rise, plateau, or fall. They can do so in unison or as some rise and others fall. Societal fitness can be measured by absolute and relative standards. A society's life expectancy, for example, can be compared to its own levels in previous years. We can visualize a landscape in which a country's fitness peak rises or falls in terms of its previous levels and in relation to its neighbors'. South Korea's fitness steadily rose for decades while the North's stagnated. Indeed, DPRK fitness relative to South Korea, Japan, and China surely declined. Its rank relative to Russia and Mongolia, however, may have experienced little change, for their HDI scores also plateaued or declined in recent years.

The fitness landscape of East Asia in the twenty-first century showed a series of peaks rising while that of the DPRK declined in absolute and relative terms. The North's leaders plodded along in a sort of Death Valley. They wished to raise their peak, but they valued regime security over public weal. Their situation resembled that of East Germany as well as the USSR in the 1980s, but with some important differences. The case of the German Democratic Republic was especially salient, because East Germany's lack of fitness contrasted sharply with the high fitness achieved by neighboring West Germany—not only much larger but also far more affluent and free. As North Koreans learn more about conditions in South Korea (as well as in China), pent-up pressures for change can only mount. Without a real parliament elected by popular vote, however, the DPRK cannot readily implement the East German model, because the GDR parliament, chosen in a free election in 1990, *voted* to end the East German state and join a unified Germany.[27] From this perspective, a gradual change in North Korea and peaceful union with the South appears less likely than a convulsive end of the road for the system and its ruling dynasty. The critical grain of sand can come from many directions. Several could emerge at the same time—a perfect storm multiplying their corrosive effect.

INTERDEPENDENCE

Complexity science sees all living things as interdependent. The South accepted the reality of global interdependence and managed to join—not castigate or stand apart from—global networks of trade, cooperation, and security. The export-led growth strategy exposed South Korean firms to global competition, which limited collusive rent seeking and promoted both learning and innovation.

The South benefited from global networks but also contributed to their ability to create values for mutual gain. The North, in contrast to the South, glorified autarky. Often scorned and denigrated by its sometime patrons in Moscow and Beijing, Pyongyang went its own way. Making a virtue of necessity, it developed WMD with marginal help from outside. A vicious cycle resulted as DPRK tests of new weaponry elicited widespread condemnation and tighter sanctions. The more that the DPRK did its own thing, the greater became its isolation.

HOW TO INCREASE FITNESS

The single best indicator of societal fitness is HDI rank. To improve human development, societies and governments must broaden and deepen education opportunities; bolster individual and public health; and raise incomes. The ROK made significant progress on the first two goals, but income inequality remained a major challenge—aggravated by worries that any redistribution of wealth would reduce economic dynamism. The DPRK provided many years of public education but vitiated its quality by its system of mind control and by permitting class origin to influence educational opportunities. Low incomes for most North Koreans, along with the deep alienation and mutual distrust experienced by many, conduced to poor public health.[28] Only a sliver of DPRK society enjoyed a high material standard of living and the health quality it permits. There could be no quick remedy for these problems. Radical, if not revolutionary, changes were needed.

Most of the societies that rank in the top twenty places on the HDI share three cultural traits that took root in Europe in the wake of the Protestant Reformation. The young Martin Luther downgraded priestly authority.[29] Equal before God, everyone can and should read and interpret sacred texts for him- or herself. This outlook led to revolutionary demands for mass literacy, free thought, and respect for individual dignity (for both sexes). Protestants led, but most Catholics (with Iberia lagging) eventually followed. Orthodox Christian leaders, however, rejected these demands, while most others—Muslim, Buddhist, Hindu, and animist—ignored or never heard of them.

As noted in chapter 2, missionary and other private schools mushroomed in Korea in the late nineteenth and early twentieth centuries. Greater use of Han'gŭl helped literacy to spread. Free thought and free expression, however, were circumscribed by authorities. Japanese occupiers declared their language the official tongue and suppressed any signs of resistance. Anti-Japanese Koreans based outside the country could use Korean, but they too had to observe the political correctness of their faction. Opportunities for free thought and expression increased in the South after 1945, but U.S. and Korean authorities labored to curb political dissent. Confucian respect for seniority also played a role. When I lectured in Seoul in 1970 I observed that (as in Taipei) only senior professors and white-haired journalists commented or raised questions, while younger professionals and students kept their views to themselves.[30] Not till the 1980s did free thought begin to flourish in South Korea. In the North, however, party-line orthodoxy ruled from 1945 into the twenty-first century. Yes, some innovations appeared under Kim Jong Un. The new leader seemed to approve Mickey Mouse; but if his whims changed, even Mickey could be taboo. A domestic Intranet was accessible for some North Koreans, but the Internet was off limits except for a narrow elite. A Russian blogger complained in 2014 that President Putin was trying to impose North Korean–type controls over Internet access in Russia, where it was already more constrained, he said, than in China.[31]

Respect for individual dignity remained a challenge for South Korea in the twenty-first century. Even with a female president inaugurated in 2013, discrimination against women remained a fact of life. Nor was artistic freedom an absolute. When an international art show opened in Gwangju in 2014, a leading South Korean artist, Hong Sung Dam, was forced to withdraw his painting of President Park as a puppet controlled by her late father. In protest against this intervention, several artists withdrew their works and a few festival officials resigned.[32]

In the North, however, there was little if any respect for any form of human rights. The powerful did what they could and others what they must—discipline and terror sustained by networks of informers and gulags. Corruption—much worse in the North than in the South—helped the top one percent to retain a comfortable lifestyle while most people suffered and many hungered.

Mocking the principle of Juche, Pyongyang relied on outside aid as a crutch, one that permitted the regime to plow precious resources into a large army and weapons development. The irony was painful: development of any kind depends ultimately on self-help, but the Kim dynasty's top-down rule prevented North Koreans from helping themselves and one another.

11

GRIT at Panmunjom?

How to Cope with Conflict

Northeast Asia takes its place in the wider debate about the roles played in world affairs by zero-sum conflict and by cooperation. The frequent volleys of bellicose words and deeds emanating from North Korea raise doubts whether outsiders can reach any accommodation with Pyongyang on issues of high politics, such as weapons and boundaries, or even the "low" politics of trade, environment, and culture. For a fragile if not failing state, nearly everything is high politics—from energy to human rights.

A medley of theories proffers guidance on how to explain conflict behavior and how to resolve conflicts in the region.[1] This chapter focuses on "GRIT"—the strategy of graduated reciprocation in tension-reduction proposed by psychologist Charles E. Osgood. To what extent have the major actors in Northeast Asia attempted some version of GRIT in past decades? Why have their efforts in this direction foundered, or even backfired? Regardless of past experiences, might a strategy of true GRIT ameliorate conflicts today and tomorrow? What can we learn from earlier versions of GRIT practiced by the United States and USSR, as well as the United States and China?

GET TO YES

Getting to Yes by the late Roger Fisher and William Ury offers a road map to negotiating mutually advantageous deals "without giving in."[2] The authors recommended that each side assess and focus on its own deep interests. The wise policymaker will ask, "What is my side's best alternative to a negotiated agreement?" To reach an accord, empathy is essential. Each party needs to understand how the conflict and its possible resolution look from the other's vantage point.

Fisher and Ury disparaged "positional bargaining" because it can obscure the deepest interests of each participant.[3] If interests conflict, then Fisher and Ury recommend "principled negotiation"—an objective examination of the case based on the *principles* at stake. This approach makes sense for a boundary dispute arising from a new curve in a river formerly divided down the middle. But what if each party starts from a very different principle? Can the "getting to yes" approach succeed not just in domestic disputes but also in life-and-death confrontations such as those that take place on and around the Korean peninsula? What if one side presses for political and civil liberties while the other sees order as fundamental? What if one side pursues regime change while the other seeks to keep its existing power and privileges? What if one side seeks to prevent the entry of more powers into the nuclear-weapons club while its opponent demands weapons equality? These questions suggest why the "getting to yes" approach must be heavily qualified if applied to negotiations with North Korea. Still, its basic ideas illuminate why negotiations with Pyongyang have failed when the parties relied on positional bargaining or disagreed on the principles at stake.

Getting to yes can be facilitated if negotiators strive to *create* values (utilities of any kind) useful to each side instead of trying to *claim* them for one side only.[4] Value-claiming is a *distributive* competition for larger shares of a limited supply of goods—for example, water. Value-creating, by contrast, is an *integrative* bargaining process to expand supply. These alternatives generate three approaches to negotiation. Hard-line unilateralists see politics as a zero-sum contest in which one side wins and the other loses. Thus, North and South Korea have long been locked into a struggle to see who will defeat whom—what Russians call *kto kovo*. The opposite approach, win-win, expects positive rewards for all parties. Conditional cooperators try to create values for mutual gain but take precautions lest other actors fail to reciprocate.[5]

Value-creators see most situations as open-ended—as "variable-sum." This means that one or even both sides can lose (as in a nuclear war), but there is also a possibility—though not an inevitability—of joint gains. So they look for ways to expand the pie to generate positive outcomes for each party. Unilateral gains are sometimes possible but are likely to be short-lived, whereas mutual gains are more likely to endure.

Fear of zero-sum outcomes leads players to reply to the other side's tough moves in kind—tit for tat (TFT). Thus, North and South Korea have long sought to match or, better still, outdo each other. When I visited Panmunjom in 1970, the South Koreans had erected an elaborate building to display ROK propaganda exhibits for visitors. Across the dividing line, the North Koreans raised a slightly higher structure—what Americans called the "ice cream parlor." They appeared to best the South.

In the early 1980s the frontline South Korean town Dae-sung dong ("town of liberty"), and the frontline North Korean town Ki-jung dong ("town of peace") engaged in a "flagpole war." The South's flagpole rose from 85 to 98 meters. But then the North raised its pole from 80 to 160 meters. The North's huge flag weighs almost three times as much as the South's. Believing the flag war silly, the South quit the race. But De-sung dong did much better in more practical terms. Only a few hundred people lived in Dae-sung dong, but—heavily subsidized and using clean irrigation water from the DMZ—they became the richest farmers in the ROK. The North's "town of peace" appeared to be occupied only in daytime by persons who seemed to do little except wash its windows.

The dangers and waste of this potentially lethal competition can be seen in rival dams. Two years before the 1988 Summer Olympics were to be held in the ROK, the DPRK began to build its huge Imnam Dam at Geumgang Mountain on a tributary to the Han River not far from the DMZ. Imnam generated much-needed electricity, but it could also flood the South if its waters were released by design or by accident. Fearing a "water bomb" from the North, the South in 1987 began constructing a "Peace Dam" some 35 kilometers downstream also on a tributary of the Han River to contain a potential deluge. The Imnam reservoir could hold 2,620 million tons of water; the Peace Dam reservoir stood empty for years, but could hold a bit more—2,630 million tons.

Large dams can be dangerous, even without war. In 2002, only months before the World Cup finals, cracks appeared in the clumsily built North Korean structure. Soon a wall of muddy water and chunks of ice tumbled from the North. The DPRK repaired the cracks, but South Korea resumed construction of its own dam, completed in 2005 at a cost of $430 million.

In September 2005 North Korea released massive quantities of water from other dams without warning, flooding the South and killing people on both sides of the DMZ.

The Imnam Dam caused other problems. It reduced water inflow in the Han River by 12 percent, threatening the ecosystem and aggravating water shortages in Seoul. Some South Koreans called for shutting the Peace Dam's four sluice gates to fill up a reservoir for drinking water. But this could cause flooding in North Korea. The Peace Dam, like its Northern counterpart, could harm the other side. A value-creating solution would be for the North to release more water to alleviate shortages in the South. This would require a willingness on both sides to create mutual gain. The South provided drinking water to Kaesong for some years, but cut back in early 2015 before North Korea announced it suffered a severe drought.

PRISONER'S DILEMMA, TIT FOR TAT, AND GRIT

Calculating what they see as self-interest, the major players in Northeast Asia are often myopic. They behave like players in a single round of game theory's Prisoner's Dilemma (PD). Accused of a crime and prevented from communicating with each other, each of two players may choose to confess or be silent. If each confesses, both go to jail. If each is silent, both are released. But a player can achieve the very best outcome—freedom plus a reward—if he or she defects and the other remains silent. Here is the dilemma: if each prisoner trusts the other to be silent, both can go free. If both fear the other may confess (defect from the common cause), each will confess and both go to jail. Mutual defection leads to mutual punishment. To minimize loss and maximize potential gain, self-preservation dictates *sauve qui peut*—each player for him- or herself. Having rationally pursued self-interest, however, each player suffers, and loses the possibility of mutual gain. If each prisoner practiced *enlightened* self-interest, each would cooperate with the other and refuse to confess.

The game-theory exercise underscores the twin problems of communication and trust that bedevil all human relations, but the real world differs from PD in several ways. In the game, the two prisoners cannot communicate with each other. Neither can be sure the other will not defect. In the real world, players can usually communicate with each other, if only though muddied and broken channels, and often sending false signals to mask intentions and capabilities. Usually there are more than two players—allies, foes, bystanders—whose responses and actions may shape the "game." Outcomes in world affairs are seldom decided by one round of play. Usually the game goes on. Each round is part of one or more larger games.

If the PD game is reiterated, players can mimic each other's move in a pattern of tit for tat (TFT). This pattern can demand rough justice—an eye for an eye. But TFT can also mean "one good turn deserves another" or "one hand washes the other" for mutual gain. In reiterated rounds of PD, the best strategy for the long run is to follow a "nice" or "generous" version of TFT: if you play first, be nice; afterward, mimic the other side. If your turn comes second, you should mimic the other player but be sure to reciprocate if he or she plays nice. Whether played by humans or by programmed computers, players learn that it pays to cooperate.

If the players embark on a nice version of TFT, the momentum of their words and deeds should take them into positive territory. The problem is that if one side fails to cooperate on every play, positive momentum will not start or will be derailed. The players will then find themselves on a treadmill of mutual defection—as has happened often in U.S.-DPRK relations. North Korean diplomats often called for a version of TFT. They insisted on the principle "a word for a word, an action for an action." The North complained that Washington, after an agreement had been reached, often moved the goalposts. For their part, Americans retorted that Pyongyang ignored the goalposts as well as the ground rules.

To break the momentum of mutual defection, one player must take a unilateral first step toward conciliation—even if the other side has just played tough. To reverse a vicious cycle of escalating tensions, psychologist Charles E. Osgood in 1962 suggested a strategy of graduated reciprocity in tension-reduction, or GRIT.

The initiator of GRIT should announce that it seeks to move step by step toward détente and better relations. The process should begin with several small steps. If they are reciprocated, then larger steps will follow.[6] Still, the initiator risks that its nice moves will be ignored or abused. To guard against this possibility, the first steps toward détente should be limited and reversible. For example, U.S. officials could regularly call the Democratic People's Republic of Korea by its chosen name (as Henry Kissinger did with the People's Republic of China in the early 1970s).[7] The initiator should announce that its moves do not arise from weakness but from a deliberate strategy aimed at shifting from confrontation to cooperation. If the other side reciprocates with nice moves of its own, the process can escalate to more substantive concessions.

GRIT differs from TFT in two ways. The initiator does not mimic the tough steps of the other side but tries to start a process that breaks from mutual defection. If nice initiatives are reciprocated, the initiator's next actions should raise the quality of the interaction, graduating from low-risk, symbolic steps to more substantive moves.

Attempts to do good can backfire. In 1970 a U.S. Army lieutenant in the United Nations Command at Panmunjom told me how he had tried to improve the atmosphere within the quanset hut conference room. Instead of standing stiffly and glaring when a North Korean indicated that he wanted to pass, the American smiled and made way for him. Shortly thereafter, the American found himself surrounded by several North Korean soldiers who began to jostle him. "Knuckle practice" nearly ensued. The North Koreans, it turned out, interpreted the lieutenant's conciliatory gesture as weakness. Reducing tensions in that situation could not begin with gestures initiated by a mere lieutenant. For a stragtegy of peace to work, the U.S. president or head of the UN team would need to announce a new strategy—and make sure that North Korean leaders and troops got the message. Ideally, DPRK authorities would show some willingness to respond in kind.

THEORY VERSUS PRAXIS

Should each party strive to match or outdo tough actions by the other side? While tit for tat can lead to mutual loss, it avoids the catastrophic loss that can happen if one party cooperates and the other defects. The worst-case scenario worried Captain Hans J. Neumann, a U.S. Army officer based at Panmunjom. As he wrote me on August 15, 1970: "I am not willing to risk leaving out a step that *may* not be necessary and find to my woe that it was in fact needed. The Communists can afford to be a bit less defensive because we have shown on a number of occasions that we will not attack first."[8]

Captain Neumann questioned the proposition that tension-reduction should commence with an announcement from on high. He believed it "logical . . . to begin reducing tensions at the level of the men who have daily, even hourly, contact with the opposition." He recalled an occasion when UN and DPRK guards played pool together in the conference area. "The harmony began at the bottom without negotiations and was ended by an order from the leaders who are [allegedly] bargaining for 'peace.'" Not long after the pool game, North Koreans ambushed a U.S. truck and killed four soldiers, shooting each four times in the back of the head. The North Koreans then towed the truck to the conference area and spit on it.

Neumann asked: "Is it unreasonable to expect to be left alone when I do not aggress? [Recently] the North Koreans tried to run over me with a truck . . . forcing me to jump aside at the last second."

Neumann believed in meeting force with force. At a meeting of the two sides at Panmunjom, he recalled, "I was seated on a bench when one of their guards walked in front of me, bumped me with his leg and continued walking. I swung at him with the camera I had in my hand and hit him the rear end. He turned, glared, and walked away mumbling." Neumann stated that UN personnel faced such provocations daily. "Our guards," he maintained, "do not provoke them."

Continuing to assail what he saw as Ivory Tower naïveté, Neumann wrote me again on April 9, 1971. He explained that "the open hatred and *eagerness* to do violence" shown by the North Koreans is a "tremendously shocking eye-opener." Speaking to them is like "talking to a stone wall while being constantly reviled to your face; it is making unilateral moves to reduce tension and being taken advantage of time after time after time; it is abiding by agreements and seeing the oponent break the rules and deny even pictorial evidence."

To ram home his viewpoint, Neumann continued: "On 9 and 12 Oct. 70, the North Koreans, completely unprovoked, attacked 14 of our guards with 30 of their guards and 30 'workers' armed with saws, shovels, and spiked clubs. They knocked one of our guards to the ground and savagely kicked him and chopped at his skull with shovels." He was dragged away, "a bloody mess with deep gashes on his neck and head and a depressed skull fracture. . . . Voila! The result of 18 years of attempting honest negotiations." Neumann said my own writings were irresponsible, destructive, and misleading. GRIT theory, he said, was "completely out of touch with reality."

U.S. Army major Edwin R. Risberg was also dismissive of conflict resolution theorizing. In a four-page letter to me dated November 2, 1970, he stated that "all of our peaceful gestures and proposals thus far have been met with violence. How can the ROK risk any tension-reducing moves when dealing with such a fanatically hostile adversary?" Risberg cited incidents like those mentioned by Captain Neumann, but added another complication—what he called the "Oriental Communist mind." Based on his experiences in Vietnam and Korea, Risberg concluded that, for Oriental Communists, "vice and corruption are a way of life.

A man is a fool if he does not take advantage of and exploit his fellow man. Fear is the greatest motivating factor. Force is the language that is understood best, and to be soft or desire to negotiate is a sign of weakness. To lose face is a terrible disgrace."

Neumann and Risberg would not have been surprised when, on August 18, 1976, some thirty North Koreans attacked and killed two American soldiers as they and a group of South Koreans tried to prune a tree that impaired vision from a UN checkpoint. A few days later UN forces returned in force and completed the task—watched by a bevy of DPRK machine gunners. A U.S. soldier who participated stated that "the world will probably never know just how close we were to World War III during those three days. Everyone in my unit just assumed on the morning of the 21st that we would never see the 22nd. It was a very profound moment in our lives and a time that we will never forget."[9]

Do these real-life experiences prove that theories like GRIT cannot work or that, in some form, they are needed? Surely political actors should try to assess each other realistically and take steps to protect themselves from abuse. But decades of tit-for-tat along the DMZ gained little for either side except preservation of a dangerous and costly status quo.

WHY GRIT IS DIFFICULT

An effort to develop GRIT confronts seven major challenges.

First, which side should make the first move? Osgood argued that the stronger party should do so, because it can better afford to take risks for peace. By this reasoning, the United States should initiate a dialogue with Pyongyang rather than vice versa. The stronger side can better afford to risk concessions, but it may ask, "Why forgo any advantage?" However, the mind-set frame of each actor can prove more decisive than the balance of power. When Mikhail S. Gorbachev launched a GRIT-like strategy toward the Reagan administration in the late 1980s, his side was the weaker—and more desperate for détente.

As we shall see in chapter 15, after the "Leap Day" accord collapsed in 2012, neither Washington nor Pyongyang wanted to take the first step. The United States demanded that the DPRK demonstrate its willingness to demilitarize before six-party talks could resume; Pyongyang, for its part, rejected any preconditions and said that Washington needed to stop its hostile behavior.

Relations between Seoul and Pyongyang in 2012 were also paralyzed by conditionality. The Lee Myung Bak administration would not discuss more food aid unless the North apologized for the *Cheonan* sinking and the Yeonpyeong shelling in 2010. The DPRK, for its part, demanded that Seoul apologize for not having sent an official delegation to the funeral of Kim Jong Il in 2011. Pyongyang also insisted on a withdrawal of sanctions before it would meet with the South. The impasse hurt both North and South. The tourist resort at Mt. Kumgang was closed in 2008 and did not reopen until 2012. Its closing for four years cost Hyundai and the ROK government some $1.6 billion and lowered tax revenues for local governments in Kangwon province by an estimated 12.5 percent. TFT can save face but cost money.

Second, small steps may lead nowhere. To be safe, the initiator usually begins with symbolic gestures. The other side may interpret these as cheap tricks and not reciprocate. Neither side wishes to be fooled.

Third, timing: The initiator may give up on GRIT before the other side absorbs the message and devises an appropriate response. The initiator cannot wait long if domestic critics attack its giveaways.

Fourth, asymmetries: If the parties' assets are asymmetrical, then it may be difficult to achieve balance with a proportional concession. Between a superpower and North Korea, nearly all assets are asymmetrical.

Fifth, the monkey wrench problem. Foes of détente or extraneous events in other realms can throw a monkey wrench into the proceedings that disrupts the process of tension reduction. As we shall see in chapter 14, Vice President Dick Cheney and his adjutants often upset the diplomacy of lead negotiator Christopher Hill even when President George W. Bush sought an accommodation with Pyongyang.[10]

Sixth, politics as usual. Bureaucratic inertia, vested interests, and conflicting priorities can throttle GRIT. Thus, as we also see in chapter 14, the U.S. Treasury in 2005 moved to strangle North Korea's illicit businesses even as Secretary of State Condoleezza Rice and Hill sought an arms accord.

Finally, momentum may be hard to sustain. The first steps toward conciliation may come cheaply, while further moves encounter profound obstacles and greater risks.

Is the strategy of GRIT naïve and infeasible? No. It is a path to reconciliation that can both nourish and draw upon a willingness to create values for each party. This was essentially the path taken by John F. Kennedy and Nikita S. Khrushchev in 1963. The administration of U.S. president Richard M. Nixon used GRIT-like tactics to open a direct dialogue with Beijing in 1971–1972. Worried about a possible rebuff from China, however, Nixon and his national security adviser, Henry Kissinger, kept their overtures to Beijing secret—even from the U.S. secretary of state. They departed from Osgood's recommendation that top leaders announce in advance their effort to change the game. But Zhou Enlai understood Kissinger's nuanced messsages and responded in kind.[11]

It is unlikely that the leaders of the great powers read academic writings about GRIT or "nice" ways to do TFT. Still, Soviet and U.S. leaders groped toward ways to temper mutual distrust and enmity. Khrushchev called for disamament by "mutual example." Short-lived thaws took place in 1955, 1958–1960, 1963–1964,

1968–1969, 1972–1973, and 1979. Not until the the late 1980s, however, did Soviet and U.S. leaders succeed in (nearly) ending the Cold War.

But fake GRIT is also possible. Reacting to signs of U.S.-Chinese détente, leaders of North and South Korea smiled at each other and, following a year of secret talks, issued a communique on July 4, 1972, committing the parties to unification by peaceful means and without external interference. Each side, however, soon showed that it had been trying to deceive and undermine the other. The North claimed a victory for its peace offensive and garnered recognition by several Western countries. ROK president Park Chung Hee explained that putting a hand on the enemy's back is the best way to feel when it may attack. In 1973 both sides gave up all pretense of goodwill. Pyongyang and Seoul terminated their dialogue and stepped up clandestine efforts to develop nuclear weapons.[12] The GRIT-like tactics of each side had not been sincere. Arrogant self-confidence ended up in a zero-sum struggle.[13] In 1974 the North tried to kill the ROK president but managed only to shoot his wife. A second round of secret North–South talks in 1984–1985 yielded some small-scale family reunion visits but ended when the North demanded an end to U.S.-ROK military exercises. As Moscow took up relations with South Korea in the late 1980s, an increasingly confident Blue House in Seoul developed a strategy aimed not at joining with the North but at absorbing it.[14]

The ROK's so-called Sunshine Policy under presidents Kim Dae Jung and Roh Moo Hyun could have been an exemplar of GRIT if it had been reciprocated.[15] From 1998 to 2008 the ROK transferred some $3 billion to the DPRK (more than the $1.9 billion delivered by China in the same period).[16] To be sure, the ROK government dragged its feet on some commitments made by Kim Dae Jung, but North Korean leaders treated both ROK presidents as patsies who could be milked for one-sided concessions. Critics faulted South Korea's leaders for not insisting on reciprocal actions by the North. Ostensibly angered by South Korean rhetoric and by ROK-U.S. military exercises, Pyongyang shut down one of the last vestiges of the Sunshine Policy, the Kaesong Industrial Park, in April 2013, only to have it reopen a few months later.

The aborted North-South détentes of the early 1970s and again in the early 2000s showed that mutual distrust persisted even when direct communication could be facilitated by face-to-face meetings with a shared language. Each side had reason to agree with Hamlet's advice to his sister, "Best safety lies in fear." *Unless each party can be persuaded to work for tension-reduction and mutual gain, neither GRIT nor any other diplomatic technique can succeed.* The very word *détente* is Janus-faced—one could say loaded. In medieval French, *détente* meant the trigger of a crossbow that, when pulled, released an arrow. Starting about 1900 détente began to signify a relaxation of political tensions. How to reduce tensions without letting the arrows fly is a crucial question in diplomacy.

High-Context Diplomacy and the Linton Thesis

Culture—the basic values of a society and its way of life—is a matrix that conditions how policymakers and negotiators perceive the world and respond to signals. Negotiations are heavily shaped by whether participants embody a "low-" or "high-context" approach to negotiations.[17] *Low-context* Americans are said to focus on the bottom line and on legalities with little regard for cultural sensitivities. Most Asians, including Koreans, are said to lean toward a *high-context* style. While Americans often push for an explicit commitment drafted by lawyers, many Asians esteem the total relationship enveloping the negotiation. For Asians, a negotiated deal requires personal bonds between the negotiators. Good rapport helped Henry Kissinger and Zhou Enlai to talk for hours in 1972 as they drafted the Shanghai Communiqué, papering over disagreements on Taiwan and other issues.

An American with vast experience in Korea, Stephen W. Linton, identified the DPRK approach to negotiations as very high context: "From the North Korean perspective, human relations should never be made conditional on something else. Problems should be portrayed as annoying obstacles to what is most important: friendship between the highest levels of leadership. . . . [Attempts] to meet leadership, resolve sensitive issues and conclude agreements, all on a three-day trip to Pyongyang, sends the wrong message." Unlike many Westerners, Koreans do not see impersonal law as the framework for action but rather the personality behind the law. According to Linton, "Proof of interest at the highest level is paramount for giving the negotiating process legitimacy."[18]

What if Linton is correct that Koreans, unlike Westerners, do not see impersonal law as the framework for action? Personal ties might help negotiators reach a deal, but if law counts for so little, how long will the deal last? Linton replies that "what appears to Westerners as 'the rule of law' can look like the 'misrule of law' to North Koreans. They would rather focus on the 'intention' rather than the wording of agreements. . . . Legalistic parsing of documents, accepted as a matter of course by Westerners, can look like insincere 'twisting,' thereby undermining faith in the written word. North Koreans' search for personality behind law is thus a search for constancy—not just emotion."[19]

Linton wrote that "more focus on atmospherics and relationships between principals would go a long way" in negotiating with North Koreans—but only if U.S. officials take these relationships seriously. "Many Koreans note . . . that while Americans are quick to use first names and slap people on the back in a display of friendship, their 'true intentions' are often 'inscrutable,' and they do not seem to take friendship itself that seriously." An apparent "obsession with being 'neutral' and 'fair' . . . can translate as a selfish reluctance to 'stand up for your friend.'"[20]

North Korean leaders have proclaimed their desire to do business at the highest level with the United States. As we shall see in chapter 12, Kim Il Sung proved himself ready to deal when former president Jimmy Carter traveled to Pyongyang in 1994. In October 2000 Number Two in Pyongyang strongly urged Number One in Washington to visit Number One in the DPRK and assured President Clinton that all problems could be resolved. Instead of the president, Secretary of State Madeleine Albright went to Pyongyang in November 2000 and, by the time she departed, thought she achieved an understanding with Kim Jong Il. She urged Clinton to go to North Korea and seal the deal, but it was not consummated as time ran out on his presidency. When former president Clinton finally visited Pyongyang in June 2009, he was greeted warmly, and allowed to bring home two detained American journalists.

Showing himself less dedicated to meeting top leaders than his father, General Kim Jong Un (one year in the job) snubbed Google president Eric Schmidt and former New Mexico governor Bill Richardson, long an interlocutor with the DPRK, when they traveled to Pyongyang in January 2013. The young general showed even less finesse when he suggested to basketball superstar Dennis Rodman that Barack Obama give him a ring sometime. Photos taken at the time showed Schmidt and Richardson looking at a computer in a room so poorly heated that everyone wore heavy coats, while Rodman basked in places warmed for Kim Jong Un's comfort.

A KOREAN WAY OF NEGOTIATING?

Contrary to the high-context thesis, Koreans can be abrasive—not only with adversaries but also with ostensible allies and fellow Koreans. Pyongyang's behavior challenges any view that North Korea's diplomacy arises from a culture that requires a feel-good atmosphere to nurture trust and smooth over differences. As we saw in chapter 6 on Pyongyang's quest for nuclear technology, North Koreans could be callous and grabby when dealing with their ostensible benefactors in the USSR. Even with Western and other foreign donors of humanitarian aid, DPRK officials are often rude and demanding. Christopher Hill's memoir records many positive personal interactions with his Chinese, Japanese, and South Korean colleagues, while his many encounters with DPRK diplomats were generally formal and businesslike.[21]

Experience shows that when Koreans negotiate, whether from the South or the North, they are often tough. Thus, one experienced U.S. diplomat pictured Koreans as "very direct and tough people." When South Koreans tried to open negotiations with Chinese representatives in Hong Kong in the early 1980s, "they made quite a hash of this. They tended to demand things up front, and to use very blunt and insulting bargaining techniques, and to misunderstand the difference between things that needed to be done with a wink and a shrug and things that could be done explicitly. And so they were getting nowhere."[22]

The legacy of Confucianism may also shape Koreans' negotiating behavior. Koreans are taught to show respect to elders. They believe that deference to superiors is proper, but they also expect that it may bring rewards. Elders are expected to take care of younger persons who, in time, will return the favor. But while it may be virtuous for a younger brother to give way to his older brother, or a wife to her husband, it could be wrong for a business or government agent to make a concession to another firm or country, because a concession might imply recognition of the other's superior standing. Accordingly, North Koreans often object to any sign of unequal treatment in negotiations with South Korea. Since the United States is so large and powerful, however, North Koreans may be more inclined to respect its authority, while it would be disgraceful to bow to South Korea.

What can be the role of high-context diplomacy or Confucian respect for authority when DPRK commentators compare George W. Bush with Hitler or Hillary Clinton with a funny old lady pensioner going shopping (as they did in July 2009) or ROK president Park Geun Hye with a prostitute working for Obama the pimp (as they did in April 2014)? DPRK diplomacy seems to be driven by forces much deeper than a desire to maintain face (*cheymyon*) and nourish the "inner spirit" (*kibun*) of negotiations. One analyst says these qualities are basic to Korean culture—in both North and South—but he also catalogs a whole series of tough negotiating DPRK tactics that are meant to coerce, offend, manipulate, confound, and obstruct.[23] The fistfights that occasionally break out in the ROK Diet also contradict any idea that Korean culture assures genteel behavior.

At times North Korean negotiators seem to play roles in what one observer has called "a theater of the absurd: Pyongyang promises, then procrastinates, then provokes, then pauses. After a long pause come new promises, and the cycle starts anew."[24] An American based in Seoul perceives a "now-familiar cycle of North Korean provocation, American warnings, North Korea follow-through and American calls for more peace talks"—which calls are mocked by Pyongyang as abject surrender.[25]

Can these contradictory impressions be reconciled? Scott Snyder's *Negotiating on the Edge* (1999) devotes an entire chapter to what could be seen as high-context diplomacy.[26] North Koreans value *punuigi* (atmosphere) and *kibun* (good feeling). If these are absent, then North Koreans practice *kojip* (intransigence)—expressed in brinkmanship, cries of wolf, demands for unilateral concessions, bluffs, blackmail, manufactured deadlines, and threats to walk away from the negotiations. All this aims to *create leverage out of weakness*.[27] Also, before a deal is possible, the lead DPRK negotiator may need to show *kosaeng* (suffering)—proof for his bosses that he has done everything possible to extract the most possible concessions. Underlying the entire enterprise is "face." An American visitor to Pyongyang was told, "For us, saving face is as important as life itself."[28] When a U.S. diplomat asked his DPRK counterpart to be sure a U.S. condition for an accord was made clear to the top leader in Pyongyang in 2012, the North Korean demurred, saying, "I'd be shot if I did that." Asked if the top leader ever made mistakes, a DPRK official said "no."[29]

Snyder argues that North Korea's crisis-oriented negotiation style manifests a pattern of drama and catastrophe. Rather than a linear process with a discrete beginning, middle, and end, Snyder suggests that North Korea's dealings with the United States should be seen as a *cycle* in which issues are revisited, points reexamined, and interpretations redefined. Expanded, the process may include new issues and deeper mutual understanding.

"Good vibes" may set the stage for developing a personal and working relationship. But conviviality can also incubate corruption. Koreans may conclude business deals at a feast that celebrates a relationship rather than in some formal setting.

While Linton emphasizes face and feeling, and Snyder drama and catastrophe, each behavior may be part of a larger and quite distinctively Korean way of negotiating. Thus, a Washington insider on Korean affairs observed: "One has only to spend time working with a South Korean company to see how similar are these strands, and how they have their own internal logic. It is inordinately frustrating for outsiders who must deal with Koreans, because the mixture of bombast, face, stubbornness, and emphasis on context and good relations may seem quite puzzling. But it's all part of a whole that has an internal logic."[30] This logic arises from the fact that Korean culture is the most hierarchic in East Asia. As a result, when discussions between two "equals" breaks down, it is a huge break, and also virtually impossible for them to back down or compromise from a stance, no matter how illogical that stance is—to do so is to lose all face and submit to the other side. In this context, a third party, usually of higher rank, is needed to intervene and find a solution. Once relations are restored, great warmth and flexibility is possible by all sides; but approached in the wrong manner, this is impossible. These patterns of conflict and conflict resolution were evident in South Korean television dramas before the 1990s.[31]

CONSTRUCTIVIST CAVEATS

While neorealists say that state behavior mirrors the hierarchy of power, constructivists emphasize the roles of perception and misperception. Reality, according to constructivists, is what we perceive and make of it. Our vision of reality is constructed. What appears to be objective can be subjective.[32] As we see in Northeast Asia, actors on the world stage tend to be self-righteous and often ignore other actors' perspectives. Thus, nuclear-weapon haves demand that other states remain nuclear-weapon have-nots. Each side elevates its own concerns and downgrades others'. The pots of this world often call the kettles black. The world's military superpower objects if others also invest in military power. To aggravate the situation, humans are fallible—they perceive or reason imperfectly. People of goodwill may disagree on what is good and bad. Even well-informed experts disagree on what norms exist; whether certain actions violate those norms; and, if so, how to respond.[33] Even if we agree that humanity has reached some consensus on what is criminal, we must still be cautious about our judgments. Piracy has for centuries been treated as a crime against all humanity, but what if the pirate is a former Somali fisherman whose livelihood has been ruined by foreign ships?

Constructivists note that Americans do not worry much about nuclear weapons in British or French hands, but they worry a great deal about nukes in the hands of states that seem to behave like rogue elephants. While most Europeans have come to assume that Washington will not use nuclear weapons except in self-defense, North Korean leaders recall how U.S. bombers flattened their country in the early 1950s and fear a repeat performance. The George W. Bush administration's espousal of preventive war and nuclear threats (detailed below in chapter 13) helped keep these fears alive.

Small things can become big when perceived in a certain light. Some observers thought that DPRK demands for the return of $25 million from its accounts in the Banco Delta Asia as a prerequisite for complying with its February 2007 arms control commitment showed that Pyongyang was insincere or petty. Given that $25 million is a trivial sum on the world scene, a cynic might say that Pyongyang was just exploiting the issue to delay meeting its obligations. Others surmised that the U.S. action against Banco Delta Asia showed that White House hawks wanted to kill the February 2007 accord.

Many Americans saw their country as a beneficent gendarme to the world, whereas Pyongyang and many other actors saw the United States as a brazen bully. On October 8, 2008, the DPRK delegate to the United Nations accused the United States of "terrorism committed by state armed forces."[34]

The deepest divergence in viewpoints concerned nuclear arms. The United States and other nuclear haves assumed they were entitled to membership in an exclusive club whose doors they tried to keep shut. DPRK leaders thought they had every right to nuclear arms, while Washington said they had none. Pyongyang also objected to expanded U.S. arms sales to South Korea, authorized by Congress in September 2008 to acquire the same kinds of weapons sold to NATO members.

There are two or more sides to most encounters—including those involving North Korea. A report issued in May 2010 by South Korean officials concluded that a North Korean torpedo sank the RCK corvette *Cheonan* near Baengnyeong Island in March 2010. This finding was endorsed by some U.S., Australian, and Swedish experts. But Pyongyang said the evidence was cooked.[35] Seoul refused requests by Pyongyang to examine and possibly challenge the evidence. The investigation took place with no input from Chinese or Russian experts, some of whom also raised questions about the conclusions. A leading Korean specialist in the United States found the ROK investigative report to be riddled with contradictions.[36]

The UN Security Council issued a presidential statement condemning the attack but did not identify the attacker. Nonetheless the official ROK view dominated media outlets in South Korea and in Western countries. Assuming that North Korea committed an act of aggression, South Korean and U.S. analysts speculated on Pyongyang's motives. Did the DPRK military strive to show its mettle? Did the elder Kim wish to promote succession of his son, Kim Jong Un?[37] Was Pyongyang jealous of South Korea's rising stature in world affairs?

A constructivist might ask: If the DPRK did sink the *Cheonan,* was this a response to a confrontation in the same area in November 2009, when several North Korean sailors died? Did Pyongyang look back to a clash in 1999 that led to the sinking of a DPRK vessel and the deaths of more than thirty seamen? In each case DPRK vessels are believed to have initiated the shooting but were outgunned. Regardless of who started the shooting in 1999 and 2009, the North may have wanted to avenge its losses.

Another serious incident occurred in November 2010. Just hours after the ROK ignored a DPRK request and commenced live-fire maneuvers close to Baengnyeong, North Korean artillery then struck the island, killing civilians as well as military personnel.

The principles at issue were strongly contested. North and South Korea challenged each other across the Northern Limit Line (NLL) established by UN authorities in 1953 after the Korean Armistice was signed.[38] The NLL aimed to keep North and South from fighting in the Yellow Sea (for Koreans, the West Sea). Instead of merely continuing the North–South dividing line close to the 38th parallel, however, the NLL bends northward along the western coast of North Korea. The NLL was drawn up at a time when a three-nautical-mile territorial waters limit was the norm, but when in the 1970s a twelve-nautical-mile limit became internationally accepted, the NLL generated competing claims by Seoul and Pyongyang to territorial waters between the ROK islands and the DPRK mainland. Starting in 1973, Pyongyang termed the NLL illegitimate. In 1999, North Korea drew up its own "West Sea Military Demarcation Line," claiming a maritime boundary farther south. It skirted ROK-held islands such as Yeonpyeong but encompassed valuable fishing grounds. Seoul pointed out that the Armistice Agreement treated Baengnyeong and four other islands as ROK territory. Pyongyang, in turn, noted that the Law of the Sea extends state sovereignty twelve miles from its land borders. Since some of the ROK islands lie within twelve miles of the North Korean coast, ROK live-fire exercises in the area could be seen as taking place in DPRK territory. Besides all this, Pyongyang in 1977 proclaimed an economic and fishing exclusion zone of 200 miles off its coast into the West Sea. This generated a boundary dispute with Beijing as well as with Seoul.[39]

Seoul and Washington stood by the 1953 NLL, but Pyongyang maintained that international law calls for extending the land line straight out into the sea. The North wanted fishing rights far south of the line. Ways forward could include creating a military-free joint fishing zone with an agreed code of conduct for fishing vessels operating there. But several ROK-DPRK efforts at negotiation ended in failure.[40]

With no agreement, fishing vessels from both North and South operated near the NLL and often crossed it, provoking angry ripostes. South Korean military exercises close to the NLL drew harsh responses from the North. A peace treaty would probably require some modification of the NLL.

A constructivist would contend that the rights and wrongs in these cases were unclear. Looking at the same facts, each side interpreted them to suit its own interests. What one side believed to be just, the other saw as unjust. To satisfy the conflicting interests could require a creative grand bargain with many trade-offs.

Is There Any Value to Theory?

As we shall see in chapter 15, U.S. and North Korean diplomacy seemed to reach an impasse in Barack Obama's second term. North–South relations remained tense, while Beijing and Pyongyang maintained at most a façade of friendship.[41] Did all this mean that the theories discussed here are useless? No. Some theories help explain diplomatic failures and suggest ways to avoid them. For example, GRIT explains why a second lieutenant's smile spawned conflict rather than harmony at Panmunjom. Charles Osgood's theory wisely suggests that, for tension-reduction to succeed, the strategy must be enunciated at the highest level. High-context culture theory and the Linton thesis help explain why the brief trip of U.S. diplomat James Kelly to Pyongyang in October 2002 (described in chapter 13) with his accusation of wrong-doing by Pyongyang and rigid instructions (no side discussions of any kind, no socializing) terminated eight years of limited cooperation.[42]

Unless each adversary can be persuaded to strive for mutual gain, neither GRIT nor any other diplomatic technique can reduce tensions.[43] No prescriptive theory can succeed unless it is earnestly and *consistently* implemented by all parties. Unless all parties wish to explore what a negotiated deal could accomplish, then no recipe for getting to yes will crack open a mountain of intransigence. For an observer to conclude that some theory has failed, *both* Washington and Pyongyang would have to act as recommended by that theory and do so together and for some time.

If both sides really want a deal and it is relatively simple, then they may not need any theory to light their way. But if things are tense, as in U.S.-Soviet relations in the early 1980s, then following insightful guidelines may remove blockages and hasten progress.

Of course the parties must be in synch and the timing must be right. As we shall see in chapter 15, it appeared in 2012 that Washington and Pyongyang were ready to exchange food for arms control. Had the deal been formalized and implemented promptly, it might have endured. Food deliveries could have begun and DPRK plans for a missile launch put on hold. Instead, momentum was interrupted by the death of Kim Jong Il in November 2011. Terms were not formalized until February 29, 2012. By that time, however, a new DPRK "General" was trying to look both tough and filial. Preparations for the missile launch were nearly complete. The launch took place in April on the centennial of Kim Il Sung's birth. As Washington saw it, Kim Jong Un had spiked the deal. Americans ignored DPRK claims that the rocket that launched a satellite was different from the kind that can carry a warhead.

Some analysts question whether laws, values, and theories endorsed by Westerners apply also to Asia. However, Singapore's ambassador-at-large, Tommy Koh, became a model for universality. His labors showed that some diplomatic techniques are useful across cultures, so long as they are adjusted to fit the particulars of each actor.[44] In April 2014 Koh received Harvard University's "Great Negotiator Award" for his work as chief negotiator for the U.S.-Singapore Free Trade Agreement, the Third UN Conference on the Law of the Sea, and the UN Rio Earth Summit.[45] Another transnational diplomat was Ban Ki-moon, former ROK Minister of Foreign Affairs and Trade, elected in 2007 and reelected in 2011 to serve as secretary-general of the United Nations.

Like Christianity and other faiths, none of the theories discussed here has received a fair trial. Given their failures or relative successes, we can better understand the historical record and what approaches might be more fruitful in future interactions.

III

Opportunities Aborted

12

The Agreed Framework Sets the Stage for a Grand Bargain

There is a tide in the affairs of men,
Which, taken at the flood, leads on to fortune.
Omitted, all the voyage of their life
Is bound in shallows and in miseries.
—Brutus to Cassius, Shakespeare, *Julius Caesar,*
Act 4, Scene 3, 218–221

Hopes for arms control and improved U.S.–North Korean relations ebbed and then flowed during the presidency of William J. Clinton. Turning back a threat of war, the Agreed Framework signed by U.S. and DPRK representatives in 1994 halted North Korea's reprocessing of plutonium for nuclear weapons in exchange for specified economic and political benefits. Late in 2000 Pyongyang invited Clinton to meet with Kim Jong Il and solve all outstanding issues, but the clock ran out, and a new president entered the White House. The 1994 accord endured until 2002, when Washington and Pyongyang accused each other of violating their commitments.

THE JOINT NORTH–SOUTH COMMITMENT TO DEMILITARIZATION

President George H. W. Bush broke the diplomatic logjam over Korea in September 1991 by announcing the withdrawal of all U.S. tactical nuclear warheads, land- and sea-based, from overseas deployment. In secret, he also withdrew from Korea all nuclear bombs deliverable by aircraft. His actions registered in both Seoul and Pyongyang. In December 1991 representatives of North and South Korea drafted a Joint Declaration on the Denuclearization of the Korean Peninsula, which was signed on January 20 and entered force on February 19, 1992. It pledged North and

South not to acquire or use nuclear weapons and not to possess facilities for pluto-nium reprocessing or uranium enrichment—commitments that exceeded obliga-tions imposed by the Nuclear Nonproliferation Treaty (NPT). The two countries agreed also to establish a control commission and permit inspections of facilities chosen by one another.

Did North Korea comply with the North-South declaration? The North never permitted the South to inspect its facilities. This led the ROK and the United States to resume their annual military exercises—which were anathema to Pyongyang, and a reason it gave for not allowing ROK inspectors into the North. Pyongyang also conditioned inspection of its facilities on inspection by DPRK personnel of U.S. bases in the South to verify that no nuclear weapons were present. Thus, each side blamed the other for nonfulfillment of its commitments. Still, neither side formally withdrew from the joint declaration (which had no provision for with-drawal), and it was reaffirmed in subsequent statements by the North. Washing-ton, Beijing, and Tokyo were glad to maintain the formal ban on nuclear weapons in North and South Korea, which implied no return of U.S. nuclear weapons to bases in the ROK.

PRESSURES ON THE CLINTON ADMINISTRATION TO ACT

Bill Clinton settled into the White House in January 1993. The second year of his presidency showed how a combination of private and public diplomacy, backed by threats and political-economic carrots, could turn a collision course into a fast track toward arms control and political détente. Clinton's memoir, *My Life* (2004), detailed how military pressures, material incentives, mediation by former presi-dent Jimmy Carter, and negotiations by Ambassador Robert L. Gallucci combined to move the United States and North Korea away from an armed confrontation to signing an Agreed Framework limiting the DPRK nuclear program. The next years would show, however, that farsighted foreign policies can fall victim to partisan politics at home.[1]

As noted earlier, the DPRK signed on to the Nuclear Nonproliferation Treaty in 1985 and the IAEA safeguards agreement in 1992. Balking at IAEA inspec-tion demands, Pyongyang in March 1993 announced that it would withdraw from the NPT in ninety days. Following intense bilateral negotiations with the United States, North Korea announced it was suspending its withdrawal from the NPT one day before the withdrawal was to take effect.

Early in 1994 the U.S. intelligence community reported that North Korea might already have produced one or two nuclear weapons. In February the DPRK finalized an agreement with the International Atomic Energy Agency (IAEA) to allow inspections of all seven of its declared nuclear facilities, thus averting sanc-tions by the UN Security Council. On March 1 inspectors from the IAEA arrived in North Korea for the first inspections since 1993. But Pyongyang seemed intent on hiding something. When the DPRK refused to allow the IAEA team to inspect its plutonium reprocessing plant at Yongbyon, the IAEA Board of Governors called on North Korea to "immediately allow the IAEA to complete all requested inspection activities and to comply fully with its safeguards agreements." On May 19 the IAEA confirmed that North Korea had begun removing spent fuel from its nuclear research reactor even though international monitors were not present. The United States and the IAEA had insisted that inspectors be present for any such action because spent fuel can potentially be reprocessed for use in nuclear weapons.[2] On June 13 North Korea announced its withdrawal from the IAEA. In theory the DPRK was no longer a member of the IAEA but was still obligated to accept IAEA inspections as a corollary to its participation in the NPT. Six years later, on October 22, 2002, a joint statement issued by the United States, Japan, and the ROK asserted that a uranium enrichment program launched by the DPRK violated the North–South Joint Declaration. Against this interpretation, some argued that the declaration explicitly allowed for each side to use nuclear energy solely for peaceful purposes—which implied some uranium enrichment or plutonium reprocessing.

The options and restraints facing the Clinton White House were similar to those that challenged the George W. Bush and Barack Obama administrations in later years. Should Washington try to conciliate the North by canceling the maneuvers conducted annually by U.S. and ROK forces? Or should it conduct and amplify the exercises to intimidate the North and please hard-liners in Seoul and in Washington? Going further, should U.S. bombers or missiles attempt "surgical strikes" to wipe out DPRK nuclear facilities, as Israel destroyed Iraq's Osiraq reactor in 1981 (and a Syrian nuclear site in 2007)? If U.S. bombs hit their targets, radiation might spread. Even without nuclear weapons, North Korea threatened to ignite a firestorm in South Korea. U.S. experts reckoned that, if war erupted, a million South Koreans and many thousands of Americans could die. Despite the risks, the Clinton administration in early 1994 geared up for a surgical strike to knock out the Yongbyon plants.

What Koreans called the "atmosphere" (*punuigi*) in 1994 was extraordinarily complex. Even as the United States beefed up its military forces in Korea with Patriot missiles and Bradley fighting vehicles, U.S. ambassador Madeleine Albright was trying to mobilize the UN Security Council to demand sanctions against the DPRK. Behind the scenes, Beijing was urging restraint on North Korea.

JIMMY CARTER ON TRACK II

As tensions mounted, several private American visitors met with Kim Il Sung. He talked with the Reverend Billy Graham, pastor to U.S. presidents; scholar Selig Harrison; and former U.S. president Jimmy Carter. These unofficial agents of "Track II

diplomacy" laid the groundwork for subsequent "Track I" negotiations by government officials. Meeting with Carter on June 16–17, Kim Il Sung, just weeks before
his death, approved an outline of what became the Agreed Framework.[3] Some of
what Carter did and promised exceeded any mandate he carried from Washington. Outflanking hard-liners in Washington and offering some international pub-
licity to Kim Il Sung, Carter brought with him a CNN television crew.

The DPRK leader avoided any sign he was bowing to pressure. Just weeks
before Carter's visit, Kim Il Sung had refused to meet with two emissaries chosen
by President Clinton, senators Richard Lugar and Sam Nunn, who were expected
to carry a blunter message than Carter.

How did Carter's intervention defuse the crisis and bring the contending parties to the table? He went to the top (as recommended by Stephen Linton) and
created a way for the parties to move beyond the impasse on special inspections.
He enabled each side to back away without losing face. Washington could retreat
from its commitment to pursue UN sanctions. Washington's counterdemand—not
to refuel the shut-down reactor—permitted it to declare victory. The North Koreans could say they had simply been seeking a secure source of electricity. Unlike
conventional mediators, Carter took actions that effectively committed the Clinton administration to resume negotiations even though he was acting virtually as
a free agent.[4]

TRACK I AND THE AGREED FRAMEWORK

Neither Washington nor Pyongyang in 1994 followed Charles Osgood's GRIT
principles precisely. Neither side issued a public declaration of peaceful intent.
Neither promised that small steps would lead to larger ones. But when Kim Il
Sung signaled to Carter a willingness to trade the DPRK nuclear weapons program for a package of economic aid and international recognition, the White
House responded promptly and positively. U.S.-DPRK negotiations began in July
and stopped only briefly after Kim Il Sung's death on July 8, 1994 (at age eighty-
two), after which his son and designated heir, Kim Jong Il, became the paramount
DPRK leader and committed his administration to continuing his father's policies.

Negotiations resumed in August. Following several rounds of talks, the heads
of each delegation—Gallucci and Kang Sok Ju—signed the Agreed Framework in
Geneva on October 21, 1994.[5] The accord was neither a treaty nor a legally binding executive agreement,[6] but a political commitment between the two countries
that was noted by the UN Security Council. A model of diplomatic finesse, it constituted a package of conditional cooperation. The agreement (just a few pages)
stipulated that, "in accordance with the October 20, 1994 letter from the U.S. President [Clinton]," the United States would lead a consortium "for the provision to
the DPRK of a LWR [light-water reactor] project with a total generating capacity

of approximately 2,000 MW(e) by the target date of 2003." For its part, the DPRK would freeze its graphite-moderated reactors and related facilities and dismantle them "when the LWR project is completed." The IAEA would monitor the freeze. The United States and the DPRK would cooperate in finding a method to store the spent fuel from the 5 MW(e) reactor and "dispose of the fuel in a manner that does not involve reprocessing it in the DPRK." To offset the energy lost by the freeze, the United States would every year supply the DPRK with 500,000 tons of heavy oil for heating and electricity production (an amount just half of what the Soviets had provided in previous times) until the first LWR unit became operational. ("Heavy" oil is viscous, like that from tar sands in Canada and Venezuela, and loaded with impurities costly to remove. Light oil, less dense but rarer worldwide, would have been easier and cheaper for North Korea to utilize.) The Americans thought that coal-powered energy plants would be more useful to North Korea, but if Pyongyang insisted on LWRs, then the Americans would go along.

The framework committed the two sides to "move toward full normalization of political and economic relations." They would "reduce barriers to trade and investment, including restrictions on telecommunications services and financial transactions"; open liaison offices in their respective capitals; and, as progress was "made on issues of concern to each side," to "upgrade relations to the Ambassadorial level." None of this happened.

The United States would "provide formal assurances to the DPRK, against the threat or use of nuclear weapons by the U.S." For its part, the DPRK would "consistently take steps to implement the North–South Joint Declaration on the Denuclearization of the Korean Peninsula"—which it had already violated by refusing to permit ROK inspection of suspected nuclear facilities—and "engage in North–South dialogue." The DPRK would remain a party to the NPT and "allow implementation of its safeguards agreement under the Treaty."

The last paragraph began: "When a significant portion of the LWR project is completed, but before delivery of key nuclear components, the DPRK will come into full compliance with its safeguards agreement with the IAEA." Spelling out this provision, the parties agreed in confidential notes that full-scope IAEA safeguards would be applied when the major nonnuclear components of the first LWR unit were completed but before the delivery of key nuclear components. Here was one way the accord bridged differences. It stretched out the schedule for inspections and linked them to delivery of key reactor components.

Looking back, we see that the DPRK shaped the structure of the negotiations more than the United States. North Korea managed to exclude both the ROK and China from the deliberations. Pyongyang was better organized for the negotiations than Washington. It excelled in orchestrating moves at and away from the table—threatening to withdraw from the NPT and to unload the reactor.

Because the winning formula was proposed by Pyongyang in 1993 and revived by Carter in 1994, some observers said that the Agreed Framework could have been concluded a year earlier. One U.S. official replied that political support in Washington would have been too weak then. The 1994 deal won support by compelling "the North Koreans to defuel the reactor [and] to have roughly 30 kilograms of plutonium sitting in this pond of water deteriorating."[7] A more sinister explanation is that some U.S. leaders counted on the collapse of the DPRK regime before the LWRs could be completed.

WAS THE AGREED FRAMEWORK A MIRAGE?

Critics—right, left, and center—found or invented many reasons to fault the Agreed Framework. Some complained that it gave too much to a bad actor—that Clinton was deceived by signs that North Korea would rein in its WMD programs. Some arms controllers said the framework weakened the nonproliferation regime the IAEA was trying to impose on Iran and Iraq. The accord required the DPRK to "can" and store its spent nuclear fuel, but did not require the North to give up its nuclear components entirely—as Belarus, Ukraine, and Kazakhstan had done following the Soviet Union's breakup. This gave North Korea easy access to spent nuclear fuel that could be reprocessed—an asset it later exploited when the Agreed Framework collapsed. Another shortfall was that the 1994 accord permitted North Korea to delay its return to the NPT by more than five years. Finally, the framework focused on a single known plant that could produce *plutonium* for nuclear weapons, but did not cover the rest of the country. What about other facilities that might produce plutonium *or* enriched uranium? Ambassador Gallucci considered including a ban on uranium enrichment but decided not to burden the Agreed Framework with additional complications. The Americans told the North Koreans that uranium could not be enriched under the agreement but did not write down this restriction in the confidential memorandum.

Defenders of the Agreed Framework argued that politics is the art of the possible. The 1994 accord was not ideal, but the Clinton team saw it as the least bad option available. It generated value for each side and avoided war. Yes, the Agreed Framework mentioned no facilities other than Yongbyon, but it reaffirmed the 1992 declaration by North and South Korea banning uranium enrichment facilities as well as plutonium reprocessing facilities in the DPRK and the ROK.[8]

The Agreed Framework promised security on the cheap. The total cost of providing North Korea with heavy oil and two LWRs was expected to be $5 billion—most of it paid by Japan and South Korea. Not small change, but trivial next to the cost of building defenses against DPRK nuclear-tipped missiles. As of 1994, the United States had already invested more than $50 billion just in researching antimissile defense. By 2015 the total bill for developing and deploying admittedly unreliable antimissile defenses was many times higher.[9]

The benefits of the 1994 Agreed Framework were no illusion. The plutonium production that the framework halted in 1994 was a much larger program than the uranium enrichment initiated later in the decade. Had the earlier program kept going, it would have yielded sufficient plutonium to make several nuclear weapons a year.[10]

THE IAEA AND DPRK UNDER THE AGREED FRAMEWORK

The International Atomic Energy Agency maintained a continuous presence at Yongbyon to verify the freeze until 2002. The agency viewed its activities under the Agreed Framework as a subset of its duties under the earlier Safeguards Agreement. It monitored the 5 MW(e) reactor, the Radiochemical Laboratory (for reprocessing), the fuel fabrication plant, and the partially built 50 and 200 MW(e) nuclear power plants. The IAEA and the DPRK continued to disagree on the legal status of the Safeguards Agreement, but the two sides held technical meetings, usually twice a year, to deal with outstanding issues. For the IAEA, the main topic was the preservation of existing information. Despite seventeen rounds of technical consultations, however, the agency reported "no progress" on key issues. In September 2000, just before high level visits by U.S. and DPRK officials, the IAEA determined it would need three or four *years* to verify the correctness and completeness of North Korea's initial report. But the DPRK refused even to discuss such a program of work. The last such technical meeting took place in November 2001. IAEA efforts to convene another technical meeting in 2002 were rebuffed.[11]

IMPLEMENTATION: SLOW AND NOT SURE

Like Henry Kissinger and Zhou Enlai in the early 1970s, Washington and Pyongyang seemed quite aware in the mid-1990s that small steps could have large consequences. Both sides began in January 1995 to dismantle the trade embargo each had imposed forty-five years before. Each side would now permit direct phone calls and financial transactions. Washington would permit U.S. steelmakers to buy magnesite from North Korea to line their blast furnaces. DPRK and U.S. journalists could now open news bureaus in each other's country. But the U.S. State Department said that further relaxation of economic sanctions would depend on progress on the "nuclear issue" and on DPRK restraint in exporting missile technology—an issue not mentioned in the Agreed Framework.[12]

The Clinton administration organized the Korean Peninsula Energy Development Organization (KEDO) with Japan and the ROK to build two light-water reactors for the DPRK. But Republicans, who won control of Congress in November 1994, balked at funding the Agreed Framework—which had never been vetted or approved by Congress. Short on funds, the Clinton administration went, hat in hand, to the European Union to gain funding for the undertaking. That is how the EU became a member of KEDO alongside the United States, South Korea, and Japan. KEDO's first director, Stephen Bosworth (Barack Obama's choice in 2009 to oversee dealings with the DPRK, even as he remained dean of the Fletcher School of Diplomacy), later commented that the Agreed Framework was a "political orphan" within two weeks after its signature.

The Agreed Framework was a bilateral accord, but one of the actors, the United States, wanted its implementation to be multilateral. Financial responsibilities were not specified. Ultimately South Korea and Japan paid most of the bill—some $1.5 billion when the last staff workers were withdrawn in 2008. The multiplicity of actors and the low priority attached to this project by Washington, Tokyo, and Brussels meant that the light-water project suffered from a lack of clear vision, persistence, and high-level attention. Pyongyang wanted to deal only with Washington and sought to exclude any evidence of South Korean equipment, know-how, or personnel. It wanted not just the reactors but also—gratis— the supporting infrastructure and communications links. The necessary upgrades for North Korea's electric grid and installation of backup facilities were among the problems left unanswered. Liability—who would pay if workers were injured— was never resolved.

North Korea charged that the United States was not fulfilling its obligations. The LWR project moved very slowly.[13] The target date for its completion was 2003, but key contracts were not let until 1997—three years after the framework was signed. In 2002 the first concrete was poured, but KEDO was still soliciting bids for some components. By 2002 it looked as though the reactors could not be completed until 2009 or later.[14] The KEDO website in 2002–2003 showed a glorious drawing of the LWR project but not much else.[15]

Responsibility for the delays fell on many shoulders. KEDO members had to resolve who would pay how much and who would build what. North Korea demanded such high wages for its workers that KEDO looked to import labor from other countries. In addition, oil shipments to the DPRK were often late. Many economic sanctions remained. Diplomatic relations between the United States and North Korea were not established. The Clinton administration said that it suspected illicit nuclear programs in North Korea, but several on-site visits by U.S. experts, including former Defense Secretary William Perry, found no evidence for these suspicions. By the late 1990s, however, evidence was accumulating that the DPRK was conducting a clandestine program to produce highly enriched uranium. Pyongyang stonewalled any effort by the IAEA to check the accuracy of DPRK reports on activities at Yongbyon. Another problem for the United States and its allies arose in August 2000, when North Korea began delivery of fifty Nodong missiles and seven launchers to Libya, reportedly procured on behalf of Iraq and Egypt as well as Libya, at a cost of $600 million.

Toward a Broad Accord in 2000

Despite real and potential flashpoints, in 2000 the North's relations became more cordial with South Korea, the United States, and other countries. In June the first North–South summit took place. Having pocketed a few million as his price for participating, Kim Jong Il met with ROK president Kim Dae Jung. Newspapers were exchanged with the South for a few days until Pyongyang ended the practice. Meanwhile, the Dear Leader's great thoughts were being published and promoted from Laos to Madagascar and Ecuador. Kim Jong Il also traded visits and pleasantries with Russian president Vladimir Putin. The KCNA reported that the Russian and the DPRK leader "forged intimate relations and deepened trust" through their Pyongyang meeting in July 2000. Putin and other sources reported that in 2000 Kim Jong Il offered to give up the DPRK rocket program if other countries would launch its satellites. The joint declaration by the Russian and North Korean leaders about the peaceful purposes of the DPRK's rocket program may have aimed at undermining the U.S. rationale for missile defenses.[16] Kim Jong Il returned Putin's visit in 2001 and toured Russian space facilities.

On October 11, 2000, the KCNA reported: "With relations between the DPRK and the U.S. dramatically improving in Washington, the [Workers'] Party's 55th birthday celebrations were held nationwide, marked by a grand parade, an evening gala, a gigantic gymnastic display and various kinds of congratulatory meetings. In a mood of reconciliation between north and south Korea after the historic inter-Korean Pyongyang summit in June, forty-two south Korean delegates, including representatives of civic and religious groups, were invited to attend the ceremony for the first time."[17]

The summit meeting between the two Kims in June 2000 ushered in a renewed effort by Washington and Pyongyang to reach a grand bargain. These efforts were spearheaded by Madeleine Albright, U.S. secretary of state since December 1997. Her experiences confirmed Linton's thesis about the importance for Koreans of high-level personal contacts.[18] Meeting the DPRK foreign minister, Paek Nam Sun, for the first time in Bangkok in July 2000, she was reportedly struck by his "smooth professionalism." Their talk, expected to last fifteen minutes, continued for an hour. She asked her opposite number if Pyongyang would dispatch a high-level emissary to Washington to reciprocate the visit to Pyongyang in 1998 by former Defense Secretary Perry. Though it took a few months to get a reply, in October 2000 the DPRK sent to Washington Vice Marshal Jo Myong Rok, regarded by some observers as the second most powerful figure in Pyongyang. Visiting the State Department, the marshal wore a gray suit; half an hour later, he appeared at the White House in a full military uniform adorned with medals. Was his costume change a sign of professionalism or a sign that Pyongyang remained unbowed?[19]

"With a flourish," according to Albright, the vice marshal presented Clinton a letter from Kim Jong Il, inviting the U.S. president to Pyongyang. When Clinton hedged, Jo pressed for a definitive reply. When Clinton suggested that Albright go first to prepare the ground, Jo did not give up. He said that if the president and secretary came together, "We will be able to find a solution to all problems." Albright commented later that "North Korea's top-down decision-making style didn't fit well with our practice of trying to 'pre-cook' arrangements . . . before committing the President." Still, Jo invited Albright to Pyongyang.[20]

Before Jo left Washington, each side pledged "no hostile intent" toward the other. The joint pledge amounted to a constructive compromise between the North's demand for a nonaggression pact and the traditional U.S. position that the UN Charter already bans aggression. The importance of the pledge was underlined in 2002 when the Bush administration refused to reaffirm it.

Both sides pointed to breakthroughs. The KCNA on October 12 published what it claimed was the full text of the joint communiqué issued at the end of Jo's three-day visit to Washington. But the North Korean version as rendered in English differed from the official U.S. text in several ways. It omitted any reference to the desirability of transparency in implementing the 1994 Agreed Framework. Instead, it said that "both sides agreed to make clearer the implementation of the commitments made in the agreed framework."

According to the KCNA version, both sides "declared that they are ready to take a new orientation in bilateral relations." Both "affirmed the commitment to make all efforts to establish new relations free from past antagonism in the future." The parties aimed to build on the "principles stipulated in the June 11, 1993 DPRK-U.S. joint statement and reconfirmed in the October 21, 1994 agreed framework." These principles included "mutual respect for sovereignty and non-interference in each other's internal affairs" and the utility of sustaining "diplomatic contacts on a regular basis through bilateral and multilateral channels." They discussed a "mutual visit of economic and trade experts in the near future to seek trade and commercial possibilities of contributing to the creation of an environment beneficial to the two peoples and favourable for expanding economic cooperation in northeast Asia as a whole."

The parties agreed that "settlement of the missile issue would make an important contribution to the radical improvement of the DPRK-U.S. relations and peace and security in the Asia-Pacific region. The DPRK side informed the U.S. that it will not launch any long-range missile while the talks are going on to discuss the missile issue as an effort to build new relations."

The KCNA version said that the communiqué "took note of the fact that an access [for former Defense Secretary Perry] to the underground facility in Kumchang-ri was useful for clearing the U.S. of its worry." ("Worry" was rendered as "concern" in the U.S. text.)

The KCNA documents said: "The DPRK side expressed thanks to the USA for its significant contribution to meeting the DPRK's humanitarian needs in food and medicine aid." The United States expressed thanks to the DPRK for "cooperating in the excavation of remains of the U.S. soldiers who were reported missing during the Korean War."

Both sides agreed to support and encourage international efforts to combat terrorism, as pointed out in the October 6, 2000, joint statement.

Discussing the desirability of converting the 1953 Armistice Agreement into a permanent peace mechanism, the KCNA alluded to "four-power talks"—which implied participation by the ROK as well as China—as an afterthought, rather than earlier in the sentence, as in the U.S. version. The DPRK version called for "denuclearization" of the Korean peninsula, whereas the U.S. text called for a "nuclear-weapons free" peninsula. Anxious to push all troubles under the rug, the DPRK text said that Albright would visit Pyongyang to "make arrangements for the President's [Clinton's] visit." The U.S. text said she would "prepare for a possible visit" by the U.S. president.

Accelerating the pace of diplomacy, Albright arrived in Pyongyang in late October 2000. She had been told that to get diplomatic results with North Korea one had to take time and build a relationship. But she had only two days—not even the three derided by Linton. When she met Kim Jong Il, the Dear Leader promptly expressed admiration for her energy (after a marathon flight) and expressed gratitude for two symbolic acts—Albright's visit to his father's mausoleum and a condolence letter from Clinton after Kim Il Sung's death—as well as for humanitarian assistance in recent years. Again expressing the hope that Clinton would visit, the DPRK leader averred that "if both sides are genuine and serious, there is nothing we will not be able to do."

During her short stay Albright found Kim Jong Il to be isolated but intelligent, well informed, and able to discuss a wide range of technical problems without consulting his advisers. He seemed amenable to a missiles-for-cash deal and did not object to the continued presence of U.S. troops in Korea, which he now saw as a stabilizing influence. The main event underscoring cultural differences was a demonstration for Albright by more than 100,000 people—what she saw as "an Olympic opening ceremony on steroids"—singing and moving to songs such as "Let Us Hold High the Red Flag." Critics later accused her of becoming a tool for DPRK propaganda, but she could hardly have refused to look at the spectacle without damaging the high-context vibes.

After her visit, Albright reported to Clinton that Kim Jong Il might accept negotiated curbs on North Korea's missile programs as well as its nuclear weapon ambitions. Clinton wanted to visit Kim Jong Il in late 2000 and try to bring to fruition the negotiations conducted by Albright and others. Incoming president George W. Bush did not object. But Clinton felt he must choose in the final weeks of his presidency between a possible deal with North Korea and one final mediation effort for the Middle East. He chose the latter. The Americans then invited Kim Jong Il to visit what was still the Clinton White House, but he declined—perhaps because the invitation came so late and could be seen as an affront to "face." But the biggest obstacle to a diplomatic breakthrough was not poor communication or cultural differences, but time. Clinton had too many items on his platter and too little time to deal with them.

The Clinton team opened the door partway to yes with Pyongyang. In 2001 the Bush White House slammed it shut.

13

Bush Gets Tough
with North Korea

After taking office in 2001, President George W. Bush did not seek an arms control accord or broader accommodation with North Korea. He and his closest advisers disparaged the ROK "Sunshine Policy" to open up the North as naïve and misguided. Having placed North Korea on a putative "axis of evil" in January 2002, the White House instructed Assistant Secretary of State James Kelly to fly to Pyongyang in October and accuse the DPRK of opening a uranium enrichment facility to skirt its obligations under the Agreed Framework. The ensuing confrontation led each side to terminate a deal that had halted the North's plutonium production for eight years. Losing this constraint and permitting—perhaps provoking—North Korea to build its own nuclear arsenal marked a major failure of U.S. policy.

The DPRK Not a Priority

Newly elected president George W. Bush and his closest advisers declared that the 1994 Agreed Framework was flawed. The president said that Kim Jong Il behaved like a petulant, spoiled child who, given what he wants, demands ever more.[1] As in earlier times, Korea was not a priority for Washington. When Bush took office, the U.S. Defense Department could not say whether North Korea's military assets had increased or diminished in recent years. The Pentagon did not know if the DPRK had nuclear weapons and, if it did, how many. Its contingency plans for dealing with North Korea had not been updated for years. As Defense Secretary Donald Rumsfeld saw it, the United States had no options except "rhetoric" and "75 sledgehammers to beat that gnat into the ground."[2]

Unilateralist hard-liners controlled U.S. policy toward North Korea and most other foreign issues in the George W. Bush administration—at least until its second term. Vice President Dick Cheney argued that regime change in Pyongyang was the only way to end the nuclear threat from North Korea.[3] Cheney and his staff demanded terms that they knew Pyongyang would refuse: "complete, verifiable, irreversible dismantlement" (CVID) of North Korea's nuclear program *before* the United States made any material concessions.[4] By contrast, Secretary of State Colin Powell thought that negotiations with the DPRK could be useful (as did Condoleezza Rice, *after* she became secretary of state in 2005); but Powell's deputy on arms control, John R. Bolton, sought to block, and often succeeded in sabotaging, any movement toward an accord.[5]

Leaders in Europe as well as in South Korea were shocked by Bush's aggressive unilateralism on a whole range of issues. The president seemed almost intent on losing friends and inspiring adversaries.[6]

HOSTILITY TO LAW AND TRANSPARENCY

President Bush and his entourage opposed any curb on his actions. Whereas the United States usually supported and tried to shape international law, the Bush White House rejected the Kyoto Protocol to the UN Framework Convention on Climate Change, "unsigned" the Rome Statute of the International Criminal Court, and abrogated the ABM treaty. It contrived legal doctrines to justify torture of alleged enemy combatants and eavesdropping on U.S. citizens.[7]

The North Korean regime also resisted any external restraint. Like Soviet Russia in the 1920s, the DPRK felt encircled by hostile powers. For Pyongyang, the United States and the United Nations were one—North Korea's foe in 1950–1953 and ever since across the DMZ. The DPRK did not trust even Moscow and Beijing. It suspected the Korean Peninsula Energy Development Organization (KEDO) to be a Trojan horse meant to deceive North Korea.

Both the Bush team and Pyongyang resisted transparency. Each played its cards close its vest. Neither communicated fully with its subjects or its potential partners abroad. The United States, of course, remained a far more open society than North Korea. But multiple revelations about the lead into the Iraq war showed how those in power could manipulate information to deceive the public, Congress, and foreign governments.

ATTITUDES TOWARD ARMS AND ARMS CONTROL

Both the Bush administration and Kim Jong Il appeared to value weapons of mass destruction (WMD) as useful instruments of policy. The Pentagon's *Nuclear Posture Review* (*NPR*), submitted to Congress on December 31, 2001, proclaimed a new strategic triad composed of offensive strike systems, active and passive defenses, and a revitalized research and development base to update U.S. forces. The *NPR* stated that the new triad, bound together by enhanced command and control and intelligence, would reduce, but not eliminate, U.S. dependence on nuclear arms.[8]

Against which targets might nuclear weapons be used? North Korea headed the *NPR* list. "North Korea, Iraq, Iran, Syria, and Libya are among the countries that could be involved in immediate, potential, or unexpected contingencies." All showed long-standing hostility toward the United States and Washington's partners; North Korea and Iraq in particular posed serious security threats. All sponsored or harbored terrorists, and all had active WMD and missile programs. Given the ongoing modernization of Beijing's nuclear and nonnuclear forces, China could also become "involved in an immediate or potential contingency."

What would be the role of antimissile systems? According to the *NPR*: "Missile defenses could defeat small-scale missile attacks intended to coerce the United States into abandoning an embattled ally or friend. Defenses that provided protection for strike capabilities of the New Triad and for other power projection forces would improve the ability of the United States and its allies to counterattack an enemy. Improved defenses could also provide the President with an option to manage a crisis involving one or more missile and WMD-armed opponents."

Championing national missile defense and withdrawing from the ABM treaty with Moscow, the Bush administration ignored the widely shared views of scientists and engineers that no defense could respond effectively to rockets equipped with multiple warheads or decoys; that no system of advanced warning sensors, radars, and defensive missiles could be regarded as reliable unless tested in battle; that the proposed system would do nothing against low-flying cruise missiles launched close to U.S. shores and that the real WMD threat to the United States could come from containers smuggled on trucks or ships. Not only was the administration investing in a system that could never work, but it was also misleading the public by promoting a false sense of security.[9]

The United States proceeded to throw much good money after bad. A dozen years after the Bush team embraced missile defense, the U.S. Defense Department conceded that the defense systems deployed in Alaska and California would not work. The Pentagon announced in February 2014 that its next budget would include funds to overhaul Boeing Company's ground-based missile defense system and develop a replacement for an interceptor built by Raytheon after several recent test failures. "We've got to get to more reliable systems," Frank Kendall, under secretary of defense for Acquisition, Technology and Logistics, told a conference sponsored by McAleese & Associates and Credit Suisse. Did the problems arise from a shortage of funding in recent years? No, Kendall said. They resulted more from decisions to rush deployment of technologies that had not been completely and thoroughly tested. "Just updating the things we've got is probably not going to be adequate. So we're going to have to go beyond that," he said—offering no details.[10]

As noted later, in chapter 20, President Barack Obama's Pentagon pushed Seoul in 2015 to buy and deploy its "THAAD" defense system to shield South

Korea from short- and medium-range missile attack. Washington pointed to the vaunted successes of Israel's "Iron Dome," heavily subsidized by the United States. Serious analysis showed, however, the dome to be quite leaky. It stopped at most 5 percent of missiles fired from Gaza—not the 85 to 95 percent claimed by Israel and the Pentagon.[11]

If defense against short-range missiles is problematic, how much more difficult to intercept an ICBM—especially if outfitted with multiple warheads? *The Economist* reported in 2014 that "not even the American military can distinguish sophisticated decoys from a warhead (though it might manage to do so if confronted with relatively crude weapons designed by Iran or North Korea)." Some analysts hoped that antimissiles fired from drones could intercept enemy missiles during their launch phase, but the problems in deploying such a system close to North Korea or Iran, not to speak of China or Russia, might well be insurmountable.[12] A survey of expert opinion conducted by *The Economist* concluded: "Even with new technology, America's multi-billion-dollar efforts to build a shield against long-range ballistic missiles look doomed."[13]

By scuttling the ABM treaty in 2001–2002, the White House antagonized the Kremlin and pressured both Russia and China to buttress their deterrent forces. Withdrawing from a treaty without obtaining congressional approval departed from abundant precedent and probably violated the U.S. Constitution.[14] It cast doubt on the reliability of the United States to stand by its agreements—an issue that later dogged arms negotiations with Iran in 2015, when forty-seven Republican senators warned Tehran that the next U.S. president could reverse any agreement signed by President Obama.

Meanwhile, the administration also embraced a doctrine of first strike. Bush and Rice averred that, in an age of WMD and terrorist actions, the United States would not wait while enemy forces prepared to attack. Instead, Americans would preempt. The White House conflated the terms *preempt* and *prevent*. The invasion of Iraq in 2003 or an attack on North Korea could be described as a *preventive* war meant to cut short a *future* threat, but not as a *preemptive* strike to neuter an *imminent* attack. None of the putative axis of evil states could conceivably attack the United States with missiles or planes for many years.

The Bush White House wanted more and better nukes for the United States and seemed not to worry much if other actors obtained nuclear weapons. Even as Washington called on its challengers to abjure nuclear weapons, the Pentagon sought to develop "bunker busters" to menace command-and-control bomb shelters and what used to be called "battlefield" nuclear weapons.[15] The *Nuclear Posture Review* advised that U.S. weapons laboratories might have to resume nuclear tests, halted since 1992. All such moves were just heavenly for Bush's backers among "rapture" evangelicals expecting an Armageddon from which only they would emerge triumphant.[16]

The Bush administration paid little deference to the Kremlin's views on world affairs even though the Russian Federation was still a nuclear superpower and a potential source of "loose nukes." Still, Bush met Russian president Vladimir Putin in Slovenia in June 2001. The American president looked into Putin's eyes and perceived a very "straightforward" and "trustworthy" partner, a Russian patriot with whom he could have a "very constructive relationship"—very surprising comments given the sovietological training of his national security assistant Dr. Rice.[17]

Following the 9/11 attacks on American targets in 2001, the Bush team sought Moscow's support for America's "war on terror." The *NPR* issued at the end of 2001 declared that a nuclear "contingency involving Russia, while plausible, is not expected." Having withdrawn from the ABM treaty, the Bush administration did not want to update U.S.-Russian arms controls with any kind of formal commitment. Bowing to Russian requests, however, Bush agreed to a Strategic Offensive Reductions Treaty, signed with Putin in Moscow in May 2002. Known as SORT (even the acronym implied disdain for arms control), the treaty filled just three pages—quite unlike its long and detailed predecessors. SORT called for reductions in U.S. and Russian operationally deployed strategic warheads to no more than 2,200 by the end of 2012, but left each side with enormous flexibility as regards its future deployments.[18]

Thus, the Bush administration pursued its own version of Juche. Confident of U.S. military superiority, the Bush team took a cavalier approach to arms control, viewing it as undesirable and unnecessary. Accordingly, the Bush team nearly ignored the nuclear programs of Iran and North Korea and focused instead on Iraq. It did so regardless of the fact that the National Intelligence Estimate of October 2002 identified only a *desire* in Baghdad to obtain WMD and saw little evidence of an existing WMD capability.[19] The Bush team invaded Iraq for reasons other than arms control, while doing very little to thwart WMD development in North Korea or Iran.

Strategic U.S. self-reliance, filliped by an aversion to treaties, led Washington to undermine efforts to strengthen the nonproliferation treaty and conventions on chemical and biological weapons. Bush allowed India to buy nuclear fuel and equipment for its civil nuclear program and persuaded the U.S. Congress and Nuclear Suppliers Group to go along. This permitted India to thumb its nose at the NPT even as Washington sanctioned Iran for its ostensibly civil nuclear program. Pakistan, of course, worried that any uranium India could import for its power reactors would free up enriched uranium for its weapons.

Demise of the Agreed Framework

Many observers thought that Bush's policies reflected an ABC complex—"anything but Clinton." The new president steered away from any kind of deal nurtured by his predecessor. Bush's choice for secretary of state, Colin Powell, did not immediately internalize his boss's demons. Powell assured Madeleine Albright in late 2000 that the Bush team would pick up with North Korea roughly where the Clinton team left off.[20] Indeed, Powell repeated this formulation when speaking to reporters on March 6, 2001, just as ROK president Kim Dae Jung—architect of South Korea's Sunshine Policy—arrived in Washington. Powell stated that "some promising elements were left on the table, and we'll be examining those elements." But this did not happen. Reading Powell's optimistic comments in the *Washington Post* early the next day, Bush was livid. He phoned Rice at 5 a.m. and told her to read page A20. Donning a robe, she went out to pick up the paper. She then assured the president that she would "take care of it." She phoned Powell and cajoled him to retract his statement. Later that day, as Bush met with Kim Dae Jung, Powell stepped out of the Oval Office to inform the press that he "had gotten a little forward on his skis." He said that North Korea was "a threat . . . we have to not be naïve about the threat." Powell underscored that Bush "understands the nature of the regime in Pyongyang and will not be fooled by it."[21] He then told the Senate that the DPRK is a "despotic regime" and that the United States might want to revisit the KEDO deal with North Korea. The former national security adviser and chairman of the joint chiefs of staff was internalizing the values of his new boss.[22]

The ROK president was aghast at Bush's way of thinking. North Korean leaders also showed disappointment and frustration. They had hoped for better ties with the United States after visits by a former president and a secretary of state. They knew that the new president's father, George H. W., had cultivated ties with China and that the elder Bush urged his son to continue negotiations with the DPRK.

In January 2002 President Bush assigned North Korea, along with Iraq and Iran, to what he called an "axis of evil." The CIA reported that North Korea was completing a uranium enrichment plant, using technology acquired from Pakistan—giving Pyongyang a second route to nuclear weapons.[23] The Clinton administration had earlier detected signs of a uranium enrichment program but had opted to watch and wait, believing it wiser to improve relations and *then* deal with the problem quietly, when Pyongyang might believe it had more to lose from a confrontation.[24]

As part of its "bold" new approach to North Korea, the White House sent James A. Kelly, assistant secretary of state for East Asian and Pacific affairs, to Pyongyang on October 3–5, 2002. His two-day meeting led to exchanges that soon killed the Agreed Framework. Following a tight script and with no authority to maneuver or explore nuances, Kelly told the North Koreans that Washington had evidence of their uranium enrichment plant.[25] His allegation seemed to catch the North Koreans off guard. The following day, Kelly later reported, DPRK diplomats confirmed his accusation and claimed that their country had every right to this facility.[26]

Seeking to keep Congress focused on Iraq, the Bush administration did not report these exchanges in Pyongyang for eleven days. DPRK representatives, however, soon denied they had admitted to having a uranium plant. Translation from Korean into English for Kelly may have led to a misunderstanding. Perhaps the DPRK diplomats meant only to tell Kelly that North Korea was *entitled* to have a uranium enrichment facility. Perhaps they had felt the need for a strong response to bad *kibun*—the insinuation their country had been cheating. But when a French official proposed taking the matter to the United Nations, Kelly replied, "The Security Council is for Iraq."[27]

Ulterior Motives?

Had the 1994 accord masked a drive by one or both sides to cheat and continue a zero-sum struggle against the other? The evidence is muddy. The United States and its partners supplied fuel oil to the North, as promised, but were often behind schedule in doing so. Progress on the two light-water reactors was so slow that Pyongyang asked whether the United States and its partners were trying to sabotage North Korea's development.

Kim Jong Il introduced his "military first" priority not long after approving the Agreed Framework. Did he plan to exploit a more relaxed mood in Washington to develop a uranium facility on the sly? Noting Republicans' disdain for the Agreed Framework, the DPRK regime may have felt that North Korea must be prepared for all contingencies. Kim Jong Il may also have wanted to appease his own country's military or other hard-liners. He may have believed that the DPRK could hide its operation and, if it were discovered, deflect any criticism.

North Korea's uranium enrichment program probably began in 1997–1998—several years after the Agreed Framework was signed and before Bush entered the White House. A clandestine operation of this kind surely ran contrary to the spirit of the 1994 accord. When the U.S. intelligence community asserted its existence in 2002, the most hawkish U.S. official, John Bolton, declared he would use the analysis "to go straight for the Agreed Framework's jugular."[28] But one authority noted that the NPT permits signatories to have *civilian* enrichment operations under IAEA inspection. Pyongyang may have felt no obligation to declare its uranium plant until the United States and its partners had built the two light-water reactors, as promised in 1994.[29]

The impasse over uranium facilities, according to Condoleezza Rice, meant that "the United States had to respond forcefully." Having informed its partners of "what we knew," the United States halted heavy oil shipments in November 2002.[30] Three days later the DPRK blamed the United States for collapse of the Agreed Framework. The DPRK then withdrew from the NPT and expelled the IAEA inspectors.

The Agreed Framework appeared to have stopped DPRK plutonium production for eight years. It also brought promise of a new page in U.S. relations with North Korea. Total outlays for work on the two light-water reactors amounted to $1.5 billion by the time the last workers withdrew in 2006—the lion's share paid by South Korea.[31] This sum—spread over more than a decade—was a fraction of what the Pentagon spent every year for R&D on ballistic missile defenses ($8.127 billion requested for fiscal year 2016), rationalized in part as a way to cope with the future North Korean threat.[32] Even if outlays for heavy oil delivered to North Korea by several countries under the Agreed Framework are included, the bills for halting DPRK plutonium reprocessing were trivial compared to the costs of coping with a nuclear-armed North Korea.

What of the other democracies?

- The European Union did nothing to halt the conflict spiral in Northeast Asia. It issued restrictions on development assistance to North Korea in November 2002.
- Japan's relations with the DPRK seemed to improve in September 2002 when Prime Minister Junichiro Koizumi (in that office 2001–2006) visited Pyongyang and elicited from Kim Jong Il an admission that North Korea had abducted thirteen Japanese citizens in the late 1970s–early 1980s, only five of whom, Kim Jong Il said, were still alive.[33] The five and some of their family members were allowed to return to Japan on condition that they later return to the North, which did not happen. Sources in Tokyo said a much larger number had been abducted and asked for proof that the eight had died. In Japan, conservatives used Kim's extraordinary confession for domestic political purposes.[34] More than a dozen years after Koizumi's visit to Pyongyang, the abductee issue was still unresolved and continues to impede better relations between Japan and the DPRK.
- A parallel issue troubled ROK–DPRK relations: Seoul charged that nearly 500 South Koreans had been abducted. Hundreds of North Koreans were also abducted from China.

Security in Northeast Asia became less stable in Bush's first term. Pressures mounted on Japan, South Korea, and Taiwan to go nuclear. Tokyo authorized Japanese military commanders to shoot down incoming missiles without consulting civilian authorities—seen in China as a worrying step toward a revived Japanese militarism.

Asked how to sum up U.S. policy to North Korea in Bush's first term, a Washington insider replied, "the failure of Condi Rice." Serving Bush as special assistant for national security, she permitted Vice President Cheney and Defense Secretary Rumsfeld to steer the president toward a belligerent unilateralism. She allowed hawks and moderates to produce an incoherent strategy.[35] Allowing (or pressing) the Agreed Framework to evaporate constituted a major policy failure for both Pyongyang and Washington.

Neither the Bush nor the Kim Jong Il governments handled their relationship in a way that improved the security and well-being of their own citizens. The Bush team should have picked up where Clinton left off in 2000, but did not—with tragic consequences that could probably have been avoided. Whatever its shortcomings, the 1994 Agreed Framework could have been saved. Besides aborting momentum toward arms control, Bush's blend of bombast and malign neglect undercut any pressures on Pyongyang to pursue accommodation with Washington and its partners. Having resumed plutonium production at Yongbyon in 2003, the DPRK tested its first nuclear device in 2006 and others later on. Whatever clandestine uranium enrichment took place, however, its product could not be made ready for use in a bomb for many years. Washington focused on a quite distant threat while failing to investigate fully a possible opportunity to reduce, if not eliminate, a more proximate danger.

14

Six-Party Hopes and Missed Opportunities

Relations between Washington and Pyongyang were more like a Bach concerto than a Beethoven symphony—not entire movements of adagio and allegro but sharp point and counterpoint. Having spurned serious negotiations with Pyongyang for two years, the George W. Bush administration began in 2003 to take part in six-party talks with the DPRK. Following several rounds of meetings hosted by Beijing, the six parties in September 2005 agreed to a basic approach: The North committed to abandoning its nuclear programs in exchange for the gradual granting of benefits (heavy fuel oil) and normalization of relations with the United States, Japan, and the ROK. The deal collapsed when the United States made clear it would never provide a light-water nuclear reactor to the DPRK.

Following North Korea's first nuclear test, in 2006, the six-party talks resumed. In February and October 2007 the six parties signed off on plans for specific steps to meet the terms of the 2005 accord. These included the shutdown of the nuclear reactor at Yongbyon, resumption of inspections, and a complete declaration of all nuclear programs in North Korea. For its part, the United States had to facilitate the return of $25 million in frozen assets and remove the DPRK from the U.S. list of state sponsors of terrorism. These understandings fell apart over Pyongyang's refusal to provide information on its uranium enrichment facility or permit on-site inspection of undeclared facilities. Despite some movement toward a grand bargain in 2005 and again in 2007, Washington and Pyongyang deadlocked in 2008. The impasse probably harmed the long-term interests of each side.

EVOLUTION OF THE BUSH ADMINISTRATION'S WORLDVIEW

The Bush team's strategic doctrines and the Pentagon's "shock and awe" assault on Iraq in 2003 only intensified the DPRK regime's quest for a nuclear-missile deterrent. Pyongyang in 2003 said that its nuclear policy embodied "the principle of self-reliant defense based on the *Juche* idea" and served to defend DPRK sovereignty and to cope with the threat of an American first strike.[1]

If Britain and France were unwilling to rely entirely on their ally, the United States, and insisted on having their own nuclear deterrent, with what greater cause would a country still at war with the United States insist on having a reliable means to keep its longtime foe at bay?

Though lukewarm toward most arms controls, the Bush administration launched a Proliferation Security Initiative (PSI) in 2003 to prevent the transfer of WMD-related materials and contraband originating from, or destined for, countries or nonstate actors of "proliferation concern." The PSI created a network of countries that shared information about suspicious air, sea, and land shipments. If the intelligence were strong, then a country might inspect the cargo or deny overflight to a suspected trafficker. The informality and flexibility of the PSI made it possible for countries as different as Russia and Japan, Australia, and Saudi Arabia to become members.[2] By June 2004 the PSI included seventeen countries, and many more signaled their support. At that time North Korea had no missiles deployed except for surface-to-air defenses and short-range attack. It did possess transport planes and helicopters capable of infiltrating at least two air force sniper brigades and assault forces deep into ROK rear areas. In 2004, however, flying hours for DPRK air forces amounted to fewer than 20 hours a year, compared to 150 for Japan and more than 200 for the United States (which decreased to fewer than 120 in 2013—less than in China, India, or some European countries).[3]

ULTERIOR MOTIVES

On many foreign problems the Bush team preferred to go it alone, joined only by an "alliance of the willing." With North Korea, however, the Bush White House demanded a multilateral approach that included U.S. allies Japan and South Korea as well as China and Russia. Having considered America's options after the demise of the Agreed Framework, President Bush concluded that "nothing would work without getting China on board," Condoleezza Rice later wrote. "He pressed President Jiang Zemin to host the talks."[4]

North Korea preferred to deal directly, one on one, with the world's only superpower, but Washington got its way, and six-party talks commenced in Beijing in August 2003. The Bush team may have demanded the six-party venue because, as one observer noted, the process was "designed to fail."[5] One against five, Pyongyang was defensive and rigid. Also, the format was cumbersome: the time required for translations meant that delegates only rarely could move beyond their prearranged talking points.

Leaders in all six countries had priorities other than arms control. Kim Jong Il's regime clearly saw its nuclear and missile capabilities as major levers not to be traded away except for substantial rewards. Pyongyang used arms negotiations to buy time. The DPRK leadership could have calculated: "If arms control does not lead to a broader breakthrough, our negotiating efforts will have shielded our nuclear buildup from attack. Sooner or later we can present our nuclear weapons capability as an accomplished fact—like China, Israel, India, and Pakistan." As in New Delhi and Islamabad, leaders in Pyongyang also wanted to demonstrate that their country excelled in weaponry, if not in other realms.[6]

North Korea wanted security before it would disarm. For the United States, this was putting the cart before the horse. Yes, Washington promised trade and aid if North Korea disarmed, but said it would withhold full normalization until Pyongyang satisfied an array of conditions.

The White House seemed not to worry much about nuclear spread so long as the United States could improve its own arsenal. In late 2000 the outgoing secretary of state believed that "many in Congress and within the punditocracy opposed a [Clinton–Kim Jong Il] summit because they feared a deal with North Korea would weaken the case for national missile defense."[7] A missile-proof astrodome had been a holy grail for many conservatives ever since President Reagan launched the Strategic Defense Initiative in 1983. So long as North Korea looked ominous, Japan would chip in and take part in missile defense. In consequence, the Bush White House probably did not want a "Libyan solution" (like that achieved in Libya in 2003–2004) by which Pyongyang would renounce its nuclear ambitions and open the country to IAEA inspectors.[8] To make such a solution less likely, the Bush team pressed North Korea to go even further than Tripoli and give up its other illicit activities, transform its economy, end restrictions on food assistance, and become a "normal" state—a package unacceptable to Pyongyang.

Bush's tough line won dollars and political support from passionate conservative donors and voters. Business analysts warned that defense spending might plateau in 2005, but prices for shares in Boeing and Raytheon, each a major National Missile Defense contractor, soared in the first days after Bush's reelection.

In 2004 the United States withdrew 12,000 troops—one-third of the existing force—from Korea for duty in Iraq, and planned to pull back most of the remaining U.S. troops from positions close to the DMZ to bases south of Seoul.[9] Concerned that Washington might be planning to attack, some DPRK strategists worried that the United States wished to spare its own soldiers and depend more heavily on long-range weapons to harm North Korea.

The off-and-on-again negotiations allowed North Korea to continue developing WMD and to sell more weapons abroad. North Korea's economic ties with China, South Korea, and Japan modulated external pressures. Far from maintaining a cordon sanitaire around the DPRK, Japan in 2004 moved toward investing in North Korea. Meanwhile, South Korean investors as well as tourists continued to expand their activities across the DMZ. Pyongyang stepped up its efforts to woo public opinion in the ROK and to strengthen animosity in the South toward the United States.

North and South Korea agreed in June 2004 to stop propaganda broadcasts along their border and to take steps to avoid clashes along the DMZ and in the high seas, but they made no moves to reduce arms or troops (1,105,000 in the North versus 687,700 in the South, with some 4.5 million reservists on each side). They did not sign a peace treaty or take any action on the North's WMD. The tank traps, gun emplacements, and minefields remained in place, with no sign of an imminent political solution to their conflict. Indeed, only a few hours after the June 2004 accord, the ROK Defense Ministry reported that two North Korean navy patrol boats, chasing Chinese fishing boats poaching in the area, crossed into waters controlled by South Korea off the west coast, and retreated when ROK warships approached. A different version came from North Korea's state-run news agency, which claimed that three South Korean warships had infiltrated the waters of North Korea and two South Korean jet fighters threatened its fishing boats as part of the South's alleged efforts to exercise jurisdiction in the area. Similar incidents continued to occur, including, for example, on November 1, 2004.

A few marginal economic gains did little to improve living standards in the DPRK. By 2004 authorities in Pyongyang were uprooting the green shoots of a market economy that had emerged in the late 1990s. Thousands of North Korean refugees crossed into China, and hundreds managed to reach South Korea in 2003–2004. The DPRK remained isolated and impoverished, with no immediate avenues to enter the global community of modernizing and prosperous nations. South Korea's economic assistance to the North remained limited in 2005 and would not be expanded so long as the DPRK retained its nuclear weapons programs.[10]

TOWARD A JOINT STATEMENT OF PRINCIPLES IN 2005

The Bush administration's approach to foreign affairs shifted after Condoleezza Rice replaced Colin Powell as secretary of state in 2005.[11] In his second term Bush and Rice looked for ways to generate a legacy more positive than the Iraq war. They adapted parts of the Powell orientation earlier quashed by Cheney and Rumsfeld. Rice sought to deepen the president's interest in serious negotiations with Kim Jong Il. Bush responded by suggesting that "we could call his bluff and offer him a peace treaty if he gives up his weapons and opens up to the world." This could be regime change by other means. Bush thought, "That place [North Korea] can't stand true sunshine." Rice wrote that the president's proposed initiative "was a little further than I was willing to go." Still, she asked her advisers to think about the idea. She then traveled to the ROK and China armed with the knowledge that the president "was willing to think big." She would suggest to Seoul and Beijing a "restart of the Six-Party Talks in which the United States would be prepared to be flexible."[12]

In Bush's second term the six-party talks appeared to reach two major accords—in 2005 an agreement on principles and in 2007 a three-stage plan for dismantling the Yongbyon complex in exchange for aid and security assurances. Two of the stages were nearly completed by late 2008, but Pyongyang and Washington deadlocked over inspection issues as the Bush administration made way for a new president.

In the interval between the 2005 and 2007 accords, the DPRK tested a long-range missile and a nuclear device. The UN Security Council condemned the tests, but North Korea's actions served to concentrate Washington's attention and added greater self-confidence to Pyongyang's quiver.

Movement toward a deal with Pyongyang was helped by shifts in attitude and top personnel in Washington.[13] Negative influences included Pyongyang's refusal to discuss its uranium enrichment and its role in Syria; DPRK rejection of U.S. demands for on-site sampling to verify plutonium production at Yongbyon; and Japan's intransigence on abductees. A new ROK president ended unconditional Sunshine in 2008.

Beneath the zigs and zags, a pattern emerged. The "agreed" language was usually ambiguous. When Washington seemed to toughen its terms, Pyongyang pulled away and raised the ante. The North Koreans threatened to expose the irony that Washington and Moscow wanted the DPRK to demolish its nuclear deterrent even as they retained and improved their colossal arsenals and China expanded its own.

THE CONFIDANTE AS SECRETARY OF STATE

Auguries in Pyongyang were not bad. In January 2005 Pyongyang's Korean Central News Agency (KCNA) said the DPRK stood ready to settle the nuclear issue peacefully and even to treat Washington as a "friend." In February, however, the DPRK suddenly reverted to bluster. Pyongyang announced that it had actually produced nuclear weapons and was suspending indefinitely its participation in six-party talks. The DPRK accused Washington of "brazen-faced, double-dealing tactics"—combining dialogue with a policy of "regime change." What sparked the tougher inflection? President Bush had made only one, rather innocuous reference to North Korea in his 2005 State of the Union speech. But Rice, in the hearings about her suitability to be secretary of state, had listed North Korea with five other "outposts of tyranny" and, twice that week, affirmed that "all options are available" for dealing with North Korea. None of this persuaded Pyongyang that Bush was making a fresh start. One wonders if America's leading diplomat publicly lambasted recalcitrant deans and department heads when she served as provost at Stanford University. Did her experience suggest that dialogue was improved by publicly insulting her opponents?[14]

But Secretary Rice now wanted a deal with North Korea. She made Christopher Hill the assistant secretary of state for East Asian and Pacific affairs and gave him some authority to conduct give-and-take negotiations with Pyongyang, unlike his hamstrung predecessor, James Kelly. As U.S. ambassador to the ROK, Hill had become popular there. A creative diplomat, he was willing—like his mentor, Richard Holbrooke—to take risks and sometimes exceed his instructions. Hill proposed to Rice that the administration assemble a package of incentives for North Korea and sell it to the Chinese, who would then sell it to Pyongyang— replaying a technique used by Holbrooke and Hill in 1995 when they got Serbian leader Slobodan Milošević to sell their ideas to the Bosnian Serbs for the 1995 Dayton Agreements.[15]

In March 2005 the IAEA declared that it remained "committed to securing full safeguards compliance by the DPRK through peaceful means." Unable to verify the completeness and correctness of the initial report of the DPRK under the NPT Safeguards Agreement, however, the Agency had concluded that since 1993 the DPRK was not complying with its obligations under the agreement. Between 1994 and 2002, the Agreed Framework had been a tool for "bringing the DPRK into compliance with its safeguards obligations. However, the reports about a clandestine uranium enrichment programme, the end of the 'freeze' pursuant to the Agreed Framework, and the expulsion of the IAEA inspectors brought this phase to an end."[16]

Unrepentant, Pyongyang became more defiant. In March 2005 the DPRK said it was no longer bound by its more than five-year-old moratorium on flight-testing of longer-range missiles. In April 2005 DPRK vice foreign minister Kim Gye Gwan told independent scholar Selig S. Harrison that Pyongyang might give nuclear weapons to other actors if "the United States drives us into a corner." Later that month Pyongyang denounced Bush and his entourage in terms that made "axis of evil" look like a compliment. The authoritative newspaper *Rodong Sinmum* declared on April 29, 2005, that the U.S. president was "the world's worst fascist dictator, a top-notch war maniac and Hitler junior waving hands stained with blood shed by innocent people." It called the whole "brutish Bush bellicose group" a "bunch of hardened thugs losing their grip on the ability to think normally and not the kind of people we should deal with in the first place."

Tough actions followed tough words. In June Pyongyang refueled its reactor at Yongbyon and said it was starting to reprocess 8,000 spent fuel rods removed in March. Washington began to flex its economic muscles. In June 2005 the U.S. Treasury froze the U.S. assets of three North Korean entities responsible for WMD and missile programs and barred U.S. citizens and companies from doing business with those firms. Washington also labored to persuade other governments to block DPRK exports of missiles and nuclear materials and to stop Pyongyang's trafficking in narcotics and counterfeit dollars. In 2005 Japan closed its waters to foreign ships lacking liability insurance against spills and other accidents. Since almost no North Korean vessels carried such insurance, the new requirement could halt most shipping traffic between the two countries. Seoul and Beijing, however, were loath to take part in any actions that would further isolate the North.

The atmosphere was not helped by U.S. allegations, later proved unfounded, that North Korea had sold partly processed nuclear fuel to Libya and perhaps to other buyers on the black market. Also, Bush's disinformation campaign regarding Saddam Hussein's WMD left the world dubious about anything the White House might say about anything. Washington had dissipated its soft power, and an impression grew that Washington's words were no more reliable than those of its adversaries.

After meeting with Ambassador Hill in July 2005, however, Kim Gye Gwan said Pyongyang would return to the six-party talks. The KCNA explained that the "U.S. side clarified its official stand to recognize [North Korea] as a sovereign state, not to invade it, and hold *bilateral* talks within the framework of the six-party talks" (emphasis added). Later that month, Kim Jong Il told a Chinese envoy of his father Kim Il Sung's dying wish for the denuclearization of the Korean peninsula. Given the traditional Korean respect for elders, this was a sign that the Dear Leader may truly have wanted a deal.

THE AGREED PRINCIPLES, SEPTEMBER 19, 2005

Having resumed their talks on September 13, the six parties on September 19, 2005, announced agreement on a set of principles to guide future negotiations.

- North Korea committed to abandoning all nuclear weapons and existing nuclear programs and returning, at an early date, to the NPT and to IAEA safeguards.
- The United Sates affirmed "no intention to attack or invade the DPRK with nuclear or conventional weapons."
- The ROK committed to the 1992 Joint Declaration on Denuclearization, which all parties said should be observed and implemented.
- The DPRK stated that it had the right to peaceful uses of nuclear energy, and the other parties agreed to discuss, at an appropriate time, "the provision of light water reactor [unclear if singular or plural] to the DPRK." All six parties "undertook to promote economic cooperation in the fields of energy, trade and investment, bilaterally and/or multilaterally." The five pledged energy assistance to the DPRK, with the ROK specifying that it would provide 2 million kilowatts of electric power to the DPRK.
- The DPRK and the United States undertook "to respect each other's sovereignty, exist peacefully together, and take steps to normalize their relations."

- The DPRK and Japan agreed to normalize their relations on "the basis of the settlement of unfortunate past and the outstanding issues of concern."
- The "directly related parties" promised to "negotiate a permanent peace regime on the Korean Peninsula at an appropriate separate forum."
- "The Six Parties agreed to explore ways and means for promoting security cooperation in Northeast Asia."
- This consensus would be implemented in a "phased manner in line with the principle of 'commitment for commitment, action for action.'"[17]

Though Washington would not offer Pyongyang a formal nonaggression treaty, the U.S. delegation declared that the United States had no nuclear weapons on the Korean peninsula and had no intention to attack North Korea. But it soon appeared that the six parties had finessed too much. Ambiguity reigned. The joint statement did not specify *how* energy would be provided to the North. It put off discussion of the DPRK demand for a light-water reactor until an "appropriate time." Though the Clinton administration had pledged to build two LWRs for the DPRK, the Bush White House now argued that North Korea could not be trusted with *any* nuclear capabilities. The statement was silent on whether, as Washington charged and Pyongyang denied, the North was running a clandestine uranium enrichment program. It also set no date for disarmament and specified no details for inspection.

On the final day of the session Assistant Secretary Hill read a closing U.S. statement that had been sent to him overnight from Washington, a message drafted by hard-liners in the National Security Council but approved by Rice.[18] Hill informed the delegations that the "appropriate time" for discussion of LWRs would come when the North had "eliminated all nuclear weapons and all nuclear programs" and after this had been verified by credible international teams, and after Pyongyang had ceased proliferating nuclear technology. Underscoring Washington's resistance to LWRs for the DPRK, Hill stated that the United States wanted to close down KEDO by year's end.

Rice in her memoirs claimed to have negotiated the delicate compromise of conflicting positions embodied in the joint statement. She gathered the Chinese, ROK, Japanese, and Russian foreign ministers when all were at the United Nations. Later, she woke Li Zhaoxing, the Chinese minister, late at night to work out compromise wording. She then phoned Stephen Hadley (her replacement at the National Security Council) to tell him that "there can't be a problem. I've committed us to the language."[19] According to Don Oberdorfer and Robert Carlin, however, she then signed off on the closing statement drafted by Hadley and Michael Greenberg at the NSC.[20]

In later years the DPRK often referred to the September 15 statement as a nearly sacred foundation for accommodation with the other five parties. But Rice in her memoirs says *nothing* about adding these killer amendments to the U.S. position, which essentially neutered the deal. In her telling, the joint statement just vanished into thin air.

Passing over the debacle of her efforts and those of Christopher Hill, Rice's memoir stressed that she hoped a peace and security mechanism could be developed for Northeast Asia once the nuclear issue was resolved "satisfactorily."[21] She also expressed her admiration for the way the Treasury Department could mobilize international financial action against North Korea without having to go to the United Nations.[22] The Treasury Department's actions, however, probably added to Pyongyang's suspicions and intransigence.

If the State Department had played the role of somewhat conciliatory cop, the U.S. Treasury stepped up its role as tough cop. On September 15 the Treasury Department designated Banco Delta Asia (BDA) in Macao as a "primary money laundering concern" under the USA Patriot Act and managed to freeze some $25 million in North Korean funds. In October the Treasury Department sanctioned eight North Korean entities for their involvement in WMD proliferation and froze their U.S. assets. In 2006 the Bank of China froze DPRK accounts containing millions of dollars.

In reply to Hill's closing statement, the DPRK on September 20, 2005, accused Washington of reneging. The North accused the United States of using the negotiations to "disarm us and crush us to death with nuclear weapons." The DPRK Foreign Ministry underscored the problem of sequencing. It declared that the North would not make the first move. Others "are telling us to give up everything, but there will be no such thing as giving it up first." Pyongyang warned that Washington "should not even dream" that the DPRK would give up its nuclear arsenal until the United States provided it with a LWR.

Regardless of these harsh words, a few days later in New York the DPRK deputy foreign minister, Choe Su Hun, told the UN General Assembly that the recent joint statement represented his country's "principled positions." Choe affirmed that the DPRK would not need a "single nuclear weapon" if its relations with the United States were normalized, if bilateral confidence were built, and if the North were no longer exposed to a U.S. nuclear threat. But he reiterated that Washington should give civilian nuclear reactors to the DPRK as part of "simultaneous action" on the North's disarmament. Adding to the momentary euphoria, South Korean media reported that the North intended to invite Rice and perhaps even Bush to Pyongyang to elevate the status of the Dear Leader and normalize bilateral ties.

Which actor should take the first step? Former ROK prime minister Goh Kun suggested that the United States issue a security guarantee to the North "concurrent" with DPRK denuclearization.[23] But the guarantee could be offered in an instant, while denuclearization could take years to complete. Once the North dismantled its nuclear machinery, however, a security assurance could be withdrawn overnight.

When six-party talks resumed in November 2005, the ROK and Japan proposed separating the outstanding issues into three categories: dismantlement of Pyongyang's nuclear program; economic and energy assistance to North Korea; and Pyongyang's bilateral issues with Washington and with Tokyo. But U.S.-DPRK disagreements blocked progress. The North Korean delegation demanded unfreezing DPRK funds at the BDA. In December North Korea said it would pursue the construction of larger graphite-moderated reactors—the kind of reactor the Agreed Framework aimed to supplant. KEDO in 2003 had stopped work on the LWRs but did not formally end the project until June 2006.

North Korea Goes Nuclear

When Rice became secretary of state, she intimated to Bush that he could match his father's accomplishment in unifying Germany by a nuclear deal with Pyongyang, a peace agreement to replace the 1953 armistice, and eventual unification of North and South. Bush liked big, game-changing ideas, and this gave Rice some room to maneuver. When China's president, Hu Jintao, visited the White House in April 2006 and suggested security assurances to the North, Bush asked, "How about I give Kim a peace treaty?" Cheney, also present at the luncheon, was stunned. Hu agreed to inform Pyongyang that Bush wanted a breakthrough, but by that time Pyongyang was preparing to test ballistic missiles and its nuclear device.[24]

Chinese mediation often played a constructive role. When North Korean and U.S. diplomats went their separate ways, Beijing stood ready to host more rounds of negotiations. Sometimes China proposed bridging language that helped the two—or the six—enter another commitment. Beijing also tried to use its material support to restrain DPRK actions, but with little effect. Counting on Beijing's devotion to stability, Pyongyang ignored Chinese admonitions.

Things got worse in 2006 before they got better. On July 4–5 the DPRK test-fired seven ballistic missiles. Six short- and medium-range missiles appeared to function as planned, but the three-stage Taepodong-2 fell apart soon after launch. The U.S. State Department called the launches a "provocative act" violating North Korea's voluntary moratorium on flight-testing, observed since September 1999. The UN Security Council unanimously adopted Resolution 1695—a compromise between the strong stance favored by Tokyo and Washington and the milder language favored by Beijing and Moscow. China insisted that the resolution not invoke Chapter VII of the UN Charter, which allows for economic and diplomatic measures (Article 41) and military actions (Article 42) against threats to peace and security. Nonetheless the resolution condemned North Korea's missile launches; called on Pyongyang to return to the six-party talks; and demanded that the

DPRK suspend its ballistic-missile activities and reestablish its flight-testing moratorium. The resolution also required states to prevent missiles and related "items, materials, goods and technology" from being transferred to the DPRK. It also required UN members to prevent the procurement of such items from Pyongyang and the transfer of any "financial resources in relation to" North Korea's weapons programs. The United States, Japan, and Australia took the lead in implementing the resolution; Seoul halted food and fertilizer assistance; but China played the paper tiger. It allowed sanctioned goods to cross into the DPRK and North Korean planes to fly over its territory regardless of their cargo.

Pyongyang responded that it would not be bound by the UN resolution. Combining a smile with a growl, the DPRK Foreign Ministry on October 3 stated that Pyongyang "will in the future conduct a nuclear test under the condition where safety is firmly guaranteed." It also said that North Korea would refrain from the first-use of nuclear weapons, "strictly prohibit any nuclear transfer," and "do its utmost to realize the denuclearization of the [Korean] peninsula."

Six days later, on October 9, 2006, the DPRK tested a nuclear device underground, with a yield under one kiloton—so small that some analysts said it "fizzled." The DPRK averred that its "nuclear test was entirely attributable to the U.S. nuclear threat, sanctions and pressure." The DPRK asserted that it had to test in order to protect its "sovereignty." Pyongyang warned that it might conduct further nuclear tests if the United States "increases pressure" on the country. The Foreign Ministry added, however, that North Korea remained committed to implementing the September 2005 joint statement. It recalled also that the "denuclearization of the entire peninsula was President Kim Il Sung's last instruction and an ultimate goal" of North Korea.

Responding to North Korea's nuclear explosion, the UN Security Council on October 16 unanimously adopted Resolution 1718—this time acting under Chapter VII, Article 41, authorizing measures *not* involving the use of force to enforce Council decisions. The resolution condemned the DPRK test and "demanded" that the DPRK not conduct any further nuclear test or launch of a ballistic missile and that it return to the NPT. It ordered the DPRK to suspend all activities related to its ballistic missile program and "abandon all nuclear weapons and existing nuclear programs in a complete, verifiable and irreversible manner" and "return immediately to the six-party talks without any precondition." The resolution authorized, but did not require, member states to stop and inspect shipments of cargo for WMD going to or from North Korea. It banned DPRK imports or exports of tanks, armored combat vehicles, heavy artillery, combat aircraft, warships, missiles or missile systems, and related materiel including spare parts. The resolution imposed an asset freeze and travel ban on persons related to the nuclear weapons program.

To monitor and adjust the sanctions, the Council established a committee consisting of all its fifteen members. However, China did not approve the practice of inspecting cargo to and from the DPRK and urged other countries to refrain from provocative steps that could intensify the tension. China repeated that the six-party talks were the best means of handling the issue and opposed the use of force.

The DPRK representative "totally rejected" the text, saying that it was "gangster-like" of the Security Council to adopt such a coercive resolution against his country while neglecting the nuclear threat posed by the United States against the DPRK. This, he said, amounted to a double standard.

Later, when North Korea launched another long-range missile on April 5, 2009, Security Council members debated whether this action violated Resolution 1718. Russia and China said no, because Pyongyang claimed merely to have launched a satellite that was sending back patriotic songs from outer space (another outright lie). In a compromise move, the Security Council issued a presidential statement—less than a resolution but more than a declaration—condemning the test and saying it was in "contravention" to Resolution 1718. Meanwhile, *the sanctions committee on North Korea had not met in the previous two years and failed to designate even a single North Korean company to be added to the UN blacklist of banned entities.* The bite of UN sanctions was proving shallow.

PROGRESS IN 2007

Pyongyang's nuclear explosion in October 2006 at first deepened the gulf between North Korea and its negotiating partners. But the test permitted North Korea to negotiate from a new sense of strength and deepened Washington's resolve to defang a would-be nuclear power. In December 2006 Hill and his DPRK counterpart happened to meet at the Beijing airport as they prepared to fly home. In the airport they agreed to hold their first bilateral in years without Chinese mediation. Meeting secretly in Berlin on January 16–17, 2007, both sides quickly agreed on terms to be finalized at six-party talks in February. Hill arranged the Berlin meeting without the knowledge of Cheney and other Washington hard-liners. Rice backed the initiative and its outcome, and Bush approved.

True to the Berlin understanding between Hill and his DPRK counterpart, the six parties on February 13, 2007, approved the most substantive accord on North Korea since the 1994 Agreed Framework—an "action plan" to implement the September 19, 2005, joint statement. North Korea would halt operation of its nuclear facilities at Yongbyon during a sixty-day initial phase in return for an initial shipment of 50,000 tons of heavy fuel oil. The sixty-day period represented a neat compromise between the initial U.S. proposal of forty-five days and the North's counter of ninety. Both sides knew how to bargain.

The plan established working groups to formulate plans for economic and energy cooperation; denuclearization; a "Northeast Asia Peace and Security Mechanism"; and bilateral DPRK relations with the United States and with Japan. Following the shutdown of facilities at Yongbyon, Pyongyang would provide a complete declaration of all of its nuclear programs and disable all of its existing nuclear facilities in return for an additional 950,000 tons of heavy fuel oil or its equivalent. Besides providing energy aid to North Korea, the United States would begin removing Pyongyang from its list of state sponsors of terrorism and stop the application of the Trading with the Enemy Act toward North Korea.

The United States gave North Korea extra time to fulfill its commitments. Pyongyang refused to act on its February 2007 pledge to shut down the Yongbyon reactor until it received $25 million in funds frozen by the U.S. Treasury in Macao. Soon, Treasury's assistant secretary for terrorist financing and financial crimes said that the two governments had reached an understanding on the frozen funds. Washington insisted, however, that the funds "will be used solely for the betterment of the North Korean people, including for humanitarian and educational purposes." Months passed. Finally, a Russian bank assisted the funds transfer to Pyongyang. On June 25 the DPRK confirmed that it had received the funds and it began shutting down the Yongbyon nuclear facilities, a process confirmed by the IAEA in July.

A new crisis arose on September 6, 2007, when Israeli bombers destroyed a Syrian facility that U.S. officials asserted was a nuclear reactor being built with North Korean assistance on the Yongbyon model. For the next year and more, the DPRK refused to discuss the issue except to deny that it was helping a Syrian nuclear project. Washington had to decide whether to press the issue as an example of nuclear proliferation by Pyongyang or ignore it and focus on Yongbyon.[25]

Notwithstanding the Syrian controversy, the six parties met again in late September 2007 and issued a joint statement on October 3. North Korea pledged that by December 31 it would provide a "complete and correct declaration of all its nuclear programs—including clarification regarding the uranium issue." Pyongyang also agreed to disable its Yongbyon and other nuclear facilities subject to the September 2005 joint statement and not to transfer nuclear material or technology abroad. In return, North Korea would receive the remaining 900,000 tons of heavy fuel oil or its equivalent as pledged on February 13. Washington agreed to begin removing North Korea from its list of state sponsors of terrorism and to "advance the process of terminating the application of the Trading with the Enemy Act" toward North Korea "in parallel with" North Korea's denuclearization actions.

Pyongyang ascribed a sacrosanct quality to the October 3 joint statement.[26] The fact that the statement had no provision for verification, however, led to huge difficulties in the following year. As of late 2007, however, both sides seemed determined to execute their commitments. In November a team of U.S. experts arrived in North Korea and began leading the disablement of the Yongbyon nuclear facilities, trying to make the December 31 deadline that had been stipulated on October 3. Funding for the disablement process was provided by the State Department's Nonproliferation and Disarmament Fund.

SUNSHINE = MOONSHINE?

For most of George W. Bush's second term, bilateral relations seemed to improve between South and North Korea. It was unclear, however, whether Seoul's Sunshine Policy served to bring the North in from the cold or reinforced its tendency to hunker down and ask for more. A second ROK–DPRK summit took place on October 2–4, 2007. Not insisting on a reciprocal DPRK visit to the South, ROK president Roh Moo-hyun traveled to Pyongyang to meet with Kim Jong Il. They agreed to take steps toward reunification, ease military tensions, expand meetings of separated families, and engage in social and cultural exchanges. They expressed a "shared understanding . . . on the need for ending the current armistice mechanism and building a permanent peace mechanism."

On December 19, 2007, the Grand National party candidate, Lee Myung-bak, was elected ROK president, ushering in the first conservative government in Seoul in ten years. Lee pledged to review the Sunshine Policy of his two predecessors and insist on reciprocity by the North. After Lee's inauguration in February 2008, Seoul stopped sending rice and fertilizer to the North. In response, Pyongyang then began to restrict cross-border exchanges with the South. In July 2008 DPRK troops shot and killed a South Korean tourist, a middle-aged woman, as she walked on the beach in the Mount Kumgang resort—after which Pyongyang demanded an apology from Seoul! The DPRK refused to allow South Korean officials to inspect the shooting scene, claiming the woman trespassed into a restricted military zone despite repeated warnings.

Following the killing, the ROK halted subsidies for civic groups committed to North–South cooperation, and Hyundai Asan immediately suspended its tours. On balance, however, Seoul's response to the killing was quite restrained. In November 2008, one day after the North threatened to close its land border with the South, the ROK Ministry of Unification announced it would resume subsidizing local civic groups to assist their humanitarian activities in the North. The ROK government expressed hope that North Korea would accept an offer to send materials and equipment necessary to improve military communication between the two sides. However, a telephone message from the ROK military to the North proposing that the two sides discuss this plan went unanswered. Pyongyang also closed its Red Cross liaison office at the truce village of Panmunjom and cut off direct telephone links with its South Korean counterpart. The DPRK intensified its refractory behavior in 2009.

MORE POINT AND COUNTERPOINT

In December 2007 President Bush wrote a letter to the DPRK leader addressed "Dear Mr. Chairman" and had it delivered to Pyongyang by diplomat Christopher Hill. Two months after Bush's somewhat cordial letter, the New York Philharmonic, with State Department approval, played and gave master classes in Pyongyang as well as performances in Beijing and Seoul. The concert in North Korea began with the DPRK and U.S. national anthems, for which the elite audience of 2,500 stood. A symphonic rendition of "Arirang," a folk song loved by Koreans north and south, brought tears to many eyes. The program included *Lohengrin* but also Americana—the *New World Symphony, An American in Paris,* and *Candide.* The audience stood and clapped for six minutes after the last piece. "Someday a composer may write a work entitled *Americans in Pyongyang,*" said conductor Loren Maazel, drawing warm applause from the audience. This visit marked the first occasion that a U.S. cultural organization appeared in North Korea and the largest contingent of Americans since the Korean War. Looking for precedents, historians recalled the triumphant visits of the Boston Symphony and New York Philharmonic to the USSR in the late 1950s and the Philadelphia Orchestra's concerts in China in 1973.

The orchestra's visit had come in response to a North Korean invitation the previous year.[27] The hosts and the concertgoers gave the Americans a warm and friendly reception. DPRK vice minister of culture Song Sok-hwan called the visit a "big stride in cultural exchange." Conductor Maazel was equally positive. "This might just have pushed us over the top" in finding a way beyond past discord, said former defense secretary William Perry after the concert, adding that Washington should reciprocate by inviting North Korean performers to the United States. But there was no replay of ping-pong diplomacy. A White House spokesman commented that a concert is just a concert—not a diplomatic coup. Indeed, U.S.-DPRK negotiations in 2008 encountered one problem after another, and no high-level invitations went to Pyongyang. U.S. officials feared "doing an Albright"—giving respectability to the enemy.

IMPASSE

How near and yet so far. The United States and North Korea in 2008 nearly got to yes on a wide-ranging agreement, only to have the year end in deadlock. Why? Each side, its supporters said, had been reasonable; each side, its critics maintained, had been two-faced and scheming. Interpreting what happened was difficult because many exchanges took place behind closed doors and some reported understandings were not put down in writing or published. For Washington, the most important problem was verification; for Pyongyang, delivery of promised fuel oil on time. The "sacrosanct" October 3, 2007, agreement laid out a three-stage program for denuclearization but provided no mechanism for verification until the third phase. State Department officials seemed ready on occasion to cut Pyongyang some slack; the DPRK Foreign Ministry also sought to bridge differences. But hard-liners in Washington (also in Tokyo and Seoul) raised the ante on several occasions, giving Pyongyang cause (and excuse) to pull back.

Though required to provide a complete and correct declaration of its nuclear programs by December 31, 2007, Pyongyang failed to produce the declaration until June 2008. Trying to explain the DPRK delay, a State Department spokesman on January 2, 2008, referred to "some technical questions about the cooling of the fuel rods." But Pyongyang offered a different explanation. Since energy deliveries to North Korea were behind schedule, the DPRK was slowing Yongbyon disablement.

In February 2008 Christopher Hill requested that Congress waive the "Glenn amendment" sanctions imposed on North Korea following its 2006 nuclear test. These sanctions, which banned nonhumanitarian assistance to nonnuclear weapons states that detonate a nuclear weapon, prevented the National Nuclear Security Administration from carrying out work to dismantle the Yongbyon nuclear facilities. Hill also informed the Senate Foreign Relations Committee that, in autumn 2007, North Korea showed U.S. officials two conventional weapons systems it claimed were the recipients of the thousands of aluminum tubes imported years before—the tubes that had raised suspicions of a uranium enrichment program. The North said the tubes were currently being used for a second conventional weapons system. But tests of the aluminum in a U.S. laboratory showed traces of highly enriched uranium. How did it get there unless as part of a uranium enrichment process? Questions remained weightier than answers.

Then, in April 2008, two former U.S. officials stated that the State Department was conceding too much by focusing on North Korea's plutonium assets and ignoring its commitments in other arenas. "It is one thing to compromise in order to craft an agreement, keep difficult negotiations going, and not let the best be the enemy of the good," Winston Lord and Leslie Gelb wrote in the *Washington Post*. "It is another thing to let the other side breach compromises already reached."[28]

In June 2008 the DPRK provided its long-awaited declaration—some 18,000 pages of documentation detailing the operations of its 5-megawatt nuclear reactor and plutonium reprocessing facility at Yongbyon, records dating back to 1986. As with the aluminum, there were traces of highly enriched uranium on the paper. But President Bush immediately announced that he would begin the process of removing North Korea from the list of state sponsors of terrorism and lift sanctions on North Korea under the U.S. Trading with the Enemy Act.[29] Justifying Bush's announcement, the State Department said that North Korea had not committed a terrorist act since 1987. The White House stated on June 26 that eight of eleven components of the disablement process had been completed and that close to 50 percent of nuclear fuel rods in the Yongbyon nuclear reactor had been removed. One day later, with CNN cameras rolling, DPRK workers blew up the cooling tower for the 5-megawatt reactor at Yongbyon.

Still, critics charged that Bush was giving away the store. John R. Bolton, now a private citizen, asserted that the North's nuclear and ballistic missile programs "materially assisted Syria and Iran, two other states on the terrorism honor roll." Bolton could not see what remained of President Bush's doctrine that those who support terrorists will be treated as terrorists. "Nothing can erase the ineffable sadness of an American presidency, like this one, in total intellectual collapse."[30] A subsequent report by the Congressional Reference Service cited French, Japanese, South Korean, and Israeli sources describing recent North Korean programs to provide arms and training to Hezbollah in Lebanon and the Tamil Tigers in Sri Lanka—two groups on the U.S. list of international terrorist organizations. Moreover, there was much evidence of a long-standing collaboration between North Korea and the Iranian Revolutionary Guards.[31]

While not denying these concerns, some security analysts advised the United States to focus on the most urgent danger and work to disable the Yongbyon facility so it could yield no more plutonium. Everything else was of secondary importance. As Roger Fisher and William Ury would have argued, focus on your deepest interests and consider the alternative if no agreement is reached.

The Bush administration had its own questions about the accuracy and completeness of the DPRK declaration. The 18,000 pages said nothing about uranium enrichment or North Korea's activities in Syria. Some experts thought the report understated DPRK plutonium production—37 kilograms versus a U.S. estimate of 50 kilograms. Washington wanted on-site sampling to determine the efficiency of Pyongyang's nuclear efforts and the likely quantities already produced.

North Korea maintained that, under the October 2007 accord, it was not obligated to address verification at this stage. But Pyongyang gave way and on July 18 signed a communiqué providing for a six-party verification mechanism that could visit declared facilities, review documents, and interview personnel. Tokyo and Seoul wanted a tougher stand. So Washington demanded a more intrusive verification system. But Washington itself was already pushing back the goalposts. On June 18, 2008, Secretary Rice told the Heritage Foundation that Washington would delay removing North Korea from the list of state sponsors of terrorism until it could verify the accuracy and completeness of the declaration. She acknowledged that Washington was moving up verification from the third phase to the second phase of the process—a move sure to spark DPRK resistance. On August 11, 2008, the State Department informed the North Koreans that they would not be removed from the terrorist list until a strong verification regime was in place. In response, the DPRK Foreign Ministry accused the United States of violating the six-party implementation accords. In late August Pyongyang announced it was suspending the work of neutralizing its nuclear facilities. In September it pledged to restore the facilities to their original state.

DPRK flexibility was probably limited by Kim Jong Il's health: he suffered a severe stroke in mid-August. No other officials would dare alter whatever course Jong Il had set. The North kept the Dear Leader's condition a secret, but U.S. and ROK intelligence grasped that a major medical emergency had occurred.[32]

Still hoping for a breakthrough in the negotiations, Washington softened its demands. On October 1 Hill brought to Pyongyang a draft protocol stipulating less intrusive inspection procedures. Hill and Kim Gye Gwan seemed to reach an understanding. Soon, the Bush administration announced that North Korea had agreed to all demands for inspection of its nuclear facilities and that it would be removed from the list of state sponsors of terrorism. The State Department cautioned, however, that the DPRK could be returned to the list if it failed to facilitate inspection. Apparently satisfied, Pyongyang resumed disabling the Yongbyon facilities.

But discord immediately erupted over the ostensible accord between Hill and Kim Gye Gwan. U.S. officials asserted that North Korea had agreed to allow inspectors to collect samples from its nuclear facilities and remove them from the country for analysis. But Pyongyang contradicted these claims and said the two sides had agreed that verification would be confined to "field visits, confirmation of documents, and interviews with technicians"—and would begin only after North Korea received energy assistance promised in 2007. The discrepancy may have arisen from differences between written and more extensive verbal understandings. Pyongyang refused to put in writing what Hill thought had been agreed to orally.[33] What U.S. officials regarded as logical modes of verification probably struck the North as espionage.[34]

Getting tougher, Pyongyang in November 2008 said it was slowing by half the pace at which it unloaded the spent fuel rods from its 5-megawatt reactor, because of "the delayed fulfillment of the economic compensation" by China, Russia, South Korea, and the United States. A Japanese source said North Korea was reducing the rate from 30 rods to 15 rods per day. By November the DPRK had removed about 5,000 of the 8,000 total spent fuel rods.

The removal of the spent fuel rods constituted one of the last of eleven steps North Korea agreed to take in 2007 to disable the three primary facilities at its Yongbyon nuclear complex. In return, the other parties (except Japan) agreed to supply one million tons of heavy fuel oil or its equivalent. The U.S. State Department reported in November 2008 that about 550,000 tons had already been shipped or would soon be delivered. In early December the State Department said that U.S. shipments of heavy fuel oil would not continue without a verification agreement, but that the United States had already finished supplying its share

(200,000 tons). South Korea indicated that its assistance would be reconsidered. Russia's envoy to the six-party talks, Deputy Foreign Minister Alexei Borodavkin, stated that Russia would complete its delivery of 200,000 tons of heavy fuel oil "in a few months." China said it would continue to implement the agreements made in 2007. Japan remained adamant that it would not supply its share of heavy fuel oil (200,000 tons) until its concerns about abductees were resolved. At Washington's request, Australia and New Zealand offered to make up for Japan's share, but they too conditioned their assistance on resolution of the verification impasse.

Some ROK and U.S. authorities said the North Koreans would allow sampling when they judged the price to be right. Given the stakes, arguing about 200,000 or even 600,000 tons of oil looked both petty and myopic. Isolated and impoverished, however, North Korea would not permit its adversaries to welsh on their promises. Pyongyang as well as Washington could be legalistic. The parties had earlier seen how the DPRK had refused to act on its February 2007 commitments until $25 million from Macao reached Pyongyang. If Kim Jong Il had suffered a serious medical problem in 2008, as widely believed, whoever was making decisions in Pyongyang could not afford to look weak.

DPRK statements implied that Pyongyang might be willing to address the question of sampling in the third and ostensibly final phase of the negotiations. As of December 2008, however, the parties remained deadlocked on verification. China generated a single negotiating text based on consultations with each of the parties. The draft did not speak of "sampling," but called for "scientific verification procedures" and "international standards" in order to find consensus. Hill told reporters that "most delegations were prepared to work with the Chinese text," although "that consensus was not shared by" North Korea.

The United States and its allies, in the opinion of at least one observer, "could have been satisfied with the fact that international aid organizations were allowed unprecedented free movement inside North Korea, that markets were given more influence, that North Koreans were interested in learning from the West." But "demands for more access, more transparency, more information, and more concessions" looked to Pyongyang like "blunt attempts at data mining and bringing about regime change. Consequently, international organizations were curtailed in their activities and most of them finally driven out of the country."[35]

In December 2008 Kim Gye Gwan warned that if the energy assistance did not materialize, "we will adjust the speed of disablement." A few days later, another DPRK source stated that "aid from China and Russia has continued and we do not intend to stop the disablement process yet."

The year 2008 ended with movement toward a deal with North Korea in paralysis. On December 12, 2008, the United States announced it would not go forward with energy assistance without progress on verification. Rice had enlisted President Bush and Stephen Hadley to support a serious attempt for the United States to bridge differences with Pyongyang.[36] However, they failed to overcome the North's aversion to inspection measures that could reveal the extent of DPRK uranium capabilities. Having made some concessions, the North may have thought that U.S. demands for verification amounted to one bridge too far. In January 2009 the DPRK stated there could be no nuclear inspections unless America's "hostile policy and nuclear threat to the North are fundamentally terminated." The DPRK Foreign Ministry appeared to have lost out to the hard-liners in Pyongyang, and the tougher orientation could not be easily changed. The six-party talks did not resume.

15

Obama and Kim Jong Un

Approach and Avoid

Despite decades of interaction, everything between the United States and North Korea roiled in uncertainty. Did the other side want to normalize relations and create joint values, or wreak havoc and seize values? Hard-liners in each camp distrusted the other side and labored to weaken the adversary. If negotiations took place, then hard-liners treated them as a way to buy time and nurture conditions for their side to win. Moderates, however, experienced an approach-avoidance syndrome. Attracted to the prospect of a peace deal, they were also repelled by its dangers. The closer they approached such an accommodation, the risks loomed larger. Diffident leaders then became more cautious. On occasion they tried to test the other side's goodwill. If the adversary failed the test, then relations could return to the norm—neither peace nor war.

The Obama administration attempted at times to signal Pyongyang that the United States was prepared to normalize relations, sign a peace treaty, and provide energy and economic assistance. The terms on offer seemed congruent with some, if not all, of North Korea's objectives. But interactions between the Obama White House and Pyongyang often stoked mutual distrust. American offers to make a fresh start often contained language Pyongyang would perceive as insulting, scolding, or threatening. Alternating between smiles and bombast, North Korea's diplomacy also evoked disquiet.

Contradictory messages produced cognitive dissonance. To resolve the dissonance, leaders could venture more steps toward conciliation or return to a hard line. Small steps and half measures, however, did not quash doubts on the receiving side. The dilemma was sharper for Pyongyang than for Washington, because the perceived dangers were greater. American and ROK armies were poised at the North's doorstep—nearly on its beaches—and were backed by huge economic as well as military assets.

Deciding which fork to take was the more hazardous because a misstep could trigger denunciation by critics wanting to crow, "We told you so." Each side felt a need to show its resolute strength against a dangerous adversary and thus preempt criticism by domestic rivals and fair-weather allies. The military-industrial complex and intelligence bureaucracies on each side had their own reasons and ways to subvert movement toward détente.

The default position was inertia—a malaise that kept each side from enhancing its people's deepest interests. Some of this infirmity was self-induced—brought on by hard-liners agitating stubborn memories and fears.[1] Usually each side seemed to be playing a broken record. Bad timing also played a role. On the rare occasions that promised change, the two sides were usually out of synch. Neither played the same music at the same time. A mutually advantageous deal was available, but stayed out of reach.

COGNITIVE DISSONANCE

Barack Obama thought and wrote about nuclear weapons issues while still in college.[2] More than two decades later, as a U.S. senator, Obama in May 2005 named North Korea as one of the "biggest proliferation challenges we currently face." Obama called for the strengthening of the Nuclear Nonproliferation Treaty so that countries like North Korea "that break the rules will automatically face strong international sanctions." Yet after Pyongyang's October 2006 nuclear test, Obama appeared on *Meet the Press* and complained that the United States had no leverage over North Korea because of Washington's refusal to hold bilateral negotiations.

Given that Obama esteemed the worldview of Protestant theologian Reinhold Niebuhr, David Brooks asked in 2007 what might be the practical implications for foreign policy of Obama's Niebuhrian instincts. In reply, Obama waxed rhapsodic about the need to get energetically engaged in the Middle East peace process. Should the United States then sit down and talk with Hamas? Obama said no: "There's no point in sitting down so long as Hamas says Israel doesn't have the right to exist." Obama disliked the grand Bushian rhetoric about ridding the world of evil and tyranny and transforming the Middle East. But he also disliked liberal muddleheadedness on power politics. Revolted by what he saw as the arrogant unilateral actions of the Bush administration, Obama called for humility. Against dovish passivity as well, he argued for the hardheaded promotion of democracy in the spirit of John F. Kennedy.[3]

In the televised presidential debate on July 23, 2008, Obama was asked, "Would you be willing to meet, separately, without preconditions, during the first year of your administration, in Washington or anywhere else, with the leaders of Iran, Syria, Venezuela, Cuba, and North Korea, in order to bridge the gap that divides our countries?" Obama replied, "I would," and added that it was a "disgrace" that the Bush administration had refused on principle to do so.

When Obama was elected in November 2008, however, a North Korean diplomat wrote off as implausible any scenario for improved U.S.-DPRK relations. He confided to a retired U.S. official, "The time for us diplomats is over. Our time is finished. Others are in charge." Another DPRK representative said that Pyongyang could no longer take seriously the efforts of diplomats like Christopher Hill in the second term of George W. Bush. Whatever sort of deal U.S. diplomats proposed, Pyongyang lost faith that it would be carried out. Here was a mirror image. Americans for their own reasons distrusted Pyongyang.

Entering the White House in January 2009, Barack Obama for nearly three years faced a North Korea still headed by Kim Jong Il. The macho rhetoric and equally tough actions taken by Pyongyang in those years probably sought to assure a smooth succession and to preempt any bullying by U.S. forces. Having made more than 300 public appearances after his stroke in August 2009, the Dear Leader passed away in December 2011 and was promptly succeeded by his youngest son and chosen heir, Kim Jong Un.

The new leader, not yet thirty years old in 2011, seemed more extroverted and perhaps reckless than his father. He appeared self-confident but had strong grounds to feel unsure how to cope with the many challenges facing the DPRK from a hostile superpower, an often critical ally, and a dynamic rival across the DMZ. Though coached by his father and others for several years, the new leader also had to master opponents within the DPRK system and secure acceptance by Pyongyang's top "one percent."

The Obama administration and Pyongyang sent each other conflicting signals—some of them conciliatory, others quite tough. If one side proffered a somewhat conciliatory approach, it was usually accompanied by words or deeds likely to lead each side to pull back and avoid the other. Tone deaf or stone deaf, leaders in Washington and in Pyongyang seemed to ignore or miss the meaning of each other's communications.

Moments of hope for better relations were usually short-lived, killed off by words or deeds that revived and perpetuated the fears, doubts, frustrations, and anger that had persisted since the 1950s. This pattern meant that the promise of graduated reciprocity in tension-reduction (GRIT) never got a fair test. Neither side was fully committed to détente, and neither had cause to count on the other's goodwill. Movement toward better relations never got beyond a few conciliatory moves. If prospects for an understanding improved, then a monkey wrench soon jammed movement—inserted by hard-liners in either camp or by the standard routine of bureaucracies.

Past memories as well as current pressures boxed in each side. Americans believed North Koreans dishonest. They had built up a uranium enrichment program in secret; balked at comprehensive verification of their facilities; invited and later expelled IAEA inspectors; issued aggressive threats; and tried to sell the same horse twice or thrice. The Obama administration needed constantly to assure Seoul and Tokyo that the United States remained a reliable ally and give no pretext for Republicans to attack what they might portray as a weak stance.[4] These constraints led the Obama team to reiterate the demand of the George W. Bush administration that Pyongyang make the first moves and demonstrate a commitment to denuclearization.[5] For Pyongyang, this demand implied it must surrender before the talks could even begin. The North Koreans complained that they had twice stopped weaponizing plutonium only to see Washington raise the bar.

Let us examine several interactions that illustrate how difficult it was for Washington and Pyongyang to overcome these restraints and reach a deal for mutual advantage.

Fists Remain Clenched in 2009

In January 2009 Pyongyang delivered three mixed signals in the days before Obama entered the White House. First, the DPRK Foreign Ministry issued a statement insisting that verification activities for nuclear disarmament should be carried out reciprocally between North and South Korea. It called for "free field access" to verify withdrawal of U.S. nuclear weapons and prevent their reintroduction. Second, North Korean officials told independent scholar Selig Harrison that the country's stock of plutonium had "already been weaponized" and could not be inspected. Third, having offered to sell 14,000 nuclear fuel rods from Yongbyon to South Korea, the DPRK demanded such a high price to a visiting ROK official that Seoul spurned the deal.

Obama's inaugural address on January 20, 2009, was far more guarded than his preelection enthusiasm for summitry. Obama promised that "we will extend a hand" to others if they were willing to unclench their fist. This pledge implied that others had been in the wrong—clenching their fist. In case there was any doubt on this issue, Obama's offer to "extend a hand" was addressed "to those who cling to power through corruption and deceit and the silencing of dissent." Obama's remarks drew applause, either for his offer or for his depiction of bad guys. Given the North's obsession with face, leaders in Pyongyang were unlikely to rejoice if Obama meant to characterize them as "those who cling to power through corruption and deceit and the silencing of dissent." Nor would they appreciate his prediction that they were on the "wrong side of history." The childhood mantra that "words can never hurt me" was untrue.

Immediately after his inauguration, President Obama had messages sent to North Korea underlining his sincerity about diplomatic negotiations; but Pyongyang appeared unmoved. In February 2009 Secretary of State Hillary Clinton named Stephen Bosworth to serve as U.S. special representative for North Korea policy.[6] Bosworth had been executive director of KEDO, 1995–1997, and U.S.

ambassador to Seoul, 1997–2001. He knew Korea and the world beyond, but continued to serve as dean of the Fletcher School of Diplomacy (2001–2013). Given his divided attentions between North Korea and Fletcher, his appointment could hardly have gratified Pyongyang's quest for top-level attention.

Pyongyang did not unclench its fist. On April 5, 2009, the DPRK launched a three-stage Unha-2 long-range rocket. The rocket quickly fell apart and failed to put its payload, a communications satellite, into orbit. Unable to agree on a resolution, the UN Security Council on April 13 issued a "presidential statement" condemning the launch and declaring it "in contravention of Security Council Resolution 1718."[7]

In response, the North's Foreign Ministry stated on April 14 that the DPRK was withdrawing from the six-party talks and would "no longer be bound" by any of its agreements. North Korea also said it would reverse steps taken to disable its nuclear facilities under six-party agreements in 2007 and would "fully reprocess"—extract plutonium from—the 8,000 spent fuel rods from its Yongbyon reactor. Two days later the North ejected IAEA and U.S. monitors from the Yongbyon complex, after which the UN Security Council (UNSC) on April 24 placed financial restrictions on three North Korean firms believed to be participating in proliferation.[8]

Was the missile test a response to Obama's overtures? Outsiders should probably reserve judgment. The test may well have been planned long before Obama's inauguration. Had Pyongyang really wanted to unclench its fist, of course, it could have delayed or canceled the test. Besides, the North may not have perceived an olive branch in Obama's rather mixed messages.

The DPRK conducted its second underground nuclear test in May 2009, producing a larger yield than the first. The UN Security Council issued another presidential statement condemning the test as a violation of its Resolution 1718. Having held back from joining the Proliferation Security Initiative, the ROK announced it would now participate. The DPRK countered that it considered Seoul's participation in PSI to be an act of war and that it would no longer be bound by the 1953 Armistice Agreement.[9]

In June the UN Security Council unanimously adopted Resolution 1874, which expanded sanctions against Pyongyang. The resolution intensified the inspection regime to prevent proliferation to and from North Korea and called for enhanced financial restrictions against North Korea and a nearly comprehensive arms embargo on the country. The DPRK Foreign Ministry then announced "countermeasures." The DPRK would weaponize all newly separated plutonium from the spent fuel at Yongbyon and continue to develop the country's uranium enrichment capability. In July the Security Council added ten North Korean entities linked to WMD programs to its list of sanctioned organizations and persons.[10]

A vicious cycle of actual and verbal fireworks ensued: North Korean missile or nuclear tests led to UN condemnation, which led to DPRK indignation. In 2006,

2009, 2012, 2013, and 2016, the DPRK responded to UN Security Council actions with a version of three arguments. First, the tests in question were produced by American hostility (though at none of these junctures did Washington make new military threats). Second, the UNSC resolutions were an attempt to disarm North Korea and render it vulnerable. Paraphrasing the Melian dialogue as recorded by Thucydides, one DPRK statement asserted that "only the strong can defend justice in the world today where the jungle law prevails. Neither the UN nor anyone else can protect us." Third, using a convoluted legalism, Pyongyang argued that it was fully within its sovereign right to test missiles and nuclear weapons because the DPRK had already withdrawn from the NPT. In the wake of the 2009 UNSC presidential statement, the DPRK argued that a rocket to lift a satellite into space could not be considered a missile. As a member of the United Nations, of course, North Korea was, and is, legally bound by UNSC decisions—period.[11]

Comprehensive Package, or "Vulgar Remarks" by a "Funny Lady"?

Notwithstanding the DPRK actions and UNSC responses, Secretary Clinton on July 23, 2009, offered a comprehensive statement of U.S. policies toward North Korea at the Association of Southeast Asian Nations (ASEAN) Regional Forum meeting in Thailand. She noted that many delegations at the ASEAN forum had expressed directly to the North Korean delegation their concerns over the North's provocative behavior in recent months. "North Korea has been on the wrong course," she said. It showed "no willingness to pursue the path of denuclearization." The United States and its allies and partners "are committed to the verifiable denuclearization of the Korean Peninsula in a peaceful manner." UNSC Resolution 1874, combined with the designations authorized by the UN Sanctions Committee, provided a powerful tool to curb North Korea's unacceptable activities and to pressure individuals and entities connected to the regime's nuclear, ballistic missile, and other WMD-related programs. The United States was prepared to work with the North Koreans if they proved willing to implement their previous commitments. "Russian and Chinese representatives have visited Washington to work together on these issues."

America's "quarrel is not with the North Korean people," said Clinton. "It was the North Korean leadership that rejected humanitarian aid from the United States and forced us to suspend our food aid program." The United States will "continue to work closely with other governments, international organizations, and NGOs to address human rights violations and abuses perpetuated by the regime. . . . And we will keep funding Korean language radio broadcasting for the same purposes, and we will soon announce a special envoy for North Korean human rights."

Clinton continued: "As we enforce sanctions, we are open to talks with North

Korea, but we are not interested in half measures. We do not intend to reward the North just for returning to the table. We will not give them anything new for actions they have already agreed to take. And we have no appetite for pursuing protracted negotiations that will only lead us right back to where we have already been."

Clinton then offered a package deal: "*We and our partners have a more ambitious agenda for any future talks. Such talks must lead to irreversible steps by North Korea to denuclearize. This, in turn, would lead us and our partners to reciprocate in a comprehensive and coordinated manner. Full normalization of relationships, a permanent peace regime, and significant energy and economic assistance are all possible in the context of full and verifiable denuclearization*" (emphasis added).

Clinton stressed that "the United States does not seek any kind of offensive action against North Korea. We have said that over and over again. The North Koreans said in a meeting today that they've been subjected to nuclear weapons on the Korean Peninsula aimed at them. That hasn't happened for decades. So I think they are living in a historical time period that doesn't reflect today's realities."[12]

But if Clinton meant to revive a dialogue with North Korea, she utterly failed. A few days before the ASEAN meeting, interviewed by ABC News, she likened the leadership in Pyongyang to "small children and unruly teenagers and people who are demanding attention." In response, DPRK Foreign Ministry spokesman blasted Clinton for what he called a "spate of vulgar remarks unbecoming for her position everywhere she went since she was sworn in." He said the DPRK could only regard Clinton as "a funny lady as she likes to utter such rhetoric, unaware of the elementary etiquette in the international community. . . . Sometimes she looks like a primary schoolgirl and sometimes a pensioner going shopping."[13] Thus, Clinton's positive words were drowned out by her nasty words, which generated still more nasty words. Before Clinton addressed the forum, the North Korean delegation attempted to take the podium to speak to the media, but was turned away by security guards. In August 2009 Hillary's husband, former president Bill Clinton, visited North Korea to secure the release of two U.S. journalists accused of spying. While there, he met Kim Jong Il. The state-run KCNA said that the former president's visit would help "bilateral confidence." A week later, UN secretary-general Ban Ki-moon (a former ROK foreign minister) appointed an eight-person panel of experts to the Security Council's 1718 committee to assess implementation of the sanctions on North Korea in accordance with Resolution 1874.

In September the State Department said the United States was "prepared to enter into a bilateral discussion with North Korea" as a precursor to resuming the six-party talks. In October Kim Jong Il informed Chinese premier Wen Jiabao that Pyongyang was ready to return to multilateral talks provided bilateral talks with the United States yielded a favorable result. The State Department reported that North Korea issued a standing invitation for Stephen Bosworth to visit Pyongyang. Following sweet with sour, the DPRK in November announced it had reprocessed the last 8,000 fuel rods from the Yongbyong reactor.

Obama Lectures the Nobel Committee on Liberal Realism

Based on hopes that Obama had created a new climate in which multilateral diplomacy and international cooperation had gained a central position, the Nobel committee awarded him its peace prize on October 9, 2009. The committee "attached special importance to Obama's vision of and work for a world without nuclear weapons. . . . Dialogue and negotiations are preferred as instruments for resolving even the most difficult international conflicts. . . . Democracy and human rights are to be strengthened."[14]

While reiterating his hopes for peace and disarmament, Obama in his acceptance speech on December 10 argued the case for a kind of liberal realism in world affairs. "We will not eradicate violent conflict in our lifetimes. There will be times when nations—acting individually or in concert—will find the use of force not only necessary but morally justified." Still, he said, "in dealing with those nations that break rules and laws, I believe that we must develop alternatives to violence that are tough enough to actually change behavior. . . . Sanctions must exact a real price. Intransigence must be met with increased pressure—and such pressure exists only when the world stands together as one."

Obama explained, "Over time, as codes of law sought to control violence within groups, so did philosophers and clerics and statesmen seek to regulate the destructive power of war. The concept of a 'just war' emerged, suggesting that war is justified only when certain conditions were met: if it is waged as a last resort or in self-defense; if the force used is proportional; and if, whenever possible, civilians are spared from violence."

"A decade into a new century," he continued, "this old architecture is buckling under the weight of new threats. The world may no longer shudder at the prospect of war between two nuclear superpowers, but proliferation may increase the risk of catastrophe. Terrorism has long been a tactic, but modern technology allows a few small men with outsized rage to murder innocents on a horrific scale."

In the nuclear age, Obama went on, it became clear that "the world needed institutions to prevent another world war. . . . America led the world in constructing an architecture to keep the peace . . . mechanisms to govern the waging of war, treaties to protect human rights, prevent genocide, restrict the most dangerous weapons."

Obama declared that the international community should not allow "nations like Iran and North Korea" to "game the system. Those who claim to respect international law cannot avert their eyes when those laws are flouted. Those who care for their own security cannot ignore the danger of an arms race in the Middle East or East Asia. Those who seek peace cannot stand idly by as nations arm themselves for nuclear war."

Obama said it was necessary to "balance isolation and engagement, pressure and incentives, so that human rights and dignity are advanced over time." Richard Nixon's meeting with Mao Zedong, according to Obama, "helped set China on a path where millions of its citizens have been lifted from poverty and connected to open societies. Pope John Paul's engagement with Poland created space not just for the Catholic Church, but for labor leaders like Lech Walesa. Ronald Reagan's efforts on arms control and embrace of perestroika not only improved relations with the Soviet Union, but empowered dissidents throughout Eastern Europe."

The speech ended on a Niebuhrian note: "We do not have to think that human nature is perfect for us to still believe that the human condition can be perfected. We do not have to live in an idealized world to still reach for those ideals that will make it a better place."[15]

As Obama's first year as president ended, point and counterpoint continued. Ambassador Bosworth led a delegation to Pyongyang from December 8 to 10 and delivered a letter from Obama to Kim Jong Il. Two days later, acting on a tip from the United States, Thai authorities seized thirty-five tons of weapons from a North Korean plane that had made an unscheduled landing in Bangkok. A North Korean diplomat reiterated a claim first heard in 2003: The DPRK has the right to make whatever it wants and sell it to whomever it chooses.

CHEONAN AND ITS AFTERMATH IN 2010

Pyongyang's New Year message in 2010 boasted of its recent underground nuclear test but reiterated its "consistent" call to establish a "lasting peace system on the Korean Peninsula and make it nuclear-free through dialogue and negotiations." North Korea proposed talks to replace the 1953 cease-fire with a peace treaty.[16] A week later Pyongyang threatened war with South Korea in response to Seoul's statement that it would invade North Korea if the North threatened a nuclear strike.

In February China's news agency reported that Kim Jong Il told Chinese authorities that Pyongyang was still committed to the denuclearization of the Korean Peninsula. A few days later, however, UN undersecretary-general for political affairs B. Lyn Pascoe said the DPRK leaders were "not eager" to resume the six-party talks.

On March 26 the ROK ship *Cheonan* sank near the Northern Limit Line. The ROK organized a multinational Joint Civilian-Military Investigation Group to analyze what happened. The investigation announced its findings on May 20.

It concluded that North Korea was responsible for firing a torpedo that sank the South Korean ship. Pyongyang denied any involvement in the *Cheonan* sinking. As noted in the discussion of constructivist theory in chapter 11, other interpretations of the *Cheonan* sinking were possible.

Pyongyang in April stipulated that any arms agreements would have to treat the DPRK on an "equal footing with other nuclear weapons states." But on May 24 ROK president Lee Myung Bak stated that South Korea would sever most trade with the DPRK in response to North Korea's actions. In July the United States and the ROK conducted a four-day joint military exercise in Korea's East Sea in response to the *Cheonan* incident. In late August President Obama tightened financial restrictions against North Korea, and the U.S. Treasury Department announced sanctions on eight North Korean entities.

Also in August former president Jimmy Carter visited Pyongyang to bring home a U.S. citizen arrested after entering North Korea from China. In September Carter wrote in the *New York Times* that during his visit to Pyongyang he received "clear, strong signals" that North Korea wanted to restart negotiations. Meanwhile, in Pyongyang, the Korean Workers' Party held its first conference since 1966 to approve the appointment of Kim Jong Un as vice chairman of the Central Military Commission, an action likely taken to smooth the transition to a new supreme leader.[17]

Then, in November, North Korea revealed that it had constructed a 2,000-centrifuge uranium enrichment facility. It showed the facility to a visiting team of foreign experts including former Los Alamos National Laboratory director Siegfried Hecker. DPRK officials claimed that the facility would produce LEU (low-enriched uranium) for a LWR (light-water reactor) already under construction. The enrichment plant was housed in the former fuel fabrication building for the graphite-moderated reactors at Yongbyon, while the LWR was being constructed at the former site of the 5-megawatt reactor's cooling tower. Hecker later said in an interview that the size, shape, and stated efficiency of the centrifuges were close to a centrifuge model known as the P2, which Islamabad's bomb maker Abdul Khan had obtained illicitly from Europe. Interpreting the pattern outlined above at the end of chapter 5, Hecker stated: "The combination of the Pakistani design, the Pakistani training and the major [Khan] procurement network they had access to" allowed North Korea to "put the pieces together to make it work."[18]

On November 23, 2010, hours after an ROK artillery exercise further south, DPRK troops fired artillery rounds at the South Korean island of Yeonpyeong, killing two soldiers and injuring seventeen others. South Korea returned fire and scrambled combat aircraft in the area. In response to the shelling, Beijing called for an emergency session of the six-party talks to "exchange views on major issues of concern." But Washington, Seoul, and Tokyo stated that North–South relations needed to improve before multilateral discussions could take place.

Americans warned Chinese officials that any future "kinetic" action by North Korea against South Korea would be met by a devastating response. Washington and Seoul seemed to be on the same page. Still, the vigor of any U.S.-ROK action was constrained by the knowledge that Seoul could be pummeled in 53 seconds by DPRK artillery.

THE RISE AND FALL OF THE LEAP DAY ACCORD IN 2011–2012

Contradictory signals continued in 2011. Pyongyang's New Year message warned that war could lead to a horrific "nuclear holocaust." It called for "unconditional negotiations" with the South, even as the message boasted that the DPRK was taking the offensive on all fronts under General Kim Jong Il. The only references to the United States were hostile, combined with assertions that the ROK government was a U.S. puppet. But most of Pyongyang's 2011 message addressed plans for bolstering the country's light industry and agriculture. The erstwhile priority for "military first" (sŏngun) acquired a different connotation. Instead of claiming all resources for the military, the single reference to sŏngun in the 2011 New Year Message implied that the slogan stood for improving living standards. Qualifying if not contradicting all this, many of the regime's boasts were half-truths or blatant lies. The factories cited in the message were working at half-speed; some did not yet exist.[19]

The 2011 message called once more for a peace treaty to formally terminate the Korean War. The Obama administration spurned this proposal, saying it might divert attention from the need to denuclearize the Korean peninsula. The Obama administration backed South Korea's rejection of the North's bid for "unconditional" talks to reverse the conflict spiral. Seoul opposed holding such talks until Pyongyang showed by actions—not just words—its sincerity. Neither Seoul nor Washington specified what these actions should be. At times they demanded more words, such as an apology for sinking the ROK warship.

More zigs and zags: in February 2011 the DPRK threatened to turn Seoul into a "sea of fire" in response to U.S.-ROK joint military exercises. In March DPRK authorities told a Russian official that Pyongyang was willing to return to six-party talks and to discuss its uranium enrichment activities. In April Jimmy Carter again visited Pyongyang, this time with three other former heads of state. They hoped to revitalize negotiations, but did not get to meet Kim Jong Il. In May South Korean president Lee Myung Bak introduced the possibility of inviting North Korea to the 2012 Nuclear Security Summit in Seoul, on condition that the North commit to giving up its nuclear weapons. A North Korean spokesperson rejected the precondition, stating that denuclearization was an attempt by the South to open the way for an invasion. In July an American warship forced a North Korean freight vessel believed to be carrying missile components to Burma to turn back off the coast of China.

Despite, or because of, these incidents, U.S. ambassador Bosworth and North Korean first vice foreign minister Kim Gye Gwan met in New York in July 2011 in an effort to revive multilateral negotiations. In September DPRK prime minister Choe Yong Rim repeated for Chinese officials what Kim Jong Il expressed to Russia in August: Pyongyang was willing to consider a moratorium on nuclear testing in the context of the six-party talks. In October American and DPRK diplomats met again, this time in Geneva, to discuss steps that could lead to resumption of the six-party process. Ambassador Glyn Davies replaced Bosworth as the U.S. special representative for North Korea policy. In December Kim Jong Il passed on to his just deserts, and Kim Jong Un took over as North Korea's supreme leader.

Dispensing with the six-nation process, American and DPRK negotiators on February 29, 2012, announced in *separate* statements an agreement by North Korea to suspend operations at its Yongbyon uranium enrichment plant, invite IAEA inspectors to monitor the suspension, and implement moratoriums on nuclear and long-range missile tests. The United States would provide North Korea 240,000 metric tons of food aid under strict monitoring.

Just two weeks after this Leap Day accord, Pyongyang announced it would send a satellite into space to honor the centenary of Kim Il Sung's birth. On April 13 the DPRK attempted but failed to launch a weather satellite using the Unha-3, a three-stage liquid-fueled rocket. The United States suspended its participation in the Leap Day accord. The UN Security Council condemned North Korea's launch as a violation of its resolutions 1718 (2006) and 1874 (2009), which banned any launch using ballistic missile technology. In reply, the North repeated its claim that a satellite launch was a legitimate part of its space program. Far from apologetic, also in April the DPRK displayed six road-mobile ICBMs in a military parade, said by some experts to be mock-ups.

American diplomats insisted that they had warned DPRK representatives that any ballistic missile launch would scupper the Leap Day accord. But they did so orally and not in any joint written statement. The Americans believed that a formal statement was not necessary, since the UN Security Council had already banned DPRK ballistic missile tests. The North's diplomats may have failed to inform Kim Jong Un of the American stipulation. Or the new DPRK leader may have decided to proceed with a rocket launch anyway, hoping that Washington and the UN Security Council would ignore their own admonitions. In oblique defense of the DPRK stance, several analysts observed that the DPRK rocket that launched a satellite differed from the type that could deliver a warhead.[20]

Collapse of the Leap Day accord deepened American reluctance to resume negotiations unless Pyongyang demonstrated a commitment to denuclearization.[21] Retired American diplomats warned North Koreans that Washington's level of distrust had increased and that few State Department officials regarded talking with Pyongyang as a way to boost their careers. Washington's outlook did not brighten when Kim Jong Un used visiting basketball personage Dennis Rodman in 2013 to suggest that President Obama give him a ring in Pyongyang sometime. By contrast, Iran's new president and his foreign minister addressed Washington and the rest of the world in constructive tones, as noted below in chapter 17.

More Vicious Cycles in 2013

In January 2013 the UN Security Council passed Resolution 2087 in response to North Korea's launch in December of another Unha-3 rocket, this time putting a satellite into orbit. The resolution strengthened existing sanctions and froze the assets of additional North Korean individuals. Unfazed, the DPRK conducted its third nuclear test in February. In response, the UN Security Council in March unanimously adopted Resolution 2094, another in the series aimed at limiting North Korea's WMD and other illicit programs. The new sanctions sought to block DPRK access to bulk cash transfers, prevent illicit DPRK activities, and restrict ties to international banking systems.[22]

On April 1, 2013, the DPRK National Assembly passed a law on the responsible use of nuclear weapons. The weapons, the law stated, were only for defense and deterrence. They could be "used only by a final order of the Supreme Commander." They were for "deterring and repelling the aggression and attack of the enemy against the DPRK and dealing deadly retaliatory blows at the strongholds of aggression." Thus, the weapons could be used on the battlefield but also against civilian targets. Both nuclear weapons states and their allies were potential targets. The law did not include a "no first use" clause, but stated that DPRK nuclear weapons would never be used against nonnuclear states unless they joined a hostile nuclear weapons state in attacking the DPRK. The DPRK "shall strictly observe the rules on safekeeping and management of nukes and ensuring the stability of nuclear tests." It will establish a mechanism to assure that nukes, their technology, and substance "may not leak out illegally." The DPRK "shall cooperate in the international efforts for nuclear nonproliferation and safe management of nuclear substances on the principle of mutual respect and equality, depending on the improvement of relations with hostile nuclear weapons states." The DPRK "shall strive hard to defuse the danger of a nuclear war and finally build a world without nukes."[23]

The content of the law implied that Pyongyang was adapting the Chinese model: first, reject efforts to constrain the country's nuclear weapons development; then, having exploded several nuclear devices, support a policy of nonproliferation. As we shall see in the next chapter, however, Pyongyang's fine words and promises were nullified by its global network aimed at circumventing limits on its own weapons programs.

Insults from a Spurned Suitor in 2014

Though no supporting documents are available, Leon V. Sigal of the New York–based Social Science Research Council reported that DPRK officials in autumn 2013 indicated their willingness to return to the principles of the Leap Day accord and possibly not exercise their "right" to launch satellites. But that was not good enough for Washington, which insisted that Pyongyang had to do more—and without reciprocal steps by the United States. In spring 2014 Washington, Seoul, and Tokyo agreed to soften this stance. Without a commitment to reciprocal steps, however, nothing happened to close the gaps between the democracies and Pyongyang.[24] Still, Sigal, Bosworth, and other former U.S. officials received a similar message from Ri Yong Ho, the DPRK diplomat responsible for six-party negotiations, whom they met in Singapore in January 2015.[25]

To see how the parties did—or did not—interact, let us review what they said and did in 2014. Kim Jong Un's New Year 2014 message again claimed that the country could have both butter and guns. The message boasted that the DPRK in 2013 had successfully followed "the Party's new line of developing the two fronts simultaneously (*byungin*) and thus achieved brilliant successes in building a thriving socialist country and defending socialism." Other key points:

- "Strengthening defense capabilities is the most important of all state affairs."
- The first job of the People's Internal Security Forces is to defend the leader; second, the system; and third, the people.
- Industry should produce weapons that are "light, unmanned, intelligent, and high precision."
- "It is imperative to establish the monolithic leadership system in the Party."
- "To resolve the reunification issue . . . we should reject foreign forces and hold fast to the standpoint of By Our Nation Itself."
- "The U.S. and south Korean war maniacs . . . are going frantic in their military exercises for a nuclear war against the north," but another war "will result in a deadly nuclear catastrophe and the United States will never be safe."
- Mutual slander by North and South should stop.[26]

North Korea's National Defense Commission (NDC) followed up on January 16, 2014, with a proposal to improve North–South relations. The NDC asserted that war would bring "unimaginable destruction to Koreans"—that is, *not only* to South Korea. Moreover, a war would help "big powers fish in troubled waters." The NDC repeated Kim Jong Un's New Year proposal for the two sides to stop slandering each other and added a start date—January 30. Second, the North suggested the South make a "political decision" to cancel its forthcoming military exercises with the United States. (A last-minute cancellation was unlikely, but in 1992 the ROK and United States did cancel a major exercise to advance dialogue.) For its own "practical step," the NDC said the North planned to make the first move and stop "all acts provoking the other side," notably in the West Sea. Finally, the NDC recommended a "practical measure to prevent a nuclear holocaust." The NDC "courteously" proposed that the South not bring "dangerous nuclear strike means" to South Korea or the surrounding areas, a likely reference to flyovers by American B-52 and B-2 bombers.[27]

A retired U.S. official who dealt with North Korean issues for decades, Robert Carlin, thought that the January 2014 proposal by the NDC aimed at relaunching a negotiation process. But Seoul and then Washington dismissed the DPRK overture the very next day, with no qualification or counteroffer. This rejection reminded Carlin of the deafening silence that ensued when the NDC in June 2013 stated that the nuclear issue was back on the table. The lack of response in each case flummoxed North Korean officials, according to Carlin, because NDC statements come directly from the supreme leader.[28]

The DPRK permitted family reunions in late February 2014 despite the imminent U.S.-ROK military exercises, but Pyongyang on March 6 rejected an ROK proposal to organize more family reunions. As the U.S.-ROK maneuvers got under way, the North tested new artillery on February 27, 2014, and short-range ballistic missiles on March 3. The DPRK failed to warn international aviation authorities of the tests, however, and one of the DPRK missiles nearly struck a China Southern Airlines jet with 220 passengers on board. The plane was flying from Tokyo to Shenyang at 33,000 feet when it crossed the trajectory of one of the rockets, which had flown by just six minutes earlier and was yet to descend. Instead of apologizing, a DPRK official said the tests were for defense and bragged about their accuracy. A Chinese general condemned the DPRK's disregard for airline safety and international norms.[29] A Chinese photographer captured Kim Jong Un at the missile launch—linking him to the reckless behavior.

Acting somewhat like a scorned suitor, the NDC on March 14, 2014, issued a much tougher statement than in January. It denounced the United States for infringing upon "the sovereignty of the DPRK, the life and soul of its people, century after century. It is again the U.S., the sworn enemy, which has resorted to crafty and foolish moves to undermine the ideology of the DPRK and bring down its social system." It advised Washington "to roll back its hostile policy towards the DPRK and lift all the measures pursuant to the policy." The NDC said the United States "aimed at undermining the ideology of the DPRK and *bringing down its social system by dint of U.S.-style democracy and market economy,* and swallowing up all Koreans and the whole of Korea by force of arms for aggression" (emphasis added). Washington talked foolishly when it said that the keynote of U.S. policy is "DPRK's dismantlement of its nukes first." Washington should "properly understand that Pyongyang's nuclear deterrence is neither a means for bargaining nor a plaything to be used for dialogue" about improving relations. The DPRK's nuclear deterrent is not a ghost that does not exist unless recognized by the United States. Washington claims to have a strategy of patience, waiting for the DPRK to make changes first, but this will never happen. As a sign that Pyongyang had given up on Obama, the NDC said the DPRK would "wait with a high degree of patience for the time when the White House is bossed by a person with normal insight and way of thinking." So long as America's nuclear threats and blackmail persisted, the DPRK would bolster its nuclear deterrent "for self-defense."

The National Defense Commission advised Washington to "stop at once its groundless 'human rights' racket." The NDC asserted that "national sovereignty is more important than human rights." Washington should not rant about others while the United States imprisons more people than any other country and brandishes "sharp swords against any forces opposed to the state and endangering its existence." Trying to denigrate the UN Human Rights report, the DPRK added this fillip: "As for [Michael] Kirby, who took the lead in cooking the [UN] 'report,' he is a disgusting old lecher with a 40-odd-year-long career of homosexuality. He is now over seventy, but he is still anxious to get married to his homosexual partner."[30]

As for the DPRK, it "also does not show any mercy and leniency towards a tiny handful of hostile elements doing harm to the ideology and social system chosen by all its people who are the masters of its sovereignty." Washington "would be well advised to mind its own business, being aware of where it stands, before talking nonsense about others' affairs. The U.S. had better roll back its worn-out hostile policy towards the DPRK as soon as possible and shape a new realistic policy before it is too late. This would be beneficial not only to meeting the U.S. interests but also to ensuring the security of its mainland"—a threat that DPRK bombs could reach the United States.[31]

On April 23 the North's Committee for the Peaceful Reunification of Korea (CPRK) sent an open questionnaire to President Park Geun Hye. What kind of "unification" did Park want? If she hoped one side would swallow the other, as happened in Germany, this would mean war. How could she talk of confidence-building when South Korea was joining with the United States in maneuvers to destroy the North? Was there any difference between Park's "Nordpolitik" and Lee Myung-bak's watchword "No nukes, opening, and $3,000"? (His offer in 2007 was to raise per-capita incomes in the North to $3,000 over ten years.[32]) "Does Park wish to drive North–South relations to a catastrophe just as traitor Lee did?" How could Park talk of a nuclear-free Korean peninsula when the South's war exercises with the United States introduced more than 1,000 nuclear weapons? "The U.S. nuclear blackmail and war drills targeting the north are the root cause of the escalating tensions on the peninsula and the worsened inter-Korean relations." Was

Park willing to cancel "the Ulji Freedom Guardian drills scheduled to be staged again between August and September?" Would she "pull down the concrete wall built by the *yusin* regime of her father south of the Military Demarcation Line and abolish his 'Security Law'?"

The Committee scoffed at the South's pledge to preserve the North's "social system." Pyongyang scorned Park's offer to provide "aid to women in pregnancy and malnourished children" as "an insult and mockery . . . [of those] who receive the greatest special benefits as the king of the country." How could she propose "NGO exchange" and "cooperation" while blocking inter-Korean relations? The Committee said Park should discard the "May 24" restrictions set out by Lee Myung Bak after the *Cheonan* sinking. She should agree to turn the five islands in the West Sea into "peace waters" instead of talking about a "peace park" in the DMZ.

The Committee added that the future of "inter-Korean relations entirely depends on the attitude of Park Geun Hye." It advised her to accept the New Year proposal (of Kim Jong Un) and not feign ignorance of it. She should respect and implement the historic July 4 joint statement, June 15 joint declaration, and October 4 declaration.[33]

On day later, April 24, the DPRK denounced "the puppet south Korean regime" for cosponsoring a "resolution on human rights in North Korea" at the UN Human Rights Council, contending that the resolution slandered its fellow countrymen. The ROK's reckless scheme to set up an "office" in Seoul on human rights in the DPRK brought "North-South relations to a total bankruptcy."

On April 27 the DPRK escalated its rhetoric. It called President Park a "wicked sycophant and traitor, a dirty comfort woman for the U.S. and despicable prostitute selling off the nation." It accused her of pandering to her "powerful pimp," President Obama.

Obama had visited Seoul a few days before the "pimp" allegation and said that the United States and ROK stood "shoulder to shoulder, both in face of Pyongyang's provocations and our refusal to accept a nuclear North Korea." Amid signs of activity at a test site in North Korea, the two presidents warned Pyongyang against conducting a fourth nuclear test. Park said that Obama's visit sent a message that North Korea's provocations would not be tolerated.[34] Neither the U.S. nor the ROK president offered any kind of cooperative program to the North.

In response, Seoul's Unification Ministry urged Pyongyang to abide by an earlier agreement to stop abusive rhetoric.[35] Its spokesman called the North's "unspeakable curses and foul words an immoral act."

Not to be silenced, the North on April 28 conducted a live fire drill shooting into waters just north of the Northern Limit Line. A similar North Korean exercise at the end of March resulted in the two sides exchanging hundreds of rounds of artillery fire after South Korea said rounds landed in its territory.

Apparently understanding every idea that might drive U.S. or ROK policy, the

North seemed to reject any sort of grand bargain premised on denuclearization in exchange for economic aid. There could be no "opening" or reform of the North that risked ideological pollution or weakening its hard line toward dissent.

2015: LESS APPROACH AND MUCH AVOIDANCE

Kim Jong Un's New Year message for 2015 repeated that the DPRK could and would improve both its economy and military preparedness. The first priority for People's Internal Security forces was to protect the leader; second, the system; and third, the people. The Worker-Peasant Red Guards and the Young Red Guards should train for "all-people resistance . . . to defend their own provinces, counties and villages by themselves." The leader promised "a radical turn in the military's supply service to improve living conditions for soldiers and their villages." As they had already agreed, the North and South "should resolve the national reunification issue in the common interests of the nation, transcending the differences in ideology and system." Kim advised South Korean authorities neither to seek "unification of systems" that incites distrust and conflict "nor insult the other side's system and make impure solicitation to do harm to their fellow countrymen, traveling here and there."

Foreign-policy makers in Washington focused on the once fertile crescent for most of 2015, but President Obama on October 16 pointed to the recently concluded Iran deal (discussed below in chapter 17) as a way for the world community to address North Korea's nuclear ambitions. Meeting with ROK president Park Geun Hye, the two leaders said they were open to negotiations with North Korea on sanctions, but that Pyongyang needed to show it was serious about abandoning its nuclear weapons program. Asked if he saw the possibility of a deal with North Korea like that reached with Iran, Obama replied that he saw no indication that North Korea envisioned a future without nuclear weapons. "At the point where Pyongyang says we are interested in seeing relief from sanctions and improved relations and we are prepared to have a serious conversation about denuclearization, . . . we'll be right there at the table," he said. However, "we haven't even gotten to that point yet, because there has been no indication on the part of the North Koreans, as there was with the Iranians, that they could foresee a future in which they did not possess or were not pursuing nuclear weapons." Park said it was important to have concerted international efforts toward a solution to the North Korean nuclear issue, but she added: "There is a saying: You can take a horse to the trough, but you can't make it drink water."[36]

The leitmotif persisted: if either side—the DPRK or the United States and its allies—extended an olive branch, it was wrapped in thorns. Neither side seemed able to make a conciliatory move without adding an insult or precondition sure to abort the offer.

16

North Korea's Weapons of Mass Destruction

North Korea's development and proliferation of WMD (weapons of mass destruction) posed a variety of challenges to regional and global security. By 2015 the DPRK had tested several nuclear devices and a three-stage rocket that put a satellite into orbit. Pyongyang claimed that it could miniaturize nuclear warheads to mount them on missiles, fire missiles from submarines, and strike targets not only in nearby Japan but also in the distant United States.

Mao Zedong once claimed that just six atomic bombs would give China a deterrent. The word *deter* means to dissuade by terror. Did North Korea's nuclear and missile tests—especially those in 2012 and 2013—provide Pyongyang with a credible deterrent? Did these displays of power compel recognition of the DPRK as a nuclear-weapons state? Despite Pyongyang's claims, doubts existed about the power and dependability of its nuclear bombs and missiles. The requirements for a reliable ICBM were far more stringent than for a space launch.

Following paths that others had blazed, North Korea could probably achieve a credible minimum deterrent. But when? Were the obstacles facing Pyongyang so severe that its boasts and threats amounted to a calculated bluff? Were the problems so formidable that the DPRK might still be willing to curtail its WMD in exchange for a grand bargain that provided meaningful security assurances and economic benefits?

A Partial Victory for Juche and "Military First"

No Communist regime had been so reliant on foreign aid as North Korea. Still, the DPRK developed nuclear weapons relying mainly on its own skills and resources. Like China, the DPRK's nuclear programs took shape with only marginal and intermittent foreign assistance. Pyongyang's first nuclear explosion was the culmination of more than half a century of determined striving and sacrifice.

After the North's requests for nuclear assistance were repeatedly rebuffed by Moscow and Beijing, Pyongyang turned to Islamabad for help in enriching uranium. As we saw in chapter 6, Pakistan's bombmaker Abdul Khan's network transferred centrifuges, sophisticated drawings, training, and other forms of know-how to North Korea in the late 1990s in exchange for missile technology, dollars, and jewelry.[1] However, Pakistan's assistance did *not* contribute to the North's nuclear devices that were tested in 2006 and 2009, both of which used plutonium as the fissile material—not enriched uranium. The ingredients for the 2013 test, however, were unknown to outsiders.

How could scientists in a poor country make a nuclear weapon with little outside help? The examples of Nicolae Ceauşescu's Romania and Muammar Gaddafi's Libya suggested that a government run as a family business could not organize everything needed to produce nuclear weapons.[2] But North Korea, somewhat like the USSR and China, showed that dictatorships could mobilize resources and inspire or compel scientists to perform at a high level.[3]

Pyongyang's leaders felt betrayed by Moscow and Beijing. The intensity of North Korea's drive for nuclear weapons probably embodied a spirit of "we'll show 'em." Kim Jong Il's "military first" slogan reflected the regime's willingness to sacrifice public weal for military strength. Other Communist autocrats—Lenin, Stalin, Tito, Mao Zedong, Ho Chi Minh, and Fidel Castro—espoused self-reliance, but none (except Albania's Enver Hoxha) made it the cornerstone of state ideology. As suggested above in chapter 2, Korea's particular Confucian heritage may have fostered risk-taking as well as obedience to authority. The Kim dynasty inculcated its subjects with chauvinism and distrust of foreigners. Finally, Communist ideology portrayed politics as a zero-sum struggle.

THE NORTH'S FOUR BASIC CONCERNS

During Barack Obama's presidency the DPRK moved ahead on all WMD fronts. It announced on April 2, 2013, that it would utilize its nuclear facilities so as to stimulate the economy *and* build up its nuclear forces. Pyongyang underscored its commitment to nuclear energy by promoting the General Bureau of Atomic Energy to the status of a government ministry. The DPRK was also expanding its missile launch facilities. It had at least one new nuclear test tunnel ready to go. It had also restarted its plutonium production reactor and continued to progress toward operation of an experimental light-water reactor (LWR).[4]

Four concerns seemed to drive Pyongyang's nuclear programs.[5] First, to protect the leader, the regime, and the state. DPRK authorities vowed they would not follow the roads of Libya and Iraq, whose regimes were overthrown, North Korea asserted, because they lacked a nuclear deterrent.

Second, to profit. The North's traders could not only acquire hardware and technology for the DPRK but they could also sell weapons and know-how for hard currency.

Third, to gain respectability and influence. The North's WMD gave the regime assets and a kind of prestige still lacking in South Korea and in most poor countries.

Fourth, to economize. Like Eisenhower in the 1950s, Nikita Khrushchev in the early 1960s, and Vladimir Putin in the 2000s, the Kim Jong Un regime appeared to see investment in nuclear weaponry as more cost-effective than pouring resources into conventional forces.[6] Pyongyang probably hoped that a convincing WMD capability would compensate for relative declines in the quality and quantity of its conventional forces. It could get more wallop for the won—"more bang for the buck," as Americans said. Of course such hopes ignored the difficulties in using nuclear weapons as a tool of diplomacy or military policy.[7] To be sure, the DPRK fielded one of the world's largest armies, but its human and material foundations were eroding. Given North Korea's nutritional deficits, its stock of strong young men ready for military service was shrinking. The low quality of DPRK conventional weapons was manifest in 2010 when only one in four artillery shells fired at Yŏnp'yŏng hit the large island, and a quarter of the rounds fired did not explode.[8]

North Korea in 2015 possessed the fourth largest military in the world. DPRK military personnel in 2015 numbered more than one million—twice the ROK total. Of North Korea's 24 million people, 4 to 5 percent served on active duty, and another 25 to 30 percent were assigned to a reserve or paramilitary unit and were subject to wartime mobilization.[9]

North Korea relied on a predominantly obsolescent equipment inventory across all three services, combined with significant capacity for infiltration and disruption operations, underpinned by its pursuit of a missile-delivered nuclear capability. Large-scale exercises were carried out—or staged, though mainly involving a single service.

Maintaining aging equipment while carrying out adequate training hours proved difficult for the DPRK and may have undermined morale. In 2013 an SO-1 patrol boat sank during naval exercises. In 2014 a military helicopter exploded in midair and at least two 1950s-era MiG fighters crashed while training, leading North Korea to suspended flight drills for a time. The nation's tanks, armored personnel carriers, and vessels were also around fifty years old. A propaganda photo in 2014 showed Kim Jong Un aboard a Romeo-class submarine, a type first produced in the 1950s.[10]

By 2016 the North–South ratio had reversed since the mid-1950s, when the ROK fielded twice the number of DPRK forces. The size of DPRK forces as well as the quality of its equipment increased dramatically in the 1970s and 1980s, perhaps to prepare for a blitzkrieg across the DMZ. But falling birth rates affected both North and South. To maintain its large army Pyongyang needed to extend the period of service and lower its physical requirements. By 2020 the North's forces

Juche implies energetic militancy. Following a Taekwondo exhibition at the Arirang Mass games in 2008, performers display the DPRK flag. (Photo by Stephen Gong)

A female soldier at the Victorious Fatherland Liberation War Museum points to a captured U.S. helicopter. (Photo by Stephen Gong)

could shrink to less than one million, while ROK forces will probably decline by one-fifth—to about 400,000. American forces stationed in South Korea declined from more than 100,000 in the 1950s to about 28,500 in 2015. However, the South counted on Washington to augment ROK forces with 690,000 American troops, 160 naval vessels, and 2,000 aircraft in the event of a need to defend the ROK.[11]

The size of North Korea's military budget was unknown, but probably approached $7 billion in 2014. Even though DPRK military spending consumed a far greater share of GDP than in the South, its absolute total was much smaller. One estimate put South Korea's military budget in 2013 at s $31.8 billion—between one-fourth and one-third of China's $112.2 billion; nearly half of Russia's $68.2 billion; and almost double Iran's $17.7 billion.[12] Another estimate for 2014 placed South Korea's outlays at $36.7 billion—tenth in the world, behind the United States ($610 billion), China ($216 billion), and Russia ($84.5 billion); Japan placed ninth, at $45.8 billion.[13]

North Korea's most capable combat aircraft were its MiG-29 and MiG-23 fighters and its SU-25 ground-attack aircraft. However, the majority of the North's aircraft were less capable MiG-15s, MiG-17s, MiG-19s (F-6), and MiG-21s. The North also operated a large fleet of AN-2 Colt biplanes, 1940s vintage, probably tasked with inserting special-operations forces into the ROK. The North's air force also had several hundred helicopters, including some made in the United States, obtained by circumventing U.S. export controls.

The DPRK possessed many small ships and a growing number of small submarines able to deliver a torpedo like the one that may have struck the *Cheonon*. The North also possessed land-based and sea-based cruise missiles that could threaten enemy shipping.[14]

Cyber operations provided a relatively inexpensive tool for conducting asymmetric and deniable military options. Pyongyang probably used cyber operations to collect intelligence and cause disruption in South Korea and other adversaries. Starting in the 1970s, the DPRK developed a modest electronic warfare capability, which it expanded after it reviewed the Pentagon's Operation Desert Storm in 1990–1991. In 1998 the cyber warfare "Unit 121" was reportedly established within the DPRK's Reconnaissance Bureau of the General Staff Department. Its staff received training in Russia and China as well as in the DPRK. Starting in 2009, it appeared that North Korean hackers mounted a series of distributed denial-of-service attacks against South Korean commercial, government, and military websites, rendering them briefly inaccessible. For two weeks in 2012 DPRK hackers jammed the global positioning systems of aircraft using Seoul's main international airports and ships in nearby waters. North Korea was probably behind two separate cyberattacks in 2013 on ROK banking, media, and governmental networks. Having defected, a former computer specialist in the North reported that some 6,000 persons were conducting cyber warfare for the DPRK, often using Internet infrastructures in other countries, such as China. When Sony Pictures was hacked in late 2014, President Obama blamed the DPRK. He did so with confidence because the United States had penetrated the North's cyber capabilities several years earlier with early warning radar.[15]

NORTH KOREA'S WMD ARSENAL

As we saw in chapter 6, the Pyongyang leadership decided soon after the Korean armistice that it would seek nuclear weapons.

The Plutonium Route

North Korea tested plutonium-fueled nuclear devices in 2006 and 2009. The fuel for North Korea's putative "nuclear" test in 2013 was unknown to outsiders. Monitors picked up little or no radiation. Without a third plutonium test, Pyongyang could have no confidence in a miniaturized plutonium design.[16] But the prospects for plutonium weapons looked dim. Pyongyang halted production of plutonium in the 1990s and again in 2007.

When Stanford University's Siegfried S. Hecker first visited Yongbyon in 2007, it appeared to him that Pyongyang was prepared to give up the plutonium production complex. The plutonium used in the 2006 and 2009 tests derived from four rounds of reprocessing that had begun in the late 1960s.[17] North Korean officials told Hecker in 2010 that they had decided to convert the Yongbyon complex from a military plutonium production facility into a civilian nuclear power facility. They said there was no more plutonium in the pipeline ready to be reprocessed. The metal fuel rod fabrication facility was gutted and turned into a centrifuge hall. Pyongyang offered to sell its remaining fresh metal fuel rods to South Korea.

In April 2013, however, North Korea announced that it would restart the facilities at Yongbyon, including the 5 MWe gas-graphite reactor, "without delay." Pyongyang did not need to rebuild the cooling tower destroyed in 2008, but could instead connect the existing reactor to a newly built pump house near the experimental LWR that was also under construction at the site. American experts estimated that this facility could produce one or two bomb's worth of plutonium per year. This would not be a game changer, but would give North Korea more plutonium if it sought warheads for missiles. It would be useful in case the uranium route encountered difficulties.[18]

The Uranium Route

Despite decades of denials and deception, the DPRK in 2009 announced it had developed uranium enrichment technology to provide fuel for a new experimental

LWR, which was under construction. In November 2010 it showed off an enrichment facility with 2,000 P2 centrifuges arrayed in six cascades intended to produce 3.5 percent low-enriched uranium (LEU) for use in a reactor. Hecker estimated that if the cascades were refigured, the facility could yield some 40 kg of highly enriched uranium (HEU) per year.[19] If the North possessed additional facilities unknown to outsiders, then it might produce a larger quantity of HEU.[20]

Hecker suggested that the United States respond to the uranium processing facility unveiled in 2010 by encouraging Pyongyang to pursue nuclear electricity in lieu of the bomb. That course would mean addressing North Korea's underlying insecurity and require Washington to stop opposing any form of nuclear power in the DPRK. In April 2013, however, Pyongyang said it would use the uranium plant to make nuclear weapons.

How did the existence of an enriched uranium facility change the security situation? Pyongyang already had a small arsenal of nuclear weapons fueled with plutonium. Its long pursuit of the plutonium route to the bomb, interrupted by the 1994 Agreed Framework and some six-party agreements, yielded a plutonium inventory of 24 to 42 kilograms—sufficient for four to eight bombs. Those tested and those that remained were relatively primitive and probably not suited for missile delivery, Hecker thought.

If Pyongyang used the new centrifuge facility to make one bomb's worth of HEU per year or augmented it with another bomb per year at an undisclosed facility, then this would provide a hedge but not dramatically alter the security calculus. North Korea could turn to HEU for a simpler, more assured path to a primitive bomb. But it could be more difficult to miniaturize a missile-capable bomb using HEU than with plutonium.

Both Hecker and the UN Panel of Experts on DPRK Sanctions believed that North Korea could not produce many key specialty materials and components for the enrichment facility indigenously. However, the DPRK had an illicit international network through which it had procured UN banned materials such as high-strength aluminum, maraging (strong yet malleable) steel, specialty epoxy, and components such as ring magnets, bearings, vacuum pumps, valves, and flow meters. Once the necessary materials and components were procured, Hecker inferred that North Korean specialists had built the centrifuges and incorporated them into working cascades. "The combination of the Pakistani design, the Pakistani training, and the major [Pakistani] procurement network they had access to" allowed North Korea to "put the pieces together to make it work," Hecker said.[21] He and other analysts were impressed by the abilities and determination of North Korean scientists and engineers.

Having violated the 1991–1992 Joint Declaration with South Korea on Denuclearization of the Korean Peninsula, Pyongyang proclaimed it void in January 2013.

Uncertainties remained about the quantity and quality of North Korea's WMD. In 2014 the DPRK probably had sufficient plutonium and HEU for approximately five to twenty-five nuclear weapons. But their number, size, and reliability were unknown. A cautious estimate credited the DPRK in 2015 with a few nuclear weapons too large to be delivered by ballistic missiles. Unless checked by a new arms agreement or by force, the North's arsenal by 2020 or 2025 could grow to fifty nuclear weapons, some mounted on ballistic missiles.

CHEMICAL AND BIOLOGICAL WEAPONS

The DPRK acceded to the Biological and Toxin Weapons Convention (BTWC) in March 1987, but many analysts believed Pyongyang violated its commitments by maintaining a secret biological warfare development program and stocks of weaponized agents. North Korea began work on chemical weapons immediately after the Korean War, while its pursuit of biological weapons began later.[22] North Korea developed its chemical warfare capabilities over time. By 2015 North Korea was believed to possess a large arsenal of chemical weapons, including mustard, phosgene, and sarin agents. The Pentagon believed that North Korea could deploy missiles with chemical warheads. The ROK Ministry of National Defense estimated that North Korea had 2,500 to 5,000 tons of chemical weapons. Eight different factories in North Korea produced lethal chemicals, such as nerve, blister, blood, and vomiting agents, as well as tear gas, stored in six different facilities. Chemical weapons could be delivered by virtually all DPRK fire support systems—artillery, multiple rocket launchers (including those mounted on ships), and mortars, plus Frog and Scud missiles.[23] With such large chemical-weapons capabilities, the North could fire ballistic missiles armed with chemical agents at ROK and U.S. military facilities in the South, including command and control centers, airfields, and ports—possibly preventing U.S. reinforcements to land.

It is difficult for any actor to use chemical or biological weapons on a large scale. Conventional weapons can hit their targets with greater accuracy than poison gas, with less risk of blowback. However, if conventional arms were scarce and the regime desperate, governments and/or rebels may turn to chemical weapons as a last resort, as happened in Syria under President Bashar al-Assad.

MEANS OF DELIVERY

The DPRK initially relied upon assistance from the Soviet Union and China to develop its missiles, but eventually became an exporter of ballistic missile systems and technology. As of 2015 the DPRK deployed both short-range Scud and medium-range missiles known as Musudan and Nodong. Its series of test launches included an upgrade to the surface-to-surface missile designated KN-02 by the

Pentagon. More than 100 Scud and Nodong ballistic missiles and other rockets were test launched during an eight-month period in 2014—all in breach of UN sanctions.[24] The Nodong tests, the first since 2006, appeared intended to demonstrate a boost in accuracy rather than range.

North Korea's real deterrent was its artillery and rocket forces poised to destroy Seoul in less than an hour. These forces were forward-deployed and fortified in several thousand underground facilities. Not only the artillery but also the rockets lacked the kind of accuracy needed to attack military targets, but they could devastate a city and terrorize the enemy population. As Van Jackson and Hannah Suh have pointed out, however, there was no reason to assume that Pyongyang would willingly plunge into a major war with a superpower and its Korean ally.[25] The regime is surely more dedicated to its survival than to suicide.

Starting in 1998, North Korea conducted four tests of missiles beyond medium range. The sole test of its two-stage intermediate-range Ŭnha-2 (called Taepo Dong-1 or TD-1 by the Pentagon) attempted in August 1998 to place a satellite into orbit but failed. The inaugural flight test of North Korea's longest-range missile, the liquid-fueled, three-stage Ŭnha-3, ended in failure some forty seconds after launch on July 5, 2006. In April 2009, the Ŭnha-3 was tested again. The first stage of the missile traveled approximately 270 km before falling into Korea's East Sea (Sea of Japan). The remaining stages and the payload landed far out in the Pacific Ocean. In February 2012 the DPRK agreed to cease long-range missile tests in exchange for food aid from the United States. Despite this accord, North Korea again launched an Ŭnha-3 in April 2012, ostensibly to place a weather satellite in orbit. It too exploded after a few minutes of flight time. Two days after the failed test, a parade in Pyongyang featured six road-mobile ICBMs on carriers that appeared to be of Chinese origin. Some outsiders thought these might be mock-ups, not operational missiles. Having learned from previous failures, the DPRK succeeded in December 2012 in launching a satellite with the Ŭnha-3.

The DPRK argued that its Ŭnha-3 rocket was a space launch vehicle, but the Pentagon regarded it as a potential ICBM, which it called the TD-2 (for Taepo Dong, a village near the Musudan-ri launch facility). A space launch, however, does not test a reentry vehicle (RV). Without an RV capable of surviving atmospheric reentry, no military can deliver a weapon to target from an ICBM. As of 2015 there was no evidence that DPRK engineers had miniaturized a nuclear warhead able to survive reentry into the atmosphere and mate it with a ballistic missile with expanded range, accurate guidance, and payload capabilities. Meanwhile, starting in 2013, articles in the officially authorized newspaper *Rodong Sinmun* forecast at least six more launches of DPRK satellites—for earth observation, communication, and lunar orbit. A facility to build a rocket larger than Ŭnha-3 was spotted by a satellite.

Table 16.1. Estimates of North Korea's ballistic missile inventory as of 2015

Missile type	Launchers	Estimated range	Engine	Initial operational capability
KN-02 (a DPRK version of Soviet SS-21)	< 100	75 miles	Solid	? 2006
SCUD-B	< 100	185 miles	Liquid *	1981
SCUD-C	< 100	310 miles	Liquid*	?
SCUD-ER	< 100	435–625 miles	Liquid*	2003
No Dong	< 50	800 miles (medium-range)	Liquid*	1999
IRBM ("Musudan")	< 50	2,000+ miles (intermediate-range)	Liquid*	?
Ŭnha-3 (space launch vehicle)		3,400+ miles	?	2012?
TD-2	Unknown	3,400+ miles (potentially intercontinental range)	?	?
KN-08 (Hwasong-13) (road-mobile)	6?	3,400+ miles (potentially intercontinental range)	?	? shown in parades but not flight-tested

Notes:
Scud missile (Hwasong in North Korea): tested, operational
 Several variants of this missile have ranges of up to 700 miles. Carrying a 700- to 1,000-kg warhead, this range would include most of South Korea. The Scud's accuracy is only 0.5 to 1 km but would suffice to wreak much destruction on a city, especially if the North developed a nuclear warhead small enough for this missile. Scuds use liquid propellants and can be transported and launched from large trucks.

No Dong missile: tested, but insufficiently to demonstrate reliability
 This missile is believed to be able to carry a 700- to 1,000-kg warhead to a range of 1,000–1,300 km, which would allow it to reach most of Japan. It uses Scud-level rocket technology and has an accuracy of several kilometers, again limiting its use to large targets like a city. It too can be transported and launched from large trucks.

IRBM (Musudan) missile: not tested, not operational
 North Korea has displayed this missile in parades but, as of 2015, there were no known flight tests. Range probably too short to reach Guam. Can be transported on a mobile launcher but needs to be filled with liquid fuel before launching.

TD-2: not tested, not operational
 Taepo Dong-2 (TD-2) is the Pentagon's name for an ICBM derived from the Ŭnha-3 space launch vehicle. If the Ŭnha-3 were modified to carry a 700–1,000-kg warhead rather than a light satellite, the missile might reach Alaska or even Hawaii. As of 2015, a ballistic missile version of the space launch vehicle had not been tested. Because of its size it was unlikely to be mobile, and instead would be launched from a large launch pad. Its accuracy would likely be many kilometers.
 As of 2015, none of the North's longer-range missiles had been flight-tested.

(continued next page)

Although data are necessarily incomplete, estimates of North Korea's missile inventory are summarized in table 16.1.[26]

ARMS CONTROLS

The DPRK joined the Nuclear Nonproliferation Treaty (NPT) in 1985; occasionally threatened to withdraw after joining; and withdrew in 2003, the only country to do so. Pyongyang acceded to the Biological Weapons Convention in 1987 and the Outer Space Treaty in 2009. As of 2016 it had not joined the Chemical Weapons Convention, the Comprehensive Test Ban Treaty, the Convention on Certain Conventional Weapons, the Ottawa Mine Ban Convention, or the International Convention on the Suppression of Acts of Nuclear Terrorism. It also did not belong to the Proliferation Security Initiative, the International Code of Conduct against Ballistic Missile Proliferation, the Missile Technology Control Regime, the Nuclear Suppliers Group, the Convention on the Physical Protection of Nuclear Material, or the Wassenaar Arrangement on Export Controls for Conventional Arms and Dual-Use Goods and Technologies.

Having claimed membership in the nuclear weapons club, would the DPRK

Cruise missiles: North Korea possessed and continued to develop anti-ship cruise missiles derived from the Chinese CSSC-3 Silkworm/Seersucker designs. The DPRK probably could produce variants of these missiles domestically.
Sea-based missiles: Satellite images indicated that North Korea had a submarine at the Sinpo South Shipyard that could be a test bed for submarine-launched ballistic missiles. In 2015 the DPRK showed a video of Kim Jong Un watching a missile launched from a submarine, but U.S. analysts said the images were manipulated.
Drones: North Korea publicized a March 2013 military live-fire drill that for the first time featured an unmanned aerial vehicle (UAV) in flight. The drone appeared to be a North Korean copy of a Raytheon MQM-107 Streaker target drone. North Korean press coverage of the event described the UAV as being capable of precision strikes by crashing into the target. The drill also featured the UAV as a cruise-missile simulator, which was then shot down by a mobile SAM. In May 2014 the ROK reported finding several UAVs that had flown from the North, passed over the DMZ, and landed in different parts of South Korea. Although the UAVs were rudimentary, at least one had photographed South Korean military installations and the presidential compound. In the future drones could carry weapons as well as cameras.
Aircraft: The DPRK in 2015 still deployed some 80 Hong-5 light bombers that could be retrofitted to carry nuclear ordnance. But they dated from the 1940s and would be highly vulnerable to anti-aircraft guns. A more plausible method to deliver WMD would be to use radiological material in the thousands of artillery tubes aimed at Seoul. North Korea possessed some MiG-29 and SU-25 jet fighters, but in-flight training was limited to about twenty hours a year.
* Liquid propellants must be filled on the field after reaching launch positions, a process that may take an hour or two.

now oppose nuclear proliferation? On April 1, 2013, the DPRK adopted a Law on Consolidating Position of Nuclear Weapons State.[27] The law pledged the DPRK to cooperate in international efforts for nuclear nonproliferation, but with a potentially crippling proviso: such cooperation was conditional "on the improvement of relations with hostile nuclear weapons states." The law required the DPRK to establish a mechanism for safekeeping and management so that "nukes [sic] and their technology [and] weapon–grade nuclear substance may not leak out illegally." From Pyongyang's standpoint, however, there probably was no law against sale of nuclear substances. On several occasions North Korean diplomats told Americans, "We can build whatever we want and sell it to whomever we choose."

ILLICIT TRADE AND WEAPONS PROLIFERATION

North Korea proliferated WMD know-how and materials for decades. It traded nuclear for missile technology with Iran. It exported missiles and missile technology to Egypt, Iran, Libya, Pakistan, Syria, and Yemen. It supplied UF6 to Libya via the A. Q. Khan network. It also began secretly to build the nuclear reactor in Syria that Israel destroyed in 2007. The DPRK may have supplied chemicals used in the Assad regime's war against rebels. In 2012 there were reports that South Korea stopped a DPRK ship and seized graphite rods that had been purchased by Syria. The DPRK also helped Myanmar's incipient chemical and missile programs. Burma's generals promised Washington to break their ties with North Korea, but Japanese news sources reported in November 2012 that Japan had intercepted proliferation sensitive items bound for Burma from North Korea. As of 2014, the Burma-DPRK connection was still expanding.[28] North Korea also sold arms and military training to several African countries.

The proliferation network established by A. Q. Khan was officially liquidated but did not disappear. It was transformed from a single-node import network into a more complex, multinode export network. Pyongyang also developed its own import nodes, such as the Nam Chongang Trading Company, an arm of the General Bureau of Atomic Energy, which bought and sold a wide range of legitimate and illicit goods, including many with dual-use nuclear potential sanctioned by the United Nations. Pyongyang successfully used intermediaries in China and other places where North Korean entrepreneurs could do business and procure dual-use equipment. The DPRK also used transshipment countries, such as Singapore, Malaysia, and the United Arab Emirates. Pyongyang employed air and land routes through China with little risk of inspection.

The UN Panel of Experts on DPRK Sanctions reported in March 2014 that North Korea operated a global network to buy and sell weapons in contravention to UN resolutions. It persisted "with its arms trade and other prohibited activities in defiance of Security Council resolutions, while activities related to its nuclear and ballistic missile programmes [also] continue."²⁹ Pyongyang used trading companies and fronts to conduct a sophisticated trading network, which proved adept at evading outside scrutiny and sanctions. To elude UN sanctions the DPRK employed "multiple and tiered circumvention techniques." According to the UN report, these included:

- Using sealed shipping containers that employed the legitimate international container trade system as cover—techniques pioneered by drug-trafficking organizations to integrate logistics operations within the global supply chain. The volume of containers flowing through the system allows physical inspection of only a small percentage of them.
- Transshipping illicit cargo on vessels operated by large international shipping companies, via a neighboring regional transshipment hub.
- Using indirect shipping routes and multiple carriers to obscure a cargo's origin.
- Hiding the real nature of the goods, the true consignor, and their origin. Reputable shipping companies will carry containers despite knowing almost nothing of what they contain. The practice of handling the cargo under a "Said to Contain" clause poses a challenge for implementation of sanction measures. In one instance, the DPRK used a European shipping company with an office in Pyongyang to send arms to Iran in July 2009. The company told the panel it lacked legal capacity to open the containers and check their contents once the DPRK customer had packed, sealed, and cleared them through customs. The panel found that the shipper, shipping agent, owners, operators, and carriers were not provided with correct information on the real nature of the goods.
- Employing overseas-based front/offshore companies or middlemen to arrange illicit shipments using legitimate trade systems.
- Making false labels or misleading declarations of cargo in shipping. Here are some examples: "construction material" for ballistic missile-related items (October 2007); "generator parts" for rocket fuses (March 2008); "oil boring equipment" for rocket fuses (July 2009); "bulldozer spare parts" for tank parts (November 2009); "mechanical parts" for conventional arms and munitions (December 2009); "lead pipe" for ballistic missile-related items (May 2012). In the *Chong Chon Gang* case, detailed below, the manifest did not list the prohibited military cargo, and there was no bill of lading for it.
- Concealing the identity of the entities involved by false or very limited information in shipping documents—for example, by omitting the address, contact person, telephone, or fax number of the entities involved in a consignment.

- Providing a slightly different name of a known or designated entity to conceal its identity.
- Making use of physical concealment techniques, such as placing illicit cargo in larger crates or hiding it behind false walls with false labeling or misleading markings. The costs of such an inspection could easily discourage member states from applying robust inspection on similar cargos.
- Reregistering or reflagging DPRK ships.
- Retaining the network despite sanctions against some North Korean entities. Sometimes Pyongyang renamed or merely replaced one banned entity with another entity, not (yet) banned.

The UN panel learned a great deal when, in July 2013, authorities in Panama inspected the *Chong Chon Gang*, a DPRK-flagged cargo ship en route from Cuba. Beneath 10,000 tons of sugar, laid out across the upper layers of freight containers, inspectors found undeclared weapons. The hidden cargo amounted to six trailers with surface-to-air missile systems and twenty-five shipping containers loaded with two disassembled MiG-21 jet fighters and fifteen MiG-21 engines, plus missile and other arms components. Reviewing the evidence, United Nations investigators found that the North Korean crew had used secret codes in communications, falsified the ship's logs, and switched off an electronic system that would otherwise have provided real-time information on the ship's location to the international maritime authorities. DPRK embassies in Cuba and Singapore had helped arrange the arms shipment, along with front businesses based in Pyongyang, Vladivostok, and Singapore Questioned about this cargo, the Cuban Foreign Ministry on July 16, 2013, said that Cuba had sent Soviet-era weapons to be repaired in North Korea. But the UN inspectors doubted that much if any of the consignment was meant to be returned to Cuba.

Documents from the UN report showing how the DPRK tried to evade sanctions are highlighted in "How to Cheat," the appendix to this chapter. But the UN panel may well have missed more illicit traffic than it unveiled. Stopping and searching the *Chong Chon Gang* could have been like discovering a needle in a haystack. This vessel did not benefit from the advantages of foreign flagging, transshipment, or chartering, and so required different concealment techniques.

Much of North Korea's banned proliferation activity took place beyond its borders, in the offshore economy of unregulated free-trade zones, ports, and financial centers. Shipments utilized offshore bank accounts, flag-of-convenience ships and passports, honorary consuls, free-trade zones, and containerization. Some vestiges of North Korean state involvement remained: businesses operated from embassies, using diplomatic passports and bulk cash transfers by trusted couriers. Most of these entities proved highly adaptable, amorphous, and resilient. They interacted with foreign-based or roaming North Korean intermediaries whose associations, experiences, and language skills dated back to the pre-1989 era, when North Korea enjoyed foreign or military-to-military relations with many single-party, Marxist-oriented states. North Korea tried to shroud these operations in secrecy, but the veil lifted slightly as they interacted with legitimate companies that shipped their goods and with the banks that held, transferred, or converted their funds. While the majority of companies and individuals identified as involved in sanctions violations were either registered abroad or held foreign passports, most international sanctions focused rather narrowly on companies and individuals registered in North Korea. This targeting took the form of "designations" by which the United Nations and the European Union, together with countries such as Australia, Japan, and the United States, ordered asset freezes on particular companies, trade bans, and travel bans against individuals traveling on DPRK passports. They missed the forest for the trees.[30]

CONSTRAINTS

The UN Panel of Experts in 2014 noted that the DPRK remained dependent on procurement from abroad for certain items needed in its nuclear weapon and ballistic missile programs. "In particular," the panel stated, the DPRK "lacks sufficient domestic precision machine tool manufacturing capability and it purchases off-the-shelf items for its ballistic missile-related programmes. The Panel also assesses that it will likely seek out foreign suppliers for components it will need to fabricate fuel rods for its reactors."

By 2016, North Korea had made great strides in its nuclear/missile development, but many uncertainties remained.[31]

- Could it miniaturize warheads and mate them with long-range reentry systems?
- Could it really produce warheads fueled with highly enriched uranium?
- Could the North accomplish these tasks if international sanctions tightened?
- What if China did more to constrain cross-border traffic in dual-use materials? Beijing showed a growing impatience with its headstrong and impetuous ally, but Chinese entrepreneurs cooperated with North Korean firms to circumvent many United Nations restrictions.
- Could the DPRK test, produce, and maintain nuclear weapons *safely*? Siegfried Hecker thought that the country's weak infrastructure, the inexperience of its scientists, and the lack of a serious regulatory agency presented dangerous risks.
- Could the North afford both guns and butter? The regime boasted that its nuclear facilities could help to raise living standards while producing a powerful deterrent. But North Korea is a tiny country beset with severe eco-

nomic and other constraints. Even much larger countries, such as France and the United Kingdom, debated whether to retain their nuclear missile forces and, if so, on what scale.

- Would the North's security not suffer if its emerging WMD forces triggered a competitive arms race that included South Korea and Japan?

If these issues worried Kim Jong Un and his advisers, might they still be attracted by some version of the Leap Day accord? A ranking DPRK government official told Hecker in November 2010 that the October 2000 Joint Communiqué, which brought Secretary of State Madeleine Albright to Pyongyang, would be a good place to resume the arms control dialogue.

The United States blundered by provoking North Korea and permitting it to develop WMD. The North blundered by doing so. Its conventional artillery provided sufficient deterrent against an ROK or American attack. Its genuine security would have gained if the resources invested in "military first" had gone to social and economic development.

It was also folly for Washington, Tokyo, and Seoul to buy, deploy, and count on missile defenses for their security Starting in 2006, South Korea labored to build and deploy antimissile systems more effective than America's, but defenses usually lose out against improvements in offensive systems.[32] It is more likely that North Korea could field a dozen missiles with nuclear warheads than that the United States and its allies could mount defenses able to intercept and destroy them.[33]

APPENDIX: HOW TO CHEAT

The following are extracts from the UN Panel of Experts document S/2014/147, with some abbreviations and elisions, and with some translations from the Korean into English by UN personnel. Spellings in English are as in the original English, or in translations from Korean or Spanish.

Annex VIII

Cargo found onboard the *Chong Chon Gang*

- Twenty-five standard shipping containers and six trailers weighing a total of about 240 tons of arms and related materials.
- Components of SA-2 (C-75 Volga) and SA-3 (C-125 Pechora) surface-to-air missile systems, along with components for the associated SA-2 and SA-3 radar systems such as the six trailers (i.e., the vans housing the system electronics, the operator stations, or the power generators); antennas, bases, transmitters, and tracking systems, as well as their supporting structures;

electric generators; and other miscellaneous equipment (reels of cables, transport trailers, control and measurements instruments, etc.).

- Four SA-2 and two SA-3 launchers, disassembled.
- Two MiG-21 jet fighters disassembled with parts packed into several containers plus fifteen MiG-21 engines and afterburners.
- Eight 73-mm rocket-propelled projectiles (PG-9/PG-15 antitank and OG-9/OG-15 fragmentation projectiles) to be fired with recoilless rifles, as well as a single PG-7VR round, a high explosive antitank tandem charge to penetrate explosive reactive armor.
- A single box of 7.62-mm cartridges (440 rounds); a machine tool for loading shotgun cartridges (12 gauge caliber ammunition); and a machine tool for manufacturing 5.56-mm cartridges.

Annex X

Unofficial translation of the "secret" instructions

Dear Captain of *Chong Chon Gang* (Secret),

Believing that it must be hard to make such a long voyage, I wish you organize everything well until arriving at Cuba safely. While you must have already received sailing instruction, I am giving you additional instructions regarding the additional cargo from Cuba to homeland as follow. *The instructions should be known only to the Captain, Political Secretary and Security Officer.* Five days before arriving at Havana, please inform the Deputy Captain so that he could make a [loading] PLAN. *After unloading in Havana, load the 26 20-foot containers. Load the containers first and load the 10,000 tons of sugar (at the next Port) over them so that the containers cannot be seen.* When you send communication in this regard, use the following description: Container → Mechanical parts; Number → number of boxes. For example

   loaded 26 boxes of mechanical parts

   While you do not need to send a daily report on this shipment of containers, if necessary, report as described above. *In principle, the containers will not be declared to Customs in Panama.* However, if it is required for you to do so, you will receive a message

   Payment arranged for 26K in Panama

which you shall understand as having to declare the containers in Panama. If you need to make a declaration, do as follows:

   Shipper—Metal Co, Havana
   Notify—Ferrous Export and Import Co;
   Consignee—To Order;

Cargo—Generators;

Quantity—26 package / 127 tons.

I will leave it up to you regarding the other matters on the declaration such as B/L and Manifest. If the containers should not be declared to customs in Panama, you will receive a message

Payment was not arranged for 26K in Panama

which you shall understand as not declaring the containers. I wish you a safe voyage.

Salute,

(PS) Please confirm to Headquarters that you have received and understood these instructions by submitting the following message

Instruction on the payment in Panama

[The source of the message and its date are not given.]

To: OCRU [Ocean Management Company], Vladivostok, Russia
CC: OCKP [Ocean Maritime Management Company], Pyongyang
From: Chong Chon Gang
11 June 2013
Today failed to establish contact with agent via VHF various times. Request to contact the Counsellor Office as soon as possible and find out how the person in charge of 26 boxes would organize the plan of the vessel's port-entry. The person in charge of the 26 boxes told us that he would locate the vessel while drifting via VHF once the loading/port-entry is arranged. But there has been no contact yet.

To: OCKP, Pyongyang, 21 June 2013
CC: OCRU, Vladivostok, Russia
From: Chong Chon Gang
re "26 boxes" and loading of containers and trailers
20 pcs out of TTL of 31 pcs were loaded.

Annex XII

Message from OMM regarding transportation fee for an "additional cargo of 200 tons"

June 24, 2013
To MV CCG
Fm Ocean [OMM head office, Pyongyang]
Transportation fee for the additional cargo of 200 tons will be transferred to K2. Deposit in cash after setting off for sailing.

Annex XIII

Application for payment submitted by Chinpo Shipping Company on behalf of OMM Russia
July 7, 2013
Remittance Application Form

Pay CCY by telegraphic transfer only US$72,016.76
Rem. Fee USD90.02 Telex USD22.38 Total USD72,130.16
Payee's Bank and Address: CTA O= [handwritten 3 short horizontal bars]
Handwritten C.R. [or B.?] Finton
En [sic] N.Y.
Applicant: Chimpo Shipping Co. Ptc Ltd [street address] Singapore
[Illegible handwritten word followed by "de cuenta."]
PLS FAX BA SLIP TO: 62962952

Annex XIV

Communication between OCRU and the shipping agent in Panama falsely stating that the ship was only carrying sugar and showing that OCRU knew of the need to declare all containers.
From: Ocean Russia D <oceanvid@gmail.com>
Sent: July 03, 2013 12:04 AM
To: Operations
Subject: RE: Materials for MV Cong Chon Gang
To: Shipping Agent
Fm: Ocen Ru
Re: MV CCG—transit Pancanal
Good day, dear Shipping Agent
Kindly be informed that MV CCG wud arrive at Pancanal by 10th July. Pls revert us best proforma d/a and any needed documents for this vsl on transit purpose. Vsl will arrive there with bgd sugar ldd at Cuba. Meanwhile, Owners had arrange bunkering of this vsl thru their channel at Pancanal. Local supplier will contact with you directly.
Brgds
Han

[The UN Panel inserted here a message dated May 14, 2013, from Operations to Ocean Russia: "Derrating certificate is expired. Please inform if you will renewal before arrive Panama. Cargo declaration must include number of containers, how stowed, their size, type, and weight."]

Annex XV

False declaration submitted to the Panama Canal authority via the local shipping agent omitting any reference to Port Mariel [where the weapons were loaded]. It lists previous ports visited: Dalian and Zhenjang, China; Kojong, Korea (South); Chongin, Hungnam in Korea (Democra); Vostochniy, Russia, 17 April; Habana, 22 June; Puerto Padre, 06 Jul. Destination: Nampo, Korea (Democra).

Annex XVI

Cargo manifest submitted to Panamanian authorities falsely stating that *Chong Chon Gang*'s only cargo was sugar.

Annex XVIII

Communication conveying letter of protest from OMM head office in Pyong-yang for Panamanian authorities stating that *Chong Chon Gang* was only carrying sugar—10,200 tons loaded in Padre.

Annex XX

Documents showing financial transactions conducted by DPRK embassy personnel in Cuba
Disbursement: Account (to the ship's agent) Cash Receipt
I confirm the receipt of 12,000 US$ in cash from commercial counsellor of the Embassy in Cuba for the transportation fee of 200 tons of sugar. Maritime Management Bureau << Chong Chon Gang>>, Captain: Ri Yong Il
Dated Juche 102 (2013), June 10 [Chongchongang Shipping Co. Ltd.]

To: OCRU [July 5, 2013] OCKP
From: *Chong Chon Gang*
Commercial counsellor said that he signed a guarantee that Disbursement Account (D/A) will be paid in one week and confirmed the vessel would start sailing upon finishing the loading. The Counsellor requested the owner to reimburse the D/A in one week.
To OCKP
We received one pouch from the Embassy to the Homeland.
RGDS

Annex XXI

Captain's list of contacts referencing "26 boxes," embassy and Cuban military personnel. Port of loading for arms and related materiel is given as Mariel. The document contains, handwritten in Korean, references to "26 boxes," "Counsellor," "Secretary," and "Cuba military person" [given in Spanish as *Artone*], and their phone numbers.

Annex XXII

Link between Tonghae Shipping Agency Pte. Ltd., Chinpo Shipping Co. Ltd., and DPRK embassy in Singapore.

Annex XXIII

Official registrations of businesses co-located with the DPRK embassy in Singapore: Chinpo Shipping Company (Private), Great Best Trading (Private), Tonghae Shipping Agency (Private).

Annex XXIV

Key management personnel and shareholders shared by Chinpo Shipping, Tonghae Shipping Agency, and Great Best Trading Company. Lim Cheng Wah, Director, since 30 April 1993; shareholder Lim Whay Yuan; secretary Ling Ai Kwong; shareholder Tan Bee Tin; and several other shareholders. Their names and addresses in Singapore were obtained from the Accounting and Corporate Regulatory Authority of Singapore (www.acra.gov.sg). However the official registration of Great Best Trading Pte., Ltd., did not name the manager(s) of the company.

Annex XXV

Stowage plan [a diagram], which does not reflect presence of containers and trailers.

Annex XXVI

Letter from captain requesting contact be made with owner and owner's operating company.

Annex XXVII

Loading check sheet possessed by captain identifying holds where containers and trailers would be placed, size of containers, and labeling trailers belonging to surface-to-air missile systems.

IV

Policy Options amid Uncertainty

17

Revolutionary Pariahs

Why North Korea Is Not Iran

Widely seen as revolutionary pariahs, both Tehran and Pyongyang faced international pressure to change their ways. However, a wide-ranging accommodation proved easier to reach with Iran than with North Korea. While North Korea seemed determined to retain and bolster its limited but growing nuclear weapons capability, Iran in 2015 accepted verifiable curbs on its ability to develop a nuclear weapon for at least ten years. With economic potential and military assets much greater than the DPRK, and with long-standing cultural ties with the West, Iran could contemplate more readily than North Korea a grand bargain with the world's great powers. Indeed, the July 14, 2015, Joint Comprehensive Plan of Action could lay the basis for broader cooperation on the multiple crises roiling the Middle East. The plan's way of finessing technical challenges and its wider political potential could set a positive example for North Korea and the world.

WHICH MUST COME FIRST—SECURITY OR ARMS CONTROL?

Barack Obama recognized that a sense of security in Tehran and in Pyongyang could be a prerequisite for arms limitations. Asked in 2007 if an Iranian bomb could be deterred, then-Senator Obama said yes: "I think Iran is like North Korea. They see nuclear arms in defensive terms, as a way to prevent regime change." Asked what would be the central doctrine of his foreign policy, Obama replied, "The single objective of keeping America safe is best served when people in other nations are secure and feel invested."[1] Continuing this line of thought, Obama in a debate with Senator John McCain in 2008 stated: "We are . . . going to have to . . . engage in tough direct diplomacy with Iran, and this is a major difference I have with Senator McCain. This notion that by not talking to people we are punishing them has not worked. It has not worked in Iran; it has not worked in North Korea.

In each instance, our efforts of isolation have actually accelerated their efforts to get nuclear weapons. That will change when I'm president of the United States."[2]

The debates with Pyongyang and Tehran over their nuclear programs recalled the conflicting priorities that stymied negotiators in in the 1920s and 1930s. In those interwar years France and its allies demanded "security first" and "*moral* disarmament" as preconditions for what the USSR called "*material* disarmament." The Kremlin under Lenin and Stalin wanted to bolster both its regime and state security by weakening the armed forces and solidarity of its capitalist adversaries. The victors in World War I, however, sought to preserve the new world order. Led by France, the anti-Communist states demanded "security first." They refused to disarm until the Bolsheviks forswore revolution. The Kremlin, however, wanted France to disarm before it would rein in the Comintern.

Penalized and ostracized by the Versailles system, Germany began in the early 1920s secretly to rebuild its armed forces. Much of this effort took place on the territory of the other pariah state, the USSR. Moscow, like Berlin, wanted to overthrow the existing order. When Hitler came to power in 1933, he demanded arms equality for Germany. If France would not disarm, then Germany would *rearm*—and did. The rise of Nazi Germany ended all talk of disarmament and forced other European countries and the USSR belatedly to energize their own arms buildups.

A dictatorship can guard its secrets and devote huge resources to military R&D. Like North Korea and Iran in the early twenty-first century, Yugoslavia under President Josep Tito showed in the early Cold War era that, as one observer put it, "the more isolated the regime and the more hostile the international environment, the less relevant are global norms regarding weapons of mass destruction. Isolated regimes also are inclined to discount the political costs of violating international taboos." One of Tito's most intellectual comrades, Edvard Kardelj, advised in 1950 that Yugoslavia must build an atomic bomb "even if it costs us half of our income for years."[3] This advice came at a time when nonaligned Yugoslavia already enjoyed U.S. support—quite the opposite of North Korea's position.

An impasse similar to that between security and disarmament arose during the U.S.-Soviet Cold War negotiations. Washington usually sought inspection first and then arms control, while Moscow again wanted real (material) disarmament before any form of inspection, or *kontrol'* (*accounting* or *counting* in Russian, as in French). Washington and Moscow finally came to terms in the 1970s and 1980s when they convinced each other that neither sought regime change and that most verification could be conducted by satellites. Still, Ronald Reagan cherished the slogan "Trust but verify." Starting in 1987, both human inspectors as well as machines checked what came out of a Soviet and a U.S. factory that had made intermediate-range missiles.

COMPARING THE TWO PARIAHS

Following the Soviet collapse, the United States led a coalition devoted to maintaining or reducing the number of nuclear-weapons states. With Saddam Hussein overthrown in 2003, the main challengers to the nuclear status quo were North Korea and Iran—each a revolutionary pariah struggling within a cage of economic and other sanctions. Pyongyang made its stance explicit: it wanted nuclear arms for security and international acceptance as another nuclear-weapons state. Each of North Korea's neighbors, as well as the United States, feared that Pyongyang's nuclear weapons would set off a chain reaction across Asia.

Iran lagged North Korea in nuclear weapons R&D, but Tehran's behavior implied that, when its nuclear programs became more advanced, it too might join the nuclear-weapons club. Tehran denied that it wanted nuclear arms and claimed to seek only the right to produce nuclear energy. Outsiders believed, however, that Iran had pursued in secret a uranium enrichment program for some eighteen years in breach of its NPT obligations. Intelligence sources in the United States said that Iran halted its nuclear weapons program in 2003, but the IAEA reported that Iran was not transparent about its nuclear past. The IAEA had tried to investigate whether Iran had conducted nuclear related tests at secret sites but was not allowed to visit suspected locations.

Compared with the worldwide ambitions of the former USSR, the revolutionary and weapons programs of North Korea and Iran were modest. Pyongyang wanted to preserve its regime and unify the Korean peninsula. Tehran too concentrated on regime security, but was also active in supporting coreligionists in Iraq, Syria, Lebanon, Bahrain, and Yemen. Some Iranian leaders continued to preach death to Israel and to the "Great Satan" in America. It seemed clear, however, that if Iran ever acquired the means to attack Israel, not to speak of the United States, its preparations might be cut short by a preventive strike. Besides issues with Washington and Israel, Iran had conflicts with antiregime forces within the country and with its neighbors.

IRAN AND THE GREAT POWERS REACH AN ACCORD

Arms negotiations between Pyongyang and Washington remained desultory; but Iran in 2014–2015 conducted intense negotiations for twenty months with the P5+1—China, France, Germany, the United Kingdom, the United States, and Germany. Despite apparent progress at the negotiating table, hard-liners on each side continued to feed one another's distrust. Iran's president, Hasan Rouhani, appeared to operate on a short leash held by Supreme Leader Ali Khamenei.[4] Many young, educated, and comparatively affluent Iranians welcomed any sign that Iran might rejoin the world.[5] But Iranians lived under a divided government in which relative moderates spoke and acted at the forbearance of conservatives.[6] In Washington, many Republicans wanted to add to sanctions—not suspend them.[7] There was little fondness for Iran in the broad American public. Democrats as well as Republicans in Congress persuaded Obama in 2014 to reject Tehran's proposed ambassador to the United Nations because of his role in the 1979 seizure of the U.S. Embassy—no matter that the rejection violated U.S. obligations as host to the United Nations. Two Republican moderates, former secretaries of state Henry A. Kissinger and George P. Shultz, set out five tough criteria for evaluating a nuclear deal with Iran.[8]

Culminating nearly two years of negotiation, Iran and the world's great powers signed a Joint Comprehensive Plan of Action on July 14, 2015.[9] Filling many pages of text and annexes, the accord met some, if not all, the objectives of each party. In return for a phased lifting of international economic sanctions, Iran pledged to reduce by 98 percent its stockpile of low-enriched uranium (which could be processed to make bomb-grade fuel) and reduce its operating centrifuges (used to enrich that fuel) to 5,000. If Iran wished to violate the agreement, then it would need at least a year to produce the weapons-grade fuel required for a single bomb—compared to two or three months in 2014–2015.

The heart of the trade-off was an Iranian commitment to substantially restrict its nuclear program for more than a decade in return for relief from European and United Nations sanctions and a waiver of U.S. secondary sanctions, which impeded other countries from doing business with Iran. President Rouhani told Iranians the agreement was a "win-win" for both sides.[10] It preserved Iranian honor and scientific achievements while ending economic sanctions. Under a new UN Security Council resolution that replaced seven prior ones, Iran would obtain relief of sanctions on conventional arms trade after five years and on ballistic missiles after eight years—less time than critics would like, but not the immediate relief Iran (and its arms suppliers China and Russia) had sought. Iran would get back more than $100 billion in oil revenue that had been frozen in foreign banks. Sanctions on banks, oil trade, and ordinary commerce were to be lifted. Iran could again purchase modern airplanes and parts from Boeing and other suppliers.

The accord did not address concerns about Iran's support for Hezbollah, its refusal to accept Israel, or its human rights abuses, but U.S. officials said the accord would block four pathways to an Iranian nuclear weapon. First, it would reduce by two-thirds the number of centrifuges Iran currently had installed—from 19,000 to 6,000—of which only 5,060 would be allowed to enrich uranium for the next decade at a facility at Natanz (a location that would remain vulnerable to military attack). Of the remaining centrifuges, a few hundred would be allowed to operate at an underground plant at Fordow but would not be allowed to enrich uranium. Excess centrifuges would be dismantled and stored under constant electronic surveillance.

Second, Iran would cap enrichment at Natanz at 3.67 percent of the isotope U-235 (far below weapons grade) for fifteen years and reduce its stockpile of 10,000 to 12,000 kilograms of low-enriched uranium by 98 percent, to 300 kilograms—a quarter of what would be required for a single nuclear weapon if it were refined to weapons grade.

Third, a heavy-water reactor under construction at Arak had to be modified so that it could produce only a tiny amount of plutonium. Iran could not build a facility to reprocess the spent fuel, which had to be exported.

The fourth pathway to a bomb—the so-called sneakout—would be addressed by intensified monitoring and verification, including the resolution of questions about past military dimensions of the Iranian program. According to an agreement with the IAEA, Iran would allow the agency to visit sites where military-related nuclear activity was believed to have taken place, including Parchin, a military base that Iran had paved over three times to hide suspected prior weapons research.

Other restrictions on research and development of more advanced centrifuges were meant to keep Iran from rapidly ramping up uranium enrichment capacity in the years 2026–2030. Iran agreed to implement the additional protocol of the NPT and provide access to inspectors "where necessary and when necessary," in the words of Obama, if Iran was suspected of illicit activity. A joint commission would be set up to supervise implementation and resolve the inevitable disputes.

The July 2015 joint plan could be scuttled by either side. Many hard-liners in Washington and in Tehran opposed any deal with an adversary that could not be trusted. But President Obama pledged to veto any legislative action that tried to torpedo the accord.

Lifting of sanctions on Iran under the joint plan depended on a clean bill of health for Iran from the International Atomic Energy Agency. In December 2015 the IAEA reported that its investigations showed that Iran (confirming the CIA analysis) had conducted nuclear weapons research until 2003 and to a lesser extent until 2009, but the agency found no evidence of such work for the past twelve years.[11]

WHY KIM JONG UN HUNG TOUGH AND PRESIDENT ROUHANI WELCOMED AN ACCORD

In Pyongyang, unity from above was the rule. Having executed his uncle in 2013 and his defense minister in 2015, Kim Jong Un seemed to exercise total control.[12] Still, the DPRK leadership faced a dilemma like that confronting Tehran. Each regime wanted the material benefits that could come with closer integration with the outside world, but some leaders in each country feared the political consequences of opening its doors to foreign influences.

Thanks in part to oil revenues, in 2014 Iran's per capita income exceeded $13,000, while North Korea's was far less than $2,000 per year. Economic growth in each country had stalled. According to the CIA *World Factbook,* North Korea's tiny economy ($40 billion GDP) grew at 0.8 percent in 2012; Iran's much larger economy ($1 trillion GDP) "grew" at minus 1.9 percent. Each country's economy was striated by sanctions on nuclear-related technology, weapons, and banking transactions. But Iran suffered greatly from bans on exports of crude oil and precious metals; the country, for example, had trouble obtaining spare parts for its Boeing airliners acquired before 1979.

Life expectancy in Iran and North Korea was about seventy years—lower than in some neighboring states. Public health in both countries suffered from sanctions as well as the inefficiencies of a government-controlled economy. Iran gave more space to the private sector than did the DPRK, but the Heritage Foundation ranked both Iran and North Korea as among the most repressed economies in the world. Inflation in Iran reached 27 percent in 2012. Nearly a quarter of Iranian youth had no jobs. To be sure, a privileged few managed to become rich. The top 10 percent of Iranians possessed nearly one-third the country's wealth. Some 20 percent of Iranians were obese, but at least 5 percent of children were underweight. Infant mortality in Iran was high—40 per 1,000 live births. A quarter of adults were illiterate, more women than men. Literacy in North Korea, by contrast, was nearly universal, and Kim Jong Un in 2013 stipulated twelve years' education for all North Koreans. Each country's assets as of 2014 are summarized in table 17.1.

Sanctions curtailed economic growth both in Iran and North Korea, though elites in each country still managed to smuggle in creature comforts. While the bosses in Pyongyang seemed to care little if their people went hungry, many leaders in Iran seemed to worry about popular unrest. Knowing that GDP growth had stalled, the Iranian government elected in 2013 strove to lift the burden of sanctions. Unlike North Korea, Iran had a large middle class, which was well informed about the world and was demanding a better quality of life. Visiting the gleaming apartments of some such persons in 1998, I listened in horror as they talked about how some had been tortured in the early years of the theocracy—one so severely that she suffered brain damage. By the time Kim Jong Un took supreme power, a privileged elite existed in Pyongyang, along with an emerging commercial sector in several other cities. MIT researcher John S. Park found that external pressures stimulated entrepreneurs in China and the DPRK to develop new ways to evade UN sanctions.[13]

Trade boomed across the Tumen River. A privileged few in North Korea could enjoy five-star cognac even as most North Koreans remained both poor and repressed. Most North Koreans had only vague ideas of life in China, South Korea, and the world beyond. A large fraction of the population had long been malnour-

Table 17.1. Comparing Iran and North Korea in 2014–2015

	Iran	North Korea
Territory	1.7 million sq. km (18th in the world)	121,000 sq. km (99th in the world)
GDP at purchasing power parity	$1 trillion	$40 billion
GDP growth	−1.9% (208th in the world)	0.8% (168th in the world)
GDP per capita purchasing power parity (PPP)	$13,300 (2012)	$1,800 (2011)
Inflation rate (consumer prices)	27% (2012)	No data available
Population	80 million, with 1.24% annual growth	25 million, with 0.53% annual growth
Arable land	10% arable	19% arable
Electricity consumption	173 billion KWh (22nd in the world)	17 billion KWh (72nd in the world)
Unemployment	15%; among youth, 23%	No data available
Exports	$67 billion (53rd in the world) in 2012	$5 billion (114th in the world) in 2011
Imports	$70 billion (43rd in the world) in 2012	$4.3 billion (137th in the world) in 2011
Trade as % of GDP	13%	nearly 25%
Life expectancy at birth	71 (149th in the world)	70 (155th in the world)
Infant mortality	40:1,000 live births	25:1,000 live births
Health expenditures	6% of GDP	No data available
Literacy	85%	99%
Social homogeneity	61% Persian	99% Korean
Religion/ideology important	Very	Yes. Public commitment to state ideology.
Ideological unity	No	?
Political system	Elections; divided, multilayered government; secular and religious authorities	Dynastic rule + cronies in a virtual Mafia
Political and civic freedom	Not free: 4.5 on 1–7 scale	Not free: 7 on 1–7 scale
Economic freedom	Statist, but with some free enterprise. Among the most repressed economies (173rd) in the world with a score of 40.3.	Statist, with some market activity. The world's most repressed economy: 178th with a score of 1.0.

(continued on next page)

Table 17.1. Comparing Iran and North Korea in 2014–2015 *(continued)*		
	Iran	North Korea
Perceived threats from outside	Sanctions by U.S. and allies; threat of preventive war by Israel and U.S.	UN and U.S. sanctions; pressures also from ROK, China, Russia, and Japan
Importance in region	High	Important as a spoiler
Dependence on Russia or China	Yes	Very high
Influenced by U.S. soft power	Yes	?
Proud of history and culture	Yes	?
Persecution complex	Yes	Yes
Nuclear weapons	Not yet	Some
Nuclear ambitions	Divided opinions among leaders	Yes, for minimum deterrent
Active duty forces	545,000 (Israel: 160,000)	690,000 (ROK: 653,000)
Reserve forces	1,800,000 (Israel: 630,000)	4,500,000 (ROK: 2,900,000)
Multiple rocket launch systems	1,474 (Israel: 48)	2,400 (ROK: 214)
Defense budget in 2015	$6.3 billion (Israel: $17 billion)	$7.5 billion (ROK: $33.1 billion)

Sources: CIA World Factbook; The Economist; Freedom House, Freedom in the World; Heritage Foundation, Economic Freedom Index; Global Firepower Index; and other sources cited in this chapter.

ished. In contrast with Iran, some 4 percent of North Koreas were obese, but more than 20 percent of children were underweight.[14] For many North Koreans, both brain and body growth had been stunted. Many North Koreans of military age were five inches shorter than South Koreans.

Starting under Kim Jong Il, the regime's "military first" orientation siphoned off resources needed for investment and civilian consumption. According to the CIA's *World Factbook,* North Korea's capital stock by 2014 had declined to levels nearly beyond repair—the result of underinvestment, shortages of spare parts, and poor maintenance. Industrial and power output had fallen to below 1990 levels. Weather-related crop failures aggravated chronic food shortages caused by systemic problems, including a lack of arable land, collective farming practices, poor soil quality, insufficient fertilization, and persistent shortages of tractors and fuel. Large-scale international food aid deliveries as well as aid from China allowed most North Koreans in the early twenty-first century to escape the absolute starvation experienced in the mid-1990s. Still, many people continued to suffer from malnutrition and poor living conditions. Starting in 2002, the government had reluctantly allowed private farmers' markets to sell a wider range of goods. It also permitted some private farming to boost agricultural output. In December 2009 the DPRK carried out a redenomination of its currency, described earlier in chapter 7. The currency reform coupled with a crackdown on markets and foreign currency use yielded severe shortages and inflation, forcing Pyongyang in February 2010 to ease the restrictions.

Starting in 2012, the Kim Jong Un regime pledged to improve the country's economic life by renewing its commitment to special economic zones with China, negotiating a new payment structure to settle its $11 billion Soviet-era debt to Russia, and developing new agricultural and industrial policies to boost domestic production. The North Korean government pledged to forge a strong and prosperous nation. It sought also to attract foreign investment. At the same time, the regime's determination to maintain centralized controls seemed likely to inhibit fundamental reforms.

Freedom House judged North Korea the least free country in the world. Iran had elections, but it too ranked among the not-free. Most North Koreans had extremely limited access to information about the outside world. Very few had direct knowledge of life beyond the North's fortified borders. A few North Koreans gained information from travel and personal exposure. A larger fraction accessed smuggled DVDs and listened surreptitiously to foreign radio broadcasts. Most depended on word-of-mouth rumors spiked by those with personal exposure or access to DVDs. Still, an increasing share of the population in the Kim Jong Un era perceived glimmers of opulence elsewhere. Some young women walked the streets of Pyongyang in high heels and miniskirts made in China from South Korean patterns. Many Iranians, by contrast, were "wired" and able to communicate with relatives and others abroad. Many Iranians had gone to school or worked abroad. Many knew in detail what they were missing.

As of 2015 North Korea's population was not one-third of Iran's, but its armed forces were larger than Iran's—more than treble, if reserves were counted. DPRK defense outlays were estimated at $7.5 billion; Iran's, at $6.3 billion. South Korea, however, outspent North Korea by more than 4 to 1, while Israel (population 8 million) outspent Iran (population ten times larger) by more than 2 to 1. North Korea had nearly twice the number of multiple rocket launch systems projectors as Iran. More important, North Korea had some nuclear warheads—probably fewer than a dozen, and of uncertain reliability; Iran—for the present—none. Considering all the factors of conventional military strength (but excluding nuclear weapons), the Global Firepower Index in 2015 ranked Iran as the world's twenty-third strongest military power (down from sixteenth in 2013) and North Korea, thirty-sixth (down from twenty-ninth two years before); Israel ranked eleventh (up from thirteenth), and South Korea seventh, up from eighth).[15] Regardless of the precise distribution of military power, however, the conventional forces and geography of

North Korea and Iran sufficed to deter any plausible threat. Both countries needed economic progress far more than nuclear arms.

Stanford physicist Siegfried Hecker concluded that Iran did not have sufficient uranium ore for a large nuclear electricity program. It would be more cost-effective for Iran to buy uranium on the international market. He recommended that Iran follow the example of South Korea and develop nuclear energy in complete transparency and with international cooperation. "South Korea worked very closely with the United States and with Japan," Hecker explained in an interview in 2014. "It spent a couple of decades learning how to master the key technologies while these countries were helping it put nuclear electricity on the grid. During that time, South Korea developed into one of the best, if not the best, nuclear reactor manufacturers and fuel fabricators in the world. The key move that South Korea made early on was to stay away from enriching uranium domestically and reprocessing its used reactor fuel, which could provide it with plutonium for a nuclear weapons effort. In other words, South Korea took the most profitable path to nuclear electricity and stayed far away from taking the nuclear bomb option."[16]

WHY A DEAL WITH IRAN WAS MORE ATTAINABLE THAN WITH NORTH KOREA

Neither Iran nor the DPRK needed to fear a foreign attack unless its nuclear weapons development or other actions provoked outsiders to mount a preventive war. However, North Korea demanded to be recognized as a nuclear weapons state, while Iran claimed to have no nuclear weapon ambitions. Iran could forgo nuclear weapons because its geopolitical and economic resources assured it a commanding position in its region.[17] North Korea, by contrast, was a speck on the map of East Asia. Apart from coal and some exotic minerals, its resources offered little to induce foreign investment or trade.

Another difference was that Americans and Iranians could understand each other far better than Americans and North Koreans. Both English and Persian shared Indo-Iranian-European roots, while Korean had no ties to any Western language. A far larger share of Iran's people understood English and other European languages than did North Koreans. Many Iranians had relatives in the West. Many had studied or worked abroad.

Most Americans and Iranians, whether Zoroastrian or Muslim, believed in one God. Zoroastrianism was the first major monotheistic faith, but it fostered a belief, shared by most Christians, that the power of good must struggle endlessly against evil. Children of the same book as Jews and Christians, Muslims believed in Satan as well as Allah.

Muslims, long before Christians, endeavored to learn from the philosophers and scientists of ancient Greece. Europeans acquired the fullest transcriptions of texts by Aristotle and other Greeks from Muslims. Muslims, Jews, and Christians learned from one another for several centuries in Andalusia. In time, however, some Islamic authorities in al-Andalus and elsewhere repressed free thought. While censors in the twenty-first century had difficulty blocking information on the Internet, they could more readily limit public access to books. In 1998 a seminary student in Isfahan begged me to send him a copy of Aristotle's writings in English. How ironic—and tragic—that a Muslim felt a need to obtain from a Westerner an English version of Greek writings the Islamic world had transmitted to Europe many centuries before.[18]

While Iranians were monotheistic, Koreans for most of their history did not believe in one supreme being. Their civilization was built on Shamanism, Confucianism, and Buddhism. Starting in the nineteenth century, however, many converted to Christianity. Although some elders in Kim Il Sung's family were Presbyterian, the Communist regime in Pyongyang banned all religion except hypernationalism and devotion to the reigning dynasty. While many South Koreans knew about Christianity, most North Koreans lacked familiarity with the West's Christian traditions. Like Korea's kings in times past, the DPRK treated Christian missionaries as subversives from an alien culture.

Many Iranians and North Koreans had a hate-love attitude to the United States. Modernizers in each country looked to the United States in the late nineteenth and early twentieth centuries as a guide to development and a bulwark against imperialist intrigues. Persia's parliament, the Majlis, backed two Americans, William M. Shuster and, subsequently, Arthur Millspaugh, as they organized the country's treasury and taxation programs just before and after World War I and again during World War II.[19] Two other Americans, Arthur Pope and his wife, Phyllis Ackerman, edited a six-volume *Survey of Persian Art* in the 1930s. Returning to Iran in the 1960s, they spent the rest of their lives there and are buried in a gorgeous mausoleum in Isfahan.

Some Iranians recall that U.S. pressures at the United Nations helped push Soviet occupation forces from northern Iran in 1946. However, any positive thoughts Iranians had about Americans were confounded by memories of U.S. involvement in the coup that restored the Pahlavi dynasty in 1953 and by U.S. support for the Iraqi-Iranian war of the 1980s, during which a U.S. ship shot down an Iranian Airbus, killing nearly 300 persons including scores of children. Given the anti-American drumbeat of official propaganda, few Iranians could know that a major impetus for ousting Prime Minister Mohammad Mossadegh in the 1953 coup came from Iran's middle classes, merchants, and mullahs, who loathed his secularism.[20]

In 1998 Iranian president Mohammad Khatami sought dialogue instead of a clash between civilizations. That summer I found myself addressing both diplomats and Islamic scholars in Tehran. When his turn came, the Iranian scholar who introduced me denounced my various "errors"—apparently to please some higher-ups, for he proceeded to give a speech not so different from mine on the need for East–West reconciliation. My best rapport emerged on a mountaintop overlooking the smoggy Tehran below. An off-duty colonel in the Iranian army and I joined in urging two off-duty privates not to pollute their lungs and the mountain air with their cigarette smoking.

Both positive and negative feelings toward the United States also existed in Korea. Some Koreans knew that Westerners brought schools and modernization to Korea and that the United States was the first country to recognize the country's independent statehood. Older South Koreans appreciated America's role in driving back Communist forces in 1950–1953. Few North Koreans knew that Kim Il Sung started the war in 1950, but most were sure that U.S. bombers flattened their country in the ensuing conflict. Compounding the misunderstandings, North Koreans were taught in the Kim Jong Un era that DPRK nukes could destroy New York.

POLICY IMPLICATIONS FOR DEMOCRACIES

In the twenty-first century the Pyongyang leadership and some officials in Tehran saw the United States as the greatest threat to their security but also as a potential key to their economic advance. What did all this mean for the United States and other governments struggling to halt and reverse the spread of nuclear weapons? Outsiders needed to offer the revolutionary pariahs security—for their regime and their country. The outlines of grand bargains that could benefit all parties were known. Why did these proposals go nowhere? Often the timing was wrong. When one side wanted a deal, the other was not ready. Often the offer was issued with a condescending or hostile tone—disregarding Lenin's advice to his diplomats in 1922: "Avoid venomous [*iadovitie*] words!"[21]

Miscommunication often played a role, but "hawks" within each government were sometimes the key obstacle. Here is one example. In spring 2003 leaders in Tehran—the Ayatollah Ali Khamenei, President Khatami, and top officials in the foreign ministry—proposed a dialogue "in mutual respect" on a broad agenda with the United States. The essential trade-off was that Tehran would abstain from developing WMD under full transparency in exchange for full access to Western technology and a halt to U.S. efforts at regime change. The Iranian proposal was given to a Swiss intermediary, who faxed a copy to the State Department. Knowing of tensions between the State Department and the White House, the intermediary also gave a copy to Bob Ney, a congressman from Ohio who knew Iran well and sought dialogue with the Khatami regime. Congressman Ney passed the proposal to President George W. Bush's adviser Karl Rove, whom he knew from college. Secretary of State Colin Powell and his deputies were joined by National Security

Advisor Condoleezza Rice in urging a positive response, but Vice President Dick Cheney and Defense Secretary Donald Rumsfeld said, "We don't speak to evil." They killed an opportunity for a major breakthrough, in part because they wanted to expand their "shock and awe" defeat of Saddam Hussein into regime-changing attacks on Iran and Syria. Adding insult to injury, the Bush administration chastised the Swiss diplomat for delivering the message.[22]

"Face" is important to many, if not all, cultures. Many North Koreans as well as Iranians believe the West often treated them rudely and unfairly. Like North Koreans and Iranians, Russians have also felt insulted by intimations of Western superiority. Their sensitivities were mollified when President John F. Kennedy praised the Soviet people in his June 10, 1963, "Strategy of Peace" speech, setting the stage for the nuclear test ban. Kennedy initiated a process akin to what psychologist Charles Osgood termed "graduated reciprocation in tension-reduction" (discussed in chapter 11), to which Khrushchev responded with what he called "disarmament by mutual example."

Starting with Rouhani's election in 2013, Tehran and Washington embarked on a process of tension-reduction. High-context diplomacy garnered some positive results. Between Pyongyang and Washington, however, contacts of any kind were thin. North Koreans and Americans could not readily forget their bloody encounters in 1950–1953 or their many confrontations since. Iran and the United States, by contrast, never fought each other. Their disputes were less serious than those that drove the U.S.-Soviet Cold War. Americans had far more in common with Iranians than with North Koreans. A shared cultural heritage, of course, could not guarantee compromise on issues of survival.

From Capitol Hill to Riyadh to Jerusalem, the opposition to a nuclear deal with Iran intensified in 2015. Presidents Obama and Rouhani could seize the opportunity created by their nuclear accord to forge a political and strategic realignment in U.S.-Iranian relations. A nuclear deal could open the door to normalization—the best way to make sure that a nuclear freeze held fast.[23]

If the democracies and Tehran reached a long-term accommodation, then what could be the impact on North Korea? If Iran's leaders curtailed their nuclear weapons program in order to lift sanctions, then Kim Jong Un might regard them as naïve and heighten his priority for "military first." Alternatively, he might curtail nuclear and missile development too, if offered a convincing array of security assurances and economic incentives. If détente worked for Tehran, could it not help North Korea as well?

18

Basic Forces and *Fortuna*
versus Human Factors

Are humans playthings of the gods? Do we determine our own paths, or are they preset by forces and structures out of our control? No single factor explains the ups and downs in North–South relations or in the six-party talks. But the record shows that ideas and determined individuals have sometimes overcome the thrust of material forces and neutered the vagaries of time and chance. Smart power can outweigh both hard power and caprices of fortune: *fortuna*. Where there is a will—on all sides—paths to mutual gain can be developed.

In the debate between voluntarism and determinism, Juche came down on the side of subjective power. Whereas this chapter focuses on the capacity of individuals to foster constructive change, Juche—as ideology and morality—promoted the belief that the subjective power of the collective can and should promote the cause of revolution, as defined by the Kim dynasts. As we saw in the first pages of chapter 2, Juche sought to mobilize the collective—not the individual—to serve the top leader.

INDIVIDUAL PERSONALITY

Graham Allison and Philip Zelikow, in their book *Essence of Decision,* showed how U.S. and Soviet behaviors in the Cuban crisis could be explained as rational strategic responses to the balance of power; by the standard operating routines of government bureaucracies; and by partisan political competition within each society.[1] Each of these three forces shaped decisions not so much by its objective content but by how it was perceived and evaluated. Both perceptions and responses were conditioned by the cultural values and patterns of each society. At bottom, how the crisis arose and passed into history reflected the personal makeup of the leaders on each side. These included Nikita Khrushchev's propensity to gamble on ventures that promised immediate gains and to ignore long-term dangers and John F. Kennedy's combination of cool deliberation and macho resolve. Kennedy's decisions were also influenced by the personalities and predilections of his closest advisers, such as his brother Robert F. Kennedy and Robert S. McNamara.

Analysis of the democracies' relations with North Korea must also include a consideration of the personal makeup of the top leaders in each country. Westerners know even less about Kim Jong Un than they did about Khrushchev in 1962. By comparison, most American presidents are nearly an open book.

LITTLE BARACK LEARNS REALPOLITIK

When Barack Obama was just four to six years old, his stepfather, Lolo, spent hours wrestling with him. Soon after they moved to Jakarta, Lolo told Barack, "The first thing to remember is how to protect yourself." This was the message after an Indonesian boy raised an egg-sized lump on the side of Barack's head. Aged eight or nine, Barack had "tussled" with the older boy after he ran off with a friend's soccer ball. The other boy "cheated," Barack said, and hit him with a rock. The next day Lolo brought home some new boxing gloves and instructed his stepson to bob and stay low. "There," Lolo said. "Keep your hands up."

In those years (1967–1971) Barack often ran in the Jakarta streets morning and night with friends from all social classes. They hustled odd jobs, caught crickets, and battled swift kites with razor-sharp lines. The loser watched his kite soar off, to be seized by grasping hands elsewhere. Lolo told Barack that a man absorbs the powers of whatever he eats and promised his stepson some tiger meat.

Barack chose not to write his grandparents in Hawaii about much that he witnessed in Jakarta. "The world was violent," he wrote later—"unpredictable, and often cruel." Since Toot and Gramps knew nothing about such a world, there was no use raising questions they could not answer.[2]

Barack's mother gave money to beggars and tried to protect the servants from Lolo's wrath. "Your mother has a soft heart. That's a good thing in a woman," Lolo said. "But a man needs to have more sense." It had nothing to do with good or bad, Lolo explained. It was a matter of taking life on its own terms.

Once, during their boxing sessions, Barack felt a hard knock to the jaw and looked up into Lolo's sweating face. Lolo said, "Pay attention. Keep your hands up." They sparred for another half hour and then sat down with a jug of water. Barack noticed a series of indented scars on Lolo's leg. "Leech marks," Lolo said matter-of-factly. You kill the leeches with salt, but you still have to dig them out with a knife. Did it hurt? "Of course it hurt. Sometimes you can't worry about hurt. Sometimes you worry only about getting where you have to go." To Barack it seemed that Lolo never showed anger or sadness. "He seemed to inhabit a world of hard surfaces and well-defined thoughts." Asked if he had ever seen a man killed, Lolo said yes. Why was he killed? "Because he was weak. Men take advantage of weakness in other men. They're just like countries in that way. The strong man takes the weak man's land. He makes the weak man work in his fields. If the weak man's woman is pretty, the strong man will take her. . . . Which would you rather be?" When Barack did not answer, Lolo rose to his feet and said, "Better to be strong. If you can't be strong, be clever, and make peace with someone who's strong. But always better to be strong yourself. Always."[3]

Thus, a child of eight or nine years old acquired the distilled wisdom of Thucydides and Machiavelli plus the neorealist distinction between "balancing" against—joining partners to resist—a strong foe and "bandwagoning" with him, basically following his lead. During his time in Indonesia Barack also learned a foreign language and how to cohabit—and have fun with—tough kids in the streets of a land shaped by Islam, Hinduism, Christianity, and animism. In later years Barack also learned how to interact with kids from rich families in Honolulu even as he scooped ice cream and did other odd jobs. Over the years, Barack attended the best schools on scholarship but often had to rough it.

Obama thought deeply about nuclear weapons in college long before he became president. While President Ronald Reagan was promoting an arms buildup against the "evil empire," Obama wrote a lead story for the Columbia College *Sundial* about the contrasting positions on arms control taken by two student organizations.[4] He also wrote a term paper about Soviet disarmament policy, for which he received an A.[5]

THE AUDACITY OF HOPE VERSUS DYNASTIC PRIVILEGE

Kim Jong Un and Barack Obama shared some characteristics. Both lived abroad for a time and attended elite high schools. Both liked basketball; but one continued to play basketball, as well as surf and golf, even as president, while the other seemed only to watch. Judging by the jowls on display as he took power in 2011–2012, still less than thirty years old, Kim Jong Un engaged in little rigorous activity in his twenties beyond gourmandism and other forms of hedonism.

Jong Un emerged as the chosen one, a younger son elevated to dauphin status in a widely revered, if also feared, charismatic dynasty.[6] Obama grew up in straitened circumstances, son of an African exchange student and a white American who later married an Indonesian, a man who taught him boxing and other skills. In Hawaii, Barack was reared for years by his mother's white parents. By dint of persistent striving and some good luck, Obama got to the Ivy League and, for a time, Wall Street. Then, with a law degree from Harvard, he chose to work as a community organizer among the poor of Chicago, where he met his wife, a corporate lawyer who was the great-great-great granddaughter of a slave. Jong Un, by contrast, was a relative purebred who led a pampered life and chose an entertainer for his consort.

Obama's education was far more sophisticated than Jong Un's—so refined that he became a law professor at the University of Chicago and wrote two best-selling, but serious, books. His leadership style was far more deliberate than Jong Un's, who sometimes appeared impetuous and reckless. Obama's style resembled JFK's; Jong Un's was more like Khrushchev's. Obama faced severe political competition at every step—many of his appointees and policies were blocked by Republicans. Having executed his aunt's husband, Jang Song Taek, and much of his uncle's entourage in 2013, Jong Un claimed to have eliminated factions in the DPRK. In April 2014 he was reelected as first chairman of the National Defense Commission by the country's rubber-stamp legislature, which also approved the leader's choices to fill some top posts vacated by recent purges. In 2015 he was reported to have executed his recently chosen minister of defense and some of his cohorts. Obama faced far more outspoken critics than did Kim Jong Un, many of whom labored to demolish his policies and presidency, but he responded only with argumentation and, when Congress did nothing, executive orders.

Obama could access the assets of a superpower but faced myriad problems at home and abroad. Jong Un presided over a near-failing state but manipulated its assets to stay in power and slowly raise his nation's strategic and economic power. The cerebral U.S. president was said to lack the human touch, while Jong Un smiled as he rubbed shoulders with soldiers and occasionally held a baby. He appeared far more confident and outgoing than his insecure and introverted father.

We do not know what lessons Kim Jong Un learned as a child from his father. We can surmise that he did not hustle odd jobs or sleep in his car but lived an indulgent existence away from the hoi polloi. He came to appreciate basketball and skiing while attending a boarding school in Switzerland. He certainly observed and learned something from the tough policies his father conducted at home and across borders in the first decade of the twenty-first century. The young general appeared far more impulsive as well as extroverted than his father. The short, bejowled young man presiding over a hungry nation seemed to admire tall basketball players. He smiled at Mickey Mouse, invested in a flashy ski resort and swim park, and showed off a picture-book wife. With all the markings of a spoiled and pampered child, he used a killer instinct to amass the kinds of power sure to corrupt. He courted the military, sometimes ordering them to take actions that approached the red lines of South Korean and American forbearance. The DPRK satellite launch in April 2012, for example, sure to nullify the Leap Day accord, showed a high level of bravado and a willingness to defy both Washington and the UN Security Council.

Considering their diverse upbringings and asymmetric assets, one of the U.S. and DPRK leaders' few links was an affection for basketball. Neither Obama nor Kim Jong Un did much to alter relations between their countries.

Having outlined the relevant personality factors, let us next consider some of the micro forces, or structures, that shape U.S. relations with North Korea. These include the strategic balance, bureaucratic routines, and some parameters of partisan politics—for example, the competition between Republicans and Democrats in Washington. After outlining the tangible factors, we examine intangible ideas and free will. Between the poles of structural determinism and voluntarism is the realm of what Machiavelli called *fortuna,* analyzed later in this chapter.

STRUCTURES OF POWER

Realists contend that world politics is best understood as a quest for power.[7] They believe that intangibles, such as ideals, do not drive this quest but rather reflect or mask it.[8] "Communications problems" are by-products—not root causes—of conflict. Neorealists (a.k.a. structural realists) go further: they maintain that individuals, domestic politics, and culture count for nothing in world affairs. International relations is a mirror of the material structure defined by the hierarchy of military and economic power. The strong do what they desire, while the weak must submit—either following the leader (bandwagoning) or seeking partners to resist (balancing).[9] Leslie H. Gelb, a former president of the Council on Foreign Relations in New York, derided soft power as mere "foreplay" to coercive power. The world, he said, was not flat but—at least for the present—pyramidal, with one country on top.[10]

Geopolitics

Geography sometimes looks like destiny. Sited where China, Russia, and Japan face one another, Korea has long been pressed either to join with or to balance against one or more of its neighbors. This kind of pressure intensified after a distant power, the United States, extended its reach to Northeast Asia in the nineteenth century. As explained in chapter 3, Korea, annexed by Japan, disappeared from official U.S. discourse and maps from 1911 until 1942. Given the fragile nature of the U.S.-Soviet alliance in World War II, realists could have anticipated (though none did) that the victorious powers would divide the peninsula in two—a Communist and an anti-Communist Korea.

When North Korea drove south in 1950, as we saw in chapter 5, the proximity of Russia and the remoteness of the United States led George F. Kennan, known as the author of President Harry Truman's "containment" policy and a devotee of geographical determinism, to advise Secretary of State Dean Acheson to consign the entire peninsula to the Soviet sphere of influence. Had the United States followed Kennan's fatalistic realism, then Korea would soon have been united under Communist rule and probably would have remained so for many years. But this did not happen. Against big odds, the United States chose to fight and soon reversed the tide. General Douglas MacArthur overcame geographic odds by landing forces at Inchon. He then ignored geopolitics by driving north toward the Yalu River, thereby provoking China to enter the fray. Having reached a virtual stalemate, the two sides agreed in 1953 to divide the peninsula close to the 38th parallel.

Geoeconomics

Material forces—military, economic, geopolitical—set the stage. As one Korea became two in the late 1940s, in the run-up to the Korean War, the North possessed significant advantages over the South. Its industrial base was more developed; its military better equipped; its political administration more cohesive; and its major patron far more committed than the South's major backer.

The ravages of war, 1950–1953, left both North and South prostrate. After the war the United States became far more engaged in Korean affairs than was Russia or China. The United States devoted major resources to help South Korea (like Taiwan) reach and go beyond economic takeoff. In the 1970s South Korea became one of Asia's "Little Tigers." From the 1970s into the twenty-first century, geoeconomics favored the South.

More than six decades after the Korean Armistice, the United States retained significant forces ready to fight in and for South Korea. American and ROK forces conducted maneuvers and operated under a Combined Forces Command headed by a U.S. general. Starting in 2007, authorities in Washington and Seoul inched toward agreement that control of South Korean forces in wartime should be shifted to the ROK. Implementing this principle, however, proved to be problematic. Recurrent crises with the DPRK led U.S. and ROK leaders to put off consummation of this plan.

The South's growing economic lead over the North exerted contradictory influences on Pyongyang—both limiting and fostering the regime's willingness to take on the risks of détente. The North Korean regime, like the Soviet in past decades, probably hoped that arms accords would lead to an easing of the economic sanctions that blocked access to Western and East Asian technology. Food shortages probably pushed the North Korean regime, like that of the erstwhile USSR, to make concessions in arms control negotiations.[11] The Agreed Framework of 1994 and the reciprocal visits by DPRK and U.S. officials in 2000 coincided with bad harvests and starvation in the North.[12] The DPRK leadership did not want its people to see and then compare developments in the North and South. Still, a regime that could indulge its elites and intimidate or brainwash most of its subjects had little reason to fear a revolution from below.

Contrary to materialist expectations, asymmetries in wealth on the Korean peninsula did not push the DPRK leadership to its knees. Instead, the Pyongyang regime tended to hang tough. Confronted with challenges on all sides, the DPRK championed self-reliance and either walked away from negotiations or tried to drive very hard bargains.

North Korea's incipient nuclear weapons capability could also push Pyong-yang in opposite directions. Though the North remained weak militarily relative to the South and its superpower ally, even a minuscule nuclear weapons capability helped to level the playing field. Confident it possessed a minimum deterrent after its first nuclear tests (2006, 2009, 2013, and 2016), Pyongyang often defied its five interlocutors. Believing that it operated from a new kind of strength, however, the DPRK on occasion seemed ready to consider a grand bargain.

The forces of global interdependence also registered contradictory impacts. While South Koreans tapped into these forces to become more prosperous, the North did not shape or benefit from the forces sweeping the planet. Isolation hurt the North and militated for joining the world, but it also widened the gaps to be bridged.

A SECOND EXPLANATION: *FORTUNA*

Neorealism verged on hubris in its confidence that scientific assessment of mate-rial factors could explain human history. Materialist explanations leave little to chance or to free will. But any review of human life shows this view to be too nar-row. Consider, for example, the consequences if Franz Ferdinand's driver in Sara-jevo had not made a wrong turn; if Gavrilo Princip's bullet had only grazed the archduke; if Hitler had been felled by an assassination; and if Lee Harvey Oswald's rifle shot had missed John F. Kennedy.

To what extent have the zigs and zags of Korean affairs been shaped by intan-gibles? Let us consider what Machiavelli called *fortuna*. Is it a mysterious power that intervenes to shape human affairs? Is it a black hole that sucks in and devours other forces? Or is it more like blind chance—coincidence that appears to bring us good or bad luck?

Fortuna, for Machiavelli, could be an angry goddess who lays waste like a flooding river that overflows its banks—a primal source of violence directed against humanity. "She shows her power where *virtù* and wisdom do not prepare to resist her, and directs her fury where she knows that no dykes or embankments are ready to hold her." *Virtù*, for Machiavelli, meant all the qualities needed to make for a strong polity—it included bravery, boldness, foresight, and ruthless-ness. *Fortuna* could be resisted by human beings, but only in circumstances where *virtù* and wisdom had prepared for her inevitable arrival.[13]

Nassim Taleb warns us to expect "black swans"—important events that could not have been expected, events so rare that they would not show up even on the tail end of a bell curve. Yes, Europeans believed all swans are white, but when they reached Australia, they found black swans—an event unprecedented for them. Taleb claims that *almost all consequential events in history come from the unex-pected*—while humans convince themselves that these events are explainable with "hindsight bias."[14] His examples include World War I, the personal computer, and 9/11/2001.[15] The list could include the near collapse of the U.S. banking system in 2008.

Some individuals and societies seem to lead charmed lives, while others encounter one disaster after another. But science denies that *fortuna* is an angry goddess. "Fate" is just coincidence and inadequate preparation for dealing with untoward events. Floods take place as a result of physical forces combined with human impacts on the environment and poor planning by humans.

Still, there are limits to what science can anticipate. Today's physical features may serve as pre-adaptations for new life forms if the environment changes. Darwinian pre-adaptations cannot be prestated or foreseen. Their evolution is not deducible from physics. The more diversity in the biosphere, the more possibilities for unpredictable adaptations.[16]

Some individuals and groups are better equipped than others to cope with challenges and make the most of opportunity.[17] As a Chinese fortune cookie reveals, "Thorough preparation makes its own luck." People whose eyes and minds are open and searching are most likely to experience serendipity—finding value in unexpected places. Persistent hard work, combined with courage, often pays off. As Virgil put it, "*Audaces fortuna iuvat, timidosque repellit*"—fortune rewards the bold and repels the meek.[18]

Chance and timing have played gigantic roles in Northeast Asia. Consider these turning points where a slightly different concatenation of events could have catapulted relationships in a different direction.[19]

- What if, in the late nineteenth and early twentieth century, anti-imperialists in the United States had resisted Japan's takeover of Korea? Many Americans working in Korea urged Washington to do so. Since Washington demanded an open door in China, why not apply the same logic to Korea? If the United States had allowed self-determination in the Philippines, as the anti-imperialists demanded, then Washington would have had less incentive to cede Korea to Japan.
- What if Woodrow Wilson in 1919 had extended support for national self-determination to Korea? His "Inquiry," led by Walter Lippmann, as we saw in chapter 3, did not even put Korea on its agenda.[20]
- What if Washington had applied the logic of the 1932 Stimson Doctrine not only to Manchuria but also to Korea?
- What if, years or months before the USSR joined the war against Japan and occupied northern Korea, the United States had recognized Syngman Rhee's provisional government and made Korea a founding member of the United Nations?

Were such moves simply not in the cards because they contradicted the premises of realpolitik?[21] No. They would have enhanced America's interests in the world and conformed to moral and legal principles long espoused by U.S. government. Washington sometimes stood on principle. For example, it refused to recognize the forced incorporation of the three Baltic countries into the USSR even though Roosevelt valued Stalin as an ally.[22] Despite Washington's efforts to work with the Gorbachev regime, U.S. diplomat Jack Matlock spoke in Latvia in 1986 reminding people there that the United States had never recognized the Soviet annexation of the three Baltic republics.

- What if Stalin in August 1945 had rejected the U.S. proposal to divide Korea at the 38th parallel? What if Stalin, knowing America had few troops in the south, had instead ordered the Red Army to occupy the entire peninsula, as it did in some East European countries? By 1946 the Soviet regime took a harder line in divided Korea. A quirk of timing may have saved the South from Communist rule.
- What if Secretary of State Dean Acheson in January 1950 had vetted his remarks on the U.S. defense perimeter with U.S. experts on East Asia? Instead, he spoke without a written script and gave the impression that the United States would let South Korea fend for itself if attacked. Half a year later, this same secretary of state helped convince President Truman to mobilize U.S. forces and the United Nations to drive back the North's forces from the South.
- What if the Soviet delegate had taken his seat in the UN Security Council when it deliberated a response to the North Korean attack? Washington's ability to activate UN collective security was aided by what looked like a freak incident—the absence of the Soviet delegate from the UN Security Council when it voted to condemn and then resist the North's actions. A Soviet veto would have complicated Washington's decisions and, even if the United States opted to fight, would have deprived U.S. actions of legitimacy.

We can also wonder what might have happened if certain assassination efforts had failed or succeeded.

- What if assassins had succeeded earlier, or failed entirely, in three attempts on the life of President Park Chung Hee? The 1974 attempt missed the president but killed his wife, Yook Young Soo, leaving Park gloomy and dispirited.[23] Jimmy Carter's inauguration and the shift of U.S. policy toward Korea in 1977 added to Park's difficulties. Park's death by assassination in 1979 probably helped preserve authoritarian rule in the ROK, which continued until the late 1980s.

- What if plots against the life of Kim Dae Jung had succeeded and not merely left him lame? The best-known challenger to Park Chung Hee's rule, Kim claimed that Park tried to have him killed in 1971 and on several subsequent occasions. He survived in part thanks to U.S. protection. On his third try, Kim Dae Jung won the ROK presidency in 1997. Had he been killed or given up hope, he would not have been able to introduce his Sunshine Policy.
- What if the Chun Doo Hwan administration, the U.S ambassador to Seoul, and the Carter administration had handled the May 1980 Kwangju uprising differently? What if other policies had prevailed and nearly 200 persons not been killed? The incident heightened provincial hostilities within South Korea and stoked anti-American sentiments.
- What if the plot against the life of ROK president Chun Doo Hwan had succeeded when he visited Rangoon in October 1983? Instead, he lived; but the explosion killed at least seventeen Koreans (including some ROK ministers) and four Burmese. The government in Rangoon blamed North Korea for the explosion and severed diplomatic ties.[24] Relations between Seoul and Pyongyang became far more tense. Authoritarian rule tightened its grip in South Korea.
- What if Kim Il Sung had not agreed to meet with Jimmy Carter in June 1994? What if he had died before Carter arrived? The Great Leader expired just weeks after his historic deal with Carter that set the stage for the Agreed Framework signed later that year. Kim's son and successor seemed to feel obliged to carry on his father's understanding with Carter. Had the father in his last months refused to see Carter (as he later turned away some Clinton stalwarts), then Kim Jong Il would have inherited a more confrontational legacy—perhaps even a war.
- What if Kim Il Sung had not passed on just before he was scheduled to meet with ROK president Kim Young Sam? "Fate played a trick on me," Kim Young Sam later wrote. "If I had met Kim Il Sung, I would have changed the nation's history."[25] But Kim Young Sam's failure to attend the funeral of Kim Il Sung and his ban on sending private condolences did not endear the ROK leader to Pyongyang, whose media did not even mention his demise in 2015.
- What if Democrats had not lost control of Congress in the 1994 elections? This happened shortly after U.S. and DPRK negotiators signed their Agreed Framework. Republican reluctance to fund the deal contributed to the long delays in breaking ground for the two light-water reactors promised in 1994. The Clinton administration felt compelled to seek funding from the European Union as well as from Japan and the ROK. All this took time. Meanwhile, some North Korean actions also delayed the whole project.

Neither side took account of its own role in the demise of what could have been a win-win operation.

- What if President Bill Clinton in late 2000 had accepted Kim Jong Il's invitation to travel to Pyongyang and resolve all issues between the two governments? The groundwork had been laid by Madeleine Albright and others, but Clinton opted to work on another worthy cause: striving to mediate Israeli-Palestinian differences. The prospects for a grand bargain with Pyongyang looked good just as Clinton lost his lease on the White House.

- What if newly elected George W. Bush had listened to Colin Powell instead of hard-liners close to the White House in early 2001? Powell wanted to build on the movement toward a deal with Pyongyang generated by the Clinton administration in 2000. Instead, harsh words from the Bush White House fostered confrontation instead of détente with North Korea. Not only did Bush's policies abort movement toward arms control; they probably also undermined movement in North Korea toward a more market-friendly economy. They helped catalyze a harder line in the North's domestic as well as its foreign policy.

- What if a U.S. armored car had not killed two high school girls in a narrow lane in South Korea in June 2002? What if the drivers had not been on maneuvers for three days with little sleep? What if villages had been forewarned of the planned military transit? What if U.S. authorities had responded to Korean grievances with greater empathy? Would anti-U.S. sentiments in the ROK have risen to such a pitch in the early twenty-first century?

- What if, starting in 2003, the United States had not become bogged down in an elective war in Iraq? Washington might have paid more attention to the DPRK and endeavored with sticks and carrots to stop North Korea's nuclear weapons development. Were it not for the war in Iraq, Pyongyang might not have wanted or dared to test a nuclear weapon.

- What if Condoleezza Rice, having left the NSC for the State Department in 2005, had not become more committed to traditional diplomacy and put a skillful diplomat, Christopher Hill, in charge of negotiations with the DPRK? What if Hill had not sometimes stretched his instructions? What if he had not crossed paths with his DPRK counterpart in late 2006 and set up their bilateral encounter in Berlin? What if Rice had not given her blessing to that meeting and its product—an outline of the accord signed by all six parties in February 2007?

- What if, instead of waiting for a new U.S. president, Pyongyang had opted to clinch a deal in 2008? As happened in 2000, the brightest prospects for a U.S.-DPRK accord took shape just as the president's term ended.

Each of these what-ifs was shaped by structure and by agency—by the configuration of forces and actions of individual players. They seem to mock any explanation based on materialistic determinism. If things had not jelled as they did—if some events had occurred earlier or later—then politics in Korea would have become quite different. As in all human relations, timing and coincidence often triggered both positive and negative developments. America's involvement in Iraq, for example, diverted Washington's attention from North Korea in 2003–2004, even as it probably deepened Pyongyang's determination to acquire a nuclear deterrent. Starting in 2005, however, as the burdens of the Iraq war became heavier, the Bush administration appeared to seek a negotiating breakthrough with the DPRK.

IDEAS AND FREE WILL

We must also consider the intangibles that shape world affairs—concepts, perceptions, beliefs, words, feelings, cultural and personal values, soft power, smart power, and—not least—willpower. These are the domains analyzed by students of ideas and ideals, culture, constructivism, psychology, and diplomatic technique.

Let us acknowledge that material forces provide basic elements of the framework for human actions and that accidents of timing often seem to block some paths and lead to others. None of us is completely free. We are all bound by nature and nurture, by life experiences, and by elements of chance and timing. As organisms coevolve with each other and their environment, however, some organisms become more fit than others—better able to cope with complex challenges. Some humans make decisions and pursue policies that enhance their objectives, while others waste their assets and opportunities.

Strong individuals and societies overcome their heritage and other barriers so as to put their lives on their chosen trajectories. To do so, of course, they must be determined and persistent. Machiavelli warned that *fortuna,* like a rain-driven flood, can lay waste to human enterprise. He also noted, however, that wise politicians can anticipate and plan for floods and other stresses. Skillful policymakers can mitigate damage and sometimes turn a challenge into an opportunity. They can even overcome material limitations and the forces released by a perfect storm.

Nothing illustrates better the ways that strong individuals can counter perfect storms than Blaine Harden's juxtaposition of the Great Leader and the fighter pilot.[26] Each did his thing against all odds. Kim Il Sung was the Soviets' third choice to lead North Korea. He stumbled at first but exploited signs of popular resistance to consolidate his position and intimidate or purge potential rivals. He badgered and cajoled Stalin until he got the Kremlin's approval to invade the South, along with the consent of a very reluctant Mao Zedong. Kim Il Sung blundered as a general and later as an economic planner, but his regime survived by milking the USSR and China. He founded a dynasty that endured for generations. Meanwhile, the teenaged No Kum Sok plotted to escape from Kim Il Sung's tyranny. To do so he had to mask his class origin and lead in praising the Great Leader. He became the youngest fighter pilot in Kim Il Sung's air force. Having judiciously steered his MiG away from dogfights with the far superior U.S. Sabre jets, No Kum Sok resolved to fly his plane across the lines and land at a U.S. air base. Everything worked for him—the weather; his place among the planes taking off; a down day for U.S. radar; and the stupefaction of U.S. pilots and ground crews, who did not shoot as he landed in the wrong direction and with no advance warning. Though his father had died earlier, No Kum Sok found his mother in South Korea. He did not know that the Americans would pay him $100,000 for a MiG-15. He flew for freedom, not money. Ignorant of English, he soon found himself enrolled in a U.S. college and in time became a successful engineer who eventually became a millionaire and retired in Florida.[27]

Idealism and Neoliberalism

Democrats (small d) contend that self-rule should be the underlying principle of politics. They believe that self-rule conduces to prosperity and peace—at home and across borders. Communist theorists, by contrast, have argued that an enlightened vanguard should lead and decide for the masses.[28] Rugged individualism, Communists have said, leads to chaos and domination by the privileged few. Until communism prevails across borders, the contradictions of free enterprise will cause war.

The postulates of democracy are supported by complexity science, which holds that the key to fitness is self-organization—in all realms, political, social, cultural, and economic. Revising social Darwinism, it maintains that the capacity to cooperate is crucial for societal fitness. Liberal peace theory takes respect for democracy one step further: it argues that a liberal consensus makes war nearly unthinkable among democracies. Experiences around the globe in recent centuries have proved that liberal peace theory is basically correct and that arguments for top-down rule are wrong.[29]

The lessons of global history have been confirmed also on the Korean peninsula.[30] The more that freedom and self-organization took hold in South Korea, the more prosperous it became and the more devoted to a peaceful resolution of issues at home and with the North. Authoritarian rule in the North, by contrast, conduced to immiserization, isolation, and bellicosity.[31] Though one-party rule remained in China, greater economic freedom there sometimes coincided with a more constructive role in world affairs, as when Beijing hosted the six-party talks. This image, however, was then undermined by China's brazen expansion into adjacent seas, as discussed below in chapter 19. Russia, by comparison, did little to shape the six-power negotiations, even when it overflowed with petrodollars. Nor did Putin's land grabs on Russia's borders enhance the country's moral stature.

Can ideas change how things work? Seeking to perform a symbolic act for peace, some thirty women from many countries crossed from North to South Korea across the DMZ on May 24, 2015—International Women's Day for Peace and Disarmament.[32] They called for an end to the Korean War and a new beginning for a reunified Korea. They held symposiums in Pyongyang and later in Seoul, where Korean and other women shared their experiences and ideas of mobilizing women for peace. They wanted to walk across the two-mile-wide DMZ, but were instead bused, flanked by ROK military and police cars at a customs area connecting the ROK and the Kaesong Industrial Zone. "We feel very celebratory and positive that we have created a voyage across the DMZ in peace and reconciliation," said Gloria Steinem, honorary co-chair of the WomenCrossDMZ group. On the ROK side, the peace walkers joined South Korean activists and held a rally at a pavilion just south of the DMZ. The Nobel laureate and North Ireland peace activist Mairead Maguire explained that their effort aimed at helping people to see their common humanity. The Liberian Nobel laureate Leymah Gbowee also took part.

Not far from the pavilion, the peace walkers got a frosty reception. Some 500 protesters greeted the group with placards telling the women to "Go to hell," "Get out," or "Go back to North Korea." In this same vein, the blogger and attorney Joshua Stanton in Washington, DC, wrote that the march detracted from human rights issues in North Korea and favored repression. Stanton noted that the website WomenCrossDMZ.org blamed "crippling embargoes" for the lack of survival basics in the North.[33] A column by Serge Schmemann (*New York Times,* May 28, 2015) depicted the women as "Talking about Peace, When Despots Don't Care." To the realist critique, Abigail E. Disney replied (*New York Times,* Letters, June 3, 2015) that the activists had no illusions that their march would change North Korea's human rights behavior overnight or topple a dictatorship. Still, "peace cannot be achieved without the will of the people. So to dismiss our group as well intended and naïve suggests that change comes only from above, which is an idea whose time has surely come and gone."

Like me, Schmemann had seen how the Soviet regime manipulated and exploited peaceniks. Still, as argued in chapter 9, campaigns for peace and for human rights generated a serendipitous and convergent outcome in the USSR. Transnational actors sometimes played a crucial role in influencing Soviet policy. By encouraging moderate instead of hard-line responses, they supplied both information and ideas to a closed society.[34] A similar trajectory could evolve in North Korea, but how long would the process take? The Nautilus Institute might serve a function in Korean affairs comparable to the Pugwash movement in the Cold War, but change can come quickly or slowly. The Pugwash Conferences on Science and World Affairs began in 1957, hoping to bring scientific insight to East–West issues,

but Mikhail Gorbachev's campaigns for perestroika and glasnost did not commence until four decades later. The Nautilus Institute, founded in 1992 to foster
security and sustainability in the Asia-Pacific region, sponsored insightful studies
and meetings on Korean issues. Two dozen years after its founding, however, there
was no sign of a commitment in Pyongyang to deep reform in North Korea.

Meanwhile, the only individual whose vision and persistence really improved
U.S.-DPRK relations was Jimmy Carter. It was he who, meeting with Kim Il Sung in
1994, worked out the outlines of the Agreed Framework concluded later that year.
Other Americans, such as Robert Gallucci, Bill Richardson, Madeleine Albright,
Christopher Hill, and Stephen Bosworth, generated both vision and energy, but
lacked the clout and independence of a retired president and the fortunate timing
that marked Carter's 1994 visit to Pyongyang.

The first (noncommunist) Americans to meet North Korea's president Kim Il
Sung likely were journalists Harrison Salisbury of the New York Times and Selig
Harrison, then of the Washington Post, in 1972. Congressman Stephen Solarz was
the first U.S. public official to meet him, in 1980, and the Reverend Billy Graham
met him later, in 1992 and 1994. Mark Berry, a member of a peace delegation
headed by the former president of Costa Rica, Rodrigo Carazo, met Kim Il Sung
on April 16, 1994. Berry recollected: "Little did I know when I met Kim Il Sung on
April 16, 1994, weeks before his death, that I would be among a very small group
of Americans ever to do so." Berry found Kim Il Sung upbeat and well informed,
but also anxious to set firm policy lines to guide and limit his successor. Once a
hunter of wild boar, the DPRK leader seemed to appreciate the suggestion of one
delegation member that he visit the United States and try sport fishing.[35]

A CLASH OF CIVILIZATIONS?

Among the intangibles shaping politics in Northeast Asia is the role of culture.
Cultural values provide a matrix from which ideas, perceptions, and decisions
spring forth. Their precise role and weight, however, are difficult to measure.

Koreans, as we saw in chapter 2, received both Confucianism and Buddhism
from China. Koreans, North and South, are still taught to respect authority, but
their Confucianism may be more aggressive in some ways than that of the Chinese. Blended with Communism in the North, Confucian ideas about authority
probably facilitated the DPRK's hard-line policies at home and abroad. Even the
Unification Church spawned in South Korea was led by an authoritarian, the Reverend Sun Myung Moon, whose whims were obeyed by thousands—perhaps millions—of people worldwide for decades.

Compared to Koreans, most people in the West in the twenty-first century
cared little for authority—even within the family. Most Westerners wanted and
demanded a great range of personal freedom.[36] Like many Koreans, North and

South, many—probably most—Americans were nationalist to the point of chauvinism. At the same time, many were becoming comfortable with multiculturalism.

If a U.S. president ever meets a top DPRK leader, their respective cultures and upbringing will shape their mutual perceptions and interactions. At bottom, however, each side will probably be guided by its strategic perceptions and calculations.

HIKING WITH UNCERTAINTY

None of these explanations—determinism, *fortuna*, voluntarism—provides all the answers. None accounts for the up-and-down patterns in the six-party talks or in North Korea's bilateral dealings with South Korea or the United States. Despite huge asymmetries of power, the DPRK has held its own in all these transactions.

How do the factors studied here interact? They do so like a hiker negotiating a rugged landscape.[37] The actual physical contours—the rivers, mountains, and so on—are like the forces that condition and constrain states. The hiker can go from point *a* to *b* along several possible routes, with some being safer, quicker, or more scenic than others. *Fortuna* may shape the journey in the form of the hiker's encountering warm, clear skies or flash floods, rainstorms, lightning bolts, fallen trees, and other hazards. Accidents of timing and coincidence—good and bad luck—can be critical.

At every juncture the prudent hiker must make choices. He or she evaluates the landscape and calculates the likelihood of *fortuna*'s impacting the journey to make it more difficult or easier. The hiker may decide that the safest route is the longest and most arduous.

All the key factors feed on one another. The structure of each society, the region, and the global system give rise to, and condition, each individual actor. Individuals, in turn, may shape the structure. *Fortuna* may intervene, helping or blocking agents of change or putting them on unexpected and unwanted trajectories.[38] The responses to structures and events of key leaders such as Barack Obama and Kim Jong Un are shaped by the nature and accidents of their upbringing and by the dynamics of their personalities.

In Korea, as elsewhere, the thrust of material forces has often been altered by apparent accidents of timing and coincidence. Both hard power and *fortuna* have sometimes been trumped by free will. Individuals have often accomplished miracles, overcoming physical, emotional, and intellectual obstacles even when everything stacks the odds against them.

Smart, skilled, and determined individuals thus may sometimes overcome all obstacles to reach a deal. Jimmy Carter did so in 1994; Madeline Albright came close in 2000; Christopher Hill also came close in the last years of the George W. Bush administration (thereby becoming "Chris Jong Hill" for some critical Republicans). Some North Korean officials and diplomats performed equally or even more difficult feats, given that suspicions of weakness or betrayal in Pyongyang could be far more lethal than in Washington.

Wise and courageous hikers for peace can blaze an uphill path over stubborn obstacles and a mischievous *fortuna*. Their efforts can help avoid the worst and foster better, if not the best, futures in Northeast Asia. Willpower—or its lack—has been crucial to the impasse in U.S.–North Korean relations. Opposed ideologies and ignorance of each other's culture also obstructed efforts to improve relations. But the ultimate problem was a lack of strong determination in Pyongyang and in Washington to develop a broad working relationship that would subordinate lesser concerns to larger ones. Distrusting one another for more than six decades, each side preferred to keep its powder dry.

19

What to Do about—or with—China?

China wants to have it both ways,
Join the world and jail its foes,
Fight corruption but hide the Web,
Ignore that opposition grows.
Capitalism, [they] say, is fine—
But freedom hates a party line

—Roger Cohen, "Annus Mirabilis 2014,"
New York Times, December 8, 2014

The changing relationship between China and the United States proved to be one of the megachanges and megachallenges of the twenty-first century. China's rise is the geopolitical equivalent of the melting polar ice caps: gradual change on a massive scale that can suddenly lead to a dramatic turn of events. The sine qua non for a peaceful twenty-first century is Sino-U.S. cooperation. If the overall relationship between the United States and China were positive—including the latter's policies regarding North Korea—then prospects for peace and prosperity would improve across Northeast Asia. Issues involving the DPRK could bring China and the democracies closer together or exacerbate their differences. China is both the dependent and independent variable in these equations.

CHINA AND HUMAN RIGHTS IN THE DPRK

Are we our brothers' keepers? Beijing tended to side with Cain's implied "no." Starting in the 1980s, however, China joined the world of international commerce with its mix of rules and norms. Had the time come for China to strengthen legal and moral codes that foster not just wealth but also human development? On paper, China was moving in this direction. China joined the World Summit in 2005 and the UN Security Council in 2006 in endorsing the responsibility to protect. In practice, China still had a long way to go—both at home and in North Korea.

China's obligations to its own people as well as to those of North Korea were underscored by the February 17, 2014, report of the Commission of Inquiry established by the UN Human Rights Council. It recommended that states with "historically friendly ties with the DPRK, major donors and potential donors, as well as those states already engaged with the DPRK in the framework of the Six-Party Talks, should form a human rights contact group to raise concerns about the situation of human rights in the DPRK and to provide support for initiatives to improve the situation."[1]

The commission also recommended the following: "The United Nations and the states that were parties to the Korean War should take steps to convene a high-level political conference. Participants in that conference should consider and, if agreed, ratify a final peaceful settlement of the war that commits all parties to the principles of the Charter of the United Nations, including respect for human rights and fundamental freedoms. States of the region should intensify their cooperation and consider following such examples as the Helsinki Process."

For China, however, the Helsinki Process could imply negative as well as positive implications.[2] The process helped to stabilize borders and foster freer trade across Europe, but it also legitimized civil-society action against governmental abuse of human rights.

Beijing, like Moscow, repressed free speech and smothered demands for greater autonomy by national minorities. Both China and Russia often aligned with regimes that abused human rights. Of course no state or society was blameless. The United States did too little to compensate its own minorities for past abuses and protect them going forward. But the U.S. government and most Americans acknowledged past and present shortfalls and tried to correct them. China, Russia, and Japan barely acknowledged their abuses, past or present, much less took corrective measures.

For China and Russia, human rights were more problematic than weapons limitations. Both Beijing and Moscow approved UN resolutions aimed at curbing North Korea's WMD programs. China, however, sometimes endorsed a UN resolution only to poke holes in its implementation. For example, Beijing did little to stop dual-use equipment from transiting into the DPRK. Beijing would be tempted to block UN agencies from acting on DPRK human rights abuses. But such an orientation would be myopic. Could not real support for human rights—along with Olympic medals, acrobatic dancing, and revived Confucianism—serve to enhance China's soft power?[3]

ARMS CONTROL OR STABILITY?

American officials often asked Chinese leaders to pull U.S. chestnuts out of the fire in North Korea, but Beijing had its own concerns there. Washington focused on denuclearizing North Korea. China began to share this goal in the 2010s, but Beijing's top priority remained stability—including assurance that U.S. troops would never again approach the Yalu. China and the DPRK were bound until 2021 by their Treaty of Mutual Aid, Cooperation, and Friendship—signed by Zhou Enlai and Kim Il Sung in 1961, then renewed for twenty years in 1980 and again in 2001. Article 2 of the treaty committed each side immediately to render military and other assistance by all means to its ally against any outside attack. That eleven years passed between the entry of Chinese forces into the Korean War (1950) and a formal alliance (1961) spoke volumes about tensions then between leaders in Beijing and Pyongyang. Strains multiplied in the twenty-first century, but China continued to furnish much of the energy and food consumed in the DPRK.

China refused to help Pyongyang develop nuclear weapons, as detailed above in chapters 6 and 16. Responding to the DPRK's first nuclear tests, China took increasingly tough stands against North Korea's WMD programs. It voted for, or acquiesced in, UN Security Council condemnations of Pyongyang's missile and nuclear tests. Starting in 2011, Beijing stopped automatically supporting North Korea in international forums, where in the past it often watered down efforts to censure Pyongyang. It no longer provided diplomatic cover for the DPRK as it did in the aftermath of the *Cheonan* sinking. Beijing appeared to recalibrate its North Korea policy, enhance its consultations with the United States and the ROK on peninsular issues, and support tighter enforcement of UN Security Council sanctions on North Korea, an area where China's performance did not match its commitments in times past.

In September 2013 Beijing issued a 236-page list of dual-use equipment and materials that it banned for export to the DPRK. In December 2013 a retired general wrote that denuclearization had become the condition for stability in North Korea. He listed the dangers that Pyongyang's WMD programs presented to China. If a North Korean rocket disintegrated, then its debris could land on China. If an accident occurred at a DPRK test site or if the United States or the ROK attacked a DPRK nuclear facility, the fallout could reach China. The general scoffed at Pyongyang's commitment to "advance economic development and nuclear weapons together." Given North Korea's resources, he said, to advance on both fronts was impossible. The North's determination to possess nuclear weapons meant that "on the quest of denuclearization there is still no way out, and instability on the Korean Peninsula will continue."[4]

Another reason for Beijing to contain North Korea's WMD programs was that gangs within China might buy or steal North Korea's weapons and threaten to use them against the Chinese government.[5]

Pyongyang's ties with China were also strained by the 2013 execution of Jang Song Taek, an elder well known and trusted by authorities in Beijing. He had taken a leading role in establishing the jointly managed Special Economic Zones on Hwanggumpyeong Island and Wihwa Island, where Chinese and North Korean interests diverged.[6]

With North Korea increasingly seen by some Chinese authorities as a liability, Beijing modified its supportive posture. As of 2015, all DPRK attempts to arrange a visit to Beijing by Kim Jong Un were politely rebuffed. By contrast, from June 2013 through September 2015 presidents Xi Jinping and Park Geun Hye met six times and their countries' foreign ministers met eight times.[7] In September 2015 the ROK president was the only head of state from a democratic country seen in Beijing at the military parade celebrating the defeat of Japan. Xi's interactions with Seoul implicitly underscored the gap between Beijing and Pyongyang. Xi probably wanted to assure South Koreans that they had a reliable friend in Beijing, stoke interest in resuming talks on denuclearization of the peninsula, and emphasize the value of trade between China and the ROK. Both countries opposed Japan's moves toward a more active military role in world affairs. China was pleased that the ROK (at that time) seemed unwilling to join the U.S.-Japanese antimissile defense system.[8]

In October 2015, however, relations between China and North Korea seemed to improve. Liu Yunshan became the first Politburo Standing Committee member to visit North Korea in four years—that is, since Kim Jong Un took the helm. Liu attended the ceremonies for the seventieth anniversary of the founding of the Korean Workers' Party. During his four-day visit he was often seen at the side of Kim Jong Un. Liu's published comments showed a greater Chinese concern for stability in the North than for denuclearization. Though Xi Jinping did not travel to Pyongyang, China's president sent a message to Kim Jong Un praising North Korea's "positive progress in developing the economy and improving people's livelihood" and expressed optimism about China–North Korea ties. Some observers inferred that Beijing might be seeking better relations with Pyongyang as a response to Washington's enhanced "rebalancing" effort to contain China.[9]

CHINA AND THE TWO KOREAS

Starting in 1992, China and the ROK developed bilateral mechanisms to govern their cultural, political, and security affairs. By 2013–2014 China had become South Korea's number-one trade and investment partner. Also, the ROK had become China's third largest export market. Total trade between the two countries was more than $270 billion in 2013. China and the ROK signed a free-trade agreement in June 2015. In 2015 some 10 million travelers from China and South Korea visited each other's countries, and around 60,000 Chinese were studying in South Korea. Authorities in Beijing and Seoul referred to interactions between their countries as the pursuit of a "mature strategic cooperative partnership."[10]

The shadow of North Korea hung over the evolving ties between China and South Korea. A few days after President Xi visited Seoul in July 2014, the DPRK government issued another call for North–South reconciliation. It noted common points between the North's call for a low-level federation and the South's proposal for a confederation. It urged that North and South establish unity with no dependence on, or meddling by, foreign powers—a possible reference to China as well as the United States. It called on the South to stop its "North-directed military exercises" with U.S. forces. In tandem with the government statement, Pyongyang's Democratic Front for the Reunification of Korea on July 7 issued a long recitation of actions taken by Kim Il Sung and Kim Jong Il to promote unification. Then, contradicting the spirit of these conciliatory statements, the North proceeded to test-fire many short-range ballistic missiles. On July 17 UN Secretary-General Ban Ki-moon condemned the missile tests as violations of Security Council resolutions. Nonetheless, the KCNA proceeded to show photos of Kim Jong Un "supervising" the firing of many artillery shells into the North's adjacent waters. Unfazed, from July 16 to 21 the ROK and United States conducted maritime exercises involving the aircraft carrier USS *George Washington*.

Despite Chinese angst about DPRK actions, many factors pressed for continuity in Beijing's policy to Pyongyang. Besides their long-standing support for stability in Korea, some Chinese leaders probably worried that if the DPRK opened to the world, then China's growing hold on the North's mines and ports would face greater competition. Trade with China helped DPRK foreign trade to rise by nearly 8 percent in the 2010s—thereby helping to stabilize the Pyongyang regime.

If the DPRK imploded, Chinese armed forces would surely try to prevent large flows of refugees into China. Chinese forces could again cross the Yalu and meet advancing U.S. and ROK troops in or near Pyongyang. Chinese troops could cooperate or compete with ROK and U.S. forces to control DPRK nuclear assets. Thoughtful analysts suggested that Beijing, Washington, and Seoul should plan together how to cooperate and avoid a collision should the DPRK collapse. But officials in Beijing were reluctant to discuss this sensitive topic. The very idea of a DPRK implosion probably unsettled Beijing leaders, since China could be the next Communist domino. Some Chinese authorities began in 2015 to listen to U.S. concerns, but provided almost no feedback.

Prospects for a cooperative scenario with Beijing would benefit from a pledge by Seoul and Washington that American forces would never be based north of Pyongyang.[11] As of 2015, however, the United States refused to make such a promise. Even if one were made, Beijing authorities would probably discount such a pledge when they recalled how NATO expanded up to the Russian border. If, however, Beijing were to establish a puppet government in part of North Korea, the costs for China would be huge.

THE SPECTRUM OF SINO-AMERICAN RELATIONS

The prospects of Sino-American cooperation on North Korea took shape in the broader context of relations between a rising power and an existing hegemon. Washington challenged Chinese claims in the South China and East China Sea, as discussed later in this chapter. Washington also expressed concern about China's theft of industrial and military secrets, cyber warfare preparations, space rivalry, resource competition, abuse of individual human rights and national minority rights, and threats to Taiwan.[12] A growing worry was China's impact on climate change and environmental degradation. Pollution caused more than 1 million premature deaths each year within China and contributed to more than 7 million worldwide. Fine particles blown from China strengthened storms over the North Pacific and generated havoc in North America.[13] Presidents Xi and Barack Obama committed their countries to lowering carbon emissions, but the target dates seemed very remote to environmentalists.

Having achieved little and lost much in Iraq and Afghanistan, the White House announced in 2012 that the United States would pivot toward the Asia-Pacific region. President Obama explained the new orientation in U.S. foreign policy to the Australian Parliament on November 17, 2011: "As we plan and budget for the future, we will allocate the resources necessary to maintain our strong military presence in this region." While administration officials insisted that this new policy did not aim specifically at China, the implication was clear. From now on, U.S. military strategy would not focus on the once fertile crescent or the global "war on terrorism," but on China.

The White House preferred engagement with China, but hedged by enhancing the tools for containment. Some Americans believed the world's oldest major democracy had to rein in the world's oldest civilization and most populous country. Meanwhile, America's defense expenditures in the Obama years were at least eight times those of China. U.S. defense outlays surpassed those of the next eight or nine largest defense spenders *combined*. Despite pressures to cut U.S. budget deficits, the U.S. Navy would not reduce its eleven aircraft carrier groups to ten. For its part, China floated one retrofitted Ukrainian aircraft carrier that could move, but was still not yet ready to land airplanes. Less expensive than aircraft carriers or feeding soldiers, the tools of cyber warfare could help to level the fields of combat. China and the United States were leaders in this domain, with Russia and North Korea following in their wake.

China was vexed by the Obama administration's pivot to Asia as well as

American pressures to open China's economy, U.S. complaints about China's treatment of human rights, and Washington's efforts to limit China's influence at the World Bank and the International Monetary Fund (IMF). Though China benefited from an open global economy, it resented that many of its rules were shaped by the United States. Thus, Washington balked at ratifying changes in IMF voting arrangements that would give China more say. The United States proved reluctant to increase the World Bank's lending capacity, provoking China to create a parallel structure with Brazil, Russia, India, and South Africa to rival the World Bank. Many U.S. allies—even the United Kingdom—ignored Washington's caveats and rushed to join the new Asian Infrastructure Investment Bank organized by China. The economist and White House adviser Lawrence Summers opined that Washington's failure to keep its allies from joining this new institution signaled "the moment the United States lost its role as the underwriter of the global economic system."[14]

In 2014 China increased its defense spending (the official numbers) by about 7 percent—approximately in line with growth of its GDP. But the official budget for 2015 showed a 10.1 percent increase over 2014, to $144.2 billion—much more than the reported 6.9 percent GDP growth. One expert said that defense spending was not a huge burden for China because it amounted to only 2 to 2.5 percent of GDP. But the same expert acknowledged that actual defense spending could be 50 percent higher than reported.[15]

China's steady advances in military weaponry, beginning with a nuclear bomb in 1964, were impressive but not surprising for a large country with millennia of technological innovation—and with extensive borders and vulnerable sea lanes to maintain.

Here was a classic security dilemma. The United States saw China modernizing its armed forces and decided it must beef up U.S. assets across the Pacific Ocean. In response, China believed it needed to do more to counter the U.S. buildup. The pattern of action and counteraction began to resemble the U.S.-Soviet arms race—dangerous, expensive, and probably unnecessary if clear minds could prevail.

THE NEXT GREAT WAR?

Harvard political analyst Graham Allison argued that China and the United States faced a "Thucydides Trap"—the "dangers that can arise when a rising power challenges a ruling power—as Athens did Sparta . . . and as Germany did Britain a century ago." Allison quoted Thucydides: "It was the rise of Athens and the fear that this instilled in Sparta that made the [Peloponnesian] war inevitable." This claim spawned a theory of hegemonic war dear to neorealists. Many of them predicted that rising powers will seek to deliver a quietus to a weakening hegemon, or that the hegemon will wage a preventive or preemptive war against challengers before it becomes too late. According to Allison, "In twelve of sixteen cases in the past 500 years when a rising power challenged a ruling power, the outcome was war." Since war was avoided in four cases, Allison conceded that hegemonic war is not inevitable. But since China was rising and, by some measures, the United States declining, Allison concluded that the United States faced a "chronic condition" that had to be managed.[16]

Proceeding from similar premises, Aaron Friedberg's *Contest for Supremacy* argued that Sino-U.S. rivalry is rooted in the evolving structure of power—a rising giant challenging the hegemon—exacerbated, as happened between Sparta and Athens, by ideological differences. Friedberg conceded that Beijing and Washington did not wish to risk an all-out war. Neither government believed war necessary to attain its ends, and each believed time was on its side.[17] In 2014, however, Friedberg cautioned that President Xi Jinping could destroy the Chinese political system by trying to weed out high-level corruption. Why? Because the system bred corruption and depended on it. Like Mikhail Gorbachev, Xi might undo the very system he hoped to save. Since Beijing liked to blame the United States for its problems, Chinese leaders, if desperate for internal reasons, might foment a confrontation with America.[18]

Did the evidence show that China and the United States had to fight? No. The case for a nearly inevitable collision rested on a distorted view of the past, present, and future.[19] Yes, Imperial Germany challenged Great Britain in the late nineteenth century, but World War I erupted for other reasons. That war began in the Balkans—between Serbia, backed by Russia, and Austria-Hungary, backed by Germany. Great Britain entered the fray only when Germany violated Belgium's neutrality.[20] One reason that Serbian nationalists targeted Archduke Franz Ferdinand was their fear that, if he became kaiser, he might reform and thus save the Hapsburg empire.[21] What about the collapse of Europe's great empires in the late 1940s–1950s? No rising power knocked them from their perches. Great Britain, France, and other colonial powers were simply exhausted and overstretched. Vietnam and Algeria drove out the French with modest or no help from China or the USSR.[22] Mao Zedong's China challenged Moscow's leadership of the Communist movement, but that confrontation in 1969 to the early 1970s led to a cold peace—not a major hot war.

If hegemonic war theorists were correct, there should have been a war between the United States and the USSR. Instead, the ailing Soviet regime in the 1980s concluded many arms and other cooperative arrangements with the West. The Soviet system was sick, and Moscow's empire disintegrated not with a bang but a whimper. Far from sowing salt on the soil of their former antagonist, the United States and other Western countries immediately provided economic and moral support for Russia and the other successor states.

What, if anything, did humans learn about world politics in the nearly 2,500 years since Thucydides wrote *The Peloponnesian War*? One lesson *not* found in Thucydides was that rivals can cooperate at the same time they compete. While such mixed relationships existed in many eras, their logic and policy implications were expressed scientifically in game theory only in the twentieth century—first by French mathematician Emile Borel, and then by American scholars such as John von Neumann, Oskar Morgenstern, Thomas Schelling, Anatol Rapoport, and Robert Axelrod. That such mixed relationships could help prevent Armageddon and conduce to mutual gain was demonstrated by U.S. and Soviet experiences during the many decades of the Cold War. Their interactions gave rise to awareness that communication can help moderate and channel conflict.

The United States and China did not find themselves locked in a Thucydidean trap. Rather, they were perched uncomfortably on the horns of what game theorists describe as a Prisoner's Dilemma. In theory, the best outcome for each party could only be reached via cooperation. Both sides could win through cooperation, but—doubting this outcome—self-interest would push each party to hedge against being suckered. If one party acted to reduce tensions and the other failed to reciprocate, then the cycle of "defect-defect" would probably resume.[23]

While many U.S. decision makers absorbed game-theory insights about managing conflict, it is not evident that top policymakers in China did the same. According to Kenneth Lieberthal, "strategic distrust of China is not the current dominant view of national decision makers in the U.S. government, who believe it is feasible and desirable to develop a basically constructive long-term relationship with a rising China." He and a Chinese academic close to policymakers in Beijing believe that many top Chinese leaders see U.S.-China relations as a zero-sum struggle in which, over time, China will prevail.[24] Sinologist David Shambaugh and Fudan University professor Wu Xinbo wrote that mutual distrust was pervasive in both Washington and Beijing, permitting few incentives for actors in either government to cooperate.[25]

Sun-tzu and other classic Chinese theorists portrayed conflict in winner-take-all terms. Given that only one side can win, they advise a shrewd leader to bide his time, deceive the other side, and wait for an opportunity to destroy his opponent. Thus, Sun-tzu declared that "warfare is the Way [Tao] of deception. Thus, although [you are] capable, display incapability to them [on the other side]. When committed to employing your forces, feign inactivity. When [your objective] is nearby, make it appear as if distant; when far away, create the illusion of being nearby. . . . Display profits to entice them. Create disorder [in their forces] and take them. . . . Attack where they are unprepared. Go forth where they will not expect it."[26]

Sun-tzu would surely endorse all the tools of cyber warfare. The corollary to being unknowable is seeking out and gaining detailed knowledge of the enemy through all available means, including espionage. The Chinese sage advised to never rely on the goodwill of others, luck, ghosts or spirits, inference from phenomena, or hope for "measures of Heaven." Know your enemy and exploit his weaknesses. Identify enemy agents, tempt them with profits, and turn them into double agents.

Hard-line policies like those advised by Sun-tzu, whether practiced by Beijing or by Washington, underscore the paradox of the Prisoner's Dilemma. A positive outcome in Prisoner's Dilemma situations requires each actor to trust the other. But even though both parties learn that joint cooperation nets gains for each side, and even after many interactions with positive results, one party can always defect and inflict great damage on the party who trusts in cooperation. To guard against this contingency, some kinds of safeguards need to be built into the relationship.

Cooperation across cultural divides should be easier for Americans than for the Chinese. In theory if not in practice, most Americans accept that "all men are created equal" and that all individuals—and nations—are equal before the law and God. Do the Chinese have any equivalent to America's greatest poet, Walt Whitman, who saw and felt the interdependence and equal dignity of every human being?[27] The closest Chinese analogue to Whitman's worldview might be found in Taoism, but this "way" does not stress the equality of each person but focuses on how to connect oneself with the yin and yang of the cosmos.[28] Chinese tradition focuses on the individual as a vitally integrated element within a larger familial, social, political, and cosmic whole.[29] Chinese propaganda sometimes referred to Whitman as a man of and for the people, but Beijing seldom practiced what Whitman preached and did.

All this made it hard for the Chinese, caught with the United States in a Prisoner's Dilemma, to be a reliable partner in a quest for mutual gain. Outsiders often spoke of China's "rise," while Chinese often referred to their recent and planned development as "rejuvenation" (fuxing). The "Chinese Dream" articulated by Xi Jinping was a return to greatness from a time of national humiliation—not as a rise from nothing. A similar dream inspired Sun Yat-sen and other Chinese leaders.[30] Still, creating Chinese territory by piling sand on top of rocks in the South China Sea (described later in this chapter) reached far beyond any claims to past Chinese greatness.

A key ingredient in building a cooperation spiral would be for China to make its national security apparatus more transparent.[31] In fact the Chinese Ministry of National Defense published white papers every two or three years after 1995.[32] The 2015 white paper noted that for a decade China's doctrine on "Preparation for Military Struggle" (apparently enthralled by IT) had emphasized "winning local wars under conditions of informationization." The 2015 white paper added that such "new security domains as outer space and cyber space will be dealt with to maintain the common security of the world community" as well as "China's overseas interests." Also, China's navy would gradually shift its focus from "offshore waters defense" to the combination of "offshore waters defense" with "open seas protection."

Foreign responses to the white paper (written in 2014, published in English in 2015) ranged across a wide spectrum. Some observers treated it as a virtual declaration of war, while others merely noted the attention given to cyber war and informationization. Indian analyst Gurpreet S. Khurana found the 2014/2015 white paper less transparent than the one in 2012. It lacked detail on China's military budget. It spoke positively about China's relations with Russia but said nothing about India. Khurana inferred from this 2015 white paper that Beijing believed that China had arrived on the world stage and displayed a "single-minded preoccupation" with "how it could challenge the unipolar world order dominated by the U.S."[33]

What did the white paper say about nuclear weapons? Before China acquired nuclear weapons, Mao Zedong termed them "paper tigers" and ridiculed respect for them as nuclear "fetishism." After China's first tests, Beijing changed its tune but pledged it would not be the first to use nuclear weapons. The 2015 white paper, however, severely circumscribed the no-first-use commitment:

China has always pursued the policy of no first use of nuclear weapons and adhered to a self-defensive nuclear strategy that is defensive in nature. China will unconditionally not use or threaten to use nuclear weapons *against non-nuclear-weapon states or in nuclear-weapon-free zones* [emphasis added], and will never enter into a nuclear arms race with any other country. China has always kept its nuclear capabilities at the minimum level required for maintaining its national security. China will optimize its nuclear force structure, improve strategic early warning, command and control, missile penetration, rapid reaction, and survivability and protection, and deter other countries from using or threatening to use nuclear weapons against China.

American officials regarded any commitment to "no first use" of nuclear weapons as unenforceable and unreliable. Chinese officials, in turn, inferred that the U.S. stance resulted from Washington's scheming to leverage its nuclear advantages. Chinese anxieties were magnified by U.S. reluctance to admit the fact of mutual vulnerability. Meanwhile, policymakers in Tokyo and elsewhere doubted that nuclear deterrence could restrain Chinese maritime excursions. They feared a stability-instability paradox in which the reality of nuclear deterrence could enable limited conventional aggression. Both sides tended, almost pathologically, to talk past each other.[34]

Given the lethality of modern weapons, war could not be a cost-effective way to resolve disputes between major powers. A combination of factors reduced the frequency of big wars and the number of war deaths per capita. Images and news reports from Syria, Ukraine, and Tibet obscured the big picture, for global trends were away from violence.[35] Still, misperceptions and misunderstandings raised the risk of a Sino-U.S. confrontation. Huge miscalculations had led to grave consequences in the past. As we have seen, Pyongyang, Moscow, and Beijing in 1949–1950 assumed that the United States would not intervene if North Korea used force to unite the Korean peninsula. Top U.S. officials believed China would not join the Korean War even if UN forces approached the Yalu River. These and many other cases remind us that rationality is bounded by lack of complete information, fatigue, competing priorities, and wishful thinking—some of the same factors that contributed to the Great War that began in 1914. As the Lord advised Mephistopheles in *Faust*, "So long as humans strive, they will err and go astray" (*Es irrt der Mensch solang er strebt*).

COMPROMISE OR FIGHT IN CHINA'S ADJACENT WATERS?

Beijing in 2014–2015 stepped up its claims over the waters separating China and its neighbors. Would this zone become a shatterbelt? China or the United States—or both—could lead the way to compromise. China's territorial claims to islands and waters in East Asia were long-standing, but Beijing became insistent and bellicose over these issues, causing a sharp rift between China and many of its neighbors. Thus, the Philippines and Japan announced that "they would become 'strategic partners' in settling their maritime disputes with China—anathema to Beijing, which [preferred] to see these disputes handled separately."[36]

China appeared to claim nearly the entire South China Sea—including resources in the territorial waters of the Philippines and other littoral nations. Indeed, Beijing claimed sovereignty over Indonesia's Natuna undersea gas field—located some 1,000 kilometers from any uncontested Chinese territory. Beijing often framed its claims in strategic ambiguity and failed to provide specific legal justification for them. Were lawyers in China's foreign ministry outdone by military or economic officials?

No country had cause to be self-righteous about its rights in the Yellow, East China, or South China seas. Seldom did any littoral state offer to share its jurisdiction with other claimants to the same resources. Since claims overlapped and legal obligations were blurred, many actors contested each other and threatened force to take what, they said, belonged to them.[37] The ensuing battles of nerves could become real battles due to misreadings or bad luck.[38]

China was far more vulnerable to exogenous forces than the United States. China depended on imported commodities far more than did the United States. More than half the world's annual merchant fleet tonnage, including four-fifths of all the oil burned in China, passed through the South China Sea in 2014. The

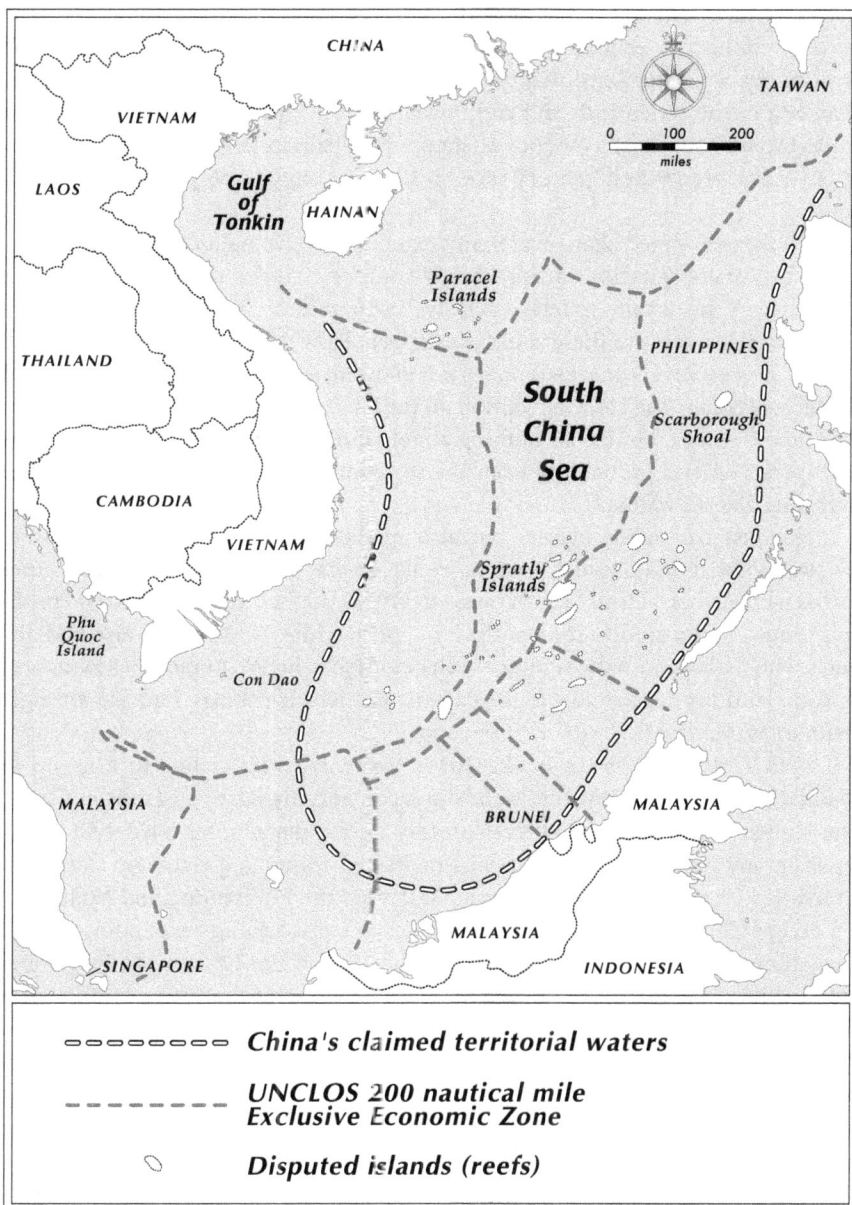

Map 19.1. Competing claims in the South China Sea

waterway functions as the throat of the Western Pacific and Indian oceans—the mass of connective economic tissue where global sea routes coalesce.[39] China's position vis-à-vis the South China Sea resembled America's vis-à-vis the Caribbean Sea in the nineteenth and early twentieth centuries. Whereas a revisionist United States could easily overpower status-quo Spain in 1898, a revisionist China in the early twenty-first century faced a superior status-quo power, the United States.

All parties agreed that sovereignty extended twelve nautical miles from the shore, but major questions arose when a country claimed an island, or even an outcropping, in distant waters. Exclusive economic zones extended 200 miles from shore. But some of these zones overlapped. How then to reconcile competing claims? There was no consensus on what is allowed or restricted in self-proclaimed air defense zones. The UN Convention on the Law of the Sea attempted to regulate maritime disputes, but it said nothing about land disputes. Disputes over islands and specks of land protruding from the sea guaranteed there would be disputes over the adjacent waters.[40]

Not just the major players but also medium and smaller countries were involved. North and South Korea, as we have seen, often challenged each other across the Northern Limit Line. A peace treaty to end the Korean War would probably require some modification of the NLL. Meanwhile, North Korea also had disputes with China about the rights of each country in the West (Yellow) Sea (as well as their land border across Mount Paektu, and which country had the stronger claim to Manchuria).

Both China and Japan in the 2010s tightened their claims to a group of islands, known as the Senkaku islands in Japan and the Diaoyu islands in China. The United States proclaimed its neutrality on the dispute, but pledged to back Japan in any war. Six or more nations registered competing claims in the South China Sea—Brunei, China, Indonesia, Malaysia, the Philippines, and Vietnam.[41] All except China looked to the United States to resist Beijing's expanding claims. Even though Washington never ratified the Law of the Sea, the United States asserted its right to sail the international waters close to the China mainland. It showed the flag there and sailed close to a Chinese-claimed outcropping to stiffen the backbone of Washington's Asian allies and partners. Some U.S. vessels kept tabs on military and other developments in China.

China's growing assertiveness could prove self-defeating. Edward N. Luttwak predicted that China's rise would drive its adversaries to balance against it. He contended that China will not—could not—change course because of its version of "great-state autism."[42] A Norwegian historian wrote that China's neoimperial policies sabotaged any Chinese hopes for soft-power influence.[43]

Competing claims at sea, in the air, and on land are difficult to negotiate. Even Canada and the United States faced disputes they could manage but not resolve. Still, there were useful precedents. The major powers agreed not to militarize or make territorial claims on the moon or in Antarctica. Some fifty counties signed onto the Antarctica Treaty, and thirty set up research bases there. But none claimed *ownership* of the rocks and ice.[44]

The stakes in the waters off China were much higher than in Antarctica. The most feasible solution to competing maritime claims, including those by the ROK and the DPRK, would be joint development of fish and mineral resources. The parties might debate whether they should divide resources 50–50 or in some other proportion. Almost any deal would seem more attractive than prolonged feuding or war. Having pressed its claims in the Tonkin Gulf for thirty years, Beijing agreed in 2000 to a settlement that allotted 53.23 percent of the area to Vietnam and 46.77 percent to China. But ostensible agreements can leave unresolved problems. In 2005 Chinese forces killed Vietnamese fishermen in the gulf.[45]

Two authorities argued that 'Washington should support the development of a rule-based regional order by throwing its full weight behind efforts to use international law and arbitration to address sovereignty disputes." They pointed to the Philippines, which took its competing claims with China to the International Tribunal for the Law of the Sea. The process tested whether the region was ready to manage disputes peacefully by legal means. The United States had reason to support this mechanism.[46] China on December 7, 2014, rejected and strongly denounced the Philippines' call for compulsory arbitration of their respective claims in the South China Sea. Beijing pointed to its prior agreements with Manila obliging the parties to resolve their disputes by negotiation. In October 2015, however, the panel ruled it had jurisdiction and began to hear arguments by the Philippines in November.[47]

Which party would put its immediate interests aside and take the first steps toward constructive compromise? China had more at stake than any other country. Its claims were far more extensive than those of other claimants.

The riparian nations needed to negotiate ways to share the resources. Unless China pulled back its extensive claims, however, it would be difficult to create value for each party. Instead of bullying smaller nations, today's leaders in Beijing—like some emperors of old—could show magnanimity and retract their extensive claims in the Yellow, East, and South Seas. Such moves could show Beijing's resolve to grow in harmony with its neighbors.

The United States could also take a leading role in fostering an accord to manage, if not resolve, maritime disputes. Unlike China, the United States had no territorial claims in these seas and did not covet their fish or mineral resources. But Washington might consider whether intelligence in the area could be collected by less intrusive means. As the senior partner in a series of bilateral alliances, Washington could press Japan and other U.S. partners to constrict or suspend their own claims for the common good. Most ASEAN members would gladly join such a

324 NORTH KOREA AND THE WORLD

bandwagon. Forging a set of constructive accords on these vital waterways could buttress peace across East Asia and demonstrate that Beijing and Washington could collaborate not only in science and business but also in limiting conflict in world affairs.

GDP WARS

Predictions of hegemonic war were reinforced by assertions that China's GDP had already or would soon eclipse America's. Graham Allison reflected in 2012 with regard to China: "Never has a nation moved so far, so fast, up the international rankings on all dimensions of power. In a generation, a state whose gross domestic product was smaller than Spain's [had] become the second-largest economy in the world."[48] If someone asked, "When will China become number one?" Allison in 2015 answered that China had already become number one in many fields. Already in 2006, for example, China became the leading emitter of carbon as well as the top holder of foreign exchange reserves.[49] Unless Americans overcame their dysfunctional ways, a respected economist predicted, China would surely dominate the United States—first economically and then politically.[50]

Contrary to those who assumed that China's continued growth and expansion were unstoppable, a professor at Beijing University detailed the internal problems—from unemployment to inequality to pollution—impeding China's development. He argued that democracy could help reduce these problems, but stopped short of prescribing Western-style democracy for China.[51] To tap China's economic potential, another professor argued, would require much greater market freedom and less state control; also, the rule of law instead of rule by law. The imbalance between market and state gave rise to widespread corruption and the widening gap between rich and poor.[52] To forgo top-down hierarchy and permit creative destruction, however, would require the Party to cede much of its role in public life.

Having started from a low base and with untapped resources, China's rise could not be extrapolated. Just as Germany and Japan made great strides as they rose from the ashes of World War II, so it was natural for China to grow richer and stronger after discarding Maoism. Official Chinese estimates suggested that the country's rate of GDP growth would decline from 9 or 10 percent per annum to about 7 to 7.5 percent—the rate in 2014. In 2015, the rate fell to 6.9 percent. But a decline to 2 or 3 percent was also a real possibility.[53]

No matter the size of China's GDP, per capita incomes in China were likely to remain low relative to those in Japan, South Korea, Singapore, Taiwan, and the West. Meanwhile, water shortages, pollution, and demographic problems would surely reduce societal fitness. The smog over Beijing became so thick in 2011 that many residents turned to the U.S. embassy for accurate reporting. Thanks to its

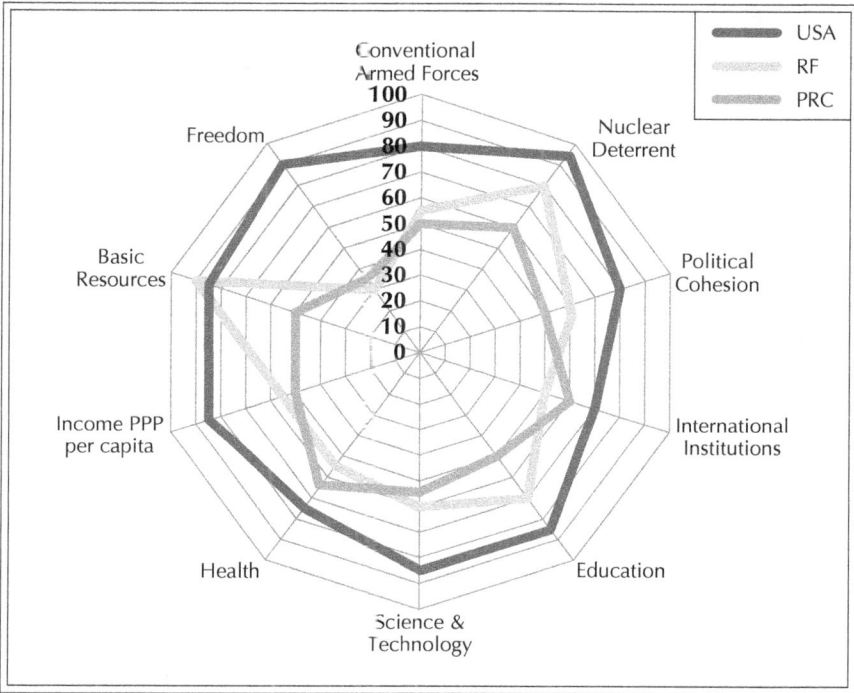

Figure 19.1. Parameters of power in China, Russia, and the United States, 2015. *Sources*: Author's estimates based on data published by the International Institute for Strategic Studies, the World Economic Forum, the World Bank, *The Economist,* and other periodicals.

one-child policy (changed to two-child in 2015), China would acquire a huge number of pensioners relative to workers. The ratio of workers per retiree could well be just 2 to 1 by 2040. Caring for the elderly by then could consume China's entire GDP.

Why declinists were wrong was spelled out by Donald Gross in *The China Fallacy: How the U.S. Can Benefit from China's Rise and Avoid Another Cold War.*[54] The United States, Gross urged, should not strive for hegemony but merely work to prevent hegemony by others—the traditional U.S. effort to prevent any foreign power from exercising regional dominance in the Asia Pacific. Gross pointed to the gains for each side if positive symbiosis replaced distrust and rivalry.

China and other countries rose quickly by various measures in the twenty-first century, but in terms of overall power—hard, soft, smart power—the United States was not in decline. Figure 19.1 outlines the parameters of power in China, the United States, and Russia in 2016.[55]

Considering the many factors that shape world affairs, one scholar reached this conclusion in 2011: "Over the last two decades, globalization and U.S. hegemonic burdens have expanded significantly, yet the United States has not declined; in fact it is now wealthier, more innovative, and more militarily powerful compared to China than it was in 1991." He noted, for example, that more than 90 percent of China's high-tech exports were produced by foreign firms.[56]

A former director of East Asian affairs on Obama's National Security Council agreed that, while China looked strong from outside, per capita income was no more than 15 percent of America's. China had the world's second largest economy but remained a developing country with enormous problems.[57] China's economy probably needed the United States more than vice versa. China needed Americans to buy its products, but Americans could get along without cheap imports. China did not place in the top 100 countries on the UN Human Development Index,[58] though it ranked 90th on the Social Progress Index.[59]

WHO WILL OWN THE TWENTY-FIRST CENTURY?

The evidence suggested that the twenty-first century would not belong to China.[60] Nor would world affairs be dominated by the United States as in much of the twentieth century. At the end of the twenty-first century, however, the United States could well be far more than first among equals. Early in the century the United States still led the world in most features of soft power as well as hard power. To be sure, America's ability to mobilize these assets with smart power was uncertain. Americans squandered great human and material resources in shortsighted policies and campaigns at home and abroad. Despite its dysfunctional politics, however, the United States remained a relatively open society with a strong potential for renewal.[61] This situation gave Washington a margin of security that permitted it to take initiatives for peace with confidence since, even if they were rejected, no great dangers would ensue.

The United States in the early twenty-first century was not declining relative to China or any other power.[62] But assertions or predictions to this effect were dangerous, because—if believed—they could help push Washington or Beijing onto a collision course. If Washington and/or Beijing acted as though both sides had to collide, then confrontation or even war would be more likely. Sober individuals in each country looked for ways to avoid the worst and promote mutual-gain policies, but they could be swept aside by the proponents of fear and hostility.

Nothing directly on the table between Washington and Beijing was worth fighting for. Neither trade disputes nor intellectual property rights nor human-rights issues could be resolved by war. Military pressure could not alter China's policies toward those who challenge Communist rule or minorities such as Tibetans and Uighurs. Basing some U.S. Marines in Australia would not alter

China's treatment of human rights or its posture toward Taiwan. On the contrary, any signs that Washington wanted to intimidate the Middle Kingdom would sharpen nationalist and xenophobic tendencies there. A relaxation of tensions with the United States would do more for freedom within China than confrontation.

THE BROAD PICTURE

Complexity science, as well as negotiation theory, recommends that competing actors pool their strengths to enhance each party's interests rather than fight for short-term gains. Partial gains by compromise are better than absolute wins that often cost more than they are worth. If the parties fight and one side seems to win, then chances are the victory will prove pyrrhic. History is full of apparent victories that appear later to have been defeats.

In the twenty-first century the United States and China became increasingly interdependent—linked so closely that they could help or hurt each other. Trade wars would be counterproductive. On balance, the free flow of goods and people benefited both sides. To be sure, most Chinese with American PhDs remained part of the U.S. workforce. They helped to sustain the quality of higher education in the United States and to keep America in the forefront of technological innovation. But many returned to China to share and cultivate the spirit of enterprise and creativity cultivated in U.S. universities, laboratories, and start-ups.

If Americans and Chinese leaders were wise, they would bolster complementary interests. Both countries needed clean energy, reliable food and water supplies, and better health-care systems. Both needed to reduce security threats in Northeast Asia and Southeast Asia. Neither Washington nor Beijing should act on the self-fulfilling expectation that conflict between them is inevitable. Each needed to help its own country and others to develop in harmony.

As in Taiwan and South Korea, the authoritarian system in China might someday become more pluralistic. One-party rule, inherently rigid and dogmatic, impeded China's capacity to cope with complex challenges. Without free access to information and free expression of divergent views, China would continue to make more huge mistakes such as the Three Gorges Dam. Chinese leaders realized that free information flows are essential for commerce and science, but feared they could activate groundswells of dissent. But repression is a losing strategy. China's one-party system faced internal pressure to evolve into something like Taiwan's multiparty democracy. If China moved in this direction, then pressures would mount for North Korea also to allow more political and economic freedom.

Many factors pushed for political and economic transformations in Northeast Asia. Reliable predictions were impossible, but it seemed likely that by 2100 mainland and Taiwan Chinese would confederate, if not unify, their polities. So, most likely, would the two Koreas. The more reconciliation between Beijing and Taipei, the less reason for tension between China and the United States, and the greater the prospects for their collaboration in Korea.

20

What to Do about—or with—
North Korea?

How should one deal with a regime that seemed to break all the rules—endangering its own subjects and the world? How should the democracies respond to sporadic calls from Pyongyang for high-level talks to resolve tensions on the Korean peninsula? Messages from the DPRK leadership did not sweep forward like the shifts from allegro to the more forceful movements in a Beethoven symphony. They resembled more the point and counterpoint of a Bach concerto, but without much overall harmony. Their contradictions did not stir concord but dissonance—often jarring and difficult to understand.

The United States and its partners faced ten major options. Could they ignore North Korea and keep a safe distance from distant dangers? Continue the Obama administration's "strategic patience"? Retreat to a Fortress America? Bomb the North's missiles and nuclear weapons before it became too late? "Hack and frack" to subvert the existing DPRK regime? Intensify international pressures? Tolerate the regime, but seek to transform the system so North Korea could join the world? Foster unification of North and South? Continue to deter and contain? Or seek to engage and negotiate ways to enhance values for all parties?

Which approach had the best prospects? A successful policy would need to address what Thucydides portrayed as the basic drivers of foreign policy: the quest for honor, security, and material gain.[1] The most promising route to arms control and human security in the DPRK, as in the Soviet and Iranian cases, was to engage and explore ways to create values for key stakeholders.

LIMITS TO RATIONAL POLICYMAKING

Life is a constant becoming of new opportunities and constraints that *enable*, but do not cause, innovations in our personal, artistic, scientific, economic, cultural, and political lives. No one can anticipate the adjacent possibles into which human

329

systems may "become."[2] Thus, Alan Turing's idealized computing machine in the 1930s set the stage for IBM giants, laptop computers, cell phones, and social media—all of which enabled the "Arab spring." Could other chains of human interactions with IT some day enable a North Korean spring?

Entire ways of life unfold over time, from unplanned and undirected behavior as well as from top-down planning. If highways are built, traffic will result, permitting fruitful encounters along with accidents and traffic jams. If buildings are erected, cities may—or may not—grow. If shopping malls are built, cities may empty out; then, if people crave city life or use phones to buy things, shopping malls may wither. Impossible-to-predict innovations generate new adjacent possibles—opportunities and constraints—that people may or may not exploit. As Rilke put it: "The future enters into us . . . to transform itself in us long before it happens."[3]

We cannot know what adjacent possibles may flow from our policies, laws, and regulations. Serendipity, as well as synergy, opens new doors. When Machiavelli wrote about *fortuna*, as we saw in chapter 18, he observed how floods can destroy the works of man unless the foresighted make adequate preparations. Scientists of his era did not know that a meteor ended life for three-fourths of earthlings. Scientists now also know that the demise of dinosaurs enabled birds, small mammals, and other life forms to survive and multiply. Extinction events destroy life but can also set the stage for life's evolution. Meteorites, for all their deadly capacity, deposited amino acids that became the seeds of earthly life.[4]

Our existence is full of such parallel truths. Some foreigners who have worked in North Korea find many of its people (at least those who live in Pyongyang) normal—not so different from people elsewhere—while other outsiders perceive a society of fear-driven robots. The recollections of the British ambassador to the DPRK in 2006–2008 help to reconcile these disparate visions. Most of his contacts were with the "outer elite" of Pyongyang—not the top, "inner elite." He found his contacts to be sharply differentiated human beings, with a good sense of humor, often fun to be with. His outer elite (most of them managers rather than leaders) ate more rice than most North Koreans, but meat for them was a rarity. Their clothes were adequate, but not smart. They lived in crowded flats, a long way from their jobs. How did they respond to long-winded political meetings? Some acted like true believers in a religious gathering. But many just switched off and entered a kind of catatonic state. After the meeting, facing a long commute home, many chose to walk, fearful that the gleaming metro might suffer another power cut and get stuck in a tunnel. Many enjoyed leisurely talk with friends (the more friends the better, in case one got in trouble). Many spoke of their parents with respect rather than affection, and chafed at the Confucian authority parents still exercised. These lives would seem dull to Westerners. The outer elite often watched reruns of locally made propaganda films, though some borrowed and watched DVDs of

South Korean and American soap operas.[5] If this was how the outer elite lived, then life for many, if not most, North Koreans probably involved great "human insecurity," as portrayed earlier, in chapter 7.

Rational planning has its limits. We must live forward not knowing what will or *can* happen.[6] The issues that drive human affairs are not prestatable, optimization problems. We cannot anticipate the novel variables that will become relevant. We can, however, try to mold what new life forms, institutions, and technologies enable. If we wish to live fully in a cosmos of unknowns, then each must do what he or she regards as meaningful—at a minimum, striving to do no harm.

With an awareness of all the imponderables and uncertainties, let us consider some policy options.

Ten Approaches to North Korea

1. Ignore North Korea?

Should Washington and its partners act as though they hear no evil, see no evil, and then speak no evil? Could the United States go on with its other business and ignore what some observers have called a rogue state? For a large country such as the United States, even nonaction is a kind of action with far-reaching consequences.

Can the United States and other democracies ignore North Korea and hope that its actions and troubles will not disturb the rest of the world? Washington since the 1870s usually assigned a very low priority to Korea and devoted far more attention and resources to China, Russia, Japan, and—at times—Indochina and the Middle East. In June 1950, however, the Truman administration concluded that U.S. security was intimately connected with Korea. The George W. Bush and Barack Obama administrations preferred to focus on other issues, ignoring dangers that did not yet explode on their doorstep.

The United States has often refused to recognize regimes it does not like. It did not recognize the revolutionary government of Mexico from 1911 to 1920, the Communist regime in Russia/USSR from 1917 to 1933, and the People's Republic of China from 1949 to 1979. Nonrecognition of these regimes brought no evident benefit to their peoples or to the United States. Given the absence of formal ties, Washington had no official presence in those countries and so lacked contacts, information, and leverage. The worst abuses of human rights in the Soviet Union occurred in the 1930s while the democracies focused on their own immediate problems and ignored those in the USSR. The greatest human rights abuses in Communist China occurred in the three decades before the exchange of embassies with the United States in 1979.

Are we our brothers' and sisters' keepers? The United States and Europe have often ignored genocide. Western governments were aware of mass killings in the Ottoman Empire during World War I and in Rwanda in 1994 but decided not to get involved. Washington did almost nothing to stop or even protest Hitler's Holocaust. Starting in the 1950s, American and European officials knew that China practiced cultural, if not physical, genocide in border regions such as Xinjiang and Tibet, but offered only mild and somewhat perfunctory protests. Having weighed the reasons to challenge Beijing against the potential harm to their own interests, they opted for near silence. But there were costs—practical as well as moral. Chinese pressures on Muslims in Xinjiang, like Russian policies in the Caucasus, helped inflame a spirit of jihad that threatened global and economic stability. The passions of the Boston Marathon bombers in 2013 became more acute due to events in Chechnya and Dagestan.

One reason to stay away from distant troubles is that interventions in other countries often fail or, if they seem to succeed, soon backfire. Even successful interventions can be Janus-faced. Thus, America's participation in the Korean War helped contain Communist expansion, but it also encouraged a major debacle—more than ten years of fighting in Indochina. Yet an ostrich posture may be impossible to sustain and can also generate costs. Having closed their eyes and ears to nuclear developments in Israel, India, and Pakistan, the Big Five placed few obstacles on their paths to becoming nuclear-weapon states—an example Pyongyang hoped to emulate.

2. More Strategic Patience?

The Obama administration offered to negotiate with North Korea if Pyongyang demonstrated a willingness to honor its earlier commitments to denuclearization. Feeling cheated or rebuffed after the Leap Day accord in 2012, Washington waited to see what happened next. The advantage to strategic patience was that it spared the United States whatever psychic and material burdens resulted from a more active policy. The downside was that, while Washington passively waited, Pyongyang improved its weapons of mass destruction and continued to repress its subjects.

3. Return to Fortress America?

Should the United States withdraw its forces from South Korea and Japan, and let China and North Korea's other neighbors wrestle with the Kim Jong Un regime? Besides saving money, an American withdrawal would diminish U.S. tensions with China and North Korea. If Pyongyang's missiles threaten the United States and its allies, then those nations could beef up antimissile defenses.

Somewhat like George F. Kennan in 1950, a researcher at the Cato Institute (who was formerly an official in the Reagan administration) argued that the United States should "begin to act as a normal nation in Northeast Asia. Washington should end its defense guarantees and withdraw its troops from South Korea and Japan." While the United States "retains an interest in a stable Northeast Asia, even more so do the surrounding nations. The best American 'leadership' would be to turn responsibility for the peninsula over to neighboring states. Let them deal with the 'North Korea problem.'"[7]

Against this proposal was the argument that the United States remained the indispensable force in preventing an anarchic war of all against all.[8] Given the challenges and opportunities posed by a rising China, it was nearly unthinkable that the United States would withdraw from Pacific and Asian affairs.

4. Bomb North Korea before It's Too Late?

Staying clear of civilian targets, the United States could try to take out North Korea's missile and nuclear facilities.[9] Assuming that the Kim Jong Un regime sought survival and not suicide, then it would probably not choose the "Samson option" and bring down the roof.[10] But even if the North fired its artillery at Seoul, some argued, the damage would be less tomorrow than if a large-scale war erupted in five or ten years.

Despite best efforts to conduct "surgical strikes," collateral damage from an attack on North Korea's WMD would probably be extensive. As was the case in Iran, the DPRK probably possesses many caches of WMD and facilities in secret locations. Thus, preventive strikes would probably miss some relevant targets. Even if the strikes did succeed, DPRK scientists would retain the know-how and motivation to rebuild their WMD programs. The regime might act more the rogue if it lacked a credible deterrent.[11]

"Preemption" applies only to a blow against an imminent attack. A "preventive" war aims to destroy a future capacity to attack. While a preventive war might appeal to purists, it had few backers among the likely targets of North Korean revenge attacks. Why risk a highly likely retaliatory blow when there is no imminent danger?

5. "Hack and Frack"

How to transform North Korea? Harvard researcher Jieun Baek suggested that the U.S. government pursue three strategies to "hack and frack" the erstwhile Hermit Kingdom. First, strengthen covert operations to hack into North Korea's information channels and support internal dissidents. Second, increase funding for NGOs in the United States and South Korea to transmit outside media into North Korea and provide business skills to North Koreans. Third, bolster training for North

Korean defectors in journalism, information technology, and social media. The more informed its citizens, the less the North's leaders would be able to eliminate "bad seeds" by relegating alleged criminals and their relatives to prison camps.[12]

In a similar vein, a former U.S. Army judge, presently an attorney in Washington, called for a strategy of guerrilla engagement to replace and reconstruct the regime in North Korea.[13]

Could outsiders provoke a grassroots revolution in North Korea? Subversion might not destroy the regime, but could surely weaken it. Broadcasts by Radio Free Asia, balloon-lifted propaganda leaflets, and smuggled electronic devices helped to inform some North Koreans about their own country and the world. Anti-regime propaganda probably shocked some North Koreans by detailing how their dear leaders siphoned off billions in state funds to store in family accounts in foreign bank vaults. Many army officers would be displeased to learn of their leaders' indulgences while their soldiers hungered.

Still, subversion could inflict little damage to the core of a pervasively totalitarian dictatorship. Regime change in North Korea would be far more difficult than in Eastern Europe or North Africa. Yes, nonviolent revolutions overthrew dictatorships in those regions; but these convulsions took place in societies with much weaker controls than in the DPRK and where many people had far greater access to communication technology and external contacts than those available to most North Koreans.[14]

Regime change could be fostered also by the demonstration effects of the Chinese and South Korean examples; by cultural exchange, tourism, and science; and by external pressure. Would such effects need years or decades to shape life in the DPRK? There was no way to know.

6. Intensify International Sanctions and Pressure?

The effects of hacking and fracking could be strengthened by intensifying sanctions that target North Korea's privileged one percent and shake their loyalty to the regime. As of 2016, elites in North Korea did not seem to suffer much from existing sanctions. Indeed, some traders made money by imaginative devices to circumvent sanctions. Still, the existing constraints and penalties could be tightened. The kinds of pressures mounted by the U.S. Treasury against Banco Delta Asia in 2005–2007 could be expanded—actions that produced bank runs not only in Macao and Hong Kong but also in mainland China. What would happen in Pyongyang if elites could no longer draw dollars from ATMs? There were signs that strong sanctions softened Teheran's intransigence in 2013–2015. Sanctions on the Putin regime in 2014–2015 seemed not to reduce its aggressive behavior, but did accelerate capital flight from Russia.

In the early twenty-first century there was a growing consensus that the international community has a right and duty to intervene against regimes that abuse their own people. But the "Responsibility to Protect" principle proved extremely difficult to implement. If outsiders did little to help the peoples of failed-state Somalia or end the strife in Syria, could—would—they do anything to protect North Koreans from their rulers?[15]

The UN Security Council condemned North Korea's nuclear and missile tests and mandated sanctions to punish and prevent these practices. The UN Human Rights Council Commission of Inquiry in 2014 recommended strong measures by the Security Council and General Assembly to stop human rights abuses in the DPRK. The commission asserted that "the international community, through the United Nations, bears the responsibility to protect the population of the DPRK from crimes against humanity using first and foremost appropriate diplomatic, humanitarian and other peaceful means. The responsibility of the international community is further warranted by the fact that the DPRK's crimes against humanity impact many persons from other states, who were systematically abducted and who continue to suffer enforced disappearance, along with the families they left behind. In a number of these cases, the abductions involved blatant violations of the territorial sovereignty of other states."

The UN Commission of Inquiry asserted that "the people of the DPRK have suffered too long. It is the responsibility of the international community to protect them from the depredations of their own government. The Commission finds that the international community must discharge its responsibility to protect by pursuing a multi-faceted strategy that combines strong accountability measures targeting those most responsible for crimes against humanity, reinforced human rights engagement with the authorities of the Democratic People's Republic and support for incremental change based on people-to-people dialogue and an agenda for inter-Korean reconciliation."[16]

Of course the DPRK was quick to reply. It rejected the General Assembly and Human Rights Council resolutions as "a ridiculous attempt to infringe upon the sovereignty of the DPRK and do harm to its dignified socialist system by abusing human rights for a sinister political purpose" and as " political chicanery which does not deserve even a passing note."[17]

How the DPRK Should Change

The UN Commission of Inquiry called for immediate implementation of far-reaching reforms that would change the essence of the DPRK polity. They recommended the following:

- Establishing genuine checks and balances upon the powers of the Supreme Leader and the Workers' Party of Korea.
- Creating an independent and impartial judiciary, a multiparty political

system, and elected people's assemblies at the local and central level that emerge from genuinely free and fair elections.

- Vetting the entire officers' corps for involvement in human rights violations and limiting the Korean People's Army to defending the nation against external threats.
- Dismantling the State Security Department and placing the Ministry of Public Security under transparent democratic oversight.
- Establishing an independent constitutional and institutional reform commission with international experts to guide and assist this process.
- Accepting a field-based presence and technical assistance from the Office of the High Commissioner for Human Rights and other relevant United Nations entities to help implement these recommendations.[18]

The commission also recommended that the Korean people foster inter-Korean dialogue in a phased approach leading up to an Agenda for Reconciliation. Inter-Korean dialogue could include friendly sporting events; academic and business interactions; scholarships and apprenticeships for young people from the Democratic People's Republic of Korea; student exchanges; exchanges between civil society organizations including national Red Cross societies; contacts between professional organizations and women's groups; the development of "sister city" relationships; and, eventually, the reestablishment of transport and communication links.

What the International Community Should Do

The Commission of Inquiry asserted that the international community had a responsibility to protect North Koreans from crimes against humanity because the DPRK government failed to do so.[19]

The United Nations had to ensure that those most responsible for the crimes against humanity committed in the DPRK were held accountable. Options to achieve this end included a Security Council referral of the situation to the International Criminal Court or the establishment of an ad hoc tribunal by the United Nations.[20] Urgent accountability measures needed to be combined with a reinforced human rights dialogue, the promotion of incremental change through more people-to-people contact, and an inter-Korean agenda for reconciliation.

The Security Council needed to adopt targeted sanctions against those most responsible for crimes against humanity. The United Nations needed to prevent recurrence or continuation of such crimes in the DPRK. "The United Nations Secretariat and agencies should urgently adopt and implement a common 'Rights up Front' strategy to ensure that all engagement with the Democratic People's Republic of Korea effectively takes into account, and addresses, human rights concerns. . . . States that have historically friendly ties with the DPRK, major donors and potential donors, as well as those states already engaged with the DPRK in the framework of the Six-Party Talks, should form a human rights contact group to raise concerns about the situation of human rights in the Democratic People's Republic of Korea and to provide support for initiatives to improve the situation."[21]

These United Nations recommendations for internal change were well conceived, but would never be implemented by the DPRK leadership. International condemnation of the DPRK could instead bolster Pyongyang's dogged pursuit of nuclear weapons and devotion to its gulag archipelago. North Korea's leaders would never choose to destroy their privileged way of life. In addition, China would never permit Kim Jong Un to be tried before an international court. To brandish him and other DPRK leaders with "crimes against humanity" would only stiffen their intransigence.

A paradox loomed: the commission's recommendations, if implemented, would either require regime change or bring it about. Knowing this, the Pyongyang leadership would fight them and become more determined to build up its nuclear weapons so as to resist external dictation. *Doing the "right thing"— condemning the Kim family dictatorship—could make things worse.*

7. Could North Korea Reform and Join the World?

How to help North Koreans overcome their estrangement from the rest of humanity? Could outsiders encourage a transition to a modernizing and reform-oriented North Korea? Could the DPRK adopt and adapt China's example to keep top-down political control but open doors to market economics and cultural exchange?

China managed the transition from Maoism to Leninist capitalism thanks in large part to the genius and other personal qualities of Deng Xiaoping.[22] In the second decade of the twenty-first century, however, no such leader appeared in Pyongyang. The closest candidate had been Kim Jong Un's uncle, Jang Song Thaek, but he was executed in 2013. Ruled by a rigid power elite and lacking a rule-breaker such as Deng Xiaoping, the DPRK faced many difficulties in opening to markets and Western ideologies.

Unless the DPRK curbed its weapons of mass destruction programs, it would still be subject to U.S. and United Nations sanctions. Unless the regime's treatment of workers changed dramatically, it would not benefit from the Generalized System of Preferences, which grants nonreciprocal tariff relief by many richer countries to more than 100 of the world's poorest countries as encouragement to grow their economies. Any sign of illicit business by the DPRK state would still be punished by U.S. and other external agencies. If a partially reformed DPRK sought to join the World Trade Organization, then Washington would probably demand that it be treated as a nonmarket economy.

Both China and Russia had reason to prefer a reformed and modernizing

Pyongyang Metro. Some features of life in Pyongyang appear quite dazzling. At an average depth of 110 meters, the Pyongyang Metro is one of the deepest in the world. It is believed to serve also as a bomb shelter. Some North Koreans, however, prefer to walk lest an electricity failure strand the metro in a tunnel. (Photo by Stephen Gong)

Dancers celebrate the regime at the Arirang Mass Games in 2008. (Photo by Stephen Gong)

DPRK to a unified Korea, especially one closely tied to the United States. Commercial interests in China and Russia might penetrate North Korea more readily if it remained independent. Authoritarians in Beijing and Moscow would face fewer challenges if freedom reigned only in South Korea.

The DPRK border with China offered North Korea a lifeline to the outside world. They share a border 1,420 kilometers (880 miles) long. From west to east, the Yalu River, the Changbai mountain range (with the Paektu volcano), and the Tumen River divide Korea and China (and, for 15.5 km—fewer than eleven miles—Korea and Russia). Visitors could see that the Yalu and Tumen rivers served as very real borders between three sovereign entities, and that sovereignty and borders matter.[23] At the western end of the border near the Yellow (Western) Sea, the Chinese city Dandong was the largest city on the border. On the other side of the river was the DPRK city of Sinuiju.[24] Their waterfronts face each other and were connected by the Sino-Korean Friendship Bridge. Much of the China–North Korea trade moved across this bridge.

In 2014 Chinese cell phone service extended 10 km (6 miles) into North Korean territory, which led to the development of a black market for Chinese cell phones in the border regions. Since international calls are forbidden in North Korea, violators put themselves at considerable peril when they acquire and use such phones.

Both the feasibility and the difficulty of implementing a Chinese model could be seen in the Rajin-Khasan project. It aimed to refurbish the Rajin port on the DPRK's northeast coast and renovate a railroad connecting Rajin to the nearby Russian town of Khasan. A double-track railway between Rajin and Khasan reopened in September 2013 after years of renovation. The state-run Russian Railways had a 70 percent stake in the joint venture, with the DPRK holding the rest. South Korean companies were expected to buy part of the Russian stake.[25] President Park Geun Hye supported South Korean participation in the project as a way to build a "Silk Road Express," linking the ROK to Europe via the DPRK, Russia, and China. In 2014 the ROK waived its May 24 sanctions established in 2010 after the sinking of the *Cheonan*, which banned all nonhumanitarian economic and social exchanges with the North. The ROK government allowed a South Korean consortium to invest in the Russian-led Rajin–Khasan rail/port project in North Korea, treating it as an indirect investment.

A modernized rail link from Siberia into North Korea opened in 2013 and conducted a test run in April 2014, carrying coal from Siberia to Rajin. By late 2014 the Rajin port, now renamed "Rason," had three wharves—one leased to Russia, one leased to China, and one for the DPRK. Some 5 million tons of Russian coal were unloaded at Rason in 2014. The Russian pier had been upgraded, and huge, brand-new cranes stretched into the sky. The Russians also renovated some 50 kilometers of railway leading to the harbor, while the Chinese completed

Map 20.1. Where China, Russia, and North Korea meet

a highway to their own territory. The situation recalled the late 1950s, when China and Russia competed on North Korean soil with Pyongyang pulling the strings.

The DPRK could also exploit its hub location to manipulate the ROK as well as China and Russia. For South Korea to become a full member (not just an observer) in the Organization for Cooperation between Railways (OSJD), it needed the unanimous support of all existing members.[26] According to the *Joongang Daily*, Pyongyang informed Seoul that it would not attend the May 2015 meeting of the OSJD—to be held in Seoul. Thus, no unanimous vote would be possible, and President Park's hopes for a Silk Road Express were impeded, if not derailed.[27]

Russian and Chinese authorities, as well as South Koreans, expressed frustration at the slow pace at which North Korea met its commitments.[28] Perhaps seeking to speed up their transactions, Russia and China were collaborating in construction of the Zarubino port on Russia's Pacific coast, just 18 kilometers from China and 80 kilometers northeast of Rason. It was expected to handle as much as 60 million tons of cargo each year—many times more than Rason. The Zarubino project gave Russia and China an alternative to North Korea's Rason. For the landlocked regions of Northeast China, Zarubino could be an outlet to the world.[29]

Having visited Rason in 2014, the economist Rüdiger Frank wrote:

Even though Rason has been an SEZ [Special Economic Zone] since

1991, and despite travel restrictions for locals, it has remained a part of North Korea that looks, smells, and feels like the original. The roads are a bit bumpy, there are villages with the typical low white buildings, kitchen gardens, surrounding walls, unpaved roads, and long wooden chimneys seen everywhere in the DPRK's northern provinces. Oxen carts pass by, children with red scarfs march to school, the city is covered with slogans glorifying the "Great Sun of the 21st century, comrade Kim Jong Un" or the Party's Military First (*sŏngun*) Policy. Public announcements on wallpapers . . . remind people that September and October are "hygienic months" (*wisaeng wolgan*) and encourage them to pay extra attention to cleanliness. A gigantic mosaic mural with the faces of the two deceased leaders sits on a hill, right next to the international telecommunications center that was once built by Loxley of Thailand. Two bronze statues of the leaders are under construction. Many windows in the apartment blocks in Rason are equipped with solar panels, and the balconies are full of red Kimjongilias. It is autumn. Long chains of red pepper dry in the warm September sun and wait to become a key ingredient of Korea's typical fermented cabbage, kimchi.[30]

The Chinese-owned Golden Triangle Bank in Rason posted on its outside wall the day's currency exchange rates. In September 2014 the rate was one euro for 10,476 won, one U.S. dollar for about 8,000 won, and one renminbi for about 1,300 won. Frank was astounded: he could actually exchange euros into domestic currency at the published rate—which was not much different from unofficial rates on the street. He could not take won bills out of the country, but that seemed of secondary importance. Anywhere else in North Korea the domestic currency was taboo for foreigners.

Comparing Rason and the Industrial Zone near Kaesong, Frank opined that Kaesong was a completely artificial world separate from the real North Korea. At Kaesong, "South Korean factories, guaranteed free of communist propaganda, stand in a previously sparsely inhabited North Korean plain. About 50,000 selected North Korean women are brought in by buses every morning, work their shifts, and then return to their living quarters outside the zone. The area is off limits for ordinary North Koreans and for Western tourists alike. Call it a zoo or Disneyland."

The tragedy of Rason, according to Frank, was that the zone opened up in ways that foreigners might like but, as of 2014, this effort brought in little foreign investment. "Here, North Korea is what it could be without major reforms or effort: more open, more human, more approachable, more honest, and obviously very much more interested in business cooperation with the outside world." Foreigners were allowed to mingle, unsupervised, with locals. The local bank published currency exchange rates close to free market rates. Regulations of all kinds were reduced. But potential investors were still put off by the country's volatile military-political environment, its unpredictable legal climate, and the human rights situation. Frank wrote in late 2014: "I leave the Rason SEZ with excitement about what is possible in this isolated country, and full of hope that the reality as I see it in this enclave will sooner or later be extended to the rest of North Korea. After all, Kim Jong Un has announced the opening of nineteen new SEZs. But in order for Rason to become a model, it has to overcome the ideological concerns of skeptical cadres. The only way to achieve this is economic success."

The Swiss businessman Felix Abt maintained a more hopeful outlook. He settled in Pyongyang in 2002 as the country director for the engineering firm ABB. During the next seven years he founded a foreign chamber of commerce; a foreign-invested software enterprise; a system of e-commerce; and a pharmaceutical chain that used extensive advertising. None of this would have been possible, Abt thought, without engagement from the country's decision makers. However, the Pyongyang Business School he founded in 2004 to train managers closed in 2010 when foreign support stopped. Still, in 2015 Abt believed that private farming and trading were increasing and repression decreasing. "Experience," he wrote, "shows that working with the North works; coercive demands do not."[31]

Abt saw change coming from on high as well as from a growing middle class. Could the DPRK evolve in a manner similar to China or Vietnam? Pressures mounted on the Kim Jong Un regime to liberalize North Korea, but top leaders hesitated to embrace that route lest the entire system collapse. The regime seemed to prefer a problematic status quo to the risks of deep reform. Its subjects, no matter their discontent, appear too weak and disorganized to challenge and alter the system. Perhaps, however, they could modify it from the bottom up.[32]

8. Could Two Koreas Become One?

Should outsiders foster unification of a divided people? Unification of the two Koreas could take place as the outcome of processes that are gradual or sudden, peaceful or violent. Authoritarian regimes in Eastern Europe and the USSR lost support for decades but then were quickly replaced by elected governments in 1989–1991. As when East Germany merged with West Germany, North Korea could virtually overnight join the world as part of a unified Korea. The two German states came together peacefully and rapidly in 1989–1990. They did so consensually—by legislative action in the German Democratic Republic as well as the Federal German Republic. They merged without the ethnic or cultural conflicts that divided peoples in Iraq, Afghanistan, Yemen, and much of Africa. As in most of the former Soviet empire, former Communist leaders in East Germany put on liberal, nationalistic costumes. By contrast, unlike Germany, North and

South Vietnam were unified only after decades of civil war and foreign intervention, with the Communists coming out on top.

Consequences of Unification

A sudden collapse of the Kim dynasty could open the door to a peaceful union of
all Koreans. As in Germany, efforts to unify the two Koreas would confront few, if
any, ethnic or sectarian divides. Many Northerners would have cause to welcome
a federal or centralized union with the South. Still, South Koreans would need to
avoid any posture of superiority and condescension. As in East Germany, many in
the North might resent that their values had been thrown onto the scrap heap of
history.[33]

A unified Korea would probably have no nuclear weapons. China, Russia,
and the United States would act to disable any nuclear weapons or facilities in the
North and convert any nuclear materials to civilian uses. Assuming that China and
Japan did not become more militaristic, a unified Korea could also reduce its conventional forces. Korea might retain its alliance with the United States as a hedge
against aggressive neighbors, but U.S. forces might well be reduced to a symbolic
rather than war-fighting stance. Korean troops might play a greater, but still limited, role in UN and other peacekeeping missions.

The costs for the South of unification would be heavy, but bearable. Given the
numbers, the burden of unification could be far greater on South Koreans than it
was on West Germans. The ratio of East to West Germans was far smaller (1:4)
than that between North and South Koreans (closer to 1:2). The East–West gaps
in wages and lifestyle were also smaller in divided Germany (1:3 in 1989) than
they are in the Koreas (1:30 or more in the early twenty-first century). To bring
the North closer to standards in the South could require investments of a trillion
dollars or more—nearly the size of the South's GDP ($1.3 trillion) in 2013.[34] This
would mean investing about $100 billion per year for a decade. Seoul could mini-
mize some of the unnecessary burdens incurred by Germans, for example, converting the East's Communist-era currency at par with that of the West.

Kim Dae Jong's Sunshine Policy may have aimed to delay unification until
North–South gaps narrowed. By the second decade of the twenty-first century,
however, South Korean elites were more confident that the costs of unification
could be managed. ROK leaders hoped for what Victor Cha called "socialization."
They retried to induce all Koreans and foreigners to think of Korean unification
as good and virtually inevitable. Unification would benefit not only Koreans, both
north and south, but also Korea's neighbors, because the peninsula would become
a zone of peace and growing prosperity.[35]

Economic growth in a unified Korea would probably slow for several years,
but, as new synergies emerged, accelerate. A larger pie would soon mitigate the
economic costs of unification. These burdens would also be eased by the joys of

having eliminated a malignant force and reuniting long-lost relatives. Fears of war or lawlessness would no longer deter foreign investors surveying opportunities in the former DPRK.[36]

Business elites in the South would profit more from economic integration than workers, many of whom might suffer from wage competition with the North. Given that a growing percentage of South Koreans is elderly, they would benefit from the larger and more youthful base of support generated by workers in the North.[37]

In a unified country, Koreans in the North would trade less with China and more with their natural trading partners in the South. Economic growth would gain as the educated and disciplined workers in the North synergized with the capital and modern technology of the South. It is unknown how quickly northerners would absorb capital and modern technology. Most northerners might be slow to accept new ways at first, but then do so with alacrity. Most northerners were taught to obey, not to innovate. Still, the engineers at Yangbyon, as well as DPRK musicians and dancers, foreign traders, and entrepreneurs abroad, displayed great ingenuity and industry in the early twenty-first century. So did the middle-aged women who opened market stalls to sell whatever they could in Pyongyang and other northern cities. North Koreans' food intake and living standards could advance dramatically if local resources were shifted from military to civilian applications.

A Chaotic Alternative

Communist regimes fell and were soon supplanted by democratic institutions in most of Eastern Europe with little bloodshed. Still, replacing the ancien régime or altering national borders can also entail violence. In Romania the president and his wife were executed—a possible nightmare scenario for the Kim dynasts. Given his alleged crimes against humanity, Kim Jong Un could not become part of a unified Korean government. If not arrested or mobbed, Kim Jong Un and his extended family might be resettled in a comfortable refuge.

Regime collapse could also lead to war—in the North, up and down the peninsula, across the region, perhaps around the globe. Former Communist elites could seize as their personal property resources and enterprises that had belonged to the state. There could be a struggle between the haves, who benefited from top-down, dynastic rule, and the mass of have-nots hopeful of a better life. Remaining hardliners might train their weapons on rivals and insurgent have-nots, or shoot across the border at the South. They could even threaten a nuclear doomsday for all.

The ensuing turmoil could be sharpened—or modulated—by outside intervention. Chinese forces as well as U.S.-ROK units could face many challenges: to establish a provisional government; to prevent pillaging and civil or cross-border war; to locate and secure all weapons, conventional as well as WMD; to shut down proliferation networks and seal borders and ports to ensure against leakage; to prevent egress by persons of concern; to provide humanitarian relief—food, shelter, medical care, and decontamination in case of leaks from weapons production or storage facilities.[38]

The interveners could fight to dominate the erstwhile DPRK or strive to harmonize their actions. As of 2015, Chinese officials were reluctant even to discuss collaborative action for this contingency. Given that rebuilding the North would be a huge and costly task, Beijing might acquiesce in a unified Korea led from Seoul—provided that U.S. troops stayed in the South or, better still, left the Korean peninsula entirely.

Thus, regime failure could lead to one of the best—or one of the worst— possible futures.

9. Deter and Contain?

Sooner or later the DPRK regime will probably implode because, like the Soviet system, it is as inefficient as it is inhuman. Since analysts cannot know when the DPRK might reform or implode, U.S. and allied policymakers have to deal with the existing reality. Containment and deterrence held back Soviet expansion and helped prevent a major war. Meanwhile, cultural and other exchanges nurtured the foundations for détente, perestroika, and glasnost. Should the democracies not rely on a similar strategy in dealing with North Korea? A cold peace would be preferable to a hot war. Against this approach, however, is the risk that containment and deterrence could imply acceptance of the DPRK as a nuclear-weapons state.

The United States and its partners needed to contain and deter in a manner that avoids undue provocation. Should they continue conducting maneuvers with landing craft that could assault North Korea's shores? Should the United States fly its bombers to Korea from distant bases to show their prowess?

If North Korea acquired a credible minimum deterrent, this achievement could conceivably ease Pyongyang's anxieties and foster a more stable policy environment. Here was a paradox like the one that confronted Washington in the 1960s as the USSR improved its missiles. If the adversary acquired a credible deterrent, the outcome could be greater stability. Recognizing the value of mutual deterrence, Moscow and Washington renounced large-scale missile defenses in 1972.

While the balance of power between two nuclear superpowers was relatively symmetrical, all the issues of deterrence and defense in Northeast Asia were very fluid in 2016. Even though conventional ROK and U.S. forces were superior to North Korea's, the DPRK artillery provided Pyongyang a more than adequate deterrent against an attack from the South. Meanwhile, the DPRK was developing a nuclear-missile force that might someday threaten the United States as well as

South Korea and Japan. As noted in chapter 16, the ROK began in 2006 to research and develop its own antimissile defenses. Meanwhile, South Korea deployed defenses with U.S., Israeli, and indigenous components. In 2016, however, the Pentagon was pressing the ROK to buy and deploy its Terminal High Altitude Area Defense. This system, known as THAAD, was billed as capable of intercepting and destroying incoming missiles within a 200-km range—further out than any existing or projected indigenous ROK defense network. Some South Koreans worried that THAAD would antagonize Beijing, because it could morph into a system able to neutralize China's missiles. Others hoped that the South could develop defenses with a minimum of foreign involvement. Some opposed any system that might link South Korea's defenses with those planned for Japan.

Cutting through the hyperbole, a Washington insider argued that effective antimissile defenses were not only expensive and provocative but infeasible. Lawrence B. Wilkerson, a retired U.S. Army colonel and chief-of-staff to Colin Powell when he was U.S. secretary of state, argued that antimissile defenses serve mainly to keep military contractors "well-fed and happy." Wilkerson said missile defense is "a form of camouflage for big contracts" to Lockheed Martin and other military contractors. Wilkerson recalled that when William Perry, an engineer, was U.S. secretary of defense, Perry's "team analyzed ballistic missile defense and came to the conclusion that it was simply too expensive and that it would simply take away budget share from other places where the military needed funds." Later, when Donald Rumsfeld became defense secretary under George W. Bush, the United States was suddenly committed to a $100 billion antimissile program—even though "every engineer we talked to still told us that the whole idea was infeasible and that it would not work the way it was described." Still, "here we are now [in 2015], building this system that at best will shoot down two out of ten targets that are coming at it. And if those missiles are loaded with nuclear devices, two of out of ten will not do very much."

Now, Wilkerson complained in 2015, "we are taking that system and we are trying to sell it to South Korea. We're pitching it to them as if it were extremely effective, and we are citing the over-hyped 'Iron Dome' system in Israel as proof that missile defense works. But if anyone actually starts launching sophisticated missiles, nuclear-tipped, it will be a complete disaster." Still, if President Park sees THAAD as "a political necessity to satisfy the Americans, she will have to have it."[39]

Deterrence and containment of North Korea could continue without THAAD. Defense systems to protect individual ships at sea might prove more feasible, but efforts to erect antimissile defenses for land targets amounted to throwing money and brainpower to the wind.[40] Worse, promises of reliable defenses encouraged false hopes. Regardless of their effectiveness, U.S. and South Korean plans for missile defense goaded North Koreans (as well as Chinese and Russians) to improve their own offenses. If these chain reactions gathered steam and if war erupted, the net result would be even more deaths and destruction.

10. Engage and Negotiate?

Which approach has the best prospects? To detach from Northeast Asia was not feasible for the United States. Strategic patience yielded no fruit. A preventive strike would entail unacceptable risks. Subversion, sanctions, and external pressures pushed the Pyongyang regime to hunker down. Indeed, the DPRK leadership was neuralgic about reform and any form of unification. Washington's default posture had to be deterrence and containment. This orientation could prevent a war but would not stop the North from improving its weapons and oppressing its people. Deterrence might be necessary, but it would not suffice to elicit positive changes in Pyongyang's behavior. The only viable route to peace in Northeast Asia was to engage and negotiate. The best hope to improve security and the human condition in Northeast Asia was probably to pursue policies that encouraged more openness in the DPRK.

The devolution of the Cold War offered lessons for dealing with North Korea. Then, the United States and its allies maintained the hard power needed to contain and deter the USSR, but they also used engagement and negotiation to cope with, and ultimately defeat, Soviet imperialism. Having given up any hope of imminent regime change in Moscow or Beijing during the Cold War, the United States identified shared interests and concluded agreements that each party believed enhanced its interests.

Symmetry and sufficiency made arms controls between the United States and USSR/Russia thinkable. Their arsenals were similar in size and quality. Even if reduced by half, the remaining forces would provide a credible deterrent. These features were absent in U.S. relations with North Korea. Washington wanted to improve and keep most of its nuclear arsenal while denying nuclear weapons to the DPRK. However, Pyongyang regarded its incipient nuclear-missile capability as its bargaining ace and insurance against foreign attack. Like Israel, India, and Pakistan, the DPRK resisted any arrangement that allowed some states to have nuclear arms but denied them to others.

Assuming that North Korea insisted on keeping its existing nuclear arsenal, the United States and its partners could try to negotiate a *freeze* on the DPRK stock of nuclear weapon and fissile materials. As with Iran, however, any agreement would require a wide-ranging inspection and verification scheme. A full disclosure of the country's present nuclear assets and facilities would be necessary, but the North could be spared any requirement to offer up a complete history of its nuclear programs.

If negotiations failed to reach an agreement, the United States and its partners would need to restrict North Korea's ability to raise the quantity and quality of WMD. The partners would need to block Pyongyang's capacity to obtain, as well as proliferate, nuclear and missile materials and technology. China as well as other governments would have to permit inspection of airplanes and other vehicles carrying goods into and from North Korea. It might also be possible to incentivize Chinese traders to desist from shipping dual-use goods to the DPRK, though it seemed doubtful that outsiders could outbid Pyongyang on matters vital to the North's leaders.

Engagement could mean expanded cultural and other exchange. The United States missed an opportunity to arrange a DPRK visit to reciprocate that of the New York Philharmonic to Pyongyang in 2008. Starting in 2011–2012, however, the Knowledge Partnership Program at the University of British Columbia brought several groups of DPRK professors to its campus for six-month periods to study business. Meanwhile, the Pyongyang University of Science and Technology permitted 500 sons of the DPRK elite to study with American and other foreign professors. The university's official aim was to equip these young men with the skills needed to modernize the DPRK and engage with the international community. The university was founded by Dr. James Chin-Kyung Kim, a Korean-American entrepreneur who was invited by the DPRK leadership to build a university similar to one he opened in northern China. Heavily subsidized by American and South Korean Christian charities, the university was far more open than most other DPRK institutions. Still, as of 2015, the only female on the staff worked in the computer room to prevent students from accessing e-mail, social media, or international news. The DPRK endeavored to prevent ideological contamination, but experiences around the world suggested that this effort would fail.

For and Against Engagement and Negotiation

Each of the three Kim dynasts called at times for serious discussions with the United States to secure peace and stability in the region. Skeptics in Washington warned that that Pyongyang used negotiation merely to extract concessions, divide its adversaries, and buy time to continue its WMD programs without outside interference. Even if Pyongyang negotiated in good faith, any engagement with the DPRK would serve to legitimize and perpetuate a regime that deserved to perish.

Many U.S. officials were reluctant to enter another discussion with the North that could lead to one-sided concessions or reduce pressure on Pyongyang to curb its WMD programs. Americans also worried lest bilateral U.S.-DPRK talks upset their partners in Seoul, Tokyo, Beijing, and Moscow. Each capital had reason to object to any schemes that exclude it from planning on matters that affected its vital interests. Of course, North Koreans also had reasons to hold back. Table 20.1 presents a summary of the reasons, pro and con, for Washington and Pyongyang

Table 20.1. Bargain or resist? Choices for the USA and the DPRK

	USA	DPRK
Interests at stake	Stop nuclear spread and reduce chances of nuclear war. Keep good relations with Seoul and Tokyo and nurture collaboration with China and Russia.	Security of the regime and the state. Support from the military elite and the public. Keep and bolster our one ace—nuclear bombs and missiles—for deterrence, image, and cash.
Possible mutual gain deals	Strategic stability and arms control in exchange for economic and political rewards.	Diplomatic recognition and economic and political rewards in exchange for arms control.
Likelihood of a deal and implementation	Good if they accept our terms for freezing or disabling nuclear weapons and facilities.	Good if U.S. Congress goes along with the White House.
Means of enforcement	On-site inspection might again be feasible, backed by international cooperation in the Proliferation Security Initiative (PSI).	If we surrender nukes, we have no way to compel the United States and the ROK to carry through with promised economic and political benefits.
Costs of conducting negotiations—including solidarity with domestic and foreign allies	Risk offending ROK and Japan and hawks in Congress and the U.S. public.	Risk offending hawkish elites in military and other circles.
Alternatives to negotiation	Ignore. Regime change. Containment and deterrence.	Carry on with nuclear-missile programs and Juche aided by China and commercial ties with non-Western actors.
Legitimacy of war	Little support in United States and ROK; active opposition from China and Russia.	War would be suicidal, although some elites might consider a "Samson option."

to meet and to bargain. Table 20.2 outlines some of the reasons why DPRK leaders might wish to stop or continue developing nuclear weapons.

Two experts on business deals claimed that the real issues in negotiation are not buying, selling, crafting deals, and overcoming bias. They quoted Ralph Waldo

Table 20.2. The debate in Pyongyang: Should the DPRK continue to develop nuclear weapons?

Yes	No
We must practice self-help since Moscow and Beijing deserted us for the West.	Our economic plight compels us to join the world economy while preserving our system.
Even a few bombs can deter enemy attack and give us leverage; the United States talks big but does little.	If we go nuclear, South Korea and Japan may follow; better to strike a deal with the United States that isolates and immobilizes South Korea.
Our foes will not dare attack us because they do not want a major war. Besides, we can attack Seoul and blow up South Korea's reactors.	Hanging tough is pointless. No one will attack us if we renounce nuclear arms. The United States promises us energy assistance and normalization.

Emerson: "Man hopes; genius creates." Ultimately, negotiation is about engaging other people, who, like all humans, are usually well intentioned but have different interests and perspectives. The only requirement to become a "negotiation genius" is "the ability to change your beliefs, assumptions, and perspective."[41]

In world affairs, however, these two experts were too optimistic. Between contending and mutually distrustful actors—states, mafias, terrorists, and other armed groups—the stakes and risks are more serious than in most domestic interactions. One cannot assume that the other side is well intentioned and just needs to adjust its lenses.

If each side maintains a rigid hard line, then serious negotiation might never begin. The Kim Jong Un regime sometimes called for talks without preconditions, while the Obama White House insisted that Pyongyang virtually surrender before negotiations could begin. Washington said it would resume talks only if North Korea demonstrated that it would live up to its obligations, including compliance with UN Security Council resolutions and, ultimately, denuclearization. Each party was concerned with "face" and the appearance of reliability. Each believed the other had acted in bad faith in times past. Each wanted to defend its "principles." The key issue, however, remained: Could any accommodation create values for each party?

Arms controllers and human rights advocates argued that negotiations with the North could stem the spread of nuclear weapons and, over time, improve the lot of North Korea's people. These potential gains, they said, outweighed the risks. The stakes were high. If the North continued its nuclear programs, then Japanese and South Koreans might also seek nuclear arms. Unless the North's isolation were eased, its people would continue to suffer hunger and repression. Easing tensions could not guarantee a better life for North Koreans, but was probably an essential gate opener.

To meet Pyongyang's quest for honor, security, and profit, a grand bargain had to be negotiated and implemented.[42] The United States and its partners had to provide credible security assurances as well as diplomatic recognition and economic and technical assistance to the North. The quid pro quo would be a freeze on North Korea's development of weapons of mass destruction. The outlines of such a deal were initiated in 1994, 2005, and 2012 but were aborted by myopic forces on each side.

Stanford nuclear expert Siegfried Hecker suggested that the United States and its partners pursue the "three nos"—no *more* bombs, no *better* bombs (no more nuclear testing), and no export of nuclear technology and materials—in return for one yes: American willingness seriously to address North Korea's fundamental insecurity.[43] A high-level North Korean government official told Hecker in November 2010 that the October 2000 Joint Communiqué, which brought Secretary of State Madeleine Albright to Pyongyang, would be a good place to start.[44]

What sort of deal could be arranged? At least seven points needed to be addressed:

1. Security assurances for the DPRK to compensate for limits on its nuclear deterrent.
2. A peace treaty to replace the 1953 armistice.
3. Adjustment of the Northern Limit Line.[45]
4. Establishment of diplomatic relations by Washington and Pyongyang and by Pyongyang and Seoul.
5. The gradual end to UN sanctions against the North in tandem with Pyongyang's acceptance of a freeze of its nuclear and missile programs.
6. Cultural, family, and information exchanges.
7. Agricultural and technological assistance to the North.

Any grand bargain would need to serve the interests not only of the United States and North Korea but also of South Korea, Japan, China, and Russia. Mutual gain could be accomplished by a few compromises and moves to "enlarge the pie." All parties—including China, Russia, and Japan—could gain from accelerated economic development and trade across the entire peninsula. Washington needed to assure Beijing and Moscow that U.S. forces would never be deployed north of Pyongyang. Security assurances to North Korea and China would not require any reduction in America's ability to defend South Korea and Japan.

All the actors in Northeast Asia needed to think of their shared concerns as interacting within a circle that could shrink or expand. How could they grow the circle of what is negotiable? More and more issues, conflicts, and situations could be negotiated.[46] Where might the circle end? How large could the circle become? If the parties focused on their deepest interests, the circle of what is negotiable could expand exponentially. For this to happen, however, all parties would need to perceive and work for outcomes beneficial to key stakeholders.

Acknowledgments

My thanks to the many individuals who have given wise counsel and encouragement for this project over the years. They include Charles K. Armstrong, Mel Gurtov, Stephan Haggard, Stuart A. Kauffman, Sun Joo Kim, Stephen Linton, Katharine H. S. Moon, Alexander Motyl, Marcus Noland, Terence Roehrig, and Yurim Yi; also the late Robert A. Scalapino. Mel Gurtov and Gregory J. Moore read the first draft and offered many insightful suggestions. Discussions by working groups led by the late Stephen Bosworth and Graham Allison at the Belfer Center for Science and International Affairs, Harvard University, enriched the book, as did seminars at the East-West Center at the University of Hawaii and Harvard's Korean Institute and Davis Center for Russian and Eurasian Studies. Fruitful discussions of several chapters also took place at annual meetings of the International Studies Association and the American Political Science Association. The research facilities of many institutions proved invaluable: the Woodrow Wilson International Center for Scholars, the US-Korean Institute at the School for Advanced International Studies, the Korea Economic Institute, the Arms Control Association, the Peter G. Peterson Institute for International Economics, and the Brookings Institution. Shiping Hua, editor of the Asia in the New Millennium Series at the University Press of Kentucky, introduced me to the press, where editors Stephen M. Wrinn and Allison B. Webster and other staff members provided valuable assistance at every stage. Donna Bouvier meticulously copyedited the manuscript (parts of it more than once). Ali Ho Clemens and Daniel Liu prepared figure 2.1. The Bertelsmann Foundation contributed figure 10.1.

Valuable suggestions came from the editors and reviewers of journals and websites in which portions of some chapters were published: *Asian Perspective, Asian Survey, Bulletin of the Atomic Scientists, The Diplomat, Financial Times, Global Asia* and *Global Asia Forum, International Negotiation, Journal of East Asian Affairs, Journal of East Asian Studies, Korean Journal of International Studies*, the *New York Times*, and *Pacific Focus*. Jennifer Knerr authorized updating of work previously published by Paradigm Publishers.

Photos in the text were provided by Jeremy Hunter (www.jeremyhunter.com) and by Steve Gong (stevegongphoto.com).

Thanks to my family, too, for their support and patience over the years.

What an American diplomat once said about Russia certainly applies also to

North Korea: "There are no experts—just various degrees of ignorance." Despite the generous input of others, any errors in this book are the responsibility of its author.

Notes

PROLOGUE

1. Quoted in David Drake, *Sartre* (London: Haus, 2005), 88.

2. The Americans later granted Lt. Gen. Ishii Shiro and his subordinates in Japanese biological warfare units immunity from prosecution for war crimes in exchange for the technical information they had gathered. See Sheila Miyoshi Jager, *Brothers at War: The Unending Conflict in Korea* (New York: W. W. Norton, 2013), 242–257.

3. Ibid.

4. Ibid., 257.

5. Frank McCourt, interviewed by Terry Gross in 1996, replayed on WBUR, National Public Radio, July 20, 2009.

6. Charles Marsh, *Strange Glory: A Life of Dietrich Bonhoeffer* (New York: Alfred A. Knopf, 2014).

7. On the Lacy-Zarubin agreement of January 1958 and its long-term consequences see Yale Richmond, *Cultural Exchange and the Cold War: Raising the Iron Curtain* (University Park: Pennsylvania State University Press, 2003).

8. "Origins of the Soviet Campaign for Disarmament: The Soviet Position on Peace, Security, and Revolution at the Genoa, Moscow, and Lausanne Conferences, 1922–23" (PhD diss., Columbia University, 1961)

9. Lincoln P. Bloomfield, Walter C. Clemens Jr., and Franklyn Griffiths, *Khrushchev and the Arms Race: Soviet Interests in Arms Control and Disarmament, 1954–1964* (Cambridge: MIT Press, 1966).

10. Clemens, *The Arms Race and Sino-Soviet Relations* (Stanford: Hoover Institution, 1968).

11. Osgood, *An Alternative to War or Surrender* (Urbana: University of Illinois Press, 1962).

12. Amitai Etzioni, *The Hard Way to Peace: A New Strategy* (New York: Collier, 1962); Vincent P. Rock, *A Strategy for Interdependence: A Program for the Control of Conflict between the United States and the Soviet Union* (New York: Scribner, 1964); Walter C. Clemens Jr., ed., *Toward a Strategy of Peace*, foreword by Robert F. Kennedy (Chicago: Rand McNally, 1965); W. Averell Harriman, *America and Russia in a Changing World: A Half Century of Personal Observations* (Garden City, NY: Doubleday, 1971).

13. Many lectures were based on Clemens, "Soviet Policy in the Third World in the 1970s: Five Alternative Futures," in W. Raymond Duncan, ed., *Soviet Policy in Developing Countries* (Waltham, MA: Ginn-Blaisdell, 1970), 313–343. Also published in Korean in *Non Dan* (Seoul) 6, no. 4 (January–February 1971): 121–148.

14. "GRIT at Panmunjom: Conflict and Cooperation in Divided Korea," *Asian Survey* 13, no. 6 (June 1973): 531–559, followed by Clemens, "The Impact of Détente on Chinese and Soviet Communism," *Journal of International Affairs* 28, no. 2 (1974): 133–157.

15. Jun Zhan, *Ending the Chinese Civil War: Power, Commerce, and Conciliation between Beijing and Taipei*, foreword by Walter C. Clemens Jr. (New York: St. Martin's, 1993).

16. Clemens, "How to Cope with North Korea and Nuclear Weapons: What Bush Could Have Learned from Lenin, Osgood, and Clinton," *Journal of East Asian Affairs* 18, no. 2 (Fall–Winter 2004): 221–247; also Clemens, "Peace in Korea? Lessons from Cold War Détentes," in *Confrontation and Innovation on the Korean Peninsula* (Washington, DC: Korea Economic Institute, 2003), 1–17.

1. Why Care about North Korea?

1. Princeton Seminars, February 13, 1954, quoted in Robert L. Beisner, *Dean Acheson: A Life in the Cold War* (New York: Oxford University Press, 2006), 323. Acheson's interest in Korea was long-standing. Yale anthropology professor Cornelius Osgood thanked Acheson (Yale 1912–1915) and Yale provost Edgar S. Furniss for their personal support in his researching and writing *The Koreans and Their Culture* (New York: Ronald Press, 1951). As acting secretary and later secretary of state, Acheson pressed Congress in the late 1940s to provide economic assistance to South Korea. Ironically, his omission of Korea from the U.S. defense perimeter in a January 1950 speech probably encouraged Stalin to approve the North's invasion in June 1950. After leaving government in 1953, Acheson served on the Yale Board of Trustees, along with his frequent critic, Robert A. Taft.

2. Osgood, *The Koreans and Their Culture*, v.

3. World Summit Outcome Document, paragraph 138: "The international community, through the United Nations, also has the responsibility to use appropriate diplomatic, humanitarian and other peaceful means, in accordance with Chapters VI and VIII of the Charter, to help protect populations from genocide, war crimes, ethnic cleansing and crimes against humanity. In this context, we are prepared to take collective action, in a timely and decisive manner, through the Security Council, in accordance with the Charter, including Chapter VII, on a case-by-case basis and in cooperation with relevant regional organizations as appropriate, should peaceful means be inadequate and national authorities manifestly fail to protect their populations from genocide, war crimes, ethnic cleansing and crimes against humanity. We stress the need for the General Assembly to continue consideration of the responsibility to protect populations from genocide, war crimes, ethnic cleansing and crimes against humanity and its implications, bearing in mind the principles of the Charter and international law. We also intend to commit ourselves, as necessary and appropriate, to helping States build capacity to protect their populations from genocide, war crimes, ethnic cleansing and crimes against humanity and to assisting those which are under stress before crises and conflicts break out." http://www.who.int/hiv/universal access2010/worldsummit.pdf, adopted by the UN General Assembly September 15, 2005 (accessed 2/24/2014) and endorsed by the UN Security Council Resolution 8710 on April 28, 2006. http://www.un.org/News/Press/docs/2006/sc8710.doc.htm (accessed 2/24/2014).

4. http://www.state.gov/documents/organization/153139.pdf (accessed 2/10/2011). Under Secretary of State Sarah Sewall reiterated Washington's commitment to the R2P in 2015, focusing on the need to prevent atrocities. See her statement at www.state.gov/j/ remarks/247827.htm (accessed 11/2/2015). The first time the UN Security Council autho-

rized coercive measures under the Responsibility to Protect was in Resolution 1970, adopted on February 26, 2011, which several NATO powers then cited to justify their military actions against the Gaddafi regime in Libya. http://www.un.org/press/en/2011/sc10187.doc.htm (accessed 4/10/2011).

    5. http://www.ohchr.org/EN/HRBodies/HRC/CoIDPRK/Pages/Report ofthe CommissionofInquiryDPRK.aspx (accessed 2/28/2014).

    6. Human Rights Council, "Report of the Detailed Findings of the Commission of Inquiry on Human Rights in the Democratic People's Republic of Korea," at http://www .ohchr.org/EN/HRBodies/HRC/CoIDPRK/Pages/ReportoftheCommissionofInquiry DPRK.aspx (accessed 2/19/2014).

    7. Ibid.

    8. Current Intelligence Staff Study, Sino-Soviet Competition in North Korea (ESAU XV-61), April 5, 1961, declassified May 2007, Summary page i.

    9. Details in chapter 5 below.

    10. Diligent searches in the National Archives and other depositories by Professor Terence Roehrig and other researchers have not found the original document. It may never have been signed by—or even shown to—DPRK representatives.

    11. Gregory J. Moore, ed., *North Korean Nuclear Operationality and Regional Security and Nonproliferation,* foreword by Graham T. Allison (Baltimore: Johns Hopkins University Press, 2014).

    12. Gilbert Rozman, "The Geopolitics of the Korean Nuclear Crisis," in Richard J. Ellings and Aaron L. Friedberg, eds., *Strategic Asia, 2003–04* (Seattle, WA: National Bureau of Asian Research, 2003), 252.

    13. Kenneth N. Waltz, *The Spread of Nuclear Weapons: More May Be Better* (London: International Institute for Strategic Studies, 1981). For the pros and cons, see Scott D. Sagan, ed., *The Spread of Nuclear Weapons: An Enduring Debate,* 3rd ed. (New York: W. W. Norton, 2013).

    14. See David E. Hoffman, *The Dead Hand: The Untold Story of the Cold War and Its Dangerous Legacy* (New York: Random House, 2009); Eric Schlosser, *Command and Control: Nuclear Weapons, the Damascus Incident, and the Illusion of Safety* (New York: Penguin, 2014).

    15. For definitions, see http://wordpress.mrreid.org/2014/01/19/bent-spears-broken-arrows-and-empty-quivers/ (accessed 5/6/2015).

    16. "Russia Prepares Nuclear Surprise for NATO," *Pravda,* November 12, 2014; Nikolai N. Sokov, "Why Russia Calls a Limited Nuclear Strike 'De-escalation,'" *Bulletin of the Atomic Scientists,* March 13, 2014; Dave Majumdar, "Five Russian Nuclear 'Weapons' of War the West Should Fear," *National Interest,* January 31, 2015, at http://nationalinterest .org/feature/5-russian-nuclear-weapons-war-the-west-should-fear-12159 (accessed 4/24/2015).

    17. Press conference, March 20, 1963. "With all of the history of war, and the human race's history unfortunately has been a good deal more war than peace, with nuclear weapons distributed all through the world, and available, and the strong reluctance of any people to accept defeat, I see the possibility in the 1970s of the President of the United States having to face a world in which 15 or 20 or 25 nations may have these weapons. I regard that as the greatest possible danger and hazard." http://www.presidency.ucsb.edu/ws/index .php?pid=9124 (accessed 10/10/2010).

    18. Graham Allison, "A Nuclear Nightmare Averted," *The Atlantic,* May 22, 2015, at

http://belfercenter.ksg.harvard.edu/publication/25390/nuclear_nightmare_averted.html?b readcrumb=%2Fexperts%2F199%2F (accessed 6/1/2015).

19. Thus, Vladimir Lenin portrayed disarmament diplomacy as a way to defend the Soviet state, divide its foes, and spread Communist revolution by other means. North Korea's leaders could have learned from Lenin how to use arms control negotiations to shield their country's weaknesses and divide enemy ranks. Soviet diplomacy tried to expose the futility of disarmament negotiations so long as capitalist regimes remained in power and pursued their vested interests. Walter C. Clemens Jr., "Lenin on Disarmament," *Slavic Review* 23, no. 3 (September 1964): 504–525.

20. http://www.crisisgroup.org/en/regions/asia/north-east-asia/north-korea.aspx (accessed 8/15/2015). For a summary of DPRK, U.S., and ROK statements in summer and fall 2015 on North Korea's WMD, see http://www.crisisgroup.org/en/publication-type/ crisiswatch/crisiswatch-database.aspx?CountryIDs=%7b12551CAA-C038-4BEB-ADE2-A9F834190F6C%7d#results (accessed 11/3/2015).

21. Gilbert Rozman, *Strategic Thinking about the Korean Nuclear Crisis: Four Parties Caught between North Korea and the United States* (New York: Palgrave, 2007).

22. General Yang Yung in *People's Daily,* October 24, 1960, quoted in Current Intelligence Staff Study, Sino-Soviet Competition in North Korea, 14.

23. Gavan McCormack and Wada Haruki, "Forever Stepping Back: The Strange Record of 15 Years of Negotiation between Japan and North Korea," in John Feffer, ed., *The Future of U.S.-Korean Relations: The Imbalance of Power* (London: Routledge, 2006), 87.

24. Katherine H. Moon, *Protesting America: Democracy and the U.S.-Korea Alliance* (Berkeley: University of California Press, 2012).

25. Selig S. Harrison, "Did the U.S. Provoke N. Korea?" *Newsweek,* October 16, 2006.

26. For references, see Walter C. Clemens Jr., *Complexity Science and World Affairs* (Albany: State University of New York Press, 2013).

27. http://hdr.undp.org/en/content/table-1-human-development-index-and-its-components (accessed 7/4/2015).

28. http://www.undp.org/content/dam/undp/library/corporate/HDR/2014HDR/HDR-2014-English.pdf (accessed 4/24/2015).

29. This thesis is argued with many case studies in Daron Acemoglu and James A. Robinson, *Why Nations Fail: The Origins of Power, Prosperity, and Poverty* (New York: Crown, 2012).

30. Walter C. Clemens Jr., *Dynamics of International Relations: Conflict and Mutual Gain in an Era of Global Interdependence,* 2nd ed. (Lanham, MD: Rowman & Littlefield, 2004).

31. See ibid. and Clemens, *Complexity Science and World Affairs.*

32. Walter C. Clemens Jr., *Can Russia Change? The USSR Confronts Global Interdependence* (New York: Routledge, [1990] 2011).

33. Clemens, *Complexity Science and World Affairs.*

34. A. A. Golovin and A. A. Nepomnyashchy, eds., *Self-Assembly, Pattern Formation, and Growth Phenomena in Nano-Systems* (Berlin: Springer, 2006).

35. Hard power is the ability to command or coerce others using military or economic assets; soft power is the ability to inspire or persuade others to act as you would like. Conversion power is needed to activate these assets and use them to shape others' behavior. See Joseph S. Nye, *The Powers to Lead* (New York: Oxford University Press, 2008). Many academic specialists believed that, of their number, Nye had the greatest influence on U.S. foreign policy.

36. See, for example, http://www.nautilus.org/energy/2006/beijingworkshop/index .html (accessed 7/15/2007). The Northeast Asia Peace and Security Network brings together nonproliferation specialists, regional security experts, and nongovernmental organizations to analyze energy and other issues of peace and security in Northeast Asia.

37. Robert O. Keohane and Joseph S. Nye, *Power and Interdependence*, 3rd ed. (New York: Longman, 2001), 9–17.

38. Peter Matthiessen, *The Birds of Heaven: Travels with Cranes* (New York: North Point, 2001).

2. How Korea Became Korea

1. Sonia Ryang, "Introduction: North Korea—Going beyond Security and Enemy Rhetoric," in Ryang, ed., *North Korea: Toward a Better Understanding* (Lanham, MD: Lexington Books, 2009).

2. Rüdiger Frank, *Nord Korea: Innenansichten eines totalen Staates* (Munich: Deutsche Verlags-Anstalt, 2014).

3. Poem by Kim Myông Ik, translated in Jae-Jung Suh, ed., *Origins of North Korea's Juche: Colonialism, War, and Development* (Lanham, MD: Lexington Books, 2013), 15.

4. Charles K. Armstrong, "Socialism, Sovereignty, and the North Korean Exception," in Ryang, *North Korea*, 43.

5. Charles K. Armstrong, *Tyranny of the Weak: North Korea and the World, 1950–1992* (Ithaca: Cornell University Press, 2013), 89–93.

6. Far from being new or revolutionary, the term Juche represented an amalgam of Confucian respect for the past, cultural identity markers, and contemporary imaging. A similar term, *chajusong*, calls for humans to develop independently and master their own destiny. The same word, *chajusong*, was also used by another nationalist, ROK president Park Chung Hee, in the 1960s. That the concept was endorsed in the South as well as the North reflected a shared heritage. Keith Howard, "*Juche* and Culture: What's New?" in Hazel Smith et al., eds., *North Korea in the New World Order* (New York: St. Martin's Press, 1996), 169–195.

7. Armstrong, "Socialism, Sovereignty, and the North Korean Exception."

8. B. R. Myers, *North Korea's Juche Myth* (Busan, ROK: Sthele, 2015); also Myers, *The Cleanest Race: How North Koreans See Themselves and Why It Matters* (Brooklyn, NY: Melville House, 2010).

9. Benedict R. Anderson, *Imagined Communities: Reflections on the Origin and Spread of Nationalism*, rev. ed. (New York: Verso, 1991).

10. Bert Feintuch, ed., *The Conservation of Culture: Folklorists and the Public Sector* (Lexington: University Press of Kentucky, 1988).

11. Korean Central News Agency (hereinafter KCNA), February 10, 2014.

12. Ryang, "Biopolitics or the Logic of Sovereign Love—Love's Whereabouts in North Korea," in Ryang, *North Korea*, 59.

13. Sonia Ryang, *Reading North Korea: An Ethnological Exploration* (Cambridge: Harvard University Press, 2012), 83.

14. Heonik Kwon and Byung-Ho Chung, *North Korea: Beyond Charismatic Politics* (Lanham, MD: Rowman & Littlefield, 2012), 85–87.

15. When two rescuers swam to help a family stranded on their roof, the worker father gave them not his children, but portraits of the long-dead president and his son, the Dear Leader. Other such exploits were proudly recorded by the KCNA on August 9, 2006.

16. Excerpts from *The Great General of Sŏn'gun and the World of Love* (2005) analyzed in Kwon and Chung, *North Korea,* 186–187.

17. Letter to the Teaching Staff and Students of Mangyongyondae Revolutionary School and Kan Pan Sok Revolutionary School on the 65th Anniversary of the Founding of the Schools, October 12, Juche 101 (2012). Paraphrased in KCNA, October 13, 2012; full text at Association for the Study of Sŏn'gun Politics UK, at http://www.uk-songun.com/index.php?p=1_357 (accessed 6/23/2015).

18. *Sourcebook of Korean Civilization* (hereinafter *Sourcebook*), ed. Peter H. Lee, 2 vols. (New York: Columbia University Press, 1993–1996), 1: 5–6.

19. "Land of Morning Brightness," in Frances Carpenter, *Tales of a Korean Grandmother* (Boston: Tuttle, 1973), 27–35.

20. Another version holds that Kija left China because the Chou dynasty had replaced Kija's relatives in the Shang dynasty.

21. Casting doubt on this story, the Bronze Age in Korea was quite different from that in China.

22. Kyung Moon Hwan, *A History of Korea: An Episodic Narrative* (New York: Palgrave Macmillan, 2010), 3–4.

23. Scott Snyder, *China's Rise and the Two Koreas: Politics, Economics, Security* (Boulder, CO: Lynne Rienner, 2009).

24. Katharine H. S. Moon, *Protesting America: Democracy and the U.S.-Korea Alliance* (Berkeley: University of California Press/GAIA, 2013).

25. Martina Deuchler, *Confucian Gentlemen and Barbarian Envoys: The Opening of Korea, 1875–1885* (Seattle: University of Washington Press, 1977).

26. *Sourcebook,* 1: 7–9.

27. Ibid., 1: 9–13.

28. Ibid., 1: 14–15.

29. George Alexander Lensen, *Balance of Intrigue: International Rivalry in Korea and Manchuria, 1884–1899,* 2 vols. (Tallahassee: University Presses of Florida, 1982), 1: 2.

30. Martina Deuchler, *The Confucian Transformation of Korea: A Study of Society and Ideology* (Cambridge: Harvard University Press, 1992), 98ff.

31. *Sourcebook,* 1: 474–475.

32. Lensen, *Balance of Intrigue,* 1: 2–3.

33. Max Weber, *The Protestant Ethic and the Spirit of Capitalism* (New York: Scribner, 1976) (first German edition, 1904–1905).

34. JaHyun Kim Haboush and Martina Deuchler, eds., *Culture and the State in Late Chosŏn Korea* (Cambridge: Harvard University Press, 2002).

35. Lucian W. Pye, *Asian Power and Politics: The Cultural Dimensions of Authority* (Cambridge: Harvard University Press, 1985), esp. chaps. 2 and 8; also Pye, "Political Culture Revisited," *Political Psychology* 12, no. 3 (September 1991): 487–508.

36. Pye, *Asian Power,* 75.

37. This sentence and several other qualifications of Pye's views in these pages were suggested by Dr. Yurim Yi.

38. Pye, *Asian Power,* 84.

39. *Yangban* filled most civil service and military leadership positions but had to qualify by passing (often aided by bribes) government exams in Confucian texts and history. *Yangban* did not dirty their hands but lived off the labors of indentured agricultural workers, who generated the resources needed for the life of a scholarly official. Lower-class persons

were eligible to take the exams but seldom had the means needed. The *yangban* class was abolished in 1894 and was soon replaced by Japanese administrators. Some former *yangban* retained their social status and wealth by collaborating with the Japanese.

40. Adam Johnson, *The Orphan Master's Son* (New York: Random House, 2012).

41. Like Columbia University's Ruth Benedict and Margaret Mead, Osgood tried to link culture and personality to the environment. He thought Korean culture less intellectual than Chinese and less aesthetic than Japanese. The personality and temperament of Koreans resembled more those of people to the north, shaped by their close ties to nature. Somewhat like the way that Mead and her colleague Geoffrey Gore depicted Russians, Osgood argued that the cycle of seasons locked Koreans and northerners into their settlements in frozen winters only to be liberated briefly in warmer weather. "First rest, then exuberance"—manifested at times in wild dancing and heavy drinking. Cornelius Osgood, *The Koreans and Their Culture* (New York: Ronald Press, 1951), 331–334.

42. Gilbert Rozman, "Can Confucianism Survive in an Age of Universalism and Globalization?" *Pacific Affairs* 75, no. 1 (Spring 2002): 11–37; and Rozman, *Northeast Asia's Stunted Regionalism: Bilateral Distrust in the Shadow of Globalization* (New York: Cambridge University Press, 2004).

43. For a list of Chinese-sponsored Confucian institutes around the globe, even at the Pontifical Catholic University of Rio de Janeiro, see http://confuciusinstitute.unl.edu/institutes .shtml (accessed 5/8/2015). The University of Chicago abolished its institute in 2014 because hiring and other decisions were made in Beijing (*Inside Higher Ed,* September 26, 2014).

44. See the debate between Patrick McEachern, "Interest Groups in North Korean Politics," and Jacques E. C. Hymans, "Assessing North Korean Nuclear Intentions and Capacities: A New Approach," *Journal of East Asian Studies* 8, no. 2 (May–August 2008): 235–258 and 259–292.

45. Gregory Henderson, *Korea: The Politics of the Vortex* (Cambridge: Harvard University Press, 1968).

46. Ibid., 347.

47. Henderson found that the Assembly spent more energy criticizing the executive than passing laws. Rhee and the Assembly struggled against each other even during the Korean War. The Assembly accused rightists of being Japanese collaborators and leftists of being Communists.

48. According to the World Intellectual Property Organization, in 2012 South Korea placed fourth in the world in the absolute number of patents awarded, 113,467; Japan ranked first, with 274,791; the United States second, with 253,155; China third, with 217,105; Europe fifth, with 65,665; next came Russia, with 32,880; North Korea had 6,520. See http://www.wipo.int/ipstats/en/statistics/country_profile/countries/kp.html (accessed 6/17/2014).

49. In the 1890s the only young men to take the state exams were the sons of nobles and wealthy merchants. An English observer asserted that schools and exams devoted little attention to science or mathematics. Instead they emphasized artful expression of philosophic and poetic concepts. Passing the state exams often required bribery. Families of exam takers made the exams an occasion for eating and drinking as their sons were called up to be examined. A. Henry Savage-Landor, *Corea; or, Cho-sen: The Land of the Morning Calm* (New York: Macmillan, 1895), 206–210.

50. http://thelearningcurve.pearson.com/index/index-comparison (accessed 5/14/2015).

51. As of 2015 Finns had won four Nobel prizes—two in science, one in literature, and one in peace; Koreans just one—in peace. Many of Finland's best and brightest chose to be teachers.

52. Mark Berry, "Meeting Kim Il Sung in His Last Weeks," April 15, 2012, at http://www.nknews.org/2012/04/meeting-kim-il-sung-in-his-last-weeks/ (accessed 6/1/2012).

53. Ra Kyung-jun, "Early Print Culture in Korea," *Korean Culture* (Summer 1999): 13–21.

54. *Sourcebook,* 1: 521–525.

55. Descended from Tungusic (Manchurian) tribes, Koreans, like the Japanese, probably migrated from the Northeast Asian mainland. Their language may be tied to the Ural Altaic family, which includes Mongolian, Hungarian, Turkish, and Finnish, and possibly Japanese. The Korean and Japanese languages share a similar grammar but little more.

56. Known as a Confucian humanist, Sejong (r. 1418–1450) also composed music for wind and string instruments that is still played in the twenty-first century on ceremonial occasions. The sixth king after him, Yeonnsangun (r. 1494–1506) is considered the worst tyrant of the Chosŏn dynasty. His reign was marked by a series of bloody purges of Neo-Confucian scholars.

57. Ch'oe Malli quoted in *Sourcebook,* 1: 519–520.

58. More than 50 percent of all Korean vocabulary is derived from Chinese loanwords. In many cases there are two words—a Chinese loanword and an indigenous Korean word with the same meaning. Compounding foreign influences, under Japanese rule (1910–1945), large numbers of Chinese character compounds that were coined in Japan to translate Western scientific vocabulary came into use in Korea. American influence since 1945 is reflected in the many English words also absorbed—often quite oddly—into Korean. For example, since Korean lacks an *f, fashion* is rendered as *passion*—as in "passion stores." Though the word *stress* can be readily rendered with Korean words, some contemporary writers prefer to use the English word *stress* spelled with Korean letters.

59. Deviating somewhat from Marxist-Leninist dogma, *Kullo-ja* includes all kinds of workers. There is a separate word for physical, or blue-collar, workers: *Nodong-ja.*

60. http://www.declan-software.com/korean.htm#Origins (accessed 7/6/2009).

61. Hymans, "Assessing North Korean Nuclear Intentions," 266.

62. Daniel H. Bays and James H. Grayson, "Christianity in East Asia: China, Korea, and Japan," in Sheridan Gilley and Brian Stanley, eds., *World Christianities, c. 1815–1914,* vol. 8 of *The Cambridge History of Christianity* (Cambridge, UK: Cambridge University Press, 2008), 493–512.

63. Kim Young-sik, "A Brief History of U.S.-Korea Relations prior to 1945," at http://www.asianresearch.org/articles/1483.html (accessed 6/10/2014). Allen wrote four or more books on Korean folktales, customs, and foreign relations. He spent his last twenty-seven years as a physician in Toledo, Ohio.

64. Kenneth M. Wells, *New God, New Nation: Protestants and Self-Reconstruction Nationalism in Korea* (North Sydney, NSW: Allen & Unwin, 1990).

65. Donald N. Clark, "Christianity in Modern Korea," at https://www.asian-studies.org/eaa/Clark-Korea.pdf (accessed 4/28/2015).

66. "Why South Korea Is So Distinctively Christian," *The Economist,* August 12, 2014.

67. http://www.forbes.com/pictures/lmh451fdj/geun-hye-park (accessed 4/28/2015).

68. A. Sung Park, "The Minjung Theology: A Korean Contextual Theology," at http://www.biblicalstudies.org.uk/pdf/ijt/33-4_001.pdf (accessed 6/16/2014); Elias Kruger, "Min-

jung Theology as a Korean Ideology of Political Dissidence," at http://www2.davidson.edu/academics/acad_depts/rusk/prima/V012Issue1/minjung.htm (accessed 6/16/2014).

69. John Charles Pollock, *A Foreign Devil in China: The Story of Dr. L. Nelson Bell, An American Surgeon in China* (Minneapolis: World Wide Publications, 1971).

70. http://www.worldvaluessurvey.org/WVSContents.jsp (accessed 7/1/2014).

71. Geeta Anand and Jaeyeon Woo, "Asia Faces 'Missing Women' Problem," *Wall Street Journal,* November 27, 2015, 1, 12.

72. *CIA World Factbook* at https://www.cia.gov/library/publications/the-world-factbook/geos/ks.html (accessed 12/1/2015); Lee Ji-yoon, "Spectre of Aging Population Worries Economists," *Bulletin of the World Health Organisation* 88, no. 3 (March 2010), at http://www.who.int/bulletin/volumes/88/3/10–030310/en/ (accessed 12/1/2015).

73. *DPR Korea 2008 Population Census National Report* (Pyongyang: Central Bureau of Statistics Pyongyang, 2009) at http://unstats.un.org/unsd/demographic/sources/census/2010_PHC/North_Korea/Final%20national%20census%20report.pdf(accessed12/1/2015); *CIA World Factbook* at https://www.cia.gov/library/publications/the-world-factbook/geos/kn.html (accessed 12/1/2015); Thomas Spoorenberg, "Niveaux et tendances de la fécondité en Corée du Nord," *Population* 69 (March 2014): 477–489. Deaths from famine in the 1990s may have been less than earlier estimates, but deteriorating economic conditions in North Korea raised the total of excess deaths to more than one million from 1993 to 2008. See Thomas Spoorenberg and Daniel Schwekendiek, "Demographic Changes in North Korea: 1993–2008, "*Population and Development Review* 38, no. 1 (March 2012): 133–158.

74. Katherine H. S. Moon, *Protesting America: Democracy and the U.S-Korea Alliance* (Berkeley: University of California Press, 2012).

3. How Korea Became Japan

1. Quoted in Yur-Bok Lee, "A Korean View of Korean-American Relations, 1882–1940," in Yur-Bok Lee and Wayne Patterson, eds., *Korean-American Relations, 1866–1997* (Albany: State University of New York Press, 1999), 1–34 at 15.

2. William Franklin Sands, *Undiplomatic Memories* (New York: McGraw-Hill, 1930), 56. On the conflicts between an idealistic American chargé d'affaires in Seoul and an insouciant State Department, see Samuel Hawley, ed., *America's Man in Korea: The Private Letters of George C. Foulk, 1884–1887* (Lanham, MD: Lexington Books, 2008).

3. The number amounted to 16,314 full texts or extracts, according to the *Korean Review* (May 1902): 223–224.

4. Isabella Bird Bishop, *Korea and Her Neighbors* (New York: Fleming H. Revell, 1897).

5. A. Henry Savage-Landor, *Corea, or Cho-Sen: The Land of the Morning Calm* (New York: Macmillan, 1895).

6. Quoted in Yur-Bok Lee, "A Korean View."

7. Quoted in Yur-Bok Lee, "Korean-American Diplomatic Relations, 1882–1905," in Yur-Bok Lee and Wayne Patterson, eds., *One Hundred Years of Korean-American Relations, 1882–1982* (University: University of Alabama Press, 1986), 23.

8. Wayne Patterson and Hilary Conroy, "Duality and Dominance: An Overview of Korean-American Relations, 1866–1997," in Lee and Patterson, *Korean-American Relations, 1866–1997,* 5.

9. Details in the next chapter.

10. The Korean title for such a regent is *Hŭngsun Taewongun*.

11. *A Historical Summary of United States–Korean Relations, with a Chronology of Important Developments, 1834–1962* (Washington, DC: U.S. Department of State, 1962), 3.

12. Fred Harvey Harrington, "An American View of Korean-American Relations," in Lee and Patterson, *One Hundred Years*, 50–51.

13. Quoted in Yur-Bok Lee, *Diplomatic Relations between the United States and Korea, 1866–1887* (New York: Humanities Press, 1970), 29.

14. Harrington, "An American View," 51.

15. http://www.presidency.ucsb.edu/ws/index.php?pid=2951st=korea&st1=grant (accessed 7/11/2009). This database permits a researcher to search for "Korea" and the name of a U.S. president or the relevant year and quickly find the full text of any relevant comments, with "Korea" highlighted in red.

16. That a U.S.-Korean treaty would be drafted in China by a U.S. naval officer and a Chinese official made it a diplomatic anomaly. Earlier Shufeldt tried to send a letter to the Korean king by way of Japanese officials. Twice the Koreans refused even to open the letter. Since Japan's good offices did not work, Shufeldt sought and got assistance from China, which saw U.S. influence on Korea as less bad than Japanese or Russian. See Martina Deuchler, *Confucian Gentlemen and Barbarian Envoys: The Opening of Korea, 1875–1885* (Seattle: University of Washington Press, 1976), 109–117.

17. *A Historical Summary of United States–Korean Relations*, 4.

18. For the context, see ibid.

19. Huang Tsunhsien quoted in Chae-Jin Lee, *A Troubled Peace: U.S. Policy and the Two Koreas* (Baltimore: Johns Hopkins University Press, 2006), 11.

20. http://en.wikipedia.org/wiki/Empress_Myeongseong#The_American_Expedition (accessed 6/12/2007).

21. http://www.presidency.ucsb.edu/ws/index.php?pid=29512&st=korea&st1=grant (accessed 7/10/2009).

22. http://www.presidency.ucsb.edu/ws/index.php?pid=29529&st=cleveland&st1=korea (accessed 7/10/2009).

23. Lee, *Troubled Peace*, 12.

24. Yur-Bok Lee, "Korean-American Diplomatic Relations," 18.

25. One delegate stayed on in Massachusetts to study at the Governor Dummer Academy. Moon-Hyon Nam, "Early History of Electrical Engineering in Korea: Edison and First Electric Lighting in the Kingdom of Corea," in *Singapore 2000: Promoting the History of EE Jan. 23–26, 2000*, 1–9, at http://www.ieee.org/portal/cms_docs_iportals/iportals/aboutus/history_center/conferences/singapore/Nam,-Early_History.pdf (accessed 6/1/2007).

26. Michael Adas, *Dominance by Design: Technological Imperatives and America's Civilizing Mission* (Cambridge: Harvard University Press, 2006), 1–31.

27. http://www.presidency.ucsb.edu/ws/index.php?pid=29530&st=korea&st1= (accessed 7/13/2009).

28. http://www.presidency.ucsb.edu/ws/index.php?pid=71083&st=korea&st1= (accessed 7/13/2009).

29. George Alexander Lensen, *Balance of Intrigue: International Rivalry in Korea and Manchuria, 1884–1899*, 2 vols. (Tallahassee: University Presses of Florida, 1982).

30. http://www.presidency.ucsb.edu/ws/index.php?pid=29535&st=korea&st1= (accessed 7/13/2009).

31. Text at http://www.isop.ucla.edu/eas/documents/1895shimonoseki-treaty.htm (accessed 5/4/2009).

32. http://www.presidency.ucsb.edu/ws/index.php?pid=29544&st=great+oriental+empire&st1=roosevelt (accessed 7/10/2009).

33. See *Krasnyi arkhiv* documents cited in Walter C. Clemens Jr., "From Nicholas II to SALT II: Change and Continuity in East-West Diplomacy," *International Affairs* (London) 49, no. 3 (July 1973): 385–401; also Clemens, "The Hague Peace Conferences," *Encyclopedia of Russian History,* 4 vols. (New York: Macmillan, 2004) 2: 625.

34. *Opisanie Korei,* 3 parts (St. Petersburg, 1890).

35. Seung-Kwon Synn, "Imperial Russia's Strategy and the Korean Peninsula," in Il Yung Chung, ed., *Korea and Russia: Toward the Twenty-First Century* (Seoul: Sejong Institute, 1992), 3–29.

36. See report from Lloyd C. Griscom, U.S. Legation in Tokyo, to Secretary of State John Hay on January 8, 1904, in *Foreign Relations of the United States* (hereinafter *FRUS*) *1904* (Washington, DC: Government Printing Office [GPO], 1905), 410–411. All editions of *FRUS* referred to in this book were published in Washington, DC, by the U.S. Government Printing Office. Editions of *FRUS* from 1861 through 1960 may be found at http://digicoll .library.wisc.edu/cgi-bin/FRUS/FRUS-idx?type=browse&scope=FRUS.FRUS1; for later volumes, see https://history.state.gov (accessed 3/20/2016).

37. William Reed, "Information, Power, and War," *American Political Science Review* 97, no. 4 (November 2003): 633–641.

38. Translation from *Japan Times,* February 11, 1904, reprinted in *FRUS 1904,* 414.

39. See Article IV of text delivered on February 26, 1904, to the secretary of state by the Japanese legation in Washington in ibid., 437.

40. Griscom to Secretary of State Hay, March 17, 1904, in ibid., 438.

41. Hay to Horace N. Allen, U.S. Legation in Seoul, April 6, 1904, in ibid., 452. The Korean minister of foreign affairs then expressed his apologies to Mr. Allen (453). As late as January 1905, however, Roosevelt sent to Congress a State Department report on reforms of the U.S. "extraterritorial judicial system in China and Korea, with . . . a draft of an act providing for the establishment of a district court of the United States for China and Korea."

42. James Bradley, *The Imperial Cruise: A Secret History of Empire and War* (Boston: Little, Brown, 2009), and Bradley's essay "Diplomacy That Will Live in Infamy," *New York Times,* December 6, 2009.

43. Tyler Dennett quoted in *FRUS 1950* (GPO, 1976), 7: 625n5.

44. Text at http://dokdo-research.com/temp25.html (accessed 6/21/2014).

45. See Rhee's letter to President Harry Truman on May 15, 1945, in *FRUS 1945* (GPO, 1968), 6: 1028–1029 and n31.

46. A. A. Gromyko, *Pamiatnoe,* 2 vols. (Moscow: Politizdat, 1988), 1: 189.

47. "*Khitryi i mudryi*" in ibid., 1: 17.

48. Anatolii F. Dobrynin, "Dal'nevostochania politika SShA v period russko-iaponskoi voiny (1904–1905)," Moscow, 1947, cited in Lensen, *Balance of Intrigue,* 1: 441.

49. In 1908 Roosevelt reported that the State Department often received appeals to stop mistreatment abroad of various groups—blacks, whites, Christians, Jews, Armenians, Koreans, and others. Only in exceptional cases, he said, should the United States act in their behalf.

50. All this was documented in Japanese government ordinances and Japanese newspa-

per accounts sent by the U.S. Legation in Tokyo to the secretary of state on January 19 and July 6, 1906. See *FRUS 1906* (GPO, 1909), part 2: 1023–1026, 1044–1046.

51. Ibid., part 2: 999–1005.

52. Japan treated Taiwan, annexed in 1895, much better, in part because many Japanese looked up to Chinese civilization but down on Korean. Equally or more important, Taiwan was administered by enlightened naval officers; Korea, by rather brutal army personnel. A century or more later, ties between Taiwan and Japan were cordial and respectful, while Korean resentments toward Japan still bristled. In 2007 Tokyo continued to deny that Japan had abused Korean and other Asian women in World War II. Taiwanese professors, with whom I hiked in the 1990s, seemed to remember their associations with Japan fondly and joked among themselves in Japanese. In the 1970s there were still Taiwanese professors who remembered their education in Russia and were glad to speak Russian again.

53. Before Cheng arrived at the colony in 1942, however, another Japanese commander treated the lepers "like his family." When he died, residents purchased a cenotaph in his memory. Norimitsu Onishi, "A Korean Bridge Must Span Years of Bias and Sadness," *New York Times*, August 9, 2007, p. A4.

54. http://www.presidency.ucsb.edu/ws/index.php?pid=29551&st=korea&st1= (accessed 7/13/2009).

55. http://www.presidency.ucsb.edu/ws/index.php?pid=29552&st=korea&st1= (accessed 7/13/2009).

56. The inquiry dealt with three issues concerning Japan—including Japanese "interests in Eastern Asia and the Pacific"—and more than a dozen issues concerning China, including the Open Door policy. *The Paris Peace Conference, FRUS 1919* (GPO, 1942), 1. The inquiry is found on pages 9–220 of this volume, but "Korea" does not appear in the index.

57. From 1878 to 1882 the founder of modern China, Sun Yat-sen, studied at Iolani School in Honolulu and learned English. (His portrait hung near the door to the headmaster's office when I chaired the foreign language department there in 1960–1961.) Sun then spent one semester at Oahu College, later known as Punahou, Barack Obama's prep school. Returning to China in 1883, Sun studied medicine and converted to Christianity. He came to picture revolution in China as similar to the salvation mission of Christianity. After his proposal for modernizing China was spurned by the Qing Viceroy in 1894, Sun returned to Hawaii and founded the Revive China Society. His subsequent political work got financing from Chinese in Hawaii, Canada, and Europe. Sun received some of his ideas about democracy from Americans, but he smuggled arms to Filipinos fighting for independence from the United States. He did so hoping to use the Philippines as a staging area to attack the Qing dynasty in China. When the Filipino liberation effort was crushed in 1902, Sun looked elsewhere. To get around the Chinese Exclusion Laws then in effect, Sun in 1904 "gained entry to the United States through the use of documents falsely attesting to his status as a U.S. citizen." http://www.archives.gov/publications/record/1998/05/sun-yat-sen.ht (accessed 5/10/2014).

58. For the instructions to the U.S. ambassador in Japan, see *The Paris Peace Conference, FRUS 1919*, 2: 462; for omission of Korea among topics of the Inquiry, see ibid., 1: 72, 90.

59. *A Historical Summary,* 8.

60. *The Memoirs of Cordell Hull,* 2 vols. (New York: Macmillan, 1948), 1: 270.

61. All quotes and paraphrasing as rendered in the report from the U.S. Embassy in Tokyo to the secretary of state, dispatched on November 27, 1918, but not received in Washington for nearly a month—on December 23. See *FRUS 1919,* 1: 490–491.

62. John K. Fairbank in 1968 quoted in Dean Acheson, *Present at the Creation: My Years in the State Department* (New York: W. W. Norton, 1987), 740.

63. The text is quoted in William J. H. Hough III, "The Annexation of the Baltic States and Its Effect on the Development of Law Prohibiting Forcible Seizure of Territory," *New York Law School Journal of International and Comparative Law* 6, no. 2 (Winter 1985): 327, and is analyzed in the entire issue.

64. This sentence is not quoted and its legal justification is omitted in David F. Schmitz, *Henry L. Stimson: The First Wise Man* (Wilmington, DE: SR Books, 2003), 102–107. The book mentions Korea once, in passing, on 103.

65. Although the Stimson Doctrine did not help Korea, it later encouraged Washington and most Western countries to defy Soviet annexation of the Baltic republics. See Hough, "Annexation," and Walter C. Clemens Jr., *Baltic Independence and Russian Empire* (New York: St. Martin's, 1991).

66. Nicholas D. Kristof, "Unmasking Horror—A Special Report; Japan Confronting Gruesome War Atrocity," *New York Times,* March 17, 1995; updated in other newspaper articles and books, many cited in the Wikipedia article "Unit 731" (accessed 2/16/2014).

4. How One Korea Became Two

1. See letters by Syngman Rhee and other Korean leaders to President Harry S. Truman and subsequent exchanges between Rhee and other U.S. officials in *FRUS 1945* (GPO, 1969), 6: 1028–1037.

2. Roosevelt gave little thought to Korea. He could hope, however, that the promise of eventual independence for Korea would appeal to some U.S. voters. See Stephen E. Pelz, "U.S. Decisions on Korean Policy, 1943–1950: Some Hypotheses," in Bruce Cumings, ed., *Child of Conflict: The Korean-American Relationship, 1943–1953* (Seattle: University of Washington Press, 1983), 97–101.

3. Notes by the Chinese delegation show that, meeting with Roosevelt in Cairo on November 23, 1943, Chiang Kai-shek stressed the need to grant independence to Korea. The next day, however, Roosevelt told Churchill he had no doubt that China "had wide aspirations which included the re-occupation of Manchuria and Korea." *The Conferences at Cairo and Tehran, FRUS 1943* (GPO, 1961), 325 ff.

4. See Soviet and U.S. sources analyzed in Walter C. Clemens Jr., *Baltic Independence and Russian Empire* (New York: St. Martin's 1991), 297–298. The extent of Roosevelt's appeasement, if not myopia and perfidy, seems not to have penetrated the minds of the many historians who rank him as one of the greatest U.S. presidents in foreign policy. One secretary of state, however, considered Roosevelt superficial as well as haughty. See Dean Acheson, *Present at the Creation: My Years in the State Department* (New York: W. W. Norton, 1987).

5. Andrei A. Gromyko, *Pamiatnoe,* 2 vols. (Moscow: Politizdat, 1988), 1: 189–190.

6. General Wang Peng sheng, an adviser to Chiang Kai-shek's government, worried about a Soviet takeover of Korea. He stressed that peace in the Far East depended on resolving the problem of Korea. Comments transmitted by the U.S. chargé d'affaires George Atcheson Jr. in Chungking to Washington on August 14, 1943, in *FRUS 1943* (GPO, 1963), 3: 1095–1096.

7. C. E. Gauss in Chungking to the Secretary of State, December 6, 1943, in ibid.

8. Chu Hein-ming, chief of the Russian Department, Ministry of Information, May 20, 1945, as reported in *FRUS 1945* (GPO, 1969), 7: 870–876 at 873.

9. For U.S. statements on April 3, 1945, and a related internal discussion on June 11, 1945, see *FRUS 1945* (GPO, 1967), 1: 191, 1242.

10. Memorandum by G. M. Elsey, Assistant to the President's Naval Aide, transmitted to Admiral William D. Leahy on July 1, 1945, and subsequently transmitted to Truman. See *The Conference of Berlin, FRUS 1945* (in 2 vols.) (1960), 1: 309–310.

11. Elsey at ibid.

12. German Communists being trained in the USSR were initially told to create a broad-based regime in the Soviet zone of Germany. As they prepared to follow the Soviet Army into Berlin, however, they were instructed to move left. Wolfgang Leonhard, *Die Revolution entlässt ihre Kinder* (Cologne: Kiepenheuer & Witsch, 1973 [first published 1956]); also Gerhard Keiderling, ed., *"Gruppe Ulbricht" in Berlin, April bis Juni 1945: von den Vorbereitungen im Sommer 1944 bis zur Wiederbegründung der KPD im Juni 1945: eine Dokumentation,* with a preface by Wolfgang Leonhard (Berlin: Berlin Verlag A. Spitz, 1993).

13. Notes by U.S. ambassador W. Averell Harriman in Moscow in *Conference of Berlin,* 1: 46–47.

14. Ibid., 1: 310.

15. Report by Harriman in Moscow to President Truman and Secretary of State James F. Byrnes, July 3, 1945, in *FRUS 1945* (GPO, 1969), 7: 912–914.

16. *Conference of Berlin,* 1: 310–315, 924–926.

17. Stimson to Truman, July 16, 1945, in *Conference of Berlin,* 2: 631.

18. This act violated Moscow's April 13, 1941, neutrality pact with Tokyo, which bound each side to respect the other's territorial integrity for at least five years. The Kremlin denounced the 1941 treaty in April 1945, but it probably remained legally binding until April 1946.

19. Rusk's recollections in a July 12, 1950, memorandum included in *FRUS 1945,* 6: 1039.

20. Sheila Miyoshi Jager, *Brothers at War: The Unending Conflict in Korea* (New York: W. W. Norton, 2013), 20.

21. *FRUS 1945,* 6: 1038n48.

22. Ibid., 6: 1038.

23. See above, note 12.

24. The United States allowed no say for Moscow in the occupation of Italy, nor did the USSR allow the West a voice in the occupation of Bulgaria and Romania.

25. Charles K. Armstrong, *The North Korean Revolution, 1945–1950* (Ithaca: Cornell University Press, 2003), 53.

26. A former minister in the provisional government based in Shanghai and then in Chungking, Yu-pil Lee (Yi), had headed the Self-Rule Council. When the Communists took control, he moved south, but died en route.

27. See, e.g., Ruth Benedict, *Chrysanthemum and the Sword: Patterns of Japanese Culture* (Boston: Houghton Mifflin, 1946); Margaret Mead, *Soviet Attitudes toward Authority: An Interdisciplinary Approach to Problems of Soviet Character* (New York: Schocken, 1951). On cultural anthropology and U.S. foreign policy, see Peter Mandler, *Return from the Natives: How Margaret Mead Won the Second World War and Lost the Cold War* (New Haven: Yale University Press, 2013). Whatever her limitations, underscored by Mandler, Mead's ideas on personality and culture were the most stimulating I encountered at Columbia.

28. Cornelius Osgood, *The Koreans and Their Culture* (New York: Ronald Press, 1951). Osgood's work was sponsored by the Yale Peabody Museum of Natural History and funded

by the Viking Fund, with freedom to investigate and material assistance granted by Lt. General John R. Hodge, who was in charge of the U.S. occupation.

29. Pelz, "U.S. Decisions on Korean Policy," 107–109.

30. *FRUS 1945*, 6: 1065–1076 at 1070–1071.

31. Ambassador Harriman in Moscow to Soviet Foreign Commissar Molotov, November 8, 1945, in *FRUS 1945* (GPO, 1967), 2: 627. His message ignored the brusque rejection of U.S. overtures by Soviet authorities in Korea.

32. Hodge in Seoul to MacArthur in Tokyo, October 12, 1945, in *FRUS 1945*, 6: 1072–1073.

33. *FRUS 1945*, 2: 699–700, 716–717.

34. Named Kim Sung Joo (or Kim Sŏng-ju) by his Presbyterian parents, the future leader took the name Kim Il Sung ("become the sun") in 1935. Some skeptics say he lifted it from a legendary hero believed to have fought for Korean independence several decades earlier.

35. *FRUS 1945*, 2: 697–705. The *New York Times* reported on July 9, 1947, that nearly 2 million refugees had moved south from the Soviet zone.

36. Andrei Lankov, *From Stalin to Kim Il Sung: The Formation of North Korea, 1945–1960* (New Brunswick, NJ: Rutgers University Press, 2002), 18; Jager, *Brothers at War*, 24–26.

37. *FRUS 1946* (GPO, 1972), 1: 1145–1160 at 1148, 1153.

38. *FRUS 1947* (GPO, 1973), 1: 736–750.

39. Hickerson to the Secretary of State, March 6, 1948, in *FRUS 1948* (GPO, 1974), 3: 779–780.

40. *FRUS 1948* (GPO, 1975), 1: 14–15.

41. In January 1950 the chief of the U.S. Advisory Group, Brig. Gen. William L. Roberts, and several ROK officers made a good case to U.S. ambassador-at-large Philip C. Jessup "for at least a few aircraft and antiaircraft guns." Tanks were less urgent. Jessup memorandum dated January 14, 1950, in *FRUS 1950* (GPO, 1976), 7: 1–7 at 2.

42. See Se-Jin Kim, ed., *Documents on Korean-American Relations, 1943–1976* (Seoul: Research Center for Peace and Unification, 1976).

43. http://www.asiasource.org/society/syngmanrhee.cfm (accessed 5/5/2009).

44. See the observations of a U.S. diplomat-scholar, Gregory Henderson, in Henderson, *Korea: The Politics of the Vortex* (Cambridge: Harvard University Press, 1968).

45. Gromyko, *Pamiatnoe*, 2: 130.

46. Sergei N. Goncharov, John W. Lewis, and Xue Litai, *Uncertain Partners: Stalin, Mao, and the Korean War* (Stanford: Stanford University Press, 1993), 84, with background at 27–28.

47. Ibid., first chapters and appendices, including messages to Stalin from I. V. Kovalev.

48. Gromyko, *Pamiatnoe*, 2: 128.

5. How a Civil War Became Global

1. The analysis here depends heavily on documents from Soviet and East European archives available at Woodrow Wilson International Center for Scholars, Cold War International History Project (CWIHP), Washington, DC, in its print publication, *Bulletin,* and online. For starters, see Kathryn Weathersby, Introduction, "New Russian Documents on the Korean War," *Cold War International History Project Bulletin,* Issues 6–7 (Winter 1995–1996), also at http://www.wilsoncenter.org/sites/default/files/Bulletin6-7_Korea.pdf. Issues 6 and 7 also include analyses of Soviet documents by Evgenii P. Bajanov, Hyun-su Jeon,

and Alexandre Y. Mansourov; a summary of research into Chinese documents by Chen Jian; a report on Soviet interrogation of American POWs by Laurence Jolidon; and a critique of the Wilson Center project by Bruce Cumings with a rebuttal by Weathersby; also "New Evidence on North Korea," *Bulletin*, Issues 14–15 (Winter 2003–Spring 2004), which includes an Introduction by Weathersby and the work of Beijing-based scholar Shen Zhihua ("Sino-Soviet Korean Conflict and Its Resolution during the Korean War," 9–24). The Wilson Center and other documents are used in William Stueck, ed., *The Korean War in World History* (Lexington: University of Press of Kentucky, 2004). Chinese, Korean, and some Russian-language sources are used and interpreted by Charles K. Armstrong, *Tyranny of the Weak: North Korea and the World, 1950–1992* (Ithaca: Cornell University Press, 2013). Sources from Russia, China, Korea, Taiwan, and Japan are used in Wada Haruki, *The Korean War: An International History* (Lanham, MD.: Rowman & Littlefield, 2013). U.S. military archives as well as the Wilson Center and Korean documents are sourced in Sheila Miyoshi Jager, *Brothers at War* (New York: W. W. Norton, 2013). Chinese materials are used extensively in Chen Jian, *China's Road to the Korean War: The Making of the Sino-American Confrontation* (New York: Columbia University Press, 1994). For some two dozen post–Cold War materials on the Korean War, see Walter C. Clemens Jr., "North Korea and the World: A Bibliography of Books and URLs in English, 1997–2007," *Journal of East Asian Studies* 8 (2008): 293–325 at 297–299.

2. Thomas Christensen and Jack Snyder, "Chain Gangs and Passed Bucks: Predicting Alliance Patterns in Multipolarity," *International Organization* 44 (1990): 137–168.

3. Long excerpts from MacArthur's and Acheson's statements can be found in Se-Jin Kim, ed., *Documents on Korean-American Relations, 1943–1976* (Seoul: Research Center for Peace and Unification, 1976), 83–89.

4. Dean Acheson, *Present at the Creation: My Years in the State Department* (New York: W. W. Norton, 1987), 356–358.

5. Rhee to the U.S. ambassador-at-large, Philip C. Jessup. See Jessup's January 14, 1950, memorandum in *FRUS 1950* (GPO, 1976), 7: 1–7.

6. Putative archival material in the *The DPRK Report* (Moscow), no. 23 (March–April 2000) quoted in Jussi M. Hanhimäki and Odd Arne Westad, eds., *The Cold War: A History in Documents and Eyewitness Accounts* (New York: Oxford University Press, 2003), 185–186.

7. South Korean troops and agents had been conducting operations along and across the 38th parallel; but because they lacked tanks and heavy artillery or U.S. military support, the North Korean invasion cannot be justified as a preemptive strike.

8. http://www.wilsoncenter.org/publication/did-stalin-lure-the-united-states-the-korean-war-new-evidence-the-origins-the-korean-war (accessed 5/17/2014).

9. Chen Jian argues that China entered the war for its own reasons—to reassert its central place on the global stage—and that it was not a passive actor responding to pressures from Moscow or threats from the United States. Chen Jian, *China's Road to the Korean War*; see also Thomas Christensen, "Threats, Assurances, and the Last Chance for Peace: The Lessons of Mao's Korean War Telegrams," *International Security* 17, no. 1 (Summer 1992): 122–154.

10. "A North Korean Officer's Story," in Richard Peters and Xiaobing Li, eds., *Voices from the Korean War: Personal Stories of American, Korean, and Chinese Soldiers* (Lexington: University Press of Kentucky, 2004), 76–84.

11. Kennan to Acheson on August 21, 1950, in *FRUS 1950*, 7: 623–628.

12. Paul Nitze, a proponent of building up U.S. forces, agreed with Kennan that the Korean War overextended U.S. forces and, with Kennan, opposed UN forces advancing into North Korea. See Nicholas Thompson, *The Hawk and the Dove: Paul Nitze, George Kennan, and the History of the Cold War* (New York: Henry Holt, 2009), chap. 8.

13. A North Korean officer briefed the Chinese on the threat posed as the Americans proceeded north after Inchon. The Chinese recognized the material advantages of the U.S. forces but trusted in the morale and combat experience of their own. See General Hong Xuezhi, "The CPVF's Combat and Logistics," in Xiaobing Li, Allan R. Millett, and Bin Yu, trans. and ed., *Mao's Generals Remember Korea* (Lawrence: University Press of Kansas, 2001), 106–138 at 114–117. The book includes chapters by Marshal Peng Dehuai and Marshal Nie Rongzhen.

14. Alexandre Y. Mansourov, "Stalin, Mao, Kim, and China's Decision to Enter the Korean War, September 16–October 15, 1950: New Evidence from the Russian Archives," *Cold War International History Project Bulletin,* Issues 6–7 (Winter 1995–1996): 94–119 at 100.

15. For details on the Korean and other wars, see John Whiteclay Chambers II et al., eds., *The Oxford Companion to American Military History* (New York: Oxford University Press, 1999).

16. See, for example, Draft Memorandum Prepared by the Policy Planning Staff, Department of State, July 25, 1950, in *FRUS 1950,* 7: 469–473 at 471.

17. Bruce Cumings, "Korea: Forgotten Nuclear Threats," *Le Monde Diplomatique,* at https://mondediplo.com/2004/12/08korea (accessed 5/16/2010).

18. Headlined in the *New York Times,* December 1, 1950, along with a report of a Soviet veto in the UN Security Council of a resolution calling for the withdrawal of Chinese troops from Korea. Another report cited an editorial in Beijing's *People's Daily* demanding the withdrawal of UN troops from Korea, withdrawal of U.S. ships from Taiwan, and the seating of the People's Republic of China at the United Nations.

19. Truman's answers to questions from the press could not be quoted, but only paraphrased, which led to uncertainties about his precise meanings. *New York Times,* December 1, 1950, p. 3.

20. David McCullough, *Truman* (New York: Simon & Schuster, 1992), 832–833.

21. A DPRK pilot in 1950 described each side's air campaigns in Blaine Harden, *The Great Leader and the Fighter Pilot: The True Story of the Tyrant Who Created North Korea and the Young Lieutenant Who Stole His Way to Freedom* (New York: Viking, 2015).

22. William Taubman, *Khrushchev: The Man and His Era* (New York: W. W. Norton, 2003), 332, 732n30.

23. Marshal Xu Xiangqian, "The Purchase of Arms from Moscow," in *Mao's Generals,* 139–146.

24. "Minutes of Conversation between I. V. Stalin and Zhou Enlai," September 19, 1952, History and Public Policy Program Digital Archive, APRF, f. 45, op. 1, d. 343, lines 97–103, trans. Danny Rozas with Kathryn Weatersby, http://digitalarchive.wilsoncenter.org/document /111247 (accessed 5/21/2015).

25. Would these be ZIS or ZIM autos? Andrei Vyshinskii's notes on the meeting are unclear. Stalin seems to say that the ZIMs are smaller than the ZIS, but quite beautiful, and that the Chinese delegation would receive ZIMs. ZIS (factory named for Stalin) cars were built on Packard senior series dies sold to the USSR during World War II at the instigation of the U.S. government and used by top Soviet officials. ZIM (factory named for Molotov) cars were smaller and used by officials of intermediate rank. Both were heavy gas guzzlers.

26. John Lewis Gaddis, *George F. Kennan: An American Life* (New York: Penguin, 2011), 413.

27. Much of what follows derives from Shen Zhihua, "Alliance of 'Tooth and Lips' or Marriage of Convenience? The Origins and Development of the Sino-North Korean Alliance, 1946–1958," Working Paper series, WP 08-09 (Washington, DC: U.S.-Korea Institute at SAIS, December 2008); and Kathryn Weathersby, "Dependence and Mistrust: North Korea's Relations with Moscow and the Evolution of Juche," Working Paper series, WP 08-08 (Washington, DC: U.S.-Korea Institute at SAIS, December 2008).

28. With State Department support, private citizen George F. Kennan held several private meetings in May and June 1951 with Jakob Malik, Soviet ambassador to the United Nations. Kennan proposed a cease-fire along existing military positions, to be supervised by an international authority. The Soviets agreed and pressed the North Koreans and Chinese to begin negotiations with the U.S. military command. Gaddis, *George F. Kennon*, 426–429.

29. The following paragraphs are based on Hungarian diplomatic reports analyzed in Balázs Szalontai, "Four Horsemen of the Apocalypse in North Korea," introductory essay in Christ Springer, *North Korea Caught in Time: Images of War and Reconstruction* (Reading, UK: Garnet, 2010), ix–xxvii. A similar picture emerges in Taewoo Kim, "Overturned Time and Space: Drastic Changes in the Daily Lives of North Koreans during the Korean War," *Asian Journal of Peacebuilding* 2, no. 2 (November 2014): 241–262, which draws on National History Compilation Committee, ed., *Hangukjeonjaeng, munseo wa jaryo, 1950–53* [*The Korean War, Documents and Data, 1950–53*] (Seoul: NHCC, 2006), as well as on DPRK, Soviet, and U.S. sources.

30. Robert Frank Futrell, *The United States Air Force in Korea, 1950–1953*, rev. ed. (Washington, DC: Office of Air Force History, 1983).

31. As described above in the prologue, a film and exhibition on these themes were shown at the World Congress of the Peoples for Peace in December 1952.

32. Jager, *Brothers at War*, 257.

33. L. P. Beria to G. M. Malenkov, April 21, 1953, in *CWIHP Bulletin*, Issue 11 (Winter 1998) at 183. The Chinese, North Koreans, and Soviets blamed each other for what became an embarrassing deception. Ibid., 180–199.

34. Minutes of Conversation between I. V. Stalin and Zhou Enlai.

35. Stueck, *Korean War*, 311; also "American President: A Reference Resource," at http://millercenter.org/president/eisenhower/essays/biography/5 (accessed 4/30/2015).

36. Roger Dingman, "Atomic Diplomacy during the Korean War," *International Security* 13, no. 3 (Winter 1988–1989): 50–91.

37. Haruki, *The Korean War*, 28–29; Dmitri Volkogonov, *Triumf i tragediia: politicheskiĭ portret I. V. Stalina* (Moscow: Izd-vo Agenstva pechati Novosti, 1989); and Volkogonov, *Stalin: Triumph and Tragedy* (New York: Grove Weidenfeld, 1991).

38. James I. Matray, "Revisiting Korea: Exposing Myths of the Forgotten War, Part 2," *Prologue* 34, no. 2 (Summer 2002); Haruki, *The Korean War*, 267.

39. The Eisenhower administration later asserted that it finally broke the stalemate at Panmunjom by virtue of its "unmistakable warning" to Beijing that it would use nuclear weapons against China if an armistice were not reached. See James Shepley, "How Dulles Averted War," *Life*, January 16, 1956, 70–72; Dwight D. Eisenhower, *The White House Years: Mandate for Change, 1953–1956* (Garden City, NY: Doubleday and Co., 1963), 179–180. But the sequence of events does not support this interpretation. The Eisenhower administration began in February and March 1953 to discuss the use of atomic bombs in Korea, but it made

no public threats until May 1953—when the three Communist governments were already moving to end the war. See Jager, *Brothers at War,* 268–277; Haruki, *The Korean War,* 257–262; Dingman, "Atomic Diplomacy"; Rosemary Foot, "Nuclear Coercion and the Ending of the Korean Conflict," *International Security* 13, no. 3 (Winter 1988–1989): 92–112.

40. Haruki, *The Korean War,* 293-294. Estimates of military and civilian casualties range widely.

41. United States official documents give estimates of between 35,000 and 55,000 servicemen and-women killed in the Korean War. The lower estimate sometimes adds that at least 8,000 were missing in action.

42. Xiaobing Li, Allan R. Millett, and Bin Yu, "Introduction," in *Mao's Generals,* 6, 25. Citing Chinese materials, they estimated Chinese outlays at between 6.2 billion and 10 billion yuan.

43. Ibid., 26–27.

44. William Dean, *General Dean's Story* (New York: Viking Press, 1954), 272–275.

45. Szalontai, "Four Horsemen," xi. The photos in Springer, *North Korea Caught in Time,* give credence to the diplomat's report and that of General Dean.

46. Tak-young Hamm, *Arming the Two Koreas: State, Capital, and Military Power* (London: Routledge, 1990), 133; Nicholas Eberstadt and Judith Banister, *The Population of North Korea* (Berkeley: University of California Press, 1992), 32.

47. Szalontai, "Four Horsemen," xix.

48. Ibid., xxvi.

49. Geoffrey Perret, *Commander in Chief: How Truman, Johnson, and Bush Turned a Presidential Power into a Threat to America's Future* (New York: Farrar, Straus and Giroux, 2007), 6.

50. As noted in the prologue, some Japanese resented a situation in which they felt compelled by economic pressures to provide blood for U.S. wounded in Korea.

6. How North Korea Got the Bomb

1. Etel Solingen, *Nuclear Logics: Contrasting Paths in East Asia and the Middle East* (Princeton, NJ: Princeton University Press, 2007).

2. Avner Cohen and Steven Lee, eds., *Nuclear Weapons and the Future of Humanity: The Fundamental Questions* (Lanham, MD: Rowman & Littlefield, 1986).

3. Jacques E. C. Hymans, "Discarding Tired Assumptions about North Korea," *Bulletin of the Atomic Scientists,* May 28, 2009, at http://www.thebulletin.org/node/7115 (accessed 06/03/2009); for more details, see Hymans, "Assessing North Korean Nuclear Intentions and Capacities: A New Approach," *Journal of East Asian Studies* 8, no. 2 (May–August 2008): 259–292.

4. Michael J. Mazarr, *North Korea and the Bomb: A Case Study in Nonproliferation* (New York: St. Martin's, 1996), 17.

5. Bruce Bennett, "The Sixty Years of the Korea-U.S. Security Alliance: Past, Present, and Future," *International Journal of Korean Studies* 17, no. 2 (Fall–Winter 2013): 15–17, http://www.icks.org/publication/pdf/2013-FALL-WINTER/2.pdf (accessed 5/24/2014).

6. The armistice obliged the signatories to "cease the introduction into Korea of reinforcing combat aircraft, armored vehicles, weapons, and ammunition; provided however, that combat aircraft, armored vehicles, weapons, and ammunition which are destroyed, damaged, worn out, or used up during the period of the armistice may

be replaced on the basis piece-for-piece of the *same effectiveness and the same type"* (emphasis added).

7. On invitation, several U.S. students, myself included, visited Dubna in 1958.

8. Document 10 in William E. Griffith, *The Sino-Soviet Rift* (Cambridge: MIT Press, 1964), 388–420 at 399.

9. Walter C. Clemens Jr., *The Arms Race and Sino-Soviet Relations* (Stanford, CA: Hoover Institution, 1968).

10. Nie Rongzhen, *Nie Rongzhen hui yi lu,* 2nd ed., 3 vols. (Beijing: Zhan shi chu ban she, 1983), vol. 3.

11. Olli Heinonen, "North Korea's Nuclear Enrichment: Capabilities and Consequences," *38 North*.org, June 22, 2011, at http://belfercenter.ksg.harvard.edu/publication/21153/north_koreas_nuclear_enrichment.html (accessed 3/5/2014).

12. http://digitalarchive.wilsoncenter.org/document/115925 (accessed 5/6/2015).

13. Liang Zhi, "North Korean Apprentices in China and the Nature of Socialist Exchanges in the 1950s," introduction to http://www.wilsoncenter.org/publication/north-korean-apprentices-china-and-the-nature-socialist-exchanges-the-1950s?mkt_tok=3RkMMJWWfF9wsRouuqvBZKXonjHpfsX56uwkUa601MI%2F0ER3fOvrPUfGjI4ATMRkNq%2BTFAwTG5toziV8R7LEJc1tzMAQXRXh (accessed 9/16/2014).

14. The following is a list of documents used here and in the rest of this chapter, and are cited in the text where appropriate. All are available from the Woodrow Wilson International Center for Scholars, Cold War International History Project, North Korean Nuclear History, archived at http://digitalarchive.wilsoncenter.org/collection/113/north-korean-nuclear-history (accessed 4/17/2014).

Document 1: Conversation between Soviet Ambassador in North Korea Vasily Moskovsky and the German Ambassador, August 26, 1963.

Document 2: Conversation between Soviet Ambassador in North Korea Vasily Moskovsky and Soviet specialists in North Korea, September 27, 1963.

Document 3: Report, Embassy of Hungary in North Korea to the Hungarian Foreign Ministry, January 11, 1964 ("!" in the original document, which should not be confused with another report by the Hungarian ambassador on that date).

Document 4: Report, Embassy of Hungary in North Korea to the Hungarian Foreign Ministry, March 13, 1967.

Document 5: Report, Embassy of Hungary in North Korea to the Hungarian Foreign Ministry, February 29, 1968.

Document 6: Report, Embassy of Hungary in the Soviet Union to the Hungarian Foreign Ministry, November 12, 1969.

Document 7: Report, Embassy of Hungary in North Korea to the Hungarian Foreign Ministry, July 30, 1975.

Document 8: Memorandum, Hungarian Foreign Ministry, February 16, 1976.

Document 9: Report, Embassy of Hungary in North Korea to the Hungarian Foreign Ministry, February 18, 1976.

Document 10: Report, Embassy of Hungary in North Korea to the Hungarian Foreign Ministry, April 15, 1976.

Document 11: Telegram, Embassy of Hungary in North Korea to the Hungarian Foreign Ministry, June 25, 1976.

Document 12: Memorandum, Branch Office of the Hungarian Ministry of Foreign Trade in Pyongyang to the Hungarian Ministry of Foreign Trade, August 9, 1976.

Document 13: Memorandum, Hungarian National Commission of Atomic Energy to the Hungarian Foreign Ministry, August 31, 1976.

Document 14: Report, Embassy of Hungary in North Korea to the Hungarian Foreign Ministry, December 8, 1976 (part of the virtual archive but not cited in this chapter).

Document 15: Telegram, Embassy of Hungary in the Soviet Union to the Hungarian Foreign Ministry, January 20, 1977.

Document 16: Memorandum, Hungarian Foreign Ministry, February 16, 1977.

Document 17: Report, Embassy of Hungary in North Korea to the Hungarian Foreign Ministry, November 21, 1977.

Document 18: Telegram, Embassy of Hungary in North Korea to the Hungarian Foreign Ministry, February 17, 1979.

Document 19: Report, Embassy of Hungary in North Korea to the Hungarian Foreign Ministry, March 12, 1981.

Document 20: Report, Embassy of Hungary in North Korea to the Hungarian Foreign Ministry, April 30, 1981.

Document 21: Memorandum, Hungarian Academy of Sciences to the Hungarian Foreign Ministry, March 7, 1983.

Document 22: Letter, Hungarian Foreign Ministry to the Hungarian Academy of Sciences, April 6, 1983.

Document 23: Report, Embassy of Hungary in North Korea to the Hungarian Foreign Ministry, March 9, 1985.

Document 24: Report, Embassy of Hungary in North Korea to the Hungarian Foreign Ministry, May 30, 1988.

Additional details of many events described in this chapter—names, official positions, dates, places, and documentary references—are given in Walter C. Clemens Jr., "North Korea's Quest for Nuclear Weapons: New Historical Evidence," *Journal of East Asian Studies* 10, no. 1 (January–April 2010): 127–154.

15. Kathryn Weathersby, "Dependence and Mistrust: North Korea's Relations with Moscow and the Evolution of Juche," Working Paper series, WP 08-08 (Washington, DC: U.S.-Korea Institute at SAIS, December 2008).

16. Ibid.

17. Heinonen, "North Korea's Nuclear Enrichment."

18. William C. Potter, Djuro Miljanic, and Ivo Slavs, "Tito's Nuclear Legacy," *Bulletin of the Atomic Scientists* 56, no. 2 (March–April 2000): 63–70.

19. Don Oberdorfer and Robert Carlin, *The Two Koreas: A Contemporary History*, rev. ed. (New York: Basic Books, 2014), 197.

20. Andrei Lankov, "The Troubled Russia-North Korea Alliance," *Asia Times Online*, December 25, 2004, at http://www.atimes.com/atimes/Korea/FL25Dg01.html (accessed 4/29/2009).

21. IAEA, "In Focus: IAEA and the DPRK," at http://www.iaea.org/NewsCenter/Focus/IaeaDprk/fact_sheet_may2003.shtml (accessed 7/15/2009). See also Christine Wing and Fiona Simpson, *Detect, Dismantle, and Disarm: IAEA Verification, 1992–2005* (Washington, DC: United States Institute of Peace Press, 2013); and Mazarr, *North Korea and the Bomb*, 25.

22. Robert A. Wampler, ed., *North Korea and Nuclear Weapons: The Declassified U.S. Record; National Security Archive Electronic Briefing Book no. 87* (2003), documents 1 and 2, at http://www.gwu.edu/~nsarchiv/NSAEBB/NSAEBB87/#docs (accessed 1/2/2009).

23. Simon Henderson, "The Nuclear Handshake: Is the Pakistani-Saudi Weapons Program for Real?" *Foreign Policy,* November 8, 2013, at http://www.foreignpolicy.com/articles/2013/11/08/the_nuclear_handshake_saudi_arabia_pakistan (accessed 5/15/2014). For more on China and Pakistan, see Chidanand Rajghatta, "AQ Letter Reveals Pak's N-tryst with China," *Times of India,* September 26, 2011.

24. An earlier North Korean attack on ROK leaders in Rangoon in October 1983 killed twenty-one persons and wounded forty-six.

25. Oberdorfer and Carlin, *Two Koreas,* 195–196.

26. Michael J. Mazarr, "Predator States and War: The North Korean Case," in Tong Whan Park, ed., *The U.S. and the Two Koreas: A New Triangle* (Boulder, CO: Lynne Rienner, 1998), 85.

27. IAEA, "In Focus: IAEA and the DPRK."

28. John S. Park, "Nuclear Ambition and Tension on the Korean Peninsula," in Ashley J. Tellis, Abraham M. Denmark, and Travis Tanner, eds., *Strategic Asia 2013–2014: Asia in the Second Nuclear Age* (Seattle: National Bureau of Asian Research, 2013), 163–199.

29. Weathersby, "Dependence and Mistrust," 21.

30. Pervez Musharraf, *In the Line of Fire: A Memoir* (New York: Free Press, 2006), 296.

31. Heinonen, "North Korea's Nuclear Enrichment."

32. The unnamed expert supplied this comment to Jeffrey Lewis, at http://lewis.armscontrolwonk.com/archive/4234/memo-from-jon-byong-ho (accessed 5/18/2014).

33. Sharon A. Squassoni, "Weapons of Mass Destruction: Trade between North Korea and Pakistan," *CRS* [Congressional Reference Service, Library of Congress] *Report to Congress,* October 11, 2006, at https://www.fas.org/sgp/crs/nuke/RL31900.pdf (accessed 10/10/2012).

34. R. Jeffrey Smith, "Pakistan's Nuclear-Bomb Maker Says North Korea Paid Bribes for Know-How," *Washington Post,* July 6, 2011, with a link to the putative letter: http://www.washingtonpost.com/wp-srv/world/documents/north-korea-letter.html (accessed 10/10/2012).

35. For his remarkable life story, see https://nkleadershipwatch.wordpress.com/leadership-biographies/jon-pyong-ho/ (accessed 5/16/2014).

7. Human Insecurity and the Duty to Protect

1. Adam Johnson, *The Orphan Master's Son* (New York: Random House, 2012).

2. To get a feel for what happens inside North Korea—for ordinary citizens and for elites—a good novel may do as well as, or better than, academic social science. Consider how professional histories of 1812 compare with Leo Tolstoy's *War and Peace.* Tolstoy often avoids or strays from historical fact, but he conveys brilliantly how Napoleon's invasion shaped family life in Russia and even how Napoleon and other leaders surveyed the chaos at Borodino. Johnson made up parts of his story to cover the inner workings of the DPRK police state, drawing on, for example, the biographical reports of persons about to be executed in Khmer Rouge Cambodia (e-mail, Johnson to Clemens, January 6, 2014). The feel of North Korean politics is also captured in Michael Malice, *Dear Reader: The Unauthorized Autobiography of Kim Jong Il* (n.p., 2014), based on publications that Malice acquired when he visited Pyongyang.

3. Bradley K. Martin, *Under the Loving Care of the Fatherly Leader: North Korea and the Kim Dynasty* (New York: Thomas Dunne Books, 2004).

4. A. Henry Savage-Landor, *Corea; or, Cho-Sen: The Land of the Morning Calm* (New York: Macmillan, 1895), 242–243.

5. Ibid., 246–247.

6. Five defectors' autobiographical stories converge in description of life in North Korea. Each includes details about forced sex in China in exchange for food and temporary security. See the review by Louisa Lim, "Fleeing North Korea," *New York Times Book Review*, November 29, 2015.

7. Kyung-Ae Park, ed., *Non-Traditional Security Issues in North Korea* (Honolulu: University of Hawai'i Press, 2013).

8. Jang Jin-sung, "I Am Selling My Daughter for 100 Won," http://www.asialiteraryreview .com/web/article/en/337 (accessed 1/30/2013). For the poet's own story, see Jang Jin-sung, *Dear Leader: Poet, Spy, Escapee—a Look inside North Korea* (New York: Simon & Schuster, 2014).

9. Stephan Haggard and Marcus Noland, *Witness to Transformation: Refugee Insights into North Korea* (Washington, DC: Peterson Institute for International Economics, 2011). The first survey of 1,346 refugees was conducted from August 2004 to September 2005 in China; the second, of 300 refugees, from August to November 2008, in the Republic of Korea. The China survey was conducted by South Korean researchers assisted by Chinese NGOs and church groups; the second, with assistance from the Association of Supporters for Defecting North Korean Residents, a quasi-governmental organization in the ROK. The questionnaires used in the two surveys were not identical. Haggard and Nolan took account of these limitations and approached their inferences with scholarly caution. Their *Witness to Transformation* offers a social science picture that parallels *Nothing to Envy: Ordinary Lives in North Korea* (New York: Spiegel & Grau, 2010) by journalist Barbara Demick, with its six in-depth portraits of ordinary persons who fled the country. An even more detailed account is that of Yong Kim, a onetime believer in the regime, in *Long Road Home: Testimony of a North Korea Camp Survivor* (New York: Columbia University Press, 2009).

10. Sharon LaFraniere, "Views Show How North Korea Policy Spread Misery," *New York Times*, June 9, 2010.

11. Ibid.

12. For analysis, see Yonho Kim, "Cell Phones in North Korea: Has North Korea Entered the Telecommunications Revolution?" presentation at U.S.-Korea Institute, SAIS, March 6, 2014.

13. Louisa Lim, "Hunger Still Haunts North Korea, Citizens Say," *NPR*, December 10, 2012 at http://www.npr.org/2012/12/10/166760055/hunger-still-haunts-north-korea-citizens-say (accessed 11/12/2014).

14. Jieun Baek, "A Human Moment from the Most Isolated Place in the World," at http://www.policymic.com/articles/62863/a-human-moment-from-the-most-isolated-place-in-the-world (accessed 3/31/2014).

15. Felix Abt, *A Capitalist in North Korea: My Seven Years in the Hermit Kingdom* (Rutland, VT: Tuttle, 2012).

16. Ralph Hassig and Kongdan Oh. *The Hidden People of North Korea: Life in the Hermit Kingdom*, 2nd ed. (Lanham, MD: Rowman & Littlefield, 2015), 1–2.

17. As we shall see in chapter 15, the United States agreed on February 29, 2012, to supply nutritional supplements to North Korea on condition that it refrain from more nuclear and missile tests. Two weeks later, the DPRK announced that it would launch a satellite to

honor the 100th birthday of Kim Il Sung. The test took place in April, and the deal was off—killing an exchange of food for arms control.

18. According to the foundation's home page, EugeneBell USA is a not-for-profit 501(c)(3) organization established in 1995 by Dr. Stephen Winn Linton, whose views on dealing with Pyongyang are discussed below in chapter 11.

19. Reported by Yonhap News Agency, November 17, 2013.

20. See Stephen Weber, Marcus Noland, and others at http://www.theguardian.com/world/series/north-korea-network, September 11, 2014 (accessed 5/7/2015).

21. According to one critic, the Swiss Agency for Development and Cooperation slashed the budget for paper and pencils for the Pyongyang Business School and for reading materials for seminars it sponsored. It then proceeded to buy at least six new vehicles, including Toyota Land Cruisers. See Abt, *A Capitalist,* 267.

22. Kyung-Ryang Kim, "South Korea's Official Development Aid and Saemaul Undong: Its Value and Limitations," EAF Policy Debates No. 25, April 28, 2015, at http://www.keaf.org/book/EAF_Policy_Debates_N025_South_Koreas_Official_Development_Aid_and_Saemaul_Undong:_Its_Value_and_Limitations?ckattempt=1 (accessed 4/27/2015).

23. http://www.ohchr.org/en/hrbodies/hrc/coidprk/pages/commissioninquiryonhrindprk.aspx (accessed 3/4/2014).

24. For an oral report by the commission chair, Michael Kirby, on September 16, 2013, in Geneva, see http://www.ohchr.org/Documents/HRBodies/HRCouncil/CoIDPRK/FINALCOIDPRK_HRC_Oral_Update17Sep2013.pdf (accessed 3/4/2014).

25. Fyodor Tertitskiy, "Songbun and the Five Castes of North Korea," February 26, 2015, at http://www.nknews.org/2015/02/songbun-and-the-five-castes-of-north-korea/ (accessed 4/6/2015).

26. The defector Shin In Geun claimed that he was imprisoned from birth; often lived on rodents, lizards and grass; and had witnessed the public execution of his mother and brother. He earlier told his story to ROK officials and to Blaine Harden, who then wrote *Escape from Camp 14: One Man's Remarkable Odyssey from North Korea to Freedom in the West* (New York: Viking, 2010). Shin later modified his account. See Anna Fifield, "Prominent N. Korean Defector Shin Dong-hyuk Admits Parts of Story Are Inaccurate," *Washington Post,* January 17, 2015 (accessed 4/9/2015). But Shin's partial retraction did not alter the substance of his narrative or that of other defectors. According to Harden, Shin continued to say "that all this happened, but . . . at different times and places." Harden said that Shin's stunted body, the skin over his pubis, his scarred ankles, and his missing finger were all due to conditions and punishments imposed at the camp where he was born and lived until his escape at age twenty. See Harden, *Escape,* 2.

27. U.S. government statistics at http://www.prb.org/Publications/Articles/2012/us-incarceration.aspx (accessed 3/3/2014).

28. For a brief history, see http://www.un.org/en/preventgenocide/adviser/responsibility.shtml, dated April 16, 2014 (accessed 7/16/2014).

29. http://www.securitycouncilreport.org/atf/cf/%7B65BFCF9B-6D27-4E9C-8CD3-CF6E4FF96FF9%7D/s_pv_7353.pdf (accessed 5/11/2015).

30. Associated Press interview quoted in the *New York Times,* February 2, 2015.

31. Anna Fifield in *Washington Post,* January 23, 2015.

32. Quoted in http://www.securitycouncilreport.org/atf/cf/%7B65BFCF9B-6D27-4E9C-8CD3-CF6E4FF96FF9%7D/s_2015_90.pdf (accessed 5/11/2015). For related devel-

opments, see http://www.securitycouncilreport.org/un-documents/dprk-north-korea/ (accessed 5/11/2015).

33. Noted approvingly by Stephan Haggard on February 23, 2015, at http://blogs.piie .com/nk/?p=13899 (accessed 5/11/2015).

34. Nobel peace prize laureate José Ramos-Horta and others at http://www.huffingtonpost .co.uk/ben/north-korea-human-rights_b_6702258.html (accessed 5/11/2015).

8. Facing Up to Evil

Epigraph sources: Jack Rendler, an American who worked in Korea and later taught English and human rights in a Buddhist monastery in Myanmar, e-mail to author, August 29, 2014. Hannah Arendt, *Eichmann in Jerusalem: A Report on the Banality of Evil* (New York: Viking, 1963). Davia Temin, "The Sociopath in the Office Next Door," referencing Martha Stout, *The Sociopath Next Door,* at http://www.forbes.com/2010/11/19/sociopath-boss-work-forbes-woman-leadership-office-evil.html (accessed 9/1/2014). Lesley H. Gelb, "In the End Every President Talks to the Bad Guys," *Washington Post,* April 27, 2008.

1. "We" here refers to the United States, the Republic of Korea, and Japan—the three democracies in the six-party talks with North Korea that began in 2003. However, the arguments presented here probably apply to other cases as well, where democracies confront regimes whose words and deeds may appear evil.

2. Robert Mnookin, *Bargaining with the Devil: When to Negotiate, When to Fight* (New York: Simon & Schuster, 2010).

3. See David Brooks, "Obama, Gospel, and Verse," *New York Times,* April 26, 2007.

4. See, e.g., Reinhold Niebuhr, *The Irony of American History,* introduction by Andrew J. Bacevich (Chicago: University of Chicago Press, 2008 [1st ed. 1952]). Niebuhr received both praise and vilification by left and right, as well as by Christians who take him as their guide and others who question his Christianity. See Paul Elie, "A Man for All Reasons," *Atlantic Monthly,* November 2007. Obama's pastor in Chicago, Reverend Jeremiah Wright—like Martin Luther King Jr. and Jimmy Carter—also claimed Niebuhr as a major influence on his thought.

5. Walter C. Clemens Jr., "Lenin on Disarmament," *Slavic Review,* 23, no. 3 (September 1964): 504–525. Morality, Lenin told the League of Young Communists in 1920, did not drop from the skies. It was whatever advanced the cause of proletarian revolution. By this logic, "evil" was anything that obstructed the revolution.

6. Cheney quoted in Leslie H. Gelb, "In the End, Every President Talks to the Bad Guys," *Washington Post,* April 27, 2008; Ivo H. Daalder, "Only Real Negotiations Can Test North Korea," Brookings Institution, February 24, 2008, at http://www.brookings.edu/ research/opinions/2004/02/24northkorea-daalder (accessed 5/10/2008).

7. Mnookin, *Bargaining with the Devil,* 15.

8. The absolutist view dominated Western thinking until the late nineteenth century, but then gradually melted. Homosexual acts once seen as evil became merely deviant and then normal. Evil in French is *le mal,* but *mal* also signifies illness, pain, sorrow, or difficulty. The exorcist or voodoo priest can be seen as a force for evil—or for good—depending on the intention and context of his acts. See Richard Paul Hamilton and Margaret Sönser Breen, eds., *This Thing of Darkness: Perspectives on Evil and Human Wickedness* (Amsterdam: Rodopi, 2004). One essay in the Hamilton-Breen anthology suggests that an evildoer is one whose reasons for his actions no longer mitigate them. Thus, if a vampire must drink

blood to live, feeding on blood may not be evil. Another view says the only acts by the vampire that are evil are needlessly violent feedings. Katri Lehtinen, "Twentieth-Century Vampire Literature: Intimations of Evil and Power," ibid., 14.

9. New York, Illinois, Louisiana, and Kentucky could claim the title of "most corrupt state" in 2015. On a per-capita basis, Louisiana led the pack, but New York competed vigorously. Three of its past four Senate leaders had been indicted, a governor was forced to resign for hiring prostitutes, and the comptroller was found to be taking kickbacks. Dean Skelos, New York Senate majority leader, became the twenty-third New York State lawmaker to be indicted or charged with a crime since 2010. Thomas Libous, number two in the Senate, was scheduled to go on trial in summer 2015 on charges of lying to the FBI. See Evan Osnos, "Daddy Issues: Corruption in New York and Shanghai," *New Yorker,* May 7, 2015.

10. Many worldviews allow a major role for Evil as well as Good in human affairs—for example, Zoroastrianism, Manicheanism, and Spinoza's teachings. How the two forces intertwine and link human and supernatural is depicted in the sacred Barong and Rangda dances of Bali. The Barang animal mask represents good, and its types include the tiger, boar, buffalo, and the mythical animal *kek*. Evil is personified by Rangda—literally "widow," but interpreted as a witch associated with spirits of the dead. Several men armed with daggers accompany Rangda when she steps onto the stage. Under her influence, the dancers enter a trance and stab themselves, but they are protected from injury by Barong's presence. Barong's eventual victory is taken to affirm his protection of the village. Though interpreted as good versus evil, the two sides are more equivocal, and Barong's victory is never regarded as conclusive. I witnessed this dance in 1970 and again in 1983. An American woman who studied dance in Bali in the 1970s departed after two years, frightened by what she perceived as evil powers in the culture.

11. Edmund White, "Divine Decadence," review of Francine Prose, *Lovers at the Chameleon Club, Paris 1932, New York Times Book Review,* April 20, 2014, 1, 22. Orhan Pamuk points out in the same issue that "Rabbit," the protagonist in four of John Updike's books, is a "demonic, ethically troubled but also entirely ordinary character" in "Updike at Rest," review of Adam Begley, *Updike,* in ibid., 10–11. William Saletan in the same issue depicts Lance Armstrong as the "perfect predator, more aggressive and proficient than any of his competitors at exploiting chemical technology." See "Taken for a Ride," review of Juliet Macur, *Cycle of Lies,* and Reed Albergotti and Vanessa O'Connell, *Wheelmen* in ibid, 18. Whereas Armstrong's parents helped him doctor his birth certificate at age fourteen to enter a race, another book reviewed in that issue describes a brother and sister raised (almost ignored) by utopian parents, who find it hard if not impossible to navigate reality. Julie Myerson, "Innocence Project," a review of Leah Hager Cohen, *No Book but the World* (ibid., 14). *The Tyranny of Experts* by William Easterly, reviewed by Howard W. French, "Spare the Advice," (ibid., 20) argues that World Bank–type experts have betrayed the world's poor by backing "the unchecked power of the state against poor people without rights."

12. The grown sons of Dean Skelos and Thomas Libous were accused along with their fathers. When Long Island was flooding in December 2014, son Adam Skelos, son of Senate majority leader Dean Skelos, was recorded cheering the profits produced by "major water problems here with all the flooding going on. . . . I love it! Keep it coming, Mother Nature!" Dean replied, "It will," as both father and son laughed. Osnos, "Daddy Issues."

13. On May 19, 2014, Credit Suisse pleaded guilty to helping American clients avoid paying U.S. taxes and agreed to a $2.6 billion fine. The same day the FBI posted mug shots of

five Chinese officers wanted for computer fraud. Putin said Russian troops were pulled back from the RF border with Ukraine, but NATO said most of them were still there.

14. Leo Tolstoy, *War and Peace* (1868), vol. 1, part 1, chap. 28. Earlier, Goethe put forward the same idea: "Denn wer einmal uns versteht / Wird uns auch verzeihn." See his "Derb und Tüchtig," in *Westöstlicher Divan* (1819).

15. Allan Bullock, *Hitler and Stalin Parallel Lives*, 2nd ed. (New York: Vintage, 1993).

16. I. Ivlev, "General'skaia lozh,'" *Voenno-istoricheskii arkhiv* 9, no. 153 (2012): 41–58.

17. Timothy Snyder, "Neglecting the Lithuanian Holocaust," *New York Review of Books*, July 25, 2011. See also United States Holocaust Memorial Museum, at http://somewereneighbors .ushmm.org/about/exhibit (accessed 5/9/2015).

18. Rudolph J. Rummel, *Death by Government* (New Brunswick, NJ: Transaction, 1994), 8; and *Lethal Politics: Soviet Genocide and Mass Murder since 1917* (New Brunswick, NJ: Transaction, 1990), 6.

19. B. R. Myers, *The Cleanest Race: How North Koreans See Themselves and Why It Matters* (Brooklyn: Melville House, 2010).

20. For the rationale, see the author's articles "Why Not Indict War Criminals in Moscow?" *Behind the Breaking News* 2, no. 1 (February 23, 2000), Institute for the Study of Conflict, Ideology and Policy, Boston University; "Russia Has No Business Holding Chechnya," *International Herald Tribune*, February 28, 1995, p. 8; also published as "Mengapa Chechnya Harus Tetar Menjadi Bagian Rusia?" *Suara Pemearuan* (Jakarta), February 8, 1995, p. 2; and "What the World Needs Now: A Genocide Court," *Christian Science Monitor*, July 26, 1994, p. 17.

21. One diplomat described the late Serbian president Slobodan Milošević as "the sleaziest person you've ever met," armed with an IQ of 160. Many mediators have felt uneasy dealing with suspected genocidists but did so as part of the job. Still, Lord Owen (trained as a physician) could not bring himself to discuss medicine with Bosnian Serb leader Radovan Karadžić, a former psychiatrist but also an accused war criminal. Owen's partner in Balkan mediation, Cyrus Vance, believed that a mediator should not see anyone as evil incarnate. But he also thought compromise with persons so evil as Hitler impossible. Vance added, however, that with Saddam Hussein "we probably should have given talks more time." Leslie H. Gelb, "Vance: A Nobel Life," *New York Times*, March 2, 1992, p. A15.

22. The juxtapositions Light (*aša*) versus Dark and Truth versus Falsehood can be traced back at least to Zoroaster, who lived in what is now Iran early in the second millennium BCE. Elements of Zoroastrianism and Mesopotamian philosophy (as in the epic tale *Gilgamesh*) influenced both Judaism and Greek philosophy. According to the Hebrew scriptures, God created the heavens and the earth and all its creatures in six days. The creator looked at all he had made and found it "very *good*" (emphasis added). He then created the first man and placed him in a Garden of Eden, adjacent to the Tigris and Euphrates rivers. Nearby was the land of Havilah, blessed with gold that is "*good*." But God cautioned the man, saying: "You may eat from every tree in the garden, but not from the tree of the knowledge of *good and evil*. If you eat from it, you will certainly die." Having seen it was "not *good*" for man to be alone, God created a woman to be his partner. Soon, the serpent came and tempted the woman, saying, "If you eat fruit from this tree, your eyes will be opened and you will be like the gods knowing both *good and evil*." The woman ate of the fruit and gave some to her husband. Their eyes were opened, but all they saw was their nakedness. The Lord God gave them animals' skins to wear but cast them from the garden, forcing them to labor and live by the sweat of their brow.

23. Free will or determinism? Zoroaster (aka Zarathustra) extolled free will. By think-

ing good thoughts, saying good words, and doing good deeds (assisting the needy or doing good works) we increase the divine force *aša* in the world and in ourselves Many Jews and Christians, however, believe that all humans are polluted by the Original Sin of the first humans. Early Christian teachers such as Irenaeus, Ambrose, and Augustine taught that all humanity inherits the guilt of Original Sin. For Augustine, this guilt is transmitted to Adam's descendants by the sexual act and "concupiscence"—taking pleasure in human flesh instead of God. Just as the law and order of Rome were being ravaged by barbarians, Augustine saw human reason and dignity degraded by sexual passion. More than a millennium later and influenced by Augustine, both Martin Luther and John Calvin equated Original Sin with concupiscence and asserted that this guilt persists even after baptism. Salvation, for them, depended on God's grace or even on predestination. Dutch and French Jansenists, condemned by Jesuits and others within the Roman Catholic church, also held that Original Sin virtually destroyed free choice. Standard Catholic doctrine disagrees. *The Catechism of the Catholic Church* promulgated by Pope John Paul II in 1992 asserts that "Adam, as the first man, lost the original holiness and justice he had received from God, not only for himself but for all humans. Adam and Eve transmitted to their descendants human nature wounded by their own first sin and hence deprived of original holiness and justice." As a result, humans are subject to ignorance, suffering, concupiscence, and death. No one is personally guilty because of what Adam and Eve did, but—apart from the mother of Jesus—all humans are *inclined* to sin. "By our first parents' sin, the devil has acquired a certain domination over man, even though man remains free." Most Muslim theologians have been even less deterministic. They agree that God expelled Adam and Eve from Eden but taught that God forgave them their sin: no one inherits their guilt.

24. Luther was sharp with all his adversaries, but most Protestant theologians treated him with respect. Most Catholics did not. See Mark U. Edwards Jr., *Luther and the False Brethren* (Stanford, CA: Stanford University Press, 1975).

25. "*Er nennt's Vernunft und braucht's allein, nur tierischer als jedes Tier zu sein*" (He calls it Reason, but uses it only to act more beastly than any animal), *Faust*, lines 285–286.

26. *La voluntad y la fortuna* (México, DF: Alfaguara, 2008), poorly rendered in English as *Destiny and Desire* (New York: Random House, 2011).

27. *Faust*, 317.

28. Peter Lanza, father of the Sandy Hook shooter, loved his son, but Adam would not see him for two years before his shooting rampage in a school on December 14, 2012. Later, the father dreamed that he saw Adam and sensed that he embodied "the worst possible evilness." The father wished Adam had never been born. Andrew Solomon, "The Reckoning," *New Yorker*, March 17, 2014.

29. Sunny Lee, "The Pleasure's All the Dear Leader's," *Asia Times*, February 23, 2011, at www.atimes.com/atimes/Korea/MB23Dg01.html (accessed 02/23/2011).

30. Steven Pinker, *The Better Angels of Our Nature: Why Violence Has Declined* (New York: Viking, 2011).

31. Ian Morris, *War! What Is It Good For?* (New York: Farrar, Straus and Giroux, 2014).

32. Regarding a woman accused of adultery, Jesus said, "Let him who is without sin cast the first stone at her" (John 8:7).

33. The same critique applies to the USSR and its ostensible ideals. See Walter C. Clemens Jr., "The Superpowers and the Third World: Aborted Ideals and Wasted Assets," in C. W. Kegley and P. J. McGowan, eds., *Sage International Yearbooks in Foreign Policy Studies*, vol. 7, *Foreign Policy: USA/USSR* (Beverly Hills, CA: Sage, 1982), 111–135.

34. Though U.S. and Canadian policies changed, the effects of past cruelties lingered. The public health of Native Americans for much of the twentieth and twenty-first centuries was worse than that of any other group in the United States. The shorter life spans and lower incomes of Afro-Americans derive in part from the servitude of their ancestors.

35. They followed the lead of former president Richard M. Nixon who, answering a question posed by David Frost in 1977, replied, "Well, when the president does it, that means that it is not illegal." Frost: "By definition." Nixon: "Exactly, exactly." Columnist George F. Will asserted that Barack Obama's executive actions revealed the same mentality. "If the President Does It, It's Legal?" *New York Post,* August 17, 2013.

36. A letter signed in 1997 by the late Archbishop Luciano Storero, Pope John Paul II's envoy to Ireland, instructed Irish bishops not to publicize suspected acts by pedophile priests but observe canon law by handling allegations and punishments within the church. Photocopy of text in *The Guardian,* January 18, 2011.

37. See the analysis of Lyndon Johnson, Robert S. McNamara, and the Vietnam War in Bruce Hamstra, *Why Good People Do Bad Things: How to Make Moral Choices in an Immoral World* (New York: Birch Lane Press, 1996).

38. For example, on President Ronald Reagan and President Hissène Habré of Chad, see Michael Bronner, "Our Man in Africa: The Dictator America Created, the Blood He Shed, and the Reckoning to Come," *Foreign Policy* (January–February 2014): 34–47, and David Rothkopf, "Course Correction," ibid., 79–80.

39. Official Washington tolerated for decades the authoritarian and rent-seeking behaviors of most Middle Eastern regimes for the chimeras of stability and oil. In June 2008 a U.S. diplomat in Tunis summarized the regime's corruption in a cable headed "What's Yours Is Mine." See Scott Shane, "Cables from American Diplomats Portray U.S. Ambivalence on Tunisia," *New York Times,* January 15, 2011.

40. Japan's apologies for its wartime behavior were qualified. The country can be seen as a "model impenitent." See Thomas U. Berger, *War, Guilt, and World Politics after World War II* (Cambridge, UK: Cambridge University Press, 2012).

41. Mnookin, *Bargaining with the Devil,* 261–265.

42. Walter C. Clemens Jr., "Soviet Disarmament Proposals and the Cadre-Territorial Army," *Orbis* 7, no. 4 (Winter 1964): 778–799.

43. Jim Wooten, "The Conciliator," *New York Times Magazine,* January 29, 1995.

44. Marion V. Creekmore, *A Moment of Crisis: Jimmy Carter, the Power of a Peacemaker, and North Korea's Nuclear Ambitions* (New York: Public Affairs, 2006).

45. Alexander L. George and Juliette L. George, *Woodrow Wilson and Colonel House: A Personality Study* (New York: Dover, 1964). Some medical professionals, however, contended that Wilson's personality reflected more his physical than any psychological problems.

46. "Negotiating the Whirlwind," *New Yorker,* December 21, 2015.

47. See Obama, *Dreams from My Father: A Story of Race and Inheritance* (New York: Crown, 2007). For years, however, Obama regularly attended church services in Chicago where the Reverend Jeremiah Wright often excoriated white America for its evil ways.

48. Black Elk offered this insight: If you want to heal the broken hoop of your own people or harmonize your people's hoop with the hoops of other peoples, you must first mend your own personal hoop. *Black Elk Speaks* (Lincoln: University of Nebraska Press, 1961).

49. Obama added: "We may ask ourselves if we've shown enough kindness and generosity and compassion to the people in our lives. Perhaps we question whether we are doing

right by our children, or our community, and whether our priorities are in order. We recognize our own mortality, and are reminded that in the fleeting time we have on this earth, what matters is not wealth, or status, or power, or fame—but rather, how well we have loved, and what small part we have played in bettering the lives of others." Text at https://www.whitehouse.gov/the-press-office/2011/01/12/remarks-president-barack-obama-memorial-service-victims-shooting-tucson (accessed 3/14/2011).

50. David Brooks, "The Tree of Failure," *New York Times,* January 14, 2011.

51. To distort or make up "facts" is also a form of evil, especially when there is no external pressure to do so. For a critique of some assertions by Brooks, see David Zweig in *Salon,* June 15, 2015, at http://www.salon.com/2015/06/15/the_facts_vs_david_brooks_startling_inaccuracies_raise_questions_about_his_latest_book/ (accessed 7/2/2015).

52. Quoted by Richard Crouter, author of *Reinhold Niebuhr on Politics, Religion, and Christian Faith* (New York: Oxford University Press, 2010), interviewed by John Blake on CNN, February 5, 2010, at http://www.cnn.com/2010/POLITICS/02/05/Obama.theologian/ (accessed 3/10/2010).

53. Neorealism, seeking to replace sentiment with science, ignores qualities such as good and evil, because all behavior is merely a reflection of the structure of material power.

54. A. A. Gromyko, *Pamiatnoe,* 2 vols. (Moscow: Politizdat, 1988), 1: 186.

55. George C. Marshall, radio broadcast, April 28, 1947, text in *New York Times,* April 29, 1947, p. 4.

56. See, e.g., the essays in Neil E. Harrison, ed., *Complexity in World Politics: Concepts and Methods of a New Paradigm* (Albany: State University of New York Press, 2006); Melanie Mitchell, *Complexity: A Guided Tour* (New York: Oxford University Press, 2009); and Emilian Kavalski, ed., *World Politics on the Edge of Chaos: Reflections on Complexity and Global Life* (Albany: State University of New York Press, 2015).

57. See, e.g., Stuart A. Kauffman, *Reinventing the Sacred: A New View of Science, Reason, and Religion* (New York: Basic Books, 2008).

58. Carl Safina, *The View from Lazy Point: A Natural Year in an Unnatural World* (New York: Henry Holt, 2011).

59. See Crouter, *Reinhold Niebuhr,* 17; also Walter C. Clemens Jr., "Whether a Non-Metaphysical Philosophy [that of Thomas Hobbes] Can Justify a Life According to Reason," senior thesis, Notre Dame University, 1955.

9. Must We Choose between Peace and Human Rights?

1. Andrei D. Sakharov, "Peace, Progress, Human Rights," Nobel Lecture, December 11, 1975, at http://www.nobelprize.org/nobel_prizes/peace/laureates/1975/sakharov-lecture.html (accessed 5/20/2014). The lecture updates Sakharov's "memorandum," published as *Progress, Coexistence, and Intellectual Freedom* (New York: Norton, 1968), also printed in the *New York Times* earlier that year. I took a photocopy to show to friends in Prague that summer, a month before the Warsaw Pact repressed "socialism with a human face." See Clemens, "Sakharov: A Man for Our Times," *Bulletin of the Atomic Scientists,* 27, no. 10 (December 1971): 4–6, 51–56. An earlier version was published in Korean in *Non Dan* (Seoul) 7, no. 3 (November–December 1970): 137–145. The U.S. Information Service suggested I write about Sakharov for its Korean-language journal, perhaps to assure South Koreans that there could be great persons living under a Communist dictatorship. I followed this up with "Sakharov: Why He Deserves the Peace Prize," *Christian Science Moni-*

tor, September 26, 1973; and "Sakharov's Legacy," *Christian Science Monitor,* December 19, 1990, 19.

2. See, e.g., Aleksandr I. Solzhenitsyn, *The Mortal Danger: Misconceptions about Soviet Russia and the Threat to America* (New York: Harper & Row, 1980). Historian Richard Pipes, an adviser to President Ronald Reagan, agreed with Solzhenitsyn. See Pipes, *Survival Is Not Enough: Soviet Realities and America's Future* (New York: Simon & Schuster, 2004).

3. Solzhenitsyn, *The Gulag Archipelago, 1918–1956: An Experiment in Literary Investigation,* 3 vols. (New York: Harper & Row, 1974–1978).

4. The zigzag evolution of human rights in the West is traced in Francesca Klug, *A Magna Carta for All Humanity: Homing in on Human Rights* (New York: Routledge, 2015).

5. See Lincoln P. Bloomfield, Walter C. Clemens Jr., and Franklyn Griffiths, *Khrushchev and the Arms Race: Soviet Interests in Arms Control and Disarmament, 1954–1964* (Cambridge: MIT Press, 1966).

6. The Lacy-Zarubin agreement in January 1958 provided for Soviet-U.S. exchanges in many fields, including a one-month tour of the USSR and United States by editors of student and youth publications and an exchange of twenty Soviet and U.S. graduate students to study for two semesters in the other's country, a number that expanded over time and came to include a larger cross-section of educational institutions in each country.

7. Jonathan Harris, *The Public Politics of Aleksandr Nikolaevich Yakovlev, 1983–1989* (Pittsburgh: Carl Beck Papers in Russian and East European Studies, 1990).

8. The transitions from Nicholas II to Gorbachev are analyzed in Clemens, *Can Russia Change? The USSR Confronts Global Interdependence* (New York: Routledge, 1990).

9. Senator Jesse Helms (R-NC) asked why the treaty did not eliminate "the part of nuclear weaponry that kills people and destroys property." The answer was that the United States wanted to recover the nuclear material and safeguard secret information about the warhead designs.

10. On all these issues, see Clemens, "Arms Control," "The Hague Peace Conferences," and "The Intermediate-Range Nuclear Forces Treaty," *Encyclopedia of Russian History,* 4 vols. (New York: Macmillan, 2004), 1: 85–88; 2: 625; 2: 672–673.

11. Alexander J. Motyl and Walter C. Clemens Jr., "From Weimar Russia to Nazi Russia," *Global Asia Forum,* April 2, 2014, at http://www.globalasia.org/Forum/Detail/40/from-weimar-to-nazi-russia.html (accessed 4/10/2014).

12. French disarmament expert Jules Moch claimed to witness at the Geneva Summit in 1955 evidence that Soviet and Western leaders were surprised to perceive that all of them feared the consequences of nuclear war. Moch, conversation with author, 1971.

13. Matthew Evangelista, *Unarmed Forces: The Transnational Movement to End the Cold War* (Ithaca: Cornell University Press, 1999).

14. David E. Sanger and William J. Broad, "U.S.-Russia Nuclear Deal Stalls as Tensions over Ukraine Rise," *New York Times,* August 3, 2014, pp. 1, 7.

15. Putin dispatched his forces against the peoples of Chechnya, Georgia, and Ukraine while keeping them in Trans-Dniestria, a province of Moldova. These forces killed between 100,000 and 200,000 Chechens; split off South Ossetia and Abkhazia from Georgia; and watched as South Ossetians carried out ethnic cleansing of Georgian villages. When Putin's forces seized Crimea, they put Tatars as well as Ukrainians at risk.

16. Clemens, "Destroy or Negotiate? Dealing with the Reality of Evil Regimes," *Global Asia Forum,* July 31, 2014, at http://www.globalasia.org/Forum/Detail/51/destroy-or-negotiate-dealing-with-the-reality-of-evil-regimes.html (accessed 8/15/2014).

17. *National Interest*, March 21, 2014.

18. See Sakharov, *Progress, Coexistence, and Intellectual Freedom.*

19. When North Korea seized the USS *Pueblo* spy ship in January 1968, however, Washington did not respond forcefully, due mainly to its deepening involvement in the Vietnam War.

10. Why Is North Korea Not the South?

1. See, for example, Stuart A. Kauffman, *At Home in the Universe: The Search for Laws of Self-Organization and Complexity* (New York: Oxford University Press, 1995).

2. Stuart A. Kauffman, *Reinventing the Sacred: A New View of Science, Reason, and Religion* (New York: Basic Books, 2008).

3. Walter C. Clemens Jr., *Complexity Science and World Affairs* (Albany: State University Press of New York, 2013).

4. Norway ranked first; the United States, fifth. The ROK tied with Hong Kong at fifteenth, just behind the United Kingdom and just ahead of Japan. See http://www.undp.org/content/undp/en/home/presscenter/events/2014/july/HDR2014.html (accessed 2/1/2015).

5. "Poor Spirits," *The Economist*, December 7, 2013; and subsequent BBC investigations.

6. Moon-Gi Suh, "Is South Korea Really Developed? The Grim Shadows of Compressed Growth," East Asia Foundation Policy Debates, October 7, 2014, at http://www.keaf.org/book/EAF_Policy_Debate_Is_South_Korea_Really_Developed_The_Grim_Shadows_of_Compressed_Growth (accessed 11/10/2014).

7. http://www3.weforum.org/docs/CSI/2012–13/GCR_Rankings_2012–13.pdf (accessed 2/27/2013).

8. *Social Progress Index 2014*, comp. Michael E. Porter, Scott Stern, Michael Green (Washington, DC: Social Progress Imperative, 2014).

9. The facts underlying each measure are given at http://www.bti-project.org/country-reports/aso/ (accessed 2/27/2013).

10. Andrei Lankov, *From Stalin to Kim Il Sung: The Formation of North Korea, 1945–1960* (New Brunswick, NJ: Rutgers University Press, 2002), 10–14.

11. Psy's video became the most watched ever on YouTube—more than 2.4 billion times—compelling YouTube to raise the limit of views for any one item. "Gangnam Style Statue Built in South Korea's Seoul," BBC World News, November 6, 2015, at http://www.bbc.com/news/world-asia-34744836 (accessed 11/9/2015).

12. They may cooperate within the group but much less so with outsiders. See Jared Diamond, *The World until Yesterday: What Can We Learn from Traditional Societies* (New York: Viking, 2012).

13. Normimitsu Onishi, "Korea's Tricky Task: Digging Up Past Treachery," *New York Times*, January 5, 2005.

14. Byung-Kook Kim and Ezra F. Vogel, eds., *The Park Chung Hee Era: The Transformation of South Korea* (Cambridge: Harvard University Press, 2011).

15. Jong-sung You, "Transition from a Limited Access Order to an Open Access Order: The Case of South Korea," in Douglas North, John Wallis, Steve Webb, and Barry Weingast, eds., *In the Shadow of Violence: Politics, Economics, and the Problem of Development* (Cambridge, UK: Cambridge University Press, 2013).

16. Jong-sung You (ibid.) shows how a comparison of the Korean experience with those of Taiwan and the Philippines reveals the critical importance of land reform. In Taiwan,

the success of land reform under the Communist threat of mainland China also helped to remove the privileged landed class and to develop the economy without excessive distributive struggle, which eased the democratic transition and consolidation processes. In the Philippines, however, the initial failure of land reform in the absence of an external threat led to continuous distributive struggles, which made democratic consolidation difficult and helped the insurgencies to continue.

17. Kyong-Ryang Kim, "South Korea's Official Development Aid and Saemaul Undong: Its Value and Limitations," East Asia Foundation Policy Debates, April 28, 2015, at http://www.keaf.org/book/EAF_Policy_Debates_N025_South_Koreas_Official_Development_Aid_and_Saemaul_Undong:_Its_Value_and_Limitations?ckattempt=1 (accessed 4/28/2015).

18. A former U.S. ambassador to Seoul sought to minimize U.S. complicity in repressing the demonstrators but rendered the date of the May uprising as August 1980. See Christopher R. Hill, *Outpost: Life on the Frontlines of American Diplomacy; A Memoir* (New York: Simon & Schuster, 2014), 191.

19. Walter C. Clemens Jr., *Getting to Yes in Korea* (Boulder, CO: Paradigm Publishers, 2010), 32–35, 224–225.

20. E-mail communication by Ezra F. Vogel to author, 2/28/2013.

21. "Risks of Intelligence Pathologies in South Korea," International Crisis Group, August 5, 2014, at https://mail.google.com/mail/u/0/?tab=wm#inbox/147a7b72c5041c28 (accessed 5/14/2015).

22. In April 2014 an overloaded ferry in South Korea sank, killing some 300 passengers. A few weeks later, in Pyongyang, an apartment building, where more than ninety families lived, collapsed. Top leaders in Seoul and in Pyongyang apologized for each incident and said they were sleepless with grief. A drive for rapid development conduced to accidents of this kind in both South and North. Media in the DPRK said ROK president Park Geun Hye should be "hacked to death" for her faked expressions of sorrow. Meanwhile, it took Pyongyang five days to acknowledge the building collapse.

23. https://www.transparency.org/cpi2014/results (accessed 11/9/2015); Transparency-International-Corruption-Perceptions-Index-2013.pdf (accessed 5/19/2014). In 2015 Denmark took first place for honesty; Singapore placed 7th; Japan, 15th; Hong Kong and the United States, tied at 17th; Taiwan, 35th; India, 85th (up by nine places since 2013); China, 100th (down from 80th in 2013); Russia, 136th (down by nine places since 2013).

24. Oh Young-jin, "Park's Worst Enemy," *Korea Times*, February 25, 2013.

25. Hours of in-flight training per year for military pilots in Japan were 148; in China, 80–130; in Russia, 25–80; in the United States, 189–365. No data were given for South Korea. *The Military Balance 2008* (London: International Institute for Strategic Studies, 2008).

26. See http://www.bloombergview.com/articles/2014–10–13/north-korea-s-elites-are-a-threat-to-kim (accessed 5/13/2015) and other articles by Andrei Lankov in Bloomberg View.

27. Clemens, *Getting to Yes in Korea*, 247n15.

28. According to a renowned epidemiologist, this is a global pattern. See Michael Marmot, *The Health Gap: The Challenge of an Unequal World* (New York: Bloomsbury, 2015).

29. Luther's views became reactionary when peasants, inspired by his rhetoric, rose up against authorities in the mid-1520s and Jews did not flock to his version of Christianity.

30. Their deference recalled the old Korean saying "One should not step even on the shadow of one's teacher."

31. newizv.ru/society/2014–09–11/207527-bloger-anton-nosik.html (accessed 5/14/2014).

32. Thirty-four years after the Gwangju massacre, Mr. Hong saw in the sinking of the Sewol ferry in April 2014 "another massacre perpetrated by a cartel of crude capitalist businesses, corrupt bureaucrats and an irresponsible and feckless government"—what he called "state brutality." Choe Sang-Hun, "An Artist Is Rebuked for Casting South Korea's Leader in an Unflattering Light," *New York Times*, August 30, 2014. Two years earlier the artist was rebuked by the ruling party for painting the female presidential candidate giving birth to a baby who resembled her father. See BBC, November 20, 2012, at http://www.bbc.com/news/world-asia-20406985 (accessed 1/3/2013).

11. GRIT AT PANMUNJOM?

1. Conflict management theories are nested within broader approaches to international studies. These approaches include realist, liberal, game theory, constructivist, postmodern/critical theory, historical materialist/world system, feminist, biopolitical, and English School. For exposition and applications, see Jennifer Sterling-Folker, ed., *Making Sense of International Relations Theory* (Boulder, CO: Lynne Rienner, 2006). Three of these approaches—realist, liberal, and constructivist—are applied to Asia by Amitav Acharya, "Thinking Theoretically about Asian IR," in David Shambaugh and Michael Yahuda, eds., *International Relations of Asia*, 2nd ed. (Lanham, MD: Rowman & Littlefield, 2014), 59–89.

2. Roger Fisher and William Ury, *Getting to Yes: Negotiating Agreement without Giving In*, 2nd ed. (New York: Penguin, 1991). For related works, see John P. Holdren, *Getting to Zero: Is Pursuing a Nuclear-Weapon-Free World Too Difficult? Too Dangerous? Too Distracting?* (Cambridge: Belfer Center for Science and International Affairs, Harvard University, 1998); William Ury, *Getting Past No: Negotiating Your Way from Confrontation to Cooperation*, rev. ed. (New York: Bantam, 1993); William Ury, *The Power of a Positive No: How to Say No and Still Get to Yes* (New York: Bantam, 2007).

3. A positional bargainer might begin by demanding $1,000 for her used car. If the potential buyer offers $500, she might be willing to split the difference at $750. But what if the seller must leave town tomorrow and the buyer refuses to bid higher than $500? The seller's *interest* may require her to ignore her bargaining position and sell the car at any price—as happened to investment bank Bear Stearns in 2008 when it was compelled to sell its stock for $10 per share rather than the recent value of $133.

4. Howard Raiffa, *The Art and Science of Negotiation* (Cambridge: Harvard University Press, 1982); David A. Lax and James K. Sebenius, *The Manager as Negotiator: Bargaining for Cooperative and Competitive Gain* (New York: Free Press, 1986); Howard Raiffa et al., *Negotiation Analysis: The Science and Art of Collaborative Decision Making* (Cambridge: Harvard University Press, 2002); Michael Watkins, *Shaping the Game: The New Leader's Guide to Effective Negotiating* (Boston: Harvard Business School Press, 2006); Max Bazerman and Deepak Malhotra, *Negotiation Genius: How to Overcome Obstacles and Achieve Brilliant Results at the Bargaining Table and Beyond* (New York: Bantam, 2007); Gary Friedman and Jack Himmelstein, *Challenging Conflict: Mediation through Understanding* (Chicago: American Bar Association Section on Dispute Resolution, 2008). For additional references, see http://www.pon.harvard.edu/hnp/; also *Conflict Resolution Quarterly*, *Journal of Conflict Resolution*, *International Negotiation*, and *Negotiation Journal*.

5. Walter C. Clemens Jr., *Dynamics of International Relations: Conflict and Mutual*

Gain in an Era of Global Interdependence, 2nd ed. (Lanham, MD: Rowman & Littlefield, 2004), chaps. 1, 2, and 16.

6. Charles E. Osgood, *An Alternative to War or Surrender* (Urbana: University of Illinois Press, 1962).

7. Obama in his first six years as president joined in more than twenty joint statements with other governments incorporating the acronym "DPRK." In more than 100 of his own statements, however, he spoke of "North Korea." Data at http://www.presidency.ucsb.edu/ (accessed 4/11/2014).

8. Captain Hans J. Neumann writing from the Joint Security Area on August 15, 1970. His letter and several others were responses to my request for comments on an early draft of this chapter.

9. Wayne Johnson quoted in an article from *Korea Times* cited by Don Lopez, at http://www.imjinscout.com/Paul_Bunyan.html (accessed 7/3/2015).

10. George W.'s father, the forty-first president, disliked Cheney's hard-line pressures on his son, the forty-third. See Jon Meacham, *Destiny and Power: The American Odyssey of George Herbert Walker Bush* (New York: Random House, 2015).

11. Clemens, *Dynamics of International Relations,* 250–258.

12. Sung Gul Hong, "The Search for Deterrence: Park's Nuclear Option," in Byung-Kook Kim and Ezra F. Vogel, eds., *The Park Chung Hee Era: The Transformation of South Korea* (Cambridge: Harvard University Press, 2011), 483–510 at 488; Walter C. Clemens Jr., "North Korea's Quest for Nuclear Weapons: New Historical Evidence," *Journal of East Asian Studies* 10, no. 1 (January–March 2010): 127–154.

13. www.wilsoncenter.org/document-collections (accessed 3/27/2013).

14. Victor Cha, *The Impossible State: North Korea, Past and Future* (New York: Harper-Collins, 2012), 398–399.

15. Chung-in Moon, *The Sunshine Policy: In Defense of Engagement as a Path to Peace in Korea* (Seoul: Yonsei University Press, 2012); Lim Dong-won, *Peacemaker: Twenty Years of Inter-Korean Relations and the North Korean Nuclear Issue* (Stanford, CA: Walter H. Shorenstein Asia-Pacific Research Center, 2012).

16. Cha, *The Impossible State,* 388.

17. Raymond Cohen, *Negotiating across Cultures: International Communication in an Interdependent World,* rev. ed. (Washington, DC: United States Institute of Peace, 2002).

18. Stephen W. Linton, "Approach and Style in Negotiating with the DPRK," lecture, Center for Korean Research, Columbia University, New York, April 6, 1995; also Linton, testimony before the Senate Subcommittee on East Asian and Pacific Affairs, June 5, 2003; also http://www.eugenebell.org/ (accessed 3/14/2014).

19. Stephen W. Linton, e-mail to author, November 8, 2009.

20. Ibid.

21. Christopher R. Hill, *Outpost: Life on the Frontlines of American Diplomacy; A Memoir* (New York: Simon & Schuster, 2014).

22. Charles W. Freeman interviewed in Nancy Bernkopf Tucker, ed., *China Confidential: American Diplomats and Sino-American Relations, 1945–1996* (New York: Columbia University Press, 2001), 429–430.

23. Richard Saccone, *Negotiating with North Korea* (Elizabeth, NJ: Hollym, 2003), and Saccone, *The Business of Korean Culture* (Elizabeth, NJ: Hollym, 1994).

24. Karen Elliot House, "Let North Korea Collapse," *Wall Street Journal,* February 21, 1997, A14.

25. B. R. Myers, "To Beat a Dictator, Ignore Him," *New York Times*, April 1, 2000.

26. Scott Snyder, *Negotiating on the Edge: North Korean Negotiating Behavior* (Washington, DC: United States Institute of Peace, 1999). Another well-balanced interpretation is that of Richard Saccone, *Living with the Enemy: Inside North Korea* (Elizabeth, NJ: Hollym, 2006) and Saccone, *Negotiating with North Korea.*

27. Charles K. Armstrong, *Tyranny of the Weak: North Korea and the World, 1950–1992* (Ithaca, NY: Cornell University Press, 2013).

28. Snyder, *Negotiating on the Edge*, 90.

29. Ibid., 38.

30. This is one view, based mainly on experiences in politics; but the author knows an American exporter of machinery (a Caucasian who knows no Korean) who finds it easy to deal with South Koreans on business transactions and difficult to come to terms with Europeans.

31. Other observations in the foregoing paragraphs reflect my conversations with Dr. Yurim Yi in 2014 and echo passages in Snyder, *Negotiating on the Edge*, 19, 31, 145.

32. Alexander Wendt, *Social Theory in International Politics* (New York: Cambridge University Press, 1999); Daniel M. Green, ed., *Constructivism and Comparative Politics* (Armonk, NY: M. E. Sharpe, 2002); Stefano Guzzini and Anna Leander, eds., *Constructivism and International Relations: Alexander Wendt and His Critics* (London: Routledge, 2006).

33. Alfred P. Rubin, "Humanitarian Intervention and International Law," in Aleksandar Jokic, ed., *Humanitarian Intervention: Moral and Philosophical Issues* (Peterborough, Canada: Broadview, 2003), 109–121 at 110–111.

34. The DPRK delegate demanded that any "antiterrorism" activities be conducted in conformity with the principles of the UN Charter and international law. Addressing the Sixth Committee of the UN General Assembly, he warned against allowing "some specified states to use the antiterrorism struggle as leverage for seeking their political and economic purposes." To remove the root cause of terrorism, he said, it was necessary to eradicate social inequality and poverty while establishing fair international relations on the basis of mutual respect, equality, friendship, and cooperation whereby all countries and nations can fully exercise their rights to live and develop independently. KCNA, October 16, 2008. Later that month, the official newspaper *Rodong Sinmun* denounced the first U.S. flight test of a B-52H bomber equipped with laser-controlled guided missiles, calling it an expression of Washington's "wild ambition for supremacy." KCNA, October 20, 2008. These and other references to U.S. as well as DPRK reports may be found at http://www.timbeal.net.nz/geopolitics/NK_US_08.htm (accessed 2/14/2009).

35. See, e.g., the DPRK Foreign Ministry statement on the attempt to refer the warship sinking to the United Nations, KCNA, June 4, 2010.

36. Jae-Jung Suh, "Race to Judge, Rush to Act," *Critical Asian Studies* 42, no. 3 (September 2010): 403–424.

37. Eldest son and presumed heir Kim Jong Nam lost his father's favor when he was detained in Japan using a fake passport to visit Tokyo Disneyland in 2001. He sometimes called for reform of the DPRK regime.

38. Terence Roehrig, "Korean Dispute over the Northern Limit Line: Security, Economics, or International Law?" Maryland Series in Contemporary Asian Studies, School of Law, University of Maryland, 2008.

39. Daniel Gomà Pinilla, "Border Disputes between China and North Korea," *China*

Perspectives, 52 (2004), at http://chinaperspectives.revues.org/document806.html (accessed 3/31/2009).

40. Several legal scholars hold that the NLL was useful as a temporary device to avoid conflict but that treating it as a permanent maritime boundary goes against international legal principles and precedents. Jon M. Van Dyke et al., "The North/South Korea Boundary Dispute in the Yellow (West) Sea," *Maritime Policy* 27, no. 2 (March 2003): 143–158.

41. Only when Moscow agreed to forgive most of Pyongyang's debts going back many decades and to build a rail link from Siberia into a North Korean port did DPRK-Russian relations tick up.

42. Secretary of State Colin Powell was angry that his turf had been invaded by talking-point instructions to Kelly drafted by National Security Council and White House hard-liners. See Condoleezza Rice, *No Higher Honor: A Memoir of My Years in Washington* (New York: Crown, Random House, 2011), 161–162.

43. If North Korean policymaking is monolithic and inexorably zero-sum, then efforts at conciliation are futile. This is approximately the position of Sue Mi Terry, "North Korea's Strategic Goals and Policy towards the United States and South Korea," *International Journal of Korean Studies* 17, no. 2 (Fall-Winter 2013): 63–92. For a very different perspective, see Yurim Yi, "Confrontation and Engagement in Relations between the DPRK and the United States, 1991–2011," PhD diss., Boston University, 2014.

44. Koh has remarked that the chairman of a large-scale diplomacy conference "is both a choreographer and conductor of an orchestra." For an annotated bibliography of his writings, see note 45 below.

45. James K. Sebenius and Laurence A. Green, "Tommy Koh: Background and Major Accomplishments of the 'Great Negotiator, 2014,'" Harvard Business School Working Paper 14–049, February 13, 2014.

12. The Agreed Framework Sets the Stage for a Grand Bargain

1. For analysis by the participants, see Joel S. Wit, Daniel B. Poneman, and Robert L. Gallucci, *Going Critical: The First North Korean Nuclear Crisis* (Washington, DC: Brookings, 2004); and, with a longer perspective and access to wider documentation, Don Oberdorfer and Robert Carlin, *The Two Koreas: A Contemporary History,* revised and updated 3rd ed. (New York: Basic Books, 2014). Carlin had for decades also been an analyst and participant in U.S.-DPRK negotiations.

2. For a detailed chronology of North Korea and disarmament diplomacy, with frequent updates, see https://www.armscontrol.org/factsheets/dprkchron (accessed 7/5/2015).

3. Carter was accompanied by retired ambassador Marion V. Creekmore Jr., who described the meetings in *Moment of Crisis: Jimmy Carter, the Power of a Peacemaker, and North Korea's Nuclear Ambitions* (New York: Public Affairs, 2006).

4. Michael Watkins and Susan Rosegrant, *Breakthrough International Negotiation: How Great Negotiators Transformed the World's Toughest Post-Cold War Conflicts* (San Francisco: Jossey-Bass, 2001), 89.

5. Text at http://www.kedo.org/pdfs/AgreedFramework.pdf (accessed 4/8/2009).

6. Executive agreements are binding under international law but avoid the ratification process required for treaties.

7. Watkins and Rosegrant, *Breakthrough,* 105, 128–129.

8. The North–South declaration by implication distinguished between facilities to

produce highly enriched uranium (HEU), suitable for weapons manufacture, and low-enriched uranium (LEU), sufficient to power light-water reactors. See Selig S. Harrison, "Did North Korea Cheat?" *Foreign Affairs* 84, no. 1 (January–February 2005): 106–107. But an enrichment facility dedicated to producing LEU can be reconfigured to produce HEU. In this sense it is misleading to speak of fundamentally different facilities, wrote former U.S. official Larry Scheinmann in 2005, commenting on a draft of this chapter. By 2005 the Bush administration worried that any "civilian" nuclear reactor could be diverted.

9. See below, chapter 13, notes 10–12.

10. For a detailed history and evaluation, see Charles Kartman, Robert Carlin, and Joel Wit, *A History of KEDO, 1994–2006* (Stanford, CA: Center for Security and International Cooperation, 2012).

11. IAEA, "In Focus: IAEA and the DPRK," at http://www.iaea.org/NewsCenter/Focus/IaeaDprk/fact_sheet_may2003.shtml (accessed 7/15/2009).

12. Dinshaw Mistry, *Containing Missile Proliferation: Strategic Technology, Security Regimes, and International Cooperation in Arms Control* (Seattle: University of Washington Press, 2003).

13. James Goodby and William Drennan, "Koreapolitik," *Strategic Forum* 29 (May 1995): 2.

14. Joseph Cirincione et al., *Deadly Arsenals: Tracking Weapons of Mass Destruction* (Washington, DC: Carnegie Endowment for International Peace, 2002), 247.

15. Huge questions remained: How would the LWR be integrated into North Korea's electric grid? Where was the necessary backup power supply? How would insurance for builders and third parties be handled and financed? How could world-class safety standards be assured? Who would take the spent fuel from the old gas-graphite reactor? How would more comprehensive IAEA inspections be arranged? David Albright and Kevin O'Neill, eds., *Solving the North Korean Nuclear Puzzle* (Washington, DC: Institute for Science and International Security Press, 2000); Joel Wit, "Viewpoint: The Korean Peninsula Energy Development Organization: Achievements and Challenges," *Nonproliferation Review* (Center for Nonproliferation Studies) 6, no. 2 (Winter 1999): 59–69.

16. Vladimir Kirillov, "The North Korean Space Program: Bluff or Reality?" *Moscow Defense Brief* [2001], at http://mdb.cast.ru/mdb/5-2001/mas/nksp/ (accessed 5/10/2012).

17. http://www1.korea-np.co.jp/pk/149th_issue/2000101402.htm (accessed 7/23/2009).

18. Madeleine Albright, *Madame Secretary* (New York: Hyperion, 2003), 459–472.

19. Albright also liked symbols: she was famous for wearing decorative pins suited to the occasion and her own frame of mind. When she saw Jo later in Pyongyang, he wore a pin bearing the image of Kim Il Sung; she, her largest stars and stripes pin.

20. Born in 1928, the marshal lived until 2010.

13. Bush Gets Tough with North Korea

1. Condoleezza Rice, *No Higher Honor: A Memoir of My Years in Washington* (New York: Crown, 2011), 34–36, 158. Her account generally dovetails with that of U.S. ambassador Christopher R. Hill; see Hill, *Outpost: Life on the Frontlines of American Diplomacy; A Memoir* (New York: Simon & Schuster, 2014), 191–192.

2. Bob Woodward, *Plan of Attack* (New York: Simon & Schuster, 2004), 31–32.

3. Cheney's view as summarized by Aaron Friedberg, Cheney's deputy national security adviser, 2003–2005, quoted in Mike Chinoy, *Meltdown: The Inside Story of the North Korean Nuclear Crisis* (New York: St. Martin's, 2008), 194.

4. Interview with John R. Bolton in 2004 quoted in Barton Gellman, *Angler: The Cheney Vice Presidency* (New York: Penguin, 2008), 373.

5. Rice, *No Higher Honor,* 158.

6. Walter C. Clemens Jr., "How to Lose Friends and Inspire Enemies," *Washington Post* Outlook, May 20, 2001, 2.

7. See the Justice Department memoranda released by the American Civil Liberties Union at http://www.aclu.org/safefree/general/olc_memos.html (accessed 4/18/2009).

8. For the *NPR,* see http://www.globalsecurity.org/wmd/library/policy/dod/npr.htm (accessed 4/19/2009); also summarized and analyzed by Charles D. Ferguson at http://www.nti.org/analysis/articles/nuclear-posture-review/ (accessed 5/10/2014).

9. Not only the public but many journalists and even some Raytheon engineers were also clueless about the effectiveness of ABM systems. See Walter C. Clemens Jr., "A Quiz for a Peaceful Sunday," *Los Angeles Times,* March 22, 1981, cited also in *Fortune,* October 19, 1981, 142 and—two decades later—"Our Missile Defense System: Safeguard—or Skylark?" *Bostonia* 2 (Summer 2000): 29–32.

10. Reuters, February 25, 2014. The Missile Defense Agency of the Pentagon requested $7.5 billion for its FY 2015 budget, upped to $8.127 for FY 2016. See http://www.mda.mil/global/documents/pdf/ps_syring_040214_SASC.PDF (accessed 4/9/2014) and http://www.mda.mil/global/documents/pdf/budgetfy16.pdf (accessed 4/6/2015).

11. Theodore A. Postol, "The Evidence Shows That the Iron Dome Is Not Working," *Bulletin of the Atomic Scientists,* July 19, 2014, at http://thebulletin.org/evidence-shows-iron-dome-not-working7318 (accessed 8/15/2014).

12. "Star Wars 2: Attack of the Drones," *The Economist,* May 17, 2014.

13. "The Unsheltering Sky," *The Economist,* September 6, 2014.

14. The president altered the law of the land without participation by the legislature (needed to make a treaty or any other law). More than thirty members of the House of Representatives sued the administration in the District of Columbia District Court for violating Article II, Section 2, of the Constitution. The court dismissed their suit as a nonjusticiable political question. See Walter C. Clemens Jr., "It Takes Two to Tear It Up: Congress and the President Share the Responsibility," *Washington Post* Outlook, August 5, 2001, B4, and "Who Terminates a Treaty?" *Bulletin of the Atomic Scientists* 57, no. 6 (November–December 2001): 38–39, 42–43.

15. Robert W. Nelson, "Low-Yield Earth-Penetrating Nuclear Weapons," *Science and Global Security* 10, no. 1 (January–April 2002): 1–20.

16. On the "Armageddon lobby," see links at http://www.conservativesfor peace.com/ArmageddonUpdates.htm (accessed 11/11/2015).

17. Caroline Wyatt, "Bush and Putin: Best of Friends," BBC World News, June 16, 2002, at http://news.bbc.co.uk/2/hi/europe/1392791.stm (accessed 7/20/2001).

18. The treaty permitted each side to keep—not destroy—the nuclear warheads withdrawn from its deployed arsenal. The U.S. Senate approved the treaty in March 2003, as did the Russian Duma three months later, when the newspaper *Moskovskii Komsomolets* (May 15, 2003) ran the headline: "A Nuclear Bomb in Stars and Stripes." The article declared that while the treaty "does not actually bind Russia to anything, the obligations for the United States under it are even less binding than Russia's."

19. Excerpts released by the White House in *Congressional Record,* July 21 and 23, 2003.

20. Madeleine Albright, *Madame Secretary* (New York: Hyperion, 2003), 470.

21. Rice, *No Higher Honor,* 35–36.

22. "Bush Tells Seoul Talks with North Won't Resume Now," *New York Times*, March 8, 2001. See also Chae-Jin Lee, *A Troubled Peace: U.S. Policy and the Two Koreas* (Baltimore: Johns Hopkins University Press, 2006), 212–214.

23. Gellman, *Angler*, 228–229.

24. Glenn Kessler, *The Confidante: Condoleezza Rice and the Creation of the Bush Legacy* (New York: St. Martin's, 2007), 65–87.

25. Rice saw the tight script and instructions to Kelly not to socialize or have dinner with the North Koreans as a necessary concession to hard-liners in Washington but as an insult to "Colin." See her *No Greater Honor*, 161–162.

26. David E. Sanger, "North Korea Says It Has a Program on Nuclear Arms," *New York Times*, October 17, 2002; see also Document 22, CIA report to Congress in November 2002, in Robert A. Wampler, "North Korea and Nuclear Weapons: The Declassified Record," National Security Archive Electronic Briefing Book no. 87, April 25, 2003, at http://nsarchive.gwu.edu/NSAEBB/NSAEBB87/ (accessed 5/10/2014).

27. Gellman, *Angler*, 209.

28. See the memoir of under secretary of state for arms control and international security, John Bolton, *Surrender Is Not an Option: Defending America at the United Nations and Abroad* (New York: Simon & Schuster, 2007), 106–107.

29. Selig S. Harrison, "Did North Korea Cheat?" *Foreign Affairs* 84, no. 1 (January–February 2005): 106–107.

30. Rice, *No Higher Honor*, 161.

31. The United States officially terminated its support for KEDO in 2005, but the last boatload of workers sailed back to the ROK in 2006. Charles Kartman, Robert Carlin, and Joel Wit, *A History of KEDO, 1994–2006* (Stanford, CA: Center for Security and International Cooperation, 2012).

32. http://www.mda.mil/global/documents/pdf/ps_syring_040214_SASC.PDF (accessed 4/9/2014).

33. For the impact on U.S. relations with Japan and the DPRK, see Rice, *No Greater Honor*, 160.

34. Rüdiger Frank, "Dreaming an Impossible Dream? Opening, Reform, and the Future of the North Korean Economy," *Global Asia* 4, no. 2 (Summer 2009): 18–32.

35. The insider's view quoted in Kessler, *Confidante*, 71. The president's father also criticized the negative and outsized influences of Cheney and Rumsfeld. See Jon Meacham, *Destiny and Power: The American Odyssey of George Herbert Walker Bush* (New York: Random House, 2015).

14. Six-Party Hopes and Missed Opportunities

1. Article in the authoritative DPRK newspaper, *Rodong Sinmun*, on September 1, 2003.

2. Condoleezza Rice, *No Higher Honor: A Memoir of My Years in Washington* (New York: Crown, 2011), 250.

3. International Institute for Strategic Studies, *The Military Balance, 2003–2004* (London: Oxford University Press, 2004), 19, 28, 163, 177–179; Julian Barnes, "Warning Sounded on Cuts to Pilot Training," *Wall Street Journal*, December 19, 2013.

4. Rice, *No Higher Honor*, 163, 248.

5. Glenn Kessler, *The Confidante: Condoleezza Rice and the Creation of the Bush Legacy* (New York: St. Martin's, 2007), 71.

6. For India, the decision to proceed with nuclear weapons derived as much from Hindu nationalism as from worries about foreign threats. See George Perkovich, *India's Nuclear Bomb: The Impact of Global Proliferation* (Berkeley: University of California Press, 1999).

7. Madeleine Albright, *Madame Secretary* (New York: Hyperion, 2003), 469.

8. Described by Rice, *No Higher Honor*, 250–251.

9. "American Forces in South Korea: The End of an Era?" *Strategic Comments* 8, no. 5 (July 2003): 1–2; James Goodby, "America's Mixed Signals in Korea," *Financial Times*, June 11, 2004.

10. According to a former ROK prime minister, South Korea's direct aid consisted mainly of food and medical supplies. As of early 2005, the industrial zone in North Korea, where fifteen ROK companies had begun operations, occupied just twenty-three acres. They paid their DPRK workers about $57 a month—a wage so low that it helped these firms compete with industries in China. Goh Kun, "U.S.-ROK Alliance and the North Korean Problem," lecture at John F. Kennedy Forum, Harvard University, March 16, 2005.

11. For her transition to secretary of state, see Rice, *No Higher Honor*, 295–318.

12. Ibid., 348–349.

13. John Bolton moved from Washington to New York where, from August 2005 to December 2006, he became what *The Economist* called "the most controversial ambassador ever sent by America to the United Nations." When Bolton called Kim Jong Il a "tyrannical rogue" in August 2003, Pyongyang branded him "human scum" and got him excluded from six-party talks that began later that month.

14. *Nomination of Dr. Condoleezza Rice to Be Secretary of State*, Hearings before the Committee on Foreign Relations, U.S Senate, January 18–19, 2005 (Washington, DC: U.S. Government Printing Office, 2005), 20; also at https://www.gpo.gov/fdsys/pkg/CHRG-109shrg22847/pdf/CHRG-109shrg22847.pdf (accessed 4/10/2005).

15. Hill later said that DPRK negotiators, though tough, were no match for the Serbian negotiators with whom he tangled in the 1990s.

16. IAEA, "In Focus: IAEA and the DPRK," at http://www.iaea.org/NewsCenter/Focus/IaeaDprk/fact_sheet_may2003.shtml (accessed 7/15/2009).

17. Text at http://www.cfr.org/proliferation/statement-principles-six-party-talks/p11748 (accessed 10/10/2005).

18. Don Oberdorfer and Robert Carlin, *The Two Koreas: A Contemporary History*, revised and updated 3rd ed. (New York: Basic Books, 2014), 406.

19. Rice, *No Greater Honor*, 400–401.

20. Oberdorfer and Carlin, *Two Koreas*, 406–407.

21. Ibid., 400, 524.

22. Ibid., 521.

23. Goh Kun, "U.S.-ROK Alliance and the North Korean Problem."

24. Rice, *No Greater Honor*, 526; Kessler, *Confidante*, 86; and interviews in Barton Gellman, *Angler: The Cheney Vice Presidency* (New York: Penguin, 2008).

25. On April 24, 2008, U.S. intelligence officials reported their assessment that the Syrian facility was indeed a nuclear reactor being built with North Korean assistance. A CIA-produced video included photographs taken from inside and around the facility at various times during its construction, as well as satellite images and digital renderings of certain elements of the reactor's operations.

26. Siegfried S. Hecker, report on March 14, 2008, at http://iis-db.stanford.edu/pubs/22146/HeckerDPRKreport.pdf (accessed 5/16/2009).

27. Details are provided in Oberdorfer and Carlin, *Two Koreas,* 419–424.

28. Winston Lord and Leslie H. Gelb, "Yielding to North Korea Too Often," *Washington Post,* April 26, 2008.

29. For a history and analysis, see Terence Roehrig, "North Korea and the U.S. State Sponsors of Terrorism List," *Pacific Focus* 24, no. 1 *(*April 2009): 85–106.

30. John R. Bolton, "The Tragic End of Bush's North Korean Policy," *Wall Street Journal,* June 30, 2008.

31. Larry A. Niksch, "North Korea: Terrorism List Removal?" Congressional Reference Service, February 2, 2009, at http://opencrs.com/document/RL30613/ (accessed 5/10/2009).

32. When Kim Jong Il recovered, he embarked on an intense work schedule. From late 2008 until his death in December 2011, he made more than 300 public appearances, including three trips by train to China and one to Russia. Though the stroke affected his motor functions, his cognitive abilities remained strong. Oberdorfer and Carlin, *Two Koreas,* 426–427.

33. Rice, *No Higher Honor,* 311.

34. Oberdorfer and Carlin, *Two Koreas,* 428.

35. Rüdiger Frank, "Dreaming an Impossible Dream? Opening, Reform, and the Future of the North Korean Economy," *Global Asia* 4, no. 2 (Summer 2009): 21.

36. Rice, *No Higher Honor,* 706–711.

15. Obama and Kim Jong Un

1. Thus, Israeli prime minister Benjamin Netanyahu appeared happy to have a reason to suspend negotiations with the Palestinians when Hamas and Fatah announced on April 24, 2014, that they would try to form a unity government—even though a united Palestinian Authority might have been a better negotiating partner than two divided factions.

2. Barack Obama, "Breaking the War Mentality," *Sundial* (Columbia University), March 10, 1983; Janny Scott, "Obama's Account of New York Years Often Differs from What Others Say," *New York Times,* October 30, 2007; William J. Broad and David E. Sanger, "Obama's Youth Shaped His Nuclear-Free Vision," *New York Times,* July 4, 2009.

3. David Brooks, "Obama, Gospel and Verse," *New York Times,* April 20, 2007.

4. Some observers admired the energy and creativity Ambassador Christopher Hill brought to negotiating with the DPRK in George W. Bush's second term, but others disliked his efforts to reach a deal with Pyongyang. Staffers for Vice President Dick Cheney called him "Kim Jong Hill." Senator Sam Brownback, Republican from Kansas, summed up Hill's record with North Korea as "no progress on human rights, terrible deal, failed diplomacy." Brownback's comments were made during Senate hearings in April 2009 on whether to approve Hill as U.S. ambassador to Iraq. Hill won approval, 73–23.

5. Thus, Assistant Secretary of State Kurt M. Campbell, speaking in Seoul on July 18, 2009, stated that if North Korea were prepared to take serious and irreversible steps toward denuclearization, then the United States and its partners "would be able to put together a comprehensive package that would be attractive to North Korea. But . . . North Korea really has to take some of the first steps." Text at http://m.state.gov/md126237.htm (accessed 10/1/2009).

6. From other sources we know that North Koreans knew of the Bosworth appointment before he did—a testimony, probably, to the efficacy of Chinese intelligence.

7. http://www.un.org/en/ga/search/view_doc.asp?symbol=S/PRST/2009/7 (accessed 11/1/2009).

8. https://www.armscontrol.org/factsheets/dprkchron (accessed 11/11/2015).

9. Ibid.

10. Ibid.

11. Stephan Haggard and Jaesung Ryu, "'Déjà Vu All Over Again': The UNSC, China, and Missiles," *North Korea: Witness to Transformation,* April 23, 2012, at http://blogs.piie.com/nk/?p=5867 (accessed 5/5/2014).

12. http://www.state.gov/secretary/20092013clinton/rm/2009a/july/126373.htm (accessed 10/1/2009).

13. http://www.theguardian.com/world/2009/jul/23/north-korea-asean-clinton (accessed 10/1/2009).

14. http://www.nobelprize.org/nobel_prizes/peace/laureates/2009/press.html (accessed 1/4/2010). Displeased by Obama's performance, many voices in 2015 called on Obama to return the prize. See, e.g., "Nobel Secretary Regrets Obama Peace Prize," BBC World News, September 17, 2015, at http://www.bbc.com/news/world-europe-34277960 (accessed 11/1/2015). Nobel committee members promptly castigated Geir Lundestad, the just-retired secretary, who had no vote on Nobel prizes, for breaching the committee's code of silence.

15. https://www.whitehouse.gov/the-press-office/remarks-president-acceptance-nobel-peace-prize (accessed 1/5/2010)

16. "North Korea Calls for End to Hostile Relations with US," *The Guardian,* January 1, 2010, at http://www.theguardian.com/world/2010/jan/01/north-korea-end-hostile-relations (accessed 2/1/2010).

17. This was the first party conference in over forty-four years and the first meeting of the KWP of any sort since the 21st Plenary Session of the Sixth Central Committee in December 1993. Despite the long interval since any party meetings were held, the 2010 conference lasted just one day. By contrast, the First and Second Party Conferences, held in 1958 and 1966, lasted four days and seven days respectively. Each was held in the context of a major purge of opponents to Kim Il Sung. See http://www.wilsoncenter.org/event/the-korean-workers-party-third-conference-what-it-all-about (accessed 5/19/2015).

18. R. Jeffrey Smith, "Pakistan's Nuclear-Bomb Maker Says North Korea Paid Bribes for Know-How," *Washington Post,* July 6, 2011.

19. Stephan Haggard, "*Juche* Steel," February 9, 2011, at http://www.piie.com/blogs/nk/?p=227 (accessed 2/10/2011).

20. The Unha's second stage had a low thrust and a long burn time—ideal to allow the rocket to reach a high altitude before placing a satellite into orbit, but a design that could reduce a missile's range by 1,000 kilometers. See Jason Hernandez, "Proliferation Pathways to a North Korean Intercontinental Ballistic Missile," *NTI,* December 20, 2013, at http://www.nti.org/analysis/articles/proliferation-pathways-north-korean-intercontinental-ballistic-missile/ (accessed 5/5/2014). For background, see Markus Schiller, *Characterizing the North Korean Nuclear Missile Threat* (Santa Monica, CA: RAND Corporation, 2012).

21. See Evans J. R. Revere, "Tough Challenges, Hard Choices: Dealing with North Korea after the Collapse of the Leap Day Agreement," National Committee on American Foreign Policy, New York, June 2012, at www.ncafp.org/ncafp/wp-content/uploads/2012/07/Revere-Tough-Challenges-N-Korea-Final.pdf (accessed 2/29/2014).

22. Resolution 2094 also strengthened existing sanctions, expanded the scope of mate-

rials covered, and increased measures for states to enforce and monitor the implementation of sanctions and the transshipment of materials to or from North Korea through their territories. The Security Council urged states to use guidance from the Financial Action Task Force (FATF) in limiting North Korea's access to finances that could be used for proliferation purposes. (The FATF is an intergovernmental body established in 1989 by ministers of its jurisdictions, thirty-four in 2015, to combat money laundering and terrorism.) No new monitoring mechanisms were included in Resolution 2094, but additional measures were provided to states to help implement and monitor the sanctions imposed against North Korea. Members of the committee on sanctions were called upon to update the list of sanctioned goods, entities, and individuals annually and report back to the Security Council.

23. Law on Consolidating Position of Nuclear Weapons State Adopted, April 1, 2013, Juche 102, at http://www.kcna.co.jp/index-e.htm (accessed 5/27/2014).

24. Leon V. Sigal, "A Nuclear North Korea vs. a Strategically Patient U.S.: Who Wins?" *National Interest*, April 24, 2014.

25. The fact of the talks was reported in the *Straits Times* and other publications worldwide but nothing about the content.

26. Text at the website of the National Committee on North Korea (a nongovernmental organization based in Washington): http://www.ncnk.org/resources/news-items/kim-jong-uns-speeches-and-public-statements-1/2014-new-year-address (accessed 11/1/2015). As noted earlier, the Kim Jong Un administration appeared in 2015 to have limited or closed off the archive of the Korean Central News Agency.

27. The NDC text was delivered to the UN Security Council as an annex to a letter dated January 20, 2014, from the DPRK permanent representative to the United Nations. See http://www.northkoreatech.org/wp-content/uploads/2014/01/N1421078.pdf (accessed 1/5/2015).

28. Robert Carlin, "Nothing Doing," *38 North*, January 17, 2014, at http://38north .org/2014/01/rcarlin011714/ (accessed 1/20/2014).

29. Wang Hongguang, "North Korean Missiles Passing through Chinese Air Routes Is Very Dangerous," *Huanqiu Shibao*, March 11, 2014. Translation by Adam Cathcart in *Sino-NK*, at http://sinonk.com/2014/03/12/north-korean-missiles-and-chinese-passenger-aircraft/ (accessed 5/26/2014).

30. Hon. Michael Kirby, AC CMG, had been Australia's longest-serving judge.

31. Text at http://www.ncnk.org/resources/publications/ndc-of-dprk-clarifies-stand-on-u.s.-hostile-policy-towards-it/?searchterm=ndc%20march%2014,%202014 (accessed 1/5/2015).

32. For analysis of the North's very hostile response to the earlier offer, see Andrei Lankov, "South Korea's 'Grand' Smokescreen," *Asia Times*, December 3, 2009.

33. Text at http://kcnawatch.nknews.org/article/ba1m (accessed 1/10/2015). In 2015 this news service, based in New Zealand, was blocked by censors in South as well as North Korea. See https://www.northkoreatech.org/tag/kcna-watch/ (accessed 11/16/2015).

34. For the full text of the April 25, 2014, press conference with Obama and Park Geun Hye, see http://www.whitehouse.gov/the-press-office/2014/04/25/press-conference-president-obama-and-president-park-republic-korea (accessed 7/12/2014).

35. I found no sign that the ROK agreed to Kim Jong Un's proposal in January 2014 to stop slandering each other, but both sides did make such a commitment on August 12, 2000.

36. Obama said the United States wanted to see a strong South Korean relationship with

China, just as it wanted such a relationship itself, but Washington wanted to see Seoul speak out when Beijing did things that weakened international rules. Reuters, October 16, 2015, at http://www.reuters.com/article/2015/10/16/us-obama-park-nuclear-idUSKCN0SA2H0 20151016#WKTAFKODXk6BBLvL.97 (accessed 11/16/2015).

16. NORTH KOREA'S WEAPONS OF MASS DESTRUCTION

1. R. Jeffrey Smith, "Pakistan's Nuclear-Bomb Maker Says North Korea Paid Bribes for Know-How," *Washington Post,* July 6, 2011; "Korea Paid Pakistan for Nuclear Weapons Tech," Associated Press, July 7, 2011.

2. Jacques E. C. Hymans, "Assessing North Korean Nuclear Intentions and Capacities: A New Approach," *Journal of East Asian Studies* 8, no. 2 (May–August 2008): 274–275.

3. ROK officials estimated that by 2001 the DPRK had nearly 3,000 nuclear experts, many of whom had trained at the Dubna facility in Russia (*Korea Times,* March 24, 2001). South Korean science proceeded at a high level. Kim Hong Suk, a research fellow at the Korean Institute of Nuclear Safety, was ranked among the hundred leading scientists, intellectuals, and educators in the world (*Korea Times,* September 4, 2009).

4. While electric power reactors require only enrichment from the 0.7 percent of natural uranium ore to about 3 percent U-235, nuclear weapons require enrichment to over 90 percent U-235. Part of the enriched uranium can be used to breed plutonium-239 for plutonium bombs.

5. Adapted from John S. Park, "Nuclear Ambition and Tension on the Korean Peninsula," in Ashley J. Tellis, Abraham M. Denmark, and Travis Tanner, eds., *Strategic Asia 2013–2014: Asia in the Second Nuclear Age* (Seattle: National Bureau of Asian Research, 2013), 163–199.

6. By giving more resources to the military-industrial complex the Kremlin hoped to end macroeconomic stagnation as well as bolster security. In 2014 Russia's outlays for defense and law enforcement consumed up to 34 percent of Russia's budget, more than double the ratio in 2010. The United States, by comparison, spent 18 percent, or $615 billion, of its budget in 2014. See Andrey Biryukov, "The Secret Money behind Vladimir Putin's War Machine," Bloomberg News June 2, 2015, at http://www.bloomberg.com/news/articles/2015-06-02/putin-s-secret-budget-hides-shift-toward-war-economy (accessed 7/1/2015).

7. President John F. Kennedy believed that the threat of nuclear retaliation could not deter a growing range of challenges. The Defense Department under Robert S. McNamara then sought a capacity for a "flexible response." See Walter S. Poole, *Adapting to Flexible Response, 1960–1968* (Washington DC: Historical Office, Office of the Secretary of Defense, 2013), 1–3. The DPRK, of course, faced a lesser range of military challenges than did a global superpower.

8. Bruce Bennett, "The Sixty Years of the Korea-U.S. Security Alliance: Past, Present, and Future," *International Journal of Korean Studies* 17, no. 2 (Fall–Winter 2013): 1–43 at 32, at http://www.icks.org/publication/pdf/2013-FALL-WINTER/2.pdf (accessed 5/24/2014).

9. Total: 1,190,000 (Army ε1,020,000; Navy 60,000; Air 110,000) plus Paramilitary 189,000. Conscript liability: Army 5–12 years, Navy 5–10 years, Air Force 3–4 years, followed by compulsory part-time service to age forty. Thereafter service in the Worker-Peasant Red Guard to age sixty. Reserve ε600,000 (Armed Forces ε600,000), Paramilitary

5,700,000. *The Military Balance 2015* (London: International Institute for Strategic Studies and Routledge, 2015). The Pentagon in 2016 estimated 950,000 in the army and 180,000 in special forces.

10. See also Anthony H. Cordesman and Ashley Hess, *The Evolving Military Balance in the Korean Peninsula and Northeast Asia: Conventional Balance, Asymmetric Forces, and U.S. Forces* (Washington, DC: Center for Strategic and International Studies, 2013).

11. Bennett, "The Sixty Years," 2–4.

12. Numbers drawn from *The Military Balance 2014* (London: International Institute for Strategic Studies and Routledge, 2014).

13. "Trends in World Military Expenditure, 2014," SIPRI Fact Sheet, April 2015, at http://books.sipri.org/files/FS/SIPRIFS1504.pdf (accessed 5/29/2015).

14. In 2014 an anti-ship cruise missile, not previously seen by outsiders, was displayed in a propaganda film. It appeared to be a sea-skimming, anti-ship cruise missile similar to the Russian 3M24 Uran, but also possessing features similar to the U.S. *Harpoon*. Its estimated range of 130 km and altitude of just 10 to 15 meters could imperil ROK vessels used for coastal defense. Satellite imagery in 2014 identified two new helicopter-carrying corvettes, the largest surface ships constructed by North Korea in twenty-five years, apparently designed for antisubmarine operations. Satellite imagery also showed an unidentified submarine type estimated to be at least twice as large as known indigenous DPRK submarine designs.

15. See Edward J. Snowden revelations at http://www.spiegel.de/media/media-35679 .pdf (accessed 5/28/2015).

16. Frank B. Pabian and Siegfried S. Hecker, "Contemplating a Third Nuclear Test in North Korea," *Bulletin of the Atomic Scientists*, August 6, 2012.

17. Park, "Nuclear Ambition and Tension."

18. Siegfried S. Hecker, "North Korea Reactor Restart Sets Back Denuclearization," *Bulletin of the Atomic Scientists*, October 17, 2013.

19. Siegfried S. Hecker, "A Return Trip to North Korea's Yongbyon Nuclear Complex," Center for International Security and Cooperation, Stanford University, November 20, 2010, at http://iis-db.stanford.edu/pubs/23035/HeckerYongbyon.pdf (accessed 5/14/2014); and Hecker, "Redefining Denuclearization in North Korea," *Bulletin of the Atomic Scientists*, December 20, 2010.

20. Feed material in the form of uranium hexafluoride ($UF6$) is needed to power the 2,000 centrifuges. While no $UF6$ fabrication plants were revealed or discovered in North Korea, they probably existed at undisclosed sites, because the DPRK shipped $UF6$ to Libya in previous years, using the A. Q. Khan network—in violation of agreements signed by Pyongyang in the 1990s.

21. Quoted in R. Jeffrey Smith, "Pakistan's Nuclear-Bomb Maker Says North Korea Paid Bribes for Know-How," *Washington Post*, July 6, 2011.

22. Bennett, "The Sixty Years," 6–7. The importance of chemical warfare was underscored in Kim Il Sung's Declaration for Chemicalization at the end of 1961. The Federation of American Scientists reported that in 1964 the DPRK concluded a contract with Japan for deliveries of agricultural chemicals. Under the guise of these deliveries, components came into the country initially for synthesis of tabun and mustard gas; later, chlorine and phosphorus-containing organic compounds were imported. See also Joseph S. Bermudez, "The Democratic People's Republic of Korea and Unconventional Weapons," in Peter R. Lavoy et al., eds., *Planning the Unthinkable: How New Powers Will Use Nuclear, Biological, and Chemical Weapons* (Ithaca, NY: Cornell University Press, 2000).

23. http://www.fas.org/nuke/guide/dprk/cw/index.html (accessed 5/24/2014).

24. Based on the Russian-made 9K79 Tochka (SS-21 Scarab), the DPRK missile had an extended range of 220 km, a sharp increase from the previous maximum range of 140 km. North Korea obtained the Tochka system from Syria in the 1990s. North Korean media said that the missile could strike military command centers close to Daejeon, in the middle of South Korea. Claims were also made about the improved accuracy of the KN-02, already the DPRK's most accurate ballistic missile, with a 100-meter circular error probability. Ibid.

25. Jackson and Suh remind us that the most dangerous scenario should not be conflated with the most likely one. "Rather than being paralyzed by the fact that anything is possible, alliance policy and military planning needs to recognize a simple reality: no matter what North Korea threatens, it will assiduously seek to avoid war-triggering actions." Van Jackson and Hannah Suh, "The Biggest Myth about North Korea," *National Interest,* July 9, 2015, at http://national interest.org/feature/the-biggest-myth-about-north-korea-13290 (accessed 7/10/2015).

26. The information in table 16.1 derives from many estimates, including *Military and Security Developments involving the Democratic People's Republic of Korea 2013: Annual Report to Congress* (Washington, DC: Office of the Secretary of Defense, 2014), at http://www.defense.gov/pubs/North_Korea_Military_Power_Report_2013–2014; Bennett, "The Sixty Years"; Global Security at http://www.globalsecurity.org/wmd/world/dprk/missile .htm; David Wright, "What Can North Korea's Missiles Reach?" Union of Concerned Scientists, April 4, 2013, at http://allthingsnuclear.org/what-can-north-koreas-missiles-reach/; Michael Elleman, "Prelude to an ICBM? Putting North Korea's Unha-3 Launch into Context," *Arms Control Today,* at https://www.armscontrol.org/act/2013_03/Prelude-to-an-ICBM%3FPutting-North-Koreas-Unha-3-Launch-Into-Context; Stephan Haggard, Daniel Pinkston, Kevin Stahler, and Clint Work, "Interpreting North Korea's Missile Tests: When Is a Missile Just a Missile?" *North Korea: Witness to Transformation,* October 7, 2014, at http://blogs.piie.com/nk/?p=13532 (all accessed 5/30/2015).

27. Law on Consolidating Position of Nuclear Weapons State, adopted April 1, 2013, Juche 102, at http://www.kcna.co.jp/index-e.htm (accessed 5/27/2014); also at http://kcnawatch .nknews.org/article/otu (accessed 11/15/2015).

28. Burma's generals in 2014 were constructing a chemical weapons facility near Pauk and a missile facility near Minbu. These were among several facilities being built by the Directorate of Defense Industries (DDI), the agency responsible for the arms trade with North Korea. Burmese journalists who wrote about the Pauk factory were arrested and the magazine with their articles confiscated. Burma signed the Chemical Weapons Convention (CWC) in 1993 but, as of 2014, had still not ratified the CWC. The government in Burma promised the Obama administration that it would break with North Korea once it had paid for the surface-to-air missiles, but it did not. Indeed, the DDI expanded after 2009, and Burmese generals remained a law unto themselves. The U.S. Treasury placed Lt. Gen. Thein Htay, head of the DDI, on its sanctions list for alleged arms deals with the DPRK. See Jeffrey Lewis and Catherine Dill, "Myanmar's Unrepentant Arms Czar," *Foreign Policy,* May 9, 2014, at http://foreign-policy.com/2014/05/09/myanmars-unrepentant-arms-czar/ (accessed 7/10/2014).

29. The Panel of Experts was established pursuant to UNSC Resolution 1874 (2009). Its report (S/2014/147) was presented on March 6, 2014. See http://www.securitycouncilreport .org/atf/cf/%7B65BFCF9B-6D27–4E9C-8CD3-CF6E4FF96FF9%7D/s_2014_147 .pdf (accessed 5/6/2014). The panel's chairman, Martin Uden, a former UK ambassador to South Korea, was dismissed after submitting the report, a possible bow to pressures from friends of the DPRK; but the panel's mandate was extended for a year.

30. Hugh Griffiths and Lawrence Dermody, "Feb. 13: Sanctions beyond Borders: How to Make North Korea Sanctions Work," at http://www.sipri.org/media/newsletter/essay/griffiths_dermody_feb13; and, by the same authors, "Loopholes in UN Sanctions against North Korea," *38 North,* May 6, 2014, at http://38north.org/2014/05/griffithdermod 050614/; updated by Stephan Haggard, "The Mu Dong," September 10, 2014, at http://blogs .piie.com/nk/?p=13474 (both accessed 9/12/2014).

31. Olli Heinonen, "North Korea's Nuclear Enrichment: Capabilities and Consequences," *38 North,* June 22, 2011, at http://belfercenter.ksg.harvard.edu/publication/21153/north_koreas_nuclear_enrichment.html (accessed 4/8/2014).

32. Benjamin David Baker, "South Korea Goes Indigenous for Its Missile Defense Needs," *The Diplomat,* November 7, 2015, at http://thediplomat.com/2015/11/south-korea-goes-indigenous-for-its-missile-defense-needs/ (accessed 11/20/2015).

33. *Defense Industry Daily* reported on June 15, 2015, that a set of serious technical flaws had been identified in the U.S. Missile Defense Agency's Ground-Based Midcourse Defense (GMD) system—the latest problem in a program whose R&D costs already exceeded $41 billion since being accelerated by President George W. Bush in 2002. The GMD got a kill in a highly scripted test in 2014—the first success since 2008. Nonetheless, these same exoatmospheric kill vehicles (EKVs) were operationally deployed on dozens of ground-based interceptor (GBI) missiles in Alaska and California. But the Missile Defense Agency (MDA) in 2014–2015 decided on a full redesign of the missile's kill vehicle—budgeted at $99.5 million in FY 2015. Overall interceptor improvements were budgeted to cost around $700 million from FY 2015–2019.

The Pentagon's director of operational test and evaluation, J. Michael Gilmore, wrote in his annual report, released January 29, 2014, that recent test failures of the U.S. GBI system raised concerns about the system's reliability and suggested that the missile's EKV be redesigned to assure it became "robust against failure." The EKV is lifted into space by a booster rocket and then uses its onboard sensors to locate an incoming enemy warhead and destroy it on impact. Some U.S. officials compared the task to hitting a bullet with another bullet. Echoing Gilmore's view, Frank Kendall, undersecretary of defense for acquisition, technology, and logistics, told a February 25, 2014, conference in Washington, "We've got to get to more reliable [missile defense] systems." Merely "patching the things we've got is probably not going to be adequate. So we're going to have to go beyond that," he said. Gilmore and Kendall quoted in http://www.armscontrol.org/act/2014_03/Missile-Defense-Tester-Calls-for-Redesign (accessed 5/30/2015).

Roger A. Mola asked: "Does missile defense actually work?" He answered, "Not 100 percent. But it's better than it used to be." *Airspacemag.com,* April 9, 2013 (accessed 5/27/2014). Anything less than 100 percent, of course, could mean catastrophe. In fact, the MDA tests of its various systems failed more than half the time—even though they aimed to intercept *individual* reentry vehicles. There was still no conceivable way a system of systems in the fog of war could discriminate and cope with multiple warheads and decoys delivered by an ICBM. Hitting lower- and slower-flying missiles with defensive missiles (e.g., Aegis systems) was more feasible than coping with the high trajectory and velocity of an ICBM.

17. Revolutionary Pariahs

1. David Brooks, "Obama, Gospel and Verse," *New York Times,* April 26, 2007.

2. Michael Cooper, "U.S. Candidates Use Iran's Missile Tests as a Chance for a Foreign

Policy Debate," *New York Times,* July 10, 2008. Obama made this point in many contexts, for example, in an extended interview with Michael Gordon and Jeff Zeleny published in ibid., November 1, 2007.

3. William C. Potter et al., "Tito's Nuclear Legacy," *Bulletin of the Atomic Scientists* 56, no. 2 (March–April 2000): 63–70 at 69.

4. For a flavor of Khamenei's worldview, see the Supreme Leader's "Speech in a Meeting with Members of the Supreme Council of Cultural Revolution" on December 15, 2013, at http://www.leader.ir/langs/en/index.php?p=contentShow&id=11367 (accessed 1/15/2014). In July 2014 he declared that Iran would not dismantle any of its infrastructure under Western pressure, but would not need a major expansion of its fuel-making facilities for at least five years.

5. Walter C. Clemens Jr., "How 'Happy' Went Viral—Even in Iran," *Global Asia Forum,* February 16, 2015 at https://globalasia.org/forum/how-happy-went-viral-even-in-iran/ (accessed 4/6/2015).

6. References to Iran as a monolith also ignored the ethnic minorities who chafed at dictation from Tehran. In 1998 I asked nomadic sheepherders in southern Iran if the United States should seek reconciliation with the Iranian government or try to overthrow it. An elder replied, "Overthrow!" Eyes flashing at the prospect, young and old in his group seemed to agree.

7. Jessica T. Mathews, "Iran: A Good Deal Now in Danger," *New York Review of Books* (February 20, 2014): 8–12.

8. "Kissinger and Shultz: What a Final Iran Deal Must Do," *Wall Street Journal,* December 2, 2013.

9. Full text in *Washington Post,* July 15, 2015, at http://apps.washingtonpost.com/g/documents/world/full-text-of-the-iran-nuclear-deal/1651/ (accessed 7/15/2015).

10. *Tehran Times,* July 15, 2015, at http://www.tehrantimes.com/largPic.asp?12317/12317.jpg (accessed 7/15/2015).

11. "Global Nuclear Watchdog IAEA Ends Iran 'Weapons' Probe," BBC, December 14, 2015, at http://www.bbc.com/news/world-middle-east-35104715 (accessed 12/15/2015).

12. The leader's New Year address on January 1, 2014, boasted that factionalism had been removed. See http://www.kcna.co.jp/index-e.htm (accessed 1/5/2014).

13. John S. Park, "North Korea, Inc : Gaining Insights into North Korean Regime Stability from Recent Commercial Activities" United States Institute of Peace, May 15, 2009, at http://www.usip.org/publications/north-korea-inc-gaining-insights-north-korean-regime-stability-recent-commercial-activitie (accessed 10/10/2010).

14. For the horrific conditions in which orphans try to survive, see the *Frontline* documentary "Secret State of North Korea" at http://www.pbs.org/wgbh/pages/frontline/secret-state-of-north-korea/ (accessed 1/15/2014). See also Adam Johnson, *The Orphan Master's Son* (New York: Random House, 2012).

15. http://globalfirepower.com/countries-listing.asp (accessed 4/12/2014).

16. Hecker interviewed by Kourosh Ziabari, "Iran Can Enjoy International Cooperation on Its Nuclear Energy Program," *Tehran Times,* May 30, 2014, at http://www.tehrantimes.com/component/content/article/93-interviews/116035-iran-can-enjoy-international-cooperation-on-its-nuclear-energy-program (accessed 7/14/2014).

17. John W. Limbert, *Negotiating with Iran: Wrestling with the Ghosts of History* (Washington, DC: United States Institute of Peace, 2009); Suzanne Maloney, *Iran's Long Reach: Iran as a Pivotal State in the Muslim World* (Washington, DC: United States Institute of

Peace, 2008); Robin Wright, ed., *The Iran Primer: Power, Politics, and U.S. Policy* (Washington, DC: United States Institute of Peace, 2010).

18. When I described this event to a Moroccan student in Boston, he wept at how far a key Muslim country had fallen from its enlightened past.

19. Millspaugh wrote two books on Persia, several more on the United States, and one on Haiti.

20. James Buchan, *Days of God: The Revolution in Iran and Its Consequences* (London: John Murray, 2012). Official U.S. government reports suggested that Kermit Roosevelt's leadership gave spine and direction to the coup. See John Cassidy, "The Lessons of Classified Information: From Mossadegh to Snowden," *The New Yorker*, August 20, 2013, at http://www.newyorker.com/news/johncassidy/the=lessons=of=classified=information=from-mossadegh-to-snowden.html (accessed 6/2/2015).

21. Lenin's instructions were not published until 1964, apparently to buttress Nikita Khrushchev's policies against Chinese criticisms. See Walter C. Clemens Jr., "Lenin on Disarmament," *Slavic Review* 23, no. 3 (September 1964): 504–525.

22. Trita Parsi, *Treacherous Alliance: The Secret Dealings of Israel, Iran, and the United States* (New Haven: Yale University Press, 2007), 243–249, with the text of the proposal in Appendix A. Some analysts doubt that all the top Iranians were behind the proposal. Condoleezza Rice later denied she had seen it, according to Glenn Kessler: "Rice Denies Seeing Iranian Proposal in '03," *Washington Post*, February 8, 2007.

23. John Delury, "Lessons from North Korea: How to Avoid a Nuclear Iran," *Foreign Affairs SNAPSHOT*, April 5, 2015, at https://www.foreignaffairs.com/articles/north-korea/2015-04-05/lessons-north-korea?cid=nlc-foreign_affairs_this_week-041015-lessons_from_north_korea_6-041015&sp_mid=48418130&sp_rid=bWFyeS5r5rYX N6QGdtYWlsLmNvbQS2 (accessed 6/2/2015).

18. Basic Forces and *Fortuna* versus Human Factors

1. Graham Allison and Philip Zelikow, *Essence of Decision: Explaining the Cuban Missile Crisis*, 2nd ed. (New York: Longman, 1999).

2. For Indonesia A to Z and a detailed bibliography, see Audrey Kahin, comp., *Historical Dictionary of Indonesia*, 3rd ed. (Lanham, MD: Rowman & Littlefield, 2015).

3. Barack Obama, *Dreams from My Father: A Story of Race and Inheritance* (New York: Random House, 2004), 35–41. Whether or not Lolo spoke precisely these words, such ideas left an imprint on the boy's consciousness. For other insights, see Obama, *The Audacity of Hope: Thoughts on Reclaiming the American Dream* (New York: Crown, 2006).

4. Barack Obama, "Breaking the War Mentality," *Sundial* 7, no. 12 (March 10, 1983): 2–4.

5. Janny Scott, "Obama's Account of New York Years Often Differs from What Others Say," *New York Times*, October 30, 2007; William J. Broad and David E. Sanger, "Obama's Youth Shaped His Nuclear-Free Vision," *New York Times*, July 4, 2009.

6. Heonik Kwon and Byung-Ho Chung, *North Korea: Beyond Charismatic Politics* (Lanham, MD.: Rowman & Littlefield, 2012).

7. For analysis of many classic and recent theories, see Jennifer Sterling-Folker, ed., *Making Sense of International Relations Theory* (Boulder, CO: Lynne Rienner, 2006).

8. Jonathan Haslam, *No Virtue Like Necessity: Realist Thought in International Relations since Machiavelli* (New Haven: Yale University Press, 2002); Michael Smith, *Realist Thought from Weber to Kissinger* (Baton Rouge: Louisiana State University Press, 1990).

9. Kenneth N. Waltz, *Theory of International Politics* (McGraw-Hill, 1979); Robert O. Keohane, ed., *Neorealism and Its Critics* (New York: Columbia University Press, 1986); David A. Baldwin, ed., *Neorealism and Neoliberalism: The Contemporary Debate* (New York: Columbia University Press, 1993).

10. Leslie H. Gelb, *Power Rules: How Common Sense Can Rescue American Foreign Policy* (New York: HarperCollins, 2009).

11. In the case of the USSR, the first breakthrough occurred in 1963, when Moscow's signature on the 1963 nuclear test ban led to large imports of U.S. grain. Of course, other factors also played a role. Moscow and Washington sought conditions that would make another Cuban missile confrontation less likely.

12. Food aid to North Korea increased by nearly seven times in 1997–1998 relative to 1996–1997 and remained at a high level until 2005, when it fell to less than in 1997–1998. It is difficult to correlate need with foreign aid because of the inherent lags between demand and supply. See the tables recording humanitarian assistance to North Korea from 1996 to 2005 in Stephan Haggard and Marcus Noland, *Famine in North Korea: Markets, Aid, and Reform* (New York: Columbia University Press, 2007), Appendixes 2.1–2.4.

13. Cary Nederman, "Niccolò Machiavelli," *The Stanford Encyclopedia of Philosophy*, Fall 2009 ed., ed. Edward N. Zalta, http://plato stanford.edu/archives/fall2009/entries/machiavelli/ (accessed 3/22/2014).

14. Hindsight bias is the inclination to see events that have occurred as more predictable than they in fact were before they took place. Hindsight bias has been demonstrated experimentally in many settings, including politics and medicine. In psychological experiments of hindsight bias, subjects tend to remember their predictions of future events as having been stronger than they actually were—in those cases where those predictions turn out correct.

15. Nassim N. Taleb, *The Black Swan: The Impact of the Highly Improbable* (New York: Random House, 2007); and Taleb, *Antifragile: Things That Gain from Disorder* (New York: Random House, 2012).

16. One polymath argues the inadequacies of any reductionism. The evolution of the universe and of humankind does not violate the laws of physics but cannot be explained by them. Stuart A. Kauffman, *Reinventing the Sacred: A New View of Science, Reason, and Religion* (New York: Basic Books, 2008).

17. Innovators in tiny Israel compete and cooperate with those in Silicon Valley.

18. Which force will decide who wins in politics—*fortuna* or skillful use of hard power? Piero di Medici could have kept his family in power in fifteenth-century Florence by brute force. Instead, he used cunning to eliminate from the voting urn the names of those not devoted to his cause. The story is told in the chapter "Games of Fortune" in Miles J. Unger, *Magnifico: The Brilliant Life and Violent Times of Lorenzo de' Medici* (New York: Simon & Schuster, 2008), 118–119.

19. For other cases, see Philip E. Tetlock, Richard Ned Lebow, and Geoffrey Parker, eds., *Unmasking the West: "What-if" Scenarios That Rewrite World History* (Ann Arbor: University of Michigan Press, 2006).

20. What if Wilson's concern for the equal dignity of "nations" had included equal rights for all races? As a historian, Wilson wrote that in the aftermath of Reconstruction white men of the South, for their own self-preservation, were driven to remove that "intolerable burden of governments sustained by the votes of ignorant negroes." Wilson, *A History of the American People* (New York: Harper, 1917), ix, 58. In subsequent pages he provided a sympathetic narrative about the Ku Klux Klan. As president, Wilson rolled back the gains made

by black officials in government service since Reconstruction and oversaw the segregation of rank-and-file workers. Andy Newman, "At Princeton, Woodrow Wilson, a Heralded Alum, Is Recast as an Intolerant One," *New York Times*, November 23, 2015. Illustrating the point about government service, see Gordon J. Davis, "What Woodrow Wilson Cost My Grandfather," *New York Times*, November 24, 2015.

21. Counterfactual history is not the same as historical revisionism (negationism) or alternative history. See Niall Ferguson, ed., *Virtual History: Alternatives and Counterfactuals* (New York: Basic Books, 1999).

22. Following the U.S. example, no Western country except Sweden and, for a short time, New Zealand ever recognized Soviet annexation of the Baltic states. See Walter C. Clemens Jr., *Baltic Independence and Russian Empire* (New York: St. Martin's, 1991).

23. Choong Nam Kim, *The Korean Presidents: Leadership for Nation Building* (Norwalk, CT: Eastbridge, 2007), 142.

24. Diplomatic relations between the two countries were restored in 2007. Soon, reports surfaced that Pyongyang had sold rocket launchers to Myanmar and increased DPRK purchases of raw materials from Myanmar. In 2011 Myanmar was alleged to be building a nuclear weapons program with the aid of North Korea. In 2013, however, Burmese president Thein Sein, a member of the military junta that had often thumbed its nose at the West, approved adoption of the stringent IAEA's Additional Protocol. A few hours later, Sein welcomed President Barack Obama as he arrived on Air Force One. After Burma's political opening, however, tentative reforms stalled and bursts of ethnic conflict suggested that the country's democracy was very fragile. Still, the military permitted a relatively free election in 2015, in which Aung San Suu Kyi's National League for Democracy won a large majority in parliament, permitting her to select the next president.

25. Quoted by Choe Sang Hun, "Kim Young Sam, South Korean President Who Opposed Military, Dies at 87," *New York Times*, November 23, 2015.

26. Blaine Harden, *The Great Leader and the Fighter Pilot: The True Story of the Tyrant Who Created North Korea and the Young Lieutenant Who Stole His Way to Freedom* (New York: Viking, 2015).

27. Not everything was perfect. His closest friend and four other pilots were executed for not discovering or stopping his defection. Later, in the United States, his son—in his forties—committed suicide.

28. The Korean Central News Agency (KCNA) on October 16, 2008 (Juche 97) assured readers that "the Korean people are entrusting their destinies entirely to the great revolutionary party and are implementing the Party's lines and policies by displaying boundless loyalty and devotion with the revolutionary faith 'the Party decides, so we do!'"

29. Immanuel Kant, *Political Writings* (New York: Cambridge University Press, 2006); Bruce Russett, "Democratic Peace," in *Oxford International Encyclopedia of Peace*, ed. Nigel Young, 4 vols. (New York: Oxford University Press, 2009), I: 559–562; and Walter C. Clemens Jr., "Internationalist Theory and Liberal Democracy," ibid., II: 450–453. On ties between self-organization and fitness, see Clemens, *Complexity Science and World Affairs* (Albany: State University of New York Press, 2013).

30. Herodotus made a similar point as he compared Persian autocracy with Athenian democracy.

31. Seeking to report on honors for its Dear Leader, the KCNA proudly reported in October 2007 that a Kim Jong Il essay on Juche (June 19, 1997 [Juche 86]) was recently published as a pamphlet in Aruba. An even greater feat was broadcast on October 16, 2008.

Kim Jong Il's work "Our Socialism Centered on the Masses Shall Not Perish" was brought out as a pamphlet by the Party for Peace and Unity of Russia. The work, first published on May 5, 1991 (Juche 80), purported to clarify the sure victory of Korean-style socialism, key to the solidity and invincibility of socialism in the DPRK and its essential characteristics. A book-releasing ceremony took place in Moscow on October 9, 2008.

32. James Pearson, "Women Activists Cross DMZ to Mixed Reception on South Korean Side," Reuters, May 24, 2015, at http://www.reuters.com/article/2015/05/24/us-northkorea-southkorea-dmz-idUSKBN0090712010524#hgeF63YASVIORpru.97 (accessed 6/2/2015). The group also reported to U.S. audiences. See, e.g., https://www.womencrossdmz.org/women-cross-dmz-historic-walk-in-the-koreas-for-peace-and-reunification/   (accessed 11/23/2015).

33. See, e.g., Joshua Stanton, "Women Cross DMZ," May 25, 2015, at http://freekorea.us/2015/05/25/women-cross-dmz-a-qa-and-closing-thoughts/ (accessed 6/11/2015).

34. Matthew Evangelista, *Unarmed Forces: The Transnational Movement to End the Cold War* (Ithaca: Cornell University Press, 1999).

35. Mark Berry, "Meeting Kim Il Sung in His Last Weeks," April 15, 2012, at http://www.nknews.org/2012/04/meeting-kim-il-sung-in-his-last-weeks/ (accessed 2/10/2015).

36. On the use of force, however, Europeans could be said to come from Venus; Americans, from Mars. Robert Kagan, *Of Paradise and Power: American and Europe in the New World Order* (New York: Alfred A. Knopf, 2003).

37. Alexander J. Motyl, e-mail from Rutgers University, October 30, 2008.

38. Malcolm Gladwell, *Outliers: The Story of Success* (Boston: Little, Brown, 2008).

19. WHAT TO DO ABOUT—OR WITH—CHINA?

1. For the text of the report, see http://www.ohchr.org/EN/HRBodies/HRC/CoID-PRK/Pages/ReportoftheCommissionofInquiryDPRK.aspx (accessed 2/28/2014).

2. The Helsinki Final Act was an agreement signed by thirty-five states attending the Conference on Security and Cooperation in Europe held in Helsinki in 1975. The multifaceted act addressed a range of prominent global issues, and in so doing had a far-reaching effect on the Cold War and U.S.-Soviet relations.

3. According to Shakespeare, the merchant of Venice was advised that "The quality of mercy is not strained; / It droppeth as the gentle rain from heaven / Upon the place beneath. It is twice blest; / It blesseth him that gives and him that takes." The limits of a Chinese court's mercy were tested in November 2015 after the seventy-one-year-old investigative journalist Gao Yu pleaded guilty to giving documents to a Chinese language news source in the United States. An appeals court reduced her sentence from seven to five years and decided Ms. Gao could "temporarily serve the sentence out of prison" as she was "severely ill." See http://www.bbc.com/news/world-asia-china-34929468 (accessed 11/26/2015).

4. Wang Hongguang, "If North Korea's Nuclear Facilities Suffer an Attack by the United States and South Korea, the Nuclear Pollution Will Be a Disaster for China," *Huanqiu Shibao*, December 16, 2013, translated by Adam Cathcart, at http://sinonk.com/2013/12/20/pla-general-incalculable-damage/ (accessed 5/28/2014).

5. Bruce Bennett, "The Sixty Years of the Korea-U.S. Security Alliance: Past, Present, and Future," *International Journal of Korean Studies* 17, no. 2 (Fall–Winter 2013): 1–43 at 33, at http://www.icks.org/publication/pdf/2013-FALL-WINTER/2.pdf (accessed 5/24/2014).

6. Remarks by Adam Cathcart, "In the Shadow of Jang Song Taek: Pyongyang's Evolv-

ing SEZ Strategy along the China-North Korean Border," Korea Economic Institute, Washington, DC, June 19, 2014.

7. http://www.korea.net/Special/Foreign-Affairs/view (accessed 9/21/2015).

8. Mel Gurtov, "Mr. Xi Goes to Seoul," *China-US Focus,* July 15, 2014, at http://www.chinausfocus.com/foreign-policy/mr-xi-goes-to-seoul/ (accessed 7/17/2014).

9. Asan Country Report: South Korea, November 23, 2015, at http://www.theasanforum.org/south-korea-november-2015/ (accessed 11/27/2015).

10. Jonathan D. Pollack, "Reassessing the Park-Xi Summit," Asian Institute for Policy Studies, September 29, 2014, at http://www.theasanforum.org/a-us-perspective/ (accessed 11/1/2014).]

11. Bennett, "The Sixty Years of the Korea-U.S. Security Alliance," 26–28.

12. See, for example, "Getting Ugly: If China Wants Respect Abroad, It Must Rein in Its Hackers," *The Economist,* February 23, 2013; Louisa Lim, *The People's Republic of Amnesia: Tiananmen Revisited* (New York: Oxford University Press, 2014); Evan Osnos, *Age of Ambition: Chasing Fortune, Truth, and Faith in the New China* (New York: Farrar, Straus and Giroux, 2014).

13. Numerous reports on the BBC, including http://www.bbc.com/news/science-environment-27027876 (accessed 4/14/2014).

14. Quoted in Jonathan Weisman, "U.S. Primacy on Economics Is Seen Ebbing," *New York Times,* April 18, 2015, pp. 1, 3.

15. Nadège Rolland, "China's National Power: A Colossus with Iron or Clay Feet?" in Ashley J. Tellis et al., eds., *Strategic Asia 2015–16: Foundations of National Power in the Asia-Pacific* (Seattle: National Bureau of Asian Research, 2015), 45–46; on China's GDP, see http://www.bloomberg.com/news/articles/2015-10-19/china-s-gdp-growth-beats-forecasts-as-stimulus-supports-spending (accessed 10/26/2015). The actual defense outlays for the United States could be twice the official numbers if allowances were made for spending on intelligence, homeland security, nuclear and space research, pensions and medical treatment for veterans, and interest on past military outlays.

16. For Allison's views and other perspectives, see Richard Rosecrance and Steven E. Miller, eds., *The Next Great War: The Roots of World War I and the Risk of U.S.-China Conflict* (Cambridge: The MIT Press, 2015). For Allison's sixteen cases, see http://belfercenter.ksg.harvard.edu/publication/24928/thucydides_trap_case_file.html; for the methodology and other potential cases, see http://belfercenter.ksg.harvard.edu/publication/25782/thucydides_trap_methodology.html (accessed 10/1/2015).

17. Aaron L. Friedberg, *A Contest for Supremacy: China, America, and the Struggle for Mastery in Asia* (New York: W. W. Norton, 2011).

18. See Friedberg, "Xi Jingping's Anti-Corruption Campaign Is Doomed to Fail," *The Diplomat,* October 7, 2014, at http://thediplomat.com/2014/10/xi-jinpings-anti-corruption-campaign-is-doomed-to-fail/ (accessed 10/1/2015).

19. Walter C. Clemens Jr., "Must the United States Fight China?" *The Diplomat,* May 13, 2015, at http://thediplomat.com/2015/05/must-the-united-states-fight-china/ (accessed 6/1/2015).

20. A survey of recent books on World War I noted that the lack of institutions to resolve conflicts led to rapid-fire interactions between autonomous power centers operating under conditions of high risk and low trust. Uncertainty within alliances also played a role. "Still in the Grip of the Great War," *The Economist,* March 2–April 4, 2014: 87–91.

21. Simon Winder, "If Franz Ferdinand Had Lived," *New York Times,* June 27, 2014.

22. Resentments born in the past as well as in the present helped motivate the North African terrorists who struck London, Madrid, Paris, and other Western targets. See Walter C. Clemens Jr., "Who Created This Monster?" *Counterpunch,* November 24, 2015, at http://www.counterpunch.org/2015/11/24/who-created-this-monster/ (accessed 11/25/2015).

23. Shannon Tiezzi, "US-China Relations: Thucydidean Trap or Prisoner's Dilemma?" *The Diplomat,* March 24, 2014, at http://thediplomat.com/2014/03/us-china-relations-thucydidean-trap-or-prisoners-dilemma/ (accessed 5/25/2014).

24. Wang Jisi and Kenneth G. Lieberthal, "Addressing U.S.-China Strategic Distrust," Brookings Institution, John L. Thornton China Center Monograph Series, no. 4 (March 2012) at http://www.brookings.edu/~/media/research/files/papers/2012/3/30-us-china-lieberthal/0330_china_lieberthal.pdf (accessed 6/1/2012).

25. David Shambaugh, ed., *Tangled Titans: The United States and China,* (Lanham, MD: Rowman & Littlefield, 2013), editor's introduction, and Wu Xinbo, "Chinese Visions of the Future of U.S.-Chinese Relations," ibid. 371–388.

26. "Sun-tzu's Art of War," in Ralph D. Sawyer, trans., *The Seven Military Classics of Ancient China* (Boulder, CO: Westview. 1993), 155, 158.

27. Whitman, *Leaves of Grass;* Matthew Aucoin's, *The Crossing,* his opera that premiered in Boston in June 2015, describes Whitman's service as a nurse in a Civil War hospital and his dealings with a soldier from the enemy's army.

28. Qianfan Zhang, "Human Dignity in Classical Chinese Philosophy: The Daoist Perspective," *Journal of Chinese Philosophy* 40, no. 3–4 (September–December 2013): 493–510.

29. Erica Brindley, "Individualism in Classical Chinese Thought," *Internet Encyclopedia of Philosophy,* at http://www.iep.utm.edu/ind-chin/ (accessed 6/6/2015).

30. Zhang Wang, "Not Rising, but Rejuvenating: The 'Chinese Dream,'" *The Diplomat,* February 5, 2013, at http://thediplomat.com/2013/02/chinese-dream-draft/ (accessed 6/5/2015).

31. Lyle J. Goldstein, *Meeting China Halfway: How to Defuse the Emerging US-China Rivalry* (Washington, DC: Georgetown University Press, 2015).

32. http://eng.mod.gov.cn/Database/WhitePapers/2000.htm (accessed 9/15/2015).

33. See G. S. Khurana, "China Challenges the Unipolar World Order: An Assessment of China's Defence White Paper 2014," New Delhi, National Maritime Foundation, June 3, 2015, www.maritimeindia.org/View%20Profile/635688797701778445.pdf (accessed 10/1/2015).

34. Jeffrey Lewis, *Paper Tigers: China's Nuclear Posture* (London: International Institute for Strategic Studies and Routledge, 2014).

35. Steven Pinker, *The Better Angels of Our Nature: Why Violence Has Declined* (New York: Viking, 2011); Ian Morris, *War! What Is It Good For? Conflict and the Progress of Civilization from Primates to Robots* (New York: Farrar, Straus and Giroux, 2014).

36. Ian Johnson, "Will the Chinese Be Supreme?" *New York Review of Books,* April 4, 2013.

37. Yeongmi Yun and Kicheol Park, "Structural Restrictions of Territorial Disputes in Northeast Asia," *Journal of East Asian Affairs* 27, no. 2 (Fall–Winter 2013): 89–113.

38. Bill Hayton, *The South China Sea: The Struggle for Power in Asia* (New Haven: Yale University Press, 2014).

39. Robert D. Kaplan, *Asia's Cauldron: The South China Sea and the End of a Stable Pacific* (New York: Random House, 2014).

40. Gregory B. Poling, "The South China Sea in Focus: Clarifying the Limits of Maritime Dispute," Washington, D.C.: Center for Strategic and International Studies, July 2013

at http://csis.org/files/publication/130717_Poling_SouthChinaSea_Web.pdf (accessed 1/7/2014). Thanks to Frauke Heidemann and Patrick Renz, Europeans studying in Beijing, for this reference and other suggestions.

41. Brunei claims a southern reef of the Spratly Islands. Malaysia claims three islands in the Spratlys. The Philippines claims eight islands in the Spratlys and significant portions of the South China Sea. Vietnam, Taiwan, and China each claims much of the South China Sea, as well as all of the Spratly and Paracel island groups.

42. Edward N. Luttwak, *The Rise of China vs. The Logic of Strategy* (Cambridge: Harvard University Press, 2012).

43. Odd Arne Westad, *Restless Empire: China and the World since 1750* (New York: Basic Books, 2012); also Howard French, *China's Second Continent: How a Million Migrants Are Building a New Empire in Africa* (New York: Alfred A. Knopf, 2014).

44. Chinese as well as U.S. and Australian ships and a Chinese helicopter (made in Russia) cooperated in January 2014 to liberate a Russian research vessel with a cosmopolitan passenger list icebound in Antarctica.

45. Zou Keyuan, "The Sino-Vietnamese Agreement on Maritime: Boundary Delimitation in the Gulf of Tonkin," *Ocean Development and International Law* 36 (2005): 13–24; Nguyen Hong Thao, "Maritime Delimitation and Fishery Cooperation in the Tonkin Gulf," *Ocean Development and International Law* 36 (2005): 25–44; Ian Storey, "Conflict in the South China Sea: China's Relations with Vietnam and the Philippines," at http://www.japanfocus.org/-ian-storey/2734#sthash.zhlZehsy.dpuf (accessed 1/7/2014).

46. Kurt M. Campbell and Ely Ratner, "Far Eastern Promises: Why Washington Should Focus on Asia," *Foreign Affairs* 93, no. 3 (May–June 2014): 106–116 at 116.

47. http://thediplomat.com/2015/11/arguments-open-in-philippine-case-against-chinas-south-china-sea-claims/ (accessed 11/26/2011).

48. Graham Allison, "Thucydides's Trap Has Been Sprung in the Pacific," *Financial Times*, August 21, 2012. Variants of this warning were posted in books by Richard Rosecrance, Richard Bernstein and Ross H. Munro, Bill Gertz, Steven W. Mosher, John Mearsheimer, and Robert Kagan.

49. Allison testimony to the Armed Services Committee of the U.S. Senate on April 14, 2015, at http://www.armed-services.senate.gov/imo/media/doc/Allison_04-14-15.pdf (accessed 5/5/2015).

50. Arvind Subramanian, *Eclipse: Living in the Shadow of China's Economic Dominance* (Washington, DC: Peterson Institute for International Economics, 2011).

51. Ye Zicheng, *Inside China's Grand Strategy: The Perspective from the People's Republic,* edited and translated by Steven I. Levine and Guoli Liu (Lexington: University Press of Kentucky, 2011).

52. China's GDP growth since the early 1980s resulted more from top-down mobilization of resources than from efficient marketization. Its GDP per capita in 2014 was only $6,000. China had about 20 percent of the world's population, but only 10 percent of world GDP. All else being equal, one-fifth of the world's population should produce one-fifth of the world's GDP. China had markets for goods and services, yet its factors of production were still mostly controlled by the state through various administrative monopolies. Fu Jun, "Institutional Learning and Innovation in Sustained Economic Growth: The Case of China," *Global Asia Forum*, May 20, 2014, at http://www.globalasia.org/Forum/Detail/46/institutional-learning-and-innovation-in-sustained-economic-growth-the-case-of-china.html (accessed 6/20/2014).

53. China's steel output was setting records in 2014, but the number of housing starts in the private sector was falling steeply. Total lending rose faster than economic output in every quarter since late 2011. China faced a painful choice: it could slow lending and accept steady declines in economic growth or continue heavy lending and risk a sharp drop in economic growth when the financial system teetered. Keith Bradsher, "China Sees a Recovery, on Paper," *New York Times,* July 16, 2014.

54. Donald Gross, *The China Fallacy: How the U.S. Can Benefit from China's Rise and Avoid Another Cold War* (New York: Bloomsbury, 2013).

55. The foundations of national power for China, Japan, the ROK, Russia, India, Indonesia, and the United States are analyzed in Tellis et al., *Strategic Asia 2015–16.* But the authors give little attention to intangible assets—soft power, an area where China and Russia are weak, as shown in figure 19.1.

56. Michael Beckley, "China's Century? Why America's Edge Will Endure," *International Security* 36, no. 3 (Winter 2011–2012): 43.

57. Jeffrey A. Bader, *Obama and China's Rise: An Insider's Account of America's Asia Strategy* (Washington, DC: Brookings Institution Press, 2012), 147.

58. https://data.undp.org/dataset/Table-1-Human-Development-Index-and-its-components/wxub-qc5k (accessed 5/29/2014).

59. http://www.socialprogressimperative.org/data/spi (accessed 5/29/2014).

60. Mel Gurtov, *Will This Be China's Century? A Skeptic's View* (Boulder: Lynne Rienner, 2013).

61. David Rothkopf, "Therapy for the Self-Hating Superpower," *Foreign Policy* (July–August 2014): 87–88; and other articles in the same issue.

62. Joseph S. Nye, "Declinist Pundits," *Foreign Policy* (November 2012): 64; and Nye, *Is the American Century Over?* (Cambridge: Polity Press, 2015).

20. WHAT TO DO ABOUT—OR WITH—NORTH KOREA?

1. *Peloponnesian War,* Book 1, 76.

2. Stuart A. Kauffman, *Reinventing the Sacred: A New View of Science, Reason, and Religion* (New York: Basic Books, 2008)

3. Rainer Maria Rilke quoted by Frank Rose, "Beyond Our Control," *New York Times Book Review,* November 29, 2015, 15 (or. Matt Ridley, *The Evolution of Everything: How New Ideas Emerge* [New York: HarperCollins, 2015]).

4. Maria Popova, "Force of Impact," *New York Times Book Review,* November 29, 2015, 14 (on Lisa Randall, *Dark Matter and the Dinosaurs: The Astounding Interconnectedness of the Universe* [New York: HarperCollins, 2015]).

5. John Everard, *Only Beautiful Please: A British Diplomat in North Korea* (Stanford: Walter H. Shorenstein Asia-Pacific Research Center, 2012).

6. Death and taxes may be inevitable, but life can be prolonged and tax burdens delayed or altered.

7. Doug Bandow, "North Korea Advances along the Nuclear Path: Washington Should Switch from Coercion to Engagement," *Forbes,* March 20, 2015, at http://www.forbes.com/sites/dougbandow/2015/03/30/north-korea-advances-along-the-nuclear-path-washington-should-switch-from-coercion-to-engagement/ (accessed 7/9/2015).

8. Michael Mandelbaum, *The Case for Goliath: How America Acts as the World's Gov-

ernment in the Twenty-First Century (New York: Public Affairs, 2005), updated in Mandelbaum, *The Road to Global Prosperity* (New York: Simon & Schuster, 2014).

9. Jeremi Suri, "Bomb North Korea, before It's Too Late," *New York Times,* April 12, 2013.

10. Van Jackson and Hannah Suh, "The Biggest Myth about North Korea," *National Interest,* July 9, 2015, at http://nationalinterest.org/feature/the-biggest-myth-about-north-korea-13290 (accessed 7/9/2015).

11. Michael Lerner, "Patience, Not Preemption, on the Korean Peninsula," *The Diplomat,* April 24, 2013, at http://thediplomat.com/2013/04/patience-not-preemption-on-the-korean-peninsula/?allpages=yes (accessed 7/9/2015).

12. Jieun Baek, "Hack and Frack North Korea: How Information Campaigns Can Liberate the Hermit Kingdom," Harvard University Belfer Center for Science and International Affairs, April 2015, at http://belfercenter.ksg.harvard.edu/files/Hack%20and%20Frack%20NK%20final.pdf (accessed 5/1/2015).

13. Joshua Stanton, at http://freekorea.us/#sthash.mjsxC3ky.dpuf, June 8, 2015 (accessed 6/12/2015).

14. Gene Sharp advised liberation movements not to use violence against dictators—or negotiate with them—because dictators control the levers of material power. Instead, he outlined nonviolent techniques to overthrow dictatorships. See his *From Dictatorship to Democracy: A Conceptual Framework for Liberation,* 4th ed. (Boston: Albert Einstein Institution, 2010). Sharp's methods have helped generate change in many countries. See, e.g., David D. Kirkpatrick and David E. Sanger, "A Tunisian-Egyptian Link That Shook Arab History," *New York Times,* February 14, 2011, pp. 1, 9–10.

15. International efforts probably helped in Kenya, but not in Somalia or Dafur. See Alex J. Bellamy, "The Responsibility to Protect—Five Years On," *Ethics and International Affairs* 24, no. 2 (Summer 2010): 143–169, and the review articles by Edward C. Luck, "Responsibility to Protect: Growing Pains or Early Promise," *Ethics and International Affairs* 24, no. 4 (Winter 2010), and Jennifer Welsch, "Implementing the Responsibility to Protect: Where Expectations Meet Reality," *Ethics and International Affairs* 24, no. 4 (Winter 2010). See also Aleksandar Jokic, *Humanitarian Intervention: Moral and Philosophical Issues* (Peterborough, Ontario: Broadview, 2003).

16. A/HRC/25/CRP.1, February 7, 2014 (accessed 3/4/2014); other excerpts from this long document may be found in chapters 7 and 19.

17. "DPRK Foreign Ministry Spokesman Flays Hostile Forces' Adoption of 'Human Rights Resolution' against DPRK," KCNA, November 20, 2013, at http://www.kcna.co.jp/item/2013/201311/news20/20131120-21ee.html (accessed 5/9/2014).

18. Other recommended changes included the following:

Dismantling of all political prison camps and release of all political prisoners under international monitoring.

Reforming the Criminal Code and the Code of Criminal Procedure to abolish vaguely worded "antistate" and "antipeople" crimes, and enshrining the right to a fair trial and due-process guarantees articulated in the International Covenant on Civil and Political Rights.

Stopping the use of torture and instituting a moratorium on use of the death penalty; ending reprisals against persons on the basis of guilt by association; stopping forcible resettling of the families of convicted criminals.

Allowing independent newspapers and other media; allowing citizens to freely access the Internet, social media, international communications, and foreign broadcasts and publications, including the popular culture of other countries.

Abolishing compulsory participation in mass organizations and indoctrination sessions.

Abolishing any propaganda or educational activities that espouse national, racial, or political hatred or war propaganda.

Allowing Christians and other religious believers to exercise their religion independently and publicly.

Ending discrimination against citizens on the basis of their perceived political loyalty or the sociopolitical background of their families.

Ending every form of discrimination and violence against women.

Ensuring every citizen the right to food with no form of discrimination.

Seeking international food aid when necessary.

Realigning budget priorities to ensure freedom from hunger.

Abolishing travel bans; decriminalizing illegal border crossings and introducing border controls that conform to international standards.

Stopping treatment of citizens repatriated from China as criminals subject to imprisonment, execution, torture, arbitrary detention, deliberate starvation, illegal cavity searches, forced abortions, and other sexual violence.

Abolishing the state's compulsory designation of places of residence and employment.

Providing the families and nations of origin of all persons who have been abducted or forcibly disappeared with full information on their fate and allowing those who survive to return to their countries of origin.

Allowing separated families to unite and providing them unmonitored mail, telephone, e-mail, and other means of communication.

Prosecuting and bringing to justice those persons most responsible for alleged crimes against humanity and launching a people-driven process to establish the truth about such crimes.

Ratifying the International Convention for the Protection of All Persons from Enforced Disappearance, the Convention on the Rights of Persons with Disabilities, the Rome Statute of the International Criminal Court, and the basic conventions of the International Labour Organization.

19. A/HRC/25/CRP.1, 365–372.

20. The International Criminal Court in March 2014 found Congo militia leader Germain Katanga guilty of war crimes—complicity in the 2003 massacre of villagers in the gold-rich Ituri province of Democratic Republic of Congo. He became just the second person to be convicted by the court since it was established in 2002.

21. A/HRC/25/CRP.1, 371.

22. Ezra Vogel, *Deng Xiaoping and the Transformation of China* (Cambridge: Harvard University Press, 2011).

23. As of 2015 there were rail crossings into the DPRK from the Chinese cities of Dandong, Ji'an, and Tumen. The bridge from Ji'an crossed the Yalu and links to Manpo in North Korea. Ji'an was a small but bubbling town not far from the Chinese cities of Tonghua and Shenyang. The link from Tumen passed over the Tumen River to Namyang in the DPRK. Manpo was comparatively dynamic, while Namyang was resolutely rural and cut off. Hundreds of kilometers to the west, Manpo was more ready for modernity: it faced a much more commercially aware space across the Yalu. See Adam Cathcart, Christopher Green, and Ste-

ven Denney, "The Tumen Triangle Documentation Project: Sourcing the Chinese-North Korean Border," at http://sinonk.com/wp-content/uploads/2015/01/TTP_AKS-Special-Edition.pdf (accessed 5/15/2015).

24. There are some 205 islands on the Yalu. A 1962 border treaty between North Korea and China split the islands according to which ethnic group dominated each island. North Korea possessed 127 and China 78. Both countries had navigation rights on the river, including in the delta. Cathcart et al., "Tumen Triangle." Due to the division criteria, some islands, such as Hwanggumpyong Island, belonged to North Korea but abutted the Chinese side of the river. China in 2012 demanded that DPRK troops withdraw from the island. Koichiro Ishida, "Troop Deployment Row Halts China-N. Korean Island Project," *Asahi Shimbun*, July 31, 2012, at http://ajw.asahi.com/article/asia/korean_peninsula/AJ201207310004 (accessed 5/2/2013).

25. In April 2014 Russia agreed to write off nearly $10 billion of $11 billion owed by North Korea since the Soviet era. The $1 billion balance would be paid off over twenty years, with the funds being used to build a gas pipeline and improved rail service into North Korea. See Russian Railways website at http://eng.rzd.ru/newse/public/en?STRUCTURE_ID=15&layer_id=4839&refererPageId=4088&refererLayerId=3920&id=106356 (accessed 4/21/2014).

26. Founded in 1956 to facilitate rail connections across Eurasia, the organization was headquartered in Bulgaria and had twenty-six members in 2015 including China, the DPRK, and Russia.

27. See Marcus Noland, "Coordination Failures," April 16, 2015, at http://blogs.piie.com/nk/?p=14041 (accessed 4/16/2015).

28. ROK president Park Geun Hye and RF president Vladimir Putin agreed to cooperate in the Russian-led project during their summit in Seoul in November 2013. Putin warned in Seoul that if Pyongyang continued to drag its feet, then Russia would work bilaterally with South Korea.

29. Michael Lipin, "China's Landlocked Northeast Turns to Russian Port as Trade Outlet," Voice of America, September 28, 2014, at http://www.voanews.com/content/zarubino-russian-port-china-trade-tumen/2461442.html (accessed 6/23/2014).

30. Rüdiger Frank, "Rason Special Economic Zone: North Korea as It Could Be," *38 North*, December 16, 2014, at http://38north.org/2014/12/rfrank121614/ (accessed 4/3/2015).

31. Felix Abt, "North Korea: Stuck in the Past or Poised for the Future?" November 24, 2015, at http://www.nknews.org/2015/11/north-korea-stuck-in-the-past-or-poised-for-the-future/ (accessed 11/25/2015). See also Abt, *A Capitalist in North Korea: My Seven Years in the Hermit Kingdom* (North Clarendon, VT: Tuttle, 2014). For parallel observations by an Australian teacher, see Stewart Lone, *Pyongyang Lessons: North Korea from Inside the Classroom* (Create Space [Amazon], 2013). Against this rosy picture, the Pyongyang regime often cheated foreign investors—Volvo in Sweden, Xiyang Group in China, Mostovik in Russia, Orascom in Egypt—as soon as their usefulness ended. See Andrei Lankov, "Why N. Korea Won't Be Worried about Its Recent Reputational Disasters," December 17, 2015, at https://www.nknews.org/2015/12/why-n-korea-wont-be-worried-by-its-recent-reputational-disasters/ (accessed 12/18/2015).

32. On how a capitalist mentality, across both Koreas and the Korean diaspora, could foster unification, see Hyun Ok Park, *The Capitalist Unconscious: From Korean Unification to Transnational Korea* (New York: Columbia University Press, 2015). On "marketization from below," see Hazel Smith, *North Korea: Markets and Military Rule* (Cambridge,

UK: Cambridge University Press, 2015). For other transition issues, see Choe Sang-Hun, Gi-Wook Shin, and David Straub, eds., *Troubled Transition: North Korea's Politics, Economy, and External Relations* (Stanford: Walter H. Shorenstein Asia-Pacific Research Center, 2013).

33. More than half of the citizens in the former German Democratic Republic sided with Putin's Russia on Ukraine in 2014. More than three-fourths were down on capitalism, which they saw as exploitation. Citizens in what had been Communist Poland and the sovietized Baltic Republics did not share these views. They liberated themselves, while East Germany was absorbed into the Federal German Republic. Many East Germans did not like that West Germans had become captains of East German fates. Many complained that Germany was still under the thumb of the United States—a charge that North Koreans might level against Seoul. See Jochen Büttner, "Eastern Germans' Soft Spot for Russia," *New York Times,* December 30, 2014.

34. Experts' estimates ranged from $50 billion to $3 trillion. See Victor Cha, *The Impossible State: North Korea, Past and Future* (New York: HarperCollins, 2012), 402.

35. Ibid.

36. Much of the analysis here follows the detailed studies of Marcus Noland, Stephan Haggard, and others associated with the Peterson Institute for International Economics. See, e.g., Noland, Sherman Robinson, and Li-Gang Liu, "The Costs and Benefits of Korean Unification," Working Paper 98-1, at https://www.piie.com/publications/wp/wp.cfm?ResearchID=142 [no date] (accessed 5/1/2015).

37. For detailed studies of public opinion, see http://en.asaninst.org/contents/south-korean-attitudes-toward-north-korea-and-reunification/ (accessed 6/23/2015).

38. Roger J. Peters, "The WMD Challenges Posed by a Collapse of North Korea," *38 North,* April 14, 2015, at http://38north.org/2015/04/rpeters041415/ (accessed 6/15/2015).

39. Lawrence Wilkerson interviewed by Emanuel Pastreich, in *The Diplomat,* December 3, 2015, at http://thediplomat.com/2015/12/interview-lawrence-wilkerson/ (accessed 12/3/2015). Other views on THAAD by U.S., ROK, Chinese, and Russian analysts can be found in earlier issues of *The Diplomat.* Wilkerson's views were nearly identical to those of former White House science adviser Jerome B. Wiesner, for whom I worked in 1965. The essentials in the debate had not changed much in fifty years!

40. See, e.g., Robert Farley, "Should America Fear China's 'Carrier-Killer' Missile?" *National Interest,* September 22, 2014, at http://nationalinterest.org/feature/should-america-fear-chinas-carrier-killer-missile-11321 (accessed 12/1/2014).

41. Deepak Malhotra and Max H. Bazerman, *Negotiation Genius: How to Overcome Obstacles and Achieve Brilliant Results at the Bargaining Table and Beyond* (New York: Bantam Books, 2007), 382–383.

42. A former State Department planner argued in 2015 that the basis for a new working relationship—a Détente Plus—with Putin's Russia had to include a highly visible recognition of Russia's status as a great power. If the United States has to soft-peddle Russian belligerence in Ukraine and elsewhere to create a Détente Plus, could not Washington afford some symbolic acts to satisfy Pyongyang's quest for status? Leslie H. Gelb, "Russia and America: Toward a New Détente," *National Interest,* June 9, 2015, at http://nationalinterest.org/feature/russia-america-toward-new-detente-13077?page=2 (accessed 7/5/2015).

43. Siegfried S. Hecker, "What I Found in Yongbyon and Why It Matters," *APS* [American Physical Society] *News* 20, no. 3 (March 2011), at http://www.aps.org/publications/apsnews/201103/backpage.cfm2015 (accessed 6/23/2015).

44. The Joint Communiqué and Albright's visit are discussed above in chapter 12.

45. For a detailed plan for implementing the 2007 North–South accord on creating a special zone in the area, see Yong Seok Chang, "Revisiting Korea's Northern Limit Line and Proposed Special Zone for Peace and Cooperation," *Asian Journal of Peacebuilding* 3, no. 1 (May 2015): 65–85.

46. Malhotra and Bazerman, *Negotiation Genius.*

Index

Kim Jong Un: assumes power at Kim Jong Il's death, 247; Christianity and, 42; compared to Obama as an individual, 294–295; fitness plateau in North Korea and, 172; as a god-king ruler, 17, 23–24; human rights violations and, 4; Korean Workers' Party appoints as Vice Chairman of the Central Military Commission, 245; New Year message of 2014, 249; New Year message of 2015, 253; North Korean missile launches and, 250, 313; possibility of détente with, 291; pursuit of military prowess and prosperity, 123; relations with China, 312; relations with Obama and the United States, 238; role of synch and timing in U.S. negotiations with, 192; snubbing of U.S. representatives, 186; tightening of border controls, 119
Kim Jun Wook, 42
Kim Young Sam, 166, 167, 301
Kim Young Sun, 41
Kingdom of Koguryŏ, 24, 25, 26
Kirby, Michael, 251
Kissinger, Henry A., 180, 183, 185, 282
Knowledge Partnership Program, 348
KN-02 missile, 261–262, 263
KN-08 missile, 263
Koguryŏ, Kingdom of, 24, 25, 26
Koh, Tommy, 192
Kojong, 38
Korea: absence from U.S. presidential statements from 1911 to 1942, 57–58; Acheson on the significance of, 3; Christian missionaries, 37–39; Confucianism and risk-taking in, 31–33; cultural values, 306–307; culture and politics, 42–44; dynastic history, 25–31; Eulsa Treaty, 55; FDR's criticism of Japanese despotism in, 61;

geoeconomics and, 297–298; geopolitics and, 5–6, 10–11, 296–297; independence in "due course," 61–64; independent statehood, 49; Japanese annexation and occupation, 56–57, 60; Japanese attack on Chinese troops in, 52–53; Japanese expansionist ambitions and, 51–59; language, 36–37; literacy and education, 35–36; nineteenth-century reform and modernization, 49, 50; nineteenth-century relations with France, 47; origins of the 38th parallel, 64–68; overview of U.S. policies toward, 5–6; police and punishment in the 1890s, 114; religions in, 289; Russo-Japanese War and, 54, 55, 56; Sino-Soviet relations and, 70–71; structure of political power, 34–35; Tonghak upheaval, 52–53; Treaty of Shimonoseki, 53; U.S. acquiescence to Japan's ambitions in and takeover of, 45, 46, 51–60; World War II, 60. *See also* U.S.-Korean relations
Korean Central Intelligence Agency (KCIA), 34
Korean Central News Agency (KCNA): imagined community and the creation of folklore, 20; response to UN report on human rights violations, 131–132; on the U.S.-DPRK joint accord of 2000, 204–205; on U.S.-DPRK relations in 200, 203
Korean Christianity: linked to nationalism and progress, 39–40; Minjung theology, 41; missionaries and the arrival of Christianity, 37–39; modern demographics, 40, 41; in North Korea, 40, 41–42; women and, 40–41

The Price of China's Economic Development: Power, Capital, and the Poverty of Rights
Zhaohui Hong

Japan after 3/11: Global Perspectives on the Earthquake, Tsunami, and Fukushima Meltdown
Edited by Pradyumna P. Karan and Unryu Suganuma

Korean Democracy in Transition: A Rational Blueprint for Developing Societies
Hee Min Kim

Modern Chinese Legal Reform: New Perspectives
Edited by Xiaobing Li and Qiang Fang

Democracy in Central Asia: Competing Perspectives and Alternative Strategies
Mariya Y. Omelicheva

China's Encounter with Global Hollywood: Cultural Policy and the Film Industry, 1994–2013
Wendy Su

Growing Democracy in Japan: The Parliamentary Cabinet System since 1868
Brian Woodall

Inside China's Grand Strategy: The Perspective from the People's Republic
Ye Zicheng, Edited and Translated by Steven I. Levine and Guoli Liu

Civil Society and Politics in Central Asia
Edited by Charles E. Ziegler

www.ingramcontent.com/pod-product-compliance
Lightning Source LLC
Chambersburg PA
CBHW031544260326
41914CB00002B/264